# THE LONG ROAD

# THE LONG ROAD

Trials and tribulations of airmen prisoners
from Stalag Luft VII (Bankau) to Berlin,
June 1944-May 1945

Oliver Clutton-Brock
and
Raymond Crompton

GRUB STREET · LONDON

Published by
Grub Street
4 Rainham Close
London
SW11 6SS

Copyright © Grub Street 2013
Copyright text © Oliver Clutton-Brock and Ray Crompton 2013

A catalogue record for this book is available on request from the British Library

**ISBN-13: 9781909166202**

Cover design by Sarah Driver
Edited by Sophie Campbell

Printed and bound by Berforts Information Press Ltd


Grub Street Publishing only uses
FSC (Forest Stewardship Council) paper for its books.

# CONTENTS

| | | |
|---|---|---|
| | Acknowledgements | 7 |
| | Abbreviations | 9 |
| | Preface | 14 |
| | Introduction | 15 |
| Chapter One | 'A Bloody Chicken Farm' | 18 |
| Chapter Two | 6 and 13 June 1944: *Truppen 1 & 2* | 25 |
| Chapter Three | 18 and 20 June 1944: *Truppen 3 & 4* | 46 |
| Chapter Four | 21-28 June 1944: *Truppen 5, 6, & 7* | 68 |
| Chapter Five | July 1944: *Truppen 8-17* | 98 |
| Chapter Six | August 1944: *Truppen 18-28* | 138 |
| Chapter Seven | September 1944: *Truppen 29-35* | 160 |
| Chapter Eight | October 1944: *Truppen 36-46(?)*; Arnhem; | |
| | move to new compound | 170 |
| Chapter Nine | November 1944: *Truppen 47(?)-50* | 189 |
| Chapter Ten | December 1944: *Truppen 51-56* | 202 |
| Chapter Eleven | The Last *Trupp*; The Camp is Struck, January 1945 | 222 |
| Chapter Twelve | 19 January-5 February 1945: Evacuation | 237 |
| Chapter Thirteen | Stalag IIIA (Luckenwalde) and Liberation | 255 |
| | Postscript | 273 |
| Appendix I | Dates of *Truppen* Arrivals at Stalag Luft VII | |
| | (Bankau) | 274 |
| Appendix II | Old German Place Names with Modern Polish | |
| | Equivalent | 275 |
| Appendix III | Sergeant Doug Grant's Repatriation via Odessa | 276 |
| Appendix IV | F/L A.H. Hammet DFM, RAAF | 279 |
| Appendix V | SAS Operation Maple, 1944 | 282 |
| Appendix VI | Stalag Luft VII (Bankau) Prisoners of War | 284 |
| | Endnotes | 348 |
| | Bibliography | 356 |
| | Index | 358 |

R.171883 Flight Sergeant Leslie Howard Stevenson RCAF
shot and killed on 27 December 1944 by a Luftwaffe guard who was obeying orders.

\*

'There's a four-engined bomber just leaving its base
Bound for alien shores
Heavily laden with cookies and such
Presents to even the score.
There's many a flak battery throwing up hell,
There's many a fighter as well,
But the unlucky bod that gets caught, the poor sod,
Shouts back for your parachutes all.

Bless 'em all, the flak batteries, fighters and all.
Bless all the AGs and bomb aimers too.
Bless all the pilots and rest of the crew,
For we're saying goodbye to 'em all
As to the escape hatch we crawl
We haven't a notion
If we're o'er the ocean
So cheer up my lads,
LET US FALL.'

*The Stalag Luft VII version of 'Bless 'em all' (from the diary of John Tomney).*

# ACKNOWLEDGEMENTS

During the research and writing of this book, Raymond Crompton was privileged to correspond with, and to meet, the following former Stalag Luft VII prisoners of war, without whose generous assistance this book could not have been written. Sadly, many of them are no longer with us:

J. R. Abbott, J.O. Ackroyd, E. Adair, P.B. Aitken, C.J. Aldred, K.C. Anderton, T.A. Applegath, T.R. Aspinall, G.J. Badham, G.Baker, S.Barlow, S. Barraclough, G.H. Bateman, C.S. Batt, G.S. Baylis, H. Bennett, A.R. Bennett, L. Benson, T.G.W. Berry, B. Bilinski, C. Birds, D.A. Blackford, W.A. Blake, H.J. Branch, K.R. Brant, A.R. Brice, P.F. Broadribb, A. Broddle, F.W. Brown, P.H. Brown, H. Bruneau, D.R. Burns, C. Bryce, K.W. Campbell, N.C. Capar, F.J. Carey, J.E. Carter, D.R. Christianson, A.W. Clarke, A.W.J. Cleeve, R.C. Clements, A.P. Cochrane, The Reverend Captain J.B. Collins, W.S. Comfort, A. Coope, V.V. Cooper, P.H. Craig, M. Crapper, I.R.B. Crawford, G. Cross, W.S. Dashwood, B.H. Davis, J.A. Davies, T.D. DeRenzy, J.M. DeLuca, Ken Dobbs, W.T. Doidge, G.E. Dunham, T. Durrant, R.D. Eadie, C.E. Eastwood, K.E. Elliott, R.R. English, H.C. Evans, E. Evison, D.A. Farrington, J.C. Fereday, W.N. Fethers, E. Finlay, J.E. Fisher, G.A. Flay, G.H. Flintoft, D.W. Foster, A.P. Franczak, J.S. Freeman, J.E.M. Fullum, G.H.P. Gibbens, C.H. Giles, C. Gillow, R.J. Goode, D.W. Gore, R.W. Gowing, A. Grant, D.R. Grant, H.R.C. Grant, D.G. Gray, K.W. Green, R.L. Griffiths, T.C. Guy, W.R. Haddon, A.F. Hamilton, M.A. Harrington, R.S. Hartgroves, G.T.H. Haworth, E. Healy, R.P. Heard, R. Heasman, I. Hewitt, L.G. Hillyard, W. Hodgson, F. Hooker, J.M. Hooper, W.R. Horner, J.R. Horton, L.E. Howard, B.J. Howarth, P. Hudson, W.J.J. Hudson, D. Hunter, E.H. Hyde, J. Ireland, P.D. Jack, A.E. Jardine, D.W.M. James, J.S. Jenkins, N.E. Jennings, J.D. Jones, S.A. Keirle, A.E. Kemp, G.H. Kilbryde, P.S. Kirby, W.H. Knox, S. Konarzewski, G.V. Korner, M.A. Laffin, D.M.D. Lambert MBE, K.A. Lane DFC, D. Lewis, P.A. Lewis, A. Lloyd, R.F. Lloyd (later Lloyd-Davies), J.W. Lovatt, W.D. Low, A.B.D. Lyon, J.F. Macdonald, D. MacTaggart, A. Madelaine, S. Malick, F.P. Mannion, R. Margerison, D.C. Matthews, A.W. Maxwell, J.D.W. Maxwell, J.R. McConnell, A. McKibben, D.N. McLaren, A.O. McMurdon, C.J. Medland DFM, W.G. Melrose, J.W. Mills, K.C. Minifie, E. Morgan, J. Morgan, D. Neal, R.A. Neills, P.J. Nolan, R. Nutter, W.A. Oakes, N.F. Oates, W.D. Ogilvie, R.P. Olsen, R.F. Osborne, N. Ostrom, A.E. Palmer, B.J.P. Palmer, H.W. Pankratz, D.S. Parker, K.J. Pendray, J.E. Penman, J.T. Pett, C.C. Pettit, J.A. Philpot, A.E. Potter, P.J. Potts, W.A. Poulton, S.R. Price, G.H. Pringle, K. Prowd, E. Quigley, E.J. Raffill, W.J. Ramsbottom, H.H. Rathband, R.F. Raymond, B.A. Reaume, J.I. Rees, C.R. Richardson, A.A. Rigby, J.A. Robertson, J. Robinson, J.E. Robson, H.P. Rose, A.J. Sargeant, E. Sargeant, L. Sargent, D.R. Scopes, E.W. Scott, P.Y. Sekine, A.E. Seller, E.G.Selwyn, J.A. Shenton, S.A. Silver, A. Simpson, M.J. Simpson, P.S. Simpson, J.G. Smith, W.B.R. Smith, V. Smyth, F.S.A. Spriggs, R.J. Stapleton, F. Stead, J.E. Stead, D.T. Stevens, V.H. Stone, G. Surgeoner, N.H. Swale, K.E. Tate, K.G. Taylor, R. Taylor, W. Taylor, T.R. Teague, M. Theunissen, W.L. Thompson, G.B. Thomson, J. Thomson, E.J. Tolhurst, B.A. Tomblin, J.F. Tomney, A.H.J. Trumble, F.J. Tudor DFM, P.S. Twynam, J.L. Umscheid, K. Valášek, C. Van de Velde, L.J. Venus, P.O. Wadsworth, H.W. Wagner, R.G Walters, H. Watkins, J.C. Watkins, C.R. Watkinson DFM, J.G. Weedon, C. Weeks, F. Wells, L.E. Westbrook DFM, J.A.B. Wetherall, J.W. Whippy, T.S. White, D.J.R. Wilcox, J. Wiles, E.T. Williams, J. Williamson, N. Wilmot, P.G.G. Wilmshurst, L.E.D. Winchester, W.G. Winkley, H.T. Winter, P.B. Withnall, L.A. Woodward, D. Worthing, S.D. Wright, V.S.J. Zucker.

Thanks also go to C.M. de Bounevialle and L. Poole (both POWs at Stalag Luft III [Sagan]), who were crew members of POWs at Stalag Luft VII; and also to two aircrew evaders, F/O Ross Wiens RCAF (crew member of James Umscheid RCAF), and Colin Fowler (crew member of Jack Wilcox RNZAF).

The support and help of the following is also gratefully acknowledged:

Air Historical Branch 5 (RAF) (particularly Messrs Sebastian Cox and Graham Day); M.R. Aldred; Michael Allman (re Sgt P.F.J. Hayes and the crew of Lancaster LL840); Amicale des Forces Aériennes Françaises Libres; Annie Arguile (for help with French translation); Caroline Barnard (South Africa); Mair Bateman; Patricia Batt; D. Bishop; Gerald and Sir Christian Bonington CVO, CBE, DL (re their father, Lt Charles Bonington SAS); Peter Capon (archivist, Museum of Army Flying); Dave Champion (researcher); Bill Chorley; Elsie Cleeve; K. Clements; John Clinch; Joan Collingwood (re her husband Cuthbert Collingwood); Richard Collins (son of The Reverend Captain John B. Collins); Dorothy Davis; Dawe Brothers (Hereford, re The Reverend Collins); Ryan Dudley (Australia, re the crew of SR384); Elva M. Durrant; Colonel Graham C.L. Du Toit (SAAF, Ret'd); Steve Dyer (re A.M. Hughes RAAF); Jon England (artist, re Ted Milligan); Mary Escott; Søren Flensted (historian, Denmark); Roger Frost (re photo of the Rev. J.B. Collins); Tony Grant (re Thomas Trimble); Janet Griffiths; Sheila Griffiths; W/C John Grogan RAF (Ret'd) (re his father F/O R.J. Grogan and Halifax MZ711); L. Harries; Bob Hills (re John Collins at Marnhull); Michael Hingston (author of Into Enemy Arms); Alan Howe (nephew of Sgt Richard Enfield); John Howes (re Dutch affairs); Mel Hughes (son of F/Sgt Ken Hughes); T. Hyde; Linda Ibrom (researcher, Canada); S.R. James; Max Lambert (historian, New Zealand); Michael LeBlanc (researcher, Canada); Slawomir Litwinski; Carol MacLean (Canada, daughter of D.L. MacLean, for the generous loan of her father's wartime diary); Errol Martyn (author, New Zealand); Nigel McTeer (son of Anthony McTeer); National Archives of Australia; National Archives of Canada; Ron Niven (re his father William Niven); Peter O'Brien (nephew of Joe Smith, 462 Squadron); Alan Orton (re 'L' Detachment SAS); Rita Quigley; Rhys Rees; Edouard Renière (historian, Belgium); Phyllis Robertson; D. Sargeant; Jean Scott; David A. Sharp (re 69 Squadron and Tom Trimble); Lynne Shenton; Kathleen Silver; John Skinner (re diary of his father-in-law Paul Decroix); Margot Surgeoner; Peter and Dorothy Sutherland; Linda Toft (re her father A.C. Law); A. Wadsworth; W. Watkins; W.R. Watkins; J. Tom Watts DFM; K. Watts; Laurie Woods (460 (RAAF) Squadron historian); Mrs Maisie Yeo (re her late husband Edward).

Special thanks go to Raymond's brother, Alan, whose continued support never faltered; to his nephew Lee Crompton; and to his cousin Ann Russell for her help with visits on his behalf to The National Archives.

Finally, we are most grateful to Grub Street Publishing, particularly John Davies, Sophie Campbell and Sarah Driver for their great help with the publication of our book.

Raymond Crompton & Oliver Clutton-Brock
August 2013

# ABBREVIATIONS

| | |
|---|---|
| AAC | Army Air Corps |
| Abwehr | Military counter-intelligence branch of the Wehrmacht |
| AC1, AC2 | Aircraftman First Class, Aircraftman Second Class |
| ADJ | Adjutant. French rank equivalent to warrant officer |
| AFU | Advanced Flying Unit |
| A/Ldg.Air | Acting Leading Airman [Fleet Air Arm] |
| AMES | Air Ministry Experimental Station [cover-name for radar] |
| ANS | Air Navigation School |
| AOC | Air Officer Commanding |
| *Appell* | Roll call, parade |
| AWOL | Absent Without Leave |
| Bf109, 110 | German single-, twin-engined fighter, fighter/bomber. 'Bf' from Bayerische Flugzeugwerke. Popularly known as the Messerschmitt Me109, Me110 |
| BG; BS | Bomb Group; Bomb Squadron (USAAF) |
| Cooler | Camp prison cells |
| D/F | Direction finding |
| DFC; DFM | Distinguished Flying Cross; Distinguished Flying Medal |
| DSC (US) | Distinguished Service Cross (United States) |
| Duff gen | False or incorrect information |
| DZ | Drop Zone |
| FAA | Fleet Air Arm |
| FAFL | Forces Aériennes Françaises Libres (Free French Air Force) |
| 'Ferret' | Abwehr guards employed *inside* POW camps looking for anything suspicious |
| FFI | Forces Françaises de l'Intérieur – organised French Resistance |
| 'Fishpond' | Radar device in RAF aircraft to warn of approach of other aircraft |
| F/L; F/O; F/S | Flight Lieutenant; Flying Officer; Flight Sergeant |
| G/C | Group Captain |
| G-H | RAF airborne radar blind-bombing device |
| Goon | POW name for German guard (derogatory) |
| HC (bomb) | see MC (bomb) |
| $H_2S$ | Ground-mapping radar carried in some RAF aircraft |
| HMCS; HMS | His Majesty's Canadian Ship; His Majesty's Ship |
| IRCC | International Red Cross Committee (*Comité International de la Croix-Rouge*) |
| Ju52 | Junkers 52, three-engined German transport aircraft |
| Ju87 | Junkers 87, the so-called Stuka, a single-engined dive-bomber |
| Ju88 | Junkers 88, Luftwaffe twin-engined bomber/night-fighter aircraft |
| LAC | Leading Aircraftman |
| LG | Landing Ground (usually in North Africa) |
| LZ | Landing Zone |
| MC (bomb) | Medium Capacity. 'Capacity' is the percentage weight of explosive compared with the overall weight of the bomb – Charge Weight Ratio (CWR). The CWR of the MC bomb was approximately fifty per cent. That of the HC (High Capacity) bomb was over seventy per cent. |

| | |
|---|---|
| Me109, Me110 | See Bf109, Bf110 |
| MP | Military Police |
| MS; MV | Motor Ship; Motor Vessel |
| MT | Motor Transport |
| NCO | Non-commissioned officer |
| NJG | N̲achtjagdgeschwader – Luftwaffe night-fighter squadron |
| OBOE | British radio-transmitter device for ground to air navigation |
| Oflag | Abbreviation of *Offizierenlager* – officer camp |
| OCU; OTU | Operational Conversion Unit; Operational Training Unit |
| Pct | Parachutist (SAS rank) |
| PFF | Pathfinder Force |
| PG | *Prigioneri di Guerra* (*Italian*, prisoners of war) |
| P/O | Pilot Officer |
| POW | Prisoner(s) of War |
| PRU | Photographic Reconnaissance Unit |
| PTC | Primary Training Centre |
| Purge | POW word for a group of POWs moved from one camp to another (noun), or moving a group of POWs from one camp to another (verb). |
| RAF, RAFVR | Royal Air Force, Royal Air Force Volunteer Reserve |
| RAAF | Royal Australian Air Force |
| RCAF | Royal Canadian Air Force |
| RCN | Royal Canadian Navy |
| RN/RNVR | Royal Navy/Royal Naval Volunteer Reserve |
| RNNAS | Royal Netherlands Naval Air Service |
| RNZAF | Royal New Zealand Air Force |
| RT | Radio Telephone (Telephony) |
| RTO | Railway Transport Officer |
| SAS | Special Air Service |
| SBO | Senior British Officer |
| SD | *Sicherheitsdienst* – Nazi secret service (see SIPO) |
| SD | Special Duty (Duties) (RAF) |
| Sgt; S/Sgt | Sergeant; Staff Sergeant (also a US rank, 3rd Grade) |
| SHAEF | Supreme Headquarters Allied Expeditionary Force |
| SIPO | *Sicherheitspolizei* – Nazi security police (see also SD) |
| S/L | Squadron Leader |
| SORB | Squadron Operations Record Book |
| SP | Service Police |
| SS | *Schutzstaffel* – literally, protection squad. Originally, Hitler's bodyguard |
| SS | Steam Ship |
| Stalag | Abbreviation of *Stammlager* – other ranks' camp |
| TAF | Tactical Air Force |
| TCG; TCS | Troop Carrier Group; Troop Carrier Squadron (USAAF) |
| TI | Target Indicators |
| Tinsel | RAF code for aerial jamming of German radio instructions. Noun or verb. |
| TNA | The National Archives, Kew |
| T/Sgt | Technical Sergeant (2nd Grade) (USAAF) |
| u/s | Unserviceable |

| | |
|---|---|
| USAAF | United States Army Air Force |
| W/C | Wing Commander |
| Wehrmacht | The German armed forces – army, navy, and air force |
| Wimpy | Nickname for the twin-engined Wellington bomber, from the cartoon character J. Wellington Wimpy. ('Wimpey' is incorrect). |
| 'Window' | Thin aluminium strips discharged from bombers to confuse German radar. Called 'chaff' by the Americans, '*Düppel*' by the Germans. |
| W/O; WO1; WO2 | Warrant Officer; Warrant Officer 1st Class, 2nd Class. |
| W/OP | Wireless Operator. Also WOP/AG: Wireless Operator/Air Gunner |

On foot: Bankau to Goldberg

Goldberg • • Prausnitz
Peterwitz
Standorf
Heidersdorf
Pfaffendorf
Langseifersdorf
Karzen
Rothschloss
Strehlen
Köchendorf
Wansen
Zindel
Konradswaldau
Schönfeld
Gross Jenkwitz
Lossen
Karlsmarkt
Alt Poppelau
Nikoline
Schurgast
Buchitz/Dom Waldhaus
Winterfeld
Karlsruhe
Konstadt
Kreuzburg
Bankau
Stalag Luft VII

Warta
Posen
WARSAW
POLAND
Lodz
Radom
g Luft III
Leignitz
Breslau
see enlargement
Kreuzburg
Bankau
Stalag Luft VII
weidnitz
Brieg
Oppeln
Czestochowa
Kielce
Sandomierz
Lamsdorf
Stalag VIIIB/344
Cracow
CZECHOSLOVAKIA
Vienna
Danube
Budapest
Szombathely
HUNGARY
ROMANIA

# PREFACE

This is the history of a Luftwaffe prisoner-of-war camp, Stalag Luft VII (Luft 7 for short), that existed for barely thirty-two weeks from its opening in early June 1944 to its closure in mid-January 1945. It was never a big camp – at the most it held fewer than 1,700 Allied airmen and other prisoners of war – and it never produced any noted moments of great excitement, for instance an escape leading to a 'home run', except for a fatal shooting two days after Christmas.

When the time came to close the camp, the prisoners were forced at gunpoint to walk out into one of the fiercest Silesian winters known for years. Each and every hungry and cold man suffered his fair share of hardship until, eventually, they reached the comparative warmth and safety of another, much larger, camp fifty kilometres south of Berlin – Stalag IIIA (Luckenwalde). But even then their trials were not over, for food and proper accommodation were lacking for many days. Dysentery was rife, but the exhausted men somehow kept going.

This, then, is the story of these Luft 7 men who, having survived the trauma of action against, and capture by, the enemy, some as far back as 1940, came from France, the Low Countries, Germany, Norway, Denmark, Poland, the Balkans, Italy, Hungary, the Mediterranean and other seas, and from North Africa. Almost ninety per cent of POWs at Luft 7 were captured after April 1944. Two-thirds of them were RAF Bomber Command aircrew who had been flying Lancasters and Halifaxes from bases in England. Joining them were fighter pilots, Coastal Command aircrew, and even a couple of airmen from the Royal Navy's Fleet Air Arm. The Glider Pilot Regiment of the Army Air Corps was also strongly represented by some 130 of its men. There was, too, a leavening of RAF ground crew, mostly members of mobile radar stations (AMES) and of the RAF Regiment: gunners, MT drivers, radar operators and so on, some of whom were caught during the fall of Tobruk in June 1942. Sometimes a few 'strays' arrived – British or South African Army, and US aircrew – but they were sorted out in time and sent to a more appropriate camp elsewhere.

Thanks to the personal diaries of some of the POWs, we are better able to understand the highs and lows of captivity at Luft 7, especially the hardships endured during the evacuation from that camp in the bitterly cold winter of January and February 1945. And we can feel the gnawing hunger on near-starvation rations in February and March at Stalag IIIA. All this was far more than any man should ever have been asked to endure, but go through it the Luft 7 POWs did, with surprisingly few casualties. At last, in the warm sunshine of April and May 1945, nearly all of them went home.

# INTRODUCTION

Though the highest authority of Nazi Germany was the *Oberster Befehlshaber der Wehrmacht* (Supreme Commander of the Armed Forces), Adolf Hitler himself, every man captured by the Germans became a prisoner of war under the blanket control of *Das Oberkommando der Wehrmacht* (OKW), the High Command of the German Armed Forces, head of which was *Chef des Oberkommandos der Wehrmacht* General Wilhelm Keitel.[1]

Subordinate to the OKW were the *Oberkommando des Heeres* (OKH), army; *Oberkommando der Kriegsmarine* (OKM), navy; and *Oberkommando der Luftwaffe* (OKL), air force, each with its own High Command.

Immediately subordinate to Keitel was General Hermann Reinecke, head of *Der Allgemeines Wehrmachtsamt* (AWA, Armed Forces General Office), within which was the *Abteilung Kriegsgefangenenwesen im OKW* (Prisoner-of-War Section within the OKW). It was this department, headed by Generalmajor Hans von Grävenitz, that was responsible for POWs for most of the Second World War.

After the fall of France in June 1940 over 44,000 British soldiers, a handful of RAF personnel, an estimated 1.9 million Frenchmen, and several thousand Poles, Dutch, Belgians and Norwegians became prisoners of the Germans. As most of these were soldiers, they were kept in hastily-prepared camps under the control of the OKH. For want of any Luftwaffe accommodation the few RAF POWs, some of whom had been captured as early as September 1939, were shoved in with the army types.

For the purposes of administration, the German Reich was divided into *Wehrkreise* (military defence districts), nineteen of which had been created by June 1944, which were administered from strategically-important centres such as Dresden (Wehrkreis IV) or Breslau (Wehrkreis VIII). The German army's POW camps took their number from that of the Wehrkreis in which they were located, the first camp to be opened in a particular Wehrkreis being given the letter 'A' followed by B, C etc. For example, the camps in Wehrkreis IV were Oflag IVA (Hohnstein), Oflag IVB (Königstein), Oflag IVC (Colditz), and so on.

It was thanks to the commander-in-chief of the Luftwaffe, Reichsmarschall[2] Hermann Göring, however, that Allied aircrew would eventually find their way to camps under Luftwaffe control, the Luftwaffe regarding themselves as being more civilised than their army counterparts. These Luftwaffe camps were simply numbered in the order in which they were opened, irrespective of the Wehrkreis in which they happened to be located.

When the war began in September 1939, the Luftwaffe had no long-term plans for the reception, interrogation, and subsequent disposal of captured enemy aircrew, and it was not until 15 December 1939 that a *Durchgangslager der Luftwaffe* (Air Force transit camp; Dulag Luft for short) was opened at a former agricultural school at Oberursel, a few kilometres north west of Frankfurt-am-Main. The few RAF and French Armée de l'Air POWs in those early days were housed in a two-storey farmhouse. By the spring of 1940, the camp comprised solitary-confinement cells and a small, separate transit camp from which, after interrogation, aircrew were sent to a permanent POW camp.

The Oberursel site continued to expand as the numbers of POWs grew but, eventually, so great was the number of captured Allied airmen POWs passing through it that on 10 September 1943 the transit camp was relocated to the *Palmengarten und Botanischer Garten* in the heart of Frankfurt. Less than a mile from Frankfurt's *Hauptbahnhof* (main railway station), a legitimate bombing target, inevitably stray bombs fell on this transit camp. Despite diplomatic protests, it was not until the end of May 1944 that a third transit camp was opened, at Wetzlar on the Lahn river, some sixty-five kilometres to the north of Frankfurt. Interrogations continued to be held at Oberursel until the end of the war, the place being called *Auswertungsstelle West*, literally *Interrogation place West*, to distinguish it from a similar one on the Eastern Front.

It was not until the beginning of July 1940 that the first permanent Luftwaffe POW camp was opened – *Stammlager der Luftwaffe* (Air Force Camp) at Barth-Vogelsang on the Baltic coast. It became Stalag Luft I (Barth), or simply Luft 1, when Stalag Luft II (Litzmannstadt) opened on the Eastern Front in 1941 (whither a very few RAF POWs were temporarily sent in 1941).

Having persuaded Hitler that the OKL should have control of airmen prisoners, Göring decided that the Luftwaffe would build its own camps for Allied airmen POWs. Furthermore, these camps would be run entirely by Luftwaffe personnel and would be administered by the Territorial Administrative HQ of the Luftwaffe (*Luftgaukommando*). Except for the camps' Kommandants, who were appointed by Göring, the staffs of each camp would be appointed by Oberst Ernst Walde, *Chef der Kriegsgefangenen der Luftwaffe*, who, as head of the Luftwaffe's POW organisation, had full responsibility for the establishment and administration of its camps.

By July 1941, when Stalag Luft I was full of both officers and NCOs, the Luftwaffe was, once again, obliged to purge non-officer newcomers to an army-run camp, this time Stalag VIIIB (Lamsdorf) and also, at the end of that year, to Stalag VIIA (Moosburg). But as the war continued and more and more prisoners of war fell into their hands, neither the army, nor the navy, nor the air force was ever able to provide sufficient accommodation for them all.

Stalag Luft III (Sagan) opened in March 1942, but it is not clear precisely when Stalag Luft IV (Beninia?) or V (Gröditz) opened. Again, they appear to have been used for POWs captured on the Eastern Front, but it is reasonable to assume that they were first used some time between the opening of Stalag Luft III and of Stalag Luft VI (Heydekrug), first opened in June 1943. When the Luftwaffe re-opened old cavalry barracks at Gross Tychow in May 1944 for captured US airmen it became Stalag Luft IV, presumably after the original camp of that number had been closed for whatever reason. Some 350 Americans, resident there by 25 May 1944, would be joined two months later by half of the POWs from Stalag Luft VI (evacuated in July 1944).[3]

The Allies' first intimation that there was to be another camp for aircrew came on 29 April 1944 when the German Foreign Office in Berlin informed the Swiss Legation there that 'Kriegsgefangenenlager 7 Der Luftwaffe (Stalag Luft 7)' had been opened 'at Bankau near Kreuzburg, Upper Silesia'. There was, however, no, repeat no, information regarding its inmates.

The Lufwaffe, employing its own workforce, had begun the construction of the new camp in the spring of 1944, approximately sixty-five kilometres or so east of Breslau (Wroclaw) in a sandy field some 200 metres from a forest. More particularly it was three kilometres from Bankau railway station, one kilometre west of the village of Bankau (now Bąków), and seven kilometres east of Kreuzburg (Kluczbork), just off the main Kreuzburg-Rosenberg (Olesno) road.

The new camp was required following the capture of hundreds of Allied aircrew during the first quarter of 1944 – 1,300 RAF Bomber Command aircrew alone during this period, and a further 865 in the second quarter. In addition, hundreds of USAAF aircrew, mostly from the Eighth Air Force flying bombers from East Anglia, England, were taken prisoner.[4] The majority of these men were sent to an already crowded Stalag Luft VI (Heydekrug). By May 1944, new arrivals were living in a large tent.

Needing, therefore, to provide further accommodation for airmen POWs the Luftwaffe, somewhat optimistically as events were to show, chose to build the new camp, Luft 7, almost directly in the centre of what, in January 1945, would become a massive Soviet offensive.

During its brief life, Luft 7 would be visited on a number of occasions by Albert A. Kadler (a Swiss citizen acting on behalf of the British and US Protecting Power), by the International Red

Cross Committee (IRCC) (also from Switzerland), and by Henry Soderberg of the YMCA (see page 233). Visiting the new campsite on 26 May 1944, representatives of the IRCC noted not only that it was not finished but also an absence of prisoners, hardly surprising as the first POWs would not arrive until 6 June 1944.

Albert Kadler, on his second visit, noted on 15 June 1944 that 'the site itself is well-chosen, pleasant and affords excellent views. It is intended to divide the camp into four self-contained compounds; at present the prisoners of war are accommodated in small huts on a piece of ground which is to form one of the said compounds.' When full, the camp was 'designed to hold from 4 to 5,000 prisoners of war'.

Kadler also noted that, on the day of his visit, there were '107 <u>British</u> prisoners of war, all RAF personnel (non-commissioned officers)'. 'All RAF' was not strictly true, for among the POWs were two NCOs of the SAS and a petty officer of the Fleet Air Arm.

The German word for a group of military men is *Trupp* (troop in English), and they applied this word to a batch of prisoners. Although the camp was far from complete, the first *Trupp* arrived at Luft 7 on 6 June 1944, eleven days after the first Red Cross visit. *Trupp 2* followed a week later, with *Truppen* being admitted at regular intervals thereafter. *Trupp 57* was possibly the last to arrive, possibly on 6 January 1945, when POW numbers 1311-1358 were issued. Although a few more POWs arrived at Luft 7 after that date there appears to be no record of any *Trupp* number for them. With the threat of a Soviet offensive looming, it would appear that the keeping of accurate records at Luft 7 was given a lower priority. In any event the camp was to be evacuated on 19 January 1945.

Note that throughout this book all airmen are RAF unless otherwise stated.

# CHAPTER ONE
## 'A BLOODY CHICKEN FARM'

## TUESDAY, 6 JUNE 1944

At 12.30 pm a train ground slowly to a stop at the railway halt at the small village of Bankau. An hour-and-a-half later, German guards appeared from the nearby POW camp, and opened the doors of the wagons. Seventy tired and dirty Allied prisoners of war, sixty-eight of them RAF aircrew, disembarked, their limbs aching from the cramped conditions of a long journey. It was two days since they had left the Luftwaffe's transit camp at Wetzlar.

F/Sgt John Ross McConnell RCAF was one of them:

> 'While waiting for more guards to come down from the camp, some English "Tommy's" came over to talk to us. These boys had been here for quite some time. They were, what they called, working "Commandos", at present moving some lumber. The guards came over and told them to get back to work, but they didn't pay any attention. They figured they would catch hell, but just laughed it off. The Tommy's figured we must be rather thirsty after our trip, so they brought over an urn of coffee. They stayed and visited us until more guards arrived.'

Formed into a column of march the prisoners stiffly made their way to *Kriegsgefangenenlager der Luftwaffe Nr.7* (Bankau). McConnell again:

> 'After a long walk in heavy rain we arrived at the camp. We didn't mind the rain – the Germans were in it as well. On arrival we were again searched, then documented and given our (POW camp) numbers. I was L7/38. Then we were shown our quarters, a definite apple box. There were no stoves or bunks in any of the huts. Getting settled in was easy – we picked a spot on the floor and that was it.'

F/Sgt John A. 'Jack' Shenton: 'We were dismayed to see the tiny huts we were to occupy, possibly for the duration. This caused someone to remark: "It's a bloody chicken farm."'

Sgt Douglas 'Don' Scopes:

> 'The huts are 18 feet long by 7 feet 6 inches wide, and have an angular roof rising from 5 feet 3 inches to 6 feet 3 inches high. The floors are wooden, and the rest is made of brown stiff cardboard with wooden supports. There are two little windows, one of which is adjustable. The hut contains six four-legged stools and one folding table. There are no stoves or bunks in the huts, so for a bed the palliasses are placed on the wooden floor. Some of the huts lacked the wooden floor.
>
> 'We called the huts "chicken huts" or "dog kennels", and gave each hut a name in addition to its number. It obviously didn't take anyone very long to get settled in, and after this we walked over to the cookhouse where we were given a bowl of soup. The cookhouse was merely one of the huts described above with a side knocked out, and which contained one field-kitchen supervised by German cooks. The latrines were just holes in the ground with a hut placed over the top.'

Sgt John Tomney:

'We marched from Bankau to our camp this afternoon, and it was an amusing sight to see twenty German guards, all old men with fixed bayonets, escorting us along the way. On arriving at the camp we saw nothing but a rye field surrounded by barbed-wire fences, with gun-posts every fifty yards, and a lighting system that had Blackpool beaten to a frazzle. A field-kitchen staffed by a German cook and volunteers from our party cooked the food, mainly soups. German camp orders were pinned up, and we found that we had to be inside the huts from 9 pm until 7 am.'

McConnell:

'Around the camp were a high barbed-wire fence, then no man's land, and then another high barbed-wire fence. About six feet inside this was a warning fence (trip-wire). We were told that if we went inside the warning fence we would be shot. At intervals around the perimeter were look-out towers and searchlights. One guard, sometimes two, were in the towers; they all had rifles, side arms, and some had machine guns. [Strictly speaking, the 'searchlights' were spotlights. The 'trip wire' was a single wire nailed to posts about eighteen inches off the ground.]

'Frank Bishop was in charge of food. For the present all food would be prepared at a field kitchen. We were told that all our supplies would come from Breslau [now Wroclaw]. It was about forty miles west of here, and the food depot for this part of the country. In the centre of the camp was a water-pump.'

Warrant Officer Ken Lane DFC:

'This new camp had been designed in a more escape-proof way, and regard had been taken of weaknesses in other older camps. The result of this was that the latrines, which normally would have been logical places for tunnels, were situated well away from the inner fence. Efforts were made to construct tunnels, but this was done as much to annoy the Germans as for any other reason.' See page 183.

After a thorough search by the guards the seventy prisoners were lined up in alphabetical order for processing – documentation, fingerprinting, and photographing. The *Trupp* number, e.g. 'Tr.1' for this first intake, was then added to the top of each man's camp record card, as was his *Kriegsgefangennummer* (POW number).

Issued with a knife, fork, spoon, mug, bowl, two dark, woollen blankets (later increased to three), a pillow and mattress cover (which they had to fill with wood-shavings) prisoners were allocated six men to a hut, equipped with only one bowl for washing. Kadler's report of 15 June also noted that the men were 'provided with good palliasses and three German blankets each', see the IRCC report of 24 August (page 156).

Sgt John Robinson:

'We were placed six to a hut set in a barley field. Nothing to do all day but talk. No facilities whatsoever. A mobile field kitchen – a boiler on wheels (*Gulaschkanonen*) to cook daily soup. Probably the first real humour was a cartoon which pictured a hut, with a tiny propeller at the front, flying over the fence. The story behind it was that, in our boredom, someone initially whittled a piece of wood in the shape of a propeller and stuck it on top of the hut, where it revolved on a nail. Not to be outdone, the bomber men whittled four propellers, fastened to a stick, which revolved in the wind. The rattling of these devices disturbed the guards during the night, and we were told to take them down. Shortly afterwards a camp news-sheet was circulated with the cartoon.'

The news sheet, edited by F/Sgt Frank Nicklin, was called *POW-WOW*.

It was W/O D.A. 'Den' Blackford who made the propeller and stuck it on top of his hut. In Den's words, it was 'essentially just a propeller that drove a crankshaft and had two wooden men with their hands attached to the cranks working it up and down'. To the Germans, however, it was a highly-suspicious object, absolutely *Verboten*, and they instructed the camp leader and the adjutant to have the fiendish device taken down. No such thing was allowed! Den duly removed it.

When Jim Goode arrived towards the end of July 1944 he noted that 'the huts do not look too impressive, more like rows of garden sheds'. He was not far wrong, for they were cheaply made 'of cardboard and tarred cloth… which are sufficient in warm weather but which will not last through the winter'. (IRCC Report, 24 August 1944.) Albert Kadler, however, had noted that they were 'new wooden "standard-huts", a kind of miniature barrack now used by many service branches all over Germany'. There were 190 of these huts, sixteen of them for special purposes: six for the *Revier* (sick quarters); two for school rooms; two for the library; and one each for the Camp Leader, Man of Confidence, padré, barber, post office, and sports equipment.

*

Camp Commander was Oberstleutnant Behr. He was described by Peter Thomson, later the POW's Camp Leader, as being 'very tall, about 6 feet 2 inches, slimly built, fine features, black moustache. He was suffering from injuries received in the last war, but you couldn't see any of them. He was about forty to fifty. He had been a sergeant-major in the last war, and when Hitler came into power he rose in the ranks of the [Nazi] party.'

Sergeant Andrew 'Mac' McMurdon wrote that the:

'German Commandant at Luft 7 had no experience of prisoners, and was very uncertain how to treat us. He would not allow us to go to the latrine-pit (a trench with a squatter pole) at night. We complained and eventually he agreed to us going straight to the latrine and straight back. We decided to put one across the Huns and, as at that time we had received our Red Cross food parcels, we took the empty cartons under our greatcoats and walked to the latrine with our backs to the guard in the tower. In the latrine we folded the cartons flat and walked back facing the guard.

'We kept this up for about an hour before the guard became suspicious. He blew his whistle, and shouted and screamed. In rushed six armed guards, with dogs, shouting "Tunnel! Tunnel!" Some guards searched under our shack looking for the tunnel, with no success. They thought we were disposing of sand in the latrine and, after some discussion, they decided the tunnel must be in the latrine. So two of them donned high-waist waders and climbed down into the shit, again with no success. The Hun was baffled and, needless to say, we were under close scrutiny for some days and given no rations, but it was worth it.

'One morning at *Appell* (roll call), the Commandant clicked his jackboots, gave the Hitler salute, and said "Good morning, soldiers"; there was a deadly silence, then an Aussie said "Fuck off". We all burst out laughing, so the Commandant gave a sweet smile. Someone must have briefed him because he never said "Good morning, soldiers" again.'

Other camp officers were Oberstleutnant Rackwitz and Major Nölle, while the accompanying officer from the OKW was Hauptmann Schade. Peter Thomson thought that by and large:

'the German staff were fairly good. The commandant Behr was a hard man but would listen to me. Having very little German I always had an interpreter with me – a Canadian called [F/Sgt J.J.] Joe Walkty and he was very good. Major Peschel, who was [later] in charge of the Abwehr [Defence] was a bastard of the first water and we were always having arguments. Captain Wiener, an Austrian, was the man I had most contact with, and he was a real gentleman. Oberfeldwebel Frank was always screaming his head off, but underneath was not too bad. Richard Erffinger, interpreter, was an extremely nice guy and passed on to me some very helpful information as to what was going on.'

It is not clear when the security officer, Major Peschel of the Abwehr, arrived, but he had been serving at Stalag Luft VI (Heydekrug), which had closed on 15 July 1944, and was in post by the time of the IRCC visit on 12 September. Universally loathed, Peter Thomson was to describe him as being:

'a very hard man to deal with, a typical Nazi. He was very strict regarding anyone that came into the camp, and he kept all the members of the Abwehr under him very strictly under control – these are the "ferrets". He is of medium height about 5 feet 9 inches, around 180 pounds, grey hair, he was going a bit bald, blue eyes.'

Thomson added that he was: 'over fifty and well dressed'. He was sure, too, that 'he had a scar somewhere on his face but I don't remember exactly where it was'.

In an affidavit sworn before the Military Department, Office of the Judge Advocate General, in London after the war glider pilot Sgt W.H. Knox declared that Peschel 'was a Luftwaffe [sic] officer.

He was aged about forty to forty-five, height about 5 foot 7 inches, weight about 12 stone, black hair streaked with grey. I believe he had blue eyes, pale complexion, round clean-shaven face, was well built, and had a very erect carriage and a smart military appearance.'

According to the British Man of Confidence, W/O Richard A. Greene RCAF, Major Peschel, formerly of Stalag Luft III [sic], was 5 foot 7 inches tall, weighed 135 pounds, was of a slight build, had grey thinning hair, blue eyes and a sallow complexion. Greene considered that most of the camp's problems could be laid at his door. His behaviour soured relations to such an extent that when prisoners were called for to help rebuild the camp's 'cooler', a row of single, punishment cells in the *Vorlager*, Greene made it quite clear to all that their services were definitely not to be offered (see page 182).

Behr and Peschel would remain at Luft 7 to the end, but other camp officers and guards came and went, among them Oberfeldwebel Frank and, later, Captain Wiener (see page 194).

F/Sgt Len Venus:

> 'Generally, the Germans in charge were strict but correct; they themselves didn't appear to be having a comfortable time. The "ferrets" or "snoops" as some guards were called regularly visited the rooms to hear what was going on, and to try and find the radio receiver. They spoke good English as they had lived in England, Ireland and America etc. prior to the war. They enjoyed chatting, the odd cigarette, and anything else they could find. Some were disillusioned, some not. I remember a German major asking a Welsh chap next to me in the sick ward what he thought of Hitler. The reply was that "He was no bloody good". The officer walked away smiling.'

*

The first prisoners' leaders at Luft 7 were the two non-RAF men who had arrived in *Trupp 1* – Jack Lloyd (Camp Leader – his 'method of running the camp went down like a lead balloon with the more easy-going air force types') and Paul Hill (Man of Confidence, or *Vertrauensmann*). Because of the word 'Air' in their regimental name, these two soldiers – 5882820 Squadron Sergeant-Major John ('Jack' or 'Red') Lloyd, and 5550150 Sergeant Paul Hill – had logically been sent to a camp for airmen – Luft 7 – where others were uncertain as to which unit they belonged. Some believed that they were from the Long Range Desert Group. One prisoner remembered them as 'Paras', while another, who arrived with them at Luft 7, even said that 'Paul Hill was a false identity for a Czech national who spoke poor English, and Jack Lloyd did most of the talking'.

.As some correctly believed, both had been serving in the Special Air Service (SAS), in fact in its 2nd Regiment (2 SAS). Thirty-three-year-old Paul Hill, from Bexley Heath, Kent, had transferred from the Hampshire Regiment, and Jack Lloyd, a thirty-year-old former miner from Wakefield, Yorkshire, from the Northamptonshire Regiment. Both men had been sent to Luft 7 after capture in Italy, on 5 February 1944 and 24 April 1944 respectively, whilst engaged on Operation Maple. (For further on Maple see Appendix V.)

The two SAS men were not at Luft 7 for long because, as Paul Hill later stated, a 'British NCO in Stalag Luft 7 made a statement to the German authorities stating that I was organising escapes, getting in touch [with] the Polish Underground Movement and was a secret service agent'. On 28 July, as a result of this statement by the unnamed NCO, Jack Lloyd's hut was torn apart by the Germans. After morning *Appell*, the main gates swung open and in 'marched twenty goons armed with rifles and fixed bayonets, led by two officers carrying sub-machine guns. They marched straight to the hut occupied by the Camp Leader, adjutant and Man of Confidence and arrested them... Beneath the floorboards two Luger pistols and maps were found.'

The two SAS men were told by the Camp Commandant that, as they were army and not RAF, they were to be sent to Stalag 344 (Lamsdorf). Most of the RAF types were not sorry to see them go, as they had devised a plan of action that would, in theory, get everyone out of the camp. In essence, the Hill/Lloyd plan was to use the two guns to shoot the guards in the towers along the south side of the camp. Having gone through the wire, they would then make for the dense forest about a quarter of a mile away, where Polish partisans, with whom they were already in contact, would hide them all. As Wilf Hodgson[6] remarked: 'How unarmed prisoners would be able to do this without most becoming casualties was difficult to imagine.'

Taken to the civil gaol at nearby Rosenberg and placed in solitary confinement, Hill and Lloyd were removed to Oppeln (Opole) civil gaol on the following day. Here they remained in solitary confinement for forty-five days. John Lloyd: 'During this period I was allowed a half an hour's exercise per day and compelled to work ten hours a day in my cell. I was given as rations two slices of black bread and one litre of soup per day.'[5]

On 9 September the two SAS men were taken by police to Lamsdorf, but were refused entry and were taken back to Oppeln, enduring the same conditions as before. On 21 October they were moved to Stalag 383 (Hohenfels), where they remained until liberation on 16 April 1945. After they had made two unsuccessful attempts to escape from the line of march they successfully escaped at the third time of asking, and made contact with the US 71st Infantry Division in a wood near Renna, Bavaria.

*

After Lloyd and Hill had been removed Jack Lloyd was replaced by twenty-eight-year-old F/Sgt Peter Thomson RAAF, who had failed to return on the night of 15/16 March 1944 (Stuttgart). He had been trying to coax Lancaster LL828 back to England when the fuel ran out over France, and all seven of the crew baled out. Four evaded capture, but the navigator, mid-upper gunner and Peter himself were eventually caught.

Peter had been told by a French woman to go to a certain village where he would find help:

'I kept walking for hours and it was pitch bloody dark by the time I got to the village. Stumbling about I could hear dogs barking everywhere. The next thing I saw was a bit of light under a door. "Bugger it," I thought, so I knocked and an old lady said, "*Entrez*". I told her I was a British airman, she offered food and wine. She said father and the boys were down at the pub enjoying themselves, getting zig-a-zag. Father and the boys came home zig-a-zag. They offered me some wine, and we all started drinking. At about 2 am they started asking questions.'

For several weeks Peter was sheltered by the Resistance but a few weeks later, after there had been a parachute drop, he was caught when the Germans were searching all farms in the area for hidden weapons. Handed over to the Gestapo, he was taken to Creil with American 2nd Lieutenant Roy Goldenberg USAAF,[6] where they were locked up in the cellar of a house:

'It was an awful place, the walls dripped with moisture and there was very little air. There was only one bed and the two of us had to share it for two nights – bloody uncomfortable. They fed us quite well and one of them gave us a couple of cigarettes, which we craved. The following day we talked them into letting us have a shave and a wash – we hadn't performed either operation for almost a week.'

From there Peter was taken to Paris, and spent the next two or three weeks being questioned by the Gestapo at their HQ in the Avenue Foch. When they had finished with him, he was moved to Frankfurt, and 'spent about eighteen horrible days in gaol… at first in solitary confinement which was soul destroying'. At last, on 18 May 1944 he was sent to Dulag Luft (Oberursel), and then to Wetzlar, arriving at Luft 7 in *Trupp 2* on 13 June.

When he had taken off on his fateful operation in March Peter had had no reason to believe that his rank was anything other than flight sergeant, but once at Bankau it became known that he had been commissioned with effect from 18 January 1944. It was usual for an officer to go to an officer camp but, in certain instances, where deemed appropriate, permission could be given for an officer to remain at an NCO camp as its senior officer. On 28 June, therefore, following Jack Lloyd's departure, Peter agreed to being elected Camp Leader. Ken Lane, who was already the appointed deputy, also agreed to carry on in that capacity. Richard Greene had already been appointed Man of Confidence on 21 June. The Quartermaster, W/O Frank Bishop, was another of the arrivals in *Trupp 1*. Jimmy McCutchan RCAF, a thirty-one-year-old gunner, had the dubious honour of being appointed the camp carpenter.

## CHAPTER TWO

# 6 AND 13 JUNE 1944, *TRUPPEN 1 & 2*

After the first *Trupp* had been lined up in alphabetical order, the first POW to be documented at Luft 7 was flight engineer Sergeant John R. Abbott. With him were five of his crew: Warrant Officer Den A. Blackford (pilot); Flight Sergeant P. 'Pud' Hudson (navigator); Flight Sergeant W.A. 'Bill' Brookes (bomb aimer); Sergeant Les J. Tuck (wireless operator); and Sergeant Jack Shenton (rear gunner). The seventh member of the crew, F/O Fred R. Singh RAAF (mid-upper gunner), was elsewhere.

Their journey into captivity had begun on 24 May with a squadron briefing for an attack on the railway yards at Aachen. For this raid, carried out by 264 Lancasters, 162 Halifaxes, and sixteen Mosquitos (eighteen Halifaxes and seven Lancasters were lost) they flew Halifax B.111, LV906, ZA-Q for Queenie, as their regular aircraft, ZA-Z for Zebra, had not yet been equipped with $H_2S$, which all the other crews were using. Two of their regular crew – Sergeant A.G.T. 'Jock' Saunders (killed in action on 23 September 1944), and Sergeant Johnny Pyle (R/G) – had reported sick and were respectively replaced by Les Tuck (on his first op), and Fred Singh who, having only ever flown as a mid-upper gunner, went into that position while the regular mid-upper, Jack Shenton, took the rear turret.

For Den Blackford and crew this was their twentieth operational sortie, including four consecutive trips to Berlin. At 2258 hours Warrant Officer Blackford eased Q-Queenie off Melbourne's runway, the crew keeping a sharp look-out to avoid collision as the sky filled with circling aircraft.

Setting course, they were soon passing high over Belgium, and could see the heavy flak in response to the Pathfinders' red and green target indicator (TI) flares. Den Blackford:

> 'We had bombed the target and were on our way back when, at approximately 0115 hours, we were hit by a night-fighter. We believe it was a Ju88. He fired two bursts – the first one set the fuel tanks in both wings on fire, and both the port engines were knocked out. Fires also broke out in the port wing bomb-bay. Luckily, the bomb-bay doors, which had not locked after I closed them, fell open, and this caused the plane to go into a very steep climb. I say luckily because the second burst from the night-fighter went by underneath the aircraft.'

With the fires out of control, Den gave the order to abandon aircraft. The navigator opened the escape hatch in the floor and baled out, followed by the bomb aimer. The wireless operator, in handing the pilot his parachute, caught his own parachute release handle on a projecting control knob, spilling the canopy in the aircraft. The silken folds were packed into his arms and he baled out. The only casualty during the attack was the Australian mid-upper gunner, Fred Singh, who was badly wounded in the leg by a cannon shell but who nevertheless managed to bale out. Soon captured, he was taken to hospital for treatment.[7]

Jack Shenton, after a short struggle with the rear turret doors, baled out through the fuselage door on the port side. He knew nothing of his descent, having been knocked unconscious by one of his parachute harness buckles as it broke away from the webbing. He woke up on the ground, with his face badly swollen, and minus a flying boot.

Den Blackford now motioned to John Abbott to bale out, but the flight engineer saw the pilot struggling to free himself from his seat-harness and turned back to help him before both baled out. Den was also knocked unconscious for a short while on landing then, hiding his parachute in some bushes, walked all night in a south-westerly direction. Captured near Voeren, Belgium, he was taken after interrogation by the local *Bürgermeister* (Mayor) to a nearby Lufwaffe airfield and introduced to the pilot who claimed to have shot him down.[8] After being fed he was put in the airfield jail, but was awakened during the night when Bill Brookes was thrown into his cell.

Meanwhile, John Abbott was having a few problems of his own:

'I never even remember pulling the rip cord, first a sensation of falling through a black void, then a sudden jerk and I was dangling on the end of my parachute harness. I became aware that my feet were cold and, with some difficulty, looked down and saw that my flying boots had gone. They must have been wrenched off when my parachute opened. Looking down again, I could see long stretches of water, my first thought was canals. I reached for the Mae West inflator when CRASH! I landed flat on my back in a ploughed field.

'My thoughts returned to a few weeks earlier when F/Lt Eric Williams – of "The Wooden Horse" fame – visited the squadron on a lecture tour after he had escaped (along with F/Lt Oliver Philpot and Lieutenant Michael Codner) from Stalag Luft 3, Sagan. He warned us about wearing loose-fitting flying boots, and suggested tying a piece of string under the soles and fastening round the ankles. Needless to say, I did not take his advice. However, shortly after this, the new escape boots with lace-up shoes were being issued, and I endeavoured to obtain a pair from the stores. I was told yes they had them in stock, but had not yet received instructions to issue them. As I sat in a field at 2 am – contemplating my bare feet – all I could think of was those nice new escape boots occupying their shelves in the stores!

'Feeling tired, I rolled up in my parachute and soon fell asleep. It was daylight when I awoke; I made a pair of moccasins out of my Mae West, and remained hidden all day in a field of mustard crop. As it grew dusk I prepared to move.'

John Abbott was captured that night and taken to a police station. The following morning, when he was ordered out of his cell, he was surprised to see 'Pud' Hudson walk out of the next cell. Neither spoke nor showed any recognition as they were taken to a nearby railway station. Shortly afterwards a passenger train with a few box-cars at the back pulled in. As their guard slid open the door and ordered them inside, they saw Den Blackford and Bill Brookes!

Ordered off the train at München-Gladbach, they were handed over to a civilian police escort. As they waited at a tramcar-stop, a queue gradually formed up behind them. It was not until a tram stopped and the airmen got on that some of the crowd recognised their RAF uniforms. The once quiet crowd now became an angry mob, and surged forward. The police escort drew their pistols and stood between the POWs and the hostile civilians. One of the policemen quickly pressed the bell and the tram moved off, taking the airmen out of their grasp.

Disembarking on the outskirts of the city, near the entrance to an airfield, the police escort handed their prisoners over to the Luftwaffe. In the airfield's cells they found Jack Shenton and two other, wounded RAF aircrew, Sergeants Arthur R. 'Chegga' Brice and Cyril Weeks, from the same crew.

Within twenty-four hours, on 30 May, Den Blackford, his crew, Chegga Brice and Cyril Weeks, had arrived at the interrogation centre for airmen (*Auswertungsstelle West*) at Oberursel, seven kilometres (four miles) north west of Frankfurt-am-Main. Following the usual solitary confinement and interrogation, and having had their identity confirmed as bona fide POWs, they were transferred to the Dulag Luft transit camp (*Durchgangslager der Luftwaffe*) at Wetzlar, forty-five kilometres (twenty-eight miles) north of Frankfurt-am-Main. Here, a permanent staff of Allied air force POWs looked after new arrivals, and issued the airmen who were on their way to a POW camp with food and clothing supplied by the International Red Cross.[9]

*

Arthur 'Chegga' Brice and Cyril Weeks had been lost on the same Aachen raid as Den Blackford and crew. They were on Halifax B.III, LW720, NP-W, 158 Squadron, which had taken off from Lissett, Yorkshire, on 24 May with a crew of: F/S John M. Roberts (pilot); F/O W. C. 'Bill' Graham RCAF (navigator); Sergeant Jim H. Wilson (bomb aimer); Sergeant W.M. Rivers (flight engineer); Sergeant Cyril Weeks (wireless operator); Sergeant Arthur R. 'Chegga' Brice (mid-upper gunner); and Sergeant Dennis Davies (rear gunner).

They had just bombed the target when their Halifax was attacked by a night-fighter.[10] Cannon shells blew the top off the mid-upper turret, leaving Chegga Brice sitting in the open air. His silk scarf, knotted at the front, was in shreds after a bullet had passed through the knot and had taken a piece of skin the size of a penny from his Adam's apple. Blood was still running down his neck when he joined John Abbott in his cell after capture.

The attack also left Cyril Weeks with five splinter wounds in his right leg and hip. He and Chegga Brice were captured by soldiers near Puffendorf. Cyril never forgot the help he was given by Den Blackford and 'Pud' Hudson, who carried him from the railway station to Dulag Luft. After his arrival at Luft 7 he spent much of the first few months in the camp's first-aid hut, a proper medical centre having yet to be built.[11]

Jim 'Jock' Wilson also baled out and arrived at Luft 7 on 13 June. Bill Graham became a POW at Stalag 6G (Berg Neustadt). John Roberts, Bill Rivers, and Dennis Davies were killed, and now lie in the large British War Cemetery at Rheinberg, near Essen.

*

158 Squadron lost a second Halifax on the Aachen raid on 24/25 May, Halifax B.III LV918, NP-O, with its crew of: F/L Ralph Reavill (pilot); F/O Walter J. Rogers (navigator); F/O Joe E. Hounam DFM (bomb aimer); F/L Cedric C. Fox DFM (flight engineer); F/S Robert E. Hardwick (wireless operator); F/S Frank A. Spriggs (mid-upper gunner); and F/S Donald A. Stewart RCAF (rear gunner).

Frank Spriggs:

'We left the briefing room feeling quite cheerful as it should not be a very hard target – just a few searchlights, a little light flak, and the usual night-fighters. That's what the intelligence officer said at his briefing! Our attack was due at 0100 hours, and a second wave at 0200 hours.

'We took off at 2255 hours, and crossed the enemy coast at about 19,000 feet. As our bombing height was to be 15,000 feet we slowly began to lose height. We were about half an hour flying time from the target when the navigator told the pilot that we would be over the target five minutes or more before our time to bomb, so we had better fly a short dog-leg. We did this, but were still a couple of minutes in front of the other kites.

'The skipper said: "The markers are going down dead ahead." The bomb aimer got into his position in the nose and set his bomb-sight. Just as we started the bombing run, I noticed what looked like sparks shooting out from the starboard inner engine. Suddenly there was a tremendous belch of flames from the same engine. Within seconds the whole engine was a mass of flames, and then the plane went into a dive with a long trail of flame and sparks behind her.

'From my turret, I looked down on the burning engine. The flames were spreading out to the outboard engine and the fuselage. All the metal seemed to be buckling and white hot. Over the intercom, I heard the bomb aimer tell the pilot to jettison the bombs. Then the pilot said, very quietly and with no sign of panic, "The bomb-doors won't open. I'm sorry chaps, but I can't hold her. I think you'll have to bale out." Then the engineer's voice "You'd better get them out quick, because she's going to blow up any second."

'The skipper's voice saying "Okay chaps, bale out" woke me up from the dream I thought I was in. God! This can't be happening to me. I climbed out of my turret, pulled off my helmet and oxygen mask, reached down and found my parachute which I clipped on to my chest. I then crawled under the turret and back to the escape exit. As I opened the door, the force of the slip-stream blew it up. I looked down – everything was red with flames. I sat on the edge of the opening and put my legs down into space. They were immediately blown back. I grasped hold of the ripcord handle with my left hand and prepared to push myself out with my right, when suddenly something hit me on my head and face, and I remembered no more.

'The bomb aimer told me, at a later date, that after we got the order to bale out, he clipped on his 'chute. Then suddenly the plane exploded and he was blown out of the nose. The rear gunner also said that on hearing the order, he rotated the turret, opened the door, grabbed his 'chute and put it on, and rolled out of his turret backwards. He was unable to get clear because one foot was caught in the door. Then the plane exploded and he was blown clear. I presume that I was also blown out by the explosion.

'When I came to, I couldn't remember anything. I found I was laying on a bunk with two German soldiers standing guard over me. Also there were six or seven boys of ages fourteen to sixteen, with white arm bands, peering at me as though I was some wild animal. They had removed my 'chute harness and Mae West, and all my personal belongings, including my watch.

'Then I found my head and face were covered in blood, and I could hardly move my neck. I felt all over myself to see if I had broken any bones but, luckily for me, I was intact. Suddenly the silence of the night was shattered by the air-raid siren. Immediately the soldiers and the boys blew out the lamps and ran outside, locking the door as they went. I presume they must have gone to the shelters. I heard the sound of aircraft, then my brain seemed to wake up and I thought "God, this is the second attack!" The roar of the aircraft increased and then the bombs began to fall. Wave after wave came over and dropped their load. The bombs came shrieking down, and the explosions were ear-splitting. The small building that I was in began to shake. Then part of the roof was smashed in, the door was blown off its hinges, and glass from a little window over my head began to shower down on me. As I was tossed up and down on the bed, I thought this must be the end.

'The attack lasted about ten minutes. It ended with the same abruptness as it started, and everything was quiet again. I got up from the bunk and tried to get out of the door, but it had been jammed by the bombs and I couldn't open it. I then heard the soldiers coming back, so I went and lay on the bed again. They had quite a job breaking the door in. After a while five more soldiers arrived. They had a good look at me, and after searching me again, motioned me to get up and go with them. When I got outside the little shack, I could see by the light of the fires that it was a signal box about 300 yards from the marshalling yards. All around were bomb craters, burning railway wagons, and twisted rails. The whole yard was a mass of flames.

'After marching along the railway lines away from the yards, we entered a house that I found was an army headquarters. I was taken into a room in which were two high-ranking officers and a young girl who, I later found out, was an interpreter. I was searched again, then one of the officers started to question me in broken English. I told him my name, rank and serial number. Then he asked me what I was flying in, how many were in my crew, and other questions pertaining to the raid. My reply was that I was instructed to give only my name, rank and serial number. At this point he took out his pistol and pointed it at my head. I got very scared and thought he was going to shoot me. The second officer spoke to him, and after a while he put the gun away – much to my relief. I was then made to pick up all my gear, taken out into the street, and then marched down the road with many guards armed with Tommy guns all around me.

'It was about 5 am and just getting light. As we marched through the town I could see it had suffered heavy damage. We passed a large group of Hitler Youth in their brown shirts with swastika armbands. They sang as they marched, and each one carried a shovel. I found out afterwards that they were going to help clear up the bomb damage. It was now getting lighter, and a lot of people who were digging through the bomb damage began to crowd around me, yelling and shaking their fists. Then some started to throw rocks. My guards raised their guns and threatened to shoot. As we continued to march the crowd got larger, and I was relieved when we entered a large army barracks.'

Frank Spriggs and Donald Stewart were sent to Luft 7. Joe Hounam also became a POW, camp not known. (Joe remained in the RAF until 1959.) The rest of the crew were killed in the attack by a Bf110 night-fighter fitted with twin upward-firing cannons (*Schräge Musik*).[12]

*

On 19 May 1944 the *London Gazette* announced the award of the DFC to 1314755 Warrant Officer Kenneth Albert Lane, 83 Squadron:

'This warrant officer was the pilot of an aircraft detailed to attack Munich one night in April 1944. When approaching the target the aircraft was illuminated by the searchlights and subjected to heavy fire from the ground defences. The starboard inner engine was hit by shrapnel and caught fire. Soon afterwards a second engine was hit and burst into flames. Undeterred, Warrant Officer Lane continued his bombing run and pressed home his attack. Afterwards, the flames in the burning engines were quelled and course was set for home with two engines out of action. A little later, as a result of a fault in the petrol system, a third engine began to fail. Warrant Officer Lane promptly ordered the crew to jettison all moveable equipment, including guns, in an effort to maintain height. Considerable height was lost, however, before one of the defective engines could be restarted, but then Warrant Officer Lane flew on at low altitude and finally reached base. He displayed great skill, courage and devotion to duty in the face of a dangerous and difficult situation.'

Less than a month after the Munich raid on 24/25 April, twenty-three-year-old Ken Lane, on his fourteenth operational sortie with 83 (PFF) Squadron, took off from Coningsby, Lincolnshire on the evening of 22 May 1944 in Lancaster B.III ND963 OL-H for Harry, with his crew of F/S A. 'Taffy' Jones (navigator); F/S Donald E. Cope (bomb aimer); F/S R.F. 'Dick' Raymond (flight engineer); WO1 J.S.A. Aspinall RCAF (wireless operator); F/S S.J. Hall DFM (mid-upper gunner); and F/S E.A. 'Dave' Davies (rear gunner). Their target was Brunswick.

En-route, Lancaster H-Harry was attacked by a night-fighter flown by Hauptmann Werner Husemann, Stab 1./NJG3, for his eighteenth victory. So severe was the damage to the Lancaster that Ken struggled to control the aircraft and, as smoke and flames filled the cockpit, he watched helplessly as the instrument panel melted. With him pinned to his seat, the aircraft plummeted earthwards. Suddenly, it exploded and, still trapped in his seat, Ken was blown out.[13] Suffering minor burns, he was captured by armed Dutch police near Roswinkel.

Dick Raymond freed the jammed nose escape hatch, and baled out just before the port wing came off, but Don Cope, tangled up with the front guns, was blown clear still holding his observer-type parachute pack by its canvas handle. He achieved the almost impossible task of clipping it onto his harness as he fell in the darkness.[14] Stan Aspinall, badly wounded in the leg, passed out, and only regained consciousness on the ground with his opened parachute by his side. Stan Hall, Taffy Jones and Dave Davies were killed, and are buried, side by side, in the cemetery at Nieuw Dordrecht, Holland.

Ken Lane had been put up for a commission before this fateful operation, but it was not promulgated in the London Gazette until 25 July, with a seniority date of 27 April 1944 and number 177324. He was promoted flying officer on 24 November 1944 but, so far as the Luftwaffe were concerned, he was still a warrant officer, and therefore went to Luft 7, as did Don Cope and Dick Raymond. Stan Aspinall, treated for his injuries at Stalag IXC, arrived shortly afterwards. He was kept in the medical compound and eventually repatriated to Canada.

*

Bob Lloyd (later Lloyd-Davies) was born in Colwyn Bay, North Wales. Having joined the Stoke-on-Trent police in January 1936, he transferred to the Chester police in 1941. Although in a reserved occupation he joined the RAFVR in March 1943, and was called up four months later. After radio school, and because he had a knowledge of German, he was posted to 214 Squadron, 100 (Bomber Support) Group. These specialist aircraft, employed on radio counter-measure duties such as the detection and jamming of enemy radio and radar equipment, usually flew in support of RAF Bomber Command's main force.

On 24/25 May 1944, Flying Fortress SR384, 214 Squadron, was supporting the attack on the Ford motor factory at Antwerp. Bob flew as a spare wireless operator/air gunner in this aircraft, with P/O Allan J.N. Hockley RAAF (pilot); F/S Tommy D. Glenn (navigator); Sergeant W.W. 'Bill' Hallett (flight engineer); F/S Paul T. 'Tom' Lyall RAAF (wireless operator); Sergeant Ray Simpson (mid-upper gunner); F/S R.Y. 'Bob' Gundy RNZAF (port waist gunner); Sergeant J.E. 'Jim' McCutchan RCAF (starboard waist gunner); Sergeant E. N. 'Nick' Lovatt (rear gunner).

Bob Lloyd recalls:

'It was early morning (25 May) and we were on our way out from Antwerp when we were hit by flak. The first shell passed through the fuselage, between Tom Lyall and me, bursting overhead. I was opening a flask of coffee at the time and that also burst. The second shell exploded below, and the third in the port-inner engine which caught fire. Our skipper, P/O Hockley, put the aircraft into a dive in an attempt to put out the fire, but without success and he ordered us to jump. I ejected the escape-door and we – Jim

McCutchan, Tom Lyall, Tommy Glenn, Bob Gundy, and I – assembled to bale out. Bob made to jump and then went back to look at the fire; this happened three times. I had had enough by this time and made to jump, but was blown back against the fuselage and got stuck in the hatch, and I had to be pushed out.

'I ditched in the deep flooded areas on the island of Tholen, and eventually made my way to an abandoned flooded farmhouse. I was making myself comfortable when I heard someone outside and, quietly looking through a bedroom window, I saw Tommy Glenn. You can imagine our delight, although we were worried about Bob Gundy, who would have been last out from our position in the waist.

'Meanwhile, Tommy and I were watching movements on the dyke about 300-400 yards away – German and police patrols! Beyond the dyke we had seen barges. There is no doubt that Jerry knew we were not far away, and on an island without food we could not get very far. However, the next morning we decided to make a try. As it was becoming twilight we made a raft for our few possessions and set off for the dyke. But we were spotted by some Dutchmen in a boat, and taken to a small farmhouse by one of them.

'We were made welcome and very well fed. Two of the family gave up their beds for us, and made us feel at home. I spoke good Dutch at that time, having worked in Holland in the early 30s, so we got on quite well together. The next morning the Germans were searching for us and picked us up. The farmer's wife was very distressed; she had earlier asked me "When are you coming?" Little did I know when I replied "Wait a while, it won't be long". I had lost one of my flying boots when I landed in the water, but she gave me a pair of Wellington boots. The Germans promised to return them when I had been supplied with other footwear.

'Our first place of detention was in a small wooden hut used as an office in a sailing-boat yard on Tholen. We were left for quite some time in this, quite unguarded. Tommy and I decided to stay put. Eventually we were taken to a Luftwaffe station at Bergen-op-Zoom, where I was given a pair of boots in exchange for the Wellingtons. From Bergen-op-Zoom we were taken by train to Venlo,[15] where about 100 of us were "billeted" in an evacuated convent, before being sent on to Dulag Luft.

'When we all eventually met up at Luft 7, we asked Bob Gundy why he did not jump in the first instance, and he replied: "I didn't want to be the first out. I'd heard of aircraft getting back after some of the crew baled out!" This is understandable, as the intercom had been damaged and he, and Jim McCutchan, had not heard the skipper. I have no doubt at all that our pilot held the aircraft as steady as he could to enable us to get out. I heard afterwards that our mid-upper gunner had lost his parachute in the dive, and the skipper would try and ditch. That is the last we heard of them. They probably ditched in the North Sea.

Records suggest the aircraft came down in the Oosterschelde, the fifteenth victory of night-fighter pilot Oberleutnant Hermann Leube, 4./NJG3, who claimed his victim was a Halifax. The bodies of the pilot and mid-upper gunner were recovered, and were buried on the island of Zuid-Beveland.

Tommy Glenn wrote later in his diary (now held by his daughter-in-law Roz Glenn):

'In memoriam P/O Hockley, Alan James Noel, our "skipper" and pilot, who gave his life, so that we may live, remaining at the controls of the aircraft, thus allowing all but one of us to parachute to safety. He was a native of Sydney, Australia, aged twenty-six, who was always tolerant, generous, sporting and certainly one of the best pilots in the RAF or RAAF.'

F/S John Ross 'Mac' McConnell, from Lanigan, Saskatchewan, Canada, was one of three brothers serving in the RCAF. Following training as an air gunner, he was posted to 196 Squadron at Witchford, Cambridgeshire, as a rear gunner on Stirlings. The squadron's operations varied from bombing and mine-laying to dropping agents and supplies to the Resistance Movement, often in the areas of Le Mans and St Etienne, France. Mac was later transferred to 425 (Alouette) Squadron,[16] RCAF, operating Halifaxes out of Tholthorpe, Yorkshire. He flew as a 'spare' gunner, operating only when one of the crews was short of a gunner: 'Rather tough to fly this way, but I wanted to finish my tour.'

On 8/9 May 1944, 425 Squadron joined others from 6 and 8 Groups in a raid on the railway yards and locomotive sheds at Haine-St-Pierre, northern France. The crew were: Flight Officer[17] L. White USAAF (pilot); F/S J.R. Lefebvre RCAF (navigator); Sergeant J.A.A. Aubrey RCAF (bomb aimer); Sergeant J.H. Chant (flight engineer); WO2 A.A. Cornier RCAF (wireless air gunner); Sergeant J.E.M. Beluse RCAF (mid-upper gunner); F/S J.R. McConnell RCAF (rear gunner); and Sergeant R.C. Brown RCAF (under gun). The aircraft took off at 0125 hours on 9 May with a bomb load of 8 x 1,000lb and 7 x 500lb MCs.

Mac McConnell:

> 'This raid was to be my sixteenth trip, and I first met the crew at our briefing. The pilot was F/O White, and Brown was from Saskatchewan, Cornier from Alberta, and Aubrey, Beluse and Lefebvre from Quebec. I don't recall their first names or their crew positions – they were new on the squadron... Our aircraft was a Halifax B.III, LK798, KW-A for Apple, and on this trip I was the rear gunner. Shortly after bombing the target we were attacked by a night-fighter.[18] I was wounded in the right leg and suffered many lacerations to my face and hands. I managed to bale out, but broke my leg and damaged my shoulder on landing. I was captured by German soldiers south of Brussels and taken to Courtrai. From there I began the long journey to Dulag Luft and Luft 7. I don't know what happened to the rest of the crew.'

Cornier evaded capture (he was flown back from Belgium to RAF Northolt on 23 September 1944), while Aubrey, Beluse and Chant went to Stalag Luft VI (Heydekrug) and then to Stalag 357. White and Lefebvre were killed. Roy Brown was betrayed and taken prisoner. Imprisoned with many other captured aircrew in St Gilles prison in Brussels, he escaped when the train taking them to Germany in September 1944 was forced to turn back by patriotic Belgians.[19]

*

On 9 May 1944 Typhoon-equipped 266 (Rhodesia) Squadron, at RAF Hurn, was detailed for an evening 'Ramrod' sortie. The SORB records that:

> '8 of our aircraft, plus 193, 197 and 257 Squadrons, bombed the marshalling yards at Rouen. The target was bombed from 11,000 to 6,000ft and the results were considered excellent on bridge and rail junctions. One small ship was hit. Sergeant McMurdon was possibly hit by light Flak and headed South at 6,000ft with glycol streaming from his engine. Two in a day! A bit much.'

Twenty-four-year-old Sergeant Andrew O. 'Mac' McMurdon from Salisbury (now Harare), Southern Rhodesia, had taken off in Typhoon JR306[20] at 1715 hours:

'Shortly after releasing my 2 x 500lb bombs on the target, my Typhoon was hit by flak. I baled out near Rouen, and when my parachute opened German soldiers on the ground opened fire on me. I took a dim view of this, especially as I was falling into their hands. I emptied my parachute and fell into a wheat field, where three Germans jumped over the surrounding wall and opened up on me again – fortunately I wasn't hit. I was then taken prisoner and locked up in a jail.

'Four days later I was taken into an underground bunker and pushed into a room where, to my surprise, there was another Rhodesian – Bill Baillie – also from my squadron. He had been shot down in the morning.'

Hence the comment 'Two in a day! A bit much.'

F/O C.W. 'Bill' Baillie had taken off in Typhoon MM981 at 1015 hours with seven other aircraft to attack an ammunition dump near Dieppe. The SORB records:

'Took off with 197 and 257 Squadrons as 24 aircraft. Target was bombed from S.S.E. to N.N.W. from 11,000 to 5,000ft. 75% of bombs were seen to fall in target area which was smothered in smoke, but no explosions were seen from the ammo dump. F/O Baillie was last seen heading South at 6,000ft streaming Glycol and saying that his radiator temperature was excessive.'

The SORB also records:

'A fine day. 8 aircraft in the morning and bombed what was supposed to have been an ammo dump, the bombing was excellent but unfortunately the dump wasn't there. F/O Baillie had engine trouble over the target area and was last seen heading inland having called up saying he was going to bale out. He has an excellent chance of being safe.'

'Mac' McMurdon continues:

'Bill Baillie and I introduced ourselves, with four Germans watching us to see if we knew each other and what we had to say. In Rhodesia (now Zimbabwe) we have a mixed native language called *chi-lapa-lapa*, which we use when speaking to the locals. I spoke to Bill in this lingo and there were looks of amazement on the Huns' faces as they hadn't a clue.

'We were later taken to Dulag Luft, and spent a grim time there in solitary confinement with endless interrogation, and mental torture to break one down. I was told that I would be handed over to the Gestapo, but this did not happen. At the beginning of the trip to Luft 7 I was given soup at a transit camp [Bill Baillie was sent to Stalag Luft 3]. I will always remember the cloth banner above the kitchen which read "I had no shoes and I murmured, until I saw a man with no feet". I believe it is an Arabian proverb.' ['I murmured because I had no shoes, until I met a man who had no feet' is a more common version of this Persian saying.]

*

Some 22,000 flight engineers were trained at RAF St Athan, South Wales, during the war, among them nineteen-year old John Robinson from West Hartlepool. He then made up a crew with P/O

John Booth (pilot); F/O Arthur L. Hill RCAF (navigator); F/S J. MacGregor (bomb aimer); F/S Derrick G. Bicknell (wireless operator); Sergeant John Terry (mid-upper gunner); and Sergeant Tom Moffet (rear gunner). Posted to 166 Squadron (1 Group) with Lancasters at RAF Kirmington (now Humberside Airport), they arrived on the squadron during the first week of 1944, and began operations in February.

They had completed twenty operations, including the very costly raids on Nuremberg (24/25 March) and Mailly-le-Camp (4/5 May), when their luck ran out. On 19/20 May they flew in Lancaster ME775 on a raid on the Orléans railway yards. 118 Lancasters and twenty-four Mosquitos of Nos. 1 and 8 (PFF) Groups carried out an accurate attack on the target, but several 166 Squadron crews reported having seen a Lancaster going down in flames near Paris on the way to it.

This was ME775, the only Lancaster that failed to return. John Robinson:

> 'Our shooting down marked the one and only time we were attacked by a fighter. It was a black night and we had made a practice of not firing at shadows. We had corkscrewed at the rear gunner's request, and were straightening out when he said that he could see a light, but could not make out if it was on the ground or in the air. A phrase he often used.
>
> 'However, he had just got halfway through the sentence when I saw tracer whipping by under my feet as I squatted in the nose dropping "Window". The starboard wing lit up, we were fully loaded and the bombs were jettisoned by the bomb aimer, who then removed the nose escape hatch. He pointed to go, and I went, losing a boot as I left. I landed between Dreux and Chartres, and was captured by Gendarmes near Arounville [Arnouville] on 21 May.'

After solitary confinement and interrogation at Dulag Luft, John Robinson went to Luft 7.

*

Derrick Bicknell remembered that 'as far as I can recall we were attacked by a German night-fighter a little after midnight. We were shot down near Jumeauville, and I was picked up by a German patrol the following day.' He went to Stalag Luft VI (and Stalag 357), while Arthur Hill and J. MacGregor went to Luft 3. Tom Moffet was hidden by a French farmer in Goussonville until being liberated by the US Army and returned to the UK on 26 August. John Booth and John Terry (aged nineteen years) were killed and are buried in France.

It is not certain who shot them down, but Oberleutnant Jakob Schaus, 4./NJG4, was the only German night-fighter pilot to claim a Lancaster on this night. Though several other Lancasters were lost on operations to other French targets they were all lost to light flak. Schaus was himself to be killed in action on 2 February 1945, by which time he had twenty-three victories to his name.

*

Having qualified as a wireless operator at No. 2 Radio School, Yatesbury, Wiltshire, Don Scopes went to No. 7 Air Gunners School, Stormy Down, South Glamorgan, Wales, to train as an air gunner. From Wales he was posted to 19 OTU at Kinloss, Morayshire, Scotland, and then to 1663 Heavy Conversion Unit at Rufforth, Yorkshire. After he had flown operations on 102 and 78 Squadrons, and after instruction at the PFF Navigation Training Unit at Warboys, Huntingdonshire, he and his crew were posted to 635 (PFF) Squadron.

On 21/22 May 1944 510 Lancasters and twenty-two Mosquitos of Bomber Command carried out the first major raid in over a year on Duisburg, the largest inland port in Germany. Though accurate Oboe sky-marking was achieved over a cloud-covered target, twenty-nine Lancasters were lost, among them Lancaster ND450[21], F2-Y for Yoke, 635 (PFF) Squadron, with its crew of F/S P.S.M. Robinson (pilot); F/S H. 'Hank' Parker (navigator); Warrant Officer Ken G. Taylor RCAF (Obs/bomb aimer); Sergeant Frank C.V. Tuck (flight engineer); Sergeant Douglas R. 'Don' Scopes (wireless operator/air gunner); Sergeant C. Shaw (mid-upper gunner); and Sergeant R. 'Shorty' Stuart (rear gunner).

Taking off from Downham Market at 2253 hours (21 May) and having marked and bombed the target, ND450 was on its way home when it was hit by flak between Rotterdam and the Dutch coast. The SORB recorded:

> '"Y" F/S P.S.M. Robinson hit by flak. Starboard outer caught fire, Nav II Warrant Officer Taylor and Sergeant Scopes baled out over Holland. Aircraft recovered, despite injuries to Pilot and Flight Engineer. Landed at Manston (0315 hrs), no pressure on brakes, and taxied off runway into petrol bowser. Pilot and flight engineer detained Station sick quarters, Manston. Remainder of crew safe and uninjured.'

Having baled out in all the confusion Don Scopes landed in a potato field a few kilometres west of Rotterdam at about 2 to 3 am (22 May). With no idea where he was, he wandered off along a rough track, as three searchlights pierced the overcast sky in the distance. The searchlights went out, and it started to rain, but it stopped soon after. Seeing a farmhouse with a light on, Don decided to take a chance. Opening the door, he was inside before anyone could stop him. To the three men in the room, he announced that he was 'RAF'. A lot of talk followed, none of which Don could understand, before one of the men said 'Come', and led him off to another farm. There he was given 'black bread (horrible) and some cheese (worse still) and some milk (very good)'.

Some while later Dutch police arrived and escorted him on foot to the German commandant at Maassluis. In the afternoon two guards took him by electric train to Rotterdam, where they changed to a steam train for Tilburg and, after a short bus ride, reached a German camp. Don was given a thorough search and interrogation. He was released from his cell after over 16 hours and, to his relief, found that 'four other RAF chaps' were there too, 'whose presence bucked me up more than it's possible to say'. The five prisoners were marched to the local railway station and caught the train to Amsterdam, and to their next prison.

Early next morning, 24 May, Don briefly saw Ken Taylor in the same prison. Three days later the RAF prisoners were assembled and taken by train to Amsterdam and then to Venlo and another prison. There was, as Don said, a lovely view from the cell window, and a crowd of Dutch folk assembled and gave the prisoners the 'V' for Victory sign. The German guards took a dim view of this and threatened to shoot anyone who put his head out of the window.

The prisoners vegetated in Venlo until 31 May, when they were taken via Cologne, Mainz and Frankfurt to Oberursel for interrogation. On 2 June they were moved to the Wetzlar transit camp, and on 4 June began the long journey to Bankau, on which Don and Ken were re-united. On the train they managed 'to get two corner seats, seats wooden, bars on window'. The carriage was very crowded and, not surprisingly, was very uncomfortable. On 6 June the train came to a halt at Bankau. *Trupp 1* had arrived.

*

Another victim of night-fighters on the Duisburg raid on 21/22 May was Lancaster ND956, AS-I for Item, 166 Squadron, also shot down on the way home, with its crew of: F/S Trevor G. Franklin (pilot), F/S Bruce F. Bird (navigator), Sergeant Stanley D. Spencer RCAF (bomb aimer), Sergeant John F. Tomney (flight engineer), Sergeant James Kiltie (wireless operator/air gunner), Sergeant Andrew A. Anderson RCAF (mid-upper gunner), and Sergeant John Moffat (rear gunner).

John Tomney:

'We took off from Kirmington at about 2230 hours to attack Duisburg. Having reached the target without meeting any enemy defences, we went in and bombed. On our return trip, when we were within two minutes of Amsterdam, we were illuminated by night-fighter flares. The next minute our port wing was ablaze, and cannon shells were exploding in the fuselage.[22] Our skipper said: "Out you get, boys." I went forward and jettisoned the escape-hatch, losing one of my flying boots in the operation – the other I lost when I baled out at approximately 21,000 feet.

'On the way down, I began to think would I drop in the sea. Remembering there was a God, I began to pray – praying that if I dropped in the sea he would make things easy. After having floated down for about two or three minutes I began to go through thick layers of cloud, and it was very cold. The cloud broke and I could see the ground coming up to meet me. Before I knew where I was, I was struggling for dear life in a dyke. After managing to rid myself of my parachute, I clambered out of the dyke, took off my Mae West, shook myself, and felt utterly lost.'

Having landed near Hardinxveld, on the banks of the River Waal:

'I began to walk along a cart track and before long I came to a mill. Having got the miller and his wife out of bed, I was able to dry my wet clothes. I slept until about 6 am when the miller handed me a cup of tea, an egg, and bread and cheese. Never have I been more surprised in my life when a Dutch policeman walked in, said "Good morning", shook hands with me, and then said "God save the King". Shortly after, another policeman arrived and I was taken to the police station at Sleivgort. At about 11 am the *Feldgendarmes* [military police] arrived and I was moved to their headquarters at Dordrecht. I believe it was there that I met Bruce Bird, our navigator.

'We were then taken on to Tilburg and put into single cells. The Germans woke us in the morning (23 May) and we were assembled at the entrance to the jail, where I saw F/O J.W. Reilly – the pilot of G-George [Lancaster ND579, letter possibly M not G]. Also among us was Sergeant Don Scopes. Following a train journey to Amsterdam, we spent six days solitary confinement at a military barracks. The food we were given was good, and there was enough of it to satisfy a body.

'In the afternoon of 28 May we were moved by bus to Venlo, and put in a prison that used to be a convent. I was in a room with Don Scopes and a Canadian, Warrant Officer Ken Taylor. On the 31 May we were moved to Dulag Luft. There I met many USAAF boys and their courage and fortitude was bang on. They just didn't give a damn for the Hun. 2 June saw us moved to the transit camp at Wetzlar. There I met John Robinson and Ron Bland who were both on the same engineers' course as me. John was also on my squadron.'

John Tomney and Bruce Bird were sent to Luft 7, as were Robinson, Bland, Scopes and Taylor, all in *Trupp 1*. The rest of the crew of ND956 were buried at Goudriaan.

**13 JUNE 1944.** *Trupp 2* (thirty-seven men) arrived, two of whom were recovering from wounds and had come from a *Lazarett* (hospital).

The first of the group to be documented was Sergeant Edmund 'Paddy' Adair from Belfast, a wireless operator/air gunner on 630 Squadron operating Lancasters out of East Kirkby, Lincolnshire. He and his crew of P/O E. 'Ted' Champness RAAF (pilot); F/S V.S.J. Stan Zucker RAAF (navigator); Sergeant G. Naugler RCAF (bomb aimer); Sergeant J. Johnstone (flight engineer); Sergeant Les 'Titch' Jones (mid-upper gunner); and Sergeant A. Pickering (rear gunner), were shot down on 22/23 May 1944 (Brunswick), in Lancaster JB546. It was Paddy's ninth operation:

> 'At 1.20 am (23 May) I spotted two fighters on the "Fishpond", and informed the two gunners. I had to take a message from base HQ and as I was taking the broadcast number the fighters attacked and cannon shells were flying around us. I immediately switched over to the intercom and heard the pilot ordering us to put on our parachutes, as the starboard inner engine was on fire. Then he had a roll call and all the crew, except the rear gunner, said they were OK. On the first attack, the starboard inner engine and the bomb-bays were on fire. The mid-upper turret (and probably the rear turret), and the rudder-bar were shot up, so the pilot could not corkscrew the aircraft. When the bomb aimer informed the pilot that the bomb bays were on fire, and asked if he should jettison the bombs, the pilot said: "No, we will carry on to the target."
>
> 'We were sitting ducks when the fighters attacked again. I believe the petrol tanks exploded, and the navigator, mid-upper gunner and I were blown out of the Lancaster. I always thought that my pilot should have been awarded the Victoria Cross. While trying to put out the fire, I was struck a glancing blow by a cannon shell on the right side of my head, and knocked unconscious. When I came to I was in the air. I immediately went for my 'chute, but it was not on my chest. I looked up and saw it above my head. The two bits of cord, which held my 'chute on to the main harness, had broken. I tried to pull the rip-cord, but nothing happened as my right hand was injured. I then ripped open the 'chute with my left hand – which had the tops of three fingers missing. My 'chute opened, but as it caught my weight I was hanging in a large tree. I reckon that I must have fallen 25,000 feet unconscious. I landed near Quackenbrück, and was captured by the Luftwaffe.'[23]

Stan Zucker:

> 'The plane was strafed from tail to nose. I made my way forward to assist the pilot, and the wireless operator and the mid-upper gunner started to go to the rear. Then the plane went into an uncontrolled dive and blew up. The wireless operator and the mid-upper gunner were blown clear when the tail broke away. I was apparently blown through the Perspex canopy above the pilot, and knocked unconscious. I regained consciousness a few seconds before an unceremonious landing on the barbed wire fence of a military camp – but on the outside, luckily! Somehow my 'chute had miraculously opened. I can still remember my panic-stricken search for the rip-cord as I touched down. My injuries were: a broken rib, left knee badly contused, right ankle sprained, and a gashed head.
>
> 'I landed near Quackenbrück (north west of Osnabrück), and I decided that I had better find a hiding place. I chose a nice thicket of brambles and bracken, and went off into a deep sleep. Sometime during the morning I was awakened by voices. I then realised that I had selected the only clump of bushes on the village green. After a nerve-racking day, as it grew dark, I moved out.'

Despite his injuries, Stan Zucker evaded capture for four days, before he was caught by police in a field of wheat near Lingen. Taken to a police station, and later handed over to the CO of a fighter squadron, he was locked up in the airfield's guardhouse. 'Paddy' Adair and Stan Zucker arrived at Luft 7 together. Together with 'Titch' Jones, who had arrived on 6 June, they were the only survivors. At the end of June Paddy and another RAF POW with a broken spine (probably Warrant Officer Geoff Haworth – see page 41) were transferred to Stalag 344 (Lamsdorf) for hospital treatment.

'Paddy', who returned to Luft 7 in October, related an interesting event which, although not directly related to Luft 7, merits inclusion:

'I was born in Wetteren, Belgium, where I lived until I was seven years old. Consequently, I could speak Flemish and understand a little German. On my second operation (Schweinfurt 26/27 April 1944) I discovered how the Germans were defeating the wireless operators' tinselling efforts. On all squadrons the wireless operators were briefed before we left on ops to search a certain range of frequencies which the German night-fighters were using that night. When we crossed the enemy coast, I was searching my band of frequencies, and I picked up two German night-fighter pilots. So I pressed my key. All British bombers had a microphone near an engine, and on pressing the transmitter key, this sent the engine noise through the air over a range of 100 miles.

'When I lifted my key the German pilots were cursing and swearing at receiving the engine noise in their earphones, and I had a good laugh to myself. They went off the air, and I marked the frequency on my transmitter with a pencil. I kept on searching, and about a half hour later a perfect English voice was repeating one to ten on the same frequency that the German night-fighters were using. It was a very strong signal, at first I thought it was one of our Pathfinders giving a tuning transmission. But then I thought the RAF wireless operators say "Fife" for Five, "Niner" for Nine, and "Zero" for Ten. So I knew it was a powerful German transmitter, controlled by the German radar system. As you know, the German and enemy territory was split up into squares, and each square was given a number. I realised that all the German night-fighters wanted to know was a few figures to find out the bombers' height, course, speed, and square number. Only a few German night-fighters in those days had radar onboard, so most of them had to get this information from ground radar i.e. 25 = 25,000 feet (height), 18 = 180 degrees (course), 24 = 240mph (speed), and 35 (square number).

'The beauty about this simple solution was that the German pilots hadn't to learn to speak English to receive essential information, but all they had to know was English figures from 1 to 10. The RAF wireless operators on a raid on hearing English spoken would not jam the transmission, but would jam German, Dutch, and Flemish being spoken. So I thought to myself if the German who was transmitting 1 to 10 started to change the figures I would press my key. He did so, and I immediately did so for a minute or two. On lifting my key the Germans were again cursing and swearing. Every half an hour this happened repeatedly, and I was enjoying myself. I entered the frequency and time of the German broadcasts in my log-book. I was unable to jam the powerful German broadcasting station, but I was able to stop the German night-fighters from receiving the message. On leaving the enemy coast, the German station stopped broadcasting.

'At debriefing, the IO (intelligence officer) wanted to know if any of us had seen any coloured lights over enemy territory, and if we had seen any bombers shot down – my crew gave him this information. After that, my pilot said I had information on how the Germans were getting round our tinselling efforts. The IO told me to inform my wireless officer, but this I could not do as he was away on a course. I then handed my wireless log-book etc. to a young pilot officer, who was standing in. He had been up all night and wanted to go to his bed, and he told me the same thing as the flight lieutenant IO had said.

'I did five more ops over France, and I got a week's leave. I was not permitted to go home to Ireland, as D-Day was soon to begin. I arrived back at 630 Squadron on Saturday 20 June, and my wireless officer still hadn't come back from his course. I should have told my story to the CO, but I did not do so, as I thought that when my WO comes back he will see my wireless log-book and report to the CO. On Sunday, 21 June 1944, we laid "vegetables" ["Gardening" – mine-laying] in Kiel Harbour, and the following day we were shot down going to Brunswick.'

*

Once the south of Italy had been made safe following the invasion, a number of bomber squadrons were based at airfields on the Foggia Plain, near the Adriatic coast, well placed for operations across the Adriatic Sea. On the night of 3/4 May 1944, 205 Group mounted an attack on the railway marshalling yards in the north west of Bucharest, capital of Romania, the object of the raid being to disrupt enemy supplies reaching the front in Moldavia. Sixty-two aircraft were sent – fifty Wellingtons, five Liberators and seven Halifaxes – but it was a difficult target to locate due to low haze, and most of the sixty-six-and-a-half tons of bombs dropped fell on the city instead.

One aircraft failed to return – Wellington HE956, 150 Squadron, based at Amendola, approximately sixteen kilometres north east of Foggia. The circumstances of its loss are not known, but all five of its crew survived to become prisoners of war. The only one of the five to be held captive in Germany (the rest were kept in the Balkans) was wireless operator/air gunner Sergeant Charles W. Finlayson, a married Scotsman from Musselburgh. He remained on the run until 21 May, arriving at Luft 7 in *Trupp 2*.

*

On 20/21 October 1943, while RAF Bomber Command's main force went to Leipzig, twenty-eight Mosquitos went to Berlin, Cologne, Brauweiler, and Emden. Two Mosquitos – DZ519 and DZ597 – both from 139 (Jamaica) Squadron, RAF Wyton, Cambridgeshire were lost. The crew of DZ597 were killed, but the DZ519 crew – F/L Archie Mellor (pilot) and F/S Philip H. Brown (navigator) – survived being lost over Assen, Holland.

It was their third consecutive trip to Berlin in as many nights, and Phil Brown's twenty-third operation:

'On my last op we were coned by searchlights over Berlin, and hit by flak. One engine decided it had had enough on the way back, and the other carried on manfully, but over north-west Holland it too decided to give up. Thus I was forced into my one, and only, parachute jump. I landed in a ploughed field, and spent the first two or three weeks with some farmers. I was then moved by the Underground to a house in Meppel. From there I went to Maastricht, Brussels, Paris, and Toulouse. Sadly, after a hair-raising attempt to cross the Pyrenees, our small party was intercepted by a German patrol on 6 February 1944. I spent the next three months in various gaols in Toulouse, Fresnes (Paris), and Wiesbaden, before the Gestapo decided to let me go.'

In this 'hair-raising attempt to cross the Pyrenees' was a party of twenty-six personnel who were being escorted to Spain by members of the Dutch-Paris escape line. Ten of the group managed to slip through the enemy cordon that had been thrown round them,[24] but not Phil Brown, another to arrive at Luft 7 in *Trupp 2*.

Archie Mellor, on the other hand, was more fortunate. Assisted by the Comet escape line (*Le Réseau Comète*), he successfully returned to England, landing at RAF Lyneham on 2 January 1944, and was Mentioned in Despatches on 8 June 1944.

\*

During May 1944 Bomber Command carried out two raids on the large German military camp at Bourg-Léopold, Belgium, the first on 11/12 May, the second, and larger, one on 27/28 May with 267 Halifaxes, fifty-six Lancasters, and eight Mosquitos. On this later raid one Oboe-aimed target indicator fell bang on the target. Though severe damage was caused to the camp losses were heavy, with one Lancaster and nine Halifaxes failing to return.

One of the Halifaxes was LK865, C8-Q, 640 Squadron, from Leconfield, Yorkshire, with its crew of F/O Frank Williams DFM (pilot); F/S Roy P. Olsen RAAF (navigator); Sergeant Tom H. Riley (bomb aimer); F/O K. Lambert DFC[25] (flight engineer); Sergeant Ian R.B. 'Jock' Crawford (wireless operator); Sergeant Hubert Messenger (mid-upper gunner); and Sergeant T. Stewart White RCAF (rear gunner). F/O Lambert, an experienced second-tour man, had volunteered to take the place of the crew's regular flight engineer, Sergeant C. Crompton, who had reported sick.

Their skipper should have been Flight Lieutenant Bazalgette Osbourn DFM[26] but, with no operational experience on type, he had been sent as second pilot with an experienced crew on an operation to 'learn the ropes'. Failing to return from his second second-pilot trip on 22/23 April 1944 (Düsseldorf), he was, however, the only survivor of Halifax LW640, and became a POW at Stalag Luft III (Sagan).

Osbourn's replacement, Frank Williams, had already completed a tour on 78 Squadron, earning the DFM (gazetted 10 September 1943) for landing a Halifax after all four engines had failed at 12,000 feet. So, it was Frank Williams who, shortly before midnight on 27/28 May, took off at the controls of LK865. The trip to the target was routine but, bombs dropped, they were on their way back when attacked by Oberleutnant Georg-Hermann Greiner, 11./NJG1, for his thirtieth victory. (Greiner would survive the war with fifty-one victories, forty-seven of them at night.)

Roy Olsen:

> 'After "bombs gone!" we had proceeded some distance on our return flight, when suddenly the intercom packed up. Flames were visible to the rear of the pilot, who was at the controls and trying to steady the plane. I pulled with all my strength to free a stubborn front escape hatch. Then Tom Riley took over and wrenched it away. I left quickly, trying to follow the escape drill procedure – count to three before pulling the rip-cord, so as not to be entangled with parts of the plane.
>
> 'After my parachute opened, I saw the burning plane on its downward course, and the explosion when it hit the ground. I landed, possibly, between Bourg-Léopold and Schoonselhof, where I was captured by two German soldiers on duty at an outpost. I was then transported to Antwerp gaol, Dulag Luft, and Luft 7.'

Roy Olsen was immediately followed out of the same escape hatch by Tom Riley and Ian Crawford. Ian landed near Wortel, and was captured by German soldiers.

Stewart White:

'The night-fighter hit us from the starboard quarter down at, I would guess, 200 yards. He got both starboard engines with a short burst. Strangely enough there were two concentrated cylinders of sparks coming back rather than flames. During the attack, the flight engineer went back to help the mid-upper gunner. He evidently got there because the two are buried in a common grave. I was the last to jump, based on the fact that I was the only one who didn't see the plane crash. I went out of the tail turret. I couldn't get my electric suit unplugged, and jumped with it still connected – it unplugged then.

'I spent a day hiding in a wood, and then went a few miles to a village, where I hoped to find a bike. I was picked up by two German soldiers, and that was the end of my escape plan. I think that the village was fifteen or eighteen kilometres north of Turnhout. I was taken to Turnhout Castle (built in 1110),[27] and locked in a room about 5 feet by 10 feet at the top of the castle. It had a door at least 3 inches thick and one barred window. That evening I was taken to Antwerp and a day or so later to Brussels – where I met Roy and Ian. The plane came down in a pond on a farm that was used as a rehabilitation centre for drunks and vagrants, near Wortel. Apparently there are still two engines at the bottom of the pond.'

Ian Crawford, Roy Olsen and Stewart White arrived at Luft 7 with *Trupp 2* on 13 June. Tom Riley, who followed a week later in *Trupp 4* on 20 June, had found shelter with the Belgian Resistance before being caught.

The other three were killed. On his second tour of ops after four years on active service, Frank Williams, who would have celebrated his twenty-first birthday on 5 June 1944, is buried in Schoonselhof Cemetery near Antwerp with F/O Lambert DFC and Sergeant H. Messenger who, in the words of Ray Olsen, 'was very young and was greatly liked and respected by the crew'.

*

Of the 108 Halifaxes, twelve Lancasters, and eight Mosquitos whose target was the Orléans railway yards on the night of 22/23 May 1944 only Halifax LL138, 77 Squadron, RAF Full Sutton, Yorkshire, failed to return. The crew were: Warrant Officer Geoffrey T. Haworth (pilot); Sergeant Charles Thiepval Hale (navigator); F/O Alvin M. Beatty RCAF (bomb aimer); Sergeant Reginald A. Rose (flight engineer); Sergeant R.G. James (wireless operator/air gunner); Sergeant R.J. Peggs RAAF (mid-upper gunner); and Sergeant John D. 'Jack' Taylor (rear gunner).

Geoff Haworth:

'Ten minutes after bombing the target, the aircraft was attacked by a night-fighter – damaging the controls, and forcing it into an unrecoverable dive. The navigator, rear gunner and I baled out – the rest of the crew were killed during the attack. I suffered a fractured spine on baling out, and landed about forty to fifty miles west of Orléans. French villagers hid me for some hours but, because my injury needed treatment, had to hand me over to German troops. En route to Dulag Luft from Paris, eight of us were surrounded by a hostile crowd at Frankfurt railway station. It was touch and go for about ten minutes before they were dispersed by our guards.

'I arrived at Luft 7 on 13 June, and was sent to Kreuzburg hospital for examination.

On my return to Luft 7, I jumped down off the motor lorry, and a young German guard told me by sign language, to be more careful – pointing at my back he said "*kaput*" – the hospital had not told me that my spine was fractured. On 20 June, I was transferred to Stalag 344 Lamsdorf hospital, and repatriated in an exchange of wounded prisoners in January 1945, via Switzerland. My navigator, Charles Hale, stayed in the vicinity of where the aircraft crashed – possibly injured or evading capture. However, he was caught, and [was] in a German troop convoy which was shot up by RAF low-level aircraft after the invasion (22 June), and was killed.'

The rear gunner, Sergeant Jack Taylor, also captured, arrived at Luft 7 in *Trupp 1*.

*

Another Halifax lost on the Aachen raid on 24/25 May 1944 was LK885, 51 Squadron. Shot down by flak after bombing the target the crew were: P/O Carl Lawson RCAF (pilot); F/S John H. Noel RCAF (navigator); Sergeant Joe Hooks RCAF (bomb aimer); Sergeant Wilfred Gosway (flight engineer); Sergeant Ken C. Minifie RCAF (wireless operator); Sergeant Bruce A.M. Fraser RCAF (mid-upper gunner); and Sergeant Stan P. Beech RCAF (rear gunner). Lawson, Gosway, and Beech were killed during the attack.

Ken Minifie baled out, but was captured at Acht (near Eindhoven), Holland, and arrived at Luft 7, accompanied by F/S John Noel, on 13 June. Bruce Fraser was captured near Tilburg on 8 July, and arrived at Luft 7 twelve days later.

Joe Hooks was soon in friendly hands. Meeting up with WO2 J.H. Frame RCAF, 405 Squadron, who had also been shot down on the Aachen raid, the two evaded capture until they were liberated in September 1944, when Allied forces overran their hiding place.

*

Shortly before reaching the target on 22/23 May 1944 (Brunswick) Lancaster ME790, 106 Squadron, was flying at around 14,000 feet when it was hit by flak and blew up. The only survivor from the crew of eight –a 'second dickie' RCAF pilot – was wireless operator Warrant Officer George H. Pringle RAAF, on his thirteenth operation. Suffering 'injuries to the face, a broken arm, and flak wounds' he landed by parachute near Hildesheim. Captured by German troops five minutes after landing, at about 2 am on 23 May, three weeks later he arrived at Luft 7.

*

Operation Tungsten was launched by the Royal Navy at the end of March 1944 in a determined effort to destroy the German battleship *Tirpitz* lurking in Kåfjord, Norway. A strong force of ships was sent to Norway to do the job, among them the aircraft carrier HMS *Victorious*. Having taken part in the successful attack on the *Tirpitz* on 3 April 1944 (though only damaged and not sunk, *Tirpitz* was put out of action for several months), she flew further reconnaissance missions from her decks on 16 May. One of the aircraft involved was Fairey Barracuda LS547, 831 (FAA) Squadron, crewed by Sub-Lieutenant (A) T. McK. Henderson, RNVR (pilot); Sub-Lt (A) V. H. Hutchinson, RNVR (observer); and Acting Petty Officer Victor Smyth, FAA/RN (telegraphist/air gunner).

As a result of particularly bad weather in the North Sea on that day the crew of LS547 became lost, and had to request D/F bearings. Against normal practice, the ship broke W/T silence and sent their bearing out many times, but it was never picked up by the Barracuda. With the fuel situation critical, Henderson decided to head east and, hopefully, reach the Norwegian coast. They were within sight of the coast when the fuel ran out, and Henderson skilfully landed the 'glider' on a narrow, sandy beach at Stave, in the south west of Norway. The crew scrambled out unhurt and set fire to the aircraft. A German radio broadcast actually reported that 'a British glider had landed in Norway'.

Following their capture the crew were taken to Oslo, and then through Denmark and on to Hamburg. After interrogation, the two officers went to Stalag Luft III (Sagan), while Smyth went to Luft 7, where he arrived on 13 June.[28]

\*

138 (Special Duties) Squadron, based at Tempsford, Bedfordshire, from March 1942 until March 1945, was employed in parachuting SOE agents, and weapons, explosives and equipment to Resistance organisations in occupied countries.[29] On the night of 31 May/1 June 1944, the crew of Halifax LL276, NF-F, were slated for Operation Osric 74, a supply drop to the Belgian Resistance. As LL276 had been specially modified by the removal of its mid-upper turret only a rear gunner was carried. Its crew were: Warrant Officer H.G.F. Murray (pilot); F/O J. Pearcey RCAF (navigator); F/S L. Peter Notton (bomb aimer); Sergeant Thomas McCluskey (flight engineer); F/S Fred Stead (wireless operator/air gunner); Sergeant A.P. Cliff-McCulloch (rear gunner); and Sergeant R. Robinson (dispatcher).

As they approached the Dutch coast they were attacked and shot down by Feldwebel Wilhelm Morlock, 3./NJG1, in his Bf110 night-fighter. Sergeants Cliff-McCulloch and Robinson were killed during the attack. Murray and McCluskey baled out, but drowned in the Scheldt (*Schelde* in French). Pearcey, Notton and Stead also baled out and were captured. Pearcey went to Luft 3, while the two NCOs, Notton and Stead, went to Luft 7.

Fred Stead:

'Having baled out, I landed in the Schelde near the town of Tholen. I was then captured early in the morning of 1 June, shortly after swimming out of the sea, by Armenian soldiers in the German army [see also Smithson page 188]. Peter Notton and I arrived at Luft 7 on 13 June. At that time conditions were basic to say the least, but in the next few weeks things began to get organised, and books and musical instruments were being supplied by the YMCA.

'In the beginning, we had no medical facilities, except those provided by the Germans. And minor injuries were occurring in the day to day activity of the camp. In addition were the men coming in who had been wounded and discharged from German hospitals, many of whom were still in need of medical treatment. An MI (medical inspection) room had been set up in one of the huts by one of the POWs (F/S Robert O. "Slim" Ellis) who had been a member of the St John Ambulance Brigade. As the camp grew rapidly in members, he soon became in need of help, and since I had also been a member of the SJAB, I joined him at the end of July. We were, of course, under the direction of the German *Arzt* [doctor], and had two elderly orderlies allocated to us – more to keep an eye on us than to help. I don't think they had much more knowledge than we had, though they did their best.

'As the weeks passed, the MI room grew and grew with men being taken ill with the normal ailments of humanity. Huts around were turned into wards, and Hut 75 was made available as living accommodation for the medical staff, which had been increased to four.

During September we were able to organise dental parades for treatment by the German dentist in their medical quarters, which were always accompanied by armed guards.'

*

By October 1942 the tide was beginning to turn against Feldmarschall Erwin Rommel and the Deutsche Afrika Korps (DAK) in North Africa. Though its lines of supply in the desert had been overstretched, the port of Tobruk was still in Axis hands, and was able to receive a diminishing supply of material from Italy. As part of the overall Allied plan, therefore, RAF bombers did all they could to deny the port to the Germans, and bombed it 'on nine nights between 6/7 and 20/21 October, with a total of 352 sorties sent to bomb shipping and dock installations or to lay mines in the harbour'.[30]

One of the bombers, Wellington DV873, 108 Squadron, was within half an hour of Tobruk on the night of 19/20 October 1942 when its starboard engine packed up. The pilot, Sgt W. Simpson, ordered the bombs to be dropped, and turned back to base (Kilo 40) with the aircraft rapidly losing height. Simpson was unable to prevent the Wimpy from heading deeper into the desert, south rather than east, and about twelve minutes later was forced to land the bomber, which he did with none of the crew being injured. Their position was estimated to have been some seventy miles south of Sollum Bay, near the Qattara Depression.

At 0210 hours on 20 October aircraft 'C' and 'Q' of 108 Squadron, flying on the same operation as DV873, picked up an SOS, possibly from DV873, but were unable to get an accurate bearing. They did, however, see red distress signals in position 30.30' N, 27.30' E, but it is not known whether these were from DV873 or not. A report to higher authority made by 108 Squadron's commander on 22 October commented: 'Two aircraft of this squadron operating against Tobruk on the following night [20/21 October] observed a steady white light burning in approximately the same position (30.22' N 28.45' E) at 0330 hours, and it is believed that this was from the aircraft DV873 missing on the previous night.'

As DV873 did not catch fire the light was unlikely to have emanated from it or its crew, as all six of them had immediately started walking in an easterly direction. They walked for six days, with the second pilot, P/O E.R. Patrick RCAF, growing weaker and weaker all the while. The others had to keep stopping every few minutes to allow him to recover, until eventually he collapsed. Setting off to find water, hopefully at the nearby Qattara spring, they had walked for barely fifteen minutes when they stumbled upon an Italian camp. Machine-gun and rifle fire pinned them to the ground, and they were soon captured.

The two officers in the crew – Patrick and P/O J. Mills (rear gunner) – were flown from Tobruk to Italy, while the other four – Sgt W. Simpson (pilot); F/Sgt J.A. Hutchinson RCAF (navigator); Sgt A.T.S. Williamson (wireless operator); and F/Sgt H.A. Martin RAAF (front gunner) – went by road to Tripoli, Libya. They were then shipped to Palermo, Sicily and, in November, sent to Campo PG 66 (Capua), a transit camp not far from Naples on the mainland of Italy.

In December 1942, while the other NCOs were sent to camps in the south, Howard Martin was moved to Campo PG 57 (Gruppignano), near Udine, way up in the north east of Italy, where he was to spend the next nine months. It was here that he heard of the death of a fellow Australian, Private Simmonds, who 'was shot whilst barracking at a cricket match being played in the [next] compound... Nothing short of murder.'

Within a few hours of the Italian armistice early in September 1943 the German army took control of the Italian POW camps, and arranged for the Allied prisoners to be moved to camps in Germany and Austria. Martin was on his way by train with other POWs on 22 September 1943 when he escaped. He was not free for long, though, and was sent, after a short stop at Stalag XVIIIB (Wagna), to Stalag XVIIIC (Markt Pongau) (also numbered Stalag 317), both of which were in Austria. Conditions at XVIIIC were bad for the first two months: 'No blankets. No paliasses. No lights. No Red X [Red Cross parcels].' He came to Bankau on 13 June 1944, the same day as *Trupp 2*.

Also arriving on 13 June was F/S V.R. 'Stumpy' Duvall, 97 Squadron, who had been shot down on 24/25 March 1944 on the last of the raids of the so-called 'Battle of Berlin'. His Lancaster, ND440, hit by flak at 20,000 feet over the Ruhr, was finally forced to ditch in the English Channel. The impact was heavy, and several of the crew were injured. Duvall's leg was so badly injured that it was later amputated, and he was repatriated from Luft 7, with fellow Luft 7 POW Stan Aspinall, in 1945.

*

**16 JUNE 1944.** On this day, the first game of cricket was played at Luft 7. Although the Red Cross and the YMCA between them were to supply many things to the kriegies, they had not yet provided cricket equipment! Being summer of course, the thoughts of the first POWs at Bankau had turned to playing, but, without proper equipment, they had to make it themselves. The ball was fashioned from the string of Red Cross parcels, wound up into a ball, and the bat from a purloined piece of wood. The 'ball' took a bashing, and during the game two or three more had to be made. Alas, history (Den Blackford's diary) does not record the details of the match.

It was not long, though, before sports equipment began to arrive at Bankau. Den Blackford:

> 'We got some softball equipment, and as soon as that arrived we had a pick-up game with the few Canadians that were in the camp, and they were the ones who showed us how to play. Of course, we got beaten pretty badly, but really from then on softball was the game to be played because at least we had decent equipment.'

It was now early July, and in the fine weather prevailing at the camp – 'it was extremely hot and very muggy' – the non-Canadians often played softball against the expert Canadians, 'and day after day we got beaten'. By this time, too, as over 250 POWs had arrived, there were enough men present to consider making up a number of cricket teams, split into 'divisions'. On 9 July Nos. 1 and 2 Divisions played a match, which resulted in a win for No. 2 Division by twenty-six runs. Den Blackford: 'We used a softball, incidentally, to play with because our homemade cricket balls didn't last too long!'

Other sporting equipment were boxing gloves, and a well-organised series of bouts was held on 15 July, attended by the Camp Commandant. Two days later, some real cricket equipment arrived, and the competition continued apace in the glorious July weather.[31]

## CHAPTER THREE

# 18 AND 20 JUNE 1944, *TRUPPEN 3 & 4*

The Bavarian city of Nuremberg was not only an important railway centre but also a major centre for war production. Many large factories were located there, such as Maschinenfabrik Augsburg-Nürnberg (M.A.N.) which was making diesel engines for U-boats and tanks, the Zündapp motor plant producing vehicles for the army, and the Siemens works producing electrical equipment for the navy. These were the main reason why RAF Bomber Command carried out twenty-two raids on the city during the war.

One of the thousands of RAF aircrew flying on the raid on 30/31 March 1944, the night on which RAF Bomber Command suffered the heaviest losses on a single raid,[32] was Warrant Officer Donald G. Gray. Joining the RAF in 1940, he was disappointed after pilot training to be posted to Flying Training Command rather than to an operational squadron, but his determination to get on ops was eventually achieved with some unauthorised low flying – followed by an official reprimand and the long awaited posting to an operational conversion unit. From there, he was posted to 50 Squadron, operating Lancaster B.1s out of Skellingthorpe, near Lincoln.

For this Nuremberg raid Don Gray flew with his crew of F/S Alan D. Campbell RAAF (navigator); F/S George Wallis RAAF (bomb aimer); Sergeant Joseph Grant (flight engineer); Sergeant Bert Wright (wireless operator); Sergeant Frank B. Patey (mid-upper gunner); and Sergeant Douglas Maugham (rear gunner). They would be flying veteran Lancaster R5546, VN-T for Tare,[33] on Don Gray's fourth op. Shortly after take-off, the 'gremlins' went to work. Bert Wright's 'Fishpond' set went u/s, then Doug Maugham had a problem with his helmet that affected his intercom and oxygen supply. Bert Wright took him another helmet, but they were unable to correct the fault, and it was not long before Doug began to lose consciousness. When Bert had to return to his wireless set to receive messages from base, Joe Grant took a portable oxygen bottle to Doug, but within a couple of minutes Bert reported that the flight engineer, too, was unconscious in the fuselage.

Suddenly, Frank Patey, in the mid-upper turret, shouted that they were being attacked, and began firing. Don Gray immediately took evasive action – 'Corkscrew Left' – until the mid-upper gunner reported that the attack was over. With the aircraft back on course, Don then had to deal with the problem of the two unconscious crew members. Losing height as fast as he could, the starboard engines suddenly burst into flames, and soon the whole of the wing was ablaze. In no time, with the aircraft out of control, Don gave the order to bale out. There was another bang, and Don felt a searing pain in his left knee from a piece of flak. Ignoring it, he clipped the parachute pack onto his harness.

Opening the bomb-doors to dump the 4,000lb 'cookie' and the incendiaries, the crew were faced with a glaring light and a searing heat. It was then that Don made the decision not to jettison the bomb load, in case it destroyed the aircraft when it hit the ground. It would also have the advantage of leaving next to nothing for German intelligence. Then there was a massive explosion.

Don recovered consciousness when his parachute pack hit him in the face. With nothing to lose, he pulled the rip-cord. At once enveloped by the still-dark night all he could feel was a slight tugging at his ankles. Puzzled as to why his arms were raised above his head, he lowered them, but they immediately returned to the raised position. Observing, to his amazement, that the white parachute canopy was above his feet it dawned on him that he was hanging upside-down, and that a fall to his death had only been prevented by the parachute harness tangled round his ankles! Unsure of how his harness came to be in this position, he assumed that when he undid his seat straps to operate the fire extinguishers he accidentally operated the release turnbuckle on his parachute harness.

No sooner had the branch of a tree brushed against his face, than his head hit the ground with a violent blow. Half-stunned, he stumbled to his feet. Checking to see if any bones were broken – none appeared to be – his parachute harness dropped off! Dimly making out that he was standing on the edge of a forest he rolled up his parachute and stuffed it under a bush. With the moon setting in the west he headed in that direction. His eyeballs felt as if they were about to burst from his head, and every time he breathed there was a stabbing pain in his chest. Within a few seconds he had stepped onto a concrete *Autobahn*, and realised that had he landed there he would have broken his neck and been killed outright.

When Don gave the order to bale out bomb aimer George Wallis clipped on his parachute and attempted to open the escape hatch, but it was jammed tight. Looking up, he saw the navigator, Alan Campbell, making his way forward. Then there was an explosion, and Alan was hurled towards him, being knocked unconscious en route. The next thing Alan saw when he opened his eyes were the stars. Everything was quiet. Pulling his ripcord, he was relieved to see his parachute canopy open above him. Below he could see quite clearly another parachute deployed.

Hitting the ground, according to his watch, at 0030 hours he decided to head west. Within a short time a faint figure appeared in front of him. Assuming that it was an armed German looking for downed aircrew he raised his hands in the air. Great was the relief and pleasant the surprise when the figure turned into George Wallis. The two of them started out together for the Rhine, but were picked up and taken to a police station in Neuwied, north of Koblenz, ending up at Stalag Luft VI (Heydekrug) on the Baltic.

As for Don Gray, while attempting to negotiate a railway crossing near Linz, south east of Bonn, he was captured by four armed members of the Volkssturm (the German equivalent of the British Home Guard), who took him to a nearby police station. Made to turn out his pockets and produce his identity discs, Don saw that his watch had stopped at 0025 hours, the time of his landing. Led across a courtyard and put into a cell, he quickly fell asleep from fatigue. The following morning, under police guard, he was put in the back of a truck next to 'Warrant Officer Hall, RNZAF, a bomb aimer who had been badly beaten up by a German policeman'.[34]

Driven across the Ludendorff Bridge (at Remagen) to the town's police station an elderly policeman kept pointing to Don's eyes. Walking over to a mirror, Don could see what concerned his captors. In the middle of each huge, black eye was a hole filled with blood. The force of his landing must have burst the blood vessels in his eyeballs. The airmen were then locked up. As Hall was in obvious distress, Don rolled up his Irvine jacket to serve as a pillow and laid Hall onto it. The noise of whimpers and groans from adjoining cells began to get on Don's nerves, when the cell door opened and four scruffy and dispirited RAF officers and NCOs entered, accompanied by a pale little man with one leg, dressed in a combination of civilian clothing and American uniform. Don managed to persuade the guard to bring them all some food but, despite this and his own battered countenance, the newcomers regarded him with suspicion, whispering among themselves.

At about 1700 hours, a party of Luftwaffe personnel arrived. Escorting Don and his companions to a lorry parked outside, they were driven to the town's railway station. Fortunately, the officer in charge knew a little English and Don pointed out Hall's condition to him. He was not unsympathetic and helped Hall up beside the driver, borrowing Don's Irvine jacket to keep the patient warm. On arrival at the railway station the officer in charge signalled to Hall to stay where he was. That was the last Gray ever saw of his jacket or of Hall.

With Hall still in the truck, the rest of the prisoners were escorted to a platform for their train. When an air-raid siren sounded, a flight of Bf109s took off from a nearby airfield and passed overhead. Though Don Gray had been flying for over three years, these were the first enemy aircraft he had ever seen.

Once at the interrogation centre at Oberursel, Don was placed in solitary confinement and given the usual fake International Red Cross form to fill in, about which all aircrew had been warned by RAF intelligence. As the questions were mainly about military information, Don filled in his number, rank and name, and drew a line through the remaining questions.

'I spent four days in solitary confinement, enduring a lack of food, washing facilities and medical attention. This situation was made even worse with my interrogators turning the cell's radiator on and off. This was followed by a second interview, during which my interrogators gave me a book containing a full list of RAF squadrons – and their personnel! I noticed a reference to my squadron, No. 50, but showed no recognition. Trying a little subterfuge, I pretended to show some interest in the details of a Spitfire squadron. I was then threatened to be shot as a spy, but was returned to my cell. After a further two days, the bandage over my eyes was changed, and I was sent to Hohe Mark hospital, POW section, and then to Stalag 9C Obermassfeld POW hospital, a multi-storey derelict factory. Conditions were poor, with overcrowding, septicæmia rife, and plumbing antiquated and continually breaking down. The food was always cold.

'From there I was sent to Meiningen POW convalescent "home", an old opera house in a lovely town. The building was on the edge of a public open space, half of which was wired off for our use. It was here that we encountered Sergeant Norman Jackson, the flight engineer who was awarded the Victoria Cross on his return to England after the war. He had been badly burned when he crawled out onto his Lancaster wing in an attempt to extinguish an engine fire.[35] Also among the prisoners was a black Bantu soldier of the South African army. His name was Wilson Majeepa, and he was popular with the lads.

'I arrived at Luft 7 on 22 June. The accommodation was in rows of small garden shed type huts to hold six men. We "invalids" from the hospital were put in huts 71 and 72. We did not attend the twice a day roll-call parades, but were counted in the huts as some of our number were limbless or crippled. The weather was beautiful, food was adequate, and conditions, although Spartan, were agreeable. One of our number, Sergeant Ted Hughes from Yarmouth, was a humorous character, and liked to have a laugh at the expense of the rather slow-witted German orderlies at roll call. When his name was called he remained silent, until it was repeated a third time, when he would ask "Do you mean Hudges?" The following day the guard would call "Hudges" – dead silence until Ted chimed up "Do you mean Hughes?" It happened day after day. The Camp Leader and his deputy were army NCOs, and were apparently members of the SAS.

'The German Commandant appeared to be a nice old chap. We rarely saw him, except at concerts and boxing tournaments etc. On one occasion the Catholics were able to borrow from the Germans a silver chalice for a religious ceremony. A rather garrulous German guard collected the chalice after the service and, presumably thinking it funny, walked off with it on his head like a helmet. He was reported, summarily dealt with, and sent to the Russian Front.'

*

Lancaster ME738, 103 Squadron, was on its way back from Friedrichshafen on the night of 27/28 April 1944 when it was set ablaze by Oberleutnant Martin Becker, 2./NJG6, at some 15,000 feet over the *Schwarzwald* (Black Forest), Germany. The navigator, WO2 L.R. Fletcher RCAF, found himself trapped at his desk, unable to go either forward to the nose escape hatch or back to the rear door. All he could do, while clipping on his parachute, was watch as the altimeter rapidly unwound to below 6,000 feet. Resigned to his fate and totally unable to do anything to help himself, the aircraft suddenly exploded, presumably after the fuel tanks had caught fire. Though he regained consciousness in time to pull the parachute's rip-cord, he nevertheless fell heavily to the ground, fracturing both ankles and, again, falling unconscious.

There was still deep snow in the Black Forest, and Leo Fletcher was covered in the stuff by the time that he was found by an army patrol wandering along a road through the trees. He spent some time in a hospital before being released to Luft 7 where, it was noticed, he walked with a pronounced limp.

*

Also arriving with Trupp 3 was bomb aimer F/S Norman Wilmot.[36] He was on 10 Squadron, operating Halifaxes out of Melbourne, Yorkshire, when he, too, was shot down on the Nuremberg raid at the end of March 1944. He was on his fifth op, in Halifax B.3 LV881, with P/O Walter T.A. Regan (pilot); Warrant Officer W.W. 'Bill' Norris RCAF (navigator); Sergeant Alan Lawes (flight engineer); Sergeant Don L. Smith (wireless operator); F/S E. Hugh Birch RAAF (mid-upper gunner); and Sergeant R. Walter Tindall (rear gunner).

They were shot down by a night-fighter (possibly flown by Hauptmann Hubert Rauh of 3./ NJG4) before bombing the target. Norman Wilmot landed in a wood near Giessen, and suffered head and facial injuries that caused severe concussion and amnesia. He is unable to remember whether those injuries were caused by the aircraft exploding, a bad landing, or by his captors. He was unconscious and semi-conscious for some ten days, receiving hospital treatment at Frankfurt, Stalag IXC (Obermassfeld and Meiningen), before arriving at Luft 7 on 18 June. While Regan, Smith, Birch and Tindall were killed, Bill Norris and Alan Lawes became POWs at Stalag Luft VI (Heydekrug) and then Stalag 357 (Fallingbostel).

*

**20 JUNE 1944.** *Trupp 4* (twenty-seven men) arrived, including two wounded from hospital.

*

One of the many air gunners to be trained at No. 10 Air Gunnery School at Barrow (Walney Island), Lancashire, (December 1941-June 1946), was nineteen-year-old Sergeant Elwyn 'Taff' Healy, of Dowlais, Merthyr Tydfil, South Wales. Once qualified, he was posted to 90 Squadron operating Stirling Mk.3s out of Tuddenham, Suffolk.

His regular crew were F/L Ken J. MacDonald (pilot); F/O Les Poole (navigator); F/S I.W. 'Steve' Bostridge (bomb aimer); Sergeant Jimmy 'Jock' Westwood (flight engineer); Sergeant George 'Slim' Jim King (wireless operator); and Sergeant Peter Broadribb (mid-upper gunner). They carried out a variety of operational sorties, from bombing and mine-laying to dropping supplies on Special Duties to the French Maquis, as Peter Broadribb remembers:

> 'Of these operational flights a number proved to be particularly difficult, through circumstances which cropped up. I recall one mining trip to Kiel, possibly that on 24 February 1944, when we iced up very badly going out over the North Sea and struggled

to maintain 8,000 feet – in fact we stooged across Denmark without interference until Flensburg when searchlights and flak left everything above us and concentrated on our aircraft once coned. On that occasion the squadron bombing officer, "Snake", was flying with us as Steve was sick, and he virtually took over and dictated the evasive action to be taken. In a steep dive, I understand we reached 400 mph, and it took three to pull the aircraft out. We got out of a tight spot, although the compass was toppled in the process, which also led to us being lost for a period.[37]

'On one other trip our aircraft was damaged by flak, with a fair proportion of the nose shot away. We came back across France on three engines, and a second failed as we neared the English coast. Whilst we got back to Tuddenham, we were not permitted to land, having no undercart. So we were diverted to Woodbridge.[38] The organisation there was tremendous, and we pancaked amidst many sparks from the belly on the runway, to be put most smartly into a blood-wagon and rushed away for a quick tot!'

Although this crew had flown on thirty ops, only twenty-six counted towards their full tour, two having been 'recalls' while two were aborted due to engine trouble. On their twenty-seventh operation, on the night of 2/3 June 1944, they carried out supply drops to the Resistance with thirty-five other aircraft, two of which failed to return – Halifaxes LL284 and LL307, 138 Squadron. Stirling EF294, WP-G for George, 'B' Flight, 90 Squadron, also failed to return.

'Taff' Healy:

'As our Stirling lifted off the runway at Tuddenham, I checked my watch – the time was 2239 hours. This was our twenty-sixth sortie and our seventh trip in EF294. We were on a Special Duties mission – dropping supplies to the French Resistance. It was a successful drop south east of Paris, and we were heading for home at around 300 feet when we were hit by flak, one burst putting my rear turret out of action. I tried to inform the pilot, but the intercom was out as well. I then became aware of a red glow behind me, and could see the fuselage on fire. I tried to get out of the turret, but the doors had jammed. Eventually I forced my way out with an axe and started fighting the fire with an extinguisher. Just when it seemed I had the fire under control, the bottle ran dry and the flames flared up again.

'I decided to jump the fire and inform the skipper of our situation, and get another extinguisher. Meanwhile I was suffocating from the flames and smoke, and could hear the cannon shells still hitting the kite as Jerry kept plastering us. On the way up front I told the mid-upper gunner, the wireless operator, the navigator, and the flight engineer, and then carried on forward and told the pilot. The pilot was looking out at the starboard wing, one of the fuel tanks was on fire, and the starboard engines had stopped. At that moment the bomb aimer took up his "crash position", and I ran back to tell the rest of the crew. We had barely taken up ours when we were ploughing our way through a corn field with thick dust coming in everywhere.

'Fortunately it was a good aircraft (made by Short & Harland, Belfast) which held together and did not break up or explode on impact. The five of us – Les, Pete, Slim, Jock and I – got out of the rear exit – Les having set the demolition charges on the $H_2S$ – while Steve and the pilot got out of the front. We never saw them again so we assumed they got back to base.[39] It was now around 2 am (3 June) and the aircraft was blazing, so the five of us started walking across country before Jerry arrived to investigate. We walked until dawn, and then decided to hide in a bean-field. We were soaking wet and lay there shivering with cold until the sun came out, and then we started to roast with the heat. It was a boiling hot day and we did not have any water or cover, so it was very uncomfortable.

'When night came we walked for about ten miles, then Pete said he could not go any further, as his back was giving him a lot of trouble. We lay down in a corn field to wait for dawn, and when daylight came we had a look at his back, and saw he had been hit by the flak and the area around the wound had turned green. That day we came to a farmhouse, where we were given some food, and bathed Pete's back. We were then taken to a derelict chateau by the farmer, and told to hide there until evening when we would have to move on to Paris. But Pete was too ill to move, so we stayed there all night and the following day until about 4 pm (5 June).

'Then some Jerry soldiers came in the house and we started our careers as POWs. We were taken to a Luftwaffe camp in Rosière [*sic – Rosières-en-Santerre*], then searched and put in solitary confinement.[40] Pete was taken to a hospital in Amiens, and Les was kept guarded in the office as he was an officer. Slim, Jock and myself were locked in separate cells – about 7ft x 4ft x 10ft with one little glazed window high up, and soundproof walls, one light in the ceiling and a bunk bed with straw palliasse. Under the corner of the palliasse was a set of playing cards someone had made out of crepe toilet paper – they were only about the size of postage stamps but were carefully marked out in pencil.

'I was interrogated (6 June) and given a form to fill in. I wrote 1836017 Sergeant Healy, Elwyn. The interrogation officer then asked me what I knew of $H_2S$; I replied "nothing" and was then returned to my cell. During the morning we heard that the invasion had taken place. The only times I was taken out of the cell was for interrogation, and for dinner at 1200-1230 hours and for supper at 1900-1930 hours. The same procedure was repeated for 7, 8 and 9 June. On 10 June I was told by the interrogation officer that the rest of my crew had been shot for refusing to talk, and if I still refused then I would be shot in the morning. I replied that I knew nothing and was returned to my cell.

'I was taken out of my cell (11 June) and, to my relief, put on a bus along with Slim, Jock and Les. On the coach we met Pete, who told us they had not done anything to his back, as they did not have any drugs or medicines. After a journey of about eight hours we arrived in Brussels, and Pete was taken away for treatment. We were put in an old jail in solitary confinement on bread and water. They interrogated us again (12 June) and told us we would be moving. This morning (13 June) we were taken to Brussels railway station and put on a train, passing through Cologne – where there was an air-raid alarm, but nothing happened – and Frankfurt. After a journey of twenty-eight hours we arrived at Oberursel about 4 am (15 June), where we were searched and put in solitary confinement. Jock and Slim were taken away on 16 June.

'This morning (17 June) at 0600 hours the guards took us to a transit camp (Wetzlar), which was a journey of about six hours. There we were given a suitcase with a shirt, one pair of pants, one vest, two bars of soap, sixty cigarettes (American), ten packets of chewing gum, two towels, one pair of boots, a tin of boot polish, one belt, one pullover, a brush and comb, a razor, toothpaste, and a US army greatcoat. All of this was given as a gift by the American Red Cross. Then we had a shave and a shower-bath, the first for two weeks, and given a meal of tinned salmon, potatoes, bread and butter and jam. This was the first time my stomach was full since we left England. Jock and Slim had been waiting for me at the camp gates, and they took me to a bedspace they had reserved for me, where I had a good night's rest.

'This morning (18 June) we were given a Red Cross food parcel for our journey to a permanent camp. We travelled by rail in a cattle truck, but who cared as long as we had someone to talk to after eleven days of talking to yourself in solitary confinement. When we arrived at this camp (20 June, Luft 7) the fellows who were already there had a cup of hot cocoa ready. Then six of us got together and came to a hut which was to be our home for who knows how long. The six of us in Hut 82 are: Sergeant R.S. "Bob" Hall RCAF (of Normal, Illinois, USA),[41] Sergeant John Hamilton (of Truro, Cornwall), Sergeant Len W. Cook (Blakeney, Norfolk), Sergeant Jimmy "Jock" Westwood (Dalkeith, Scotland), and Sergeant Walter S. "Scotty" Rowan (Gowkshill, Scotland). They are a good set of boys and we get along quite well.

'The next morning we got up at 7.30 am, had breakfast, which was porridge and cocoa. Then played about until dinner time when we had soup and tea. Then we had a Red Cross food parcel, and a bread ration – 1/6th of a loaf. We made up what we liked for tea, so we had tinned salmon, bread and butter, and tea. For supper we had some bread and butter and jam, and cocoa. At 9 pm the curfew sounded and we had to go to bed. We sung songs, and talked about our different adventures for a while. Then when it got dark we went to sleep.

Sergeant Peter Broadribb:

'Having made three crash landings in Stirlings it was, I suppose, unfortunate that the last occasion should be in a ploughed field (near Bayonvillers) in France. We had completed our mission to a drop south east of Paris, and on such occasions we operated in bright moonlight and flew at a height of 100 feet. We had to climb to a safety height of 1,000 feet to cross pylons at St Quentin, and in dropping back down we had some six positions of light ack-ack open up on us – a crossfire! – a searchlight having coned the aircraft. I remember clearly firing from my mid-upper turret down the searchlight beam – one moment my turret was complete and next it had been shattered, with the Perspex blown away and a tremendous gale blowing about me. Two engines were alight and the intercom had broken down. The skipper obviously decided to crash-land the plane, which he did most successfully.

'Whilst I knew I had been hit quite heavily in the back, I did not appreciate until at the escape hatch by my turret that I was partially paralysed. Fortunately for me two of the lads pushed me through the escape hatch. Once we were out of the aircraft, the five of us who had escaped through the mid-hatch, got as far as possible away from the burning plane. I was able to shuffle but not raise my feet from the ground; in consequence as we moved away and kept to the fields, the other lads manhandled me over or around hedges. Whilst my memory is not too distinct as to the time, I recall that it was around 2 to 2.30 am when we came to grief. I also remember seeing two or three other aircraft, and thinking that before long they would be on the right side of the Channel.

'However, we kept moving until daylight when we hid in a field of flax. During that Saturday, 3 June, we kept our heads down, and Slim our wireless operator, a qualified St John's Ambulance man, did all he could in applying dressings to my back wounds. Throughout the period from being shot down we were aware that Jerry was searching for us. Once dusk descended we got on the move again, moving inland, hopefully towards the Maquis areas where we had been involved previously.

'Sunday I was in rather a bad way, and on reflection I have always felt the other lads should have left me, as I was in urgent need of proper medical attention and delaying their progress. Late that day it was decided to approach the French for help. We were taken to a farm and contact made with the Underground Movement; the schoolboy French of three of us proved better than the English of a French school teacher. The message we had was that if I was attended by a doctor they would need to give me over to Jerry. In the event we were given food and taken to a nearby chateau at Beaucourt-en-Santerre which, whilst empty, had been used by the Germans as a barracks. We stayed overnight and through the Monday, it being a wet day. Food was provided, but shortly after midday Germans were seen outside, and eventually as they moved into and searched the building we were found on the top floor; however, we did conceal in a chimney food given to us by the French.

'Having been taken out of the chateau we were placed against a wall and each of the five of us was covered by German field police but, fortunately, the intention was merely to search us. In due time we were taken by the army to Rosières where we were interrogated in a straightforward manner, but prior to leaving the grounds of the chateau a German officer had examined my wounds which, in the words of the lads, had turned green. Having been searched and all valuables removed, they were placed in an envelope which was sealed in my presence; these were later returned to me at Wetzlar. I was then taken to a nearby airfield and placed in sickbay; the other lads, I gather, stayed in Rosières.

'I was running a considerable temperature and clearly the Germans wanted this reduced before moving me elsewhere. I stayed in the sickbay until the Tuesday evening of 6 June when I was taken out to a half-track vehicle and placed in the rear on my back. My first shock was when being helped into the vehicle an American Thunderbolt flew down the road and, to this day, I do not know why he did not open fire, yet French people nearby were waving.

'From here I was taken to Amiens, but when on the outskirts of the town the half-track pulled off the road – I knew why when the bombs started to whistle down unpleasantly close. However I managed to scramble from the back of the vehicle and join my German escort already in the ditch – we were opposite the marshalling yards being raided by American Mitchells. After the first wave I was taken to air-raid shelters, and but for my German corporal guard pulling a pistol I would have been lynched by Todt workers in the marshalling yard who pointed to the bombers above.

'When the journey was resumed after the raid ended, I was taken to the Military Hospital in Amiens. As I was taken up the drive my corporal guard, who spoke very good English, told me the invasion had started that morning, in his words "at Cherbourg and Le Havre". On entering the hospital I was handed over to a German doctor who told me he had been in practice in Hampstead before the war. However I received only limited treatment, bandages being of paper. I was placed in a room at the top of the building with an American pilot who had lost a leg. On telling him the invasion news this went round the top floor at great speed, and all the airmen prisoners' morale was greatly boosted.

'As a result of this news I appeared to be a marked man, because I had no further treatment and food was limited to rye bread, often green with mildew. I stayed in bed until the following Saturday morning when my dressings were changed. I was told to dress, and was put on a coach which went round northern France picking up airmen prisoners before going on to Brussels. En route the four crew members captured with me were picked up, but we were not allowed to talk. The journey for me was a nightmare, and I was in a state of collapse on arrival at some barracks in the centre of Brussels, opposite a canal.

'After a night when I truly thought I would die in the absence of medical attention, I was taken for interrogation and had a phoney Red Cross form placed in front of me, which I could not complete in any event being unable to write. However, after giving my number, rank and name, I eventually also gave my home address and civilian occupation. I was told consistently that without answers to the remaining questions I could not have hospital treatment; nevertheless in the absence of further response on my part a telephone call was made which resulted in the interrogators determining I had been flying in a Stirling, and not a Lancaster or a Halifax as they had suggested originally. I was staggered when they referred to an indexed filing cabinet and subsequently told me of the squadron, the wing co's name, the fact he picked his trips, and correctly with one exception the names of the members of the crew.

'Following this I was taken by lorry to St Gilles Hospital in the suburbs, used exclusively by the Luftwaffe. From this moment I was treated splendidly. I was in a ward with other airmen prisoners, the majority of whom were Americans. The attention and food were first class, food much better than that I had on the squadron before being shot down. I was X-rayed on the Monday and operated on the next morning by a Luftwaffe lt col, who had been a house surgeon in a hospital in Boston, Mass., USA, before the war. Apparently I was a very interesting case having lost control of my body, which was being pulled up and down to the right involuntarily, and in consequence, prior to the operation to remove flak from beside my spine and lung, a lecture to some twenty-plus students was given.

'I owe much to the wonderful surgery and good luck, as part of the transverse process of my spine was sheared off by flak which was two inches inside me; suffice to say I lived to tell the tale! After six weeks plus in hospital, once I was on my feet I was returned to the barracks and from there shipped to Dulag Luft at Frankfurt-on-Main, thence to Wetzlar transit camp and so to Stalag Luft 7 (arrived 5 August). Although handicapped to a degree, the sojourn at Luft 7 was a period of my life when I learnt lessons which one could not learn other than in adversity. The odd Red Cross food parcel was received from time to time to supplement the meagre German rations, and we fared reasonably well until January 1945.'

*

Arriving at Luft 7 in *Trupp 4* with Healy was Sergeant Stanley A. Keirle, another casualty of the Nuremberg raid on 30/31 March 1944. Stan Keirle was a wireless operator on 550 Squadron operating Lancaster B.IIIs at North Killingholme, Lincolnshire. The Nuremberg raid would be his seventeenth op. The rest of his crew (on their nineteenth op) for that night's sortie in Lancaster BQ-N for Nan, LM425, were: F/S Arthur Jeffries (pilot); Sergeant Harold Simpson (navigator); F/S Dennis S. Jeffrey (bomb aimer); Sergeant Robert Paxton (flight engineer); Sergeant W. George Upton (mid-upper gunner); and Sergeant James W. Whitley (rear gunner).

Stan Keirle:

'We were mortally hit by predicted flak (before reaching the target) from the Liège defences at almost exactly midnight. The time is fixed in my mind because I had just gone over to the group frequency to receive their hourly broadcast when all hell was let loose. We had been hit in the starboard wing, the outboard engine being on fire. The pilot and engineer used the fire extinguishers and tried to feather the prop, but I am not sure whether they managed it or not. The skipper ordered parachutes on. I found mine in its stowage compartment, and clipped it on my harness. I returned to the astrodome, still plugged in to the intercom. The fire died down for a while, then suddenly broke out afresh with increased intensity and crept back into the wing itself – which burnt through very quickly.

'I stood there and watched the outboard engine and outer wing fall off – at which time the aircraft dipped a wing and started to spiral downwards with all engines at maximum revs it seemed. The g force was tremendous, and before passing out I remember floating through the air past the navigator's position and getting my feet all tangled up with the cockpit controls. The skipper was still in his seat struggling to get control of the plane. I then passed out having concluded that the situation was hopeless – mentally regretting that my mother would have to handle the news of me being listed as missing while my father was seriously ill.

'What happened next is a very vague memory, which could even be imagination. I found myself in open air with wind rushing past my face. Slowly, the realisation came that I was falling through space and that I should pull the rip-cord of my parachute. The 'chute was not on my chest, it was dangling around my feet. Having hauled it up via the loose harness, I pulled the cord and something came up and hit me under the chin – knocking me out again! I woke up tumbling through trees feeling that my right arm was entangled in a bulky object. I finally landed on my back with the object I was entangled with across my back – my bottom and legs on one side of it and my head and shoulders on the other side. I think I passed out again. Gradually my head cleared enough to know that I was stretched across something, and that all around me was quiet except for the thunder of aircraft engines overhead.'

Stan had landed close to Duren, near Liège, while his aircraft crashed at Gilippe, eight kilometres east of Verviers:

'At that moment the truth dawned that I was still alive, and the noise overhead was the bomber force on its way to Nuremberg. My parachute canopy was caught in a tree, and I could not breathe too easily. My left leg was doubled under my bottom and ached, and my back hurt very much. Gradually I forced myself to turn over and push the "object" away – my right arm was through the thing which turned out to be the cockpit canopy – all ten feet of it, or whatever its length was. My back hurt like hell! I lay there for what seemed to be ages before the noise overhead faded away in the distance. I thought to myself "Go get them fellers". Very soon I began to feel cold, and then I started to shiver but could do nothing about it. My back felt very painful, and I could only move very slowly, certainly not enough to keep warm, or to walk and find shelter. Nobody would find me in this forest even if they knew a bod was in there I reasoned, and for the second time that night thought that the outlook was not too rosy.

'I wondered how the other fellows had fared, but was fairly convinced that their chances of survival were slim, and reckoned that I was very lucky indeed to be alive. At that point I became determined that I was going to survive come what may, and set about evaluating the situation and at the same time try to keep warm. Some time later, I saw a torch waving about, so I blew the whistle attached to my battledress tunic. Gradually the light got closer, and then shone directly on me. A German soldier was holding the torch. Using sign language, he asked me if I had a gun. When he was satisfied that I was telling the truth, he propped me up and proceeded to gather sticks and wood, and then lit a fire in a clearing. That soldier carried me to the fire and made me as comfortable as possible. When I had warmed through I remembered that I had a packet of cigarettes in my tunic, so I offered him one and we smoked together. He spoke no English and I no German, but we did manage to communicate a little, and I learned that he had found two others close by but they were "*kaput*".

'The soldier left me for a short while as dawn was breaking. He returned, picked me up and carried me across his shoulder for some distance where he had a motorcycle and sidecar parked. He dumped me in the sidecar, and off we went. I think that must have been the most painful ride I have ever experienced. I was taken to a village and put in what appeared to be the village hall. There I was joined by George Upton our mid-upper gunner and Dennis Jeffrey the bomb aimer who, I seem to remember, was limping badly because of sprained ankles. George had hit a tree on landing and was bloodied around the face, I seem to recall. An officer appeared – Gestapo I think – who did not like us smoking and went into a rage immediately. He ranted and roared for a while then left us, never to be seen again. We left by truck and finished up in Aachen, I believe. I say believe because by this time I was apparently in a bad way, and Dennis and George had to support me to walk.

'I think it was George who told me, after the war, that we were made to walk through the streets of Aachen, which had been attacked that night as a diversionary raid to the main force. Seemingly the civilians were angry and wanted to get at us, and the guards fixed bayonets to their rifles in case of trouble. He told me that I was shouting back at the people, calling them all the names under the sun and they – Dennis and George – could not shut me up, which did not help the situation at all. I remember nothing of that at all! I was taken to a hospital at Aachen, and put into a wooden hut in the grounds of the hospital. Whether my two crew members were there or not, I do not know. It must have been several days before I became interested in my surroundings again. Day by day I felt better as the cuts healed, and the bruising everywhere came out. My skin had many shades from dense black, through purple and all the way to yellow, changing almost hourly. By this time I had a plaster cast on my left foot and my left knee was strapped to a board, but it was my back which was so painful.

'My German guard was quite friendly and tried to talk to me, but we could only resort to sign language – sometimes it worked, other times not. One night, the air raid sirens started to wail, and I could already hear the sound of Merlin engines. Within a couple of minutes all hell was let loose with the whistling of falling bombs and the crunch of them exploding. Then it became impossible to hear individual bombs falling; it was a crescendo of fiendish screaming and explosions. I decided that I should be under the bed instead of in it, and somehow managed to do that, throwing an incendiary bomb out of the window en route. I was bounced up and down many times, the roof of the wooden hut collapsed, but I was all right being protected by the bed. Gradually the horrendous noise faded away. After a while I could hear scraping noises and talking – it was my German guard looking for me. After hauling me out of the wreckage, he carried me to the basement of the main hospital and found a bed for me. I kept absolutely quiet, not daring to talk in case the German people milling around would resent my presence and do something about it.

'I suppose I stayed in that hospital for several days. One morning I was told to dress, and was put on board a small truck with about three other people – probably Polish people – and driven to the station. En route I could see some of the damage inflicted, which was quite considerable. The train took us to Bonn, from where we walked to Stalag 6G on the hills overlooking the city. The walk itself was absolute agony, the guard detailing two of the guys who were in the party to support me. Later it was discovered that I had three fractured lumbar vertebræ. The cure was to be strapped to a wooden bed for a week or two. For company in that room was one other Englishman – Leslie somebody – who had crashed his aircraft and received multiple fractures of both legs. (Later we were both at a medical rehabilitation unit at Loughborough College, and I was glad to see that he was mobile again.) There were, I think, five American fellows suffering from different ailments. One had walked for miles on frostbitten feet to the extent that he had lost all his toes, and others had bullet wounds and fractures. We were under the care of an elderly, apparently quite famous, Polish surgeon who eventually died in a POW camp, so Leslie told me. He was a fine gentleman and did all he possibly could for us. Our constant companion and the butt of many jokes was Aldo, an Italian soldier, who somehow became a POW in German hands. He was our batman come nurse, a great guy who did his best to make us comfortable under miserable circumstances.

'One day, early in June, I was judged to be well enough to be sent on my way, by train to Frankfurt-on-Main, and into solitary confinement at Dulag Luft awaiting interrogation. In my case, when I refused all but my name, rank and service number, the interrogator pooh-poohed my stupidity and proceeded to tell me that they knew all about 550 Squadron – naming the CO and others together with other pertinent information. He also said that they had known the Nuremberg raid was to take place before it actually happened, whether in fact they did or not I suppose I will never know.

'Around the middle of June, a whole group of RAF kriegies were assembled for transportation to a POW camp. We were told that the German population were a little annoyed at our past activities and should we be foolish enough to try to escape, we would be well and truly looked after by them! Of course that all pre-supposed that we would escape without being shot by the guards who had strict orders to show no mercy if anyone should attempt to do so, we were told! On the train, we indulged in a little guard baiting, our fellow blowing his top quite frequently at our insinuations that the Third Reich was *kaput* etc. etc. On arrival at Luft 7 I shared a hut with F/S Charles Medland DFM, Sergeant George "Slim" Jim King, F/S James "Jack" Mills, Sergeant Ronald "Spike" McGraw RCAF, and Warrant Officer Hendrik B. Vogel of the South African Air Force.'

Dennis Jeffrey and George Upton also survived, to become POWs at Stalag Luft VI (Heydekrug) and, later, Stalag 357. But Arthur Jeffries, Harold Simpson, Robert Paxton, and James Whitley, the rest of Stan Keirle's crew, were killed when the aircraft exploded.

*

One of the stories to go the rounds at Luft 7 was of the miraculous survival of a Pathfinder pilot. It seems that he was flying back across Holland at low level when his aircraft simply disintegrated, reckoned to have been the result of a direct hit in the fuel tanks. While the rest of his crew were lost in the explosion the pilot, who was not wearing his parachute, landed in a dyke in which there was barely a foot of water but below which were six feet or so of mud. He suffered no broken bones, no cuts, no bruises, just covered in mud.

Only one Luft 7 POW appears to fit the bill – pilot F/S W.J. Ward, the only survivor of Lancaster ND559, 156 (PFF) Squadron, the forty-first victim of Hauptmann Martin Drewes, Stab III./NJG1, on the night of 21/22 May 1944 (Duisburg). Though Ward and most of his crew were fairly new to the squadron, flying as rear gunner, on his sixty-sixth operation, was S/L J.E. Blair DFC, DFM, the squadron's gunnery leader.[42] As so often, experience counted for nothing.

It would seem, however, that Ward *was* injured, which was why he was handed over by the Dutch to the Germans. But if he were indeed injured, seriously as is suggested, then it is difficult to see how he could have recovered from those injuries in time to have arrived at Luft 7 in *Trupp 4* on 20 June, less than a month after he was blown out of his Lancaster. Perhaps Ward was the lucky mudlark after all?

\*

F/S Charles James Medland was awarded the DFM on 2 June 1944 after the raid to Chambly rail yards in northern France:

> 'This airman piloted an aircraft detailed to attack Chambly one night in May 1944. Soon after leaving the target area the aircraft was struck by machine-gun fire from a fighter. The starboard inner engine was so badly damaged that it became completely dislodged from its mountings. In spite of this Flight Sergeant Medland succeeded in out-manoeuvring the attacker which was finally evaded. The port engine now began to vibrate so violently that it had to be put out of action. Subsequently the aircraft was attacked on three occasions by fighters. In the last of these attacks the bomber became uncontrollable, and went into a steep dive. It seemed as if the aircraft would have to be abandoned, but Flight Sergeant Medland succeeded in regaining control and afterwards flew the badly-damaged aircraft to base. He proved himself to be a skilful, courageous and resolute captain and pilot.'

As so often happened an award was gazetted long after its recipient had been lost in action, but in Charles Medland's case the gap was only some twelve days. He was shot down on 21/22 May 1944 (Duisburg) when 514 Squadron, stationed at Waterbeach, Cambridgeshire, lost three of its Lancasters. From DS633 and DS781 there were no survivors, but from LL695, JI-A for Able, there were four. Its crew were: F/S Charles J. Medland DFM (pilot)[43]; F/O Dennis F. 'Johnny' Walker (navigator); F/S Leonard J. Venus (bomb aimer); Sergeant Anthony R. 'Tony' Sealtiel (flight engineer); Sergeant Leslie Shimmons (wireless operator); Sergeant Charles E. 'Chuck' Rose RCAF (mid-upper gunner); and Sergeant Benjamin R. 'Ben' Williams (rear gunner).

They were shot down after bombing the target, but there was disagreement amongst them as to the cause. The bomb aimer believed that they were the victim of a night-fighter, whereas the pilot believed it was flak. They were almost certainly the fortieth victim of the experienced night-fighter pilot Hauptmann Martin Drewes, Stab III./NJGI (who was to claim two more Lancasters before his night's work was done – see Ward above).[44]

Charles Medland:

> '"A" for Able aircraft were unlucky for no apparent reason. Speaking from memory the previous incumbent was Peter Hood.[45] He had two mid-upper gunners cut in half on two consecutive trips by machine-gun bullets, and failed to return soon afterwards. I understand that Peter survived, so no doubt did his crew, but I have no first-hand knowledge. I took

over the new "A", did its acceptance trials and flew it regularly until I lost it. During that time we were attacked fairly regularly, my gunners claimed three fighters destroyed and I think their claims were allowed. We were only damaged on one occasion, by a Ju88 firing rockets – that was one we claimed. At the time we were at 700 feet and nearly went into the deck as we climbed away from the target. Not particularly funny at night either. Anyway, we got back to Woodbridge for the second time of asking. "A" for Able was three weeks out of service being repaired, and we lost her on the next trip!'

Charles continues:

'I have no recollection whatever of the last moments [of A for Able]. The first thing I can recall was regaining consciousness in the pilot's seat in the cockpit sometime during the night. I can still see the instrumentation and the gyro instruments which had toppled. I thought I was back at base and wondered where the crew had gone. I tried to get out of my seat, and although it was apparent I wasn't held down, I was unable to move either of my legs. I then lost consciousness. I always understood we had been set on fire by flak.

'When I met my wireless operator, Les Shimmons, at Birmingham soon after getting back, he told me that the aircraft engines were burning and he was the last one to leave the aircraft, which I was then flying on the port outer engine only. He said that as he fell clear of the forward escape hatch the aircraft was passing just above him, the fuel tanks blew, and that I couldn't have got out. He said, and this was confirmed by Len Venus, that they had been told the pilot had been recovered from the wreckage of the aircraft, and assumed I was dead. I know that Len Venus was most surprised to see me when he arrived at Luft 7.

'The order in which my crew would have escaped in the circumstances would have been for the two gunners to have left by the rear end. The order at the front would have been Len Venus, who travelled on the escape hatch anyway, then Tony Sealtiel, who it seems likely his 'chute failed, and then Johnny Walker and Les Shimmons. Johnny Walker got hung up in a tree and, on dropping out of his harness, fell some distance and broke his ankle. He crawled to a Dutch farm house where, after a lot of hesitation, he was taken in. He was seen by a Dutch doctor the following morning who decided that it would be necessary for him to be taken to a hospital to have it set. He was taken by farm cart to Eindhoven Hospital and later to a German family, who had been evacuated from the Ruhr to Holland. When fit he was passed on to the Dutch Underground Movement, where he apparently found Les Shimmons.

'Les had come down safely; he said that after landing he sat on the ground wondering what the hell to do. He heard an aircraft flying low overhead, and when landing lights came on he realized he was sitting on a German airfield. He ran off apparently unseen and fell into a dyke; he followed this and managed to get off the airfield, and later got in touch with the Dutch Underground. Johnny and Les stayed with the Underground Movement until the Allied Armies advanced into Holland. They then managed to get behind the Allied lines, and I believe they made it back to England in August 1944.'

Johnny Walker and Les Shimmons were re-united on 26 June in a wood near Geldrop, having been taken to a hide-out where there were twenty-six Dutchmen – the only person bearing arms was the Dutch leader, Wim Gippard, but none took an active part in the Resistance – and eight Allied airmen – F/S S. Sparkes (578 Squadron); F/Sgt R.H. Punter RCAF (626 Squadron); F/S E. Grisdale (626 Squadron, same crew as Punter); Sgt J.M. Trend (15 Squadron); F/S R. Gardner (10

Squadron); Sgt William C. Kinney USAAF (ball turret gunner), and 2/Lt Harry F. Cooper USAAF (bomb aimer, from the same crew as Kinney).[46]

It is probable that most, if not all, of the RAF evaders were back in England in September, not August as Johnny Walker thought, as some of them were interviewed by MI9 on 23 September 1944. Charles Medland again:

'I have no idea where the wreckage hit the deck, but it could have been in the region of Weert, wherever that is.[47] In the morning, well after daylight I would have thought, I regained consciousness and found I was being gently shaken by some quite young girls who talked to me in a language I did not understand. They obviously saw that I was severely injured and, whilst some stayed with me, some went away. I must have lost consciousness again, but came to and found that I was being lifted, in a sitting position, through the starboard side of the aircraft where the engineer's panel and the fuselage was missing. As they lifted me clear I saw that the fuselage forward of the cabin was intact, but the fuselage was broken from where the windscreen would normally have been to the trailing edge of the port wing. As they laid me down again I lost consciousness again.

'My next recollection is waking up in a small bed in a small room. Sitting in the doorway was what I now know was a Kriegsmarine, and outside the sun was shining brightly through the leaves and white flowers of a horse-chestnut tree. I could have only been conscious a matter of seconds. My next recollection was being on an operating table with green clad persons with white caps bending over me, but that too was just a fleeting moment. Some days later I regained full consciousness in not an overlarge square room with several beds packed tightly together, much to the relief of the occupants who were fellow aircrew, who told me that I had been driving them up the wall with my incessant ramblings. I gathered that I had been there over a week. I was later told that I had a fracture/dislocation of numbers 2 and 3 cervical vertebræ, with further dislocations of a less severe nature.

'The hospital was the Wilhelmina Gestern at Amsterdam, part of which was apparently requisitioned by the Luftwaffe. One morning a German orderly came into our room and told us the Allies had landed in France during the night, adding "but already we have thrown you back into the sea". We remained there for several more days, during which time I found that my legs would not respond very well, my left one being the worse as I could not lift my foot off the ground, and my neck was troublesome and difficulty was experienced in trying to move it forwards and backwards, which caused shooting pains down my arms and legs, akin to the feeling one has when a "funny bone" is knocked, whilst turning from side to side was impossible. Movement of my head also gave me a lot of pain in the right of centre of my back under the shoulder blade, and still does to this day.

'Some time later we were warned that we would be moving at 0600 hours the following day to Germany. We were taken by coach to a railway station where we were put on a train en route for Frankfurt-am-Main. It was a delightful trip down the Rhine valley on a beautiful day. It was noticeable at all the Dutch stations the train stopped that most of the station staff were bold enough to give us the V sign accompanied by a large grin. We eventually arrived at Frankfurt and were taken by coach to Dulag Luft where the party was split up. I was taken to an underground cell, the door was unlocked and I was pushed inside, where there were at least twelve American aircrew who were either leaning against the walls, or sitting or lying on the cement floor. One can best describe the accommodation as a cement box with a steel door, which was lit by an extremely high-powered electric bulb, with a plain glass window about 18" square, the bottom of the window being about 6 feet from the floor and on a level with the ground outside. There was no ventilation and the cell smelt strongly of unwashed bodies, sweat, bowel products, both solids and gaseous, and urine. After a while one's sensory organs became accustomed to the stench and it no longer mattered.

'In the morning we were allowed to go upstairs to a toilet, and returned again downstairs. As the morning went on, the Americans disappeared one at time, and by midday I was the only one left. Early in the afternoon I was taken upstairs where a German Unteroffizier handed me a pen and a foolscap form marked in English across the top "International Red Cross". The top section related to one's personal particulars and from thereon down most of the questions related to military matters, such as squadron and flight, group, radio call signs, names of station commander, flight commanders, etc, etc., and details of one's training and other units and duties where one had served. After reading the form I inscribed my rank, name and number, drew two lines from top to bottom, and handed it back. The German ranted and raved at me and I found myself being propelled back to the downstairs cell which, after the semi-fresh air of the first floor, was most nauseating. Later in the afternoon I was taken upstairs and placed in a small room; this had a wooden bed with two dirty smelly blankets and a large frosted glass window which was locked.

'My personal property had been taken from me, consisting of a gold signet ring, cigarette case, cigarette lighter, watch, fountain pen, and a large pocket knife, and I never saw any of it again, so it was difficult to keep check of time and day. Sometime that evening an orderly came with a cup of black coffee, a piece of sausage, a thick slice of black bread. This was the first food and drink I had had since the previous day, which had been given us on leaving the hospital in Amsterdam. To the best of my knowledge, I spent nine days at this establishment in my little cell. After a couple of days I was nearly climbing up the wall. The place was hot and smelly, the window was locked, and the general conditions were dreadful. One was taken to the ablutions area in the morning, and thereafter had to rely on being able to attract attention of the guards the best way one could. There were three meals a day, breakfast consisted of barley porridge, and the elderly guard, a man of about sixty years of age, used to come back with a second helping nearly every day I was there. Dinner was served at midday and consisted of vegetable soup, complete with beetles and goodness knows what else. Still, I suppose it was filling even if it wasn't fattening. Tea varied a bit, black bread and sausage, sometimes with sauerkraut, black bread, and a very smelly cheese similar to cottage cheese encased in a gelatine casing about two inches in diameter, and sometimes black bread and carrot jam, washed down with water or black coffee.

'After about a week, I was taken out of the cell and escorted to an administrative block, where I was handed over to a German officer who took me to his office and sat me down in a chair by his desk. He sat down and introduced himself to me, and held up the form I had been given when I first arrived. He said in good English "You didn't like our Red Cross Form" and laughed. He said that his job was to find out all about me, and it was my job not to tell him. He said that since I had been in the establishment, enquiries had been made and these had traced me back to the remains of my aircraft; which was JI-A of 514 Squadron of 3 Group. After telling me more about the Royal Air Force, he threw a book across the table which contained a wealth of information about the service as far as it related to bases, groups, conversion units and training generally, adding "You have suffered in vain". That was the end of my interrogation.

'He then asked me if I was married, and whether I had written home since I was captured. When I told him no, he opened a drawer of his desk and handed me a *Luftpostkriegsgefangenen Karte* and a pen. I wrote the card and addressed it to my wife at her mother's home at Ilfracombe, although at the time we were living at 126, Kings Hedges Road, Cambridge. He read it and said "You live in Devon; one of my officers here knows your part of the country well. Would you like to see him?" I said I would, and he called an orderly and told him to take me to Room 44. On entering the room, the occupant was a German pilot and we recognised each other. He was a representative for a German firm marketing machinery for glove manufacturing, and in the course of his business used to call at Bideford and stayed at Tanton's Hotel, next to Bideford Police Station.

'He told me that he had been trained by the Luftwaffe and was a reserve officer, and had been recalled to Germany about two months before the war broke out, and that he had been flying first against the Czechs and Poles and later against the Russians. But because of his knowledge of English and England, he had latterly come to Dulag Luft on rest. I complained bitterly about not being able to wash and shave, and about the food. I did get a good wash and shave that afternoon, and the following day I was moved out to Wetzlar into a small compound furnished with tents, with a contingent of about twenty other RAF personnel whom I had not previously met. At Wetzlar the food was mainly from Red Cross parcels, which was a delightful change from the barley porridge and insect ridden soup and black bread. Here we were given a clothing parcel together with boots, shaving gear, soap, tooth powder, pencil, pipe and two ounces of tobacco, needles and cotton, tooth-brush, and one or two other odds and ends courtesy of the American Red Cross, as were the brown boots and khaki underclothes and shirts.

'On leaving Wetzlar the occupants of our tent stayed together and were in the same railway wagon. It did not hold many passengers; the seats were not upholstered but wooden slats. Each seat carried two passengers with an alleyway through the middle. The engine was driven by two quite young men dressed in Kriegsmarine uniform, probably from a ship's engine room staff. The train was made up with our coaches, I think it was two or perhaps three, and the rest appeared to be goods destined for the Russian Front. It seemed an endless journey to Bankau. During our travels, we saw that, as we moved eastward, the towns and villages showed less and less signs of warfare compared with the west, where bomb damage was colossal and whole towns appeared to have been completely devastated without a living soul in sight, and where the rubble had been bulldozed into heaps either side of the street. We also saw our first Russian prisoners. They were gaunt, physically weak, dressed in rags and so thin that one wondered how a civilised nation could reduce fellow humanity to such a state of degradation. It also provoked considerable speculation as to what the future held for us. During the journey I suffered a great deal of discomfort as I had no neck support, and the coaches, which were not upholstered nor close-coupled, were constantly shunted forward and back, and in desperation I spent much of my time lying on the floor.

Charles and his travelling companions arrived at Luft 7 on 20 June 1944:

'Finally we reached a platform beside the railway line with an indication board announcing that we had at last reached Bankau. We then set off on foot for the last two or three miles to the camp, a somewhat slow progress with those, like me, with two speeds, slow and very stationary. On arrival we found that we were to be housed in the rabbit hutches, six men to a hut. The detached residence which contained me and five others was on the far side of the compound. There was a communal water tap nearby, and a lavatory block to the rear. Sanitation was a large hole ten feet deep with a low wooden rail fitted for the sedentary jobs. There was nothing to stop one having a backward somersault if one so desired! Lime was occasionally spread over the top between which times it was the Valhalla for flies of all shapes, colours and sizes, undreamed of, drawn from all parts of Prussia and the rest of Eastern Europe.

'On the arrival of our intake at Luft 7 we found very few prisoners in residence, and at that time the camp was thoroughly unorganised. The weather being very hot, we slopped around in underpants only, or some might have worn vests as well. This did not go down well with the German officers who took the two parades a day, morning and afternoon, when we were counted. The Camp Commandant, Oberstleutnant Behr, didn't go much on it either, and we were ordered to parade fully dressed as we would at home. The first parade thereafter, the Oberstleutnant stood looking at us with a great smile on his face, obviously pleased with what he had seen and shouted out "Good Morning, Soldiers".[48] Full dress, whatever it might be, was the order of the day thereafter, though most of us only possessed a miscellaneous collection of wearing apparel at that time. My own gear was an oil-stained battledress practically worn out, no head-dress, khaki American issue shirts, khaki American socks and brown boots, and finished off with an American army greatcoat. All underwear and socks were also GI issue.

'To the best of my knowledge there were no attempted escapes from Luft 7. When we were in the compound with the mini-huts there was a "gash" pit near the safety wire, a single strand stretched around the perimeter about 15 metres inside the main fence. This pit was about 10 feet deep and all our empty food cans and similar rubbish were thrown in and, when full, buried. One of the lads got a post from somewhere to which he nailed a bedboard upon which a hand had been drawn with a pointing finger in the direction of this pit, with the words "To the tunnel" inscribed thereon. There was no apparent sign of the "ferrets" and the guards showing any interest in this undertaking, so one brave soul did a bit of digging but, as it seemed to have been written off by the Germans as a prime example of British stupidity, it was not continued with. Furthermore, with the Germans being rolled back towards the Fatherland on every front, it was obvious that the duration would be minimal, and bets were being taken in the summer of 1944 that we would be free by September 1944. However, this was extended to Christmas and then spring of 1945, which did in fact signal the end. Consequently the risk of being shot as an escaper was far greater than the risk incurred in sitting it out behind the wire. From my own point of view I was quite unfit physically, still suffering from the effects of the crash, and had to report daily for treatment, which I received in the German quarters some 800 yards away. To get there, the two German medical orderlies who had a "surgery" in the compound would take me to the gate, where we were joined by three armed guards and together we would slowly walk to the German sick bay. Five German personnel, all carrying arms, to escort a very sick kriegie and bring him back!

'The initial issue of blankets was three per man, but later on there was an order that two per man was sufficient and one had to be surrendered. I believe that most of the men who received an initial issue of three managed to retain them in spite of spot checks, as we normally knew in advance about the checks and what was likely to be confiscated if found, so that commodity was always carefully hidden. There were many things subject of search from time to time but, the Teutonic mind being what it is, articles that were forbidden could be left lying about with impunity provided that was not what the search was for, and it would be ignored.'

Charles Medland's bomb aimer, Len Venus, recalls that the:

'Duisburg raid was my twelfth op, and we were shot down after bombing the target by a night-fighter. I managed to bale out and landed near Borkel en Schaft, Aalst Waalre, near Eindhoven. I was hidden by the Dutch Underground Movement, and eventually captured by the Gestapo at a flat in Antwerp on 22 July. I arrived at Luft 7 on 26 July, and was pleasantly surprised to be greeted by my pilot, Charles Medland.'

*

James W. 'Jack' Mills joined the RAF at Uxbridge on 6 June 1940. On completion of his training as a bomb aimer he was posted to 619 Squadron, operating Lancasters out of RAF Dunholme Lodge, Lincolnshire. His seventeenth operational sortie was to Schweinfurt, the home of Germany's main ball-bearing factories, on 26/27 April 1944. 206 Lancasters and eleven Mosquitos of 5 Group, and nine Lancasters of 1 Group took part. Unfortunately, 'low-level marking provided for the first time by Mosquitos of 627 Squadron was not accurate. Unexpected strong winds delayed the Lancaster marker aircraft and the main force of bombers. German night-fighters were carrying out fierce attacks throughout the period of the raid. The bombing was not accurate and much of it fell outside Schweinfurt.'[49] Twenty-one Lancasters were lost.

On this raid, unsurprisingly classified as a failure, F/S Mills flew in Lancaster LL919, PG-W, with F/L Guy Godfrey Charles Gunzi (pilot); F/O Nickolas Vlassie RCAF (navigator); Sergeant E.G. 'Bill' Cass (flight engineer – 'spare bod'); Sergeant Alan Pickstone (wireless operator); Sergeant Les Feindell RCAF (mid-upper gunner); and Sergeant Ken Frank (rear gunner).

Jack Mills:

'We were flying an almost-new Lancaster, "W" for Willie, as our own Lancaster "V" for Victor was undergoing a "major" (service), and we were on our seventeenth op with 619 Squadron. Our aircraft was attacked by a night-fighter, and blew up before reaching the target. I was blown out unconscious, and must have pulled the parachute handle unknowingly. I landed near Landeville, Doulaincourt, France, and was captured the same day (27 April at Landeville) by Luftwaffe personnel. I arrived at Luft 7 on 20 June.'

Their assailant was probably Oberleutnant Dietrich Schmidt of 8./NJG1, who claimed his twentieth victory, a Lancaster, at a height of 4,400 metres somewhere south west of St Dizier. Jack Mills, badly wounded during the attack on his aircraft, was the only survivor.[50]

*

635 (PFF) Squadron was formed on 20 March 1944 at RAF Downham Market, Norfolk, from 'C' Flight, 97 (PFF) Squadron and 'B' Flight, 35 (PFF) Squadron, in time to participate in the disastrous Nuremberg raid on 30/31 March 1944. One of the crews, formerly of the said 'C' Flight, on that raid was that of F/L J.H. Nicholls DFC, RAAF, with his twenty-three-year-old mid-upper gunner F/S William D. Ogilvie:

'My thirty-fourth trip was the Nuremberg raid on 30/31 March 1944. Our aircraft on that raid was Lancaster B.III, JB706 (194 hours), and the rest of the crew, on their thirty-fifth op, were: F/L Johnny H. Nicholls, DFC, RAAF (pilot); F/O Ronald Easson, DFC, RAAF, (navigator); Warrant Officer Kenroy A. Jolley, DFC, RAAF (bomb aimer); F/S Sidney A.C. Smith, RAF (flight engineer); F/S Jack Gardener, RAF (wireless operator air gunner); and F/S Alfred Whitehead, RAF (rear gunner). Our function was a blind (target) marker – illuminator. Flak got us. We were at the head of the (bomber) stream, so we were not protected by "Window", and we were also a "Wind Finder", so we got it when we were flying straight and level for an exact fix to calculate the winds. The flak battery was an isolated one near Westerburg, and got three of us in quick succession. The rear gunner was killed in his turret, and the rest of us got out. But the bomb aimer's parachute did not work; he may not have had his leg straps fitted. The aircraft subsequently blew up when the "Cookie" 4,000lb [bomb] went off.

'Upon landing, I suffered a fractured ankle, and received initial treatment at Hohe Mark (Oberursel), where we were housed in the mental block for security. I was then sent to Obermassfeld Lazarett in Stalag 9C with British doctors, and then on to Meiningen for convalescence, and to receive some of the most excellent physiotherapy at the hands of Captain Laurie. We could never escape, so my walking and ankle became 100% again. I arrived at Luft 7 on 20 June and remained there until we started the forced march to Stalag 3A, my companion being Sergeant Mieczysław Cytulski, PAF. He was a real tower of strength, and when I was all in he kept me going.'[51]

Nicholls and Easson were POWs at Stalag Luft 1, while Smith and Gardener went to Luft 6 and Stalag 357. Sidney Smith was one of the many who were seriously injured on 19 April 1945 when, on the march after their camp had been evacuated, they were attacked by RAF Typhoons near Gresse, east of Hamburg, in north Germany. In a tragic loss of life with the war's end so near twenty-five airmen POWs, at least twelve British soldiers, and six German guards were killed. Eight more airmen were seriously wounded, and a further twelve less so. All were admitted to hospital.

*

On 15 February 1944 the *London Gazette* announced that 1063420 Flight Sergeant Frank Joseph Tudor, 35 [PFF] Squadron, had been awarded the DFM 'in recognition of gallantry and devotion to duty in the execution of air operations'. The unpublished citation for his award read as follows:

'This NCO has been on many operations as a wireless operator in a crew engaged in a most vital role. The targets have been in some of the enemy's most heavily-defended areas. At all times this NCO has demonstrated his skill and reliability as a wireless operator with great coolness in spite of very heavy opposition. His devotion to duty and enthusiasm to operate against the enemy are worthy of the highest praise and set a fine example to other aircrew in the squadron.'

Frank Tudor:

'In Pathfinder Force (PFF) Bomber Command, aircrew either volunteered or were picked from Bomber Command Stations. The number of missions you were required to complete was forty-five.[52] If you completed the missions you were not required to do any more in the European Theatre of Operations. In Bomber Command you may complete thirty missions, and then have a rest, probably instructing somewhere. Then you may be recalled to do another tour of thirty missions. The main point was that in PFF you were always first over the target. Forty-two of my ops were with my original crew. Unfortunately I missed out on three operations, one when my pilot, S/L Everett, went on his first mission as a co-pilot (for experience), and two due to sickness. This meant my original crew had completed their forty-five missions and I had three more to do. My pilot volunteered to do more missions so as to complete my trips, but this was not allowed, plus I would not have liked this to have happened anyway. Incidentally, S/L Everett, DSO, DFC, did volunteer to do more missions, but unfortunately "Failed to Return" after a raid on Hemmingstedt on the night of 7/8 March 1945.'[53]

Frank himself failed to return on the night of 22/23 May 1944, when 361 Lancasters and fourteen Mosquitos of RAF Bomber Command undertook the first large-scale raid on Dortmund for a year. One of the eighteen Lancasters lost was ND762, 'E' for Easy, 35 (PFF) Squadron, RAF Graveley, Huntingdonshire, with its crew of: F/L E. Holmes DFC (pilot); P/O D.E. Coleman DFC (navigator); F/O A.T. Maskell (2nd bomb aimer); Warrant Officer Frank J. Tudor DFM (wireless operator); F/S A.W. Cox (mid-upper gunner); F/L J.K. Stewart (navigator); Sergeant A.S. McLaren (rear gunner); and Sergeant J.R. Cursiter (flight engineer). It took off at 2247 hours tasked as 'Visual Centerer' with, as Frank Tudor recalls, an eighth member of the crew, a:

'Civilian Air Ministry "Boffin" working on Radar experiments... In my case this was to be my forty-fifth and last mission. I went as a spare wireless operator with a different crew. The wireless operator from this crew was not available. I had waited weeks for this occasion. In fact during the day of take-off, I had prepared myself for fourteen days' leave. My uniform etc. was spruced up and my leave pass was made out and signed with effect from 2359 hours of that day. After bombing the target, we were shot down by two Focke Wolfe 190s[54] over Holland, at approximately 0230 hours, and I landed on top of a tree in a field. I was captured at 0400 hours at a farmhouse by Dutch police. Being injured, they handed me over to the German army. They took me by an army lorry to what looked like a small convent run by two nuns. Out of sight of the German guards, one of the nuns took blood from the arm of her friend and squirted it over my face where I was injured. In broken English they explained that they wanted me to look more hurt than I really was, so that I could stay there longer with them and maybe escape. Unfortunately the ruse did not work as the next day I was taken to the Herman Goering Luftwaffe Hospital in Amsterdam. It was a great pity because I never did get to thank them for their bravery and kindness towards me.

'I arrived at Luft 7 on 20 June. As food and especially cigarettes were in short supply, one had to conjure up something to obtain these necessities. I was fortunate in being a member of a good combine (hut mates), who thought up a scheme of washing prisoners' clothes. Thus we became known as the "Dhobi Wallahs". Mind you it wasn't that much of a good job, as we had to use cold water and ordinary soap bars. Obviously we could not press or iron clothes. "So what!", these customers were not going to the Ritz. We folded the washing in orderly fashion; this was my job as I was the delivery boy. I used to take the names and hut numbers, and collect the payment. Examples of charge were as follows: one pair of socks – one cigarette; one shirt – two cigarettes; one pair of trousers – four cigarettes; one coat – six cigarettes. Chocolate and food would also be accepted for certain articles. Most of the prisoners washed their own clothes, but the remainder came to us – those that could afford it! It was amazing how prisoners kept themselves clean and tidy. There were not a lot of lice found in the clothes that we washed. To us we were doing a good job, and I am sure our customers were satisfied. I might further add that our business folded up when the Russian army attacked from the East, and the Germans took us on the forced route march – let's say our business went into liquidation.'

F/L Holmes and F/O Coleman were betrayed to the Gestapo in Antwerp on 17 June 1944, and were kept in Antwerp and Brussels jails before being sent to Stalag Luft 3. The other five were killed.

## CHAPTER FOUR

# 21-28 JUNE 1944, *TRUPPEN 5, 6, & 7*

**21 JUNE 1944.** *Trupp* 5 (two men) arrived – F/S George H. Cross and Sgt Ronald W. 'Spike' McGraw RCAF.

\*

On the night of 11/12 December 1942, forty-eight Halifaxes, twenty Lancasters, eight Stirlings, and six Wellingtons of RAF Bomber Command set off to bomb Turin, Italy. Over half turned back before attempting to fly over the Alps because of severe icing conditions, and though twenty-eight crews claimed to have bombed Turin the official report stated that only three bombs (two of them duds) and a few incendiaries fell on the city. The Italians suffered no casualties, but three Halifaxes and Stirling BF379 were lost.

Stirling BF379, MG-D, of 7 Squadron had departed RAF Oakington at 1704 hours with its crew of F/L W.T. Christie DFM (pilot); S/L V.C. McAuley DFC (navigator); Pilot Officer W.R. Jaggar RNZAF (2nd navigator);[55] F/S J.C. Jeffreys (flight engineer); F/S O. Falkingham DFM (wireless operator); F/S I. McDonald (bomb aimer/front gunner); Sergeant F.K. Nightingale (mid-upper gunner); and Sergeant R.W. McGraw RCAF (rear gunner).[56]

Christie had taken the Stirling down to around 7,000 feet over the target because of haze when it was hit by flak, and set on fire. Though the bombs were jettisoned BF379 continued to lose height. Deciding that it would be inadvisable to try to cross the Alps, course was altered to the south-west in the hope of reaching France, but they were still over Italy when Christie gave the order to bale out. What happened to him after his crew had jumped is not known, but it is likely that the Stirling was too low for his parachute to open and so paid the ultimate price for saving the rest of his crew, all of whom were taken prisoner. The squadron Form 540 recorded: 'One of the squadron's best crews, F/L Christie, was missing on this raid. He was a most experienced captain.'

Though an officer Jaggar went to the 'other ranks' camp at Stalag 344 (Lamsdorf), presumably because the Germans were unaware of his elevated status; F/S Falkingham went to Stalag VIIA, and F/S Jeffreys to Stalag IVB. F/S McDonald, camp not known, was held in a camp in Italy at some point. S/L McAuley and Sergeant Nightingale, both of whom were injured after baling out, were taken to a hospital in Rome, from which they escaped on 14 April 1944. They managed to seek sanctuary in the Vatican City and, though neither was a Roman Catholic, were granted an audience with His Holiness Pope Pius XII. On 7 June, they were repatriated by air from Rome to Spain. Taken to Madrid, they were then flown to Lisbon, and on by flying boat to Poole, England, where they landed on 9 June 1944.

Sergeant Spike McGraw, born in Truro, Nova Scotia, Canada, captured near Cuneo, a dozen miles south of Turin, arrived at the Italian POW camp PG 78 (Sulmona) on 31 December 1942. Spike McGraw:

> 'Joe Gordon and I were originally prisoners in Italy, and after Italy capitulated in September 1943 we lived with Italian people behind the [German] lines. We were recaptured in March 1944 trying to get through their lines. We were held in various camps on our way north (Sulmona 14 March, Latrina 16 March, and Mantua 12 May). I arrived at Stalag 7A Moosburg on 20 May, and finally ended up in Stalag Luft 7 on 21 June 1944... Sergeant Bob Hall was from Normal, Illinois, USA. He went to Canada to join up, and we were among some of the first kriegies in Bankau. That was when we

lived in little huts with five other guys.[57]

'Some reveries that come to mind are thoughts about Jock Campbell of Torphichen, West Lothian, Scotland, singing at night as we were lying in our little huts. My favourites were "The Old Rugged Cross" and "The Old Oaken Bucket". On Tuesday, our Red Cross parcel day, a fellow used to come around to trade his cigarettes for our chocolate and sugar bars. We used to call him "See ya Tuesday" because as soon as he had our candy etc. he would say "See ya Tuesday" and be gone. Vignettes of camp life and of the (forced) march were drawn by a fellow named Eric, for fifty cigarettes. When we moved into the larger permanent barracks, we were there only a short while when the cooks were accused of taking baths in the huge cooking vats – big trial, no verdict!'

\*

**21 JUNE 1944.** *Trupp 6* (one man) arrived – Sgt Richard A. Greene RCAF.

\*

In 1942, the quickest way to get an aircraft from Britain to the Middle East was to fly it there. The procedure generally was, having been detailed to collect an aircraft from No. 1 Overseas Air Delivery Unit, for a crew to fly from south-west England out into the Atlantic, round Spain and on to Gibraltar. Here, refuelled, the aircraft was then sent on to Malta for another stop before continuing to, usually, Egypt. All sections of the long route were fraught with danger, either from simply getting lost, running out of fuel (surprisingly common), or being attacked by enemy aircraft.

It was this latter danger that struck Wellington HX580 and its crew of five as they flew towards Malta having departed Gibraltar at 11.41 am on 30 July 1942. In fact two enemy aircraft attacked and shot down the Wellington into the Mediterranean. The rear gunner, Sgt G.W.S. Crompton RAAF, was severely wounded by the fighters, but refused to leave his post during the engagement. Such bravery would cost him his life, for the rest of the crew were unable to free him from his turret after ditching.

The only one of the survivors to end up at Luft 7 was the Wellington's observer, Sgt Richard Greene RCAF, who was an American citizen from Buffalo, New York. Following his capture on 31 July, he remained in a military hospital in Bizerta until November 1942, when transferred to PG 66 (Capua) on mainland Italy. Next month he was moved again, to PG 59 (Servigliano), and stayed there until the Italian capitulation on 8 September 1943. He escaped a week later with an American, Cpl Yax, and they spent the next six months being hidden at a farm, 'though we were forced to move around the area continually owing to the activities of the Fascists'.

At the beginning of May 1944, having heard that two Americans had been shot by Fascists, Greene and Yax decided to head north, but were captured by a band of partisans, and only managed to escape when they were attacked by more Fascists. On 8 May they were betrayed and captured again. Greene went to Stalag VIIA (Moosburg), where he remained until transferred to Luft 7 in June. As seen, he would be elected Man of Confidence.

\*

**28 JUNE 1944.** *Trupp 7* (sixty-two men) arrived.

\*

When Lancaster LL782, 622 Squadron, was abandoned on the night of 31 May/1 June 1944 (Trappes) one of the gunners discovered that his parachute had gone up in flames and elected to bale out clutching onto the wireless operator, Sgt Tom Cloran. Sadly, when Tom's parachute opened, the gunner was torn away from his helper. (See the similar incident on page 197.)

On his very first night at Luft 7, at around midnight, Fred Carey 'heard terrific screams coming from the hut next door… I went and knocked on the door thinking that the Jerries were up to something only to be told by some chap not to worry, he would see me in the morning'. Fred was then told the awful story of how the gunner 'couldn't hang on and screamed his way down to earth'. Tom suffered dreadful nightmares for many a night, and so disturbed by them were his room mates and those close by that he was moved to another hut, probably to the *Revier*.

*

James and Jeannie Comfort from Alford in Aberdeenshire, Scotland, had three boys in the armed forces: F/S William S. 'Jock' in the RAF; James in the Royal Artillery; and Alexander (Sandy) Charles, an RAF pilot officer on 80 Squadron, Desert Air Force, who was killed in action on 25 May 1942 in Hurricane BE707. Jock sailed from Glasgow on Armistice Sunday, 1941 aboard the *Arundel Castle*, and did his pilot training in South Africa before being posted to the OTU at Ismailia. Eventually he joined 111 (Fighter) Squadron which by May 1944 was stationed at Lago airfield in Italy, a landing strip near the mouth of the Volturno river, and was equipped with clipped-wing Spitfire IXs.

One day in the middle of May 1944, Jock was on patrol with his squadron when he:

> 'spotted two enemy aircraft flying below us. The flight leader told me to lead down. I fired at the first one which blew up. I then chased the other one; he kept flying into cloud and then out again. I waited below, and the next time he came out, I shot him down. He baled out and I took a picture of him with my gun camera. I was credited with two Me109s destroyed.
>
> '4 June 1944. Sunday morning was just another warm Italian day and we took off on patrol from Lago. This was more of a bore than anything else as the Hun was in full retreat to the north. Ten minutes to go and the CO would call up and say "Let's go home boys". Then one more landing done, bind a bit to the IO, and the rest of the day would be mine. However, fate intervened in the form of flak. It was light stuff, but it was so thick that there was no getting out of it, except by climbing. I remember the CO saying "Climb up aircraft or we will be over Rome". Then it happened. Robbie, decent chap he was, received a direct hit, burst into flames, half-rolled and went straight into the deck, where the petrol tanks blew up. Jed called up saying "Christ! Robbie's had it",[58] and at that moment my aircraft was hit. All I heard was a bang, I opened up the motor but it sounded so hellish that I throttled back. It was then I observed my airscrew was gone.
>
> 'I jettisoned my hood, tore off my helmet, undid my seat straps and started to climb out. However, all this had taken time, and on looking at the deck I knew I had very little height, so I decided to crash-land. The windscreen was all covered in oil, so I stuck my head over the side. Without seat straps the landing was risky, however it was too late. Gliding down I crossed over a wood at zero feet, stuck my feet on the instrument panel, checked and shut my eyes.
>
> 'Eventually, the aircraft [Spitfire MJ189] came to a standstill. I got out as quickly as possible and started to run. However a few bullets whistled over my head and put paid to that idea. I thought soldiers! But they proved to be members of the Luftwaffe

who came to me, so I had no option but to stick my hands up. The first one was rather annoyed, fixed me by the throat and then tore off my Mae West. However the others stopped his antics, and I had a good look at my aircraft. The airframe and the engine had not parted company on hitting *terra firma*, the tail assembly was at right angles to the fuselage, otherwise the aircraft seemed to be OK. It was 1020 hours, and I was a few miles north west of Rome.

'I was then taken by car to an Italian farmhouse, where the HQ seemed to be. The CO asked me the usual questions, and I gave him my name, rank and number. Meanwhile a Jerry attended to my legs which had been lacerated and bruised. Then all the company had a good look at me – some laughing, and others with looks of contempt on their faces. During all this I lay on the grass smoking my "Senior Service". When I was shot down all I had on was a vest, pants, a light khaki flying overall, shoes, socks, twenty Senior Service cigarettes, a box of matches, and a watch. I wore these clothes until I got to Dulag Luft.

'Time dragged on, and then came the Thunderbolts etc. strafing and bombing the main road, which was only a few hundred yards away. It was a lovely sight to see them diving down, the bombs being dropped, and the flashes and smoke as the guns were firing. The remainder of the day was spent in a stable, where I was crowded in with twenty or so Germans. At last night came and I was allowed to wash my face, and given a plate of soup. Incidentally, I heard the news from London, some of the Jerry's turned on their wireless and I heard Vera Lynn singing "We'll meet again". One of the officers allotted me to a truck and kindly informed me that escape would mean shooting. With two guards in front and two guards behind me, all armed with Tommy guns, I started my trip to Germany.

'We moved off and gained the main road, where there were two rows of traffic, both going north. Tanks, trucks, private cars, horse drawn transport, men on the march, and a few on bicycles. Dusk was falling, and for once the sound of aircraft engines was not to be heard. At last we started to move at snail's pace. Trucks which had been strafed only a few hours beforehand were still burning. Dead horses lay in distorted forms of death, some with split stomachs and their intestines spread across the road. The smell was hellish, but as I said to the guard "*C'est la Guerre*". Somehow or other we made some progress, and we stuck to the right and passed on. Then the throb of a multi-engined aircraft would be heard and the flares started to drop. At once all movement ceased, out we jumped, ran over the fields and lay down. The grass was damp and being in KD [khaki drill] I felt cold. One of the guards gave me his overcoat which I greatly appreciated. At last we were on the move and so we travelled through the night.

'At dawn we halted, hid the trucks in some scrub and slept. I shared my grassy bed with a German on one side and an Italian paratrooper on the other. I slept well but at 10 am I was told to get in a truck. Well off we went, but had not gone a quarter of a mile when the boys came over. It was a grand sight, but I was none too happy as the bombs and bullets came too close for my liking. One truck, which we passed half a minute before, blew up and the debris went up to 700 feet or more. A few Italian civilians were standing at the roadside, women weeping, men smoking, and a few hundred yards away was their Lancia burning fiercely – for them I had no sympathy whatsoever. A puncture delayed us at a small town, but I had a drink of Vermouth which bucked me up a lot.

'At last we reached another HQ where I was handed over to a corporal who searched me. The HQ was an old paper mill in a small town south of Viterbo. Then I was led to an Italian motorbus and seated myself beside a German sergeant. In this vehicle were twenty or so Germans and four Italian women. The women were to act as cooks, which they did, and I never saw them associating in an intimate manner with any of the Germans. That night I slept on the floor of the bus, but before I did I had a drink of cognac, vino and vermouth, which made me sleep much sounder.

'One day was spent there and then we moved up north. Travelling by night and hiding by day made progress slow. Viterbo was passed, the previous day being spent in a wood. The roads were still as crowded and the number of horses increased. I remember seeing a dead Italian civilian lying on the roadside stretched out on his back and stiff as a poker. The flies were crawling all over him, feeding on the congealed blood spattered over his clothes.

'It was a sad feeling to see my comrades flying overhead, and one day I saw my own squadron. Every bridge across the Tiber had been bombed, so we had to wade across and wait for the bus. Food was plain but there was ample of it. Main diet was brown bread, butter and sausage, plus coffee, minus sugar and milk. At one farm they killed a pig, so we had soup and fried pig. Water I seldom tasted as vino was plentiful. Cigarettes were so-so; one day we were very short and my guard – an Austrian chap – halved his one and only cigarette with me.

'At last we started to travel by day and covered quite a considerable mileage. One day the sergeant major told me I would be seeing the general. We had spent two days at a farmhouse, then I was taken to see him. His HQ was a villa, the rest of the time being an old Italian hospital. Through an interpreter, I was asked the usual questions, the majority of which I declined to answer. At last I was dismissed and put into another car with two guards. The countryside was lovely and I enjoyed the journey, although it was interrupted by dive-bombers.

'Arriving at Siena I was put in a guardroom, and there I met an American pilot. At first I thought he was a plant, but found out in due course he was OK. Charlie Landis was his name. A day was spent there then we walked five miles to a lovely Italian house, and there we waited for transport to take us to Verona. Three days spent there passed monotonously, we slept in the billiard room and often had a game. Transport being non-existent we hitch-hiked taking three days. We passed through Florence at night. At one small town the sergeant i/c got drunk but treated us OK, sharing his cigarettes and vermouth, and bought us ice-cream. Then it started to rain and did so all the way to Bologna. The scenery was mountainous which I enjoyed very much. The last part of the journey was completed by train, arriving in Verona at 12 pm on Saturday 17 June. I was interrogated on the first night, stripped naked and then allowed to dress. A small German who spoke English was pretty tough. I always will remember the stacks of English cigarettes on his desk.

'On the Sunday afternoon, when I was being interrogated again, an RAF flight sergeant came in, and what attracted my attention to him was he was smoking a cigarette. The new interrogator informed me of D-Day, and tried me for information. They had my squadron number, as my aircraft was behind enemy lines and had the code JU-C on it. He told me quite a bit about 111 Squadron, and the flight sergeant told me it was all right to tell him what I knew – I told him to go to hell. I remembered the sergeant from Gioia del Colle in Southern Italy. It was a former Italian air force grass aerodrome, west of Bari, and when I was there it was a pilot's "pool" where we flew Spits, low flying etc., before joining a squadron. I never saw him again until I was being repatriated at Halle, where I arrived courtesy of the American army. We were all checked out by our British airborne troops. We gave our number etc. and it so happened that I was a few places behind the flight sergeant. When he gave his details, he was put under close arrest.

'Following my interrogation, I shared a room with another RAF type, and met Cpl Parry-Jones[59] who also went to Luft 7. On Tuesday we started on our way to Germany, escorted by numerous members of the Luftwaffe. The trip was good, but the seats were hard. Chugging our way through Italy we saw the Alps covered in snow. Then we went through the Brenner Pass and saw all the old villages. The people were changing and already their appearance suggested they were not Italians. Mountain torrents rushed beneath us with the pine trees on either side. Each village had its church and steeple, also by the roadside were images of the crucifix. Innsbruck was reached and the valley was really beautiful. The roofs were all red, and the crops were on the turn. Soon we were in Germany, every field was cultivated and the countryside quite similar to England.

'Munich was reached then Frankfurt, and after a short time we reached the interrogation camp at Oberursel. I was left in solitary confinement for three days, and then awaited transport for two days. On 25 June I left for a transit compound [Wetzlar] and arrived there on the same day. There we received a Red Cross parcel consisting of chocolate, cigarettes, soap, towels, clothes, in fact everything. Next day we left for the POW camp. The journey took three days; the food was good as two men shared a Red Cross food parcel.

'Arriving at Bankau we walked to the camp, the date was 28 June 1944. The first week or so was a sort of recuperative period, during which we ate all our food and slept solidly for ten hours. A Red Cross parcel was issued one to a man per week, plus German rations. These were: bread 1/6th loaf per man per day, margarine, jam, cheese, and at times soup or potatoes, cabbage, meat, carrots, and sometimes turnips or peas. Two pumps supplied the water until the new cookhouse was ready. The weather was grand and all wore the minimum of clothing. Gradually things were organised, first a sports store with quite a bit of equipment, then a library, barbers and laundry. With Red Cross parcels we had ample food and managed to save some for a rainy day. I was in charge of ours and had the esteemed rank of quartermaster for the hut. Of course we had our arguments, but on the whole we all pulled together.'

*

Sergeant Peter H. Craig was twenty years of age, and from Sutton Coldfield. Following his training as an observer, he and his crew were posted to 1675 HCU at Lydda, Palestine. Conversion completed they were posted to 178 Squadron which, in June 1944, was operating Liberators out of Foggia, Italy. The rest of the all-RAF crew were Sergeant S. Tom Gill (pilot); Sergeant R. McLean (bomb aimer, on his first op for familiarisation); Sergeant Malcolm 'Sprog' Charlish (flight engineer); Sergeant Frank Cooney (wireless operator); Sergeant A.W. 'Bill' Billing (mid-upper gunner); and Sergeant P. 'Jock' Cameron (rear gunner).

Peter Craig:

'In contrast with the preceding days 13 June 1944 was dull and overcast. Huge grey cumulus clouds rolled across the Apennines, covering their summits, and swept out over the Adriatic. The wind whipped up the dust of Foggia Plain, blinding everyone.

'As the crews walked across from the mess towards the tents that constituted flights at nine o'clock in the morning, the rumour spread that tonight's operation would be something out of the ordinary. At flights however the flight commander could tell us nothing. We sat around talking and smoking, waiting for the phone to ring. Twenty minutes went by before it rang shrilly cutting off the chatter like a knife. The flight commander answered, his deep Canadian voice the only sound in that small tent "Hello, Lewis here!"

'We gathered nothing from his conversation as it consisted of mainly "OK Sir" repeatedly. Before speaking to us he rang up again: "Hello 'B' Flight Maintenance. That you Andy? Thirteen kites tonight" and he reeled off the letters of each aircraft needed. He rang off and turned to us. "Well chaps, you know as much as I do. It's a big effort – six of our kites, and seven from 'A' Flight. Target unknown. That's all for now." "Thirteen Liberators on the 13th of the month, Jesus Christ!" stage-whispered a big South African pilot.

'We poured out of the tent joking, and crowded onto the lorry waiting to take us to dispersal in order to carry out a pre-flight inspection of our aircraft. I found an electrician and asked him to check the heaters which had failed on a previous trip. As I checked my other instruments the tea lorry came round, and I sat with the armourers and riggers chatting, smoking and drinking tea. The rest of the crew had disappeared. But after a while Bill Billing, the mid-upper gunner, came back with his guns and I helped him fix them in his turret. I checked the heaters before walking back to the mess with Bill in time for lunch.

'After lunch the battle order appeared on the mess notice board. We were carrying 1,000 gallons of fuel which meant a long trip, probably the Rumanian oilfields, although that was nothing new, Ploesti being a well-known target. Take-off was 1845 hours. I sat in the mess listening to the wireless, read a magazine, and discussed with Tom Gill, my skipper, the whereabouts of the target. His guess was as good as mine. About three o'clock I had a bath in our homemade wash tub, improvised from a dinghy, before going to the navigation briefing. At this briefing we learnt the target was Munich (railway station), which was no joke, although we laughed about it. Navigational details complete we went across to the operations room at wing headquarters. Wing was located in an old Italian farmhouse and smelt of manure and sweet hay.

'After the usual lecture on our bomb load, the collecting of escape kits, radio and beacon flimsies, the main briefing began. First the Met information, followed by the wing commander's talk. He always gave the latest intelligence himself rather than have a separate intelligence briefing. "Well, chaps'" he began, "We have a hot target for you tonight. Munich will give you some idea of what the Blighty crews have to combat. I'll be frank with you; it's going to be tough. Tougher because it will be such a big contrast to Italian and Balkan targets. The latest 'gen' from our intelligence is that there are 240 guns, both heavy and light, defending Munich. There are approximately half the guns in that district which includes several towns such as Augsburg and Innsbruck. Searchlights number 150. Your target is the railway station and marshalling yards in the north-east corner of the city." He paused to indicate the spot on the target map and suggested various approaches to the target for evading flak and searchlights. He continued "Bomb on a track of 040 degrees, I repeat Zero-Four-Zero. Your time on target is 0026 hours, again I repeat Zero-Zero-Two-Six hours. It is most important that everyone is on target at the correct time simultaneously."

'He then went over the route; the height at which to fly, the ETAs at each turning point, defended areas and take-off and landing procedure. Altogether his briefing lasted three quarters of an hour, a time unheard of during his term as CO. He continued

"Finally, but most important, you are going in two minutes ahead of the Pathfinders who will be going in low. Thus your object is to divert the attention of the defenders whilst the main force attacks in strength." He ended with his familiar epilogue "Good Luck, boys, I'll be with you all the way." The group captain then said a few words stressing the importance of the target and wished us luck.

'Briefing finished, we crowded into the lorries and bumped along to the mess for our evening meal. After dinner, I prepared my flight plan; changed from khaki drill into long silk underwear, a polo-neck sweater and battle dress, and smoked too many cigarettes. More than the usual number of men visited the latrine.

'Transport to dispersal arrived on time and we bundled on our gear. The met officer gave me a new set of winds, which was a nuisance because we had to alter the flight plan. It was still light as we clattered over the metal runways to the aircraft. The sun, which had only put in an appearance during the late afternoon, was a huge red ball in the west, silhouetting the purple hue of the mountains against the orange of the sky.

'I checked and signed for the bombs; checked the intercom and sat in my cabin making out a new flight plan with the latest winds. The rest of the crew, their gear on board, sat on the grass, smoking, and watched the sunset. Everything prepared, checked and rechecked, I climbed out for a last cigarette. Everything was beautifully still. The sun's rays turned the tiny particles of dust in the air to purple. There was a clean smell of aircraft paint and petrol, of green grass and dung rotting in a deserted farm nearby. The sun perched on top of the Apennines. The silence was broken by an engine starting and roaring to life. The aerodrome awoke as one by one motors started up.

'Tom Gill, our skipper, climbed on board (Liberator EW277). I watched his face through the Perspex, serious and intent as he started up. The starboard inner engine spluttered and started, then one by one the others roared. As he throttled up, testing each in turn, the sound rose to a shrill crescendo, kicking up the dust and blowing back the grass till it lay flat along the ground, and then died down again. Tom waved to us; we climbed on board, all huddled together on the flight deck, and awaited our turn to taxi out. "Phut-phut on; generators off; Hydro Booster on."

'These preliminaries attended to, we moved out, fourth in line, to the take-off point. The green light on the control tower flickered and we turned onto the runway. Slowly Tom opened the throttles. We gathered speed, the wheels clattering on the steel runway as though we had 10,000 tin cans tied to our tail. With the throttles wide open the runway indicator lamps whipped past giving one a terrible sensation of speed. Suddenly, imperceptibly, we were airborne.

'We climbed over base, gaining as much height as possible before the set course time. The sun disappeared behind the mountains suddenly, as if it were pulled down by an invisible hand. The sky was full of the twinkling lights of many aircraft, their circuits almost overlapping. The rear gunner goes back to his turret, the beam gunner to his position and I crawl down to my table in the nose. I fastened my parachute harness and settled down; plugged in my intercom and told the skipper I was all right. The rest of the crew called him in turn. Everyone is ready. Every five minutes I told the skipper the number of minutes before the set course time.

'"HELLO TOM, NAVIGATOR CALLING, TEN MINUTES TO GO." "O.K. PETE" he replies "FIFE MINUTES.....FOUR MINUTES.....THREE. THE FIRST COURSE IS THREE-FIFE-SEVEN", I spoke slowly emphasising the figures. He repeats the course correctly. The minutes tick past slowly. "ON COURSE," Tom calls. "DEAD OVER BASE;

HEIGHT 7,000 FEET: CLIMBING AT 400 A MINUTE. AIRSPEED ONE-FIFE-FIFE."

'I repeat each detail, making sure that each is correct before settling down to work, checking our track with a drift from the rear gunner. In seven minutes we reached the coast over start point, altered course over the sea and continued climbing to 18,000 feet. The navigation lights were switched off. The night is now completely black; the hour of twilight and sunset, the most beautiful hour of half-tones and reflections, had gone leaving the void and intangible blackness. We flew on parallel to the coast climbing steadily, a minute part of the terrible force which nightly carries death and destruction to Germany.

'With the coast behind us the gunners asked permission to test their guns from which, being granted, they each fired a short burst. The aircraft, rattling with the vibration, filled with the acrid smell of cordite. The rear gunner reported a stoppage but, after trying to remedy it, announced that one gun was unserviceable. Tom decided to keep going.

'We reached the second turning point one minute ahead of time and altered course for a position on Lake Venetia. The sea was dotted with flame floats, a very reassuring sign, proving we were in the stream of aircraft. Navigational details correct as far as I could judge, I selected and fused the bombs, checking and rechecking my bombing panel. Two hours flying time from base brought us to Lake Venetia, with Venice on our port, and I estimated that we were two miles to starboard of track. The altimeter was registering 18,000 feet but we were four minutes ahead of ETA but that could be easily remedied. Through the darkness the snow on the Alps was just discernible. We were dead over the Alps near the Brenner Pass when we reached 24,000 feet and levelled out, but I could not distinguish snow from the clusters of cumulus clouds below. This being the last leg it seemed the longest, and I asked the engineer how the petrol was lasting, but he assured me we were well within our limits. The cold was extreme, the temperature being about minus 24 degrees, and the heaters failed again. Ice was falling on my chart, probably off the astro-dome as my face felt quite warm. Tom decided to lose 1,000 feet.

'Five minutes before reaching the target landmark, a small lake south west of Munich, I could just see it smooth and deep black against the purplish blackness of the surrounding countryside. I gave Tom last-minute details for the run in over the target. We would be exactly one minute late on the target, but that was a good thing, as the chances were that Jerry would be occupied with other aircraft and we would be in and out before he had time to predict us.

'As I wrote a last-minute entry in my log, I noticed my writing wavering and spreading down the page. It was impossible to write on the lines. I felt as though a dead weight was pressing down on my head. I pulled myself together and realised my oxygen supply had failed. I switched on my emergency supply and took four or five deep breaths. The sickness passed and I made sure the oxygen tube was securely attached.

'We turned dead over the lake and headed for Munich, a black smudge six minutes away. Tom put the nose down until the needle was registering 190 mph. This meant a true air speed of about 300 mph and a ground speed of 350 mph. Suddenly, as if at the touch of a single switch, hundreds of searchlights stabbed the darkness; searching, slowly and relentlessly searching the sky. A belt of them stretching half way round the city lay in front of us. Miraculously we flew through that solid wall of light untouched as though the silver beams parted to let us through. Several thousand feet below us I could see an aircraft – a Wellington I thought – coned by about thirty searchlights. Immediately afterwards I saw two other aircraft caught and held.

'All the time I searched the blackness beneath for the target, but everything was blurred. Here and there a gun flashed. Then a flare went down illuminating the target area. I saw the ribbon of railway lines reflecting the light. Then I saw the target so obvious I wondered why I had not noticed it before.

'"LEFT LEFT STEADY!" I called out directions for the bombing run. "BOMB-DOORS OPEN." The wireless operator does so and repeats "BOMB-DOORS OPEN."

'"RIGHT....STEADY....BOMBS GOING, ONE, TWO, THREE"......I call the bombs out as I press the tit. Finally all twelve are gone.

'The warrant officer calls up. "ALL BOMBS GONE. BOMB-DOORS SHUT."

I yell through to Tom, "TURN ONTO ONE-EIGHT-ZERO AND WEAVE LIKE A BAT OUT OF HELL!" Hardly had I finished speaking than I saw the blue beam of a radar controlled searchlight swinging towards us. It caught us as if it were really too easy, and dozens of others immediately coned us. I was blinded by their brilliance. Suddenly there was a terrific crump and I found myself sitting on the roof of my cabin. I realised the aircraft was on its back. She rolled over and started spinning. I was thrown all over, hitting my head and bumping my body. Faintly over the intercom I heard Tom telling everyone we had been hit and to bale out. He started to say something else but his voice was cut dead.

'I tried to reach my parachute but the centripetal force was so great that although my hand was only three inches away, I could not touch it. The aircraft lurched and I was catapulted against my 'chute. I unfastened the strap holding it, but it fell away into the nose-wheel compartment and I was flung onto the bombsight. I tried to crawl back to the nose-wheel; it was like crawling drunk up a mountain. After what seemed hours, I found my parachute and fastened it onto my harness. As I did so, I realised my harness was not secured correctly. Panic seized me. I started screaming, shouting, blaspheming, and praying. Terrible and profane words came to my lips. Ridiculous thoughts entered my mind. I wondered if I could jump out without my parachute when we were near the ground. I even thought of giving up altogether and just waiting for the end.

'However, I managed to pull myself together and finally re-fixed my harness and parachute after a terrible struggle against the intangible forces arraigned against me. I was about to pull the emergency handle to open the nose-wheel doors when I wondered if there was anyone left in the plane. I pulled out my torch and shone it into the pilot's seat above and behind me. Tom was still there although he had told us to jump what, to me, seemed a lifetime ago. I could not see Sprog, the engineer. The roar of the engines rose to a scream then died away to nothing as Tom tried to pull her out of the spin.

'Then, quietly, smoothly but suddenly the aircraft straightened out into level flight. I glanced at the altimeter. After spinning down 20,000 feet Tom managed to pull her out. I crawled back to the flight deck. Bill, the mid-upper gunner, was sitting astraddle the cat-walk with the bomb-doors open. Frank, the wireless operator, and the engineer were sitting on the flight deck. Tom was at the controls. Somehow or other we organised ourselves so that Bill got back in his turret and yelled out to me – the intercom was unserviceable – directions for evading flak and searchlights. I passed them on to the warrant officer, who in turn, passed them on to the skipper.

'It seemed that every gun, both heavy and light, was trained onto us. Green and red tracer hose-piped up, seemed to reach us, and then fall away. The orange and yellow bursts were all around us. I heard the terrible crump of one hitting our belly and I wondered if the bomb-doors would still open. I smelt something burning. All the while

Bill yelled "TURN STARBOARD.......TURN STARBOARD FOR CHRIST'S SAKE!" I kept repeating it to Frank. I saw his lips forming the words, but could not hear him calling Tom. Although we kept repeating these instructions there was no response. The controls must have been jammed as the plane kept a steady climbing course.

'A shell hit and exploded in the port outer engine. The engine disappeared as if into thin air; the rest of the wing outwards crumpled and fell away. The machine rolled over and began to dive towards the earth. It was the end this time. Bill was out of his turret in an instant and opened the bomb-doors. He sat down on the cat-walk, his legs hanging in space. His eyes were protruding and I know he was afraid. I kicked him off and he fell away legs first. As I sat down on the cat-walk, I realised why Bill had been afraid. I saw Frank shouting at me, and then he kicked me away.

'Instantly I experienced a soothing feeling of peace and quiet. Paradise must be like this. Automatically and unconsciously, I pulled the rip-cord. At first nothing happened, and then I felt a jolt in my groin. I watched the canopy open and checked my descent. Immediately afterwards there was an explosion and a blinding flash directly beneath me. I felt the waves of air from the explosion wafting upwards and jerking my 'chute. It took several seconds for me to realise that it was our aircraft burning below. At first I thought for one terrible moment that I was going to fall into the flames, but I slowly drifted downwind. I could see the outline of some trees and the dark ribbon of a road. Was this countryside Bavaria or Austria? The chances were wherever it was it meant captivity – the slow, monotonous, rotting life of a prisoner of war.

'I landed on the edge of a field of grain. My feet touched the ground first, and forced my knees up into my chest, winding me, but in a few moments I regained my breath. I unfastened my harness, disentangled myself from my parachute canopy and shrouds, rolled them into a bundle, and jumped into a ditch which took the place of a fence, dividing the field from a good second class tarmacadam road.

'About 150 yards away, in a field on the other side of the road, the aircraft burned furiously, while at intervals the ammunition exploded with a futile bang. In the distance a motorcycle barked and then died down again. Apart from the fire the night was still, although when I listened more carefully it was full of those quiet noises and peculiar to darkness. About a dozen yards away, I could see where a stream ran under the road. This would be a more secure hiding place than the ditch, where the white silk of my parachute would give me away. I half crawled, half ran along the ditch to the tunnel. The stream proved to be dry and the tunnel, a concrete cylindrical affair about three feet in diameter, was more comfortable than the ditch. I threw my parachute and harness inside and barely crawled inside when a motorcycle and sidecar dashed past going to the plane. The combination stopped near it and everything went quiet again. I suddenly thought about the time, looked at my watch and found it to be 0045 hours. Nineteen minutes ago we had just been running onto the target.

'I lit a cigarette and noticed my hands were steady, although in the plane I had been shaking like a leaf in a breeze. Then I thought it was time I took stock of my situation. The road ran almost due east and west, whilst a mountain range seemed to run on three sides, on the south, the west and further away on the north. A mile up the road to the west stood a village, whilst down the road about the same distance away there seemed to be a smaller village. About a quarter of a mile away between the southern hills and myself there was another road running parallel to the one under which I was hiding. Switzerland lay about eighty miles away to the south-west.

'By this time people were coming from the villages, walking or on bicycles, to view the blaze. Sometimes they were nearly on top of me before I had time to duck back into hiding. In half an hour more than 200 people were standing idly and stupidly in groups, talking and gesticulating. Two hours went by before they became disinterested and slowly made their way back to their beds. Intermittently I smoked cigarettes, carefully cupping the flame of my lighter, as I lit each one. I wondered how the civilians would treat me if caught, as I knew they would not have peaceful intentions towards RAF aircrews, even though they were country folk.

'I decided that the best course was to make for the hills before daybreak and hide there during the day as my present hiding place was not very secure. Although the thought of getting to Switzerland was foremost in my mind, I was not very optimistic about walking there over rough country in flying boots and clothing. At the same time, I did not want to give myself up so early in the game.

'When I thought the way clear, I made my way along the bed of the dried-up stream, away from the road, but after traversing about 100 yards found myself bogged. I retraced my steps some twenty yards, and then cut across the field south-east away from the larger village, but the going was very rough. The grass was wet and the ground very soggy. I turned south again, but again went into the bog. I seemed to be making a terrible noise; my boots squelching in the mud frightened me in case they gave my presence away, so I turned back towards the road, came to a grass field alongside and then walked parallel to the road. I wondered where Bill was; had Frank baled out; were Tom and Sprog dead? The latter two could not have possibly got out in time.

'Presently, I heard voices. I lay flat on the grass and after a few minutes a youth with his arms around two girls walked past laughing and joking. Although I was barely twenty yards away they did not even look my way. When the sound of their voices had died away I restarted, but fifty yards further on I came to a hedge surrounding a cottage. Opposite, on the other side of the road, stood a large two-storey cottage in a beautiful garden. I decided rather than go round the cottages, to walk along the road. About twenty yards beyond the cottages there was a T-shaped junction where the road met another road. In the middle stood a triangular piece of ground, with two or three trees growing there. Crouching in the shadow of the cottage hedge I decided to make for those trees, make sure the way was clear, dash across the road and turn south through the fields away from roads and other signs of habitation.

'Quite openly I walked towards the trees. When I was within two yards of the first tree, a command rang out. It sounded like "Halt!" I took a further step and saw someone standing, back to the truck, in the shadow of the overhanging branches. My first instinct was to hit him – I could see it was a man – but the instinct of self-preservation made me hesitate. That probably saved my life because as I did so, I saw the pistol in his hand. "*Englischer Flieger?*" he asked. "*Ja*" I replied, although it must have been obvious.

'He asked if I spoke German and I told him only a few words. Satisfied that I had no pistol or ammunition, he told me to sit down as we had to wait until the army men came. He was obviously only some kind of Home Guard as he was dressed farmer style, with a white band marked 'LANDWACHT' around the sleeve of his long tweed coat. I offered him a cigarette – he admitted they were better than German – and asked him if any of my crew had been captured. He told me one had been picked up along the road. I was very relieved to hear that at least one was alive.

'Then he asked "*Wo ist seiner Fahnschein?*" but I did not understand. By signs he made me realise he meant parachute. I shrugged my shoulders. He sat down and we spoke generally. Evidently he had been a prisoner somewhere in the Balkans in the last war and had had a pretty rough time. He thought the war was nearly over, but that Germany would win. He also thought Hitler was a genius. I contradicted him, told him we were winning the war, and spoke of Stalingrad, Alamein, Tunis, Rome and the Second Front which had just started. I told him Hitler was a "*Dummkopf*" and a "*Schweinhund!*" He got quite mad at this and I had to placate him with chewing gum and another cigarette. I learnt from him that this was Bavaria and that Berchtesgarten [Berchtesgaden] was only about twenty miles away.

'Presently, two girls rode up and stopped to speak to him. When they saw me and he had explained who I was, they backed away as though I might shoot or maybe rape them. Soon afterwards two German army men rode up on bicycles. They seemed to take my presence for granted, although they both unslung their automatic rifles and kept me covered. After a hasty consultation with the Bavarian, the taller of the two soldiers asked me where my parachute was. Again I shrugged my shoulders as if I did not understand. He called me one or two impolite things in German and poked his rifle in my chest. That was enough. I told him it was in the tunnel up the road.

'We set off back up the road, collected the parachute, and continued up the road towards the village. The sun began to peep above the horizon as we entered the village. I suppose it was typically Bavarian. It reminded me of any English village except that the cottage roofs were a trifle too steep. We rounded a green, went up a lane, to a two-storied house slightly larger than the rest. The larger man knocked at the door and it was opened by a man in faded German army uniform, who was, perhaps, one of the most brutal-looking men I have ever had the misfortune to meet. Of medium height with strong shoulders, his deeply lined face and cropped hair, thin cruel mouth and thick neck made him almost terrifying to look upon. The sallowness of his skin, accentuated in the early morning light, gave him a debauched appearance.

'He pushed me upstairs. On the landing a woman, looking as though she had just got out of bed, stood with a child in her arms. I went into a room fitted out as an office, and everyone, including the woman and child, trooped in after me. The brutal looking man pointed me to a chair, where I sat for the next three-quarters of an hour and did nothing except smoke. I thought they might relieve me of my cigarettes so I was making the most of them.

'In the meantime the chief of police – I suppose that was his office – had several phone calls with different people, smoked evil-smelling cigarettes and joked with his comrades and wife. They seemed to have forgotten my presence altogether. I amused myself winking and making faces at the baby, who thought it was a great joke until his mother scolded him. On the desk were some British cigarettes and some other odds and ends presumably from Bill's pockets.

'Their conversation at an end, the others shook hands with, and saluted – Nazi manner – the police official. When they had closed the door he told me to take off my clothes. I looked at his wife but her face remained as blank as if it were an everyday occurrence seeing young men strip. I complied and started to undress. As I divested each garment, the brutal official very minutely inspected each. When at last I stood in my long underwear, the woman obligingly left the room. The search completed I dressed again but he would not let me have my leather service jacket, nor my cigarettes and lighter back. He put on his hat and we both went out.

'He led me to a school on the other side of the village. We went through the front door, then downstairs into the basement, along a dismal corridor to an iron door fastened by an enormous lock. He took an outsize in keys from his pockets and unlocked the door, making a great deal of noise in doing so. The door swung back disclosing a small cell, three quarters of which were taken up by a palliasse on the floor. Sitting on the palliasse, wrapped in a dirty blanket, was Bill. I made no sign of recognition, but walked inside. The door was shut and not until his footsteps had died away did we speak.

'Bill had not known a thing from the time he had baled out until he had been awakened by a Jerry kicking him. He had a pretty nasty time when a crowd had tried to get at him at the police headquarters. One angry gent smashed his fist into his eye grazing it. We must have continued talking for over a half an hour about our experiences before crawling under the one worn, dirty blanket. We spent the day dozing and talking. Thus began and ended Wednesday 14 June 1944.

'Only one or two incidents of those dreary, monotonous three days and two nights spent in the cell underneath the school for Bavarian children in Bad Tölz, are worth remembering. One, the longing for food and drink, or even just a smoke. This torture was aggravated by the presence, four or five hours a day, of a pack of typical Nazified children, whose ages ranged between six and fourteen. One specimen in particular, dressed in Hitler Youth uniform and evidently the ringleader of the band, spoke some English. He tantalised us by speaking of food and drink repeatedly. He would shout: "YOU LIKE SOME CHEESE OR BEER, YOU ENGLISH PIGS?"

'He repeated these variations on the same theme until they became monotonous. We had to ignore these remarks until he became tired and went away. Once he appeared at the bars with a glass jug: "YOU LIKE SOME WATER?" Naturally, we replied in the affirmative, but at our appearance he got a great deal of amusement in showing us that the bottom of the jug was missing. His prestige among his comrades was greatly enhanced at this deed.

'On the Friday afternoon a new guard appeared. After a great deal of persuasion to get us a drink of water he disappeared. Five minutes later he returned with the schoolmaster who was carrying two lemonade bottles full of water. We swallowed the contents of one bottle and kept the other bottle for future use.

'Early on Friday evening we heard a lorry draw up at the school gate. This was followed by a great deal of commotion above us. We could hear hobnails scraping on the corridors and stairs. They echoed down the basement, and presently someone unlocked the door. Several guards lined the corridor outside the cell. The chief of police entered and told me to pick up the bucket which served as a latrine, and which had not been emptied since we had first entered the cell. He took me outside followed by two guards, made me empty the contents in a hedge and wash it out before replacing it in the cell. Then he led Bill and me up the stairs and out through the front doors. Half-a-dozen guards lined the path whilst a couple more kept a crowd of villagers away from the tailboard of the wagon. What a spectacle we must have looked! Two dirty, dejected, and bearded airmen. Typical looking *Terror Fliegers!*

'A young, brutal-looking guard, wearing thick glasses, motioned us onto the wagon. We climbed on board. On the floor were three oblong boxes approximately 6 feet long. I recognised them as coffins. Bill looked at me and was about to speak when the guard informed us in guttural English that talking meant death. He made us sit down on the coffins facing the cabin of the lorry. There was a nauseating stench of burnt flesh. What humility to have to sit on the coffins containing the burnt remains of our comrades.

'For two or three hours we travelled up and down hills with frequent stops. The lorry, running on coal or some kind of burner, found the going rather difficult. At one stop we picked up someone else who sat between us. By signs he made me understand he was in the Australian air force, and had also been shot down over Munich. Soon afterwards we passed through the country town of Fürstenfeldbruck. I knew this from peering through a rent in the canvas covering the lorry. After leaving it behind we pulled up again and were ordered to descend. Evidently this was a Luftwaffe training aerodrome judging from the biplanes overhead. We went inside a modern, red-bricked building and were given a separate cell each. Although they were bare they were clean, with a single wooden bed and straw palliasses in each. Presently, a youth of about seventeen brought a bowl of soup, a piece of dry black bread and a cup of yellow amber liquid like weak tea without milk. This was the first food I had eaten for three days and I can honestly say I never appreciated it more. Although I had no blanket, I must have dozed off to sleep.

'The next morning I was awakened by the guard bringing another cup of tea and one piece of bread. Although I call it tea it was in reality something brewed from herbs, marjoram I thought, and the bread tasted of wood pulp, as I afterwards learnt was true. Breakfast over I was called out before a very immaculately-dressed, even foppish, German-commissioned pilot. I told him my number, rank and name, but to all his other questions I politely refused an answer. I returned to my cell and the guard came inside and we had a chat. He was seventeen years old and had not been in the Luftwaffe long. He had to serve a short time to enable him to get used to the service discipline before starting training as a pilot, which he said was his ultimate ambition. He was cheerful, very friendly and interesting, and had he not spoken gutturally, I would have taken him for a Britisher.

'Halfway through the morning I was called out again. On entering the office or guardroom, I was surprised to see four other aircrew besides Bill. We were all marched outside, formed up in threes, and began marching down the road. The road, bordered by thick coniferous woods, was surfaced with chipping and Bill, who had no boots, they having been whipped off by the slipstream when baling out, was soon in agony. We were not allowed to speak but managed to talk out of the corners of our mouths when the two guards were not looking.

'It was very warm and we were soon perspiring in our flying clothing. Algy, one of the other crew, had no boots either, but had protected his feet with two pads made from his parachute harness tied on with string. These somewhat makeshift shoes were not too secure and we gained thankful rests each time Algy stopped to fasten them. A three-quarters-of-an-hour walk brought us to a small town where we entered the waiting room of the railway station. Perhaps a dozen people were awaiting the next train, mostly peasant women with baskets, and a few young men in uniform. We sat on the floor and waited for about half an hour before the train arrived.

'When the guard heard the train – an electric – approaching we went out onto the platform, and as it came to a standstill chose a third class compartment. It was packed, some soldiers standing. We had to stand. There were several quite pretty women travelling and I marvelled at their make-up and the shortness of their skirts, as I had been led to believe such things were forbidden under the Nazi regime. Also they were remarkably well dressed, usually in a two-piece costume with perhaps a cheeky hat.

'Some thirty minutes travelling took us to Augsburg, bearing traces of bomb damage. Again we had to wait on the platform, this time for the Rhine express. When it arrived we had a second-class compartment, and soon after starting the German sergeant in charge brought out a brown loaf, some butter and a Frankfurter sausage some 18 inches long. He divided each into six equal portions and gave us each one part. I found out that he could not speak English and caused some fun swearing at him, which he thought quite funny and joined in the laughter.

'When we reached Ulm on the Danube which was not blue but extremely muddy and dirty, I asked him for a cigarette. He took from his pocket a two-ounce packet of tobacco and a sheaf of cigarette papers. Alec, the Australian, rolled us each a cigarette, the finest and most delicious I have ever tasted. It was the first smoke I had had in four days. Funnily enough I had had no craving for a smoke during the past few days, but after tasting one my palate was not satisfied. Throughout the day he gave us each four smokes.

'The journey for the most part is really not worth recounting. We travelled mainly through the Black Forest, passing through Stuttgart, Karlsruhe, and the university town of Heidelberg; through Darmstadt and Mainz where the rivers Main and Rhine meet. All the towns showed signs of bomb damage although none was as bad as I was expecting. Mannheim was, perhaps, the worst. We had to make a detour around it, after first of all entering the station, which was in a terrible state. At one point along the line, in open country, the fields on either side of the line were pitted with bomb holes.

'We arrived in Frankfurt about midnight. The station was badly scarred by bomb blasts. There was no glass in the roof which was entirely blacked out. In fact it struck me as being more dismal than Crewe Station, which is the most depressing I have ever been in, although under different circumstances.

'After arguing and quibbling with various officials, we were herded into a cellar, underneath the main platform, in which there were about forty Frenchmen. The cellar measured about 20 feet square and looked as though it had not been cleaned since the start of the war. After more officials had been to inspect the place, the Frenchmen filed out. The six of us then lay down on the table and covered ourselves with cardboard to keep off the draughts. Soon afterwards the sergeant, who had left us, came back with a mug of soup each, for which we were very thankful. Throughout the night the cellar slowly filled with other British and American aircrew. Several badly wounded, and all dirty and bearded. About seven in the morning we were all shepherded onto the train again; after half an hour's train journey and five minutes on a tram we arrived at Oberursel, the interrogation centre for soliciting information from Allied airmen.

'The seven days I spent at the interrogation centre, the worst days of my life, are the ones I wish to forget. Briefly, I lived in a small cell into which a bunk just fitted. On the bunk were a palliasse and one blanket, flea ridden and lousy. The windows were never opened and the only time I left the cell was to be interviewed by a German officer or to attend the lavatory. I never once washed or shaved. A day's menu consisted of a bowl of soup at midday and a piece of bread and a cup of "Ersatz" tea in the morning and the evening. I was interrogated six times. After trying persuasion, bullying, threats and enticement the officer, at the last interview, took from a drawer a folder containing my squadron number, and proceeded to tell me more about my own squadron and my personal history in the RAF than I knew or remembered myself. He then showed me several photos of our wrecked and burnt plane, as well as some gruesome pictures of the unrecognisable bodies of three of my crew. He then handed me over to a guard who led me to a bathroom where I shaved off fourteen days growth of beard and had a cold shower. There were several marks on my body where the lice had bitten me.

'The next morning we, Bill and I, with about 200 British, American and Colonials, boarded the train for Wetzlar, a transit camp for prisoners of war about eighty miles north east of Frankfurt. After two days at Wetzlar spent in comparative comfort, eating good, but never enough, Red Cross food and having a hot shower, and at least one wash per day, sixty-four RAF commenced the two-and-a-half-days journey across Germany through Leipzig and Breslau to Stalag Luft Seven, near Bankau, Upper Silesia.'[60]

*

The target for the thirty-eight Wellingtons of the RAF's Italian-based 205 Group on the night of 29/30 May 1944, beyond the mighty River Danube (Donau), was the Luftwaffe airfield Fels am Wagram, near Feuersbrunn, fifty kilometres north west of the Austrian capital, Vienna. Thirty-five of the Wimpys attacked. Bombing was concentrated, with sticks of bombs seen to fall across the airfield.

Only Wellington LN318,[61] 142 Squadron, from Amendola, failed to return with its crew of five. Rear gunner Sgt Brian Halligan RAAF:

'Aircraft was coned and subsequently hit by heavy flak while over the outskirts of Vienna, returning from bombing airfield. Aircraft repeatedly hit by flak while evading searchlights. Three fighters attacked immediately after dousing of searchlights. Aircraft's controls hit. Cannon shells burst outside turrets; rear gunner sustains slight shrapnel injuries. Plane now out of control. Captain orders bale out. All members of crew acknowledge and subsequently bale out. I baled out from the front hatch at about 2,500 feet. Aircraft was then diving and out of control. Pilot was just able to obtain sufficient control to enable crew to clear aircraft.'

The aircraft crashed 'some miles S.W. of Vienna', at Hofstetten, near St Pölten, Austria.

The two officers in the crew, F/O H.B. Keen RAAF (pilot) and F/O W.K. Todd RAAF (navigator), were captured and sent to Stalag Luft III (POW numbers 5660 and 5661 respectively). Two of the three NCOs, Sgt J.D.F. Gallagher and Sgt E.R. Yeo, were sent to Luft 7 in *Trupp 2*.

Brian Halligan, however, who had been hit by splinters in the legs and was unable to walk on landing, was found by dairy-farm hands, and was sent to Stalag XVIIB (Krems-Gneixendorf), his POW number 104259 being an indication of the large size of the camp. Just over a fortnight later he, too, arrived at Luft 7, in *Trupp 7*. Admitted to the camp Lazarett, he was visited there by the German flying officer who had shot down LN318, who said to him in perfect English: "You are too young to be fighting the war. You should be home with your mother." Brian replied: "Sir, I couldn't agree more."

*

Taking-off from Foggia Main airfield at 2117 hours on the night of 13/14 June 1944 in Wellington Mk.X LP234, 40 Squadron, were P/O Malcolm R. Denson RAAF (pilot); F/S Alex Goodman-Jones RAAF (navigator); Sergeant A.L. 'Tony' Sorzano (bomb aimer); Sergeant Phillip S. Kirby (wireless operator/air gunner); Sergeant Reg Haughton (rear gunner); and Sergeant Albert W.G. 'Archie' Belverstone as a second wireless operator/air gunner. Their target was the Bavarian city of Munich.

Phillip Kirby:

'On 13 June 1944 we were detailed for an attack on Munich. We were shot down by flak on our run in to the target, and all the crew managed to successfully bale out.

Archie was on his first trip, and I was "showing him the ropes". I was lucky to find him a parachute, otherwise he would have had to share mine! I landed in a wood – probably not too far from Munich. I got too close to a camp, and as dawn was breaking I was captured by German soldiers with dogs.'

Alex Goodman-Jones was free for twenty-four hours before being caught at dusk by civilian police. He noted, too, that their Wellington had been 'damaged by heavy concentrated flak', and that the order to put on parachutes was acknowledged by the whole crew, no-one was injured and all baled out safely at around 6,000 feet.

Another pilot, Maurice Lihou, in a 37 Squadron Wellington, wrote of the loss on this same raid of a Wellington in his book *Out of the Italian Night* (in which he called himself 'Lee'):

> "Wimpy caught up in a searchlight behind, Skipper," called out Jock. A sudden chill ran through Lee's spine. That's Bobby, he thought.
> "They've got him, Lee. It looks as if they've shot him down."
> 'Christ, I hope I'm wrong, thought Lee. There was deathly silence inside the aircraft. Outside, above the noise of the engines, could be heard the dull thuds of the flak.'[62]

It was not long before all of LP234's crew were captured, and sent to Dulag Luft via Frankfurt.

Philip Kirby: 'We were in Frankfurt railway station when the RAF bombed it, and our guards had to protect us from the hostile crowds. I've never seen railway engines jump in the air before, but Reg said "Don't worry old boy, that bomb was one of ours!"

The only officer in the crew, Malcolm Denson, was sent to Stalag Luft III, the rest to Luft 7, where they arrived on 28 June (*Trupp 7*).

After a crew had been lost it was the painful duty of their squadron commander to write to their next-of-kin. The letter of 26 June sent by the squadron leader commanding 40 Squadron to Goodman-Jones's father, however, was hardly encouraging: '… There is the possibility, of course, that he made a successful parachute descent behind enemy lines, but I'm afraid it is a slender possibility, and I would not advise you to place much faith in the chance.'

*

F/S H.C. 'Bill' Evans RAAF was a bomb aimer on 466 (RAAF) Squadron, operating Halifaxes out of Leconfield, Yorkshire. On the night of 2/3 June 1944, he was flying on his fifth operation with his crew of P/O A.L. Smith RAAF (pilot); F/O D.R. Campbell RAAF (navigator); Sergeant F.W. Sowerby (flight engineer); Warrant Officer M. Max Bettington RAAF (wireless operator/air gunner); F/S V.W. Phillips (mid-upper gunner); and F/S Leslie J. 'Lyle' Pulbrook RAAF (rear gunner).

Airborne in Halifax Mk.III HX271 at 2222 hours course was set to the target (Trappes, France). Soon after bombing the target HX271 was shot down, probably by Hauptmann Hubert Rauh, Stab II./NJG4, who claimed a Halifax in the Dreux-Chartres area at the appropriate time. Sadly, four of the crew failed to survive the attack. The other three baled out and were taken POW. Bill Evans injured his knee while landing and was captured near Dreux, while Lyle Pulbrook was captured on 10 June. Both went to Luft 7, where they arrived on 28 June and 29 August 1944 respectively. F/O Campbell went to Luft 3.

At Luft 7 Bill Evans's roommates were Sergeant David Brown RCAF; Sergeant H.V. 'Fred' Scully; CQMS A.G. 'Sandy' Clark, 1st Battalion Gordon Highlanders; and Warrant Officer Arthur J. Owen 'a Welshman of Cardiff, and one-time member of Don Bennett's Pathfinder crew'.[63]

The attack on the synthetic oil plant at Sterkrade/Holten (near Duisburg), Germany, on the night of 16/17 June 1944, was to prove costly for Bomber Command with thirty-one bombers lost from 162 Halifaxes, 147 Lancasters, and twelve Mosquitos. Twenty-two Halifaxes were lost. One of them was MZ537, 431 (Iroquois) Squadron, RCAF, based at Croft, Co. Durham, with its crew of: Flight Lieutenant Mervyn M. Johnstone RCAF (pilot); Flight Lieutenant John C. Burns RCAF (navigator); F/O Cliff 'Dinger' Bell RCAF (bomb aimer); Sergeant John C. 'Jack' Fereday (flight engineer); F/O L.O. 'Stan' Stanley RCAF (wireless operator); F/O Milford B. 'Steve' Steeves RCAF (mid-upper gunner); and F/O R. Jack Oates RCAF (rear gunner). They were possibly shot down by a Leutnant Kristopher (?), 3./NJG7, who claimed his second victory on this night.

Merv Johnstone:

'Although my grandfather was born in Scotland, I had second thoughts about the friendliness of Scottish people in 1941. Picture the troopship *Louis Pasteur* easing its way up the Clyde after crossing the Atlantic in late November. It is a very foggy morning with the shores of the river barely visible. The boat is loaded with thousands of young Canadians – still "wet behind the ears" feeling mighty important – there to help save the "old country" from Hitler.

'The first glimpse of a native is a young lad rowing a boat alongside. A roar of greeting goes up from the Canadians. In the din it is difficult to pick out any actual words. The lad kept on rowing slow methodical strokes and looking straight ahead. Suddenly he stopped rowing, looked towards us, spat, looked away and continued rowing. The complete silence on board ship proved that the lad had made his point. The figurative "slap in the face" was just what we needed to re-examine our importance and fetch us out of the clouds.

'Our last operational trip (with 431 [Iroquois] Squadron) was on 16/17 June 1944 (in Halifax SE-L, MZ537), and was the eighth of the second tour for most of us – some of the crew were on their first tour. The target was Sterkrade in the Ruhr valley. The attack was successful. On the return route across Holland, in a relatively relaxed fashion, tins of orange juice were opened to wet the dry lips. Suddenly, what was later reckoned to be a radar-controlled night-fighter gave us a short burst of gun-fire with tracer. This set the port inner engine on fire – and us a shot of adrenalin. Engine fire procedure and a crew check confirmed that we seemed to be in fair shape excepting the fact we were now on three instead of four engines. Frantic evasive action must have been most disconcerting to Jack Fereday, our engineer, who would be monitoring damage, and also Jack Oates, the tail gunner, who wouldn't know whether to look up, down or sideways for enemy aircraft.

'Moments later, a second burst raked the aircraft, perforating the bomb aimer position, and the navigator's table; some flight instruments disappeared; a piece of the windscreen was punctured; the port-inner engine was again on fire. Major structural damage was apparent because the left wing began to vibrate and full aileron could not keep the aircraft level. Bale out!

'The navigator, bomb aimer and I contacted the local Underground organisation at once. These most remarkable young people were operating between the Maas and Waal rivers near the village of Alphen-en-Maas. They immediately put Cliff Bell, the bomb aimer, into the care of a most competent and friendly doctor. A bullet had shattered a left rib and loss of blood had left him unable to travel. Within two weeks John Burns, the navigator, and I were passed by the Underground from one hiding place to another by train, bicycle and on foot. On 16 July at the Belgian border a bad link in the Underground chain deliberately passed us to a concentration of German troops in a small village.'

Jack Fereday:

'This was to be our sixth [sic] operational mission together, and our last! We took off in "SE-L" for Love, set course in the usual manner, and I carried on with my log. It seemed just like another trip. We crossed the Dutch coast with little extraordinary happening and, after a short while, we could see in the distance, the flak over "Happy Valley" (the Ruhr). This is when I had to start pushing "Window" down the 'chute, which I didn't mind for then I couldn't see the flak, but there were plenty of flashes underneath the aircraft which I could see when the "Window" 'chute was open. We made our bombing run and, after I felt the bombs leave the aircraft, I pulled the jettison handle to make sure there were no hang-ups.

'The skipper had almost got us clear of the target area when the kite shook as flak hit the port inner engine, and I felt a stinging sensation in my right leg, but no pain. I got up and cut the engine, which was now on fire and leaving a trail of flames. I then went back and turned off the fuel supply. I then thought that the skipper must have been hit, because he couldn't seem to feather the prop. I started to go forward and saw streams of tracer shells shooting past the cockpit window. The next moment a fire started in the rest position. The skipper shouted "Abandon Aircraft", and while the navigator tried to open the escape hatch, I went back with a fire extinguisher. I put out the fire in the rest position, and then saw that the escape hatch was open, and the bomb aimer, navigator, followed by the wireless operator, left the aircraft. I followed them immediately, expecting the skipper to be right behind me. I never saw him again. He was one of the finest men I have known.

'Everything happened so quickly, I never had time to worry about the jump. I somehow managed to strap on my 'chute and slid through the hatch clutching the release handle. I pulled it after a few brief seconds and, with a jerk, I found myself floating in the air, without the slightest sensation of falling. Suddenly an aircraft roared overhead, dropping his flares and scaring the hell out of me. I noticed that somehow my Mae West had inflated, and the aircraft's slip stream caught me, causing my 'chute to swing, and I had to twist about to stop it. I had no idea how long I would be falling, and although it was pitch dark below, I thought for a moment I could see the sea. Then all at once the ground came rushing up to meet me, and I landed in the soft earth of a ploughed field of beans.

'I undid the release catch, took off my parachute harness and pulled in the 'chute, and then took off my Mae West. It was too dark to move away safely, so I took cover as best I could, wondering if the flares had given my descent away. I lit a cigarette in my cupped hands and checked my watch; it was 2 am. Then it began to pour with rain. My right leg began to ache and as soon as it became light, I was able to take a close look at it and found a small shell splinter in my thigh. I was able to pull it out and felt a little relieved, having expected it to be much worse. I now realised that to remain where I had landed had been the right decision, because only a few yards away was a deep dike surrounding most of the field. Perhaps that aircraft's slipstream had done me a favour after all!

'Removing my escape kit from my flying suit, I buried the suit, 'chute and Mae West in the field, and started walking to try and find out my location. I managed to cross the dyke all right, followed by another dyke every few fields. It was still pouring with rain, when after crossing about ten fields I came to a farmhouse. There was a notice-board by the gate, from which I found out I was in Holland. I approached the farmhouse with caution, and after knocking on the door for a short while, the farmer opened the door, took me inside and gave me a cup of coffee. By his attitude I thought I had struck lucky, but after a while a Dutch policeman arrived. I didn't know how he came to be there, but after taking me outside he explained, by sign language, that the farmer had talked too much.

'The policeman took me to his house in a nearby village, and it seemed as if everyone in the village turned out to see me. Then, with a young girl interpreting, I found out that Jerry had been sent for, so I gave them everything I had. Eventually German soldiers (military police) arrived in a car, in which there was another airman. We were both taken to a police station in another town, where Jack Oates and Stan Stanley were brought later. After waiting from 10 am until approximately 11.30 pm, a lorry arrived to take us to another gaol – in the back of the lorry were five coffins! On arrival at the gaol my number, rank and name were taken down, and I was thoroughly searched and all my remaining possessions were taken from me.

'On Sunday, 18 June, we were escorted by armed guards by train to Venlo, a journey of around three hours, and placed in solitary confinement. The next three days were spent like this, with the only interruptions being irregular interrogations and the three regular "meals" a day. We were not allowed any decent washing facilities. I was then taken to the railway station and after a train journey of about ten hours, via Cologne, we reached Frankfurt. Both cities showed signs of extensive air-raid damage, and we had to walk through Frankfurt, from one railway station to another, in order to catch another train.

'22 June: On arrival at Oberursel I was thoroughly searched, and once again placed in solitary confinement, to await further interrogation. I was awakened early in the morning and had my finger-prints and photograph taken for my POW record card. Afterwards I was given a small bowl of soup for breakfast. Later in the morning, a Luftwaffe officer visited my cell and asked me several questions, to which I replied with my number, rank and name. He then told me that London had been bombed flat with radio-controlled bombs, and gave me my first cigarette in a week, which almost knocked me out. Just before leaving he said that perhaps they would interrogate me later in the day, not that I expected it!

'That evening a guard came to my cell and took me to see an interrogation officer, he spoke perfect English and gave me a cigarette, my second in one day; I was starting to feel pampered! He checked my number, rank and name, and then started to ask me different questions, at the same time observing my reactions to each question. I replied once again, with my number, rank and name, and to my surprise he just nodded his head and then proceeded to tell me the answers. He also told me that my pilot had the "chop", and I didn't know if I should believe him or not. After about twenty minutes of interrogation he said that would be all and, if possible, I would be moved this evening. I had just finished my supper when, around 8 pm, I was taken from my cell and given back my belongings, except for my money and penknife. I was then escorted into an outer compound, where there were a lot of blokes, mainly Yanks. Today we were given the opportunity to get cleaned up. I had a shave and a shower, and washed my clothes – certainly felt a lot better for it.

'25 June: This morning I was moved to Dulag Luft at Wetzlar, where I was given my first decent meal since I was shot down nine days ago. Although it was only corned beef, potatoes, German bread and coffee, it felt like one of the best meals I have ever had. Afterwards we were issued with some clothes, our first Red Cross food parcel, and a postcard to send home, which certainly helped cheer me up.

'26 June: Started a journey by rail to my permanent POW camp, we travelled in Italian railway carriages with nine men in each compartment. We were issued with one Red Cross food parcel between two men for the trip, which took two days to complete. I arrived at Luft 7 at 8 pm on 27 June, and was documented the following morning.'

Merv Johnstone, Cliff Bell, John Burns, and Milford Steeves went to Stalag Luft I, and Jack Oates and Stan Stanley to Stalag Luft III.

*

The only good news for 77 Squadron, if it can be called that, was that of its seven Halifax aircraft that failed to return from Sterkrade on 16/17 June 1944 one managed to ditch off the Suffolk coast without loss of life. Of the forty-three crew aboard the other six only sixteen survived – fifteen POWs, one evader.

Twelve of the POWs were NCOs, and all went to Luft 7 in *Trupp* 7 (28 June 1944). Four of the twelve came from Halifax MZ711 'T-Tommy' – Sgt J. Crump (flight engineer); F/S C.S. Cork RAAF (wireless operator); Sgt G.A. Hewitt (mid-upper gunner); and Sgt A.L. Hudson (rear gunner). One of MZ711's two officers to survive, F/O R.J. 'Ron' Grogan (bomb aimer), wrote of the last flight of 'T-Tommy':

'So we went out to "T-Tommy" each feeling we needed luck and feeling apprehensive, but grinning and chatting to hide our feelings. We all asked ourselves – "Will we see tomorrow dawn?" Some will, some won't!

'After we got to "T", did our final check and smoked a cigarette. We got in and Stan [Goodman, pilot] gave the order, "Start engines". Tommy [Cusson, navigator] is fluttering about checking this and that... arranging his charts etc, whilst I have checked my bombsight, my bombs, my charts, maps, the "G" set, my gun – everything in fact! We're all set to go. I went up to the second pilot's seat to help start the engines. P.O., S.O., S.I. (port outer, starboard outer, inner etc) all started, but the P.I. would not start! "Is this an omen?" It took ten mins to start the confounded thing. Eventually she started with a roar. So we proceed with engine check etc. Everything is OK.

'Slowly we started to roll forward – we were under way! We taxied round to the head of the runway ready to take off – There goes the green for "T-Tommy". We opened the throttles and we started to shoot down the runway!

'10.54 [pm] Airborne.

'11.00 Circling to get height!

'11.15 Set course. On our way!

'The trip was fairly successful until we got to the coast. After that we could not get our position correctly – continually south of track – why? I checked and checked and rechecked but still south of track – so it went on!

'Tommy: "Hello Ron – should make the target in about twenty-five mins."

'" OK Tom." " ETA 01.15".

'At 01.10 I saw flak on our port bow! – I said: "I think we're off track Skipper – what about it then? There's the target on our port bow!"

'Skipper – "Is that the target?"

'Me – "Sure is chum! Better alter course pronto!"

'Skipper: "OK – Tom! Altering course 30 degrees port."

'Tommy: "OK skipp!"'

'Five minutes to ETA. The flak is coming up ahead – we're just getting to the outskirts! "Jesus it's hot!"'

'There was quite a lot of it at that. We started on our bombing run. We could see the TIs below the clouds; we could also see bombs burst! The met [meteorological] people said there would be no cloud. (Duff gen!) We started our run up.

" Right, right, ri…..ght, right, steady – steady – bombs gone!"

'The run-up was grand – couldn't be bettered at any time – Then it came! A stream of tracer hit us from underneath and one started from the starboard bow down. Tonight, for some reason, I have stood and sat down all the way – I usually lie down on my bed in the front – the tracer cut my seat stays and left me without a seat – shattered my B/Sight – I had a shot at the EA but whilst doing so I heard Stan shout, "Bale out". I grabbed my 'chute and as I was putting it on we started to spin. Tommy fell on top of me. I had to push him off and start to open the hatch. God, it was awful! I was terrified – I couldn't get the hatch open. The damned thing stuck. After a great deal of tugging and pulling the hatch started to open. Tommy seemed funny! Suddenly the a/c pulled out of the spin. I thought "Good old Stan, at the wheel again". Tommy started to get out first, he got stuck in the hatch – I pushed him out!

'Jack [Crump] then jumped, then Cliff [Cork], then Stan. Left me all alone! I could not get my helmet plugs off and so I literally tore it off in a frenzy and stepped over the hatch and kicked it closed. I thought – "I've had it". I managed to get it open again and dropped out on the second attempt to get out, the first attempt I got into the wrong position, so I got back and had another try. This time I got out and counted four and then pulled the rip-cord.'

Ron Grogan made a subsequent note of events in his diary:

'Shot down by fighters at 01.20 this morning. There were two FW190s. One attacked from stbd low down and one from under the fuselage. The elevators and the ailerons were shot away. The a/c was completely out of control. Spun to 8,000 feet from 22,000 feet, then she straightened out. The rear gunner shot one of the EA down. We saw it go down in flames. Baled out and I was the last to go. 'Chute opened and it was a very eerie sensation, so silent! The target was still being attacked; the flak was terrific and the bombs were still falling. Landed OK but I had no chance to escape at all. Some soldiers and civilians captured me! The soldiers were polite but the civilians were very antagonistic. I was put in a hut for the rest of the night. They had no water but they gave me "beer". It was good too!'

Later that morning, in the pouring rain, Ron Grogan was marched at bayonet point to a village some five-and-a-half miles away, and then taken to a nearby Luftwaffe HQ, where he was re-united with Stan Goodman and Jack Crump. That evening they were put in a truck, together with bits of their aircraft and a long wooden box that proved to be the coffin for the only one of the crew to lose his life, Tommy Cusson. (Thirty-two-year-old Thomas Frederick Cusson is buried in the Reichswald Forest War Cemetery.) Eventually reaching Düsseldorf via Duisburg – 'We passed through both cities. The damage was terrific. Stupendous! Literally, streets and areas are devastated. People look very pallid and unhealthy.'

On the way to Frankfurt-am-Main by train Stan decided to escape. Jumping out of the window, he had failed to take account of the speed of the train, and succeeded only in knocking himself out. He was put back on the train, and from then on the guards covered the prisoners with their Luger pistols. On 23 June, at Dulag Luft, the fifteen members of 77 Squadron lost on that dreadful night were to see each other again. Ron Grogan was particularly delighted to see the other NCOs of his crew, having been told earlier by a Luftwaffe officer that four had been killed: 'Taken to another camp across the road. Met Stan, Cliff, George [Hewitt] and Arthur [Hudson]! So they are not dead. A great relief! It is a relief to talk to somebody. No wash or shave yet! They took away our boots and belts before we went to bed!'[64]

On 26 June, while the two officers went to Stalag Luft III (Sagan), the twelve NCOs left for Luft 7, arriving in *Trupp 7* on 28 June.

*

Another *Trupp 7* arrival was twenty-two-year-old F/S Geoffrey A. Flay RNZAF, who had been flying Beaufighter Mk.10s on 489 (RNZAF) Squadron at Langham, Norfolk (16 Group, Coastal Command) with his navigator F/S Thomas Ransley Clegg.

On 14 June 1944 Langham's 'ANZAC Wing' – 455 (RAAF) and 489 (RNZAF) Squadrons – set off in their Beaufighters to attack shipping between Gravelines and the Hook of Holland:

'The aircraft took off at 03.35 hours, aircraft A, X and B/455 proceeded in formation in company with aircraft of No. 489 Squadron whilst the remaining aircraft proceeded independently. The formation made a good landfall and swept north-east along the enemy coast at 4,000 feet.

'Some five miles west of Westhoofd, four M-class minesweepers were sighted, and aircraft A/455 and X/455 attacked with bombs in the face of intense light flak, but no damage was claimed. After the attack, the No. 455 Squadron aircraft flew to a rendezvous position while No. 489 Squadron proceeded on and made contact with the North Coates Wing, and carried out a further bombing attack with them.

'All our aircraft returned safely to Langham; No. 489 Squadron lost one aircraft on the operation.' (455 Squadron War Diary).

489 (RNZAF) Squadron's War Diary was briefer:

'Six aircraft of our squadron, along with six aircraft of No. 455 Squadron, patrolled from Gravelines to the Hook but formations lost contact at rendezvous. The six 489 Squadron aircraft sighted off the mouth of the Scheldt (51°49'N 03°45'E) four M-class minesweepers and attacked with 2 x 500lbs MC bombs each in the face of considerable heavy and light flak from the ships. Several bursts were seen among and to rearward of the ships. Y did not return.'

None of the four heavily-armed enemy ships – *Vorpostenboot* (patrol boats) VP2007, VP2009, VP2011 and VP1306 – was sunk, but their combined firepower was enough to force Geoff Flay's Beaufighter, LZ543, P6-Y, to ditch in the North Sea shortly after 0500 hours. Managing to inflate his dinghy and paddle ashore, Geoff was captured by German soldiers. Standing behind anti-tank barriers they had watched him drag his rubber dinghy through a minefield!

The body of Geoff's navigator, Tom Clegg, was recovered from the sea near Rockanje on 18 June

1944, and is interred in the Rockanje (Zeeweg) General Cemetery.

Geoff was taken by train that afternoon to Rotterdam, where he spent the night in an army camp. On the following day, he was taken via Deurne, Horst, Sevenum, and Blerick to Venlo, where he spent four days in solitary confinement. Leaving there on 19 June, he passed through Cologne and Frankfurt to Oberursel. After three days of interrogation and solitary confinement he was purged on the morning of 21 June to Wetzlar, and was at Luft 7 on 28 June.

*

Rear gunner Sergeant Elwyn J. 'Taff' Morgan, from Porthcawl, South Wales, had completed six operational sorties by the time he was nineteen-and-a-half years of age. He was flying Lancasters on 550 Squadron at North Killingholme, Lincolnshire, with his crew of F/O Geoff H. Packham (pilot); F/S Jim Matthews (navigator); F/S Johnny S. Jenkins (bomb aimer); F/S Cyril C. Pettit (flight engineer); F/S Frank A. Wilson (wireless operator); and F/S Jack Jackson (mid-upper gunner). On 16/17 June 1944, in Lancaster B.I LL747, BQ-P for Peter, they were detailed for the raid on Sterkrade/Holten synthetic oil plant.

Elwyn Morgan:

'I can't remember too much about our previous ops, but before going to a squadron we did quite a few solo trips in Wimpys dropping leaflets. We then flew for a short while on Halifaxes with 425 (Alouette) Squadron, RCAF, before being posted to a Lancaster Finishing School, and then on to 550 Squadron.

'Friday, 16 June 1944: It was about noon when the flight commanders announced that operations were taking place that evening. After hearing this we walked slowly toward the mess where lunch was awaiting us. Not much was spoken between us, and after we had finished we decided to go down to the flights to check the aircraft for the night's work. I had already cleaned the guns the day previous, so I didn't have much to do. We arrived there to find the armourers changing the ammunition, as we had operated on Le Havre (14 June, E-Boats) a couple of days previous in daylight, and night tracer had to be put in. I checked the turret and the guns, and after completion of this I talked a while to the armourers who had finished their various jobs. They told me that 'P for Peter' was the oldest plane (291 flying hours) on the station and that it had just completed its sixty-fifth operation. The radio operator (Frank Wilson) and the navigator (Jim Matthews) had completed their inspections, so we walked back to the mess to sit down and listen to the radio.

'At 1700 hrs we went into the dining hall for tea where we met the bomb aimer (John Jenkins). "We're carrying a cookie (4,000lb HC bomb) tonight boys", he said. We all realised then that the attack would probably be on Germany. We ate our tea and then went back to the billets to put on our flying underwear. I wrote a letter home, and at 2000 hrs we went back to the dining hall where we ate our flying supper, which consisted of egg and chips, followed by jam and coffee. We then went down to the briefing room. Briefing was at 2100 hrs and, just before it began, all the crews crowded around the large-scale map of Europe which hung on the wall of the briefing room. On the map a coloured cord indicated the route of the night's operation. The target which was in "Happy Valley" lay surrounded by huge red and blue blobs, which represented anti-aircraft fire and searchlight batteries. From previous experience I knew what lay ahead. As the briefing proceeded and various officers had their say, the importance of the mission being successful was greatly stressed. After handing in our personal belongings we proceeded to the locker rooms to put on our flying kit. On arrival at the locker rooms we were greeted by the usual "bee hive" activity. Everyone was keen to be out at the aircraft as soon as possible. New crews were especially keyed up as this was their first blow against Germany. This was our seventh operation and previous raids had installed confidence in us.

'Entering the crew transport fully clothed for the night's work we found that friendly rivalry resulted in wisecracks passed quickly between the various crews. Everyone knew the seriousness of our job and that some of us would not ride that bus again, but it did no good to think about these things. The crew bus stopped and the driver called out "P-Peter". We got out and made our way to the Lancaster which stood awaiting us a few hundred yards away. We climbed aboard for a final check. The motors roared into life one by one and every member of the crew tested their various instruments. This being done we got out for a last cigarette. The ground crew sat around with us chatting; they were good lads and our lives depended so much on their work.

'We got in once more and settled ourselves in our positions. I loaded the guns, and once more tested my intercom; no longer were we seven lads but a bomber crew whose success and existence depended on their cooperation and efficiency. The four engines were started once more along with the other aircraft of the squadron. We taxied out of dispersal and around the perimeter track to await our turn to take off behind the other Lancasters. I looked around, the weather was fair. When our turn came to take off we taxied on to the runway. A crowd of WAAFs and ground staff always congregated at the side of the runway to wave us off. Almost 7,000 horse power was unleashed as the skipper opened the throttles. With the exhausts flaming we gathered speed as we tore down the runway; coming near the end we gradually lifted off the deck. "Undercarriage up" said the skipper, and we were airborne. It was now 2315 hours.

'We circled Spurn Head (at the mouth of the Humber estuary) in Yorkshire, gradually climbing. Oxygen was on and everyone looked weird when we donned our masks. I kept rotating my turret looking for other Lancasters to warn the skipper – this was to prevent collisions. Over the aerodrome about 12,000 feet we set course and I at once took up my search for enemy fighters. We crossed the English coast gaining height all the time, and then saw that the North Sea was hidden from our view by a thick layer of cloud. The engineer announced that all the engines were over-heating, so we could not climb higher than 18,000 feet. It was very cold so I switched on the heating for my electrical suit.

'Time passed and everything was going well. Several alterations of course were made until we turned on to the target. The bomb aimer sighted the marking flares ahead, and he gave some corrections to the pilot – we were all set for a good "prang". I kept up my search for fighters, as they usually waited for us to drop our bombs and then attack. Suddenly there came a loud explosion followed by a flash of flame which came past my turret. I knew we had been hit, and the calm voice of the skipper told us that our port inner engine was u/s. We continued to the target to drop our bombs. The navigator announced that the cabin was full of smoke, and that he was carrying out an inspection for fire – luckily there was none. Before the target was reached, the bomb aimer found that the bomb-doors wouldn't open. The navigator and the engineer tried to pump the doors open with the emergency pump, but that too was broken, covering the floor with a thick layer of oil. There was nothing to do but head for home.

'The skipper turned on course, but we were going down fast due to the heavy bomb load which we still had on board. The engineer's leg had been hurt from flying pieces of shrapnel from the flak burst, so the navigator helped bandage it up, and then he and the bomb aimer tried to get rid of the bombs. We were then down to 13,000 feet, and going along the tops of the clouds. The mid-upper gunner sighted an enemy fighter above us. His turret was out of order and we could not take evasive action due to the two bad engines, but luckily my turret was still in good order. I proceeded to give the fighter a few bursts while the pilot took our Lancaster in and out of the clouds. After about three attacks the fighter sheared off.

'It was evident we could not make our base. Ditching was out of the question as we still had our bombs aboard. We were losing height rapidly, so the only alternative was to jump. The skipper gave the order to abandon the aircraft – no panic reigned among us, although we knew that a tough time lay ahead. The engineer jumped first, then the navigator, the bomb aimer, the wireless operator, and the mid-upper gunner. Then it was my turn. The escape-hatch was just a black hole through which nothing appeared but a dark void like the mouth of a great well. Never again do I want to live through those seconds. With the parachute handle held in my right hand I dropped head first into the night. I pulled the handle and a few seconds later my 'chute opened. I held the harness straps firmly to stop myself swaying. I kept looking down but could not see the ground. A few minutes elapsed and then I saw the ground coming to meet me. With my feet together I hit the ground, and the wind started to pull me along. I got up, pulled my parachute in and proceeded to hide it with my flying kit in a ditch.

'It was raining hard and all around were ditches. I looked in a northerly direction, a fire glowed in the sky and later I learned that it was our crashed aircraft, and that several Dutch people had perished due to our bombs going off. I started to walk in a south-westerly direction, but after walking about 200 yards I found that a wide ditch confronted me. I followed it for a while until I came to a place where I could cross it. Continuing across another field I found another ditch not so wide. I jumped this one only to find ditches surrounding that field also. I had now been walking about an hour and had only covered about a mile. Coming to a narrow road I followed it down. Soon a house came in sight and I saw someone standing outside. I approached the house carefully, keeping to the side of the road. When I was within about 300 yards of the house I recognised the person outside as Frank, our wireless operator. He recognised me and I cannot say how glad we were to meet each other.

'We then decided to keep walking south-westerly. Frank had lost one of his flying boots and had hurt his neck when baling out. We continued walking in this direction and after keeping this up for about a half an hour we found that day was dawning, and that if we wanted to stay free we would have to find somewhere to hide for the day. There were no woods around to offer any cover whatsoever. Seeing a farm lad walking nearby, we both approached him and, with the aid of a small card with different languages on, we made him understand that we were English airmen and needed somewhere to hide. He took us to a small barn and told us to stay there for a while. Twenty minutes later he returned with a woman who could speak a little English. We told her who we were and asked her for some "civvy" clothes, and also somewhere to hide for the day. She then tried to explain that the Germans surrounded the whole area and would probably be searching for us. She also told us that her father had been shot some months previous for aiding British airmen. We talked a while and later she asked us if we wanted something to eat.

We said we were a little hungry and she took us to a small bungalow where we met the rest of her people.

'They prepared a small meal for us consisting of raw bacon in between a dark brown kind of bread. Against our will we ate this only to hear the sound of a motorcycle coming down the road. Before we had time to get away two German police dismounted and produced their revolvers. They took us back inside the bungalow and made us sit down. The old lady of the house made us some coffee and, believe me, it was nothing like our English coffee. We waited for about thirty minutes and then a car pulled up outside. They took us in this car to the local gaol, and I was surprised to see the number of Dutch folk who waved to us as we passed through the village. When we reached our destination, we were searched and all our personal belongings were taken off us and we were put in separate cells. The cells were pretty deadly and their furniture consisted of a wooden bed and a stool. I was so tired that I lay down on the hard boards and fell asleep immediately.

'I awoke in about two hours, my clothes were still soaking wet. Taking most of them off, I hung them around the cell to dry off a little. I sat on the stool thinking for a while. I was now getting hungry so I rang the bell on the wall which summoned the guard. He opened the door and I asked him for some food. He didn't understand me so I started pointing to my stomach. He understood me only to return with the words "*Nein speise*" (no food), and he slammed the door and locked it. It was getting dark and the only thing I could do was to try and get some more sleep. The boards were hard and over an hour passed before slumber came. I awoke several times during the night, and at last morning came. I pulled the shutters down from the window, and stood a while inhaling the fresh air. I heard someone in the next cell whistling "Men of Harlech" and "Did your Mother come from Ireland?" I knew this was one of our crew, and I whistled "I'm in love with you, Honey", a song greatly sung by our crew. Someone shouted "Is that you Taff?" and I answered "Yes". "This is Jimmy" (the navigator) the answer came back, and from then on we talked. I told him that Frank was in the next cell to him.

'We were now very hungry, and I told Jim I would ask the guard for some bread. I rang the bell and the guard appeared. I talked to him the best I could, and in the end persuaded him to give me a small piece of dry dark brown bread. I broke it in half and tried to throw one half to Jimmy, but a screen covering the window prevented this and a piece of bread was lost in the attempt. About noon movement outside my cell indicated new arrivals. I heard Jimmy at his window shout. I got up to the window and he told me that our engineer (Cyril Pettit) had arrived and he had plenty of bread. I rang the bell and the guard took me to the engineer's cell. I did not speak to him, but gladly accepted some bread and butter. I ate this and afterwards stood by the window chatting to Jimmy.

'From time to time a guard passed the cell and we had to be quiet. Shortly after this I was taken to the guardroom where I met three crew mates and another lad besides. We were then taken on another stage of our travels. We were taken in a passenger train, which was a very poor effort with wooden seats, to a place called Venlo. The prison, this time, was an old convent; again we had each separate cells. These were much better than the last due to straw mattresses and windows through which we could watch the people on the road. It was Sunday evening and very quiet and still. A church steeple over the tops of the trees added to the peacefulness of the scene. How difficult it was to think of this as a country producing so much sorrow as it had during the last few years.

'Along with my crew mates, and about twenty Allied airmen I left the convent the following morning. All day we travelled enjoying the company of each other. Cologne was the first city we passed through, a sight like this I will not forget for a long while. It was horribly gutted with not a whole building to be seen anywhere. There was a large and beautiful cathedral which had been gutted with fire. The scenery going down the Rhine (Valley) was marvellous. Endless miles of vineyards clothed the banks at the foot of the cliffs. At Frankfurt we disembarked to await another train. The railway station at Frankfurt was in a terrible mess, and the city in ruins. Civilians cast their vengeful eyes upon us; for once we were glad of our German guards.

'Oberursel, our next prison, was the dreaded interrogation centre. The place had a bad smell about it due to there being no ventilation in the cells. Being tired I slept very well the first night. Breakfast consisted of two pieces of very mouldy bread. They gave us some tea which was horrible – I learned later it was made out of mint. Following this I was taken in front of the interrogation officer. By kindness, by pleading, and finally by threats he tried to make me fill in a form giving details of my crew, squadron etc. I would not have anything to do with it. He threatened me with being a saboteur as I had taken down my stripes while I was in Holland. With his threats ringing in my ears I was taken to my cell.

'At the interrogation centre the Jerries had used a few tricks including the one of false Red Cross forms, but as far as I could gather they knew more information than I did, but just wanted me to confirm it. For dinner I had a bowl of soup – at least it looked like soup. Time hung very heavily on my hands. Previous occupants of my cell had marked their days spent there on the walls. I was pleased to see that one chap had spent eleven days there. I grew tired of listening to the voices of the guards in the corridors. Several times I dozed off on my wooden bed. Tea came at last – two pieces of bread!

'Three days passed without anything happening. I prayed for the time when the sun struck the further wall when I knew the day was ending. I felt and I am sure I looked dirty. A week had passed and I had not even had a wash. At the end of the third day a guard came for me. He took me into another building where a Lufwaffe officer sat behind a desk. We were going in the morning so he said; he must have seen the look of relief on my face. He asked me a few more questions and, when he saw I had no intention of answering him, he brought some folders for me to read. By the look of the date on these forms a good spy ring must have been in existence at home. I was taken out into another compound where I met the rest of my crew. The joy of speaking to one another after our solitary confinement was great.'

The twenty-one-year-old flight engineer, F/S Cyril C. Pettit, from Battersea in London, had joined the RAF early in 1942 as a Wop/AG, but had been put on deferred service until offered the position of flight engineer. He was finally called up on 9 July 1942. He remembers the day on which they were shot down:

'It was about 1100 hours when we first learned that operations were on for that night, Friday 16 June 1944. It was too late to do a daily inspection on our aircraft before lunch, so we continued to the mess to await that meal. After lunch we proceeded down to the locker-room where I collected my 'chute, harness, Mae West, tool-kit, log, and various other things which I would need for the night's trip and then, with the rest of the crew, boarded the "bus" which took us around the perimeter to the dispersal of "P for Peter".

'I then did my usual external and internal inspection of the aircraft, checked the fuel state etc., and notified our skipper that everything was OK, and I was ready to start up. The ground crew were also ready for starting, so we soon had the four engines roaring into life. Once started, I let the engines idle at 1200 rpm to warm them up, and then tested each in turn. It did not take many minutes to do this and, after assuring that they were OK, and that the navigator had checked his instruments, the wireless operator his radio equipment, and the gunners their turrets and found them to be OK, I cut the engines, turned off the fuel etc., and with the others, climbed out on to the "deck".

'We then returned to the flight office and hung around until we learned the time of briefing, which we were finally told was at 2100 hours. That meant that our flying meal would be at 2000 hours and take-off about 2300 hrs. Having about an hour or so to spare before tea, we cycled back to our billets where I wrote my usual letter to Doris, my wife, whom I had great hopes of seeing during the weekend. We were due for a day off on Sunday and I was going to Manchester to bring her back with me to the lodgings which I had, after many miles of cycling and making enquiries, at last succeeded in obtaining for her near the camp. The other boys were either writing home or as usual, trying to guess the whereabouts of the night's target. We were all hoping that it would be somewhere in France, but our bomb-load of one 4,000 and sixteen 500lb bombs led us to believe that the Reich was in for a heavy blow that night.

'Our flying meal was egg and chips as usual, and that, as events turned out, was to be the last we were to have in England for some considerable time. However, after the meal we filled our flasks with tea and lost no time in getting down to the briefing room for we were anxious to learn the location of our target. We were not left long in doubt, for as soon as we entered the door our searching eyes alighted on the large pin which was marking the target on the European map – which covered the entire wall at the end of the room.

'We could see at once that the target was in the Ruhr Valley, which was usually referred to as "Happy Valley", and from previous experience we knew just how warm our reception would be. According to the map, the Ruhr Valley is the most heavily-defended area in the whole of Germany, and I for one will never dispute that fact nor, I think, will many who have experienced it.

'After handing in our valuables and collecting our escape aids, we sat down to await the start of the briefing. We could see from the wall map that there were two routes to the target – a very unusual thing and a failure as things turned out – one for each wave. The second wave, which included our crew, was to take the longer route of the two. Briefing only lasted about thirty minutes and was concluded by the CO wishing us all the best of luck.

'Then amid the usual rabble of wisecracks and so on, we made our way on our cycles to the locker room where most of the chaps commenced to do their flying kit. The gunners wore the most because the turrets are the coldest positions in the aircraft. I only wore an extra pullover and a scarf for it can become very warm in the forward end of the Lancaster, even without the heaters on.'

## CHAPTER FIVE

# JULY 1944, *TRUPPEN 8-17*

**2 JULY 1944.** As a shovel was missing from the cookhouse, the Germans stopped an issue of cocoa.

**3 JULY 1944.** By the afternoon, the missing shovel had still not been found. The Germans threatened reprisals if it was not returned. At a camp meeting Lloyd and Hill resigned, but Lloyd agreed to continue as Camp Leader after the man responsible for the loss of the shovel agreed to return it. The Germans said that if it happened again those responsible would be jailed. (F/S T.D. Glenn, *P.O.W. Wartime Log…*)

*Trupp 8* (forty-five men) arrived.

\*

Before joining up David Yardley, from Cambuslang, Scotland, had been a professional boxer and a steel erector. Now, on the night of 27/28 May 1944 (Aachen), he was the mid-upper gunner of Lancaster JA712, 550 Squadron, with a tough fight on his hands when JA712 was hit by a night-fighter at around 20,000 feet. Of the seven-man crew only he and Sgt Elie J. Molnar RCAF (bomb aimer) survived. Soon found by the Belgian Resistance Molnar evaded capture until liberated early in September, but Dave Yardley, on the other hand, woke up in a German hospital suffering with several broken bones.

The Lancaster had crashed close to the Belgian village of Rebecq, some of whose inhabitants rushed to the scene in the hope of rescuing any surviving airmen before the German soldiers arrived. They found two dead in the wreckage, and then, about fifty metres from the fuselage, the very badly wounded and unconscious figure of Dave Yardley. Remarkably, it seems that he had still been aboard the Lancaster when it crashed.

Also attending the crash was the village doctor, Doctor Dupureur, who 'asked that someone bring a board or something able to serve as a stretcher so that they could carry the wounded airman at once to the hospice (the village's hospital).' One of the villagers reported Dave's whereabouts to the Germans, who removed him from the hospice to a prison in Nivelles, at the same time arresting twenty-two of the villagers, three of whom were to die as a result of their imprisonment.

There is a fascinating postscript to this story. The 'stretcher' that was used by the villagers to carry Dave from the crash site to the hospital was, in fact, JA712's rudder. It was found in the 1980s in the bell tower of the hospice's chapel where it had been hidden all those years before.[65]

Dave had still not completely recovered by the time he reached Luft 7, in *Trupp 8*: 'You could see the marks on his face where he had been blown through the turret. He had lapses of memory and forgot where he was. One day, he rose from the table, a vacant look in his eyes, and walked outside.' (Bill Taylor.) Jack Broad and Bill, sensing danger, rushed out of their hut to find him walking towards the trip wire while a guard, watching from his tower, had his machine gun trained on him. Racing after him Bill rugby-tackled Dave about a yard before he stepped over it.

Dave had recovered sufficiently to escape during the evacuation in January 1945 (see page 244).

\*

'It is with deep regret that I am writing to confirm the unhappy news that your son, 1895854 Sergeant Hamilton, Arthur Frederick, failed to return from operations carried out against HASSELT on the night of the 11 May, 1944. Your son was mid-upper gunner of an aircraft which left base [Binbrook] at 22.00 hours and I regret to say nothing has since been heard of either the machine or any members of the crew.'

Thus wrote the officer commanding 460 (RAAF) Squadron to Arthur Hamilton's father in Barking, Essex.

Happily, victims of night-fighter pilot Leutnant Hans Schmitz, 4./NJG1, Arthur Hamilton and the rest of the crew of Lancaster ND674, 460 (RAAF) Squadron, survived. Six of the crew, including Arthur Hamilton, were taken prisoner. The seventh, F/Sgt D.J. Dyson RAAF, evaded capture and, after he had been liberated, was flown back to RAF Northolt on 10 September.

Arthur Hamilton was captured at Ghent, Belgium, on 13 May: 'I was taken to a barrack and interrogated by a drunk Luftwaffe officer. I gave him my name, rank and number and he wanted to know who gave me civilian clothing. I refused to tell him and he hit me in the throat with the butt of his revolver.' He spent the next six weeks in St Gilles prison, Brussels, on a very poor diet. Having arrived in Belgium weighing around twelve stone, he was to return to England in May 1945 weighing only six.

ND674's flight engineer, Sgt Andrew Law, suffered injuries that also confined him to the Luftwaffe's St Gilles hospital. A report dated 9 June stated that he was 'suffering from laceration of the nerves of his arm'. Although Andrew would eventually reach Luft 7, he was taken away for an operation to his damaged arm, but the operation never took place, and he ended up at Stalag VIIA (Moosburg).

*

69 Squadron RAF flew specially modified Mk.XIII Wellington aircraft with a crew of four. Engaged on night-reconnaissance flights the aircraft carried no radar, while the front gun-turret was replaced by a Perspex nose. Instead of bombs, there was stowage for up to fifty-four flares, and the aircraft carried an open-shutter moving-film camera.

It was in one of these modified Wellingtons, MF231, on the night of 14/15 June 1944, that F/O C.L. Merrill RCAF (pilot), F/O K.R. Prentice (navigator), F/O R.H. Riding (bomb aimer), and F/S T. Trimble (air gunner) were given the task of reconnoitring the River Seine up to Le Havre. Thomas Trimble, inevitably called 'Paddy' given his Irish roots but Tom to his family, wrote: 'At about 8 pm we were called for briefings and got all the "gen" on the job we had to do. Actually we all thought it was going to be one of the easiest trips we could have. However things didn't work out that way.'

It was a beautiful evening as they departed RAF Northolt and set course for France. Tom:

'stood in the astrodome watching the runway fade away. Little did I think that it would be the last time I would see it for a long time and so much would be happening in between. However we set course for our target and in a short time were in sight of the French coast, where we could see fires burning on targets which had been visited earlier by our aircraft. They sure had done their work. On approaching the French coast we were informed that one plus bandits were in the vicinity but we could see nothing of them. Just before crossing the coast I tested all of my guns and everything worked perfectly.

'As soon as the coast was crossed some flak came up which certainly was at our height but about 100 yards astern. From then until we reached our destination we encountered slight flak but none very close, so everything went very well till we reached our target. Well, things did not go very well from then on, and after a few mishaps things began to happen. The first I knew of it was when I saw a sheet of flame licking past the turret. Well, just as I switched on my mic to inform the pilot, the navigator yelled out we were on fire and for someone to come and help him put it out. By this time we were well on fire and I could see nothing outside the flames so, as the pilot knew this, I set my turret dead astern and opened the doors to go back into the kite and see if I could help in any way.'

Tom was wearing a new type of flying boot, which somehow caught in the turret's mechanism. Having unplugged his intercom to get out of the turret, he plugged it in again, and was just in time to hear the pilot give the order to bale out. After a struggle to free himself, that seemed all of two minutes, he was free. Looking up the fuselage towards the front of the aircraft, though he could see no-one, he assumed that the pilot was still at the controls as the Wellington was flying straight and level. All the while the flames grew in intensity and Tom quickly clipped on his parachute. Opening the escape hatch he saw to his horror, through all the flames, that the aircraft was only some 50 feet [sic] off the ground:

> 'I didn't seem particularly to like the idea of a slow painful death by burning so I decided to jump out and make it quick and painless. So out I went and luckily I had my 'chute on when I made the decision, so immediately I was clear of the flames I pulled the cord but strange enough I didn't expect it to open. The next thing I know was when I felt a terrific jerk and I imagined I was caught in the aircraft. Well, to my delight when I looked up I saw my 'chute fully open and I was dangling in space about 1,000 feet from mother earth.'

Tom realised that he was drifting and swinging a lot under his 'chute but, while trying to correct these problems, heard the sound of an approaching aircraft, 'and on looking round found my own a/c had done a left-hand circuit and was coming back right under me. I was very low at this time so she went in about 300 feet beneath me. For a few moments I thought I was coming down into the burning wreck as it covered a very large area.' In the event, Tom landed a good half mile from the wreckage, in a field that 'was more like a cliff face'. But he had hurt his back when he landed, and it soon became so swollen that he was unable to walk. Leaving the field would have been difficult anyway, as all night long a German horse-drawn convoy made its way down the road that ran along the edge of the field: 'As I could not walk any more I sort of crawled back to where my 'chute was and rolled myself in it for the night.'

When it was light Tom saw an old Frenchman and shouted out to him that he would like some water. The old man, who didn't seem too friendly, walked away. An hour or so later German soldiers entered the field and went straight to the spot where Tom was still lying. As he had been well hidden, Tom concluded that the old man had given him away. When the soldiers saw that he was unable to walk, they sent for a stretcher. One was eventually brought, along with a German officer who spoke perfect English. He:

> 'asked me my name, but I refused to tell him. However he proceeded to tell me that I was from the crashed a/c a very short distance away. Also, to my surprise, he told me the names of all the crew and the type of "kite". Of course I thought he had picked up the other members or found some of them in the a/c but, no, he said I was the first and that there were no bodies in the a/c. Also that he had found a "document" which had all the names of the crew on it. Just then he was looking over my Mae West and discovered my name. Of course he was sure then that I was out of the a/c a few fields away.'

Of the rest of his crew, F/O Merrill was taken prisoner (Stalag Luft III), but the other two evaded capture.[66] Tom, meanwhile, was carried away on the stretcher, and put in a car. He was then driven to the wreckage of his aircraft, where the Germans scoured it for any useful pieces. Driven over to Rouen Tom was examined by a doctor, who pronounced that there was little wrong with him. Hitherto, he had been well treated by his captors, but now he was told that he would have to walk, even though he was still unable to do this unaided.

Put in a prison at Rouen he was joined by a number of American airmen: 'They were a really good lot and they helped me all they could for the next few days.' About three days later six of them were put aboard a lorry, which was also carrying six coffins. 'Well, we thought the worst was about to come but, no, they drove around for about an hour and picked up a lot of other prisoners and took us to a prison outside Paris, where we stayed for about four days. The food was pretty grim, this was the first time I had ever eaten raw potatoes and enjoyed them.'

This may well have been the notorious Fresnes prison, in which hundreds of prisoners were locked up pending their fate. Here Tom met a F/O Cullen [not identified]:

'who was very unfortunate to be there at all. He took over from the Yanks and helped me around from then until we parted. I was beginning to walk a bit then but still felt pretty weak. Well, one fine morning we were all kicked out about 5 am and crowded on a bus on our way to Brussels. This journey took about sixteen hours and was very uneventful, apart from the fact that our guard threatened to shoot us every few moments. When at last we arrived there we were thrown into separate cells, where we remained for a week. If I live to be a hundred I never want to experience anything like that again, the food was terrible and very little of it, and being all on your own didn't help a lot.'

Ironically, on the very day of his departure from the prison (probably that at St Gilles), having spent a week in solitary with nothing to read, a guard came round with some books. In no uncertain terms Tom told him what he could do with his books! When it was time to go he was lined up in the corridor 'with a lot of other POWs, mostly Yanks. However, they brought out a lot of chaps in civilian clothing who we were very suspicious of as they all had English names and seemed to know all about Blighty; also there was a Polish F/O in uniform who needed watching.' Taken to a station, when Tom got aboard the train that was to take them to Frankfurt and to Dulag Luft he found himself with four of the 'civilians' and the Polish officer. Tom became very suspicious of them when they kept asking questions, but realised that they were genuine when he discovered that 'they had been shot down earlier and had tried to escape. They did manage to get civilian clothes but were later picked up by the Gestapo and had a pretty rough time.'

The train took them to Aachen, where 'we saw the result of the RAF heavies and what a sight; you could "stand on a chair and look all over the city"', and on to Düsseldorf. Here too 'there was nothing but rain, and we had to spend the night in an air raid shelter, but the raid was not very heavy, thank heavens. I should hate to be on the receiving end of one of those raids.'[67] It took all of the next day to reach Cologne, and once again they had to go to an air raid shelter:

'but there didn't seem to be very much air activity and an attack did not develop. We got under way next morning and reached Frankfurt about midday. Here again was nothing but devastation, and I must say the people here were very hostile. This was the only time I was thankful for a guard. They certainly treated the civilian population very rough, but we didn't mind that. One of the civvies actually did hit a Yank with an umbrella.'

Soon they were at Dulag Luft:

> 'Here again we were searched, photographed, fingerprinted and pushed around in
> general, and of course, once again, put into solitary. Before this I thought the food was
> bad, but this was the last straw – two slices of the most horrible bread and a small bowl
> of watery porridge, at least it looked like porridge, but I'm afraid it would be very hard
> to say what it was, also a cup of tea without milk or sugar.'

This was all part of Luftwaffe intelligence's softening-up process of course but, within a couple of
days, he and fifty or so others were off via Wetzlar to Luft 7 in *Trupp 8*.

*

On the very costly raid on Wesseling on 21/22 June 1944 thirty-eight Lancasters of 5 Group failed
to return, six of them alone from 44 (Rhodesia) Squadron. A seventh Lancaster from that squadron,
NE138, nearly came to grief, too, on its way to the target when the control column jammed in a
forward position after being hit by a night-fighter. NE138 went into a steep dive and the pilot, S/L
S.L. Cockbain DFC, ordered the crew to bale out. Four of them did so before he regained control of
the bomber and flew back to England with the three remaining crew members.

F/S Albert 'Bert' Bracegirdle, mid-upper gunner, was 'on the seventeenth trip of his second tour'[68]
when he jumped. Another to go was the second-dickie pilot, and also Rhodesian F/L I. Rademeyer
DFC, a highly-experienced signals leader in 5 Group. Unfortunately, when he jumped NE138 was
at such an angle that he hit the tail fin, shattering his thigh. He was soon captured, but refused to
answer questions. Medical treatment was withheld accordingly, and it was ten days before he was
released to Obermassfeld hospital. It was now too late for the British surgeons there to do anything
for the now badly-infected leg, which had to be amputated high towards the groin. Bert saw him in
a wheelchair when they were briefly at Dulag Luft.

Bert, too, was soon captured, and was being taken to look for his parachute by a German official
when they were passed by a German truck in which were two more aircrew prisoners – W/O A.J.
Sargeant RAAF and Sgt F.J. Such – both of whom were also from 44 Squadron and in the same crew
of Lancaster LL938. Allan Sargeant had broken some of his ribs and had scratches to his face, but
he and Frank Such were not, all things considered, in bad shape. All three, together with LL938's
mid-upper gunner F/S Charles Phillips, arrived at Luft 7 in *Trupp 8*.

*

F/S Stanley Alfred Silver RAAF had celebrated his thirty-fourth birthday less than a fortnight
before he flew on what would prove to be his last operation as a replacement bomb aimer with
the 49 Squadron crew of P/O H.J. Carrington RAAF. Taking off from Fiskerton, near Lincoln, in
Lancaster LM539, bound for Duisburg on 21/22 May 1944, they were shot down over Holland,
possibly by Oberstleutnant Günther Radusch, Stab NJG2. With the aircraft on fire and in a steep
dive Carrington gave the order to bale out. Being the bomb aimer, and thus positioned almost on
the nose escape hatch, Stanley was the first and only member of the crew to bale out. But he was
in such a hurry to leave that he forgot to remove his flying helmet. Somehow the intercom cord
had wrapped around his left arm and, catching something as he jumped, wrenched an arm out of
its socket. He lost consciousness before his parachute became fully operational but, landing near
Roosendaal, Holland, he crawled approximately half a mile to a farmhouse, where he gave himself

up, and the police were summoned.

After a few weeks in St Gilles hospital, Brussels (26 May-30 June), Stan arrived at Luft 7 in *Trupp* 8. For further treatment he had to go on a number of occasions to Stalag 344 for physiotherapy for his injury – traction lesion of left brachial plexus which caused paralysis of his left arm. Stan records that on one of these trips:

> 'it was necessary to travel by rail. I was seated in a carriage next to a German soldier. As was customary, he wore his number on a flash on his shoulder. I noticed it and immediately pulled my [RAAF Service] disc out of my pocket and laid it on his lap. The numbers were identical – 419348! We could not speak each other's language, but our expressions spoke volumes.'

Accompanied by his guard, they went into a café: 'A near riot ensued when the occupants saw I was an Australian airman.' The guard pulled out his gun, 'and would have used it, as it was more than his own life was worth not to return me to the camp unharmed.'

*

Another Irishman in *Trupp* 8 was rear gunner Sgt P.F.J. 'Jimmy' Hayes. Born in Dublin in December 1924, he had moved to Brixton, London before the war, where he worked as a joiner. He was captured after baling out of Lancaster LL840 on the way back from Scholven-Buer, Germany, on the night of 21/22 June 1944. For reasons that will become clear, he baled out long before the pilot had in fact given the order to do so though, as the aircraft was on fire and in a steep dive at the time, Jimmy had possibly mis-heard him say: 'Prepare to bale out!'

Two months earlier, on the way back from bombing the railway marshalling yards at la Chapelle, in the northern suburbs of Paris, he was in the rear turret of Lancaster ND582, 57 Squadron, when it overshot Croydon airfield and crashed into a row of houses at Wallington, Croydon. Though ND582 had been shot up by a night-fighter, with both port engines severely damaged the pilot, F/O H.J. Young RCAF, had managed to coax the bomber back to England. Too low to bale out, they tried to find the airfield designated for 'lame ducks', possibly RAF Manston, Kent, but with the radio out of action and with airfields not showing perimeter lights due to the presence of an enemy intruder they decided to press on for their base at East Kirkby in Lincolnshire.

But, groping their way through the inky darkness, the crew were relieved when some perimeter lights were suddenly switched on. After firing a Verey Light and receiving a 'Green' from the airfield's Aldis lamp giving permission to land, F/O Young brought the damaged Lancaster in to land at Croydon. Jimmy Hayes in his rear turret thought that they were about to touch down, and said over the intercom: "Wizard landing, Skip." Back came the reply, "Don't be too sure", followed by a warning to brace for impact. Jimmy quickly curled himself into a ball as best he could to avoid being smashed against his guns and gun-sight. He remembered little of the crash before being knocked out.

Regaining consciousness, all he could see were flames and people running about and shouting. Adding to the nightmare scene was exploding ammunition, set off by the heat. Still trapped in the rear turret Jimmy thought he was going to be burnt to death but, seeing an elderly man running past, he shouted out to him for help. The man, surprised to hear a voice, looked up and saw the rear turret half way up a tree with Jimmy in it. The man was able to climb up what was left of the rear part of the Lancaster and, with the help of gravity, pull Jimmy out. Unfortunately, Jimmy landed on top of the man, pinning him down, but the man was able to extricate himself and get help, as

Jimmy recalls:

> 'Two RAF medical types arrived and with their help I got to my feet and, with one on
> each side, began to walk towards an ambulance that was parked up the road near to the
> scene of the disaster. It was only then I saw to my horror that everyone in the front of
> the plane must have perished and anyone in the two houses too. I remember calling
> out names of my friends and imploring the rescuer to try to get to them, and being
> restrained against trying, but it was a futile gesture. It was obvious nothing could be
> done. The medics were going to put me in the ambulance when one of them said "Don't
> put him in there" and they put me on the front seat next to the driver. It was a very old
> vehicle and I remember being asked to hold the choke open so the driver could get the
> engine to start, and why I should remember in the midst of such carnage I don't know,
> but it seemed so normal.'

Having overshot Croydon airfield (the old airport) the Lancaster had crashed at 2.20 am on Friday, 21 April 1944, first striking chimneys in Foresters Drive, before hitting Nos. 55, 57 and 59 Lavender Vale, Wallington, Croydon,[69] killing one civilian at No. 55 and another at No. 57. There was a third casualty, coincidentally also named Hayes. Henry Alfred Hayes, aged fifty, a keen amateur photographer, lived a few doors away at 41 Lavender Vale. According to his wife, Eva Muriel, he rushed home to get his camera but suffered a fatal heart attack as he did so.

Though three others survived the loss of ND582, the Scottish wireless operator, Sgt William Fyfe, died of his injuries that very day. The bomb aimer, Sgt D. Barber, and mid-upper gunner, Arthur Lester, were the other survivors. When Arthur and Jimmy were declared fit enough, they were sent back to 57 Squadron at East Kirkby to continue operations. They requested some leave, and this was granted provided that they did some flying before taking it. Though neither of them was keen, they agreed, and started with 'circuits and bumps' – local take-offs and landings on the airfield.

Jimmy Hayes:

> 'The first part was no problem, but when it came to landing the unreasoning fear of an
> accident left us both breaking into a cold sweat and for Arthur this was to present a problem,
> so much so that he refused to carry on flying. For me after a time I began to feel much
> better about things and so the memory of fateful times seemed to recede. They did not take
> very kindly to Arthur not wanting to fly and demoted him to aircraftman and marked his
> documents LMF (Lack of Moral Fibre), which is not very nice, but I suppose they cannot
> allow aircrew to refuse to fly even if there were mitigating circumstances, or we all would
> be at it. After Arthur's demotion he was re-mustered to ground staff and posted to another
> airfield. I also was posted to 50 Squadron at Skellingthorpe but as a spare.'

Joining the crew of one of the flight commanders, thirty-four-year-old S/L T.B. Cole DFC, Jimmy was worried that the others of his crew would think badly of him, but the opportunity to show them what he was made of soon came on an operation. The wireless operator picked up signals indicating that another aircraft was rapidly closing in on them from the rear, and urged Jimmy to open fire. Jimmy had been trained not to shoot until an approaching aircraft had been identified, but the wireless operator persisted in his urgings. Still young Jimmy resisted, and eventually S/L Cole put the Lancaster's nose down. The other aircraft skimmed past only a few feet overhead. It was another Lancaster. When they got back the skipper said that it was a good show.

So, on the night of 21/22 June 1944, two months after the Croydon tragedy, twenty-year-old

Jimmy Hayes was sitting in the rear turret of 50 Squadron's Lancaster LL840 when it took off at 2317 hours for the synthetic oil plant at Scholven/Buer, a few kilometres to the north of the vast Essen complex of factories and refineries. With Jimmy were: S/L T.B. Cole DFC (pilot); F/S K.H.C. Ingram (flight engineer, twenty-one); F/O John Craven DFC (navigator, twenty-nine); F/S A.G. Beresford (bomb aimer, twenty-two); F/O E.J. Blakemore DFM (wireless operator, twenty-five); and F/S F.H. Shorter (mid-upper gunner, twenty-four). Going with them as a 'spare bod' was twenty-two-year-old navigator W/O J. F. Lane. Though not detailed for operations that night, he went so that he could get in the thirtieth – and final – operation of his tour, following which he would be rested from operations.

They were for the most part an experienced aircrew, with five of them on their second tour. 'King' Cole had been awarded his DFC on 12 January 1943 when a flying officer (on 50 Squadron), while John Craven's was awarded on 10 September 1943 (on 61 Squadron). Eric Blakemore's DFM was gazetted as far back as 23 December 1941, when a sergeant on 9 Squadron. But, as so often, experience counted for nothing, as bomb aimer Arthur Beresford was to discover:

> 'It was a lovely evening and very clear. The flight out was uneventful and map reading from the [bomb aimer's] position I was able to fix our point of crossing over the English and Dutch coasts. Bang on track. The target was the oil refineries at Buer near Gelsenkirchen in the Ruhr. As we drew nearer we saw the green-coloured target indicators, dropped by the Pathfinder Force. There did not seem to be much flak activity, which usually meant fighters were about.
>
> 'The bombing run went well. I picked out the six spot markers which I had to bomb. A few slight calculations and directions to the skipper and I was able to say "bombs gone". With the bombs automatically went a photo flash. It was necessary to fly straight and level for a few seconds in order to get a good picture of the target from which your accuracy was ascertained. During these few seconds there was a terrific "bang" and the aircraft went into a steep dive. We think we had been hit by flak. King Cole got the plane back level at 9,000 feet (our operating height was about 23,000 feet). He did a tremendous job.'[70]

After bombs had been dropped and LL840 was on its way home King Cole:

> 'opened up the taps to increase our air speed, put the nose down slightly and suddenly we were hit by several bursts of flak. We lost 4,000 feet in a few seconds but I regained control of the aircraft after hitting my head on the roof of the cockpit. We made a quick examination of the aircraft and found that both our starboard engines had been hit. The starboard outer was feathered but the starboard inner feathering button failed to feather the engine and it over-revved to 4,000 rpm. I managed to get the aircraft on to our course for home but the trim tabs must have been damaged because extreme pressure was necessary on the rudder to keep the aircraft on anything like a straight line. We continued on our way home fighting with the aircraft the whole way.' [S/L Cole, via Michael Allman.]

After the flak had hit S/L Cole called up the crew to see how they all were. With no response from the rear gunner, Jack Lane went back to see what was wrong with him, and found the rear turret empty. Jimmy had baled out. Jack Lane was then asked to sit in the vacant rear turret, which he would never leave alive. Commenting on Jimmy's departure Arthur Beresford wrote: 'I don't blame him one little bit. I for one certainly thought it was curtains.'

The stricken bomber had staggered on until Hauptmann Ernst-Wilhelm Modrow, 1./NJG1, found it somewhere over The Netherlands.[71] To what extent he was responsible for the end of LL840 is unclear, for the Lancaster was already falling slowly out of the sky after the starboard inner engine had caught fire. It was no doubt the fire that caused the controls to cease functioning as designed, and when the starboard wing dropped and the bomber began heading earthwards S/L Cole ordered the crew to bale out. Not long after he himself had baled out, the last to do so, LL840 crashed in the Oenerbroek, a rural area south east of the Dutch village of Oene.

After the bodies of Jack Lane and Fred Shorter had been discovered in their respective turrets, Jan Willem Dalhuisen, a carpenter living in Oene, and Henk de Boer, a trainee-carpenter, were given the job of making the coffins for the two dead airmen. Jan: 'I helped to lay out the corpses in the coffins. Both victims were mutilated, they were unrecognisable. It was a terrible job.'

The coffins with the bodies were transported to the mortuary at the old cemetery of Epe, Tongerenseweg where, next day, they were buried by undertaker Van Putten in the north-west corner of the cemetery. The numbers of the graves, in sector II, are 704 (Lane) and 705 (Shorter).

The other five baled out more or less safely onto Dutch soil. S/L Cole reckoned that he got out of the Lancaster with some 600 feet to spare. His parachute had barely opened before he hit the ground, the only damage being to his left leg.

Arthur Beresford 'landed, fairly gently, in the corner of a field' in his stockinged feet, though with some damage to a foot. Hiding his parachute as best he could in a ditch he quickly left the area before getting some sleep. In the morning he tried his luck at a farmhouse: 'The door opened and a woman with a little girl appeared. She first of all looked startled and then beckoned me inside.' After making it clear that she was a loyal Dutch woman, the mother went off for a few minutes and came back with Herman Arensten, her husband. He disappeared, but several minutes later returned 'in a car with three other men. One of them who was the local doctor could speak English'. The doctor, Doctor Van Reekum from Geesteren, tended to Arthur's injured foot; the other two were Broek Roelofs, the local pastor, and, probably, L. J. Bastiaans, a medical student hiding out with the doctor, who had refused to sign a declaration of loyalty to the occupiers.

Much discussion followed among the Dutch, but Arthur gathered that they were talking about him. Eventually, after an hour or so, they 'decided that as the war was drawing to a close (it was just after D-Day) and they had had several people executed recently for helping British airmen, they did not think it worth risking any more lives for the sake of spending two to three months in a prison camp.' All Arthur wanted was a pair of boots so that he could get on with his evasion, but the Dutch took him to the police station at Borculo:

> 'The Dutch Police seemed to be annoyed that I had been turned in; I think if they had found me with no one else knowing it would have been a different story. They helped me, however, by taking me to Arnhem and handing me over to the Luftwaffe [at Deelen airfield]. I did not appreciate this until later in prison camp. I met men who had fallen into the hands of other German officials. The police also gave me a pair of clogs.'

Before he was taken away on 21 June Arthur gave his precious watch to Doctor Van Reekum for safe keeping. After the war a package arrived at Arthur's home in Wallasey, England. It was from someone called E.W. Brown writing on behalf of the doctor, who hoped that Arthur had found conditions not too bad in the POW camp. With the letter came the precious watch, carefully guarded by Dr Van Reekum. There was a 'PS' to Brown's letter: 'I would be glad if you would kindly acknowledge receipt of the watch so that I may tell the doctor that the watch is now in your possession.' Happily, this was done, and the watch is still in the possession of the Beresford family.

Arthur arrived at Luft 7 on 13 July (*Trupp 12*), ten days after Jimmy Hayes (*Trupp 8*). It will be recalled that Jimmy, for whatever reason, had left his turret whilst still more or less in the target area. Baling out somewhere near Gelsenkirchen, and descending under his lovely big canopy, he was thinking that all was well when, suddenly...

> 'there was a hell of a lot of flak bursting around and with lots of metal whizzing past in the air too close for comfort. Fortunately I drifted through the flak bursts quite quickly, and things were quieter, and I drifted through dense cloud into darkness underneath. I could see I was drifting over water, and thought I was going to get wet, but I cleared the water and landed on the grass just beyond. I was lucky because the 'chute was over a fence and I was on the other side. Had I landed on it I might have hurt myself.'

In a short while he was captured by German soldiers guarding, Jimmy thought, the reservoir near to which he had landed.

The rest of LL840's crew – Ken Ingram, John Craven, and Eric Blakemore – were soon in friendly Dutch hands. Craven and Blakemore stayed at the home of chocolate manufacturer de Vries at Frieslaan 5, Apeldoorn, until the town was liberated by the Allies several months later.

Ken Ingram, who had landed near Emst, half a dozen kilometres north of Apeldoorn, was found by the Dutch Resistance group 'Vrije groep Narda' (named after its leader Meinarda van Terwisga). Taken to the home of Mrs Juliana Catharina Bitter-van de Noordaa at Jachtlaan 134, Apeldoorn, he was joined there by Sgt Robert W. Zercher USAAF, who had baled out several kilometres to the east of Apeldoorn.

Bob Zercher was the ball-turret gunner of B-17G 42-39920, *Karen B*, 452nd Bomb Group, 729th Bomb Squadron, that had been hit by flak over Berlin on 29 April 1944. With No. 2 engine badly damaged *Karen B* limped back towards its base at Deopham Green, England, but when two more engines malfunctioned the pilot, 2nd Lieutenant Hal J. Nelson, ordered his crew to bale out. Nelson eventually put the bomber down, while he still had some control over it, at 1.30 pm at Het Vellert, some five kilometres south of Ruurlo with the crew still aboard. No-one was injured.

A member of the Dutch Resistance, Hendrik Wieggers, took the crew to safety.[72] Bob Zercher and four others went to the Slagman family in Harfsen until, in the middle of August 1944, Bob found himself on his own at the home of Mrs Meijer de Vries on the Jachtlaan, Apeldoorn, blissfully unaware of the tragedy that would shortly unfold.

Dutchman Willem l'Ecluse, a member of the Narda group, was in hiding to avoid being called up for forced labour in Germany, but was arrested and, possibly under torture by the *Sicherheitsdienst* (SD), betrayed the Narda group. In the late afternoon or evening of 30 September, SS-Hauptsturmführer Karl Fielitz and his second-in-command, SS-Untersturmführer Hubert Wigger, both from the SD's Antwerp office, caught the Narda group at the house at Paul Krugerstraat 30, Apeldoorn: Wim Aalders (born 18 February 1914), Jan Barendsen (11 September 1882), Reinier van Gerrevink (4 March 1907), Wim Karreman (5 August 1925), Jan Schut (8 June 1918) and Hans Wijma (5 February 1917). By way of a bonus they got Ken Ingram and Bob Zercher, who just happened to be in the house at the time. In the confusion one of the Narda group, Joke (Joop) Bitter, son of Mrs. Bitter-van de Noordaa, slipped away.

The matter of what the SD should do with their captives was referred to SS-Obergruppenführer Hanns Albin Rauter, SS-General and Höherer Polizeiführer, who was in command of both the Waffen-SS, the ordinary police, and the SD in The Netherlands. It was on his orders that the two airmen and the six members of the Narda group were taken to the back garden of the SD HQ at

Van Rhemlaan 9, Apeldoorn. There, at about 7 am on the morning of 2 October, they were shot by a company of NCOs recruited from a Waffen-SS Landesschützen-Battalion. Their bodies were left at various points on the streets of Apeldoorn with the label 'Terrorist' around their necks. Ken's was put by the Deventerstraat bridge over the Kanaal Noord, and Bob's some 400 metres away on the same street near Hoofdstraat, opposite the post office.

Narda van Terwisga and Juliana Bitter-van de Noordaa were also arrested, and were sent to Ravensbrück concentration camp. Juliana died there, aged sixty-six, on 6 January 1945 but Narda, surviving the horrors of that camp, was liberated by the Allies on 25 April 1945.[73]

On the night of 7/8 March 1945 Rauter was wounded in his car when it was attacked by the Dutch Resistance. He was still in hospital when found by the British Army after the war. Handed over to the Dutch, he was sentenced to death by a special court in The Hague on 12 January 1949, and was executed by firing squad near Scheveningen on 24 March 1949.

*

**6 JULY 1944.** Huts were searched for a missing shovel, which may or may not have been used in the digging of a tunnel. Sports equipment arrived, including footballs, cricket bats and balls.

**7 JULY 1944.** The camp's paper *POW-POW* was issued for the first time.

**9 JULY 1944.** *Trupp 10* possibly arrived – three wounded men from Obermassfeld Lazarett. A library was opened with the arrival of 200 books.

*

According to Sgt Pat Nolan, his room-mate WO2 George W. Sharpe RCAF 'had the annoying habit of flexing his shoulder muscles every night and kicking any article of furniture that got in his way'. Sharpe had a good excuse for this annoying habit – he had been shot in the shoulder by a German soldier as he landed from his stricken Halifax bomber HX282, 433 (Porcupine) Squadron RCAF, which had been hit by flak on the night of 18/19 March 1944 as it was returning from Frankfurt. Six of the eight-man crew survived, including the station commander of RCAF Skipton-on-Swale, G/C L.E. Wray AFC, RCAF.

The story at Luft 7 was that George Sharpe, the navigator, was using an assumed surname. Apparently, so upset was he at being 'washed out' of pilot training that he went AWOL, but immediately re-enlisted as a navigator under this assumed name. But, he gave his name as Sharpe when the nominal roll of Luft 7 POWs was compiled in April 1945, and stated that he was married and that his wife lived at The Croft, 151 Kirk Deighton, Wetherby, Yorkshire.

Whatever his name his shoulder injury was severe enough for him to be hospitalised, and it was not until 9 July 1944 that he and two other hospital cases arrived at Luft 7 in *Trupp 10*, the others being Sgt Ernest Sawyer and F/S Sydney Simes, shot down on 18/19 March 1944 and 22/23 April 1944 respectively. Simes would later be repatriated via Odessa.

*

**10 JULY 1944.** *Trupp 11* (forty men) arrived.

*

Before the war the small town of Bagnères-de-Luchon, in the Haute-Garonne *département* in southern France, was a pleasant watering-hole, its several grand hotels (including the Angleterre and the Bristol) catering for rich visitors coming to take the waters. But in April 1944 it was a frontier town occupied by German frontier guards, bad news for five airmen evaders who had managed to get half way across the Pyrenees when they were captured near Bagnères.

The airmen had jumped out of Lancaster LL791, 50 Squadron, when it was attacked by two night-fighters on the night of 25/26 February 1944 (Augsburg). Incendiaries in the bomb bay caught fire, with the flames being fed by fluid from the aircraft's hydraulic system. Rear gunner Sgt T.J. Taylor 'saw a mass of flames shooting upward between the mid-upper turret and the bulkhead door. The pilot [P/O W.H. Taylor] was unable to pull the aircraft out of the dive as the control column came up loose in his hands, and he ordered the crew to bale out immediately. The bulkhead door gave way, and smoke came pouring into the cockpit.'

First to jump was the bomb aimer, F/Sgt D.T. Balmanno RAAF: 'Left a/c at 19,000 [feet]. Six members of crew still in a/c. A/c out of control. On fire. A/c crashed near Lunéville in France.' All except the navigator, Sgt K.E. Gilson, landed safely near the village of Emberménil. It is not known what happened to Gilson, but he was 'found dead on the ground some distance from the aircraft with his parachute spread open over him. The pilot had noticed him looking about his table with a torch in the aircraft and had jumped before him.' It seems likely that Gilson was looking for his parachute and, having found it, was too low by the time he jumped for it to have deployed properly. None of the others – F/Sgt J. Ansell RAAF (W/OP); Sgt J. Acthim RCAF (mid-upper gunner); and Sgt H.S. Cammish (flight engineer) – were injured, but Sgt Taylor's flying helmet had been 'ripped by cannon or machine-gun fire'.[74] Stan Cammish was on his sixteenth operation, P/O Taylor on his fifteenth, and the rest on their fourteenth.

After a series of adventures – Acthim and Balmanno lived in a cave for a month or so – four of the six survivors (excluding Acthim and Balmanno) found themselves in the hands of the French Resistance, staying in a farmhouse in Mazerulles (a dozen kilometres north east of Nancy) which belonged to Robert Durand, head of the local Resistance. Joining them was Captain McMahon USAAF. After several weeks, the five airmen were taken by train to Nancy, and hidden in rooms over a café. Two hours later they were joined by Acthim and Balmanno, and by F/S C.W. Jackson, 76 Squadron, who had been shot down in Halifax LW629 on an operation to Stuttgart on 1/2 March 1944. He was the sole survivor.

On 4 April, using false papers provided by a chief of police, the now large group of airmen was registered as a football team and put on the overnight train to Paris, where they were dispersed into several 'safe' houses. They were now on their way down the escape line run by the redoubtable 'Françoise' Dissard, leader of what was left of the so-called PAT line. The PAT escape line, that had run from the Swiss border to Marseille and on to Perpignan via Toulouse, then over the Pyrenees to Spain, had been almost destroyed by the Germans after many of its top agents, including the Belgian officer Pat O'Leary (after whom the line was named), were arrested in March 1943. Françoise Dissard, managing to keep one step ahead of the Germans, rebuilt the line as best she could in the south west of France, with a network of other agents scattered around the country.

Thus it was that on 17 April 1944 the six survivors from LL791 found themselves on the overnight train from Paris to Toulouse, and were taken to:

'the club room of a youth organisation. Here a large party of evaders was assembled. They were given bags of food and led by a number of young girls two at a time to the railway station. They had tickets for Lannemezan but left the train three stations before that [at Montréjeau]. There were now thirty-five in the party. They were taken to an unused hotel behind the station where they met their guides, and from here an American called Frisco took them eight at a time in a Ford lorry into the foothills… The guides and all the Frenchmen in the party were armed.'

After spending the night in two cabins they began the climb over the mountains on the morning of 19 April, and spent the night 'in a combination house and barn'. On the move from 9 am until sunset on 20 April, they stopped briefly on 'the outskirts of a village where six Germans were known to be posted'. Resuming the trek at around 8 pm, having skirted the village in single file they 'came to a second village where six armed Frenchmen met them to escort them through the village'. Here an American pilot (name unknown) fell into a gulley. There was concern that the noise made by the searchers and the lights of the torches which had to be used to find him might have alerted the Germans, but the large party pressed on to yet another cabin, which was reached at around 4 or 5 am next morning, 21 April.

Here they rested while the three guides and a Frenchman went back down to the village for food, one guard remaining with the party in the cabin. At 3 pm a woodcutter appeared, and said that he had seen the Frenchman talking to a German in the village. Two look-outs were quickly posted – Sgt Stan Cammish and an American officer, 2nd Lieutenant James L. Liles USAAF, who had also been shot down on 25 February, but in daylight. An hour or so later Liles gave the alarm that the Germans were coming. Twenty or twenty-five of the party ran up the hill to the left of the cabin, with the Germans in hot pursuit. Shortly afterwards they opened fire on the would-be escapers, but when shots were heard coming from two directions, one from higher up, it was concluded that a second German patrol had arrived. S/Sgt William B. Hendrickson USAAF was one who ran the other, safe, way. A while later, whilst hiding in a gulley near Bagnères-de-Luchon, he 'saw twenty-two Germans come down the mountain trail towards Luchon with twenty-two prisoners from his party'.[75]

Five of the prisoners were from Lancaster LL791, only Cammish getting clear. He joined up with two of the American airmen in the party and, despite a scare when six German soldiers were seen below in some trees, they made their way together into Spain. Cammish was flown back from Gibraltar to Whitchurch, near Bristol, on the night of 5/6 June 1944.

For those captured, however, a tough time lay ahead, not least at the hands of the Gestapo, who were anxious to get all the information they could on the people who had been helping them. After prisons at Toulouse and Fresnes (Paris) they were held for a month or so in the civilian prison at Frankfurt, as Canadian John Acthim recalled: 'Here we were interrogated by the Gestapo. I was interrogated twice, but I refused to answer any questions. I was hit over the head and face with a rubber truncheon, once being beaten to my knees.'

While P/O W.H. Taylor joined fellow officers at Stalag Luft III (Sagan), the others made their way to Luft 7 in *Trupp 11*, together with two others from the party captured in the Pyrenees, F/S W.M. Gorman RCAF and F/S Jackson.

*

**13 JULY 1944.** *Trupp 12* (forty-five men) arrived.

*

Following their country's occupation in May 1940, a number of determined Dutchmen joined the RAF in sufficient numbers for three dedicated squadrons to be formed – 320, 321, and 322.

By the summer of 1944 320 (Dutch) Squadron, formed on 1 June 1940 for maritime general reconnaissance, was flying the twin-engined Mitchell medium bomber. On 20 June its Mitchell FR151, NO-C, was shot down by flak near Amiens in northern France. Four of the five crew were killed in action: Officier-vlieger der 2e klasse Cornelis Joan den Tex Bondt; Officier-zeewaarnemer der 3e klasse Herman Lüschen; Korporaal-schutter Leendert den Hollander; and Korporaal-schutter Johannes Hendrik Velleman. So far as the German authorities were concerned, the name of the only survivor was Harrie Groendyk.

A virtual newcomer to the squadron, Harrie was on only his second operation. Having flown with a different crew on his first operation, he never knew the names of the rest of the crew of FR151, nor did he know the name of the target, only that it was a V1 site.[76]

Harrie Groendyk was the *nom-de-guerre* of Wilhelmus Michael Theunissen. When his country was invaded by the Germans on 10 May 1940 Michael, from Hunsel in the Dutch province of Limburg, was a nineteen-year-old doing his National Service in the army. Though the fight against the invader lasted only three days, Michael fought on two of them with his comrades near Gouda before being taken prisoner.

While the enemy was deciding what to do with their Dutch prisoners, they were sent home. In due course, the Germans rounded-up the prisoners and shipped them off to Germany for forced labour. Michael, though, had other plans, and made his way through occupied Belgium to occupied France. But, crossing the Demarcation Line into unoccupied France, he was arrested and imprisoned: 'I was then given three choices – to sign on for the French Foreign Legion – go to a concentration camp – or be handed back to the Germans. I signed on for the Foreign Legion.'

Having no intention of serving in the Foreign Legion, he jumped off the train that was taking him to their camp. Though he reckons that the train was doing some 30 mph at the time he was unhurt, and started walking to Perpignan. From there, taking three days to do so, he crossed the Pyrenees into Spain, but was caught by Spanish frontier guards who sent him back to France. He tried again, and this time reached Barcelona before being arrested:

'I was put into prison for seven days, with thirteen other prisoners of all nationalities who had also crossed over, in a primitive cell about 10 ft by 10 ft. Our daily food consisted of one cup of soup with one roll of bread. After a period of seven days, we were all roped-up together and put on a train, which took us to the infamous concentration camp – Campo Miranda.'

Situated at Miranda de Ebro, in the north of Spain, the *Depósito de Concentración* had been opened in 1937 to house Franco's enemies during the Civil War (18 July 1936-1 April 1939). Some of them were still there when Michael arrived. He was appalled by what he found: 'The camp conditions were terrible, and after seeing two Polish prisoners shot and left for dead by the wire for two days, as a warning not to approach the outer fencing, we started a hunger strike. After a week of this, they gave in to our demands, and started releasing 100 prisoners a week.' Michael was eventually released in the spring of 1943. He sailed from Gibraltar to Britain, docking 'at Greenock, in Scotland in the middle of May 1943. At last, after eleven months, I was finally free again.'

Generally, no-one was allowed into Britain during the war without undergoing a thorough investigation, and it took the authorities in London three weeks to be satisfied that Michael was a loyal Dutchman. Once cleared he was then able to join the Free Royal Netherlands Naval Air Service, training as an air gunner at No. 4 Air Gunners' School, RAF Morpeth, Northumberland, from 16 September to 9 October 1943. He then spent four or five days in November at 1482 (Gunnery) Flight at RAF West Raynham before, after a five-month delay, moving on to 13 OTU at RAF Bicester (6-29 April 1944). After further training in May he was at last ready to join a front-line squadron, and was posted to 320 (Dutch) Squadron with its North American B-25 Mitchell bombers.

Thus, on only his second operation, he was shot down over France. So far as he was aware he was the sole survivor: 'I was on my own after I parachuted out and, when I landed, hid in a barn, and from there was betrayed by the French, and once more captured by the Germans. Taken to a bunker in France for about three or four days, I saw the V1, which had been our target, being launched to England.'

With him in the bunker were two Canadians and an American, and all 'were transferred to a prison somewhere in Belgium'. It was there, for the purposes of his interrogation and to protect his family still in Holland, that Michael assumed the name Harrie Groendyk, of South African nationality. When the time came for the prisoners to be sent on to Germany they travelled 'by cattle wagon (sixty per box) in appalling conditions, no sanitation, no food, and no medical aid'. Finally, on 13 July 1944, 'Harrie Groendyk' and forty-four others reached Luft 7.

*

The navigator had just called ten minutes to the Belgian coast when Lancaster LM115, 57 Squadron, was hit by two Ju88 night-fighters on the night of 21/22 June 1944 (Wesseling). Flight engineer Sgt Ray Heasman, on his twenty-ninth operation, believed that both were shot down, one by the rear gunner and one by the mid-upper gunner. If so, then it was a remarkable, and quite rare, achievement, but too late to prevent fatal damage to the Lancaster, which was on its way back from the target. The skipper, Flight Lieutenant A.F. 'Bill' Bayley, ordered the crew to bale out. Ray Heasman was next to the pilot: 'When I gave him his parachute, he pushed it away. After I put mine on I did push the other one on to him. Obviously I don't know if he tried later, but I've always thought that his was a VC job.' Bill Bayley, together with the wireless operator and the rear gunner, did not survive.

Of the four survivors, F/O J.R. Maunsell (navigator) was the only one to evade capture, being hidden on a Belgian farm until it was overrun by the Allies in September 1944. He later flew a tour on Liberators 'doing some Radar work', and was awarded the DFC in September 1945.

Ray Heasman parachuted out of LM115 into a tree near a farm close to the Belgian town of Turnhout. A Belgian woman kindly put him on a tram to Antwerp but, as Ray says, 'a "Papers" check cut the journey short'. In due course he would join the other two survivors – F/S V.L. Marshall RCAF (mid-upper gunner) and F/S A.D. Naysmith (bomb aimer) – at Luft 7, Archie Naysmith arriving in *Trupp 11*, the other two in *Trupp 12*.

*

**16 JULY 1944.** *Trupp 13* (twelve men) arrived from Stalag VIIA (Moosburg).

*

Arriving from the Mediterranean conflict was F/Sgt Arthur Kemp RNZAF, a New Zealand pilot flying Beaufighters on 47 Squadron, Mediterranean Air Command. After Operation Husky, the Allied invasion of the island of Sicily which began on the night of 9/10 July 1943, 47 Squadron was called upon to continue strikes against enemy shipping in that area. Their target on the morning of 2 August 1943 was an enemy tanker. It was sunk, but not before one of 47's Beaufighters had been shot down into the sea. The crew, Canadian pilot Reneau and his radio/navigator Len [full name not known but possibly Dennis Leonard], took to their dinghy. Arthur Kemp and Sgt R. Fisher, who had taken off from Protville airfield in the north of Tunisia at 7 am in their Mk.10 Beaufighter, JM323, circled over the dinghy for an hour or more until a rescue seaplane arrived.

But intense enemy fire shot down the seaplane and caused such damage to JM323 that Arthur was also forced to ditch the Beaufighter:

'It was a hazy morning when Bob Fisher (radio nav.) and I landed in the drink in Cagliari Bay, Sardinia. Fortunately, we were not injured in any way, and after scrambling into the dinghy, which was on the wing waiting for us, spent a fairly pleasant day. "Spanky" Reneau, who had also come down, was a few miles out to sea from us and our boys were buzzing around him all day long, although they were interfered with from time to time by Itie [Italian] fighters. Although we pooped off a few colours [signal flares], we were not seen, and consequently no one knew what had happened to us, although they must have seen us come down.'

Later that evening, having drifted well into Cagliari Bay, Arthur and Bob 'were picked up by an Italian fishing boat, and taken into Cagliari'. Locals had a good ogle at the pair of prisoners before they were 'whipped smartly into a staff car and driven to a fighter drome for interrogation'. Next stop was a prison a few miles north of Cagliari, where they joined a Wellington crew. On the following day 'Spanky' and Len arrived. They were badly sunburnt, and Len had a nasty gash across his forehead.

It was not until early on the cold morning of 14 August that they were moved on, without breakfast, to an airfield west of Cagliari, where Tenente Obino and his Savoia-Marchetti S.M.81 No. 803 were waiting to take them to Rome. By 9 o'clock they were over Rome, and two hours later found themselves at Campo PG 54 (Fara Sabina), some forty kilometres north east of the Italian capital in the province of Rieti. The camp was well organised, and food was adequate thanks to the addition of Red Cross parcels to the Italian rations of '200 gms of bread a day with sugar, oil, cheese ration, two bully tins of rice or macaroni and one brew'.

But the news was full of the impending Italian armistice, and it came as no surprise to the prisoners when it was signed (on 8 September 1943). It was two or three days, though, before the prisoners were allowed to leave the camp, by which time German paratroops had occupied nearby Palombara airfield. Together with four South Africans and three American airmen (the latter from a B-17 Flying Fortress that had ditched in the sea) Arthur set off into the hills, after hiring a donkey for the price of a pair of English boots.

The going was tough over the hilly terrain, and much of the time was spent dodging German search parties. Food was hard to come by, too, and it was decided on 29 September to split into smaller parties. Arthur set off with George McDonald (South African) and Bill Hayes (American). Bill, one of the B-17 crew, had spent twenty-six hours afloat in the Mediterranean before being rescued.

They were at large until 19 October 'when who should bowl up but six Jerries who immediately took charge of us'. They were locked up in the jail in Palombara, which was 'a castle right in the centre of the town with huge iron gates and bags of sentries. It was really a barracks for 3,000-odd Jerries who were in training there. We were locked in a cell of our own with two English [RAF] lads and a sentry posted outside the door.'

Three days later, at around 9 pm on 22 October, the prisoners escaped through the window bars and, with the classic knotting of (eight) blankets to make a 20-foot rope, climbed down to the road below. It was the luck of the draw that Arthur was last down the rope, which was a few feet short of the ground. With no one to hold it for him he jumped and sprained an ankle. Two of his fellow escapers helped him out of the town and up once more into the hills. His ankle proved more than troublesome, to such an extent that he was virtually bed-ridden for the next fortnight.

On 5 November 1943 the first snow fell. A week later the decision was taken to move on but, with Arthur's ankle still weak, he was unable to travel very fast. Nevertheless, thanks to the generous hospitality of local Italians, progress towards the Allied lines was made as the weeks passed. On 27 February 1944 they occupied a hut near Augusta, east of Rome, 'where we met Dick, Jim, Horry and Titch. Just over two months were spent on this side of the valley with an occasional trip into Augusta.'

5 May 1944, 'Mother's Day', 'began with Jerry knocking on our front door with hand-grenades, and our subsequent capture. We were taken to Subiaco and the following day were taken to Fiuggi.' Four days later they found themselves back at Campo PG 54 (Fara Sabina), where the first thing that 'caught the eyes were the barracks which had been well and truly knocked around by RAF bombs. Of my old hut, No. 2, only one end remained, but [huts] 16 and 17 were not to be seen.'

With no escaping this time, Arthur and many others were taken to Campo PG 82 (Laterina), where they stayed until 21 June. Packed onto a train they arrived three days later at Stalag VIIA (Moosburg), a large camp, with over 25,000 French prisoners: 'Our brief stay at Stalag 7A was quite a pleasant one with Red Cross food parcels arriving regularly. We were equipped with new boots and a weird assortment of clothing.'

*

Also at Moosburg was W/O Wilbur 'Mac' McCoombs RCAF, who hailed from Nova Scotia. He was a merchant seaman on the great liner *Empress of Britain*, 42,348 tons, when she was bombed and set on fire by German aircraft off the Irish coast on 26 October 1940. Two days later, still afloat, U-boat U-32 (Kapitänleutnant Hans Jenisch) administered the *coup de grâce* to the great ship. Mac was off watch below decks when the torpedoes struck. Although the ship sank in three minutes he and others were able to take to a lifeboat, and were rescued some nine hours later. Back in Canada Mac joined the RCAF. He was married in March 1942, less than two weeks before he was due to leave for service overseas.

He was on 9 Squadron when RAF Bomber Command crews were detailed to bomb a transformer station at Reggio nell'Emilia in northern Italy. On the night of 15/16 July 1943, somewhere in the dark skies over the Italian town of Mirandola, Lancaster JA679 (9 Squadron) collided with Lancaster DV167 (50 Squadron), and both plunged to earth. All seven aboard DV167 were killed, but only Sergeant E.W. Edwards from JA679; Mac and the five others were taken prisoner.

Mac was at the Italian POW camp PG 78 (Sulmona) when the Italian armistice came on 8 September 1943, and was one of the many to become a prisoner of the Germans six days later. Though dozens of POWs had already cleared off into the Italian countryside, Mac and the rest were sent by rail to Germany. Along the way he jumped off the train with two other airmen, and avoided re-capture for some eight months, most of that time with Italian partisans, but in May 1944 was recaptured. This time he was sent to Stalag VIIA (Moosburg) which, he said, was 'pretty grim'.

On 11 July 1944, Arthur Kemp, Mac McCoombs and ten others were purged from Moosburg to Luft 7. They arrived on 16 July, one year to the day after Mac was first captured. As with so many others, first impressions of the camp, with its 196 small, wooden huts 'in a wide expanse of nothing', were not good but, like it or not, *Trupp 13*, POW numbers 333-344, had arrived.

*

**17 JULY 1944.** Musical instruments and books arrived.

**18 JULY 1944.** Rained all day. First rain since camp opened. Red Cross parcels issued. Those who had been passed for repatriation due to their wounds left the camp. They eventually left for Sweden on 7 September 1944.

**20 JULY 1944.** *Trupp 14* (thirty-four men) arrived. First issue of clothing.

*

Much has been written about the raid on the German army's *Panzer* camp at Mailly-le-Camp, France on the night of 3/4 May 1944. Suffice it to say that it was, in terms of RAF bombers lost, an unmitigated disaster, no fewer than forty-two Lancasters failing to return, together with a Mosquito and a Halifax of 100 Group, the electronics wizards.

Lancaster ME586 UL-B[2] ('Baker Twice'), 576 Squadron, was shot down near Oeuilly, in the Marne *département* of eastern France. Five of the crew were killed, with only Sgt Cyril Van de Velde (flight engineer) and F/S J.D. Ward (navigator) surviving. Ward was caught in Paris trying to pass counterfeit money, and ended up at Stalag Luft III, but Cyril found refuge with a local Maquis after he had come down near Epernay in the Champagne region.

He joined 'them on raids on the Boche supply dumps of food, using a very large charcoal-burning car, which was later changed to a petrol car after the Maquis shot the collaborator who owned it… we were constantly on the move to evade, at least, capture. I was finally caught (along with an American airman).' They had been sheltered by M. and Mme. Aubossu and their son in their farmhouse until 19 June, when they were captured. The Aubossus' son was put on trial after the war as he was the prime suspect in giving them away. According to Cyril, 'he protested his innocence, but I believe he did it, because the two Alsatian dogs they kept for alarm purposes were silent. No way could a stranger have approached that farmhouse without being detected.'

Cyril was fortunate not to have suffered the fate of many of the French Resistance, for when captured he was wearing some civilian clothes and had lost his identification 'dog tags'. Accusing him of being a saboteur the Gestapo locked him up for ten days or so in Châlons-sur-Marne [today Châlons-en-Champagne] prison, before he was sent to their large, central prison at Fresnes, Paris: 'I did have a hard time until I was taken to Dulag Luft.'

The Gestapo had also picked up Monsieur Bouché, the senior police officer of Vertus, a large village twenty-five kilometres south west of Châlons, who was working with the Maquis and was also brought to Châlons prison, as Cyril recalls: 'I saw him being tortured and blinded. He subsequently died soon afterwards.' There is now 'a monument in Vertus to M. Bouché and other Resistance members, along with a couple of French farmers who were hiding us. The Boches killed them too.'

Cyril reached Luft 7 in *Trupp 14*.

*

RAF Coastal Command's 'Anzac' Strike Wing moved down on 12 April 1944 from RAF Leuchars, Scotland, to RAF Langham on the north Norfolk coast to be nearer enemy shipping off the Dutch coast. On 6 July 1944 the wing 'made a daylight attack on a considerable convoy – eight merchant vessels escorted by eleven armed minesweepers and trawlers'. (*The Story of 455 (R.A.A.F.) Squadron*, p.111, J.H.W. Lawson, Wilke & Co Ltd, Melbourne, Australia, 1951.) The wing on this day comprised some thirty torpedo-carrying Beaufighters ('Torbeaus') of 489 (RNZAF) Squadron and ten more Beaufighters armed with cannons and machine guns of 455 (RAAF) Squadron, whose role it was to provide 'anti-flak protection for the torpedo-carrying Beaufighters'.

The attack off the Frisian Islands was successful in as much as two 'merchant vessels of 7,000 and 3,000 tons respectively were sunk, a 1,900-ton vessel was seriously damaged, and a 2,000-ton merchantman and three of the escorts were damaged', but two of 455's aircraft were lost. Both the crew of one were killed, while the other crashed into the sea taking its pilot, P/O John Costello

RAAF, down with it, after it had been hit in the starboard engine whilst flying at only 50 feet. The navigator, F/S Robert 'Bluey' Taylor RAAF managed to escape into his dinghy, and was found some six hours later 'when a German patrol saw me and picked me up'. The German patrol, in fact one of their navy's fast and heavily-armed E-boats, took him to a port on one of the islands. Via Oberursel he, too, arrived with *Trupp 14* on 20 July, a fortnight after coming down in the North Sea.

\*

**21 JULY 1944**. American Red Cross parcels arrived.

**26 JULY 1944.** *Trupp 15* (forty-seven men) arrived.

\*

German night-fighter crews called it *Leichentuch* – when enemy bombers were silhouetted against a layer of cloud lit up by the moon – and this is what Oberleutnant Heinz Rökker, 2./NJG2, and his night-fighter colleagues found over Normandy early on the morning of 7 June 1944 when sent up against a raid by Bomber Command over the Allied bridgehead. Rökker claimed five *Viermots* (four-engined aircraft) in the space of twenty-six minutes with his *Schräge Musik* cannons. He received no return fire, and landed back at Châteaudun airfield having been airborne for two-and-a-half hours.[77]

One of his probable victims, Lancaster LL783, 619 Squadron, was on its way home from the target (Caen) when the wireless operator, F/S J.H. Tucker, asked the rear gunner, F/O Guy Wyand, if he could see an enemy night-fighter behind. Wyand replied that all he could see were more Lancasters. John Tucker was convinced that there *was* a night-fighter close by – he could 'see' it on 'Fishpond' – and no sooner had he asked Wyand to keep a sharp lookout than shells slammed into the bomber. In no time both starboard engines were on fire. The pilot, F/L Kim Roberts DFC, RAAF, ordered the crew to bale out, but only two survived – F/S Reg De Viell (bomb aimer) and Sgt J.F.J. Forrest (flight engineer).

Already below 2,000 feet when they jumped, they landed in marshy ground near the Normandy town of Carentan. When daylight came they decided to make a move, and succeeded in avoiding capture by German troops until, on 10 June, hungry and thirsty, they were caught by a soldier relieving himself in a hedge. Their journey away from the battle zone was not as quick as they would have wished, with 'friendly' bombers and fighters prowling overhead, but eventually they began the long journey from Périers to Dulag Luft and, ultimately, to Luft 7 in *Trupp 15*.

\*

162 (BR) Squadron was the RCAF's most successful anti-submarine squadron of the Second World War, with five U-boats destroyed, one shared sinking and one damaged. During June and July 1944, flying Canso aircraft, the squadron, operating from RAF Wick, Scotland, sank four U-boats (and shared a fifth) that were attempting to break through the North Transit Area to attack Allied shipping bringing supplies to Normandy. (The US-built PBY Consolidated Catalina was called Canso by the RCAF in accordance with the British practice of naming seaplanes after coastal port towns, in this case Canso in Nova Scotia.)

One of the four successes fell to F/O Laurence Sherman RCAF and crew in Canso 9842. On 11 June 1944 they sighted *U-980* (Kapitänleutnant Hermann Dahms) and, despite heavy fire from the U-boat's gunners, Sherman pressed home the attack, sinking the U-boat with four depth charges. There were no survivors.

F/O Sherman was awarded an immediate DFC for the sinking (the *London Gazette*, 11 June), but he had little time in which to celebrate, for just before 6 pm on 12 June he took off from RAF Wick to patrol Area 'Scarlet' in the North Sea, way beyond the Shetland Isles. At 1.20 am on 13 June a report was received from Canso number 9842 that they had sighted another U-boat running on the surface, this time *U-480* (Kapitänleutnant Hans-Joachim Förster). Accurate fire from the U-boat's gunners forced Sherman to ditch 9842 in the sea off Norway. Sherman, who had been badly burned, and two others of the crew were killed in the crash. The other five managed to get into the aircraft's inflatable dinghy. With not enough food or drink they drifted aimlessly for day after day, and after a week or so one of the five died from exposure. Three others, unable to resist the temptation, drank the salty sea water and over the next few days, their minds unbalanced, threw themselves into the sea.

The last man alive, Sgt J.E. Roberts RCAF (flight engineer), was found alive on 22 June by the crew of a whaler some 135 miles off the Norwegian coast. After the whaler had reached the Norwegian port of Ålesund the fishermen tried to find a doctor who would treat Roberts, who was in need of urgent medical attention. When no doctor was prepared to take the risk there was no alternative but to hand him over to the Germans. (See *Proud to Serve: An Operational History of Number 162 [Bomber Reconnaissance] Squadron, Royal Canadian Air Force, 1942-1945*, Jeffrey David Noakes BA [University of Western Ontario, 1994]).

A little over a month after his rescue a very fortunate John Roberts arrived at Luft 7 with *Trupp 15*.

*

Flight engineer Jim Goode was never told why he had been awarded the DFM, but thought that it 'was probably due to an incident on our third trip when we were shot up by a fighter'. On this occasion, on 25/26 June 1942 (Bremen), he was flying in Halifax R9387, 76 Squadron, with S/L 'Jock' Calder (pilot) when they were shot up by a night-fighter. When one of the crew was wounded in the leg, Jim gave him first aid which, the medical officer said on their return, had saved the man's leg. It was more probably awarded, as Jim suggests, for completing 'a tour of ops, and refusing a commission'. The award was in fact made on 20 April 1943 'for gallantry and devotion to duty in the execution of air operations', and was almost certainly awarded for the fact that he had completed his first tour of thirty operations on 8/9 March 1943 (Nuremberg).

After a 'rest' at 1658 Halifax Conversion Unit, RAF Riccall, Yorkshire, he returned to operations on 35 (PFF) Squadron at Graveley in April 1944, flying the first trip of his second tour on 30 April. On the eighteenth operation of his second tour, however, his guardian angel deserted him. Having returned from leave the crew were informed that their usual rear gunner, F/L C.A. Fraser-Petherbridge,[78] had been replaced by P/O Francis O'Connell RAAF. For O'Connell this would be his first and, sadly as events were to prove, only operation. Despite the crew's protests at this change, they were stuck with it, and an hour or so before midnight on 4/5 July they set off in Lancaster ND731 to mark the railway yards at Villeneuve-St Georges, not far from Paris.

Having successfully carried out their duty and called-in main force to bomb the yards, S/L G.F. Lambert DFC (63419), an Australian,[79] set course for home. Much night-fighter activity was observed when, at around 1.40 am, the novice rear gunner called out 'Corkscrew Port!' then, immediately correcting himself, 'Sorry. Starboard.' Lambert began the tried-and-tested defensive sequence of manoeuvres, but it was already too late.

Lancaster ND731 was hammered by the guns of the night-fighter.[80] With the port wing, both port engines and the fuel tanks ablaze George Lambert wasted no time and gave the order to bale out. Exiting from the nose escape hatch F/O Patrick Moorhead (bomb aimer) was the first to go. He evaded capture and, after his return to England at the end of August, flew Mosquitos on operations on 109 Squadron. On 20/21 April 1945 he and his pilot, F/O A.E. 'Bunny' Austin, had the distinction of being the last aircraft to bomb Berlin.

Moorhead was quickly followed out of ND731 by Jim Goode, F/L Frank Salt (first navigator) and F/L D.R. Hall (second navigator). The fate of the other four is unclear, though there is a story that German troops on the ground, following the blazing Lancaster in their truck, machine-gunned to death four of the crew, including the pilot and rear gunner.[81]

Sadly, this was not a unique occurrence. Frenchman Sgt Jean Vaissade, who arrived at Luft 7 in *Trupp 34*, baled out of Halifax NA616, 347 Squadron, on 3 September 1944 near the Dutch target of Venlo together with four others of his crew, three of whom 'Lieutenant Allègre, Sergent-Chef Witzmann and Sergent-Chef Souillard were murdered on the ground by the Germans'.[82]

Frank Salt was one of many aircrew betrayed by a Belgian working for the Germans who had infiltrated an escape line. On 7 August Frank was told that he was being moved by car from one 'safe' house to another, but was taken to the Gestapo headquarters in Paris, and then confined in Fresnes prison. When the prison was evacuated on 15 August 1944 he was one of the 168 airmen sent to Buchenwald concentration camp (see page 119). After a grim two months there he was sent to Stalag Luft III (Sagan), where the other navigator, F/L Hall, was also being held.

Jim Goode landed safely in a cornfield, a dozen kilometres west of Rambouillet, and spent the rest of the night hiding in a thicket. In the morning, no sooner had he broken cover than he was greeted by a hail of machine-gun bullets, and doubled back into the corn. Moving off he was seen by more Germans, all of whom were very much on the alert, until, rounding a corner on a road, he was once again machine-gunned. Flattening himself in a ditch he was quickly picked up by two German soldiers and led off to their commanding officer. In the afternoon he was taken to Chartres and put in a room with a number of paratroopers and a fighter pilot, all prisoners of war. The room was on the third floor of what appeared to have been some sort of school, as it had a chapel and dormitories, with barbed-wire across all the windows and a guard posted at every door.

The paras had been poorly treated since their capture on or soon after the D-Day landings on 6 June, and some still had bullets and other pieces of metal about their persons. A Major Church, 'who is their medical man', told Jim that he planned to remove these bits whenever possible.

After a local air raid, the Germans moved their prisoners into the chapel. Two friendly guards said that the RAF contingent were to be moved to Dulag Luft early on 8 July to avoid any strafing by Allied aircraft. They left by bus at 3 am after a so-called breakfast, and four hours later were in Paris. That evening they were put on a train and given food which, they were told, was to last for the two to three days' journey to Dulag Luft. The train finally pulled out at around 4 am on 9 July, but the journey across France was slow as the train had to halt on a number of occasions while the track was repaired following damage by Allied aircraft.

The men slept wherever there was space, 'on the floor, under the seats, on the seats and on the luggage racks, anywhere one could lay down'. Progress quickened the further east they went, and Dijon was reached at around 5.30 pm on 10 July. At Metz early on the morning of 11 July the Red Cross provided soup for the prisoners, whose rations had more or less been finished by now. The men persuaded the guards to let them have a wash at a pump in the sidings, which raised morale somewhat. More soup was provided before the train got under way again that evening. A few hours later, past Saarbrücken, they enjoyed a fast run to Frankfurt-am-Main. Stopping shortly after 10 pm they were kept on the train until the morning (12 July), when they were taken the short distance to Dulag Luft.

Jim was sent to Wetzlar on 17 July, but while there suffered stomach ache, possibly brought on by the change of diet. He was well enough, however, to go with the rest of the NCOs to the station and board a train bound for Bankau on 22 July. They reached Leipzig around midday on 24 July, Dresden and Görlitz on the following day, and Bankau late that same evening. As usual, they were kept on the train overnight until guards from Luft 7 arrived.

On the day of his arrival Jim 'met up with Jerry from Ingram's crew' – F/S D.G. Gerrard, also of 35 Squadron, who coincidentally had also been shot down on his forty-eighth operation.[83]

Another airman in this batch, who nearly got away with it, was Sgt Tom Sparks, rear gunner of Flying Fortress SR382, 214 Squadron. Like Frank Salt, he was betrayed while in the hands of the Dutch Resistance. Put into a van to be taken to a 'safe house' Tom found, on reaching his destination, that he was in fact surrounded by a dozen or so German soldiers, each one pointing his rifle at him!

With him on the train was F/S J.H. Whatton, his wireless operator. Another of their gunners, Sgt Norman Abbott, should have been with them, but he baled out too late. His parachute was seen to deploy, but he was hit by the falling aircraft.

\*

Another victim of night-fighters on the Villeneuve raid was Canadian-built Lancaster KB727, 419 (Moose) Squadron RCAF. Mid-upper gunner Sgt James Pett RCAF: 'We had already been attacked seven times before on this night when we finally got hit near Chartres, France.' Their unknown assailant made a head-on attack, a rare thing for a twin-engined night-fighter to do. Though the result was the loss of another 419 Squadron Lancaster, all seven crew survived – six RCAF, one RAF (Sgt F.S. Vinecombe, flight engineer).

When the American pilot, F/O J.M. Stevenson RCAF, baled out they were already down to 800 feet. Jim Pett, last to jump and standing by the rear door, saw the skipper's parachute open. It was to be the best part of seven months before Jim met up with him and the rest of the crew, who all believed that Jim must have been killed when their bomber crashed, about fourteen kilometres north east of Chartres. He was able to put them right on that score!

Jim was, luckily as events would prove for the others, captured near Evreux by soldiers of the SS Regiment *Adolf Hitler*. While he made his way to Bankau, where he arrived on 26 July in *Trupp 15*, the rest were being looked after by the French Resistance until betrayed in Paris. On the morning of 15 August, with the Allies closing in on Paris, the Germans evacuated Fresnes prison, where the six crew from KB727 and 163 other captured aircrew were being held. Together with hundreds of other prisoners, they were forced by tough SS guards into cattle trucks in the Pantin freight yards in north-east Paris for transportation to Germany.

As a result of the Allied bombing of main railway lines in the north and east of France progress was slow, slow enough on 17 August for F/O Stevenson and a number of Frenchmen, having loosened the floorboards of their cattle truck, to drop out. It did not take the Germans long to re-capture all of the escapers except Stevenson and one of the Frenchmen. The journey continued, with the guards very much on the *qui vive*. On 18 August, when a snap inspection was made after the train had stopped, a French lad looked out of a window. One of the guards saw the movement and opened fire with his automatic weapon, and shattered one of the young Frenchman's hands. Also caught by the burst, but only suffering a grazed forehead, was KB727's rear gunner, Sgt W.R. Gibson RCAF. Another of KB727's crew, F/O J.E. Prudham RCAF (navigator), suffered a violent epileptic fit brought on by lack of sleep and a month of solitary confinement at Fresnes. The SS guards offered him no help.

After three days the train had reached Germany, but it was not until six days and five nights had passed that the train with the airmen on board stopped at Weimar. The trucks with the women in them were removed and the men's trucks, connected to a local train, were pulled up the hill through the lovely beech woods to Buchenwald on Ettersburg hill. Kicked, punched, pushed, beaten off the trucks, the men arrived at the gates of Buchenwald concentration camp. It was 20 August.

For the next eight weeks they endured the truly hellish world of a Nazi concentration camp, where death and violence were the norm rather than the exception. Worse still was the fact that the Luftwaffe had no idea that they were there.

Four days after their arrival, the USAAF bombed the factories close to the camp – it was mostly the camp's inmates who provided the slave labour for these factories – and for once the bombing was accurate. Only one of the airmen, Frank Salt, was injured when he was hit in the back by a splinter. He was removed to the so-called 'hospital' for treatment.

Fortunately for the airmen there was a strong Communist group in the camp, who agreed to smuggle a letter to the Luftwaffe telling them of the whereabouts of the airmen. A trusted prisoner who worked at Nohra airfield, some twenty kilometres away, delivered the letter to a Luftwaffe officer there. Wheels were set in motion, and on 19 October most of the airmen were marched out of Buchenwald and put on a train for Stalag Luft III (Sagan), which they reached on 21 October. Two of the 168 never made the journey, one (RAF) having died three weeks earlier and the second (USAAF) succumbing in 'hospital' to purulent pleurisy on 29 November. This was also the date on which the last ten of the sick airmen POWs arrived at Luft 3.

So, it was not until the evacuated POWs from both Luft 3 and Luft 7 were brought to Stalag IIIA (Luckenwalde) in February 1945 that Jim Pett was re-united with his amazed comrades.

*

Courage was displayed by many aircrew on many occasions, and frequently went unrecorded, usually because at the time it was nothing unusual. F/S Harry Pollard, pilot of 70 Squadron Wellington LN806, was one of those to remain at the controls of his stricken bomber to give his crew a chance. Pollard and crew were on their way back from bombing the Milan marshalling yards on 12/13 July 1944 when they were in collision with Wellington MF120, 142 Squadron. Bill Taylor (bomb aimer): 'The front of the aircraft was smashed in, stopping the engines and jamming the door. I handed the parachute to the pilot... and he told me to get out by the emergency hatch in the rear. He would hold the aircraft in a dive and not let it corkscrew.'

W/O Jack Broad (wireless operator), F/S Arthur Roberts (rear gunner), and Bill Taylor (bomb aimer) were the only survivors from either aircraft. All three were captured and sent to Luft 7 in *Trupp 15*. Shortly after his parachute had opened Bill saw LN806 hit the ground and blow up. Landing in a field, he decided to head for Lake Como and Switzerland, but after three days he was captured by two German soldiers.

*

The operation to Villeneuve St Georges rail yards near Paris on the night of 4/5 July 1944 would be yet another bad night for the Canadian squadrons of 6 Group – of the eleven aircraft shot down on this raid, nine were Canadian. It was one of those times when the German night-fighter controllers got it right. Though they had already assembled a number of night-fighters over the Abbeville area of northern France, and were thus too far away to prevent the bombing of the Villeneuve rail yards, the controllers were able to direct the night-fighters onto the bombers as they headed for England.

One of the nine Canadian losses was Halifax HX353, BM-X, 433 Squadron, with a crew of six RCAF and one RAF airmen: P/O G.A. Wolstencroft (actually an American) (pilot); Sgt S.J.

Chambers RAF (flight engineer); P/O H.P. Pergantes (navigator); Sgt P.A. Reeve (bomb aimer); F/S H.R. Brewer (wireless operator); Sgt A.R. Hutchinson (mid-upper gunner); and Sgt D.L. MacLean (rear gunner), who was only eighteen years old.

Born on 23 November 1925, Laird MacLean was so keen to join up that he forged his older brother's birth certificate to show that he had reached the minimum required age of eighteen. Armed with his forgery he called at the recruiting office at Sydney, Cape Breton, Canada, on 12 November 1942. Accepting the certificate as proof of his age, he was sworn in to the RCAF eleven days short of his seventeenth birthday!

Later, on operations in England, he was not so young that he couldn't enjoy a spot of leave. He was 'on the back of a truck with a bunch of other RCAF guys in Leeds in England, on leave one night, and passing a Canadian soldier walking down a street with a young girl. The RCAF guys were whistling and shouting to the girl and the soldier took offence and started shouting back. Someone on the truck asked where he was from and he said Cape Breton. Laird said, "I'm from Glace Bay". The soldier turned and kissed the girl then ran to the truck, jumped aboard, and they continued into town.'

The Wolstencroft crew were on their way home from the Villeneuve raid on 5 July when they were attacked by a night-fighter. The wireless operator was killed, but the rest baled out and were captured. Wolstencroft went to Stalag Luft I, while Chambers and Laird MacLean arrived at Luft 7 together three weeks later.

Laird MacLean's parachute snagged on a tree, temporarily knocking him unconscious. He woke up to find himself lying close to a large tree, and by a stream. Strangely, he was not wearing his parachute harness, and reckoned that a Frenchman must have removed it. Taking off his flying clothes he hid them under the bank of the stream: 'I then stuffed my boots under my pants and took my stripes and wings off my tunic. Then I pulled my sweater over my jacket and started off across fields.' With the aid of a small compass he walked across the fields all night, dodging flak gun emplacements and an airfield.

Heading for 'the glow where our ship had hit the ground about two miles ahead over a hill', he came across a signpost that told him that Caen was seventy-five kilometres away. His Halifax 'was a burnt out mass of wreckage and still smoking'. Continuing his travels through a thick forest, where his hands were badly cut by brambles, at about 10 o'clock in the morning he came to 'a village called St Pierre and which was lousy with Jerries'. He crawled across several fields to get around the place and also a large house, which a French girl whom he had met earlier had told him was a Jerry HQ.

A few miles later he was fired at by a German sentry: 'I slipped to the ground and waited till he came up and [poked] me. I then took a stick and hit him over the head. He dropped with a funny look on his face and kept hitting out.' Laird made sure that the German would trouble him no more. Somewhat sickened by what he had done, a day later he had an encounter with another German sentry who was blocking his path: 'So I crept up behind him and grabbed his head with my left hand and cut his throat. That made two in two days, but this time I didn't mind it at all. It was as if I were killing a pig, and I guess there wasn't much difference.'

A day later the Germans caught him, in a most undramatic way:

> 'Around three o'clock in the afternoon I was standing on top of a hill and I could see our own boys fighting the Jerries on the next hill, and all in between us there were dug-in troops and machine-gun posts. I sat down beside a stream to think it over, and I must have fallen asleep, because the next thing I know there was a Jerry standing over me with one of their famed Luger automatics.'

The German took him to his officer, who told him that he was 'a gangster and a spy'. Laird could hardly have looked the part, for he was only 5 feet 7 inches tall, and appeared to be so young that when he eventually got to Luft 7 German guards gave him the nickname 'Baby Bandit' – 'baby' on account of his age and size, and 'bandit' because other POWs used him to steal whatever he could from the guards. But back in France, after sleeping on a kitchen table in a farmhouse, where there were eighteen captured Canadian soldiers, he was 'moved the next day to a small camp with about 100 men in it'. That night he slept on hay in a stable, before being moved to Alençon and Chartres. Another night was spent there, on hay again, but this time on the floor of a church. His journey continued by train to Paris and on to Metz, encouraged from time to time by the French people making the 'V for Victory' sign. He and Sidney Chambers arrived at Luft 7 in *Trupp 15* on 27 July 1944.

Hutchinson, Reeve and Pergantes, meanwhile, were found by the local Resistance and were taken to a disused farm near the town of Trun, a dozen kilometres north east of Argentan. Joined by three more airmen evaders, they were captured by a German flak battery that was moving back, though it is believed that they were betrayed to the Germans by the mayor of a nearby village. The prisoners were being taken under guard to Rouen when, at the Forêt de la Londe on the very edge of Rouen, two American P-38 Lightnings, looking for an ammunition dump in the forest, spotted the small convoy in which they were travelling and dived in to the attack. An American major, severely wounded in the head, died a few days later, while Pergantes was seriously wounded in the chest and shoulder. Hutchinson and Reeve, who was slightly wounded in the foot, took advantage of the chaos and escaped. They were sheltered at a farm by Polish refugees, staying until 27 August, when liberated by Canadian soldiers.[84]

Pergantes, meanwhile, and another of the group, P/O L.W.C. Lewis, who had also received injuries, were taken to Rouen for treatment. Pergantes ended up at a hospital at Tournai, just into Belgium, and remained there until the German staff left on 2 September, leaving their enemy patients behind for the advancing Allies to deal with. Pergantes was found by the Americans on the following day. Lewis, on the other hand, remained in captivity, and went to Stalag Luft I (Barth) for the rest of the war.

*

During the evening of 30 December 1943 an RAF high-speed rescue launch discharged a tired bomber crew onto the quay at Great Yarmouth, Norfolk. It had taken four hours for the launch to travel the seventy-odd miles from the pick-up point in the icy, storm-tossed North Sea: 'It was described by the Air Ministry as being the roughest Air Sea rescue of the war at that time.' (Fred Carey, mid-upper gunner.)

F/O L. Greenburgh and crew's Lancaster, DS821, 514 Squadron, had been hit by flak during the raid on Berlin on the night of 29/30 December 1943, shell fragments rupturing the fuel tanks. They 'ran out of juice finishing up in the North Sea at 2.30 am in the morning'. (Fred Carey.)

While the crew waited in their small dinghy for the high-speed rescue launch to arrive another aircraft dropped a second dinghy and packages of warm clothing, one of which fell onto the bare foot of the Australian rear gunner Colin Drake as it was being heaved into the dinghy. After fifteen hours afloat, the crew were admitted to the Royal Naval hospital at Great Yarmouth at 9 pm that night. The navigator, Sgt P.G. Butler, had received a nasty bang on the head when the Lancaster hit the sea, but apart from that and Colin Drake's injured foot all were in remarkably good shape. While Colin Drake remained in the sick bay for a further week, the rest of the crew enjoyed a long leave, tradition being that you got one day off for every hour in the 'drink'. They rejoined their squadron during the last week of January 1944.

On 14 March 1944 Lou Greenburgh was awarded the DFC, part of the citation for which read: 'Whilst they were adrift, Flying Officer Greenburgh did everything possible to cheer his crew, all of whom suffered severely through being buffeted by the heavy seas. Since then, this officer has made two more attacks on the German capital, pressing home his attacks with his usual thoroughness.'

Further dramas awaited the Greenburgh crew when they flew on the last major bombing raid on Berlin, 24/25 March 1944, in Lancaster 'C-Charlie' LL727. They had just released the bombs over Berlin when they were attacked head-on by a night-fighter. Luckily the young flight engineer, Sgt Les Weddle, had spotted the dark shape below and shouted to the pilot to go "Starboard for Chrissake!" The second he did so, a cannon shell slammed into the starboard inner engine. Fred Carey, having instantly swung his turret forwards, saw the bang as the cannon shell struck home.

No sooner had the heavy bomber turned onto its back and gone into a flat spin, than Lou ordered the crew to bale out. The two nearest the front escape hatch – Les Weddle and bomb aimer Don Bament RAAF – wasted no time in leaving, and both parachuted to safety and into captivity. For the five remaining in the out-of-control bomber their horrible fate seemed certain, especially for the navigator – Sgt P.G. Butler – whose parachute had disappeared through the open front escape hatch along with all the tools of his trade.

Suddenly, a bump was felt under the Lancaster, and for some inexplicable reason the aircraft's attitude changed to almost-level flight, having fallen from over 20,000 feet to barely 8,000 feet. Greenburgh and Butler, believing that they were the only two left aboard, got a shock when three others of the crew appeared. It transpired that Colin Drake had got stuck in his rear turret, and that Fred Carey and young Gordon 'Strommy' Stromberg, the wireless operator, had gallantly stayed behind to assist him. So it was that a tired and shaken crew landed back at base, Waterbeach, some while later after coming back on three engines. Sgt Butler and Colin Drake were given a rest, the latter going home to Australia and Butler to an Air Ministry establishment to be trained as a meteorologist.

Still on 514 Squadron, Lou Greenburgh (on his twenty-sixth operation) and his largely new crew, with W/O L.J.W. Sutton as second pilot, set off to bomb Massy-Palaiseau, France on the night of 7/8 June 1944 in their faithful Lancaster LL727. According to Sutton they were attacked, over the target, by an FW190 at 7,000 feet and the starboard wing fuel tanks set on fire. Then Lou Greenburgh reported that they had just dropped their bombs at 10,000 feet when 'the mid-upper gunner saw a Ju88 approaching from the rear and shouted "Corkscrew port". I waited a second or two to let the last bomb go on to the target and as I made a violent corkscrew the starboard wing burst into flames.'

Four of the crew jumped, but Lou thought that he could get the Lancaster home as the fire didn't seem to be getting any worse. After a while the bomber was coned by searchlights and hit by light flak, but they had already been spotted by Hauptmann Herbert Lorenz, 1./NJG2, who applied the *coup de grâce* to LL727. Lou gave the order for the others to go before he, too, jumped at barely 1,200 feet. LL727 exploded over St Eusoye, twenty kilometres north east of Beauvais.

Although he was the last out, Lou landed before the others, but in the end all eight crew parachuted onto French soil. Four of them – Lou, W/O Sutton, F/S R. Fox (navigator), and F/S E.G. Rippingale (bomb aimer) – evaded capture, but Fred Carey, Sgt Frank Collingwood (flight engineer), Sgt R.J. 'Andy' Woosnam (rear gunner) and young Strommy – he was only nineteen – were captured. According to a French woman who had helped Lou, Strommy 'had been caught up in the telegraph wires, was injured and taken P/W'. The only one to lose his life, he died on 9 June in a hospital in Amiens, and after all he had been through.

Fred Carey was looked after by a gamekeeper and his wife in a large château, but a month or so later he 'was nabbed, taken to a concentration camp at Compiègne and eventually finished up at Bankau', in *Trupp 15* with Andy Woosnam. Frank Collingwood, who had arrived with *Trupp 9* on 9 July, retained his Compiègne POW number 80059.

**27 JULY 1944.** The POWs were told that, as the Camp Leader (Lloyd) and his adjutant (Hill) were paratroopers [sic] and would therefore have to be moved to another camp, the POWs would have to elect replacements.

**28 JULY 1944.** Red Cross parcels issued.

**29 JULY 1944.** A stage production of well-known characters was put on for the POWs' delectation by the Debating Society. Called 'The Balloon Goes Up' the idea was that one of the celebrities in a balloon had to be ejected, the loser decided by the audience's vote. Represented were Marie Stopes, Walt Disney, Molotov, Charles Lindbergh, Eamonn De Valera, George Bernard Shaw, the Duke of Windsor, Lady Astor, and Sir Alan Cobham. Lindbergh was 'ejected' with seventy-four votes. 'Paul [Hill] was to stand for Gen. De Gaulle, but of course Paul is no longer here!' (Tom Glenn.) 'Very good entertainment, enlightening in many ways.' (John Tomney.)

**30 JULY 1944.** Camp struck by thunderstorm and heavy rain.
   *Trupp 16* arrived (ninety-four airmen from the army-run camp Stalag 383 [Hohenfels]). With the opening of Luft 7 came the opportunity for the OKH to get rid of nearly 100 airmen from Stalag 383 (Hohenfels), long-term POWs originally from Stalag VIIA (Moosburg).
   The German guards at Hohenfels were glad to see the back of some of them, particularly W/O Tadeusz Baranowski PAF, Sgt Adrian Heath, Sgt Percy Sekine, and Sgt B.J.P. 'Jim' Palmer, all keen escapers. At Stalag 383 escapers were known as 'Gallopers', and the start of the escaping season, after the snows and frosts of winter had gone, was the 'Spring Handicap'. Once caught, as most were sooner or later, the failed escaper was placed in solitary confinement in the Stalag bunker to contemplate the errors of his ways. Apparently 'Baron' Baranowski (see also page 239) was a regular occupant of the said bunker: 'While doing one of these stretches, Baron managed to raise the floorboards of his bare, whitewashed cell and start a tunnel with his pocket knife!' (*Barbed Wire. Memories of Stalag 383*, page 108.) As for Adrian Heath, he was actually caught down a tunnel. When the camp 'ferrets' appeared he was, according to fellow POW and artist Terry Frost, 'sort of curled up, hanging up on something, and he just barked like a dog and frightened them to bloody death'. (*The Barbed-Wire University*, page 96.)
   Before the war Percival 'Percy' Yasushi Sekine (born in London in 1920 to a Japanese father and English mother) had gained a black belt at Judo. At 383 he 'organised a judo club, negotiating with the guards for canvas and sacking to make a mat and jackets. He was soon running regular training sessions and even an occasional tournament; but his wartime judo career was brought to an end when he was moved from the camp after an escape attempt. Indeed, he escaped three times in all (once "disguised" as a Japanese) only to be recaptured.' (From his obituary in *The Daily Telegraph*, 19 October 2010, published four days after his death at the age of ninety.)
   He escaped from Stalag VIIA by climbing over the wire at night, as did Jim Palmer: 'I waited for a dark night... Climbing the first fence was easy but on going down the other side of it I got my seat and sundry other things hung up on one of the many wires.' Jim was able to get away without the guard in his box immediately above being able to see him and on the fifth morning of his escape he 'could see the Alps, snow capped and beckoning'. At around 2 am on the following morning 'I was just beginning to pass through a small town called Walgau when a light was flashed in my eyes and I realised that I had walked right into an armed guard. I had travelled approx. 120 miles in six nights, which is almost exactly the same as Percy Sekine, who also climbed the wire shortly after I was returned to VIIA.' Percy's other two escapes were made from Stalag 383, one by tunnel and the other via the gate. As he put it: 'Over, under and through.'

Damaged and losing height, Whitley Z7565, 58 Squadron, was on its way back from Hamburg on the night of 30 November/1 December 1941 when the pilot told the crew to bale out, as they had no chance of reaching England. The navigator, Sgt John H.K. Deane, disagreed, but the pilot and second pilot baled out anyway over Germany, leaving John to take the controls. With him were the two gunners, Sgt N.S. Bidwell RNZAF (mid-upper) and F/O F. Ivins (rear).

John headed the Whitley out over the North Sea but, as they were still losing height, turned back over Holland. Only after he had managed to land the bomber in the dark did he discover that the rear gunner was still in his turret and badly injured. All three were taken prisoner. Only John Deane went to Luft 7, via Stalags VIIA and 383, with Ivins and Bidwell going to Luft 3.

The two pilots died, though it is not known how, after they had baled out near Bad Oldesloe, to the north east of Hamburg.

*

On 21 December 1941 Reg Hartgroves was authorised to undertake a daylight nuisance raid to Oldenburg, some thirty kilometres west of Bremen, in Germany. His Hampden, AE151, 106 Squadron, was hit by flak, forcing Reg to land it near the village of Oude Schoonebeek in east Holland, close to the border with Germany. P/O Anthony Carter (navigator) was killed by the flak, but Reg and the other two crew 'were immediately surrounded by about 100 Dutch people. We were taken into custody by a very pleasant Dutch policeman who spoke perfect English.' The policeman, van Damm, offered to let Reg 'tap him on the head' so that they could make a break for it, but Reg thought it was too risky, especially as Sgt Ron Yearsley's back 'was well peppered with shrapnel'. So, Reg, Ron (wireless-operator), and Sgt Doug Martin (rear gunner) were taken into custody.

While Doug Martin eventually went off elsewhere, Reg and Ron were to follow the path that led via Dulag Luft to Stalag VIIA, Stalag 383 (Hohenfels) and, finally, to Luft 7, in *Trupp 16* (30 July).

The train of cattle trucks carrying the airmen POWs from Hohenfels, which had left on 27 July 1944, was just pulling in to Regensburg when an American air-raid started. They stopped alongside another train pointing the other way, which Reg Hartgroves could see was 'crammed full of terribly maimed and bandaged German troops. In the deathly quiet, staring at the shocked victims of the Russian Steamroller, we threw caution to the winds.'

As the bond of fighting men, albeit enemies, was too great for the RAF POWs not to do what little they could to help the wounded, they 'had a quick whip round and passed a small quantity of cigarettes across through the open windows of the ambulance train'. The recipient of Reg's meagre donation, barely two feet away, had a tiny vase of wilted flowers above his bunk. He explained to Reg that it was '*Mein Geburtstag*' – his birthday! No sooner had the all-clear sounded than an officious Hauptmann, rushing the length of the train, collected all the donated cigarettes and handed them back to the RAF. For German soldiers to take cigarettes from the enemy was, of course, '*Verboten*'.

*

Another of the ninety or so men in *Trupp 16* was a twenty-year-old Frenchman, Henri Bruneau, a sergeant WOP/AG attached to 45 Squadron, 202 Group RAF. He, his pilot, and navigator had come from the Groupe Réservé de Bombardement No. 1 (GrB1), a unit of the Free French Air Force that had been formed in Chad a year earlier on the orders of Général de Larminat. It was not officially formed, however, until 24 September 1941 at Damas in Syria, when it was placed under RAF command for operations in support of the British Army in North Africa.

On 28 November 1941 Henri and crew, in Mk.IV Blenheim V6142, were on their way from LG

75 in Egypt to bomb Ain-el-Gazala airfield when they were hit by flak as they crossed the coast. The lone aircraft was then spotted by Leutnant Hans Remmer, 1./JG27, in his Bf109, who reported that it was 'wearing the "Cross of Lorraine" markings of the Free French Lorraine Squadron, and shot it down'.[85]

The Blenheim crashed in flames, with the navigator, Lieutenant Charles Pougin de la Maisonneuve, dying of burns two days later. The pilot, W/O Raymond Jabin, also seriously wounded, was taken to a hospital in Italy. When well enough he was transferred to a POW camp, but escaped and joined the Italian Resistance under the name 'Marcel'. Eventually captured, he was killed by the Germans on 4 December 1943.

Henri, with minor burns and bruises, was flown in a Ju52 on 29 November to a hospital in Greece, where he remained for a week or so before being taken to Dulag Luft (Oberursel) and on to Stalag VIIA (Moosburg), where he was given POW number 90095. He, too, managed to escape, through a sewer, but was recaptured (see Ernie Moore, page 134). Henri and others were then transferred, after a spell at Stalag 383 (Hohenfels), to Luft 7.

*

Following Henri Bruneau from the Desert war, and lost on the same day, was navigator Ray Heard. In May 1941, Ray had been posted from 201 Squadron, Coastal Command, to the maintenance unit at RAF Kemble where, in June 1941, he joined a crew ferrying a Bristol Bombay for 216 Squadron to Heliopolis, Egypt: 'We were told we would be returned to the UK but we soon discovered that aircrew were needed more in Middle East Command than at home, so we were "retained".'

For the next five months, on 216 Squadron, Ray and his crew were mostly engaged on supply dropping and transport duties across the Middle East until, on 16 November 1941, they were detailed 'to fly some paratroops to sabotage German and Italian aircraft at a German airfield at Tmimi, south of Tobruk, in Libya. This was to be a softening up operation for a general attack by the 8th Army which was to clear the Jerries out of the desert! We had had no practice for the drop, so it was very much a "guess and by God" operation.'

The 'paratroops' were from 'L' Detachment, Special Air Service (SAS), the 'L' being of no significance other than to confuse the enemy. The idea for the creation of this unit came to Captain David Stirling as he lay in hospital following a parachute accident. Once out of hospital he persuaded General Sir Claude Auchinleck, Commander-in-Chief Middle East Command, that small bodies of highly-trained specialists, infiltrated secretly behind enemy lines, could do far more damage to the enemy than a much larger body of men, and was given the go-ahead to raise a force of sixty-five men: 'The idea was that his force should be dropped by parachute behind the Axis lines two days ahead of the launching of Auchinleck's planned major offensive against Rommel, Crusader, which was to take place in November.'[86]

'L' Detachment had been training for three months prior to the big offensive to relieve Tobruk (Operation Crusader) on 18 November 1941. Their first large-scale raid, Operation Squatter, was set for the night of 16/17 November. The plan was for fifty-five men of 'L' Detachment to be flown in five Bombay aircraft[87] of 216 Squadron to points behind enemy lines, where they would parachute out, each of the five aircraft flying a 'stick' (as a troop of parachutists was called) of roughly equal size. Three of the Bombays were to head for airfields near Gazala, two to Tmimi.

Once they had landed the five 'L' Detachment 'sticks' were to make their way to the airfields on 17 November to observe their targets, and that night were to attack simultaneously, blowing up as many Luftwaffe aircraft as they could. Having laid their explosive charges, they were to proceed to the pre-arranged rendezvous, some forty miles away, south of Trig el Abd, where vehicles of the

Long Range Desert Group would be waiting on 19 November to take them to Siwa Oasis, from whence they would be flown back to base.

That was the plan, but no-one could have known that the worst storm for thirty years was about to break over the precise area of the planned operation. A hint of it had come with a forecast for the night of 16 November of strong winds of thirty knots or more. As this was too strong for safe parachuting, the decision to go or to abort was left to Captain Stirling, who was advised by Brigadier Sandy Galloway to call the whole thing off. Stirling talked with his lieutenants but, so great were the pressures on him to make a success of his fledgling SAS, that he decided to take the risk and go.

'The last day before setting off on our mission, we had a final check-up on equipment. We wore overalls. Each man carried a 50lb pack, containing a blanket, socks, a dozen Lewisite [sic] bombs, ammo for revolver and tommy gun, hand grenades, bully-beef, biscuits, raisins, nuts and chocolates. We had no rifles but relied on grenades and tommy guns.' (Lt Charles Bonington, *War is Half Luck*). The Lewesite bombs were the result of various experiments by the SAS using their own chemicals. It was Jock Lewes 'who invented the best – we called it Lewisite [sic] after him. It was plastic explosive – the Germans later used the explosive captured from us to try to blow up Hitler at his headquarters. Jock mixed thermite taken from an incendiary bomb. This was put in a linen bag the size of a glove, a length of fuse, and a time pencil.' (Bonington.)

On the afternoon of 16 November, 216 Squadron flew the SAS to the advanced landing ground at Daba, on the Mediterranean coast, in their five Bombays, all fitted with a long-range fuel tank in the fuselage. Three of the Bombays, L5825, L5838, and L5847, were flown respectively by F/L Whitaker, Sgt Ford, and F/S Charlie West. The pilots of the other two, serials unknown, were F/L T.H. Archbell (later DFC, and wing commander CO of 24 Squadron), and F/O Priest. Lt Bonington and his troop 'flew in an aircraft called Bermondsey [L5847]. The pilot and crew knew us well.'

At around dusk, after a cooked meal, each of the five 'sticks', led by Captain Stirling (nine men), Lieutenants R.B. 'Paddy' Mayne (eleven), J.S. 'Jock' Lewes (Welsh Guards) (eleven), Charles J.L. Bonington (twelve), and twenty-year-old Irishman Eoin C. McGonigal (R. Ulster Rifles and No. 11 Commando) (twelve), climbed aboard the aircraft. In Bonington's stick there was also a Major F.C. 'Tommy' Thompson, 'an Indian army officer who had been training with us. He was coming for the ride, to see us bail out over the target and then fly back' (Bonington). The sticks of Paddy Mayne and Charles Bonington were the two designated to attack Tmimi, the other three Ain el Gazala. At around 7.30 pm the slow Bombays headed west for their drop zones behind enemy lines, nearly 300 miles away.[88]

Ray Heard and his crew, in Bombay L5847, were due back at base at 0330 hours on the 17th. After an hour or so they saw flashes on the horizon, where German aircraft were bombing Tobruk, then 'out of the darkness there came a crackle of automatic fire... A stream of red and white tracer shot under the aircraft...' (Lt Bonington.) Surviving the night-fighter they were well into the flight and nearing their targets when, as Ray Heard said, 'we hit thunderstorms, high winds and the sort of sandstorm which was terrible even for the Middle East'. Bombay L5847, with the Bonington troop aboard, was quickly lost. At around 2 am the pilot, F/S Charlie West, passed back a message that they were almost out of fuel and would have to land: 'He said he thought we were back behind our own lines. The night was pitch black. He switched on his landing lights and came down in the desert – a marvellous three-point landing.' (Bonington.)

The decision was taken to make no move until daylight, not just because it was raining steadily. A message from the aircraft at 4.30 am on 17 November stated that a forced landing had been made, it was undamaged, and requested a bearing to fix its location. This was given, and at dawn a flight of Hurricanes searched the Sidi Barrani-Tobruk area, but failed to locate the missing aircraft.

At first light, through his binoculars, Lt Bonington spotted a main road some two miles away, observing that the trucks moving along it were not British: 'An armoured car had the familiar German cross painted on it. Still nearer was a row of tents. Somebody came out of them and walked towards us.'

Ray Heard: 'We were unnoticed until a little Italian cook, on his way to base to get the breakfast going, sauntered along to have a look at this strange aircraft. He was immediately pounced upon by the commandos [sic], who were out doing a recce.' The Italian told them that they had landed only a few kilometres from Tobruk.

Ray Heard:

> 'We all got into the aircraft, took off again, and then, looking out of my navigator's window, I saw two Messerschmitts taking off from the airfield [Tmimi]. The next minute they were pumping their cannon shells into us and, as we were flying very low to keep under the radar and the ack-ack, we crash landed, being wrecked in the process.'

Ray failed to mention that they had actually flown over the German airfield at around 500 feet. After HQ had received a further message from L5847 saying it was 'in the air', another followed saying: 'Stand by. Will call you later.'

Oberfeldwebel Schulz, the German pilot who claimed the Bombay as his victim, had taken off at 0712 hours on 17 November, shot it down and had landed again, all within the space of three minutes! (See *Fighters Over the Desert*, pages 60-1.) The Bombay was not done yet, however. Charlie West managed to point it in an easterly direction but, with the port engine on fire and fuel running out, it was only a matter of time before a forced landing was necessary. Then the fighter(s) attacked again:

> 'The familiar crackle of automatic fire came. But this time bits flew out of the sides of our plane. One or two slumped forward. Tommy was sitting opposite me and I saw him put his hand up to his head. Our air gunner was lying on the floor of the aircraft. Our pilot had brought the aircraft down to about 100 ft off the desert. There were large sand dunes all around. Then the crackle came again. It seemed to creep nearer and nearer. Nobody panicked except the Italian. He started to scream. Bits began to shoot out of the sides of the aircraft into the plane.
>
> 'I felt a thud on my back behind the right shoulder and arm, as if a man had struck me with a lump of wood. I felt numb at the back. A bullet must have struck the spare petrol tank, because there was a flash of flame inside the plane... There was an almighty crash...' (Bonington.)

L5847 crashed at Tawilat al Ghazalah, barely ten miles east of El Gazala and 500 yards from the coast. The front of the Bombay was badly damaged and Charlie West was knocked unconscious, fracturing his skull, ribs and shoulder, and rupturing his diaphragm. (*The Regiment...* p.67.) The second pilot, twenty-four-year-old 740668 Sgt D.S. Martin, was killed,[89] as were A.400122 Sgt J.H. Pott RAAF (wireless operator) and 649662 AC1 William Humphries (fitter/air gunner). Pott was known to the SAS boys as 'No jump Yabbie' – 'he always stood by the door of the aircraft on practice jumps to see us out – "to kick us out" if we baulked, he said.' (Bonington.)

Two others of the crew survived – LAC Russell W. 'Rusty' Gowing (rigger/flight engineer); and Ray Heard (navigator). One of the SAS men, Platoon Sergeant Ernie Bond, found himself lying in the sand several yards from the wreckage, as did Lt Bonington. Ray found that he 'was on top of the heap formed by their bodies [Martin and Pott] and suffered nothing worse than being pinned to the floor

*Top left*: Photograph of Stalag Luft VII taken on 5 September 1944 from 28,000 feet. Clearly visible are the small huts (top right) and the new compound under construction below. [*Air Photo Library, Dept. of Geography, University of Keele*]

*Top right*: German 'mugshot' of John Tomney.

*Above left*: Stalag Luft VII Camp Leaders, circa August 1944. Left to right: Ken Lane DFC (Deputy Camp Leader); Dick Greene RCAF (Man of Confidence); Peter Thomson RAAF (Camp Leader); Joe Walkty RCAF (Adjutant and Quartermaster). [*Pat Batt*]

*Above right*: First registered POW at Luft 7 – John Abbott and his 'dog tag' (inset).

*Top left:* Den Blackford and crew, left to right: Bill Brookes; Jack Shenton; John Pyle; Den Blackford; Jock Saunders; Percy 'Pud' Hudson; John Abbott. Pyle and Saunders were not on the last operation. [*Percy Hudson*]

*Top right:* 83 Squadron crew at Coningsby. Left to right: E.A. 'Dave' Davies (KIA); J.S.A. 'Stan' Aspinall RCAF; Ken Lane DFC; Stan Hall DFM (KIA); Don Cope; R.F. 'Dick' Raymond. Photo taken by seventh crew member J.A. 'Taffy' Jones (KIA). [*K. Lane*]

*Above left:* Edmund 'Eddie' Adair, showing signs of his facial injuries.

*Above right:* Acting Petty Officer Victor Smyth, Fleet Air Arm. [*V. Smyth*]

*Inset:* The crew of SR384, 214 Squadron. Seated, left to right: Bob Lloyd; Tom Glenn; Allan Hockley; Bill Hallett. Standing, left to right: Tim McCutchan; Paul 'Tom' Lyall; Ray Simpson; Bob Gundy; Nick Lovatt.

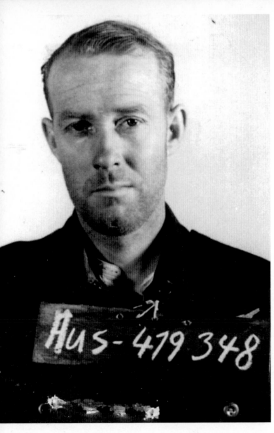

*Top left:* Some of 111 Squadron in early 1944: 'Jock' Comfort, front, with, behind (left to right), Don Hilbert, Harry Coates, Bob Brook, 'Spud' Murphy, Alf (a Scottish mechanic), and 'Hank' Hall. [*J. Comfort*]

*Top right:* Crew of LN318, left to right: Halligan, Yeo, Keen, Todd, Gallagher. [*Maisie Yeo*]

*Middle:* Bob Zercher, kneeling by the ball-turret of a B-17. [*Mrs Ruth Rumsey*] [http://www.monument.apeldoorn-onderwijs.nl/lv%20sgt%20zercher.htm]

*Above left:* F/S Stanley Alfred Silver RAAF. [*Kathleen Silver*]

*Above right:* Chief Petty Officer W.M. Theunissen, RNethNAF, London 1944. [*W.M. Theunissen*]

*Top left:* On leave at the Monte Carlo, Tel Aviv, 13 June 1943. Left to right: Ron Whitington RAAF; Arthur Kemp RN-ZAF; Bob Fisher (or Travell?) RAF; 'Hank' (USA). [*Arthur Kemp*]

*Top right:* Cyril Van de Velde and (left) M. Aubossu hiding out in the marshes near Mourmel-on-le-Grand, 7 May 1944. [*C. Van de Velde*]

*Middle left and above:* Cyril Van de Velde, 1943, and with M. And Mme. Aubossu at Mormont, France, August 1945. [*C. Van de Velde*]

*Inset:* D.L. MacLean RCAF. [*Carol MacLean*]

*Above left:* Judo class in front of the camp 'cooler', Stalag 383, August 1943. Those identified are: (front row) 2nd from right Percy Sekine, 1st from right Rothman (Army); (middle row) 2nd from right Graham Scott RNZAF, 1st from right Harold Bennett; (standing) 1st from right L. Williams (Welsh Guards). [*P.Y. Sekine*]

*Above right:* Russell 'Rusty' Gowing. [*R. Gowing*]

*Below:* Stanislaw Konarzewski (standing, 2nd from left) arrived in *Trupp 16* with another Polish airman, 'Baron' Baranowski. Three months after this photograph was taken Konarzewski was a POW. [*The Polish Institute and Sikorski Museum*]

*Right:* 'Baron' Baranowski leaning on a Mk.V Spitfire. [*The Polish Institute & Sikorski Museum*]

SGT. WZIATEK.  SGT. KONARZEWSKI.  SGT. PIEKARSKI.  SGT. GAJEK.  SGT. STIKS. (L.T. INSTS) SGT. PLASKURA.

SGT. BURCHARD.  SGT. GALAS.  SGT. PECZKOWSKI.  P/O. LUCKI.  SGT. MORYN.  SGT. BOSEK  6/8/41

*Top left:* Stalag VIIA (Moosburg), Barrack 35B, July 1942. Back row (left to right): Kerry Cobb; Tom Barnett; Stan Barraclough; Don Godard RCAF; Tom S. Jones; Sam Archer. Front row (left to right): Johnny Dutton; George Porrett; Bill Gilbey; Kim Cometti RNZAF. All arrived at Luft 7 in *Trupp 16* except Godard, who went to Stalag Luft IV (Gross Tychow). [*Harold Bennett*]

*Top right:* Stalag 383 (Hohenfels). Standing (left to right): Army; George Edwards; Doug Muirhead; Army; Sid Davidson; Army; Charles Kelly RCAF. Crouching (left to right): Wally French;

Georgie Duckham; Adrian 'Toggle' Heath; Army. Sitting (left to right): Army; Stan Barraclough. All airmen arrived at Luft 7 in *Trupp 16*. [*Harold Bennett*]

*Above:* Stalag VIIA (Moosburg), 1941/1942. Left to right: Ken Laing RCAF; unknown; Charles Kelly RCAF; unknown; Winfield Johnson RCAF. [*Harold Bennett*]

*Inset:* Dashwood and Rousseau at Varde Police station. [*Jørn Junker*]

*Top left:* Kuranstalt Hohe Mark, Oberursel, where many Allied airmen were treated for their injuries. This photo, from a postcard, was sent from Oberursel to Wetzlar on 15 August 1940, a journey that was to be undertaken by thousands of Allied POWs up to the end of the war.
*Top right:* Harry Winter.

*Middle left:* Sergeant Bill Niven.
*Middle:* Halifax NP706. Left to right: Al Zacharuk, Harry Oakeby, Leo Butkewitz, J.H. Cooper DFC. Zacharuk and Oakeby evaded capture.
*Above:* Bob Burns and his Orchestra
[*D.R. Burns*]

*Top left:* Allan Poullton. Identity card made for him by his Belgian helpers.

*Top right:* 158 Squadron crew, RAF Lissett, summer 1944. Back row, left to right: Sgt P.A. Tarlton; Sgt J.W. Perkins; Sgt S.W. Smith (KIA); F/O F.J. Dwyer (killed when parachute failed to open). Seated, left to right: Sgt W.L. Thompson; F/O B.R. Garnett (pilot, failed to bale out); F/O W.B. Nelson (POW, Stalag Luft I). Tarlton, Perkins and Thompson went to Luft 7. [*Louis Thompson*]

*Above left:* Left to right: Bruce Davis (note eyepatch); the daughter of Mr Anconee; Ted Moran. [*Mrs Dorothy Davis*]

*Above right:* Bruce Davis, photo taken in Australia in 1942. [*Mrs Dorothy Davis*] by the navigating table'. The only fatality amongst the 'L' detachment men was thirty-one-year-old Sergeant S.J. Stone, Scots Guards and 8 (Guards) Commando, who died of wounds on 5 December 1941. Several were seriously injured, the worst being Danny Hill, but they later recovered.

The awful weather that hit Operation Squatter also 'did' for the sticks of the other Bombays. Of the fifty-five SAS men on the operation, only twenty-one returned to Allied lines. Five were either killed in action or died of wounds, among them young Eoin McGonigal. Twenty-nine became POWs,[90] though one of them was lost on 9 December 1941 when the Italian ship *Sebastiano Venier* (formerly the *Jason*) was torpedoed off the Greek coast by HM Submarine *Porpoise* (Lt. Cdr. E.F. Pizey DSC, RN). Of the 2,000 or so 'British' POWs on board 309 were lost, together with eleven Italian soldiers. The loss of life would have been greater but for a German engineer officer. Taking command of the *Sebastiano Venier* after the Italian crew had abandoned her he put the ship aground a few yards from shore.

All the survivors from L5847 were captured by the Italian gunners who had shot them down. They were really only interested in looting. Lt Bonington protested to the Italian who was stripping 'Yabbie' Pott's body, but the man said he would shoot him. Fortunately, a German officer wearing the Iron Cross appeared in a Volkswagen car and told the Italians to clear off, which they did. Noting that Bonington and Tommy were officers he separated them from the men, and put them in his car, Bonington with cannon-shell splinters in his back and Tommy with 'bits of shrapnel in his head'.

The survivors of Bombay L5847 were collected by a Luftwaffe party from Gazala airfield, home to JG27 fighter squadron, commanded by Hauptmann Lippert. The two British officers were now separated. Tommy was being flown from Gazala to Derna, when his aircraft was attacked by British fighters en route: 'The German pilot had landed in a wadi and Tommy hit him over the head, took his Luger pistol, and ran away. But he ran north instead of south, and walked straight into a body of German troops.' (Bonington.)

Reunited at Derna Ray Heard, Bonington and Thompson 'faced some very abrasive questioning from a high-ranking German officer whose first impulse was to have us all shot as saboteurs. In khaki shorts and shirt, and with no insignia or flying badges, it took some fast talking on Bonington's part (he could speak some German) to establish our bona fides.'[91] Bonington said that this officer was none other than Generalfeldmarschall Albert Kesselring: 'Kesselring said, "Do you speak any German?" I replied, "No". He said, "Well, you are being taken to Germany, where you will have a long time to learn it." He left. I was glad I could not salute him, anyway, as my arm was in a sling.' This meeting must have been at the very end of November 1941, for Kesselring had only just been appointed Oberbefehlshaber Süd (C-in-C South) following his transfer from the Eastern Front. As he wrote in his *Memoirs*: 'I arrived in Rome [from Berlin] in advance of my staff on 28 November 1941.' (William Kimber, London, 1953).

The prisoners were then flown to Kephisia airport, Greece:

> 'The journey there was eventful, as we flew to Greece in a Junkers 52, among the passengers of which were some German aircrew who had been badly wounded in an encounter with a Beaufighter. One of them had his head swathed in bandages and called us "*Englische Schwein*" but was mollified somewhat when Bonington helped him get water to his lips.'

The German was a fighter pilot 'who had been shot down in flames, and had been badly burned about the face, and there was only a gash in the bandages for his mouth. He was offered an orange. I peeled it for him and popped pieces into his mouth.' (Bonington.) Enquiring as to the identity of his feeder, the German was told that he was an English prisoner of war. '*Schwein!*' was his response.

Rusty Gowing and Ray Heard were then separated from the others, and reached Dulag Luft towards the end of November 1941. Shortly after, in a group of some 140 POWs, they were purged by rail to Stalag VIIA (Moosburg) rather than to Stalag VIIIB (Lamsdorf) which, they were told, was currently closed to new admissions due to an outbreak of typhus.

In the summer of 1942 the airmen were purged to Stalag 383 (Hohenfels) and eventually, in July 1944, to Luft 7. Ray Heard:

> 'This was for us a most traumatic experience as we "old sweats" suddenly found ourselves amongst young aircrew who had been shot down only days, weeks or months previously. Most of them were flying the four-engine bombers and to talk to them about a Bristol Bombay dated one as a complete anachronism. We were to them like aircrew of a different war.'

But, from Stalag 383, Ray Heard brought with him a secret radio – the 'canary'. It was never found, but on one occasion, had the German guards bothered to look inside a dried milk tin on the table in the middle of the room, they would have discovered it. A snap search had been ordered, but the word was that the guards were looking for missing bed boards, which could be used for shoring up tunnels. Luckily the 'goons' had a one-track mind, and if they were ordered to look for missing bed boards then that was what they looked for. Appreciating this, the Man of Confidence on this particular occasion said to leave the radio inside the milk tin on the table in full view. They got away with it, too.

*

In the autumn of 1941 57 Squadron were the proud recipients of a new Wellington bomber, Z1097, named Gorakhpur after an Indian Rajah who had generously paid for it. It was in the hands of an experienced pilot, W/O Tom Purdy DFM, when it took off at 5.15 pm from Methwold on the night of 27/28 December 1941 bound for the marshalling yards of Düsseldorf. With Purdy were Sgt Max Cronin RNZAF (2nd pilot); F/O Ron Scarlett RAAF (observer/bomb aimer); Sgt Stan Barraclough (wireless operator); Sgt Bob Aldous (front gunner); and Sgt Jimmy Poulton (rear gunner).

Light flak over the Dutch coast was nothing to worry about, but as they approached Düsseldorf they could see trouble ahead. Stan Barraclough: 'There were umpteen searchlights, lots of light and heavy flak, and aircraft were already dropping their bombs.' Ron Scarlett had just dropped their bombs when the 'cockpit was suddenly filled with the overwhelming brilliance of searchlights. We were in the process of being "coned" and knew what the result would be if we didn't shake 'em off.' Unhesitatingly Tom Purdy pushed the Wimpy's nose down, and the crew 'hung on as the aircraft dived like a bat out of hell'. Tom levelled out at around 7,000 feet, after losing the searchlights, but that was when it happened.

Stan Barraclough: 'Streams of incendiary shells ripped through the bottom of the aircraft setting fire to a large section of the fuselage below the astrodome... Immediately the aircraft began to lose height. Tom knew that she was finished and gave the order to abandon aircraft.'[92] With great difficulty Stan managed to clip on his parachute, and followed Ron Scarlett out of the hatch: 'Hanging on the end of my parachute I saw the burning aircraft continue on its downward course until it exploded on contact with the ground. I did not see anyone else get out and there was no sign of Ron Scarlett's parachute in the sky below me.'

Landing on a snow-covered field in Holland Stan was unsure of his location, and set off to look for help. After a few miles he came to a large farmhouse, the occupants of which made him welcome. After a good meal, he was shown to a bed, and was soon asleep: 'Not for long though; I woke to find two uniformed men beside the bed. The younger man, who spoke English, explained somewhat ruefully that they were members of the Dutch police.' When Stan was asked to go with them, he had no choice but to comply. As he did so, he realised that his hosts had turned him in. The friendly police later told him that he had been unlucky, as the family were well-known collaborators.

Taken on the following morning to a nearby Luftwaffe base, he was then transferred to the military prison in Amsterdam. In adjoining cells were Sgt Donald Godard RCAF, the sole survivor of Whitley Z9306 (77 Squadron) also lost on the Düsseldorf raid, and P/O Charles P. 'Len' Hall, pilot of Spitfire AA804, 1 PRU, shot down by flak on 28 December whilst attempting to photograph the results of the Düsseldorf raid.[93]

On 30 December 1941 Stan Barraclough, together with four other sergeants and two pilot officers, entrained for Dulag Luft. After interrogation he was moved into the transit camp, where he 'joined Tom Barnett, Bill Gilbey and Tom Jones. The remaining bunk in our room was taken by Kerry Cobb when he arrived on 10 January [1942]. Kerry had been flying in Glenn Martin Marylands. He had been captured during the Greek campaign and brought to Dulag Luft from an army prison camp at Marburg in Yugoslavia.' Marburg-an-der-Drau (today Maribor), officially Stalag XVIIID, had been opened to house the 4,500 or so British and Commonwealth POWs captured during the defeats in Greece and Crete. Barnett, Gilbey and Jones were from the same 144 Squadron crew lost on 28/29 December 1941 (Hüls) in Hampden AD804.

From Dulag Luft, apart from Godard who ended up at Stalag Luft IV (Gross Tychow), Stan and his room mates were released to Stalag VIIA, Stalag 383 and Luft 7 (*Trupp 16*).

*

The crew of 'P-Peter', Wellington R3295, 101 Squadron, were on their way to bomb Hamburg railway station on the night of 30 November/1 December 1941 when one of the engines started to splutter, the suspicion being that it had iced up. The pilot, Sgt Paul Winfield, asked the crew whether they should drop the bombs and return, or press on regardless. The vote was five to one to press on, the only opposition coming from the observer, whose wife was pregnant. So they continued and, amidst the customary flak, bombed the target, brilliantly illuminated by the full moon, before setting course for home.

But, as they crossed the Dutch coast heading for England across the North Sea, the Wellington started to run out of engines. It 'was decided to turn back to Holland with the prospect of baling out and contacting the Underground, however slim this might be. "P-Peter" was, however, losing height rapidly and it was obvious the chances of reaching our goal were diminishing.' Terry Cooke (wireless operator) had managed to bash out the message 'Landing in sea near coast', 'but just as a ditching in the sea was being contemplated a strip of sand was observed and a belly landing was made without any due mishap. No injuries were incurred by any of the crew.' (Sgt Bill Cleeve, mid-upper gunner.)

As it was dark, the crew agreed to lay up for a few hours until daylight, then split up into pairs. Their arrival on the Dutch island of Schiermonnikoog had gone unnoticed, however, until the pilot of a German aircraft had spotted the virtually intact 'P-Peter' sticking out of the water on the beach! (An excellent photograph of Germans swarming all over the Wellington appears on page 106 of *The Wellington Bomber* by Chaz Bowyer.) It was not long after midday on 1 December that all six of the crew had been rounded up by German marines stationed on the island.

Adrian 'Toggle' Heath (rear gunner) and the American second pilot, Sgt Winfield L. 'Johnny' Johnson RCAF, came across a man gathering firewood. Through his artist's eyes Heath saw him as a 'Van Gogh peasant'.[94] Though the man could speak only Walloon, which neither airman could understand, by use of their map and sign language the two airmen understood well enough that the island was swarming with Germans. And it was not long before they met some. Johnson suggested that they should take no notice, and pretend that they hadn't seen them, but when shots were fired over their heads they put up their hands in the accepted manner.[95]

The night was spent as guests of the marines in the officers' mess. Heavily escorted to the mainland next day the crew were put into solitary confinement in Amsterdam prison.

Bill Cleeve:

> 'Eventually we were taken by road to Utrecht in a coach filled with guards equipped with rifles, bayonets, machine guns and bazookas. One or two voices wished us "Good luck" in English on the station and we were on our way to Frankfurt and Dulag Luft, little knowing we were to enjoy three-and-a-half years as the guests of the Reich.'

So, Winfield Johnson RCAF, Idwal Gwyn Davies (observer), Terry Cooke (wireless operator), Bill Cleeve and Adrian Heath, after the delights of Stalag VIIA and Stalag 383, reached Luft 7 in *Trupp 16* on 30 July. Oddly, nothing is known of 1191178 Sgt Paul Winfield's time as a POW.

*

Sergeants Vic Cooper (2nd pilot/navigator/bomb aimer), Tom Berry (wireless operator/upper gunner) and Jim Palmer (rear gunner) were the three survivors of Hampden AE123, 106 Squadron, lost on the night of 21/22 January 1942. The only one to be killed was their pilot, Sergeant Aubrey 'Johnnie' Deere. Strictly speaking, all four were on 83 Squadron at RAF Scampton but, having completed only one operation, they were ordered to report to 106 Squadron at RAF Coningsby on 18 January 1942. The reason for their move, which they were assured would only be temporary, was due to 83 Squadron re-equipping with the Avro Manchester, and only half of the squadron could be trained at any one time.

On the afternoon of 21 January the Deere crew were hurriedly called to the Coningsby crew room for a briefing on their target for the night – the submarine base at Bremen, Germany. Shortly after 5 pm Johnnie Deere took off from the snow-covered airfield, and course was set via Orfordness for Bremen.

Vic Cooper:

> 'Darkness fell rapidly as we left England behind us and we climbed to about 18,000 feet. There was a moon and the sky was clear. It was very cold.
>
> 'We crossed the Dutch coast and began to weave. We had not gone far before searchlights opened up and sent their beams sweeping across the sky – looking almost solid. When they picked us up we twisted and dived in attempts to escape into the darkness again... As we left the searchlights behind and approached Bremen, which was defended by heavy anti-aircraft fire, the port engine began to run very roughly and, soon, so unevenly that it set up a violent shaking of the whole aircraft. We flew on to the outskirts of Bremen but could do nothing to stop the shaking. We dropped the bombs, turned for home and, after two or three minutes more of its violent convulsions, which I thought would tear it from its bearers, the engine crunched to a violent stop. In a moment all the shuddering ceased. There was the port propeller stark and clear in the moonlight.
>
> 'We were flying smoothly now on one engine and had been losing height. We were down to about 10,000 feet. I worked out a new course and we turned a degree or two

to make our route to England as short as possible. We approached the searchlight belt again. Suddenly Jim shouted: "There's a 110 after us – he's just flown across to our starboard side – look out for him."'

Suddenly, several loud bangs came from the starboard engine, which stopped. Johnnie Deere, well knowing that a Hampden with no engines flew like a brick, shouted "Jump! Jump!"

The Hampden crashed on the side of a dyke near the Dutch town of Zwolle. A farmer who rushed out to the burning wreckage found close by the body of Sergeant Deere, unable to escape from the falling aircraft.

Vic Cooper and Jim Palmer landed close to each other:

'We buried our parachutes and hurried into a wood. Eventually we walked out of the wood heading west. Shortly before dawn we found a shed in the middle of some snow-covered fields. It was full of blocks of straw and various farm implements. Jim and I made a sort of box of straw and got in. It was freezing cold. From what we had read on a signpost during our walk to the shed we discovered on our escape map the rough position of where we were. We were in Holland, a few miles from Zwolle.'

On the night of 22 January, seeking help from several farmers, none would open the door for them. They continued to head westwards before deciding to go their own way, but it was not long before they were to meet again, at the Germans' headquarters at Zwolle. Re-united with Tom Berry, all three made the journey via Stalag VIIA and Stalag 383 to Luft 7 in *Trupp 16*.

In early 1940 Vic Cooper, a member of the Methodist Church, had become an ordinand, a candidate for ordination, 'the process by which individuals are consecrated, that is, set apart as clergy to perform various religious rites and ceremonies'. Though ordinands were exempt from military service, records show that of the three, including Vic, who volunteered for aircrew duties, two were killed in action. With a dispensation from the Methodist Church Conference, at Luft 7 Vic took 'communion services, preached regularly at the camp Sunday morning services', and also 'conducted several courses of Bible Studies'.

Finally ordained in 1947, he continued to serve as chaplain to various organisations for many years until, in 1991, he was: 'honoured by being invited to preach the sermon at the Annual Service of Commemoration and Dedication held in St Clement Danes, London.'

A week or so after his arrival at Luft 7 in November 1944, the Reverend John Collins wrote home to his wife on 20 November: 'I am sharing a room with a young pilot who is a W/O. He is training for the Ministry in the Methodist Church & was acting padré here before my arrival. His name is Vic Cooper.'[96]

*

Sergeant Harold Bennett had been a POW for over two-and-a-half years before he came to Bankau. Since August 1941 he had been flying Spitfire Mk.Vs on 603 (City of Edinburgh) Squadron, firstly from Hornchurch and then from Fairlop. He flew on convoy patrols, Channel sweeps, bomber escorts, and ground attacks; nothing glamorous but, nevertheless, always potentially dangerous, as he was to find out on 8 December 1941. That particular day, he noted, 'started bright, sunny and cold. I was just back from a couple of days leave. We went off on a sweep down to Le Havre with some Blenheim bombers. I was No. 2 to a tall South African P/O. We had been warned of the approach of FW190s. One minute I was weaving to protect his tail, the next I was spinning down out of control and all hell was let loose.' The tall South African pilot, F/O S.G.H. Fawkes RAF, was also shot down in the dogfight, and killed.

Landing in the cold waters of the English Channel, Harold was fished unconscious out of the sea by the German navy. Regaining his senses he found that, while one sailor was cutting off his clothes, another was massaging him to get his circulation going, and a third was spooning hot liquid into him. They told him that they were on their way to port. Harold was impressed by their kindness: 'Cannot speak well enough of them. Super chaps they were.'

Landing at Boulogne, Harold was joined in the ambulance to St Omer hospital by P/O J.A.R. Falconer, a third member of 603 Squadron to be shot down on 8 December. Leaving 'Hamish' Falconer behind (he later went to Stalag Luft III), Harold was well enough to be taken by car on the following day to Lille. From Dulag Luft, he began the journey to Moosburg on 13 December.

Arriving there shortly before midnight on 16 December, he described Moosburg as 'a French and Yugoslav work *Lager*. They had it well organised, with theatre, shop, male prostitutes and various other trades. While in this camp, 'Toggle' Heath [Sgt Adrian L.R. Heath] and myself decided to go home. We had the French tailors make us a natty suit apiece out of army blankets then, with a fortune in cigarettes, we bribed the French in the shop to leave a space in the centre of the barrels on the beer wagon.' History records that they did not get home and, indeed, both ended up at Stalag 383 on 15 September 1942, before being purged to Luft 7 on 27 July 1944.

*

The experienced crew of 106 Squadron's Hampden P1341, on their twenty-eighth operation, crashed in Denmark on the night of 14/15 January 1942 (Hamburg). They were: W/O W.S. 'Bill' Dashwood RNZAF (pilot); Sergeant R.C.O. Rousseau RCAF (observer); Sgt A.W. 'Dobs' Horseman (WOP/AG); and Sgt E.A. 'Ernie' Moore (rear gunner). Incidentally, according to Bill Dashwood, Dobs was nothing to do with horses but stood for 'Doddering Old Bastard', the said Horseman then being a very ancient thirty-three years old!

The squadron was experimenting with dropping target indicators (TIs) – the precursor of the so-called Pathfinders – and on the night of 14/15 January 1942 Dashwood's crew was one of the three that was to drop TIs approximately ten to twelve minutes prior to the arrival of the rest of the bombers. The 106 Squadron aircraft carried the TIs in four containers, each weighing 500lbs, in addition to a 250lb bomb under each wing. The plan was for the three bombers to drop their markers in a triangle round the target, with main force dropping their bombs in the middle. The plan did not, however, take into account the possibility that one or more of the three marker aircraft might not reach the target.

Shortly before reaching Wilhelmshaven, P1341's starboard engine was hit by flak and burst into flames. With the engine shut down the aircraft lost so much altitude that it was clear that they would not be able to get back to England across the North Sea. Having decided to head for Sweden, course was set northwards to Denmark, while the bombs, ammunition, machine guns, radio, and anything else removable were jettisoned from the Hampden to try to keep it flying.

Over Denmark the crew realised that they would not be airborne much longer, and baled out at around 900 feet near Nordenskov. Moore jumped first, then Horseman, Rousseau and Dashwood. Moore's landing site is uncertain, but Horseman came down on a frozen field belonging to Villads Pedersen in Heager. Rousseau landed on a field belonging to Rasmus Rahbæk of Oved, and saw Dashwood parachute onto the same field clearly illuminated by the burning Hampden, which was completely destroyed.[97]

Horseman hurt his shoulder and sprained his foot on landing, but at about 11 pm he knocked on the door of Kristen Kristiansen's farmhouse at Bolhede, not far from the landing site, and was invited in. But, as no-one in the family spoke English, Kristen's daughter, Tora, was sent to find the couple who taught at Hostrup School. When Tora learnt that they were at a party at a neighbour's house she cycled there, and told everyone about the English airman. Shortly afterwards, Horseman was arrested by the Danish police and handed over to the Germans.

Dashwood and Rousseau were also handed over to the Danish police, at Varde police station, on 17 January.

The fourth member of the crew, Ernie Moore, was determined to evade capture. Sleeping in bushes during the day and walking by night, he lived off snow and a 2-ounce emergency ration of Cadbury's chocolate. After six days, weak from exposure and near starvation, he collapsed just as he knocked on the door of Peter Petersen's farmhouse in Farup, near Ribe. Petersen opened the door to find Ernie lying on the ground and, helping him into the warm house, gave him food and coffee. It was estimated that Ernie had walked at least 150 kilometres. A message was sent to the parish executive officer, who in turn contacted the police in Ribe.

All four airmen were flown from Esbjerg airfield to Germany and from Dulag Luft to Stalag VIIA, where they joined about 150 British, Australian, and New Zealand soldiers captured in Greece and Crete, together with a few RAF.

In late July 1942 Ernie Moore, with others (see Henri Bruneau, page 126), tried to escape through the camp's narrow sewers, but were caught after a long crawl. Some of the French prisoners had reported the escape to the Germans but, so the story goes, these informers were eliminated shortly afterwards. Ernie was given a severe beating with rifle butts. He was further punished with twenty-eight-days' solitary confinement, from 30 July to 27 August, having nothing to eat but bread and water, though every third day he was given a little watered-down soup.[98]

After most of the RAF contingent at Moosburg were moved on 15 September 1942 to the much smaller Stalag 383 (Hohenfels), Roger Rousseau was retained for the time being as an interpreter on account of his language skills. He later went to Stalag Luft III, Luft VI and Luft IV.

*

**31 JULY 1944.** *Trupp 17* arrived – seven men from hospital.

The Hohe Mark that Don Gray mentioned (page 43) was, to give it its full military title, *Reserve Lazarett Kuranstalt Hohe Mark*. A large building in its own grounds, which prior to the war had been a private, psychiatric clinic, it was situated a kilometre or so west of Dulag Luft, Oberursel. Many seriously-injured airmen were sent there (one of the first, F/O Don Blew, had been shot down on 11/12 May 1940), and some would later be especially grateful to the chief physician, Oberarzt Dr Ernst Waldemar Ittershagen, an orthopædic specialist, for his pioneering technique of 'pinning' broken limbs. One of his patients at the end of October 1943 was wireless operator Sgt Harry Winter, 427 (Lion) Squadron RCAF, shot down on 22/23 October 1943 (Kassel) in Halifax LK633.

There had been a few moments of panic back at base – Leeming – when, after the engines of their regular Halifax had refused to start, the crew rushed over to the spare Halifax, LK633. In the short time available the ground crew had not managed to load the full amount of 'Window' and, once airborne, it was also discovered that the 'Monica' tail-warning device was out of order. Now that much more defenceless against enemy night-fighters they were caught by one over Holland on the way to Kassel at 9.20 pm. The two gunners, Sgt H. Russell RCAF and Sgt R.A. Wells RCAF, shot it down, but not before communications from the front had been lost. Harry Winter was told to go and find out what had happened: 'There was no response from the MUG so I proceeded to the rear turret… [it] was in shambles and jammed.' Both gunners had been killed.

While Harry was on his way back to his post LK633 was attacked again. By the time he had returned to the cockpit, both port engines were on fire, and the wing too. The American pilot, P/O J.R. Harrison RCAF, screamed for the crew to bale out but he, too, was fated to die along with his gunners. Harry Winter and the three others of his crew were captured.

Sent to the Hohe Mark for treatment to his broken femur Harry was cared for by the kindly staff of German medical orderlies – Unteroffizier Vogel, Obergefreiter Karl (an Austrian, surname not known) and Obergefreiter Adolf Dufau – and by several members of the RAF and USAAF, whom Harry Winter recalls as 'W/O Stanley[102] from Liverpool, a [rear] gunner on Manchesters, a civil USA ferry pilot Capt. ? supposed to have been picked up from the sea whilst ferrying Catalinas, and two Welsh paratroop medical orderlies, ex 1st Airborne, captured in North Africa, Rhys Jenkins from Cwmavon, Port Talbot and the other, name forgotten, from Swansea.'

When Harry arrived at the Hohe Mark he was one of seven upon whom Dr Ittershagen could practise his technique of inserting stainless-steel pins into the broken limbs and extracting them when the limbs had knitted together. The others were: Sgt Donald S. Ford USAAF (left-waist gunner) shot down in B-17F 42-30785, 351BG/508BS, on 4 October 1943 (Frankfurt); S/Sgt Mike Szewyck USAAF (ball-turret gunner), B-17F 42-30817, 95BG/334BS, 10 October 1943 (Münster); Sgt R.R.A. 'Jock' Little RAF (mid-upper gunner), 77 Squadron, Halifax JD301, 23/24 September 1943 (Mannheim); Sgt R.L. Shelshar RAF (flight engineer), 78 Squadron, Halifax LW266, 23/24 September 1943 (Mannheim); Sgt T.L. Bowlby RCAF (rear gunner), 620 Squadron, Stirling BF576, 27/28 August 1943 (Nuremberg); and Sgt W.A. Grant RCAF (bomb aimer), 432 Squadron, Wellington HE817, 27/28 September 1943 (Hannover).

They were known as the 'Pin Boys', and would remain together for the next seven months or so until the restless Mike Szewyck 'decided that it was time that he moved on toward France'. An escape was planned. Having made a rope out of window-blind cords, 'on 4 June, Bill Grant, Ted Bowlby and I lowered him from the second floor in the afternoon and made up his bed to look occupied, as he had a habit of laying down after our afternoon exercise in the grounds… We heard later that Mike was free for a few days, which caused a lot of inconvenience.' (Harry Winter.) Mike probably got home before the others anyway, as he was repatriated in an exchange of prisoners from Stalag Luft IV (Gross Tychow) aboard MS *Gripsholm* in January 1945.

Once Mike's absence had been discovered his three accomplices were marched off to the cooler at Dulag Luft. On 9 June they were sent to a hospital at Bad Homburg to have their pins removed, and sent to Obermassfeld Lazarett to convalesce, and finally, to Luft 7. Shelshar and Little arrived in *Trupp 14*, Ted Bowlby and Harry Winter in *Trupp 17*, and Bill Grant in *Trupp 32 or 33*.

*

Another airman whose injuries had been patched up at Reserve Lazarett IXC (Obermassfeld) was 1525609 F/S Denis Robert 'Bob' Burns. He was the navigator of Lancaster ND853, ZN-J, 106 Squadron, which exploded after it had been attacked immediately after dropping its bombs on 26/27 April 1944 (Schweinfurt – this raid was devastating for 106 Squadron, which lost five of its aircraft with twenty-two killed, four evaded capture, and ten taken prisoner).

Bob Burns and Sgt J. Pickstone (bomb aimer) were the only two of the seven aboard ND853 to survive. Jack Pickstone went to Stalag Luft VI, while the injured Bob Burns went to Obermassfeld hospital for the best part of ten weeks for treatment to a severe wound to his upper thigh. His wound was stitched up within a day or two of baling out, and he was then sent from Schweinfurt to Dulag Luft. It was a long walk to Schweinfurt railway 'station' – 'nothing to tell it was that except barriers with guards checking tickets' – and this began to loosen his stitches. While he was waiting at the station he noticed a burial taking place close by. One of Bob's guards explained that it was for a night-fighter pilot who had been killed in the Schweinfurt raid. This was of great interest to Bob 'because my rear gunner had shot down a night-fighter which unfortunately got us too!' The night-fighter pilot who shot down Bob's Lancaster was Hauptmann Walter Bornschein, of the *Führer Kurierstaffel*, who was himself killed on the night of the Schweinfurt raid, probably 'by return fire of 106 Sqn Lancaster ND853'.[99]

By the time Bob had reached Dulag Luft after a further walk to get there 'needless to say all the stitches tore away and my leg was a right mess'. For several days, in isolation, he received no medical attention, though clearly in need of it. After a week or so, taken to the Hohe Mark hospital, he 'insisted on attention to my leg wound. By now it was all colours of the rainbow.' Within a day or two he was removed to Obermassfeld Lazarett, where he stayed for the next ten weeks before being purged to Luft 7.

On their way from Dulag Luft, however, Bob and his companions came close to being lynched by a mob at Erfurt railway station. The town had only very recently been bombed by the Americans,[100] and 'a mob incited by plain-clothes Gestapo' nearly threw them off the platform, which happened to be on a bridge some 80 feet from the ground! Bob reckoned that he was nearer death then than he had been when his Lancaster disintegrated.

What are the odds of two aircrew with the same rank, initials and surname – F/S D.R. Burns – being at the same POW camp at the same time, and being the only two in captivity in the whole of Bomber Command with said rank and name? The Bob Burns above was 1525609 Denis Robert Burns, while the other was 545186 F/S Douglas Robert 'Bob' Burns, who arrived with *Trupp 38*.

545186 Bob Burns was a musician. When he left the RAF at the end of 1946 he 'only really knew two things – how to fly and how to play in bands'. With his knowledge of bands he set about creating one at Luft 7: 'Somewhere, I know not from where or from whom, two decrepit violins and a piano were produced... The violins were the worst I've ever used. They were like sawing through wood, and the piano falling apart after use.' As there was no printed music but plenty of blank manuscript music paper, Bob undertook the task of writing the music for his band, the Bob Burns Orchestra.

Shortly after moving from the 'chicken huts' to the new camp the prisoners 'were provided with a large and excellent assortment of band instruments, enough to get up a twelve-piece dance band with five or six piano accordians and miscellaneous baritone, soprano and bass saxophones as "spares". Again, however, there was no music and, therefore, the band's entire repertoire was written and arranged by me.' Assisting Bob with writing the music was 'Tom Bell, a Canadian guitarist, who had played with several large American bands including Xavier Cugat.'[101]

Given that it took Bob and Tom Bell a long time to write enough music for the band, pressure was put on the musicians to provide entertainment of some sort, and so 'the accordianists had got up a show themselves. This was mainly several variety acts with the accordianists as background. Apart from the leader of the band, who was an excellent musician, the other players were, in the main, buskers who did not require music.' In *Massacre over the Marne* (page 216) there is a quote from kriegie Don Gray that another show by Bob Burns and his orchestra 'failed to reach the standard of the previous shows'. Bob Burns has put the record straight by saying that, as the show had had to be hurriedly staged, Don Gray's comments about this show were most unfair.

## CHAPTER SIX

# AUGUST 1944, *TRUPPEN 18-28*

**1 AUGUST 1944.** Red Cross parcels issued. *Trupp 18* (twenty-three men) arrived. Sixteen of the men – two corporals and fourteen leading aircraftmen – had been captured at Tobruk on 21 June 1942. They were mostly ground gunners, radar operators, and MT drivers of the RAF Regiment (created on 1 February 1942). One of the fourteen LACs was George Badham.

*

George Badham enrolled in the RAFVR on 28 March 1940 at RAF Cardington, Bedfordshire. As was the way, he was immediately sent home to await the call, which finally came on 28 June 1940. Anxious to do his bit for king and country he wanted to be a wireless operator/air gunner but, as there was a problem with his left eye, he could only be a wireless operator, and so was sent to No. 1 Wireless School at Yatesbury, Wiltshire, to learn the trade. Having completed the course on Boxing Day 1940, he was sent to the Scottish port of Gourock, on the Clyde, where he boarded the New Zealand Shipping Company's MV *Rangitata* for service overseas.

The ship sailed on 5 February 1941. A month later, having endured conditions which George described as 'frightful', the *Rangitata* reached Freetown, Sierra Leone, and eventually Durban, South Africa. After a few days ashore George and his colleagues boarded an old coal-burning Belgian ship, the *Elizabethville*,[103] getting to Suez in Egypt in April.

Here the left and right hands lost contact with each other. George spent a week at a transit camp on the Great Bitter Lake before he was sent to form a so-called Wireless Intelligence Screen (later, George thought, re-named Wireless Observation Unit). But in the middle of the night he and another wireless operator, Bernard Schofield, found themselves 'on the wrong end of a train, and so we parted company with the unit – never to rejoin it!' The two strays ended up at Heliopolis, a peacetime RAF station, and were to remain there for nine weeks: 'Apart from a money shortage' wrote George, 'life was quite comfortable in a hut with a crowd of aircrew, mostly ex-Malta being rested after the turmoil there.'

George and Bernard were posted to another unit 'somewhere in the Sinai desert'. Reporting to Alexandria for instructions the RTO informed them that their unit had moved elsewhere a couple of months earlier, and so they were sent to a radio reserve post at Aboukir on the Mediterranean coast. Finally, on 10 August 1941, after a month spent on the beach, they sailed for Tobruk aboard the Royal Navy destroyer HMS *Decoy*, the only way in to the besieged garrison at that time being by sea. Accompanying the *Decoy* was another destroyer, HMS *Havock*.[104]

Off Mersa Matruh a squadron of Ju87 Stuka dive-bombers greeted the two warships, their bombs straddling the *Havock* but not damaging her. At midnight the two ships sailed into Tobruk harbour in the middle of some intensive shelling but, once again, all was well. At last, George and Bernard found their unit, 235 AMES (Air Ministry Experimental Station). Effectively a radar station, their role was to plot enemy aircraft and to report any 'sightings' to the Tobruk gun operations room by landline.

Strangely enough, George enjoyed his time in Tobruk because, as he put it, there was 'never any boredom because of the almost continuous shelling and bombing... Swimming was good until Christmas [1941] and again from mid-February [1942].'

The end for Tobruk came on 21 June 1942, when 235 AMES noted intense Ju87 activity on their radar screens on the south-east perimeter of the Tobruk defences: 'By midday German tanks were visible at the top of the escarpment and by about 6 pm it was virtually all over.' George and company destroyed their equipment, but unfortunately for Bernard Schofield he 'got the sole of his foot torn off by a shell from a tank'. George wasn't to see him again until after the war.

On the evening of 21 June, with the enemy ever closer, George and about eighty other personnel made their way to the beach in the hope of being picked up by the navy. Instead, in the morning they were rounded up by the enemy. George was put on an Italian truck with about forty others, mostly army, and taken to a POW cage in a wadi at Benghazi. After enduring a fortnight of a very uncomfortable existence in the cage George and the others were put aboard the Italian ship MV *Rosolino Pilo* (7,530 tons) and battened down in the holds.[105] (Tobruk remained in Axis hands until 11 November 1942, when the Allies re-captured it after the Second Battle of El Alamein, and were never to lose it again).

After three days at sea the *Rosolino Pilo* arrived at Brindisi, Italy. Thereafter, George and his fellow POWs were moved from one camp to another, including Benevento which was, he says, 'a temporary cage in a ploughed field'. Conditions were appalling, and were not helped when, in a terrific thunderstorm one night, most of the tents were blown down and rainwater filled the furrows.

At the beginning of November 1942 the POWs were moved to a permanent camp, PG 78 (Sulmona), in the Abruzzi mountains, roughly halfway between Rome and Pescara. It was not a bad camp by Italian standards, and for a while the prisoners enjoyed white sheets on their bunk beds. They were eventually removed as a reprisal for Italian POWs in England not having them! Then, after an armistice had been agreed on 3 September 1943, the Italian surrender was announced five days later, and the Germans took over. Though the Allied prisoners at Sulmona were ordered to stay put once the Italian guards had departed, many ignored the ridiculous order and cleared off into the hills.

There was not enough time, though, to get far enough away before the Germans arrived and came after them. George and many others were caught in the mountains and, after a week or two, were packed off by train to Germany. In their ranks were two famous England cricketers, Freddie Brown and Bill Bowes, who had also been captured at Tobruk. It took seven nights and six days for the train to grind its way to Germany, depositing George and his colleagues at Stalag VIIA (Moosburg), Bavaria, where they spent a month living in vast tents – 'horse lines' – with as many as 200 men jammed in each. With winter approaching George was happy enough to be moved on, to Stalag XIA (Altengrabow) near Magdeburg – 'again housed in stables and an awful lack of washing facilities and food'. Then came the cold weather: 'The barbed wire surrounding the camp became an almost solid sheet of ice, and in other circumstances could have been a fascinating sight – we did not appreciate it!'

On Christmas Eve 1943 George was in a group of around 200 men who were sent by train overnight to Salzgitter, only to find that they were at a work camp. Surprisingly, the RAF men in the group had only vaguely heard that RAF POW camps existed and, more in hope than expectation, put in a request to be transferred to one. George: 'To my surprise, on 26 July [1944] I was told to get ready to leave for a Stalag Luft, not having the slightest idea where.' The journey took them, in the comparative luxury of a passenger train, to Berlin then, after changing stations, to Frankfurt-on-Oder. George was asleep on a baggage trolley in the middle of the night when he was woken up by footsteps coming down the platform. There before him was the party from Sulmona, among them W/O Ronald Mead, which had gone to Stalag XIB (Fallingbostel). They all reached Luft 7 on 1 August in *Trupp 18*.

\*

In January 1944 12 (SAAF) Squadron changed aircraft from the Douglas Boston to the twin-engined B-26 Martin Marauder II medium bomber. Since June 1944 it had been based at Pescara, on the Adriatic coast of Italy, and mostly flew against transportation targets to the north of that country.

On 13 July 1944 the target was Montevarchi. One aircraft, FB437, blew up on the bombing run, and another Marauder, aircraft 'B', was also missing. From a third aircraft, FB518, WO2 D.P. De Kock SAAF (rear gunner) baled out. Taken prisoner, he arrived at Luft 7 in *Trupp 21*.

On 14 July 1944 the target was the marshalling yards at Prato, a few kilometres to the north west of Florence. On this operation the squadron's aircraft 'Z', FB425, was crewed by Lt C.E. Parsons (1st pilot), Lt D.W. Barnard (2nd pilot), Lt A.F. La Grange (navigator), WO1 J.L.W. Rodgers (top turret gunner), Warrant Officer Martin Zerff (wireless operator/air gunner), and W/O James Lees (rear gunner), all SAAF.

Over the target 'Z' was hit by intense, accurate flak. Miraculously no-one was killed, but Barnard was 'wounded ("shrapnel up the arse" was how he put it – it was a flesh wound high up on the rear of one thigh)'.[106] The rear gunner was also hit – blood in his turret – as was the navigator, who La Grange was hit in the leg. As the situation appeared to be desperate Parsons left the bombing formation, ordered bombs to be dropped, and decided it was time to bale out. The top turret gunner, though, Rodgers, said that he was unable to move. 'Barney' Barnard was sent to help him, and pulled the injured man out of his turret. It is not clear whether Rodgers was already wearing his parachute or whether Barney put it on for him, but Barney rolled him out of the open bomb-doors pulling the parachute's rip-cord as he did so: 'The parachute opened, but they were flying over a German machine-gun emplacement at the time, and the [German] gunner shot the parachute out of the air.'[107]

The other gunner, James Lees, baled out and is believed to have been taken prisoner, and Martin Zerff was also taken prisoner. From Stalag XIA (Altengrabow) Zerff was moved to Stalag XIB (Fallingbostel), arriving at Luft 7 in *Trupp 18* on 1 August 1944.

Marauder 'Z', however, was not shot down, and staggered back to base, where a safe landing was made. Barnard recalled that the aircraft was peppered with more than 400 holes from shell bursts, and that it was consequently deemed a write off.

*

By the time he got to Luft 7 with *Trupp 18* Peter Simpson had been a POW for three months short of three years, having been shot down in November 1941. When, in May 1941, six squadrons were posted to the Middle East it was decided that two pilots from each squadron would go to Takoradi on the Gold Coast of West Africa and fly an aircraft across to the Middle East, while the rest of the squadrons' personnel would continue by ship to Egypt. Chosen from 46 Squadron, one of the six, to fly from Takoradi were Peter Simpson and Charles Alpe. They were dropped off at Takoradi by the *Highland Princess* (see also page 277), while the rest of the squadron continued aboard the SS *Almanzora* (16,034 grt). In the event, 46 Squadron, which had become non-operational on 1 May 1941, would effectively cease to exist for the next year as its pilots were drafted from Egypt to Malta as reinforcements, and posted to whichever squadron needed them at the time.

Having made his way across Africa, Peter spent several weeks there before flying as second pilot, on 24 August 1941, on Sunderland N9029,[108] 230 Squadron, from Abu Qir (Aboukir), Egypt to Kalafrana, Malta. Once there he was posted to 126 Squadron.

On 12 November 1941 Peter flew what would prove to be his last operational sortie, against Gela airfield on Sicily. In company with ten others he took off at 6.45 am in Hurricane Mk.II Z3158, laden with 250lb bombs under the wings. Having dropped his bombs Peter then engaged in some ground strafing:

> 'Several [Italian] aircraft appeared to have been set on fire, and I foolishly lingered too
> long to assess the damage and was intercepted by three Macchi 202s. I engaged them

and then found I had used up all my ammo in ground attack, so made off. The Macchis were much faster and easily caught me up before I could disappear into cloud. My aircraft was set on fire and I baled out… I was much closer to the water than I thought. The 'chute had barely opened when I was in the sea at 0740 (when my watch stopped). I had a dinghy, inflated it and climbed in. I was about ten miles from the Sicilian coast.'

Italian aircraft noted his position, and after four or five hours a steam pinnace arrived and picked him up. The Italians, he noted, 'were extremely correct and looked after me well'. Once ashore, when he met the vehicle carrying his body, he was able to pay his respects to Wing Commander M.H. 'Hilly' Brown DFC and Bar, CdeG, Czech MC (37904), who had been shot down on an earlier mission.[109]

Peter was then taken to a hotel in Messina 'where I met some Fleet Air Arm chaps', Petty Officer (A) Arthur Jopling (pilot) and Lieutenant J.S. Manning RN (observer), 800X Squadron. They had been shot down by flak on the night of 7/8 October over Sicily in Blackburn Skua N4004.

From Messina they were taken to the Italian mainland, and then by train to Centocelle airfield (today, Rome-Centocelle Airport). They were put in comfortable quarters, but separated, and incompetently interrogated 'by a large Italian who claimed to be a Red Cross representative'. After a few days they were sent to a permanent POW camp, PG 78 (Sulmona). There Peter stayed until 8 October 1943. Unlike Arthur Jopling, who had disregarded the order to stay put following the Italian armistice, Peter was one of the many who were unable to get away from their camps before German troops arrived to take them over, in Sulmona's case on 14 September.[110]

By the end of the month the Germans were removing the 'British' POWs in batches to camps in Germany. The fourth batch went off on 3 October. Peter was due to have gone with them, but hid in the roof of his hut with a few others, in the hope that they would be abandoned by their guards and found by the Allies as they advanced northwards. Their hopes were shattered five days later when they were discovered, possibly after a tip-off, and sent by rail in cattle trucks to Stalag VIIA (Moosburg), where they arrived on 12 October.

On 4 November 1943 Peter was one of several to be purged to Stalag XIA (Altengrabow), where there were already a number of Free French and Vichy French POWs. Peter took the opportunity of spending time with them to improve his French, as did Sergeant Jimmy Cosgrove of the Middlesex Yeomanry (Royal Corps of Signals). Eventually, in July 1944, leaving his army colleagues behind, Peter and eight other RAF POWs were told that they had to go to a Luftwaffe camp, and set off on the long journey to Luft 7.

Two of the eight others, Warrant Officers G.H. 'Pee Wee' Cluley and F.R. Conner DFM, had been prisoners for almost four years. Cluley had had the misfortune to be on a delivery flight from England to Malta when, on 26 August 1940, Blenheim T2058 ran out of fuel near the Italian island of Pantellaria. Fred Conner suffered a similar fate a month later, in Blenheim T2176, but this time his pilot force-landed out of fuel in a field on the Italian island of Lampedusa.

*

**2 AUGUST 1944.** Heavy rain. As one man could not be accounted for at *Appell* the POWs had to stand in the pouring rain for over an hour until he was found. (Phil Rose recalls two *Appell*-related incidents. One when a hole was dug prior to one *Appell*, and it was filled with water. It was aimed at a particular Unterfeldwebel 'who always looked at faces when counting. In consequence he fell face down'. The second incident involved the 'placing of an extra pair of boots for a corporal who always counted feet – consequence, we were on parade for over two hours…').

**3 AUGUST 1944.** The bad weather continued.

**4 AUGUST 1944.** Red Cross parcel issue.

*Trupp 20* arrived (twelve men) in a purge from Stalag Luft III (Sagan). Six of the new boys were Polish NCO airmen transferred from Stalag Luft III (Sagan). Having already been POWs for two or three years they had somehow been left behind at Sagan when the rest of their fellow NCOs had been moved to Stalag Luft VI (Heydekrug) in June 1943. Their stay at Luft 7, however, was not to be long, and they were moved on to Stalag Luft IV (Gross Tychow) after a few weeks.

Also arriving was Acting Leading Airman H.C.G. Griffin of the Royal Navy's Fleet Air Arm. He was on board one of the six Fairey Albacores that were lost by 827 Squadron flying from the aircraft-carrier HMS *Victorious* on the ill-fated attack on Kirkenes harbour, Norway, on 30 July 1941. Of the eighteen crew lost, four only were killed, the rest being taken prisoner. 827's fellow *Victorious* squadron, 828, lost five Albacores (seven killed, five POW). Griffin was wounded by a bullet in the left foot, and spent some time in hospital as a result.

Another purged from Luft 3 was W/O Eric Jones, 32 Squadron. It is not clear when exactly he arrived at Bankau, but in his post-war questionnaire he says that he arrived in August 1944. This was over four years since he had been shot down, on 11 June 1940, whilst on patrol in his Hurricane over Le Tréport, France. Somehow he must have made his way to Jersey in the Channel Islands, no doubt in the hope of getting back to England, but was caught there on 1 July 1940. Sent to Germany he escaped from a train in Czechoslovakia in September 1940, before spending the next sixteen months at Stalag Luft I (Barth). He was one of the NCOs to transfer to the newly-opened Stalag Luft III (Sagan) in March 1942, where he remained until the end of July 1944. He was sent to the hospital at Stalag 344 (Lamsdorf) in October 1944 suffering with 'sacro-iliac arthritis from an ice-hockey fall' sustained three years earlier.

One of the others purged from Luft 3 was Warrant Officer Ross Breheny RAAF, 145 Squadron, who had been captured at Gabes, North Africa, on 27 March 1943. He had been pursuing a Ju88 over enemy territory when the engine of Spitfire ER199 failed.

A fellow Aussie from Luft 3 in the same purge, and also captured in North Africa, was W/O W.N. Fethers RAAF, pilot of Wellington DV562, 148 Squadron, lost on an anti-shipping raid to Tobruk harbour on 5 October 1942. All the crew survived as POWs but, knowing that officers received better treatment, Fethers told his captors that he was an officer though at the time he was only an NCO. He went to PG 75 (Torre Tresca) and PG 78 (Sulmona), Italy, before being sent to Oflag VA (Weinsberg) and Luft 3, where his POW number was 2733.

*

**5 AUGUST 1944.** *Trupp 21* arrived (seventy-three men).
Rumours went round the camp that the Russians were quite close, in the Krakow area, 'which was only about sixty or seventy miles from us, and also that they were north and south of Warsaw'.

The Luftwaffe's airfield at Fels am Wagram in Austria was a regular target for Allied bombers based in Italy. On the night of 6/7 July 1944 205 Group RAF despatched sixty-one aircraft to bomb the place. Though 'there was a fair concentration [of bombs] on the airfield' losses were heavy, with thirteen aircraft (twenty-one per cent) failing to return. 'Enemy fighters were very active, and many aircraft were seen going down in flames.'[111] German night-fighters were visible in the brilliant moonlight, and it is believed that they were responsible for the loss of the thirteen bombers – eleven Wellingtons and two Liberators. On the other hand, a large number of enemy fighters were destroyed or damaged on the ground, which helped a USAAF daylight raid from being intercepted later.

One of the Wellingtons that failed to return was MF241, 37 Squadron. It had taken off from Tortorella airfield at 2151 hours on 6 July with F/O C.W. Keighley at the controls. On board was the squadron bombing leader, F/L C.J. Burnell DFC, who had already completed a tour on 10 Squadron (on which squadron he had won his DFC, gazetted 9 November 1943). MF241 crashed in the Unterradlberg area near St Pölten, Austria at 0120 hours, 7 July. Sgt James A. Mitchell survived the crash with serious burns to his arms, but the rest of the crew – Keighley, Burnell, Lt T.V. Vlok SAAF, and Sgt L.J. Guest – were killed, and were buried at the Klagenfurt War Cemetery. Barely four weeks later, James Mitchell was at Luft 7 with *Trupp 21*.

*

The population of Canada according to the 1941 Canadian Census was only 11½ million. Such was the number of aircrew volunteers, however, that in late 1943 6 (RCAF) Group was formed within RAF Bomber Command. By the end of the war over 8,000 Canadians had lost their lives flying on operations from England, and almost one in every three RAF Bomber Command POWs was Canadian.

On the morning of 18 July 1944 some of 6 Group's Canadian squadrons were briefed for an attack on the stubborn German defences in and around the French city of Caen. As the planned Allied breakout from the Normandy beachhead was in danger of stalling, Operation Goodwood was set in motion. 667 Lancasters, 260 Halifaxes and fifteen Mosquitos of the RAF were called upon to break the enemy's resistance. It was a massive attack on five German strongpoints in the Caen area. German resistance was unquestionably loosened by it, but at a cost of one Lancaster and five Halifaxes.

One of the latter was NP706, 432 (Leaside) Squadron, based at RCAF East Moor in North Yorkshire. Its crew were F/L John H. Cooper DFC, RCAF (pilot); Sgt Dawson Wright RCAF (second dickey pilot); Sgt Harry Oakeby (flight engineer); F/O Bob Dryden RCAF (navigator); WO2 Al Zacharuk RCAF (bomb aimer); T/Sgt Leo Butkewitz USAAF (wireless operator); F/S R.E. Burton RCAF (mid-upper gunner); and WO1 Ken Elliott RCAF (rear gunner).

They were an experienced crew, as Dawson Wright recalled: 'This was the last trip of two tours and we were going to have a party after that. The crew were to be posted out as instructors. This flight was to be thirty-seven seconds over enemy territory. We made the first thirty OK, but the last seven took a few months.'[112]

NP706 arrived over its target at around 7 am and at a height of 9,000 feet. With bombs gone John Cooper turned for home, but not before accurate light flak had caught the Halifax in the mid section, killing the mid-upper gunner, Bob Burton. John Cooper: 'Fire broke out and the control cables from the pilot's control column to the rudders and elevators were severed. As the fire was beyond control and as I had no control of the aircraft I ordered the crew to jump. I was the last out after our engineer, Harry Oakeby.'

Harry Oakeby and Al Zacharuk evaded capture. Harry was liberated after a month in hiding, but it is not known how Al was liberated. He was, however, Mentioned in Despatches in the 1946 New Year's Honours. The other five were soon captured, and sent to a temporary 'cage' at Alençon. Dawson Wright was lucky to get that far for, while descending by parachute, he realised that someone was shooting at him: 'They can't do that to me, so I turned the 'chute around to see who was doing this. (Wasn't anything I could do about it anyway, but it seemed the thing to do at that time).' He was captured when he decided to shelter for the night in a clump of bushes. He was crawling on his stomach 'through the bushes when OH! OH! – it was a German field HQ. They were surprised to see me. I offered to leave but they had other ideas.'

The two officers, Cooper and Dryden, went to Luft 3 and Luft 1 respectively, while Wright and Elliott went to Luft 7 (*Trupp 21*). Leo Butkewitz eventually followed Wright and Elliott but, having been wounded in his right foot and leg by splinters (for which he was awarded the US Purple Heart), he went for treatment to a Lazarett before continuing to Luft 7.[113]

*

Bomb aimer F/S Keith Campbell RAAF was, as usual, leaning on his parachute 'and moving around to see the target more clearly, when the left clip of my harness clipped onto the hook in my 'chute.' The target for Keith and the rest of the crew of Halifax LV833 'P-Peter', 466 (RAAF) Squadron, on the night of 24/25 July 1944, was Stuttgart. Bombs gone, and the pilot had just turned for home when splinters from nearby flak bursts started rattling against the bomb-bay. Keith was just about to unclip his parachute 'when there was what seemed to be a heavy dull explosion behind me and someone saying "Bloody hell --". The next thing I knew I was in midair, floating down on one strap of my harness! The explosion, a stray flak shell which scored a direct hit on "Peter" blew me straight out through the nose and just blew the kite to hell.' Keith suffered only a few bruises and scratches. None of the seven others stood a chance.

Estimating his position as thirty miles south of Stuttgart, Keith set off for Switzerland, but was still close enough to the city to see it being attacked again on the next night. Walking along a road on the third day of his travels, a gas-powered lorry stopped, and the driver and his mate offered him a lift. Keith tried to pass himself off as French, but the driver's mate knew more French than Keith, and so the game was up. Also in the vehicle was a young girl, to whom Keith proffered his chocolate ration. This went down well with the two men, and when they stopped on the outskirts of Tübingen one of them 'went into a beer garden and came out with three bottles of beer… It was excellent beer, ice cold and tasted A1.' After the lovely beer Keith was handed over to a policeman.

At Dulag Luft he was informed by the English-speaking Luftwaffe interrogation officer, who of course knew everything about Keith and his squadron, that another aircraft from 466 Squadron had been found a few miles away, adding: 'You are damned lucky – the only one out of both of them.' (The seven crew of the other Halifax, HX243, were indeed killed.)

*

The Hamburg raid on 28/29 July 1944 was to prove a bad night for the Canadians, when thirteen of their squadrons between them lost twenty-four bombers – 143 aircrew were killed (among them over twenty RAF and one American), and twenty-nine taken prisoner.

Halifax III MZ816, 433 (Porcupine) Squadron, having bombing the target, was hit by flak near Kiel and set on fire. With the pilot possibly wounded or already dead, MZ816 went into a steep dive. F/O W.A. Martineau RCAF (navigator), F/O R.W. James RCAF (bomb aimer), and WO1 J.A. Robertson RCAF (wireless operator) were struggling to open the escape hatch when the Halifax exploded. They were the only ones of the seven crew to survive.

Alex Robertson's parachute opened just before he hit the ground, and he suffered a bruised back, later discovering that he had broken a bone in it. He and Martineau had landed near each other, and managed to hide in a field while the Germans searched the area but, as Martineau had lost both of his flying boots, they decided on the following night to steal a pair from a nearby house. They were caught by a French worker but, realising who they were, he did not report them. The next night the two hungry Canadians returned to the house to get some food, unaware that they had also been spotted the previous night by the woman of the house, a German, who *had* reported them to the authorities. It was, therefore, a considerable shock to the two airmen when guns appeared from every door and window as they approached the house for the second time.

While Martineau went to Luft 3 (Sagan), Alex Robertson went to Luft 7. Surviving an air-raid on or near Wetzlar Alex and several others were put on a train, six to a compartment, and spent the best part of three days getting to Bankau, on 5 August. Ralph James, the only other survivor, went to Luft I (Barth).

\*

Another Canadian airman to arrive at Bankau with *Trupp 21* was Sgt William 'Bill' Mackenzie Niven RCAF. Events were to prove that he, too, was very fortunate to have got that far. There is a saying in the forces that one should never volunteer, but sometimes a request is put in such a way that it becomes an order, as was the case with Bill Niven.

He was a 'spare' gunner on 431 Squadron when, late on the evening of 28 July 1944, the wing commander telephoned him. Explaining that a mid-upper gunner had been taken ill with appendicitis, he asked if Bill would take his place on ops that very night? Bill could not, of course, refuse: 'I had a feeling that something was going to happen, so I told one of my room mates how I felt. He had just come back off leave, so he didn't have to go on this op. I had a kit bag with a camera and chocolate, [and] 950 cigarettes in it. I told him if I did not come back he could have it.'

With take-off imminent, Bill climbed into his flying suit and rushed off to join his new crew: 'I had no idea what target we were going to, as I did not have a chance to go to a briefing.' The crew, all RCAF apart from the RAF flight engineer, were: F/O Robert Gray Holden (pilot); Sgt C.C. Newton (flight engineer); F/O A.L. Cameron (navigator); F/O George Johnstone (bomb aimer); F/O E. Dawson (wireless operator); Bill Niven (mid-upper gunner); and F/Sgt Francis James Clay (rear gunner). Airborne around 10.30 pm in Halifax B.III NA550, SE-U, it was not until they had crossed the English coast that Bill asked the skipper where they were going. Hamburg.

In what seemed to be no time at all to Bill they had crossed the enemy coast and were on their bombing run when suddenly a Ju88 night-fighter attacked. Bill:

> 'There was a big flash of light behind my turret. The plane went into a dive and I heard the pilot give the order to bale out. Somehow I managed to release my seat. I got out of the turret and left my helmet dangling by the oxygen tube and intercom wire. I got my parachute from the rack, hooked it on, then I went to the entrance hatch. The metal by the door had been hit by flak and it was bent over the door, but after giving the door a good pull, I got it open.'

F/O Holden ordered the bombs to be dropped, and gave the order to jump. George Johnstone and Bill Niven wasted no time in leaving. The navigator, F/O Cameron, had already taken off his helmet, with its earphones, and so never heard the pilot cancel the order to abandon the aircraft.

Bill Niven was in a cold sweat as he faced the prospect of jumping out. Eventually:

> 'I sat down on the step and pushed my feet out into the open. As soon as the slipstream came in contact with my boots, it pulled them off. I pushed myself off the step, and the next thing I knew I was floating down to mother earth. The cloud base was right down to the deck that night and I could see the searchlights shining through the clouds. It was quite an experience being the first time I had ever jumped. We had practised quite a bit

at OTU and conversion unit, but never in the air. It was a queer feeling to look up and
see the big pocket of silk above my head. When I finally got down, pretty close to the
earth, there was a burst of sparks directly below me. At first I thought it was flak then,
to my surprise, my head went under the water. When I had collected my senses, it was
a mad rush to release my parachute and inflate my Mae West. My wristwatch stopped
at 1.20 am.'

He was lucky that his flying boots had come off, for the extra weight of sea water inside them
might have posed a problem. But there he was floating around in the ice-cold water of the North
Sea, watching the searchlights come on every time another wave of bombers passed overhead.
Worryingly, though, the tide was taking him further out to sea. Waiting for the noise of the bombers
to pass he blew as loudly as he could on the whistle attached to the collar of his battledress:

'After hours of floating around it started to become light. It was a misty grey morning as I
looked around the water. Right at the mouth of the bay, I saw what I thought were three
buoys in the water and I seemed to be floating towards them. As they got nearer I could
see little red and green lights on them. When one of them came within a few yards of
me, I could see it was a freighter. I sounded the whistle, then I yelled for help. The boat
slowed down, then it turned around and pulled up alongside of me. By this time, another
destroyer and gun boat pulled up a few yards from the freighter. They started flashing
messages to each other. Then the destroyer sent out a small motor launch to pick me up.'

Taken to the destroyer, Bill was given a hot shower:

'The doctor was there and kept taking my pulse. He spoke perfect English. I asked him
what time it was and he told me it was about 8.40 which meant that I was approximately
seven hours in the water. After the shower they gave me a towel and blanket to put round
me and then took me back to the room again. The captain asked me a few questions
which I would not answer. He gave me five *Bucharest* cigarettes and a few moments
later, a little boy aged about fourteen brought me a cup of black coffee and some slices
of bread and jam, which I appreciated as I was so hungry. When I had finished they
brought me in some more. The boy came back into the room again, carrying my clothes
over his arm, which were warm when I put them on, so I thought that they must have
dried them in the boiler room. Then they brought my personal belongings and my wrist
watch, which was completely ruined.
   'The next thing I knew, two Luftwaffe officers were being ushered into my room. They
told me that I would have to go with them. Before leaving the boat, I thanked the captain
for all he had done for me, as they were really good to me. I told the air force officers that
I had no shoes, but they said that was all right. They said they had a car waiting by the
harbour. I asked the officer which city we were in; he said "Wilhelmshaven". Boy, what
a mess it was in! Our air force had really hit it!'[114]

Treading gingerly over broken glass, bricks and rubble, Bill made it to the car, which took him to
the nearby Luftwaffe HQ. Six days later he was at Luft 7.
   As for Bill's Halifax, after losing some 10,000 feet of height following the night-fighter's attack,
and with no immediate prospect of the bomber falling out of the sky, F/O Holden carried out a
check on his crew. Receiving no reply from the gunners, Sgt Newton was sent to find out what had

happened to them. He reported back that the mid-upper had baled out but that the rear gunner was wounded and dazed. Setting course for home NA550 landed at Strubby, Lincolnshire, at 0335 hours on 29 July. These few words fail to tell of the drama that took place aboard the Halifax as it clawed its way back to England, and for their actions this night the pilot and rear gunner were awarded the DFC and DFM respectively. The citation in the *London Gazette* stated:

> 'Sergeant Clay crawled to the nose of the aircraft where he remained during the return flight helping Flying Officer Holden to navigate his aircraft through a most heavily-defended area of Germany. Only when the aircraft was being landed in England did Sergeant Clay indicate that he was injured by requesting Flying Officer Holden to have an ambulance to meet the bomber on the airfield. Flying Officer Holden and Sergeant Clay displayed unswerving devotion to duty and set an example of the highest standard.'[115]

\*

There were seventy-three POWs in *Trupp 21*, but probably none had evaded capture for as long as Sgt W.A. Poulton, known as Allan to his family but as Bill to others. Shot down on 21/22 June 1943 (Krefeld), it was a good thirteen months before he fell into enemy hands.

Allan Poulton had flown on only one other operation before he was shot down, and that could so easily have been his last. It would seem that Allan's skipper, Sgt Fred Heathfield, through no fault of his own, was an unlucky pilot. He had had three crews, 'some of whom were killed, but none I am happy to say while flying with me'. He lost his second Whitley crew when he was injured and off ops, and selected his third, who had lost their pilot, after he had come out of hospital. He and his new, third, crew were posted to 51 Squadron at Snaith, Yorkshire.

But problems continued when the bomb aimer, F/O Harry Arthur 'Nick' Nock, broke a finger falling off a bicycle. Nick was back in action on the night of 3/4 July 1943 (Cologne) with Sgt Garnham and crew, but their aircraft, Halifax JD262, was shot down. Nick was the only one of the two survivors to evade capture. For his subsequent adventures with the Belgian Resistance he was awarded the MC on 12 June 1945.

A spare bomb aimer was allocated to Fred's crew, but this man refused to fly with any pilot other than his own. Even though warned that by refusing to fly he could be court-martialled, he failed to join Fred's crew for an operation one night. This was when Allan Poulton, on his first operation, joined the Heathfield crew as a replacement bomb aimer.

It was a quiet trip, so quiet that Fred decided to call the crew roll. When Allan failed to respond Fred guessed that he was probably suffering a lack of oxygen, and took the Halifax down to the thicker air. The navigator discovered that Allan's 'oxygen tube had frozen up with the moisture from his breath (even on a June night the temperature is below freezing at 18 or 20,000 feet) and he was unconscious.' He was soon revived, and was well enough to fly on the next, fateful operation.

The crew of Halifax JD244, MH-K, was Sgt F.J.H. Heathfield (pilot); Sgt D.G. Keane (flight engineer); P/O H.J. Dothie (navigator); Sgt W.A. Poulton (bomb aimer); Sgt W.C. Beresford (wireless operator); Sgt R.H. Masters RCAF (mid-upper gunner); and Sgt R. Cooper (rear gunner). They took off from Snaith a few minutes after midnight on 21/22 June 1943, and had just bombed the target and turned for home when flak hit the port wing, stopping both engines. The Halifax was flipped onto its starboard wing by the blast and, with the starboard outer engine also ablaze, lost a good 5,000 feet in seconds. With little or no hope of reaching England, Fred gave the order to bale out.

Thinking that everyone else had jumped Fred suddenly heard Bob Cooper saying that he was unable to get out of his turret. As Fred was unable to leave the controls to go and help him, as they were the only two left in the aircraft, Bob was spurred on to greater efforts, and managed to bale out. What he had not told Fred, though, was that he had been seriously wounded in his left arm.

Fred gave what he thought was enough time for Bob to bale out before turning to the small matter of his own survival. The Halifax was practically unflyable, and almost out of control: 'When I got it back under control I found I was flying just above the tree tops; in fact I was soon clipping the tops. I was lucky to put it down in a small clearing, and I was knocked unconscious and thrown across the cockpit and down into the nose of the aircraft.'[116]

Extraordinary that he had not been killed, all he suffered were 'an injured leg, a broken nose and a deep gash in my scalp'. He was fit enough to make off into Belgium, where the aircraft had crashed, and found help from the Belgian Resistance. Unfortunately, Belgian traitor Prospère Valère Dezitter had managed to infiltrate the escape line that was looking after Fred, who was caught in a Paris hotel room on 7 August. Fred survived the war at Stalag IVB (Mühlberg). Dezitter also survived the war, but was caught, tried, and then executed on 17 September 1948.

All seven crew of JD244 survived to be taken prisoner of war. Dothie, who landed in the courtyard of the Leopoldsburg power station, went to Stalag Luft III, while Beresford (given away to the Germans by excited children), Keane (betrayed by the farmer who had given him shelter in his barn), and Masters (caught at Besançon, France on 23 December 1943 trying to cross into Switzerland) went to Stalag Luft VI (Heydekrug).

By chance Bob Cooper and Allan Poulton met each other soon after landing. Finding a café in a town, they knocked at the door. After the owner had let them in, Allan made running repairs to Bob's arm. Not wishing to linger they headed for the railway station with the idea of going to Brussels, and there met an ex-Belgian army sergeant. Allan was able to converse with him in French, and was told that, as there were too many Germans about, they should give themselves up. An appeal for Bob to be taken to a doctor brought the response that, if he were, then 'the gunner would certainly be handed over to the Germans', as Allan stated in his post-war report. On closer inspection the arm looked so bad to their untrained eyes that they thought that Bob would have to hand himself in if he were to save it. This he did, and so joined his other three crew members at Luft 6.

Belgian helpers took Allan by train to Brussels, and after a week in one of the helpers' house he 'was taken to the house of an English woman who was a member of an Underground organisation. For the next six months I remained in Brussels, staying at various addresses in the city, where I was continuously assured that I was just about to leave and would be back in the UK shortly.' The English woman, who lived at 54 Rue Théodore Roosevelt, Schaerbeek, Brussels, was Madame Edith Hardy,[117] who had married a Belgian and remained in Brussels during the war. Other safe houses at which Allan briefly stayed were those of Eleuthère Thiryn, at 328 Rue de Noyer, Etterbeek, Brussels, and of Mariette Gorlia at 2 Rue de la Longue Haie, also in Etterbeek.

In February 1944 Allan was moved to Charleroi, where he was once again assured that his return to England would be imminent. These were troubled times for the Belgian Resistance, notably for the brave helpers of the Comet line (with which Allan spent much of his time), which was infiltrated by agents of the German secret police with fatal results. In consequence, Allan made no progress, and was so fed up that on 1 July 1944 he returned to Brussels, where he stayed in the Boulevard de Waterloo, St Gilles, with Madame Irène Radermackers-Balieux, who had sheltered him earlier.

A couple of weeks later he was told that this time he really was on his way home, and was moved to Antwerp. Unfortunately, this was all part of an elaborate deception engineered by Dezitter and his henchwomen, who had penetrated the Resistance to such an extent that they were able to hand over dozens of aircrew, Allan among them. Dezitter also betrayed hundreds of civilian Resistance workers, including the brave Edith Hardy. Sent to Germany, she died of dysentery on or about 15 March 1945 at Mauthausen concentration camp.

After his arrest Allan spent the next two weeks in a civilian jail at Anvers, and was released from Dulag Luft to Luft 7, where he eventually arrived with *Trupp 21* on 5 August. In his post-war interrogation report he stated that he was captured on 16 August 1944 but, as he was safely inside the wire at Luft 7 eleven days earlier, this date is impossible, and was possibly, therefore, 16 July.

*

**7 AUGUST 1944.** As if to support the rumours of two days earlier the camp had its first, and second, air-raid alert around midday. Today was also designated sports day – as it was August Bank Holiday! The alerts delayed the start of the first England v Australia Test Match, which eventually got under way at 2 pm. The match was not completed by 'curfew'.

'During the afternoon side-shows were erected – "Knock the cans off", skittles, hoop-la, "count the raisins", buried treasure, Crown & Anchor, "Throw your cigarettes on the squares to win", dice throwing etc. It was good fun.' (Tom Glenn.)

There was also a boxing match in the evening with seven bouts. During the Needlematch between the Two Clowns (F/S F.A. Sturgess and Sgt W.H. Lynch), who of course knocked each other out, a bucket of water was thrown 'accidentally' at the crowd, some of it hitting the Oberfeldwebel chief ferret – who was not amused.

During the 'sports' two unknown prisoners escaped, but were recaptured at Bankau station, and put in the cooler.

**8 AUGUST 1944.** Another Red Cross parcel issue. The Test Match ended in victory for the English, who scored 65 and 111 in their two innings to the Australians' 68 and 56. (England won the next Test, but the Aussies fought back to level the series after the fourth game. It never proved possible to fit in a fifth 'decider'.)

Date unconfirmed but possibly the day on which three GPR men arrived as *Trupp 22*.

**9 AUGUST 1944.** The prisoners noted that there were now two guards in every box, whereas previously there had been only one.

**11 AUGUST 1944.** One unknown prisoner took a chance when he jumped over the safety-fence. Ducking under the inner barbed-wire fence he turned round to see a guard pointing his rifle at him, and flung himself to the ground just as the guard opened fire – and missed. He was only trying to retrieve the cricket ball!

*Trupp 23* (forty men) was processed.

*

'It was snowing hard. I could not stand as my right leg was broken and folded back behind the knee of my left leg and hurt intensely. In a very short time I was covered over by snow.' For twenty-year-old Sgt Peter Wilmshurst the immediate future did not look too promising, but at least he was alive.

A short while before, in Halifax LK795, 76 Squadron, he had been on his way with his crew to Nuremberg on the night of 30/31 March 1944, on his thirteenth operation. His skipper, F/L H.D. 'Roger' Coverley, was on his fortieth, the tenth of his second tour, the first having been on 78 Squadron. A Ju88 night-fighter was the first to attack LK795, and Peter had just returned to his seat when they were attacked by Unteroffizier Otto Kutzner, 5./NJG3, in his Bf110 (he was to claim three victories on this long night). The '6,000lb load of incendiary bombs exploded causing a massive fire'. Listening out for a group broadcast on his wireless set Peter failed to hear the order to bale out, and realised all was not well when he saw the flight engineer, Sgt George Motts, heading for the nose escape hatch with his parachute clipped on, closely followed by the pilot.

When the Halifax went into a steep dive, Peter had great difficulty trying to reach his parachute in its stowage and clip it on. Having succeeded in this he found that he was then unable to leave his seat: 'For some unknown reason the dive became more shallow. This allowed me to get out of my seat and make my way forward to the escape hatch.' There he found F/S W.A. 'Archie' Blake (bomb aimer) who had also been unable to jump because of the g forces. But Archie got out, and Peter took his place. As soon as he too had jumped, realising that he must have been low to the ground by this time, he pulled the ripcord. After two or three swings under his parachute he hit the ground with an almighty thump, breaking his leg.

The only fatality was the twenty-year-old flight engineer, George Motts, whose body 'was found three days later suspended in a tree, the burnt remains of his parachute canopy draped around him'. The rear gunner, Sgt Dave Bauldie, was to be tragically killed, with many others, by 'friendly' Typhoon fire when they shot-up a column of kriegies at Gresse, North Germany, on 19 April 1945.

Peter, meanwhile, discovered that he was in the middle of nowhere: 'Despite my shouts no one seemed very interested and I had visions of not being found and dying of exposure.' A while later the snow stopped, and he could just make out the outlines of a house not too far away. Further shouting proved fruitless, until Peter remembered the whistle attached to his battledress collar: 'After several blows I heard a window open and a voice call out something quite unintelligible to me.' Soon, a man appeared, ran off, and about fifteen minutes later reappeared with two soldiers, 'one of whom advanced towards me with a fixed bayonet. He was quite elderly and I think more scared than I was.'

Taken inside, Peter was made as comfortable as possible. The lady of the house made some coffee, while explaining that an ambulance would not be able to get to them until daylight. When it arrived Peter:

> 'was most surprised to find my bomb aimer [F/S W.A. Blake] on a stretcher next to me. He had spent several hours dangling on his parachute which had become entangled in a tall pine tree. Unable to reach the trunk of the tree and starting to suffer from frostbite he had turned the quick-release buckle on his parachute harness and fallen about thirty feet to the ground. Consequently he was suffering from a fractured pelvis.'

The injured pair were taken to the hospital at Wissen, on the River Sieg, run mainly by Roman Catholic Sisters, but with German doctors and medical orderlies, and Red Cross nurses.

They shared the hospital with many German wounded, mostly from the Eastern Front, but regardless of their status the RAF pair were treated equally with the soldiers: 'The medical attention was first class. The army doctor who attended to us always gave a Nazi salute whenever he entered the room, until one morning he came, saluted, gave a broad smile and said "To hell with it!", and never saluted again.' On the day that Peter and Archie left they were given meat sandwiches for their journey, and most of the nurses and Sisters came to say 'Auf Wiedersehn'.

Some nineteen weeks after they had been shot down Peter and Archie arrived at Luft 7 in *Trupp 23*.

*

It was through the vagaries of war that Maurice Simpson, a young, injured Canadian airman from Creighton Mine, Ontario, would be operated on in a north German hospital by a French surgeon, Pierre Michaud, from Lyon. Maurice 'will always be grateful to him for saving my life, as I was in extremely bad shape'. He was not exaggerating.

Flying as mid-upper gunner of Lancaster ND522, 207 Squadron, on an operation to lay mines in Kiel Bay on the night of 21/22 May 1944, the bomber was attacked by a night-fighter flown by Hauptmann Franz Buschmann, Stab IV./NJG3. The Lancaster, on its way back to base, blew up and crashed into the sea near Mandø Island, just off the Danish coast south of Esbjerg. Only two of the seven-man crew survived – F/O Paul Walshe RNZAF, and Sgt Maurice Simpson RCAF. Despite having a broken shoulder and five machine-gun bullets in his back – one of the bullets 'tore a hole as large as a teacup through my bladder' – Maurice was able to take to his parachute. After four hours he struggled ashore, and was picked up by German soldiers. Three days later he was in a hospital in Schleswig, Germany, where Pierre Michaud was able to perform life-saving surgery.

After five weeks in Schleswig and Wetzlar hospitals, Maurice was on his way in *Trupp 23* to Luft 7. Paul Walshe went to Stalag Luft III (Sagan), and when he and Maurice met up again in the camp at Luckenwalde, to which both had been evacuated in 1945, Maurice discovered that Paul had also been wounded, in the legs.

Remarkably, despite the hammering his body had taken, Maurice helped to dig a number of tunnels at Luft 7 but, as he says, 'these were usually discovered'. In fact, there was to be no break-out from the camp via a tunnel.

*

Somewhere over the town of Zombor, in northern Yugoslavia, Halifax JP179 FS-P, 148 Squadron, was attacked by an unseen night-fighter[118] whilst returning from an SOE supply drop, Operation 101A, to southern Poland on the night of 3/4 July 1944. The first burst hit both starboard engines, setting them on fire, and severing the controls. The intercom was also damaged, which made it difficult for the pilot, W/O L.J. Blattmann RAAF, who had also been hit by splinters in his crutch, to give the order to all the crew to bale out. Whether four of the crew heard the order or not will never be known, for they did not survive. F/S L.W. Davey RAAF, however, heard later from the only other survivors – Blattmann and the navigator, F/S W.F. Wicks – that they suspected that the flight engineer, Sgt T.W.H. Tomlinson, had been 'killed by civilians when baled out but cannot confirm as no cannon injuries seen'. Davey was able to confirm, though, having seen him in the aircraft, that the wireless operator 'was badly mutilated with cannon fire and parachute badly holed'.

Having landed awkwardly, spraining both ankles and knocking his spine, Leonard Davey was heading south-west to cross the River Danube 'into Partisan area of Yugoslavia' when he was picked up in a wheat field by the Hungarian equivalent of the British Home Guard, and taken to military barracks at Zagred [sic – possibly Szeged], where he spent the next five days and also met up with Walter Wicks.

He was then moved to the Budapest state prison, where he was to languish for the next three weeks. It was probably here – Davey's report is unclear at this point – that a number of minor atrocities were committed against him and Walter Wicks, and possibly against another two 148 Squadron crew – F/S J.E. Taylor and F/O N.C. MacPherson RCAF, who had been captured when Halifax JP247 was shot down on the same night as JP179 and in roughly the same area. They eventually went on to Stalag Luft III (Sagan).

Leonard Davey:

'Confined to dark cell for thirteen days on little food. Taken out for interrogation several times. Refused to give information so beaten up by gaol guards on return to cell. Beatings with rifle-butts, fists, boots, under stressed condition. Confined to chains for several days.....

'Taken from cell on seventh day with others. Interrogation. No information. In blacked out cell during which time interrogated about four times. Still refused to give information during each interrogation so returned to cell where I was beaten up by gaol warden under instructions of German interrogation officer after each interview. Water changed twice, no bed or blankets, slept on floor, latrine bucket in cell. No light whatsoever. Bowl of soup a day (when it suited them).'

The nightmare ended on 31 July when Davey and Wicks were sent to Dulag Luft. It took three days to get there and, after five days at the Luftwaffe's interrogation centre and transit camp, another five days to get to Bankau. W/O Blattmann joined them on 22 August in *Trupp 27*.

*

Lancaster LL846, PO-V 'Victor', 467 Squadron, was on its way back from Stuttgart on the night of 28/29 July 1944, when the navigator reported to the pilot, F/O S. Johns DFC, RAAF, that they were dead on track and would be over the French coast, near Cabourg, in half a minute. Barely had he spoken than V-Victor was hit by a burst of flak. The port outer engine was set alight, but the crew could do nothing to prevent the fire from spreading to the rest of the wing. Johns had no option but to order the crew to their ditching positions but, before they could get there, he had put down on the waters of the Baie de la Seine. The nineteen-year-old flight engineer, Sgt D.K.J. Phillips, suffered a severe head injury in the ditching and was unable to get into the dinghy. Despite Johns' valiant efforts to pull him aboard, he drowned.

The rest of the crew, cast adrift in their rubber boat, lost the struggle against wind and tide to gain the shores of England, and were picked up by the enemy on 1 July after two days afloat. Three of the crew went to Luft 7 – F/S M.J. O'Leary RAAF in *Trupp 23*, and F/Sgt B.P. Molloy RAAF and Sgt B.R.J. Pring in *Trupp 27* – while the three others of the crew, all officers, went to Stalag Luft III (Sagan). Most of them were on their twenty-ninth operation. So near, yet so far…

*

Another Lancaster on the Stuttgart raid on 28/29 July 1944, NE164, 550 Squadron, was lost on the way out near Strasbourg in eastern France, shot down for his sixth victory by Oberleutnant Gottfried Hanneck, 5./NJG1. Though later wounded when shot down himself, Hanneck would survive the war, unlike NE164's pilot, F/O Harry Jones, one of those gallant airmen who gave his life to save his crew. Perishing with him was the mid-upper gunner, who died 'when the cord of his intercom tangled with his parachute cords and he was strangled'.

Also lost was the bomb aimer, Sgt F.H. Habgood. Having parachuted safely to earth, he was captured near the village of Niederhaslach, Alsace, and taken first to Schirmeck security camp then to Struthof-Natzweiler extermination camp, and executed. Two of those responsible for his death, brought to justice after the war, were hanged on 11 October 1946.

The navigator, F/O W. Dinney RCAF, after help from Ste Odile convent and the French Resistance, got back to England, but the rest of NE164's crew were captured, and arrived at Luft 7 in *Trupp 23* – Sgts J.R. Drury (flight engineer), Don Hunter (wireless operator), and R.B. Cumberlidge (rear gunner).

*

**12 AUGUST 1944.** Very hot day. It was noted that the guards now had machine guns in their sentry boxes.

This was possibly the day on which just one man, Sgt Harry Hoyle, arrived from the Polish/Balkan conflict. *Trupp 24?*

**14 AND 15 AUGUST 1944.** *Truppen 25* and *26* possibly arrived on these days, but names of new arrivals not known.

**15 AUGUST 1944.** Gramophone record recital (mostly classical) in the evening.

**16 AUGUST 1944.** The POWs had to remain on the parade ground after morning *Appell* while the Germans searched all the huts for unopened tins of food. Those that they found were punctured to avoid the contents being used for escape purposes.

**17 AUGUST 1944.** Prisoners confined to their huts while the Germans checked up on identity cards and photos.

**18 AUGUST 1944.** Red Cross parcel issue.

**21 AUGUST 1944.** Whilst on parade one of the prisoners made a dash for a football which was between the huts. When a guard aimed his rifle at him the rest shouted to watch out. He just made it behind a hut in time.

**22 AUGUST 1944.** *Trupp 27* (109 men) arrived.

*

Lack of nourishment was a constant worry for prisoners and, even though the International Red Cross moved mountains to provide the hundreds of thousands of Germany's captives with food parcels, there was never enough. F/S Norman Oates noted on his arrival on 22 August 1944 that his food 'was a daily bowl of boiled "grass" and a small ration of boiled potatoes. I heard that the "grass" was shredded sugar-beet tops. At first I could not eat it, but after a few days I was so hungry I managed.'

*

F/S William Ernest Egri RCAF, though born in Borsod, Hungary, on 23 December 1919, was working on a farm in Canada when war came. Having enlisted in January 1941, his first brush with death came on the night of 11/12 August 1942 when Stirling N3756, 15 Squadron, having been shot up by two Ju88 night-fighters on its return from Mainz, crashed into a pond at Potash Farm, Brettenham, Suffolk and burst into flames. It was only the brave and immediate action of three local men – Jim, John and Stan Arbons – that saved Bill Egri's life when they cut their way into the rear turret and dragged him out.

For his actions on this night Bill was awarded the DFM in the *London Gazette* on 15 December 1942. This was the original draft for the citation:

> 'Flight Sergeant Egri was a rear gunner in a Stirling aircraft which was attacked by two Junkers 88s. Our aircraft sustained extremely heavy damage and the mid-upper gunner

was mortally wounded. Flight Sergeant Egri maintained his fire in the face of heavy cannon opposition, probably destroying one of the enemy aircraft and causing the other to break off the engagement.

'It now became apparent that our aircraft was on fire and Flight Sergeant Egri left his turret and with his gloved hands and a fire extinguisher, assisted by other members of the crew, extinguished the fire. His hands sustained serious burns. Flight Sergeant Egri then returned to his turret which, together with the mid-upper, was unserviceable. He rotated it by hand, however, keeping watch for further enemy aircraft. The aircraft returned safely to friendly territory where the captain gave the crew the option of baling out as they had been unable to release their bombs owing to the damage sustained. The crew stayed with the captain, but the aircraft crashed in flames whilst attempting to land, probably owing to damage the captain had been unable to assess.'

Almost two years later, on 3 August 1944, WO1 Bill Egri was flying as rear gunner aboard Lancaster LL716, 514 Squadron, when it was lost on a daylight raid to the V1 storage site at Bois de Cassan in northern France. Flying at 15,000 feet the Lancaster was hit and damaged by 'friendly' bombs, leaving the pilot, F/O J.B. Topham, no choice but to put LL716 down on French soil. Two of the eight-man crew, including the pilot, managed to evade capture (it was not until 8 October that he set foot once again on English soil), but the remaining six were taken prisoner. Egri and two others – F/S Harold Gilmore and Sgt James Scully – would eventually join the other 106 men of *Trupp 27* at Luft 7.

*

Navigator Sgt John Watkins had the distinction of being captured by *White* Russians and of being liberated by *Red* Russians. He was shot down on the ill-fated two-pronged attack on the Blainville and Metz railway yards in north-eastern France on the night of 28/29 June 1944, when eighteen Halifaxes of the 202 despatched by 4 and 6 Groups were lost. Eleven of the Blainville Halifaxes were shot down by rampaging night-fighters, and five of those were from 102 Squadron.

It was one of those nights when the Nachtjagd controller got it right, and was able to put his night-fighters in the right place at the right time. The first contact with the bomber stream was made when it was east of Rouen. Half an hour after midnight, still on its way to the target, MZ646, 102 Squadron, with John Watkins on board, was hit from behind and below in the classic *Schräge Musik* attack, by the upward-slanting guns of a night-fighter. With the Halifax soon ablaze, Sgt F. John Higman baled out of his rear turret, while John Watkins simply dropped out through the hatch below his seat.

MZ646 was shot down in the Compiègne area, with the loss of five of the seven crew, one of whom died of his injuries within hours of being admitted to a hospital in Beauvais.

John Watkins and the rear gunner, Sgt F.J. Higman, were taken prisoner, and went to Luft 7. John Higman was soon captured, but John Watkins, having made contact with the French Resistance, was hidden for about three weeks in a wood some forty kilometres north east of Paris with six other evaders – F/S C.W. Schwilk RAAF; F/O P.G. Agur RCAF; and 2/Lt John E. Hurley USAAF (co-pilot), Sgt Leo Williams USAAF, S/Sgt Harry G. Pace Jnr USAAF, and 2/Lt Peter D. MacVean (pilot) USAAF, four of the crew of B-24H 42-50344 *Red Sox* (448 BG, 714 BS) shot down on 27 June 1944.

The French Resistance had, at this time, been issued with instructions that any aircrew evaders who were in hiding close to the front line in northern France should, if possible, be taken to a 'holding camp' behind enemy lines in Fréteval forest, south of Châteaudun and south west of Paris. In accordance with these instructions, therefore, these seven evaders were moved to Paris en route to the camp. On their way there, however, John Watkins became separated from the other six in Paris,[119] and was caught on 10 August with five other evaders (one RAF, one RCAF, three USAAF), when White Russian soldiers fighting for the Germans attacked the Maquis group who were looking after them, and handed them over to the SD at Chartres. They were doubly fortunate as, having been captured without any French people being present, it was accepted that they were just a bunch of aircrew evaders, and word reached the Luftwaffe that the SD were holding prisoners who were rightfully theirs.

After the usual stops at Oberursel and Wetzlar, John Watkins reached Luft 7 in *Trupp 27*.

*

**24 AUGUST 1944.** The camp was awoken early by the sound of two rifle shots. Fred Stead and Jim Goode recall that it was 7 am on 24 August when an Australian crossed the trip-wire, and one thing George Pringle RAAF remembered clearly of his time at Luft 7 was rescuing a fellow countryman who had lost his reason:

> 'Not sure of name. W/O Davis, I think. Came to L7 after some months in Gestapo hands and was out of his mind. I helped to bring him back from over the warning wire [at] 5.30 am when a German guard was shouting at him. He was taken from our camp that day and sent to hospital according to Germans.'

The poor chap in question was W/O Bruce Hamilton Davis RAAF. A bomb aimer shot down on 21 May 1944 at Hasselterdijk, near Zwolle in The Netherlands, he spent the first seven weeks with the Dutch Underground. He had been struck in the right eye by a flak splinter when the Lancaster was hit but, despite treatment from a doctor in the Resistance, he never regained the sight in it. Initially hidden in the bell tower of the Catholic church in the town of Oldenzaal with his navigator, WO2 E.S. 'Ted' Moran RCAF, they were moved a few kilometres away to a safe house in the village of Lutterzandweg while arrangements were made for their return to England. But plans to help them get away were thwarted one day when a truckload of German soldiers suddenly appeared. Bruce and Ted, clearly having been betrayed, were captured in civilian clothes.

Shortly afterwards they were parted, but Ted must have been processed quite quickly, for he arrived at Luft 7 on 10 July with *Trupp 11*. Bruce, on the other hand, was to suffer extensive questioning by the German Secret Police (probably the SD) who, to get him to talk about his Dutch helpers, pulled out his toe nails. Then, playing with his mind, they tormented him with a photo of his wife, Dorothy, that they had found in his pockets, saying what they would do to her when they got hold of her. Bruce then 'spent a lot of time in solitary confinement, and after one interview with the Gestapo [sic] was placed in a cell where he looked out of a small window onto an exercise yard'. The yard was also a place of execution and, as intended, Bruce witnessed several shootings. All of this continued to play on his mind.

Having been moved to several other places – he never knew their names – he arrived at Luft 7 on 22 August with *Trupp 27*. His state of mind on this day is unclear but, in view of his walking into the forbidden area beyond the warning wire only two days after his arrival, he must already have been close to a breakdown. Removed to the hospital at Loben (Lubliniec, forty kilometres south east of Luft 7), and then on to Stalag 344 (Lamsdorf), he was eventually repatriated to Australia in the POW exchanges in February 1945.

Once back in his native country, weighing just over 7 stones, he remained in hospital in Adelaide for three years. The doctors told his wife, Dorothy, 'that they considered him to be a hopeless case, and his future looked very grim'. Three years later, though, a brain surgeon from the UK, who was visiting Adelaide, was referred to Bruce's case.[120] He decided to try an operation that 'was the first of its type done in South Australia. It all made news in the medical journals.' For Dorothy there was 'a lot of heartache but we finally made it', and after ten years of marriage they started a family (two boys and a girl), which proved a great joy to both of them. In 1977-78 Bruce returned to Oldenzaal, with Dorothy, to thank those who had helped him: 'They made us very welcome and it was a wonderful experience for both of us.' After a long illness, Bruce died on 6 February 1987.

*

A representative of the IRCC, Dr M. Rossel, visited the camp on 24 August for a routine inspection. Resident at this time were 1,028 POWs: 738 British; 172 Canadians; six Rhodesians; twelve South Africans; five Americans; nineteen New Zealanders; sixty-nine Australians; three Dutch; four Free French. His report did not portray the camp in a good light, discovering that the men 'sleep on the ground on sacks of straw insufficiently filled. There are not enough blankets.' Additionally, there were no lights in the 'chicken huts' and, he reported: 'Sanitary arrangements are primitive, there is not sufficient water only four taps being available. The pump in the middle of the camp is out of order… This deplorable state of affairs as regards the huts will be improved when the prisoners are able to move into the new part of the camp…'

Cooking facilities for food from Red Cross parcels were non-existent:

'Cooking is done in old tins on makeshift fires, the only fuel often available being straw or paper. Reserves of food, stored nearby, were found to consist of 4,042 British Red Cross parcels and 569 diet parcels; 182 USA parcels and seventy-five diet parcels; fifteen medical parcels; and sixty British tobacco parcels. The percentage of theft remains very small and such thefts are nearly always of cigarettes.'

Rossel also noted that three men, who had been sentenced to ten days' detention, were serving it in one of the small huts. 'They receive bread and water for three days and on the fourth day the usual camp rations.'

Rossel noted, too, that there had not yet been any attempts to escape. His conclusion was: 'In spite of poor conditions, the camp was adequate in summer and the prisoners were satisfied. Small huts which necessitate grouping six or seven men together suit British tastes.' [121]

*

Probably around 24 or 25 August, mid-upper gunner Sergeant Raymond Davies Hughes arrived at Luft 7. He was on his twenty-first operation when shot down on 17/18 August 1943 (Peenemünde) in Lancaster ED764, 467 Squadron. Captured, and interrogated at Dulag Luft, he offered his services to a grateful Luftwaffe, who thereafter employed him with some success. Usually calling himself Herr Becker, he persuaded many new aircrew arrivals to complete the bogus Red Cross form. On 16 October 1943, however, he was moved from Dulag Luft to the civilian prison at Frankurt, and put in a cell on his own, apparently because the Germans believed that he was warning prisoners not to talk.

On the last day of October 1943 he was sent to Berlin where, until it was bombed, he was to live comfortably in the Auto Hotel, Charlottenburg, using the alias this time of John Charles Baker. For a time he worked at the Radio Metropole Broadcasting Station at Wannsee using yet another alias, Raymond Sharples. Berlin at this time was being heavily and regularly bombed by the RAF, and he claimed that he took advantage of the air raids to commit various acts of sabotage throughout Berlin. Seemingly a 'bolshie' character he was arrested by plain-clothes police, and sent to Zehlendorf-West camp on 9 August 1944. On 22 August he was taken by two guards to Luft 7, where he was questioned by Peter Thomson and by W/O George B. Edwards SAAF, who spoke German. Neither, according to Hughes, seemed particularly interested in his previous activities but, as he had become a fluent German speaker, he was given the job of advanced German instructor, and also did some interpreting for the Germans. He was, however, regarded as a collaborator from the outset, particularly because on arrival 'at Luft 7 his uniform was immaculate and a German carried his luggage'.[122] This sort of behaviour simply never happened to POWs.

At his General Court-Martial at RAF Station Uxbridge on 23 August 1945 Hughes was charged under section 4(5) of the Air Force Act with voluntarily aiding the enemy, and with accepting a salary from the enemy, whilst a prisoner of war. He was found guilty, reduced to the ranks, and 'Discharged from the RAF with Ignominy'. He was also given five years' penal servitude. His case was later reviewed, and on 7 June 1948 the Secretary of State for Air recommended to King George VI that he exercise clemency. A month later it was announced that 'His Majesty the King has now been pleased to command that the unexpired portion of the penal servitude remaining to be completed be remitted'. As Hughes had lost twenty-six days remission for insolence and misconduct the earliest date for release from Dartmoor was 20 January 1949.

The postscript to Hughes's story is that after the war he apparently married the daughter of a wealthy director of Plymouth Argyle FC, and did well for himself. Later, when former Luft 7 kriegie Frank Sturgess applied for a job with a certain company, he found himself facing a panel of directors, one of whom was Hughes, who failed to recognise him. Frank was left in no doubt that, despite his court-martial and discharge from the RAF, Hughes's career did not appear to have been blighted by his past record. (For a fuller account of Hughes's activities see *Footprints on the Sands of Time*, pages 187-90.)

*

**27 AUGUST 1944.** Another air raid in the morning. Flak could be seen to the south.

**29 AUGUST 1944.** *Trupp 28* (forty men) arrived.

*

F/Sgt A.J. 'Dick' Holden, was caught attempting to cross the Pyrenees (see also Phil Brown, page 39). In Dick's case, the pill must have been all the harder to swallow as he had been shot down over Holland just over seven months before, on 27/28 September 1943 (Brunswick). Taken to Belgium by Karst Smit, he arrived in Brussels on 27 October, and was placed in the hands of the organisation EVA, together with American airman Sgt Robert D. de Ghetto, rear gunner of B-17G 42-37737, 91BG/401BS, shot down on 10 October 1943 (Münster).

After the two had been separated, de Ghetto was captured at Beaumetz-lès-Loges (near Arras) on the night of 8/9 April 1944. Holden, meanwhile, having been passed on to the Felix escape line, slowly made his way to the Pyrenees hoping to cross into neutral Spain. His luck, and that of six others, ran out when they were caught on 8 May by a German patrol near the Pyrenees.

*

At 5 pm on the afternoon of 1 August 1944 a bomb exploded at Gestapo headquarters in Warsaw. It was to signal the start of the Warsaw Rising: 'The news arrived in London on the following day and immediately the Poles started to urge the Allies, and above all the British, to send the capital the utmost possible help.'[123] This was easier said than done, for Warsaw lies 1,500 kilometres/950 miles from London, and it would have been suicidal for aircraft laden with weapons and ammunition to fly there and back safely in the short summer nights. Permission was, therefore, sought from Stalin to allow the supply aircraft to fly to Warsaw, drop the supplies, and continue on to Russia before returning to England. But Stalin refused, the only reason given being that 'the Soviet government did not wish to encourage "adventuristic actions" which might later be turned against the Soviet Union'. So, it was clear that Stalin would offer the Poles, whom he basically regarded as enemies, no help whatsoever.

The only other possibility, therefore, was to use the recently-captured airfields at Foggia, some 240 kilometres/150 miles north of Brindisi. Warsaw was now that much closer for the big, four-engined aircraft. What followed – the aerial supply of the Polish Resistance in Warsaw from the Foggia airfields – proved to be, *pro rata*, one of the RAF's costliest campaigns of the Second World War.[124]

As the supply drops had to be precise enough to ensure that the precious supplies did not fall into enemy hands, aircraft had to fly very, very low and slow, thus becoming easy targets for German light flak – of which there was plenty. Research by author Jozef Garlinski reveals that between 3 August and 21 September 1944 PAF, RAF and SAAF aircraft flew 196 supply sorties on behalf of SOE from Italy to Warsaw and the surrounding area, of which only eighty-five were completed (forty-three per cent). The cost, though, was huge, with thirty-nine aircraft lost at a rate of almost twenty per cent.

Two of the squadrons involved were No. 148 flying Halifaxes from Brindisi, and No. 178 with Liberators at Amendola, also in Italy. 148 Squadron lost Halifaxes EB147 and JN926 – six of the survivors ending up in Luft 7 – while 178 Squadron lost Liberator KG933, two survivors also going to Luft 7.

In the small hours of 17 August 1944 the citizens of the Kazimierz district of Kraków, Poland, were awoken by a violent explosion. An RAF Liberator had crashed into the women's barracks at Oskar Schindler's Emalia factory at 4, Lipowa Street, Kraków, today the Telepod electronics factory.

A plaque on one of its walls commemorates the loss of the three crew who died in the aircraft – F/L W.D. Wright (pilot); A/S/L J.P. Liversidge RAAF (navigator); and F/Sgt A.D. Clarke (air gunner), who are buried in the Kraków Rakowicki Cemetery. Their Liberator, KG933, had taken off from its base at Foggia, Italy, at 1925 hours on 16 August 1944 on Operation Nida 504 to drop supplies on the DZ near Piotrków, some 120 kilometres north of Kraków. On its way home, KG933 was shot down by, it is believed, Oberfeldwebel Helmut Dahms, 1./NJG100, who claimed a 'Lancaster' in the approximate area at 0157 hours on 17 August. Three survived, F/L A.H. 'Digger' Hammet DFM, RAAF (see Appendix IV), Sgt Leslie J. Blunt (flight engineer) and Sgt F. Walter Helme (air gunner). By 29 August, the two sergeants had arrived with *Trupp 28* at Luft 7, some 150 kilometres north west of Kraków.

Another captured airman on 178 Squadron to arrive at Luft 7 was Sgt D.C. 'Des' Matthews, the sole survivor from Liberator KG938, which was lost on 20/21 August 1944 on an attack on the Reichswerke Aktiengesellschafte für Erzbergbau und Eisenhütten Hermann Göring at St Valentin and on the nearby Nibelungenwerk tank factory, near Linz, Austria. The raid was a failure. The factories suffered only slight damage – most of the bombs falling on woods two miles to the north – and four of the sixty-seven Wellingtons and two of the twenty Liberators despatched were lost.[125]

Des baled out through the manually-operated bomb-doors after KG938 had been coned by six searchlights and then hit by predicted flak. Three hours later he found himself hanging in a tree, with two broken ribs and a dislocated shoulder. Deciding, despite the pain from his injuries and one missing flying boot, to walk to Switzerland he was arrested by two Germans on their motorcycle combination. After a painful ride, he was thrown into the local prison, and was amazed, a while later, to be handed his missing boot. On the following day, after he had been patched up by a local doctor, he was escorted by a one-armed Luftwaffe officer to Frankfurt for interrogation and, after almost four weeks, was released to Luft 7, arriving with *Trupp 34* on 25 September.

\*

At 0326 hours on the morning of 25 July 1944 F/O C.M. Corbet RCAF landed a badly-damaged Lancaster, KB740, 428 (Ghost) Squadron, at RAF Woodbridge, Suffolk, an emergency airfield for crippled aircraft. Though the aircraft was a write-off, all the crew survived. The rear gunner, however, was missing. The rest of his crew feared that he must have somehow fallen to his death, for in the wreckage of the Lancaster were seven parachutes, one for each of them including the missing gunner. It was over a year later that they learnt of his fate.

Having taken off just after 9 pm on 24 July bound for Stuttgart with a load of 1,000lb bombs, Corbet and crew were flying at well over 20,000 feet en route to the target when they collided with another aircraft. KB740's bomb-doors were torn off, the starboard inner engine caught fire, all the propellers were bent, and the landing gear jammed. After bombs were dropped, the flight engineer, Sgt R.G. Enfield, calculated that there was sufficient fuel remaining to reach England provided that there were no leaks.

With flames streaming past his turret from the starboard wing rear gunner Sgt John Sandulak RCAF, hearing talk that a bale out was in order, needed no second bidding. Grabbing a parachute from its stowage in the fuselage, he clipped it on and jumped – too soon to hear Cecil Corbet say that there was a chance that the fire would go out, and that the order to jump was cancelled. Sandulak floated to safety and into the hands of an escape line, and was eventually taken to the special holding camp for evaders in Fréteval forest.

Back on the squadron, after leave, the Corbet crew acquired a replacement rear gunner, P/O R.E. Good RCAF. On 18/19 August, a month after the controlled crash at Woodbridge, the Corbet crew were on their way in Lancaster KB743 to bomb Bremen when the aircraft was hit, some of the crew believing by bombs from above, but it would appear that the Lancaster received a direct hit from heavy flak, and was set alight. Corbet this time had no hesitation in ordering the crew to bale out. All succeeded in taking to their parachutes, except for the rear gunner, whose turret had been blown off.[126]

Corbet and the two other surviving officers were taken prisoner and went to Stalag Luft III. Dick 'Shorty' Enfield and the other two NCOs – wireless operator Allan MacNaught RCAF and mid-upper gunner Tom Davidson RCAF – went to Luft 7 in *Trupp 28*.

**2 SEPTEMBER 1944.** A concert was held in the mess hall. 'Jock' Campbell was one of the solo singers. No water available in the evening as the system had 'gone for a burton'.

**3 SEPTEMBER 1944.** A cold but fine day. The 3 pm parade was prolonged when one man was found to be missing. A search revealed him fast asleep in his bunk.

Roman Catholic service held by Bob Lloyd.

*Trupp 29* (two men) arrived – Sergeant R.F. Gannon, and Sergeant Brian Wynne-Cole. Ronald Gannon had been shot down on 18/19 July 1944 (Revigny).[127] Two others of his crew – F/S E.H. Wells and F/S S.R. Ashton – had already arrived at Luft 7 in *Trupp 27*. Brian Wynne-Cole was lost on 5/6 June 1944 on Special Duties over France during the grandly-named Operation Titanic in support of the D-Day landings in Normandy.

As Gannon's POW number was 70445 and Wynne-Cole's 70217, it is possible that these were allocated at the same place, a camp in France. Another Luft 7 POW, F/Sgt D.A. 'Don' Farrington, had POW no. 80140, which was issued at Frontstalag 133 (Chartres), France, while Frank Collingwood, whose POW number was 80059, had spent some time at Frontstalag 122 (Compiègne). At least six other Luft 7 POWs, all captured in France, had POW numbers in the 80015-80162 range.

Don Farrington had been on the run for over three months when, on 11 June 1944, 'he and five other British servicemen were captured in woods' near Romorantin-Lanthenay, 'after they and the Resistance were surrounded by a force of 2,500 German troops, tanks, and artillery'.[128]

*

**4 SEPTEMBER 1944.** Labour Day, USA. All-day sports carnival in the camp. Began at 10 am and finished at 4.30 pm. John Tomney won the 100 metres and came second in the 200 metres.

*Trupp 30* (thirty-nine men) arrived.

*

Flying in support of main force on the night of 25/26 August 1944 (Rüsselsheim) were one or two of the specially-equipped B-17 Flying Fortresses of 214 (SD) Squadron based at RAF Oulton, Norfolk. The ten-man crew of Flying Fortress HB763 were in for a nasty shock when they were intercepted and shot down by a night-fighter.[129] Four were killed, and six taken prisoner. The pilot, W/O J.R. Lee, went to Stalag Luft 1 (Barth), and the wounded Sgt P. Barkess to Lazarett IXC (Obermassfeld). Navigator WO2 Gerald Gibbens RCAF suffered a compound fracture of the third lumbar vertebra on landing, though not sufficiently bad to warrant hospitalisation. Just over a week after being shot down he was at Luft 7 (POW no. 706). Three others of the crew joining him at Bankau were F/S John E.M. Pitchford (754), Sgt Patrick J. Curtis (697), and F/S A.C. Smith (720). Curtis and Smith were also in *Trupp 30*, but Pitchford for some reason followed them a fortnight or so later in *Trupp 33*.

*

South African squadrons, 31 SAAF and 34 SAAF, equipped with B-24 Liberators, flew fifty-five Warsaw supply missions between 13/14 August and 21/22 September 1944, completing twenty-one for the loss of nine aircraft.[130] A few flights had already been made earlier in August before it was the turn of ten Liberators of 31 (SAAF) Squadron on the night of 13/14 August 1944 to fly their first hazardous mission from Foggia to Warsaw.

Liberator EW105, flown by 2/Lt R. Klette SAAF and second pilot 2/Lt A. Faul SAAF, reached Warsaw, which the crew could see burning from forty miles away, without undue difficulty, but for the drop Klette had to come in at the detailed height of only 500 feet (150 metres) and at the slow speed of around 130 mph. Over the burning city the Germans opened up at the proverbial sitting-duck with everything they'd got, from pistols upwards. On board EW105 was the twenty-year-old English-born wireless operator, WO1 Eric Winchester SAAF: 'On fire and completely out of control the aircraft did an old-fashioned "belly flop" on what we later found out to be an airfield. We were machine-gunned on the ground and lost crew before being captured trying to reach the Poles.'

By 17 August Eric and his colleagues were at Dulag Luft. Eric's memories of his time there were bad:

> 'For instance, to be told that you are going to be shot as a saboteur because you won't or can't tell them what they want to know, and then to be taken back to a different cell than the one you had been in previously, and convinced that it is a cell for the condemned, you spend the next two or three days with your mind in dreadful turmoil while waiting to be taken out and shot. Eventually you realise that it was all a part of getting you to tell them what they wanted to know, in my case information about the acoustic mines we had dropped in the River Danube, and about which I knew absolutely nothing, and they never intended to shoot you anyway.'

On 29 August Eric and two of his crew, Henry Upton SAAF[131] and Ted Davis, were on their way to the Wetzlar transit camp, and on 1 September were escorted to Luft 7 in *Trupp 30*.

*

F/Sgt Daniel Dunkley, shot down on the night of 25/26 August 1944, landed some fifteen kilometres from Darmstadt. After walking for a few hours he was captured at around 3.30 am on 26 August. He was beaten up, and hit over the head with a rifle by the Bürgermeister of Leeheim. Another man, Adam Doerr, used his fists, a spade and a rifle butt so violently that the butt broke, while a third man, Wilhelm Reinhardt, viciously kicked him. Daniel, needless to say, was knocked unconscious.

Several hours later he was put aboard a passing lorry and taken to the outskirts of Darmstadt, where he was made to get out of the vehicle. As intended he was, again, attacked by the local population, but was rescued by a uniformed policeman and, at about 6 pm, handed over to a Luftwaffe Obergefreiter. Again attacked by this NCO and by yet more civilians, he was fortunate to reach the safety of Dulag Luft, where it was discovered that he had two broken ribs.

After the war Daniel's ill-treatment became the subject of a minor War Crimes trial, which resulted in Doerr and Reinhardt receiving five and two years' imprisonment respectively.

*

**5 SEPTEMBER 1944.** Red Cross parcel issue.

**6 SEPTEMBER 1944.** A very hot day. Den Blackford was sitting in his hut, reading, when he heard a voice saying: "Hello Den. How are you?" He looked up and there, standing before him, was Theo or 'Ted' Davis who, in happier times, lived at No. 89, Yew Tree Road, Southborough, Kent. Den lived at No. 69. Small world.

**7 AND 8 SEPTEMBER 1944.** After the first tunnel had been dug in July/August, a second was found in the refuse pit and under one of the huts. As a result, the camp was patrolled twenty-four hours a day, with more guards and dogs doing the rounds.

**10/11 SEPTEMBER 1944**. 'My gosh, it was cold last night and this morning (what's it going to be like in the winter? – hell's bells!)' (Tom Glenn.)

**11 SEPTEMBER 1944**. Just after dinner the air-raid siren went, and a large force of 'Yanks' were heard but not seen, flying high above the clouds.

**12 SEPTEMBER 1944.** Albert A. Kadler made another inspection of the camp, and was not unimpressed by what he found: 'Once the shortcomings, materially speaking, have been overcome by the removal of the prisoners of war to the new barracks, this camp can no doubt be considered as very good.' Kadler was told by Behr that the prisoners 'should be able to move to their new quarters on 20 September, 1944'. Kadler also observed that 'once completed [the new barracks] will give the best accommodation so far found in any prisoner of war camp in Germany'.

At Luft 7 on this day there were '890 British prisoners of war, RAF, RAAF, RCAF personnel (non-commissioned officers), of which seven are at Lamsdorf Lazarett, one at Kreuzburg hospital and one mental case at Loben hospital [Bruce Davis]'. Another prisoner, F/S Stan Silver RAAF (see page 102), was shortly to go to Stalag 344 (Lamsdorf) Lazarett for an operation on his left shoulder 'since the nerve specialist, Major Henderson, is again at Lamsdorf'.

*

**13 SEPTEMBER 1944.** After lunch the air-raid sirens went, and hundreds of American aircraft were seen, closely followed by heavy flak. Sure enough, one of them was hit, and the prisoners watched in horror as the stricken kite, in flames, dived vertically towards the ground.

*Trupp 31* (forty-three men) arrived.

*

Beaufighter-equipped 227 Squadron began disbanding on 15 July 1944. Four weeks later, on 12 August, the squadron would 'disappear', only to be re-born as 19 (SAAF) Squadron at Biferno, near Termoli, on the Adriatic coast of Italy. Though now officially a South African squadron it began its reincarnation much as before, that is to say with the RAF contingent leavened by South Africans.

Two days after the change, four of the squadron's Beaufighters, led by S/L Joseph Blackburn (43196), flew as fighter escort to 39 Squadron RAF on an attack on shipping in Senj harbour, across the Adriatic Sea in what is today Croatia. During the attack the starboard engine of the squadron leader's aircraft was hit, and he and his navigator, F/S Cecil Boffin, were forced to ditch about three kilometres east of Prvić Island. They were captured and interviewed in Sinj, and then in Budapest on 20 August. Ten days later Cecil was at Dulag Luft, Frankfurt, where he remained until 10 September. On 13 September he was walking through the gates of Stalag Luft VII in *Trupp 31*.[132]

*

**BETWEEN 14 AND 17 SEPTEMBER 1944**. *Trupp 32* (one man) arrived. F/S C.J. Collingwood was hot and tired after his long walk from Kreuzburg to Luft 7: 'As there were no other arrivals I was given a thorough search… I was billetted in a small wooden hut with six others who had all been captured since the invasion in June.'

Bert Collingwood had been shot down on the Schweinfurt raid on 24/25 February 1944 in Lancaster LM310, 61 Squadron. Most of the crew were on their twenty-ninth trip – just one more and they would have been tour expired: F/L Norman Webb DFC (pilot); P/O Pat Walkins (navigator); F/S Jack Bailey (bomb aimer); Cuthbert Collingwood (wireless operator); Sgt Johnny Brown (flight engineer); F/S Frank Emmerson DFM (mid-upper gunner); and F/S Jimmy Chapman (rear gunner). Emmerson, who was on his second tour and who had flown with F/L 'Jock' Reid VC, was a replacement for their usual mid-upper, 'Bluey' Purcell RAAF, who had been wounded on the Leipzig raid a few weeks earlier.

They were half an hour from Schweinfurt when trouble started: 'The only warning we had was the rattle of guns beneath us and we were in flames.' Bert Collingwood 'saw a flash, then something hit me in the face'. He managed to bale out, but remembered nothing until he found himself 'standing over a table with a uniformed German close by'. Soon the rest of his crew appeared, all that is except for Johnny Brown, who was killed, and Jack Bailey.

When Bert's face and head were heavily bandaged, he appreciated that he was in a bad way. After interrogation at Dulag Luft he was taken to the Hohe Mark hospital for treatment, but had to go to a hospital in Frankfurt for an operation on 17 March. After a further spell at the Hohe Mark he was sent to Obermassfeld, to be looked after by 'British' doctors, notably Major Cuffley and Captains Barley, Cooper and Leake (all Australian). With his eyes requiring attention, Bert was moved again, to Bad Soden hospital where Major Charters, a Scottish eye specialist, was in charge. Eventually, considered well enough to go to an ordinary POW camp, Bert left by train for Luft 7 with a solitary guard for company.

Somewhere along the route, having to change trains, Bert met a group of British soldiers. With Bert's home town being Hull, he asked them if anyone was from Yorkshire. It transpired that one amongst them was also from Hull, and he asked Bert if he knew anyone there called Collingwood. When Bert replied that that was his name the soldier said: 'Was Corporal Aidan Collingwood a relation of yours?' Yes. Aidan was Bert's brother, and had been killed in the fighting in North Africa on 14 or 15 June 1942. The soldier and Aidan had been pals together in the East Yorks Regiment.

Down the line the train stopped at Breslau, where the guard made it quite clear that this was his home town and that having a POW in his charge wasn't going to stop him from nipping off to see his wife and child. Bert went with him, and slept on the sofa in the guard's flat. In the morning the pair of them finished the journey to Kreuzburg, one no doubt happier than the other.

\*

**16 SEPTEMBER 1944**. Percy Sekine won the Stalag Luft VII Table Tennis Championship.

An evening concert given by the camp band and by a mouth-organ band was deemed to be a great success. Frank Sturgess sang a few songs, Jock Campbell sang The Holy City and Trees and, amongst other acts, there was a comic monologue on The Second Front.

**18 SEPTEMBER 1944**. Some deer were seen wandering past the camp. 'A nice piece of venison would go down very nicely right now' was the thought of Tom Glenn.

An England v Scotland soccer match ended in a 2-2 draw. It was reckoned by some to have been the best match ever seen at the camp, others that England were lucky to get the draw.

*Trupp 33* (forty-three men) arrived.

Rear gunner F/S Jim Bray thought that flak was the cause of their demise, but bomb aimer Sgt Lloyd Brooks RCAF reported after the war to his home-town newspaper, *The Paris Star*, that 'suddenly a plane rose out of the darkness and crashed into us'. The damage was serious enough, however, for the skipper, F/O Ralph Arnold RCAF, to give the order to bale out, which all seven of the crew were able to do. Lost in Lancaster LM638, 44 (Rhodesia) Squadron, on the night of 12/13 July 1944 (Culmont/ Chalindrey), they crashed near Recey-sur-Ource, a dozen miles north west of Mortière in eastern France, having possibly collided with Lancaster LM221 (F/O W.A.M. Hallett RCAF), 9 Squadron.

Five of them – Arnold, Bray, Brooks, Sgt Bill Lamb RCAF (mid-upper gunner), and Sgt Leslie Wharton (navigator) – managed to evade capture. Sgt Ken Green (wireless operator) and Sgt Ron Royle (flight engineer) did not. Ron:

'landed unhurt in a thick wood near Langres at about 0200 hours. After hiding my parachute etc., I lay up until first light and then made my way along a path through the wood until I reached a woodman's hut. Here I lay at a safe distance until a man came out and walked along the path in my direction. I intercepted him and told him who I was. He was quite friendly and took me to his hut where he gave me some food and articles of civilian dressing.

'A few hours later he fetched his brother who was a member of the local Resistance movement. Unfortunately he spoke no English, so he left after promising to return in the evening with an interpreter.

'That afternoon I went out with my friend, who was a charcoal burner, to help him with his work and on our return a patrol of about ten German soldiers surrounded the hut and I was captured.'[133]

During his evasion Ralph Arnold was 'told by members of the FFI that Sgt Green of my crew together with two of his helpers had been captured by the Germans'. It was on 17 August that Ken 'entered the bag'. A month later he was at Luft 7 in *Trupp 32* or *33*. Ron's progress, though, had been much swifter, having reached Bankau on 26 July in *Trupp 15*.

*

When crossing the Jylland peninsula on the return flight from Königsberg on the night of 28/29 August 1944 Lancaster PB436 was hit by flak and crashed at Gunderup Gaard farm, Denmark, just after 2 am. All seven crew managed to bale out before the aircraft crashed. Sgt E. Harris (flight engineer), Sgt F.E. Finch (bomb aimer), Sgt D.A. Bragg (wireless operator), Sgt J.C. Longhurst (mid-upper gunner) and Sgt W.G. Winkley (rear gunner) were soon captured and, after about a week at Dulag Luft, were sent to Luft 7, possibly arriving with *Trupp 33* on 18 September.

The other two of the crew – F/Sgt B.F. Loneon RAAF (pilot) and Sgt H.W.D. Wilson (navigator) – were helped to Sweden on 12 September 1944 by members of the Speditørerne group, specialists in helping people to escape to Sweden.[134] Within days the British Consul had arranged for them to fly back in a Mosquito to Britain.

*

**19 SEPTEMBER 1944.** Camp visited by German generals.

**22 SEPTEMBER 1944.** More Red Cross parcels arrived. Another tunnel was found in one of the school rooms. The Germans simply boarded it up, and the commandant said that if it happened again he would close the library and remove all musical instruments.

**23 SEPTEMBER 1944.** 'We have a lot of air raids around here and the other day, while a formation of American Fortresses was going over, one of them got hit by flak and came straight down. I don't think anyone got out because we didn't see any parachutes. So I guess another good crew went west.' (Laird MacLean RCAF.)

This B-17 has not been identified, but at this time they were being used on supply missions from England to Warsaw. For example, B-17G 43-38175 (1/Lt Francis E. Akins USAAF), 390th BG/568th BS, Eighth Air Force, was shot down by flak on 18 September 1944 over Poland flying on the seventh and last of the Frantic supply missions to Warsaw. Six of the nine crew were killed in action, two became POWs, while the ninth (the tail gunner) was murdered on the ground.

**24 SEPTEMBER 1944.** 'Low-hanging clouds, rain and very cool. These conditions will be no help to the boys already down with colds and the flu... An alert at noon. The Forts were heading north-east. During the alert someone made a dash for the latrine. A guard shot at him.' (John McConnell RCAF.)

**25 SEPTEMBER 1944.** A strong gale blew in the night, prisoners wondering whether or not their huts would take off! It was later reckoned that this was the coldest day so far.

*Trupp 34* (around eighty men) arrived.

\*

'I can still remember quite clearly the perfect weather conditions, and the parachute descent was like being in the front stalls at the theatre!' Thus observed former navigator Dr Deryck Lambert almost fifty years after he had had to bale out of his Lancaster. With F/O George Bradburn at the controls Lancaster ND702 'G-George', 35 (PFF) Squadron, was airborne from RAF Graveley, Cambridgeshire, at around 4.30 pm on the afternoon of 11 September 1944 on a daylight raid to the oil refinery at Gelsenkirchen. It was a measure of the Allies' aerial supremacy that RAF Bomber Command was now able to fly over Germany in broad daylight, just as the USAAF had been doing for two years, though latterly heavily escorted by fighters.

Nearing the target F/O Bradburn took 'G-George' up to 18,000 feet, but then:

> '... as we started our run on to the target, diving to 17,200 feet, the flak began to come up at us – huge brown puffs of smoke. We could hear the dull "woofs" and felt the concussion of the explosions – it was very near. The bomb aimer reported that he could see the [target] markers and we started our bombing run, being continually hit by flak. At 1826½ we bombed our target and started our photo run. The flak was too accurate for this so we turned for home, weaving all over the sky.' (Deryck Lambert.)

The two gunners – twenty-year-old Sergeant Frederick John Feakins (mid-upper) and F/S Randolph 'Dusty' Rhodes (rear) – reported that the 'kite [looked] like a pepper pot full of holes' and that one of the engines had stopped. Then, at 6.31 pm, immediately behind ND702, another bomber blew up (probably Lancaster ND534, 156 [PFF] Squadron, with no survivors). The terrific explosion shook G-George. A fire broke out behind Deryck's navigation table, and by the time that the skipper had ordered the crew to bale out the aircraft was in a dive. As it was too hot in the nose for Deryck to bale out from the front hatch he made his way with extreme difficulty to the rear door. Just as he reached it Dusty Rhodes jumped out, leaving Arthur Britchford (wireless operator) and Freddie Feakins 'frozen' by the door. Deryck signalled frantically for them to go but, when they didn't, he 'knelt on the step, put my hand on the rip-cord and let myself go'.

As he came down 'the noise from the ground and the sky around was terrific. I saw the kite flying in a shallow spiral dive towards the target, but no more 'chutes appeared. I could see Dusty's 'chute about fifty feet below.' Despite the tremendous volume of flak shells bursting all around them and, nearer the ground, small-arms fire passing very close to them, Deryck and Dusty were the only two to survive. It will never be known why the mid-upper gunner and wireless operator never jumped, but they died with their skipper, bomb aimer and flight engineer.

ND702 and ND534 crashed close to each other. On 27 December 1944 the Air Ministry Casualty department wrote to George Bradburn's wife regretting that they had no news of her husband: 'Reports have been received from the International Red Cross Committee at Geneva regarding the occupants of two aircraft which were missing as a result of the attack on Gelsenkirchen.' The Air Ministry letter added that, unfortunately, 'the reports have mixed the crews and state that Flight Sergeant R. Rhodes and Flight Sergeant D.M. Lambert were captured on 11 September...'

Deryck Lambert landed in a wood, surrounded by flak batteries. His only problem, physically, were his hands, which were numb from the cold and which were agony when blood started to flow through them again. Managing to light a cigarette, he was contemplating his future when he heard shouts and whistles, and made off deeper into the wood, his progress slowing somewhat as it grew darker. After three or four hours he emerged into a clearing but, without realising it, had stumbled into a German sentry guarding one of the searchlight batteries. The guard took him to a hut where 'in one corner of the floor lay a heap of flying clothing with Dusty's name on it'.

Another guard was summoned, and he 'put one up the spout' in such a way as to make it quite clear to his prisoner, as they began to walk off into the distance, that he would stand no nonsense. Deryck for his part thought that his last hour on this earth had come. Happily, he was quite alive when he was taken to the HQ of 24th Battery, 4th Flak Division where, to his delight, he found Dusty, who had already been there for two hours.

In the morning, having spent a very cold and uncomfortable night on the hard floor, they were put in a lorry and taken to Essen. With them was a very badly-wounded French airman whose condition – he was wounded to his head and hands and had a badly-strained side – made their 'blood boil... as he should have had medical attention long ago'. The Frenchman was probably Adjutant R.N. Oger, rear gunner of Halifax NA606, 347 (Tunisie) Free French Squadron, which had also been shot down on the Gelsenkirchen raid.

Oger's survival was something of a 'miracle' ('...se sauva par miracle'). Only able to extricate himself from his turret with difficulty he free-fell thousands of feet from his doomed Halifax while attempting to clip his parachute onto its harness. Barely feet from the ground he succeeded – 'quelques secondes avant le contact fatal avec le sol'.[135]

After they had been searched and questioned, to no effect, the three were taken to an airfield near Düsseldorf where, at last, the Frenchman was removed to a hospital. On 13 September Deryck and Dusty 'were taken by two Luftwaffe goons through Düsseldorf to the station. It was a wizard sight. Every building had been hit and the place was in a hell of a mess.' Next day they were in Frankfurt, which had had a visit from Bomber Command only the night before. It was, as Deryck noted, 'worse than Düsseldorf – the only bricks that were left standing were those in piles on the roadway! Here a goon officer said he would take no responsibility for the actions of the civilian population, one of whom gave me a hell of a kick up the backside.' These were bad times for Allied aircrew in Germany, when many a prisoner was lynched by civilians and soldiers, deliberately provoked to take such action by their demented leaders.

At Dulag Luft, Deryck and Dusty were given the usual interrogation and the 'if you don't tell us everything, I'll have you shot as a spy' routine. They both went to Wetzlar transit camp on 18 September, before reaching Bankau on 25 September in *Trupp 34*. It was a shock to see that their quarters were 'huts the size of hen huts, six men to a hut'.

René Oger, after a spell in hospital, arrived at Luft 7 with *Trupp 39* on 12 October.

\*

After all he had been through one man who was, perhaps, quite glad to be at Luft 7 was Czechoslovakian fighter pilot Karel Valášek, another to arrive with *Trupp 34* His harrowing story began on the morning of 21 May 1944, when he took off in Spitfire MJ663, NN-B, on 'Ramrod 905' to northern France (basically, an authorised rampage against a number of enemy targets). The primary objective of Karel and his fellow 310 Squadron pilots was Caen airfield, after which they were free to attack German transportation – goods trains and lorries etc – in the Caumont-l'Eventé area. His day's duty done, Karel was on his way home at zero feet when the engine of his Spitfire was hit by light flak near the town of Balleroy. With smoke billowing from the now useless Merlin engine, Karel was forced down in the Forêt de Cerisy.

A little bruised, but otherwise unhurt, he hastily departed in a southerly direction. After two days he stopped a lady cyclist in a country lane. When he enquired about the number of Germans in the area she asked why he wanted to know. Telling her that he was an RAF evader she cycled to a nearby village and, about three quarters of an hour later, came back with a man with a horse and cart. Hidden in the cart with straw and potato sacks, Karel was taken to a farm where he was met by three slightly nervous men: 'They questioned me, fed me, and then locked me up in a room in the loft. The following evening, I was brought down, and introduced to the chief of the Resistance in that area, named Monsieur Pique.'[136]

Once his identity had been confirmed, Karel was welcomed and invited to stay, but when German troops were billetted in the area after the Normandy landings he decided to head for Gibraltar, as one of his flight commanders had managed to do in 1942.[137] On 20 June M. Pique showed Karel and two evading Canadian soldiers the way to Caen but, after M. Pique had left them, a German officer and a number of soldiers suddenly blocked their path. The officer demanded to know who they were and what they were doing there. Karel replied that they worked there. Not satisfied with that, the officer had them put under guard in an empty house.

They had gone in through the back door, which was then watched, leaving the front door without a guard! Seizing their chance the three prisoners simply crept out through the front door. When the alarm was quickly raised Karel jumped into a thick hedge, and never saw the two Canadians again. He spent an uncomfortable night there, with Allied artillery bombarding nearby fields. In the morning, as he crawled away, he noticed that he was on the edge of a minefield, in which there were a number of dead animals. Hearing German voices he tried to hide once more in the undergrowth, but his feet were sticking out, and he was caught – on the front line in civilian clothes. An SS officer who had been brought to interrogate him handed him over to the Gestapo as a spy. The future for Karel did not look good. Put in the dungeon of a fort at Alençon, he spent ten days 'in a black cell with unpleasant bouts of interrogation' before being moved to Fresnes prison, Paris. He endured further interrogation at the Gestapo HQ in Avenue Foch, Paris before he and a number of other 'civilian' airmen were taken to a prison in Wiesbaden, Germany. Finally moved to a civilian prison in Mainz, by which time there were about forty of them in civilian clothes, Karel's weight had fallen dramatically from fourteen stone to barely eight.

At the end of August the forty or so airmen were taken to Mainz railway station, handcuffed in two 'chains' of twenty. Despite instructions from a member of the Feldpolizei to go to another part of the station, the Gestapo man in charge of Karel's chain mistakenly put them on a train which already had POWs aboard. The train eventually took Karel and his fellow prisoners to Frankfurt, and to Dulag Luft. As for the other chain of twenty, Karel was informed after the war by the Air Ministry that they were sent to a civilian concentration camp where they perished.

By the time that Karel finally reached Luft 7, on 25 September, he was officially an officer. He had been commissioned (176089) by the AOC of 84 Group, 2 TAF, a month before he was shot down, but this was not shown in the *London Gazette* for fear of compromising family and relatives in his homeland. It is likely that the Germans never got to know that he was an officer, and should, therefore, have been removed from Luft 7.

Joining him there in due course were two more of his countrymen, Antonín Ocelka and Gustav Přístupa, both shot down by flak whilst serving on 312 (Czechoslovakian) Squadron. Ocelka had been escorting Dakotas to Moerdijk Bridge at Eindhoven on 18 September, and Přístupa was strafing two trains on 11 August 1944 when he was hit. His drop-tank was still attached when he went in to attack, and as a result he was unable to recover from the spin induced by the flak blast. His Spitfire, ML240, turned over when it touched the ground and came to rest upside down and on fire in a field. Though injured, he managed to get out, but was taken prisoner. After treatment at a Lazarett he was released to Luft 7 in what was possibly *Trupp 41* (22 October).

Antonín Ocelka had arrived at Luft 7 a fortnight earlier in *Trupp 38* (7 October).

\*

Lancaster ND613, 103 Squadron, was barely 2,000 feet above Normandy on 14 August 1944 when it blew up. The only survivor was F/S Dugald MacTaggart, the bomb aimer. Their targets, which they were told to bomb from a height of only 6,000 feet, were enemy Panzer units at Fontaine-le-Pin.

As ND613 arrived over the target a fierce bombardment was under way on the ground. Needing to achieve accuracy following an earlier bombing attack that had gone wrong, the skipper, F/L J.P.D. Bartleet told his crew that he was taking ND613 down to 2,100 feet, and bombs were dropped.

Dugald MacTaggart: 'Within seconds [Sgt K.] Chiles, our mid-upper gunner, called out that the a/c had been hit and the starboard engines were on fire. It was immediately evident that the situation was hopeless, and the pilot gave the order to bale out.' After removing the escape hatch with some difficulty Dugald jumped, but no sooner had he pulled the parachute's rip-cord than the Lancaster exploded. None of the others stood a chance.

Unfortunately for Dugald he landed on the wrong side of the lines, and was quickly captured. At a nearby château, which was being used as a medical centre, Dugald was treated for minor burns to his left leg and right hand. He was still with his German captors when they slipped through the so-called 'Falaise Gap', eventually reaching a hospital at Bernay: 'There I met up with five Allied troops including S/Ldr Tommy Brannagan, an RCAF pilot who had operated from an airfield at Bayeux.'[138] Several days later the wounded, under constant attack from the air, found themselves at a hospital (St Katherine's?) in Brussels: 'This hospital,' said Dugald, 'had a ward in the form of wooden huts for Allied airmen.'

They were evacuated on the very day on which Brussels was liberated, 3 September. Despite the Belgian Resistance believing that they were Germans and giving the Allied wounded 'some hair-raising experiences!', MacTaggart and Brannagan were escorted via Venlo, Holland, to a POW camp at Düsseldorf, before going to Dulag Luft (then in the park in Frankfurt-am-Main) and to Wetzlar. Here they parted, Tommy Brannagan going to Stalag Luft III (Sagan), while Dugald MacTaggart arrived at Luft 7 with *Trupp 34* on 25 September.

On 13 June 1944 the first Fieseler Fi103, the V1 'buzz bomb' or 'doodlebug', exploded on English soil. 9,521 V1s were fired at England, until the last site in range was overrun in October 1944. A further 2,448 were then directed against the vital port of Antwerp and other Belgian targets, and it was only on 29 March 1945, when the last site had been captured, that the V1 attacks finally ended, having caused almost 23,000 casualties, mostly civilian.

On 28 August 1944 550 Squadron, at RAF North Killingholme, Lincolnshire, was ordered to put up ten aircraft for an attack on the flying-bomb site at Wemaers-Cappel, in northern France. For the crew of Lancaster PA991, 'E-Easy', it was to be their tenth attack on a V1 site, and their thirty-third whilst on the squadron, after which they would be tour expired.

P/O S.C. Beeson (pilot); Sgt K.J.R. 'Red' Hewlett (flight engineer); Squadron Leader Kevin MacAleavey (navigator, and 'A' Flight commander); F/S Derrick 'Ted' Neal (bomb aimer); Sgt J.K. Norgate (WOP/AG); Sgt H.S. Picton (mid-upper gunner); and Sgt J.A. Trayhorn (rear gunner), had joined 550 Squadron from No. 1 Lancaster Finishing School on 24 May 1944, and had flown their first operation on 5/6 June (Crisbecq coastal battery) in support of the Normandy landings. Kevin MacAleavey had been commissioned on 5 May 1942. Already a flying officer by December of that year, his promotion to squadron leader came in March 1944.[139] Stanley Christmas Beeson was commissioned (175515) on 13 June 1944.

It was still daylight at about 7 pm on the evening of 28 August 1944 when the skipper of E-Easy made a 'dummy' run over the target at 9,000 feet. Coming in again the Lancaster received a direct and fatal hit from a flak shell on its port side. For the three crew in the rear of the aircraft – Norgate (aged twenty), Picton (twenty-two) and Trayhorn (age not known) – it was the end of their young lives.[140]

Bomb aimer Ted Neal baled out at around 6,000 feet. His first contact with something solid proved to be the window of a French farmhouse near the village of Esquelbecq, a dozen kilometres north of Wemaers-Cappel, near Dunkirk. Though he saw the farmhouse looming large before him and tried to break his fall on a small bush, he overshot and hit the window with his head and right arm. Suffering cuts from the glass to his head and wrist, he was otherwise OK when captured by German soldiers.

Two days after the loss of E-Easy, Esquelbecq was overrun by the British Army, too late for the four survivors, who had been captured. The two officers went to Stalag Luft I (Barth), while Red Hewlett and Ted Neal went to Luft 7 in *Trupp 34*.

*

**28/29 SEPTEMBER 1944**. The POWs finally received their 'dog tags'. Mail also arrived for the first time for the first seventy kriegies.

*Trupp 35* (possibly two men) probably arrived around the end of the month. It is believed, whoever they were, that they were given POW numbers 828 and 829. The latter, though, may have been given to F/S J.S. Tames RCAF, who lost some of his toes after falling asleep in snow after he had baled out on 19/20 February 1944.

**30 SEPTEMBER 1944**. Weather getting noticeably colder. Another concert was held, and again it was well received.

CHAPTER EIGHT
# OCTOBER 1944, *TRUPPEN 36-46(?)*;
# ARNHEM; MOVE TO NEW COMPOUND

**1 OCTOBER 1944.** *Trupp 36* (possibly only two men) arrived. As with *Trupp 35*, no names are known for sure.

It was a windy day, and several POWs who had been making kites decided to give them an airing. The guards greatly enjoyed the activity, pointing out the ones that caught their eye.

During the course of the week Red Cross parcels began to arrive – 'none too early either – there are 2,000 of them down at Bankau station. Also some American sports kit such as softballs and netballs.' (Elwyn Healy.)

Rained late in the day and most of the night. Darkness now falling by 6 pm.

**3 OCTOBER 1944.** *Trupp 37* (approximately fifty, including ten GPR, men) arrived.

*

The airmen-soldiers of the Glider Pilot Regiment (GPR) of the Army Air Corps, were trained to fly gliders and to fight as infantrymen once they had landed their aircraft. Most of the Luft 7 arrivals had been captured in late September 1944 following Operation Market, the broad objective of which:

'Was to capture and hold the crossings over the canals and rivers that lay on the British Second Army's axis of advance from inclusive Eindhoven to inclusive Arnhem. The British and Poles were to capture the bridges at Arnhem and to establish a bridgehead around them so that the Second Army, led by the Guards Armoured Division, could pass through without delay on their advance northwards.'

The British forces for the Arnhem part of Market were HQ Airborne Corps (commanded by Lieutenant-General 'Boy' Browning); 1st Airborne Division (Maj-Gen R.E. Urquhart CB, DSO); and 1st Polish Paratroop Brigade (Maj-Gen S. Sosabowski). The other part of Market involved the area to the south of Arnhem being seized and held by the US Airborne 82nd Division (Brig. Gen. James M. Gavin) and 101st Division (Maj. Gen. Maxwell D. Taylor): 'The 82nd was to capture the crossings at Nijmegen and Grave and to hold the high ground between Nijmegen and Groesbeek. The 101st was to seize the bridges and defiles between Eindhoven and Grave.'[141]

Operation Garden – the British Second Army's advance from the general line of the Albert and Escaut Canals in Belgium – would be carried out in conjunction with Market. The planned finish of this advance would be at the Zuider Zee, a distance of about 158 kilometres (ninety-nine miles). The Second Army had already advanced some 280 miles/450 kilometres in the fortnight up to 11 September 1944, but the advance to Arnhem 'was to be made on a very narrow front, with only one road most of the way'. (Brereton.) This single road would prove to be the undoing of the combined operation.

The British element of Market began at around 0940 hours on 17 September 1944, when the first wave of gliders were towed off English runways. Taking off forty-five minutes later were twelve Stirling aircraft carrying 186 men of the 21st Independent Parachute Company, who were to mark the drop zones (DZ) and landing zones (LZ) for the airborne forces who were to follow. Between 0940 and 1140 hours on 17 September:

'304 Horsas, thirteen Hamilcars and four Hadrians were lifted from the operational glider airfields. The combinations [of tug aircraft and glider] were bound for LZs 'S' and 'Z', and the gliders were carrying Divisional Headquarters; 1st Air-Landing Brigade Headquarters; elements of 1st Battalion, the Border Regiment, 2nd Battalion, the South Staffordshire Regiment, and 7th Battalion the King's Own Scottish Borderers (KOSB); 1st Air-Landing Anti-tank Battery; 1st Air-Landing Light Regiment RA; 9th Field Company RE; 17-pounder anti-tank guns; heavy American radio equipment in the Hadrians; and Field Ambulance units.'[142]

As there were insufficient aircraft and gliders to take everyone in one lift the operation would have to be spread over three days.

In Brereton's words 'Market was the greatest airborne operation ever attempted. The Troop Carrier fleet which took off numbered 1,544 planes and 478 gliders. In all, twenty-six bases, nine British and seventeen American, were used. It took an hour and a half for all the aircraft to be airborne.' In support of this vast aerial armada were bombers and fighters of the RAF and USAAF:

'54 Lancasters and 5 Mosquitoes started working over the known flak positions. Then 85 Lancasters and 15 Mosquitoes attacked three coastal batteries on Walcheren [Island]. Then came 816 Fortresses, escorted by 161 Mustangs and 212 P-47s from the Ninth [Air Force] attacking 117 flak positions just before the Troop Carriers arrived. The airborne armada was protected by 371 Tempests, Spitfires, and Mosquitoes, and 548 Thunderbolts, Mustangs, and Lightnings.' (Brereton.)

Facing these aircraft were some thirty German fighters, seven of which were destroyed.

The air lift started badly on D-Day, 17 September, when an explosion blew the tail off Horsa glider RJ113. In the resultant and inevitable crash near Paulton, Somerset, twenty-one sappers of No. 1 Platoon 9th (Airborne) Field Company Royal Engineers and the two GPR pilots, S/Sgt L.J. Gardner and co-pilot Sgt R.A. Fraser of 'D' Squadron, were killed. The tug, Stirling LK148, 299 Squadron, returned to its base at Keevil, Wiltshire.

Considering the enormity of the air lift, however, it went reasonably smoothly, though nineteen-year-old GPR Sergeant Bill Oakes got quite a shock. When crossing...

'the North Sea on tow at 3,000 feet with the first pilot [S/Sgt Bert Watkins] in control I left the cockpit [of the Horsa glider] to make the usual inspection in the fuselage and was horrified to see the Air Landing Brigade Troopers [of the KOSB] making a brew of tea in a dixie can. Considering it was a plywood floor and there was a cargo of mortar bombs close by I reckon we were fortunate to reach the LZ in Holland.'

After landing safely at LZ 'S' near Wolfheze, and while waiting 'to group up for the march into Arnhem', Bill Oakes 'collected a picture postcard as a souvenir, showing a photo of a local chicken farm'. When taken prisoner a couple of days later his captors, having found the incriminating postcard about his person, kept him in solitary confinement and interrogated him 'for a whole week in an attempt to find out the significance of the photo'.

After he had landed safely with his first pilot S/Sgt Edwin Healey GPR at the controls of their Horsa, LH288, Sgt Arthur Rigby, second pilot, was wiping the dust from his face when he saw two other gliders arrive. The first was a Hamilcar which, for some reason, came in cross-wind. The moment it touched down its wheels dug in to the soft ground and its tail flipped over the nose – 'no-one escaped that crash'. The second 'was a Horsa that overshot, leapt over the railway embankment [on the edge of the landing zone], and ended up in some trees on the other side'. The two pilots were killed, but those in the fuselage survived.

At RAF Tarrant Rushton, Dorset, Sgt George H. Kilbryde GPR had watched as the four-engined Halifax tugs took off with their attached gliders on D-Day and D+1, 17 and 18 September. All the tugs returned to base. On D+2, 19 September, with the weather at first not good for flying, it was George's turn to go: 'Rose at 7.30 am. Had breakfast. Everyone is at fever pitch but try not to show it.' An hour and a half later they had their final briefing. The first two lifts had reported only light flak and no fighters to speak of, so today's mission would be a 'NAAFI' trip. Confidence was sky high, heightened even further by the news that 'Arnhem and the bridges are reported to have been taken already. All we want now is for the 2nd Army to get up there in time.'

At the briefing George, his first pilot, Lieutenant R.H. Conchie (304609),[143] and the other pilots were told that the first of twenty-eight Horsa gliders (pilot Major E.H. Leschalles, flight commander) would take off at 12.20 pm, the rest following at ten-second intervals. Further orders would be given on landing at their destination, Strip 'L', where fifteen Horsas from RAF Keevil would be joining them. George Kilbryde describes the scene at Tarrant Rushton airfield:

> 'Sandwiches and tea on the runway. All gliders and tugs drawn up on the runway. Tugs (Halifaxes) already warming up. The whole station has turned out to see us off. A WAAF truck driver whose boy friend is a gunner in our tug is crying. Our glider is in perfect condition (it's a brand new one). The cargo is well lashed in – one Jeep, one trailer (both loaded), two motorcycles. We are also carrying a cpl and three privates, all Poles. They are already in their seats, and as we watch the first glider "train" take off we start to move ourselves. Well, this is it, and we will soon know what's what.'

The gliders from Tarrant Rushton were to carry men of the Polish Parachute Brigade, and their equipment, but only twenty-one of the gliders were going, not the twenty-eight as briefed, and towing them were ten Halifaxes of 298 Squadron and eleven Halifaxes of 644 Squadron. Take-off, according to records, lasted from 12.05 to 12.16 pm. The earlier poor weather had only relented somewhat in the West Country. Others elsewhere in England who were scheduled to go to Arnhem that day had to abandon.

After forming-up over Tarrant Rushton the twenty-one tug and glider combinations set course, via Hatfield, to the north of London before swinging south and out over the North Sea, where they were joined by, probably, only twelve of the fifteen tugs (nine Stirlings of 196 Squadron and six of 299 Squadron) and gliders that had taken off from Keevil in Wiltshire. One of the 196 Squadron combinations had parted company over Buckinghamshire, and another two suffered engine trouble and did not leave British airspace.

Over the sea the weather began to deteriorate, low cloud forcing Lieutenant Conchie and George Kilbryde to follow their tug down to only 300 feet above sea level. 'This left us on our own, for the others went above it. We saw three American Wacos[144] and two Horsas go down into the sea. A German "flak" ship was engaged by British destroyers, but did not attempt to attack us at all. Passed over the coast at Ostend at 200 feet. There was still no sign of the others.'

Even had they spotted them, there were now even fewer tug/glider combinations heading for Arnhem. The tow rope of Stirling LK505 (196 Squadron) and its glider broke, forcing the latter to ditch some thirty-five kilometres off the Belgian coast. This may well have been one of the two Horsas that George and company saw going down into the sea. The other may have been one that was on tow with a 190 Squadron Stirling from RAF Fairford and which was obliged to ditch off

Ostend when its tow-rope snapped. Though four other tow ropes parted, the gliders managed to land in Belgium.

After a while, the Conchie/Kilbryde glider and their tug re-established contact with the rest of the lift, and 'we climbed to 2,000 feet and were now at the rear of the flight'. As they neared their destination at Arnhem they 'ran into fierce flak. All the tugs and gliders began weaving but two combinations were hit, one of them smashing itself to pieces on the ground. Its tail-unit had been shot away and its nose dived in, a pretty sickening sight, no hope at all for the occupants.'

This awful sight could have done nothing for morale, which was not to be improved when the remaining gliders landed near Arnhem, as George noted:

> 'In all I saw five gliders come adrift and go down before we reached the LZ [Landing Zone "L"]. Then they really let us have it. One glider after another was hit, including ourselves; they struck us somewhere near the main wheels, but nothing serious. The LZ was a ploughed field. It was marked by paratroops with red and green flares and a smoke-signal. At 3.30 pm we made a bumpy landing, smashing in the nose-wheel. All on board were unharmed however.'

Covering the landing of the gliders were a corporal and the thirty-eight men left out of a company of 7th (Galloway) King's Own Scottish Borderers (KOSB), part of 1st Airlanding Brigade.[145] The enemy, though, were already firing on the LZ. As George and his team tried to unload their Horsa they were greeted by a hail of bullets:

> 'They hit the bike and the glider but none of us was hit, and we took cover. The Hun was in possession of the top end of the field. He kept up his firing, so Lt Conchie and I dashed across the field to the edge of the wood and took up position, he with a Sten gun and myself with a rifle. The Poles were not keen to follow us and soon they disappeared. The KOSB then retreated, but Lt Conchie elected to stay.'

The already-poor situation for George and his lieutenant, caught between the fire of friend and foe alike, worsened when a nearby farmhouse was set alight. Then the trees under which George and Conchie were sheltering caught fire, and burning branches began to fall on them. At this point they decided to withdraw to Divisional HQ, but not until darkness. The Germans were continually mortaring the area but, despite the noise and confusion, the two tried to get some sleep.

At around 6 pm, with one last look at the LZ strewn with lifeless bodies, they moved off, taking only their weapons and a little food: 'We had hardly gone fifty yards before Lt Conchie, standing on a slight rise, was called upon to surrender.' Spotting four Germans the two glider pilots realised they had no chance. As they were led away, on pain of death should they try to escape, they 'passed dozens of Airborne chaps, dead, and plenty of dead Germans too'.

They then met up with S/Sgt Charles Bryce GPR, who had also flown from Tarrant Rushton and who was also destined to go to Luft 7, in *Trupp 38*. George gave Charles Bryce a hand with a wounded paratrooper, Cpl Wright, who had been hit in the lungs and arms, taking him to a German first-aid station. The prisoners, some fifty or so and mostly Airborne, were taken to an unoccupied villa and searched. There was one other glider pilot there, Sgt Maurice R. Pepper.

Having spent an uncomfortable night on the stone floor of an air-raid shelter, George and the other prisoners were marched off towards Zutphen, some twenty-five kilometres away: 'There were about 150 of us; RAF, AAC, and even one or two sailors who came as wireless mechanics, also a war correspondent.' One of the RAF lads walked the whole way in a pair of slippers – 'he stuck it out well' was George's comment. At around 5 pm that evening the tired and hungry party arrived at a barn at Zutphen: 'There were quite a number there already, under the orders of a British major. There was no food for us, but there was some straw for us to sleep on.'

On 21 September, having been fed at last, the 400 or so prisoners were crammed into a train of cattle trucks, fifty or so per truck, minus their boots which they had had to remove. Two hours later the train began its journey to Germany. There was little room in which to sit down, and the floor was covered in dust and potato peelings. No food was issued throughout 22 September, and the only water collected was rain water. Sometime on the morning of 23 September the train made its way through Cologne. Peering through cracks, the prisoners could see it 'was absolutely devastated'. Food was provided in the afternoon, one loaf of black bread per truck and a little water.

Progress through the war-torn country was painfully slow, and on 24 September it was reckoned that they were travelling south and parallel to the Rhine. Even though they were given five more loaves and more water morale was beginning to waver, and then 'the guards fired at someone. We don't know who. We have given up guessing about when we are likely to arrive.' One more night, their fourth, was spent in the trucks before, mercifully, the train came to a stop at Limburg an der Lahn. 'What a sight everyone looks. Got our boots back and marched one mile to a transit camp (Stalag 12A, Limburg).'

The glider pilots were separated from the RAF, and put on a coach for the Luftwaffe interrogation centre at Oberursel, some fifty kilometres to the south east of Limburg. They arrived at around 9 pm.: 'Divided into groups of 5 and put into a heated cell for the night. It had no beds at all, just five or six stools.' In the morning, 26 September, George and his fellow prisoners were put on a train to the Luftwaffe's transit camp at Wetzlar, 'heaven itself. Had a hot shower (three mins), new underclothes, two towels, shaving tackle, soap, forty cigarettes, and had first good meal in a week.'

Two days later George Kilbryde and the others – fifteen glider pilots and thirty-three RAF aircrew – embarked by train on the last leg of their long journey to Luft 7: 'It is a good train, plush seats and plenty of them. We each have a Red Cross parcel, plenty of bread and hot drinks.' George also had 150 cigarettes. But all day next day they headed eastwards until, late on 1 October, the train came to a halt at Bankau. As usual, it was not until the morning that they were let out and marched to the camp, when *Trupp 37* was registered.

*

Arriving in Cairo in the summer of 1944 a number of RNZAF and RAAF pilots found themselves billetted on the Heliopolis Hotel, which was largely reserved for aircrew on leave or for those in transit. They had not long been there when a notice was posted on the hotel's famous notice board to the effect that twelve pilots were required for operations in Italy. In the words of F/Sgt J.E. 'Nick' Carter RAAF 'that's where we made our big mistake – we volunteered!' Nick, six New Zealand and five Australian pilots were duly posted to fill the vacancies in 21 (SAAF) Squadron.

Based at Pescara, Italy, in July 1944 the squadron was replacing its Martin Baltimore aircraft with the bigger Martin Marauder, which required an extra crew member – a second pilot. Nick was posted as second pilot to the crew of Lt George van der H. Whitehouse SAAF.

Then came 13 September 1944. 'It was,' said Nick Carter, 'one of those days when nothing seemed to go right – we had flown our fifth op in five consecutive days and this was the sixth, our second op on 13 Sept. 1944 about the middle of the afternoon – clear weather.' 21 (SAAF) Squadron was putting up twelve aircraft in three 'boxes' of four, their target being German army positions on the Gothic Line, Field Marshal Kesselring's line of defences across the Appennine mountain range to the north of Italy.

George Whitehouse and Nick Carter in Marauder HD591:

'were accorded the signal honour of leading the third box... The target was strong points – army – near Rimini, not far up the [east] coast. Getting a dozen Marauders off the ground and into close formation quickly is no mean feat... After take-off we must have turned the wrong way – by the time our No. 2, 3 and 4 had formated on us we were miles behind the other two [boxes]. The CO, Lt Col [A.C.] Jandrell, up front over the RT – "Catch up! Catch up! Catch up!" By the time they turned in over the coast at Rimini (we always flew up over the Adriatic) we were still a long way behind, but we could see what they were copping and we knew with some trepidation that when we got there we were going to cop the lot, and we did...

'Whilst running up on target with the bomb doors open at 13,000 feet, we were hit by German 88mm flak. A fire started and roared up the corridor through the crew room to the flight deck. I looked back and saw the petrol transferring system, from outer to inner tanks via 2" diameter rubber pipes, was squirting neat avgas [aviation gasoline] everywhere like elephants' trunks. Bedlam over the RT and some screaming – I think poor Horscroft [WO1 H.E. Horscroft SAAF, mid-upper gunner] not only copped some flak but was getting roasted as well.

'The fire also prevented the release of three or four of the ten 250lb bombs. Observing the blazing aircraft the others in the "box" did a magnificent peel-off left and right – didn't blame them one little bit. We were due to go up any second.'

As the fire began to spread rapidly, Lt Whitehouse ordered the crew to bale out. Wireless operator WO1 N.H. 'Norm' Swale SAAF saw the rear gunner, WO2 J. 'Tug' Wilson SAAF, crawling out of his turret looking for his parachute pack.

Three days later one of the squadron flight commanders, Major R.U. Aitchison, reported HD591:

'being operationally serviceable took off from Pescara aerodrome at 1505 hours as formation leader on a day raid with three other aircraft in formation to bomb enemy strong point near Rimini. Heavy, moderate to intense, accurate A.A. was encountered. While leading the box over the target the aircraft was hit by flak and fire started in the bomb bay. The pilot broke formation and jettisoned the bombs. When last seen the aircraft was spinning down over the sea and burst into flames just prior to hitting the water approximately five miles S.E. of Rimini, near the coast. Three parachutes and another object were seen leaving the aircraft. It is believed from Army sources that two parachutes landed safely in the Canadian lines and two in the German lines, and so far this report is still unconfirmed despite all enquiries instituted up to this date [16 September].'

The other object reported by Major Aitchison was no doubt a fourth person with parachute, as George Whitehouse, Nick Carter, Lt Chris van Trotsenburg SAAF (navigator), and Norm Swale all baled out. The way in and way out of a Marauder was through the nose-wheel aperture, and if that failed to lower when asked... Fortunately it *was* still functioning, and when Nick had opened 'the little bi-parting manhole doors in the flight deck' three of the four survivors were able to jump past the nose-wheel. Norm probably squeezed himself out via one of the waist gun ports. Floating down Nick 'saw the aircraft explode just before it hit the sea'. It left 'a huge fire on the surface... and a perfectly circular, enormous black smoke ring spiralling outwards – and that was it'.

According to one source[146] Greek troops saw three of the crew bale out before the Marauder hit the sea eight kilometres south east of Rimini: 'One of the parachutes failed to open, a second floated down into the water and disappeared, and the third descended a stone's throw offshore on the enemy side of the line.' One wonders whether one of the three was Tug Wilson.

Unfortunately for Nick, he landed 'just on the German side, grabbed almost immediately by a Jerry platoon'. The two officers were also captured, but their POW camps are not known. Norman Swale, too, was swiftly captured, and was re-united with Nick in Bologna two days later. Nick arrived at Luft 7 in *Trupp 37*, Norm four days later in *Trupp 38* with eighty-nine others.

*

**4 OCTOBER 1944.** 'Parade was over quickly, as we had the two master-counters on – "Rommel" (the W/O) and "The Berlin Bomber" (Private 2nd Class).' (Tom Glenn.)

**5 OCTOBER 1944.** Fog drifted in during the morning. With it came extra guards and dogs. 'The fog lifted about noon, but settled in again. This was real "pea-soup fog", just like back in England.' (John McConnell RCAF). In between, the third England v Australia cricket Test Match began.

**6 OCTOBER 1944.** The Test Match concluded with a win for the Aussies by an innings and thirteen runs.

**7 OCTOBER 1944.** American Red Cross parcels issued in the morning – one per person to last a fortnight. After supper the air-raid siren went for a full-scale Allied raid. There was much excitement with the sky full of kites, and then the roar of flak and bombs. Morale rose, only to drop when one of the bombers was seen to have been hit, everyone praying that all the crew got out.

*Trupp 38* (ninety men) arrived, including sixty GPR men from Arnhem.

*

A number of airmen POWs were travelling in an open-topped truck from the Frankfurt interrogation centre when the driver swerved violently to avoid hitting another vehicle.

> 'We were all thrown into the field at the roadside together with our guards… I landed fairly well only to have a very irate German land heavily on top of me. His rifle accidentally hit me in my back which, believe me, was very painful… The guards were very agitated, and we all had to be very careful not to create further difficulties. Rifles were being cocked. I saw the funny side of it afterwards.' (Frank Mannion.)

*

With the GPR pilots was W/O Keith Prowd RAAF, shot down over Arnhem flying his usual Stirling EF248 ZO-V, 196 Squadron, from RAF Keevil, Wiltshire, on 19 September 1944. Hit by ground fire – small arms and light flak – whilst in the process of dropping supplies from a height of 1,500 feet, Keith gave the order to bale out. He managed to do so himself with only 500 feet remaining, and landed in a pine forest near the Klein Kweek farm. Though all the crew had baled out, only he, P/O J.J. Wherry RAAF (wireless operator) and F/S Jim Gordon RCAF (rear gunner), survived. Captured by 'front-line German troops', John Wherry went to Stalag Luft I (Barth), while Keith and

Jim Gordon ended up together at Luft 7 in *Trupp 38.*

The bomb aimer, F/O Reg C. Gibbs RCAF, shot at and wounded on the way down, was taken to the Arnhem Municipal Hospital, but was killed two days later when German soldiers threw several hand-grenades into the building. F/O Mike Powderhill (navigator) was also killed, still in his parachute, and Sgt D.A. 'Lofty' Matthews (flight engineer) was killed after landing, his body being found on the Amsterdamseweg. One of the two RASC air despatchers on EF248, Driver F.G. Smith, was never seen again, while Driver W.J. Chaplin, taken prisoner, died of wounds on 11 November 1944. Also on board were two 'passengers' – F/O F.D. Chalkley and Air Mechanic 2nd Class L.A. Hooker FAA (RNAS) – neither of whom survived. Hooker had been working at Keevil to gain experience on the Hercules radial engine. Chalkley, the navigator from another crew whose pilot had refused to fly any more, 'was shot by German soldiers shortly after landing by parachute in the meadow in front of the Groote Kweek farm near Arnhem'.[147]

*

One of the tug/glider combinations to take off from RAF Manston, Kent, on the second lift of men and material to Arnhem, on 18 September, was Albemarle V1785 with Horsa RJ221 in tow. Flying the Albemarle was F/L Sidney Francis 'Trader' Horn,[148] 296 Squadron, with S/Sgt C.R. 'Ron' Watkinson (1st pilot) and Sgt A.L. Jones (2nd pilot) in the Horsa. In addition to four Royal Artillery men of the 1st Airlanding Brigade – Sgt H.P. Clarke, Gunners Don Ackerman and Jeff Tyson, and Driver Joe Spence – they were carrying a Jeep, a 75mm howitzer, and a trailer of ammunition. After crossing the English coast, according to 296 Squadron's Operations Record Book, Ron reported to the tug via the communication wire:

> 'that his aileron control was unserviceable and was instructed by F/L Horn to hang on however much out of position he found himself. The glider pilot made a valiant effort to keep in correct position but could not avoid pulling the tug aircraft about and jerking the rope. For all that the combination flew on until forty miles inside Holland, when the rope gave way under the strain.'[149]

F/L Horn suggested returning to England to ditch if necessary, but Ron reasoned that if they could go back then they could just as easily continue, which they did.

Matters were not helped when the Horsa was hit by flak when flying over Walcheren Island off the Dutch coast. Though some of the Horsa's controls were cut, surprisingly no-one was hit, but twenty minutes or so later the tow-rope broke, and Ron had to make a landing as best he could without an air speed indicator, no flaps and no ailerons: 'I managed to get it down close to a farm, near the village of Fijnaart, in the province of Noord-Brabant. The nose-wheel broke and came into the cockpit, but no-one injured.' Though still a long way short of Arnhem they were, nevertheless, in enemy territory, and were attacked by German troops: 'Arthur Jones was severely hit, and one of the gunners [Joe Spence] took a bullet through his face and we were captured whilst attending their wounds.' The uninjured were led away to Dordrecht, and to POW camps. It was not until after the war, whilst visiting Arthur Jones's step-parents, that Ron Watkinson learnt that Arthur had died of his wounds on 22 September.

Though an 'immediate' recommendation for the award of the DFM to Ron was approved on 3 November 1944, it was not gazetted until 11 April 1946, shortly after his thirty-third birthday. Ron, born in Adelaide, Australia, on 3 April 1913, had returned to England with his family in 1916. He was an 'old soldier', literally, for no sooner had he reached his eighteenth birthday than he enlisted in the Royal Regiment of Artillery, and at the end of 1932 was serving with the 2nd Mountain Battery in India.

Returning from that country in November 1937, he was transferred to the Army Reserve, and was called back to the colours on 26 August 1939. After a spell at Gibraltar, he was in Plymouth on the first night it was bombed (6 July 1940). In March 1941 he volunteered for RAF aircrew, but his CO turned down his application. Undeterred, Ron tried again in August, successfully, but was not called up until April 1942. The RAF told him, though, that they had enough aircrew, but he could re-muster as a glider pilot, which he did.[150]

*

Also on the second lift were S/Sgt Dick Nutter (1st pilot) and Sgt Ray Wilson (2nd pilot) GPR. Shortly before 3 pm on the afternoon of 18 September, despite the bad visibility, they encountered heavy flak, and their glider crashed in a field. Dick was slightly injured when he was pinned in the wreckage – 'found myself with my chin in the ground, feet still on rudder bar doubled up behind me' – and was helped by men of a Royal Artillery Battery. As the glider's load was undamaged, they drove off in the Jeep to the appointed rendezvous in the woods.

Several miles past Wolfheze on the next day, Dick and his companions were strafed by Bf109s. Watching the third lift come in he 'saw four of the tugs (Stirlings & Dakotas) come down in flames by flak. Very heavy fighting, tremendous opposition.' The heavy fighting continued on 20 September, with the Germans throwing everything at the British – tanks, mortars, flame-throwers, and rocket-launchers. Dick and Ray Wilson were captured by an SS patrol 'who came on us by surprise', and were roughly treated before being marched to the town of Ede, several kilometres to the north west of Arnhem.

Dick later learnt that his section officer, Captain Iain Colquhoun Muir, had been shot dead while a POW. On 25 September, as the prisoners were being marched away, a German soldier, allegedly mistaking them for 'active' troops, fired a single shot, and Muir fell dead.

It was not just the soldiers who paid the price, however. On 21 September, being marched to a temporary prison, Dick and the others passed through several villages, where Dutch people gave the 'V' for Victory sign. Some of the Germans took offence and opened fire on the Dutch 'killing several'.

Four days later, having received little food along the way, the GPR prisoners also arrived at Stalag XIIA (Limburg) and 'stood on a parade ground with British and American aircrew for several hours, bitter cold, nearly fainting'. An American airman who could speak German was elected to tell the Commandant 'to either feed us or shoot us, either way would satisfy our hunger'. This prompted the Germans to produce Red Cross parcels, before putting the prisoners on the train to Frankfurt and Dulag Luft.

After a brief stay, ninety men left Wetzlar on 3 October, having had to wait at the station for seven hours for a train 'without overcoats or extra clothing. Damned cold.' They were beyond Breslau on 6 October when Czechoslovakian fighter pilot F/S Antonín Ocelka (see page 168) announced that they had 'passed within a couple of miles of his home'.[151] *Trupp 38* was soon at Luft 7.

*

**8 OCTOBER 1944.** The prisoners had just gone to bed when they heard a short burst of machine-gun fire, followed by a terrible scream, and much shouting.

**9 OCTOBER 1944.** A violent storm broke over the camp during the night – 'wind, hail, snow and some sleet. The hut shook and groaned. Lots of hail on the ground in the morning.'

No-one knew who it was who might have been hit last night. The general feeling was that it was one of the Russian prisoners in the adjoining compound.

**10 OCTOBER 1944.** The medical staff went down to the lower camp, a sign to the others that the move to the new camp was imminent.

The fourth cricket Test Match got under way.

**11 OCTOBER 1944.** The Test Match continued in the morning, but bad weather prevented any play during the afternoon. Australia were 97 all out and 26 for 3 in their second innings, England making 88 in their only innings.

**12 OCTOBER 1944.** *Trupp 39* (forty-four men) arrived including, from Arnhem, twenty-three GPR men and F/S Alan W. Clarke (second pilot) and F/S Harry Sorenson (navigator) from Dakota KG444, lost on 21 September. Their skipper, F/L Jimmy Edwards, who was to receive the DFC for his actions on this day, and their wireless operator, Bill Randall, managed to evade capture.[152]

*

Jettisoning the front escape hatch bomb aimer Jack Wilcox RNZAF struggled in vain to clip his parachute onto the second hook on his harness. So intense was the heat from the blazing Lancaster that he knew he had to get out whatever, trusting that the instructor had been right when he had said that he would be OK on one hook. And right behind him was flight engineer Colin Fowler, the only RAF member of the otherwise all-RNZAF crew, also waiting to get out.

Four-and-a-half hours earlier, at 7.35 p.m. on 11 September 1944, they had taken off from RAF Mepal in Lancaster LM268, 75 Squadron, to drop mines in Danzig Bay: 'The trip was uneventful and our mines were dropped as ordered. Everything went well until we were about to cross the coast at Vordingborg [on the south coast of Sjælland, Denmark] on the return trip.' Without warning, cannon shells ripped open the bomber's fuel tanks, the fuel pouring into the fuselage, where it caught alight. The two Lancaster gunners returned fire on their assailant, Oberleutnant Arnold Brinkmann, 8./NJG3, but were killed when their blazing Lancaster crashed onto a farm, killing farmer Carl Pommersgaard, his wife Edith, daughters Edith and Gerda and son Leo.[153] Only Jack and Colin Fowler survived.

As he floated down Colin noted that it was five minutes past midnight. Landing in a field near Ellerød he stuffed his parachute into a hedge before moving off to look for a church – where he had been told he would have the best chance of getting assistance. Finding Ørslev church he sat in the cemetery until morning, when the local gravedigger, Frederik Petersen, came to unlock the church. Petersen contacted someone, and eventually, on the evening of 14 September, Colin was smuggled to Sweden. On the evening of 27/28 September he was flown back to RAF Leuchars in the bomb bay of a Mosquito, finishing the war in RAF Transport Command flying between the UK and India.

When Jack Wilcox baled out he clearly remembered seeing the coastline far below, but then lost consciousness, and crashed hard into a field on Lundegaarden Farm, just east of Ørslev, badly injuring his right shoulder. Having regained his senses and in considerable pain, he injected himself with a tube of morphine: 'As the pain did not ease I guess I must have made a mess of the injection.' So severe was the pain from his damaged shoulder that he couldn't even contemplate hiding his parachute: 'I was able to shuffle in a hunched position and managed to get to a cowbarn where I lay on some hay and tried to get things sorted out.'

At dawn he went over to the nearby farmhouse that he had seen, resting under a plum tree: 'The plums were falling off the tree on their own accord... I started tossing plums at the window nearest me until an elderly couple opened the window.' Eventually getting them to understand that he was an injured Allied airman, they called the Danish police, who took Jack to the hospital at Vordingborg, where he was expected: 'They bandaged my arm and shoulder and cleaned me up generally. By then a couple of German soldiers had arrived and I was taken into a private room where I stayed until mid-morning.' Later, four more soldiers appeared 'with a stretcher and their machine guns around their necks. As they were carrying me out, the nurse who had attended me put a lighted cigarette in my mouth and a bunch of flowers on my chest.'

Jack was taken to a German military hospital, where they took off his plasters and put his arm 'in a wire frame arrangement which stayed on for a considerable time'. Shortly afterwards he was transported to Germany, and to Dulag Luft: 'After a brief interrogation I was taken by covered truck with about six American airmen, who were terribly wounded as well as severely burnt, to a hospital at a place called Hohen Hohen [sic – the Hohe Mark].' He was there for a week or so until removed to Wetzlar, where he met up with 'some English glider pilots who were tremendous chaps'. Jack and the GPR men made it to Luft 7 in *Trupp 38* on 7 October.

*

**13 OCTOBER 1944.** At 5.30 am the POWs were called for *Appell*. After four months, the 'new' camp, largely built by the toil of the Russian prisoners, was ready for occupation in the lower field:

> 'Moved into new camp. It was like going on holiday, everyone happy to leave the old camp. We had been told what hut and room had been allocated to us. This gave those who had not got on well together the opportunity to change. A space in the wire was cut, and under supervision we moved in groups... What a change, double bunks, no sleeping on the floor, and only twelve men to a room. Over 1,000 men were moved in the space of the morning, and the gap in the fence closed off.' (Fred Brown.)
>
> 'One division moved first with all personal gear, tables and bedding being moved by truck. Our hut 46 was all complete with beds and I found the room to be much larger than I had imagined with plenty of room for seven two-tier bunks and a large-size table. Two double windows on the eastern side of our room and a white electric light in the centre are our means of light during the day and night... A small stove in the end room of each hut is the sole means of heating and cooking as no fires are allowed between the barracks outside.' (Arthur Kemp.)

Tom Glenn noted: 'It's "wizard" in the new place – lighting, more room, no bending heads, grand lavatories, fourteen in a room...'

It was, however, only a fortnight or so after the move that the stoves were installed, at the same time as some of the beds: 'The beds have arrived, and so have the stoves. At the moment we are allowed fifteen brickettes of coal a day which is a good allowance.' (Elwyn Healy.)

In the new compound there were eight barrack blocks (or 'divisions', numbered 1 to 8), each divided into fourteen rooms, with eighteen men in each, more than sufficient space for the 1,600 or so prisoners who would eventually be resident there (see Don Gray's sketch plan). The barrack blocks were set either side of the football pitch, which was aligned on an east-west axis. Those on the south side of the pitch were numbered 42-46, with number 43 being the ablution/latrines hut,

The new compound drawn by Eddie Finlay.

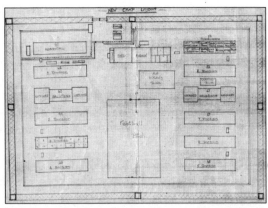

Contemporary pencil sketch of the new compound.

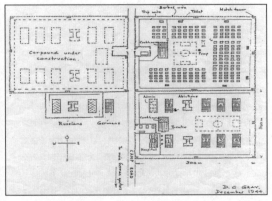

Luft 7 drawn by Don Gray, dated December 1944.

Inside of a new hut drawn by Eddie Finlay.

while on the north side there was a similar pattern for huts 48-52, hut 51 being their ablution/latrines block. Hut 47 contained the theatre/hall and kitchen. Hut 41, in the south-west corner, was the hospital, and hut 53 the headquarters block, with individual rooms for the Camp Leader, Man of Confidence, stores, club room, band room etc.

\*

**14 OCTOBER 1944** (approx). With the POWs in their new quarters, the 'ferrets' found a tunnel lined with tin cans. As a result the prisoners were ordered to hand over all tins and razor blades. This may have been the tunnel that had been started by W/O Snowden and his room mates in Barrack 52, Room 12. As all the huts were on stilts so that the 'ferrets' could see what, if anything, was going on underneath, the vertical shaft for the tunnel went down through the hollow brick column that supported the stove above: 'The stove was moved, the cement base lifted, and the tunnel went down.' (Bill Taylor.)

Tools for digging the tunnel, apart from those 'pinched from the chimney sweep', had, inadvertently, been provided in the guise of gardening tools by the Germans, who had agreed that the strips of land between the barrack huts could be cultivated for fresh vegetables. The Germans weren't fools, for the gardening implements were counted in and out of the *Lager* on a daily basis. Soil from the tunnel was put in sacks which, when lookouts gave the all clear, were passed through the barrack window and mixed with the freshly turned earth in the vegetable plot.

The shaft was dug to a depth of 24 feet, and bed boards were donated by the kriegies to shore it up. The tunnel itself, which needed to be an estimated 120 yards long to clear the wire, had reached 40 feet when, at around 2 am one morning, armed guards suddenly burst into Barrack 52. Knowing exactly where to go, they went straight to Room 12, where they moved the stove and exposed the tunnel. The occupants were paraded outside while the goons made a thorough search of the hut. 'Snowy' Snowden and three of his mates were sent to the cooler.

Clearly the tunnel had been given away to the Germans, and suspicion immediately fell on Raymond Hughes (see page 156) who had, for some unknown reason, been put in Snowy's room. The prisoners convened a 'court' in the Camp Leader's room, to which Hughes was brought 'under arrest' by two fellow prisoners. Hughes was charged with collaborating with the enemy and of passing on information to them, particularly the whereabouts of the tunnel. He was further told that if found guilty the punishment was death. Hughes broke down at this, and was kept under POW guard overnight. In the morning the Camp Leader and Man of Confidence decided that, as the Germans might take reprisals, it would be best if Hughes were handed back to the Germans, and so the wretched man 'was escorted to the main gate, accompanied by most of the camp, and thrown back to the Germans'.

Snowy and his accomplices, meanwhile, had not been forgotten by their room mates, who smuggled some matches into the cells with their meals. Shortly afterwards the cooler caught fire and burnt to the ground. The Germans rushed to get the prisoners out. When Snowy was questioned about the incident, he replied that he was cold, so he had lit a fire to warm himself.

'Right', said the Germans more or less, 'you burnt down the cooler, you rebuild it,' and a dozen or more non-NCO kriegies were instructed to do this using prefabricated sides. The story goes that, after arguing the case, it was agreed that twelve men *would* work, but not necessarily those originally chosen by the Germans. In fact, a dozen of the bolshiest NCOs were selected by the kriegies themselves. One version is that the prefabricated sides were being held up to the timber frame by the kriegies 'when someone asked for a hammer (this was planned). They all let go to search for the hammer and the sides collapsed in pieces. There was much hilarity, much to the Germans' annoyance.' (Bill Taylor.)

John Ackroyd's version was that on:

> 'the morning for the work to begin, the NCOs were there at the main gate. The work that they were set to do was the erection of two of the hen huts [sic] that we had lived in the old compound in a small compound in front of the main gate. They set to work levelling the site, digging holes and then filling them up with soil dug from other holes. This went on for some time until the German guards got a bit fed up and told them to get on with the erection of the huts, and just where they had to be! So the floor was laid, one wall was lifted and the guards were asked to hold it in position while the end was lifted. Instead of lifting the end the lads went over to the wire near the gate and started talking to all who were looking on.'

To add to the confusion the necessary bolts had somehow disappeared. All in all it was a very pleasant four days spent 'goon baiting' and, needless to say, the POWs were never asked again! The Germans finished off the rebuilding of the cooler, and the dubious honour of being the first resident of the Mk.II cooler was Bill Taylor: 'Walking past the cookhouse I encountered Captain (Hauptmann) Schultz. He was the SS officer for the camp and a nasty piece of work. I did not salute him as I passed. He shouted me back, made me stand to attention, and ordered me to salute him.' When Bill refused, Schultz withdrew his pistol from its holster, poked it into Bill's back and marched him off to the cooler, where he served seven days.

Only a few details have surfaced about the tunnels dug by the POWs at Luft 7, but 'Mac' McMurdon, with his mining experience, was asked to help with one:

> 'We dug from a refuse pit – nothing elaborate like the Great Escape – no lights, boardings etc. We kept it very narrow to avoid cave-ins in the sand… We had almost reached the fence one Sunday morning when a Pole, sitting on a horse-drawn mower, came in to cut the grass in the "no go" area. To our dismay and the utter amazement of the Pole the large horse's legs disappeared into our tunnel.'

As for escapes on the ground – through the wire, over it, or by any other cunning means – there were several attempts, unfortunately none of which resulted in a 'home run', for example see the diary entry for 7 August (page 149). The best effort involved the coal wagon which, pulled by a number of kriegies, was allowed out of the camp to collect coal brickettes for the huts. There happened to be a box built into the wagon driver's seat, large enough to hold a man. The plan was simply to put a kriegie in the box and take him to the coal depot. Distracting the guards' attention with cigarettes and conversation, the kriegie would slip out of the box and make his way to freedom. His absence would be covered by his room mates for long enough to give him a good headstart. The first man chosen, apparently called 'Fred Donald' (not known), got as far as Leipzig. A second attempt was made – again unclear as to the identity of the would-be escaper – using the same method, but this time the prisoner was stopped at Bankau station when the Gestapo were making a spot-check on personal papers. Both 'Fred Donald' and the other man were put in the cooler.

**15 OCTOBER 1944** (approx). The breakfast porridge was burnt, resulting in two of the eight divisions having to go without. A meeting was called at which each hut was represented. The decision was made that the quartermaster and cooks would be put under control of a messing committee, its members being one man from each division.

**17 OCTOBER 1944.** There was an air raid during the night, though the bangs and thumps of bombs and guns could be heard but not seen. In the morning, the kriegies 'discovered the ground covered with "Window". It was the American-type "Window", very narrow strips of aluminium.' One of the guards fired at a POW, but missed.

**18 OCTOBER 1944.** The Welsh Club was formed. Names were sent to the *Daily Mail* and *South Wales Echo* for publication.

**19 OCTOBER 1944.** When a workman inside the camp discovered that his hammer had been stolen he called the guards. It was a cold day, and every prisoner was made to stand in the open, on the sports field, for one and a half hours. At the end of this period it was dark, and very cold. When, inevitably, the hammer was not found, the Commandant informed the POWs that unless it was returned there would be no further issues of coal, and no lighting in the huts. Peter Thomson, Camp Leader, pointed out that that would be tantamount to a collective punishment, and said he would report the matter to Geneva – 'that sort of finished that'. (Den Blackford.)

**20 OCTOBER 1944.** A lorry bringing food into the camp got stuck in the mud. The prisoners had great fun getting it out.

**21 OCTOBER 1944.** The 'ferrets' returned in the morning, but never found the hammer. Typically, reprisals were taken by the Germans – no lights at certain times; no parcels distributed on Sunday because, they said, they didn't work on Sundays; and the banning of the singing of the British National Anthem.

Camp concert was held. A new song called Remember Me, composed by one of the POWs, was sung for the first time. At the close of the concert, as the Germans had banned the singing of God Save the King, the prisoners defiantly stood to attention and sang Land of Hope and Glory as loudly as they could.

*Trupp 40* (approximately forty-five men) arrived.

*

'I am very sorry you have been caused so much anxiety in awaiting definite news of Joe… We were attacking the Ruhr in daylight on Friday afternoon & on the run-up to the target [Sterkrade] received two direct hits. The first set the main bulkhead on fire & as we had our full bomb load aboard I gave the crew the order to abandon aircraft. Joe & Eric (the MU/AG) left through the rear escape hatch & although we did not see it ourselves other crews reported that their parachutes opened and that they were floating safely down at 16,000 feet.'

These reassuring words were written on 9 October 1944, three days after the events related, to the father of Sgt Joe Smith, rear gunner of Halifax NP990, 462 (RAAF) Squadron, by its pilot F/O Ed McGindle RAAF. No doubt the parents of the mid-upper gunner, Sgt W.E.L. Offley, received a similar letter.

No sooner had the two gunners jumped than a second burst of flak hit the nose of the Halifax, seriously wounding the navigator and slightly wounding the bomb aimer. With the aircraft on fire and with the navigator lying across the escape hatch McGindle could do nothing, especially as his parachute and the engineer's were being consumed by the fire, which was eventually put out. McGindle flew the bomber back to England and 'managed to make an uneventful landing at an emergency landing ground [RAF Woodbridge]'. The award of his DFC and of the DFM to three NCOs of his crew – 1452215 F/S C.F. Baldwin; Aus.434231 F/S E.G. Whelan RAAF; and 1159268 Sgt S.L. Soames – were published in the *London Gazette* on 12 December 1944:

'This officer and these airmen were captain, air bomber, wireless operator (air) and flight engineer respectively of an aircraft detailed to attack a synthetic oil refinery at Sterkrade in October, 1944. In the vicinity of the target the bomber was hit by anti-aircraft fire. A fire commenced in the fuselage behind the main bulkhead. Promptly and resolutely, Sergeant Soames attempted to quell the flames. As he fought, the aircraft was again hit. The navigator was seriously wounded; Flight Sergeant Baldwin was also wounded but withheld the fact from his captain in order to help Flight Sergeant Whelan who had gone to the assistance of their stricken comrade. Meanwhile, Sergeant Soames succeeded in putting out the fire. During this trying period Flying Officer McGindle had shown the qualities of a fine captain and his coolness and able directions greatly inspired his crew. One engine had become defective and, a little later, ceased to function completely. The airspeed indicator was unserviceable and much other damage had been sustained. Nevertheless, Flying Officer McGindle flew the aircraft safely to base. This officer displayed great skill and determination throughout.

'Flight Sergeants Baldwin and Whelan and Sergeant Soames also proved themselves to be devoted and resolute members of aircraft crew. They did everything possible to assist their captain in his endeavour to reach home, whilst their efficient first aid and constant attention to their grievously wounded comrade undoubtedly played a prominent part in saving his life.'

Joe Smith's family would have been spared the gory details that, on landing, their son 'was beaten up by German civilians and his tongue partly severed', before being rescued by German soldiers. Known to his crew as 'Dad' – he was two months short of his thirty-second birthday – Joe and William Offley joined the others at Luft 7 in *Trupp 40*.

\*

Flight Sergeant Neil Ostrom,[154] on his twenty-first operation, was second navigator of Lancaster ND929, 156 (PFF) Squadron, also on the raid on the Sterkrade synthetic oil refinery on the afternoon of 6 October 1944. Turning at Wesel for the run-in to the target the Lancaster:

'attracted flak on the way in, which it was our job to do, i.e. take the heat off the marker bombers, but on this occasion we were early, about two minutes, and therefore alone. We were hit hard and dropped the whole bomb load and immediately after, despite evasive tactics, hit again.

'I don't recall actually jumping, nor the descent and certainly did not pull the cord [to open the parachute]. When I came to about an hour later my 'chute had gone. I was lying bundled in a blanket with two "elderly" Volkssturm prodding me, to see if I would move I suppose.'

Neil's Lancaster had been hit by predicted flak, which wounded the pilot, F/O L.N.B. Cann, who nevertheless pressed on to the target. He was in such a bad way that he was removed from his seat by the first navigator, Sgt R.V. Fisher. The wireless operator then 'moved the half-fainting captain to the rest bed where he passed out'. While all this was going on Neil and the flight engineer, Sgt Charles Shaw, baled out. Sgt Fisher thereupon did the only thing that he could and took over the controls, and heroically flew the crippled bomber back to within sight of base, RAF Upwood, when Cann, having sufficiently recovered, landed the aircraft safely.

On 25 October Cann and Fisher were awarded the DFC and DFM respectively (gazetted 1 December 1944). Fisher's citation gives a little more detail: 'A shell exploded near the bomber and fragments smashed through the pilot's windscreen. Flying Officer Cann was struck in the arm and shoulder. Although bleeding profusely he continued his [bombing] run.' Flying Officer Cann and all his crew, including the valiant Fisher, now commissioned (on 20 November, but not gazetted until 19 December), were killed in action on an attack on Ulm on 17/18 December 1944.

There but for the grace of God went Neil Ostrom and Charles Shaw, both of whom had found their way, in a fortnight from baling out, to Luft 7 in *Trupp 40* on 21 October.

\*

Twenty-three FAFL aircrew (Forces Aériennes Françaises Libres, the Free French Air Force) altogether would end up at Luft 7 after parting company with their aircraft, but the majority, fourteen, were from 346 (Guyenne) Squadron flying from their Yorkshire base at Elvington, where it was formed on 16 May 1944.

Four of the fourteen came from NA555, which was also lost on the daylight raid on 6 October 1944 to Sterkrade oil refinery. It was not often that an entire bomber crew was taken prisoner, but such fortune was to befall the crew of NA555. They had bombed the target and were on their way home when attacked by a German fighter. Lt J. Hablot (pilot) and the two gunners, Sgt Nicolas Manick (mid-upper) and Sgt Raymond F. Yvars (rear), were unharmed. The navigator, Lt L. de Saint-Marc, was hit in the foot, and Adjutant-Chef Albert J.M. Philippe (wireless operator) in the shoulder. Sergent-Chef Louis Pons (flight engineer) was hit by splinters in the chest and in the right eye. Lt J. Wuillemin baled out uninjured, but was fired at as he came down. His parachute was badly holed and, consequently, he 'hit the ground heavily and was severely injured, his pelvis being fractured and his bladder perforated'.[155]

It is not known to which camps the three officers were sent after capture. Wuillemin presumably went to a hospital, while the four NCOs went to Luft 7, three in *Trupp 40*. The fourth, Pons, arrived possibly in *Trupp 55*, probably after treatment for his injuries.

*

**22 OCTOBER 1944.** *Trupp 41* (possibly twenty men, mostly ex-hospital cases) arrived.

*

It was a little over seven months after Australian F/Sgt F.J. Brown RAAF had been shot down that he arrived at Luft 7. He had been through his own private hell to get there, starting on 3 March 1944 when Baltimore FW300, 454 (RAAF) Squadron, was shot down over the Aegean Sea by two Bf109s when on a reconnaissance over the Aegean Sea and Melos Island. After the first attack, the intercom was put out of action. After two further attacks, the starboard engine stopped and the port engine caught fire, leaving the pilot, F/Sgt A.W.J. Kempnich RAAF, with no alternative but to effect a landing in the sea. Three of the crew – Brown, Kempnich and W/O J.D. Seymour RAAF – managed to climb into the aircraft's dinghy, but Francis Brown was suffering with broken ribs, a broken arm, broken jaw, and broken nose. When FW300 sank it took with it F/Sgt J.E. Stapleton RAAF.

For the next five days the dinghy drifted at the whim of the currents. With food and drink running out, Allan Kempnich decided to swim for help when he saw an islet off Antiparos. He was never seen again, and is presumed to have drowned. Both Brown and Seymour were so impressed by his courage that after the war they tried to get it recognised with an award: 'Both... spoke highly of their captain's efforts both during the attack and until his death and they feel that for such efforts the captain, F/Sgt Kempnish [sic] warrants recommendation for an award.'

On the sixth day the dinghy drifted ashore on a small island south of Antiparos, where they were found by Greek fishermen and taken to the larger island of Paros. Two days later Brown was picked up by the Germans, and taken to the Luftwaffe hospital in Athens on 9 March. Presumably at this point he and Seymour were parted, the latter ending up at Stalag IVB (Mühlberg). After sixteen days in Athens, Brown was transferred for further treatment to Obermassfeld Lazarett (26 March-1 August) and from there to Meiningen Lazarett (1 August-20 October). Two days after leaving Meiningen he arrived at Luft 7 with other wounded aircrew in *Trupp 41*.

*

**24 OCTOBER 1944.** When one of the Russian POWs escaped from his compound, the Germans went after him with their dogs. All fellow POWs hoped he didn't get caught.

A new notice appeared on the camp's notice-board addressed 'To All Prisoners of War'. It ended with the warning that: 'Escaping from camps has ceased to be a sport.' The kriegies expected things thereafter to get tougher.

**25 OCTOBER 1944.** The POWs felt a cold edge to the wind, though the weather remained good.

**26 OCTOBER 1944.** Red Cross parcel issue. 'A hell of a cold wind blowing; may snow at any time.'

George Kilbryde noted in his diary: 'Two new chaps arrived today. One, Jock Thompson, Spitfire pilot shot down over Germany or Belgium fourteen months ago. He was badly burned about the face, and is at the moment covered with plastic surgery scars. The other was Fred Townsend [sic - Townshend], Lancaster bomber engineer. He has been injured in the left eye and probably permanently disfigured. This makes us short of a bed, so one will have to sleep on the floor tonight...'

Scotsman F/S J.McK.V. 'Jock' Thompson, 222 Squadron, was shot down in Spitfire MH429 in the Lille area on the morning of 31 August 1943 on Ramrod operation S16. Londoner Sgt Fred C. Townshend was injured when Lancaster DS815, 514 Squadron, was lost on the night of 22/23 March 1944 (Frankfurt) after it had been attacked by experienced night-fighter pilot Hauptmann Ludwig Meister, 1./NJG4, for his thirty-fifth victim.[156] After the pilot of DS815, F/L Cyril William Nichol, had skilfully landed the stricken bomber near St Omer in the north east of France, the two gunners evaded capture. The wireless operator was killed while, of the other four (two officers and two NCOs), all taken prisoner, only Fred went to Luft 7.

The *Trupp* number for Jock Thompson and Fred Townshend is not known (German records are confused on this matter), but they arrived after *Trupp* 40 and before *Trupp* 47.

*

**28 OCTOBER 1944.** *Trupp* 45? arrived (thirty-nine men approximately).

*

Appearing on 28 October were several more GPR men captured at Arnhem. One of them, Sergeant William H. Knox, joined George Kilbryde in his room in Hut 48. Bill Knox bore the scars of the fierce fighting by the bridges at Arnhem: 'He had been wounded in the leg on the way over. The bullet entered his heel, travelled up his leg and came out behind the knee. Most amazing as he is now almost fit again.'

Bill Knox also brought further news of some of the GPR men who had fought so strongly at Arnhem, among them one of their officers, twenty-three-year-old Lieutenant Kenneth Trevor Chittleburgh, 'D' Squadron, who was killed by a mortar bomb on 21 September. George Kilbryde noted: 'The list of killed is getting very long and we realise just how lucky we are to be all in one piece.' A few weeks later a list of over fifty GPR men killed at Arnhem had been compiled by survivors at Bankau. Though some were reckoned to be doubtful 'there seems to be no doubt about poor old Cyril Fisher. He was a Jew. If all Jews were like him, then Englishmen would have a lot to learn.' Twenty-four-year-old S/Sgt Cyril Fisher, also 'D' Squadron, was killed on 20 September. Of the 1,262 GPR men who flew in to Arnhem, 219 were killed and 511 were taken prisoner.

On 29 October George wrote: 'One member of the room, Al Midlane, received his first letter. He has been a prisoner for eight months. This meant a cigarette all round to celebrate, instead of a drink.' Alan Midlane, though, from the Southampton area, was fated never return to England (see page 261).

Two more GPR men at Luft 7, S/Sgt Arthur Newton and Sgt Douglas Smithson, first and second pilots respectively of a Horsa glider, never even got to fight. They were towed from RAF Fairford, Gloucestershire, by Stirling LJ943 (P/O R.B. Herger RCAF), 190 Squadron, on the second lift to Arnhem, on 18 September 1944. They took off ten minutes after midday heading almost due east, crossing the English coast just north of Canvey Island, Essex. With a slight change of course LJ943 and its Horsa made for Holland, with Douglas flying the Horsa across the North Sea until the enemy coast was sighted, when S/Sgt Arthur 'Spinner' Newton took over.

Flying a glider on a tow rope behind a 'tug' aircraft was difficult enough at the best of times, with the glider pilots constantly having to maintain a tight rope in either the 'high' or 'low' position. Nearing the Dutch coast the Horsa pilots heard the rear gunner of the Stirling urgently calling to his pilot to climb right, fast, as a Dakota was heading towards them. Douglas looked out of the cockpit and, sure enough, barely forty yards away, was a USAAF Dakota/Waco glider combination closing rapidly in their direction. He shouted to Newton to go up and right, but it was too late. The wing of the Dakota caught the tow rope, and that was the last those aboard the Horsa saw of the American tug.

In climbing, the Horsa had lifted the Stirling's tail and, consequently, LJ943 began to dive towards the sea 1,000 feet below. Newton lifted the Horsa's nose in an attempt to arrest the dive but, inevitably, the tow rope snapped under the strain, and the tug and glider parted company.[157] They were near the islands to the south west of Rotterdam at that moment, and Spinner Newton made the decision to put down on land rather than on the sea, even though there was a chance of being picked up by one of the stand-by rescue launches.

He made a perfect landing near the town of Oude-Tonge in the south east of the Dutch island of Overflakkee, but someone informed the Germans of their arrival, and before long a detachment of German soldiers from the neighbouring island of Schouwen was seen heading in their direction, and took them prisoner. While waiting for transport one of the German soldiers, after some confusion, managed to make Douglas Smithson understand that he was not a German but an Armenian, and pointed to the badge on his shoulder. He was from the 812th Armenian Battalion.

After a series of long and hungry journeys Newton and Smithson arrived at Stalag XIIA (Limburg am der Lahn) on 30 September and 'found it to be an awful place. The compound was tiny and held about 1,500 men in absolutely shocking conditions. We had some food and a wash at some taps outside the huts. We hoped our stay would not be long.'[158] Only when another GPR man captured at Arnhem, Sgt K. Travis-Davison, appeared in their midst (see page 193) did they learn that Operation Market had failed.

Enduring three weeks at Stalag XIIA, Newton and Smithson were overjoyed to learn that they were to be moved to another camp. After Dulag Luft and Wetzlar, they left on 24 October for the long journey to Bankau, arriving there four days later with twenty-two RAF aircrew.

*

**29 OCTOBER 1944.** Fog and rain. POWs lamented that had the fog been a bit thicker they could have climbed the wire! Germans issued a coal ration.

**30 OCTOBER 1944.** Weather very cold and dry. Guards searched the men's huts, 'checking up on tins of food in our possession'. Red Cross parcels issued in the afternoon.

## CHAPTER NINE

# NOVEMBER 1944, *TRUPPEN 47(?) – 50*

**1 NOVEMBER 1944.** Poured with rain for much of the day. Hospital staff increased to ten. Beds for the POWs arrived, see page 180.

A further issue of Red Cross parcels brought the week's total to some 3,000, but as the camp's population was approaching 1,100 it was estimated that the parcels, on half-rations, would run out at Christmas.

The camp's first dance was held in the evening, several of the men dressing up as women.

**2 NOVEMBER 1944.** Last of the stoves were finally put into the huts. 'Some wood was issued. This was the first time we had been warm since early August.' Some of the men, too, had been without bunks since the move to the new compound, and these also arrived.

**3 NOVEMBER 1944.** Rain. The International Red Cross paid another visit to Luft 7, and this time counted 1,028 POWs, mostly British.

**4 NOVEMBER 1944.** YMCA paid a visit to the camp. The Ilag (civilian internment camp) at Kreuzburg sent over a stage and effects. A brand new piano and a worn-out trumpet also arrived.

**6 NOVEMBER 1944.** More parcels.

**7 NOVEMBER 1944.** A party of POWs went to Kreuzburg for delousing. Cold wind, rain at night.

**8 NOVEMBER 1944.** 'First snow. My word it began to get cold after that. With little food we felt the cold more than we would have done had we been well fed.' (Fred Stead.) Snow later turned to rain.

It was noted that a lot more traffic than usual was heading west, a mixture of civilians and German soldiers.

**9 NOVEMBER 1944.** One of the POWs went to hospital with jaundice.

**10 NOVEMBER 1944.** Parcel issue. Eight hours of snow. After 'Lights Out', a guard dog jumped through the window of the night latrine in one of the barracks. It roamed through the barrack until the dog was grabbed by its guard handler. This was not, apparently, the first time that this had happened, and Oberstleutnant Behr, who had already warned the guard about it, promised that it would not happen again.

Arthur 'Red' Madelaine remembered a previous occasion of a dog entering a barrack hut:

> 'At Bankau we had three-tier bunks and one night, it being so hot, we decided to leave the double window open to try and get some air in the room. Well, the ground was patrolled by guards with Alsatian dogs at night. We had all been in our bunks about half an hour when all of a sudden this big Alsatian came and jumped in the open window. Well, it was one mad scramble for the top bunks, which resulted in the bunks and occupants all crashing to the floor as the dog ran around the room. After that the window was closed every night!'[159]

**11 NOVEMBER 1944.** The men paraded at 9 am in snow and sleet. A simple Armistice Day service was held. To most it was 'just another twenty-four hours behind barbed wire' but, to Laird MacLean, the Remembrance Parade in the morning 'was the best parade so far on this camp'. The Last Post 'was sounded [by F/S Jeff Allen] on a trumpet (all we could get). It coincided with [another] fall of snow and the result was quite sombre.' (Ted Milligan.)

Probably the first new arrival at Luft 7 in November was the Reverend John Brenton Collins, a Church of England padré. John Collins ('Jack' to his family) was born in London on 26 May 1906 to Brenton Robie Collins (born in Canada in 1870) and to Evelyn Annie (née Dawson, born 1877). Educated at Eton College, he went up to Trinity College, Cambridge, where he gained a BA in 1929. He rowed in the University Boat Races of 1928-30, which Cambridge won each time. He was not only the tallest man in both boats – he stood 6 foot 7 in his bare feet – but was also the heaviest, weighing between 14 stone 3lbs and 14 stone 6 lbs. (One of the talks he later gave at Luft 7, on 10 December, was entitled 'Putney to Mortlake'. Coincidentally, another three-times boat race winner for Cambridge, in 1934-36, J.N. Duckworth, the cox, also became a padré in the forces and also became a prisoner of war, but of the Japanese. The lightest man in the crew, he weighed a mere 8 stone 7lbs in the 1936 race).[160]

In 1929 John attended Ridley Hall, the Church of England theological ordination training college in Cambridge, and left the University with an MA in 1931. He was ordained a deacon in 1933, and a priest in the following year in the Salisbury diocese. From 1933-35 he was the curate of St James, Poole, and was appointed chaplain of Canford School in 1935.

He was in Devizes, Wiltshire, when granted an emergency commission, service number 111558, as a chaplain to the forces, 4th Class (the equivalent rank of captain).[161] After various postings throughout England, he sailed for the Middle East from Avonmouth on 29 July 1941. The voyage took him via South Africa to Port Tewfik (Suez), where he landed on 4 October 1941. 13 June 1942 found him attached to the 67th Medium Regiment, Royal Artillery, at Tobruk, where he and the majority of the regiment were captured eight days later.

With many others, he was sent from Benghazi on 27 June to Lecce, on Italy's 'heel', arriving on 30 June 1942. He was at several Italian camps – PG 75 (Bari), PG 63 (Aversa), PG 66 (Capua), PG 19 (Bologna), and PG 47 (Modena) – until, after Italy's surrender earlier in the month, he was sent to Stalag VIIA (Moosburg), Germany, on 13 September 1943. A week later he was transferred to Stalag VC (Malschbach), and then to Oflag VA (Weinsberg) on 9 October 1943.

Transferred to Stalag XVIIA (Kaisersteinbruch-bei-Bruch), Austria, on 19 August 1944 he went to Luft 7 on 11 November 1944, probably the only one in *Trupp 46*. He noted in a letter home dated 13 November 1944: 'Arrived here Sat night after thirty-hours journey... Over [number censored] RAF personnel here, average age very young. Am the only officer here at present, though a doctor is expected. There seems to be a great opportunity for a padré here.'

*

**12 NOVEMBER 1944.** *Trupp 47* (forty-five to fifty men) arrived.

*

F/S George Cross was a rare bird – a Mosquito NCO navigator. He and his pilot, F/S George Roan 'Jock' Irving, had already completed forty missions together when they took off shortly after 7 pm on the night of 30 September 1944, from RAF Little Snoring, Norfolk. They were on a night interdiction sortie in Mosquito VI HR201, YP-K, 23 Squadron. George Cross: 'Jock and I... had just finished our duty when we saw a train. We decided to turn and attack it. The train turned out to be a flak train and they started a short duel out of which we came a very poor second best with the port wing ablaze outboard the engine, and the port elevator flapping, at 500 feet.'

For George it was clearly time to get out but Jock wanted to carry on if possible, and asked George to press the fire extinguisher button. It was stuck. 'Never mind,' said Jock, 'we'll climb and bale out.' But it was too late, and the last words that George heard from Jock were 'Bale out quick.' In a panic George forced himself through the Mosquito's notoriously small escape hatch. He never remembered pulling his parachute's rip-cord, and came down lop-sidedly with his intercom wires tangled round one side of his harness, thus preventing the 'chute from clipping on properly: 'This fact did not, however, prevent me from making a good descent.' He then made a good landing on soft ground: 'Just after I hit the deck our aircraft crashed with an explosion of petrol (300-400 gallons) and burnt fiercely for about ten minutes.' George was fairly sure that Jock would have had the time in which to have baled out himself.

Reckoning that he was a dozen or so miles north of Brunswick George set off towards the Allied lines many miles to the west. As luck would have it, he was walking through a belt of flak batteries when he was spotted by a Luftwaffe private armed only with a bayonet. Discretion being the better part of valour, George allowed himself to be propelled to a nearby hut. Seated therein was a sergeant, who took George to his officer, who tried ineffectually to question his prisoner:

'When he saw that he was getting nowhere he took me outside and with the two guards marched, or rather walked, with me to Wagum aerodrome about three miles away. When we got there no one seemed to be about and after consultation with the guard he took me to a POW camp – Oflag 79 – and so at about 3 o'clock on the morning of October the First 1944 I started life as a Kriegsgefangene in Germany.'

After a night in a foul-smelling cell George was given the news that his pilot was '*kaput*'. They had found a piece of flying boot with 'Irving' written on it. There could be no mistake: 'The realisation of this fact knocked me completely over, for Jock and I had been flying together for well over a year and had done all our operational flying together, both overseas and at home. He was in fact the best friend I have ever had in the service or ever will have.' Jock was just twenty-one, and married.

George arrived at Dulag Luft on 2 October, and endured the usual solitary confinement and interrogation, except that his lasted for the best part of five weeks, an unusually long time. At last, on 6 November, he joined fellow prisoners in the transit compound: 'Boy! It's wizard to be able to talk to someone at last. Lots of Yanks in this compound and they spout gen never realising the building will be wired for more than lighting.'

Next day he was off to Wetzlar, leaving on the following day with forty-four other NCOs for Luft 7. Their journey lasted from 10 pm on that day until 7 am on 12 November: 'Told to hurry with breakfast as we are at Bankau. 7.00 [hours] piled out very relieved to stretch our legs. Did quick three kilometre march to camp. Bags of barbed wire, guards, counting and once again searched. Tins pierced, forms filled up and photograph taken.'

*

W/O Freddie F. Turner (pilot); F/S Keith J. Pendray (navigator/bomb aimer); F/S Jimmy Warren (WOp/AG); and Sgt Douglas Backhouse, had bombed the railway bridge over the Ijssel at Deventer, Holland, on 15 October 1944, and were on their way home in a 'box' of Mitchells when, near Arnhem, their Mitchell, FW106, 226 Squadron, was hit by 88mm flak.

Jimmy Warren had just asked if he could remove his flak suit – to which Keith Pendray said 'No. We're too near Arnhem' – when 'the first four bursts – dead accurate for height – appeared... the next lot got us.' The two gunners baled out, but Freddie Turner and Keith Pendray (on his thirty-sixth operation) 'went down with the aircraft into the biggest field in Holland near Den Dungen', a couple of kilometres south east of 's-Hertogenbosch. 'The gunners landed just on the wrong side of the lines in the Eindhoven salient. Freddie and I were picked up by some very young soldiers within minutes of landing.' (Keith Pendray.) The four airmen were reunited at a camp in Amersfoort before beginning the long road to Bankau together.

*

On arriving on 37 Squadron at Foggia, Italy, at the end of August 1944 Sgt K.W. Saxton and crew were told that a few days earlier an American B-17 Flying Fortress 'had landed on the runway strip and had exploded due to a bomb failing to release over the target. A few days later,' continued Bill Haddon:

> 'and it was our first operational flight. When we met to be taken to the plane our rear gunner was missing. He had gone AWOL. The squadron commander, a group captain [sic], said he would be the rear gunner. Nearly half-way down the metal strip runway the plane veered to starboard off the runway and into scrubland, and after a few bumps we came to a standstill. The group captain said "Run for it lads" and he was the first one out closely followed by the rest of us. I contend that he was unofficially the first man to cover 100 metres in under 10 seconds, but it could be argued that it was "wind" assisted! However, the plane did not explode and was recovered by the ground crew the next day. The rear gunner was captured in Naples and later faced a court martial.'

The Saxton crew were on their thirteenth or fourteenth sortie when they were part of a force of eighty-three aircraft, twelve from 37 Squadron, detailed to bomb Maribor rail yards in northern Yugoslavia on the night of 21/22 October 1944. The raid turned out to be a failure, due to 10/10ths cloud over the target, but the Saxton crew, in Mk.X Wellington bomber LP259 'Y', never even got that far, their Wimpy having developed engine trouble due to icing.

Saxton was killed, but Sgt J.G. Weedon (navigator), Sgt W.R. 'Bill' Haddon (bomb aimer), Sgt Robert English (wireless operator), and Sgt John H. 'Jimmy' James (rear gunner) survived. Bill Haddon landed in bushes, receiving facial lacerations, before being caught by local police in the town of Luttenberg (today Ljutomer), and taken to the Luftwaffe base at Pulco. On 23 October he was moved to another Luftwaffe base – Graz in Austria – and, bunged into a cell in the guardroom, was delighted to discover that Gordon Weedon and Jimmy James were already there. They were joined next day by Bob English. All four would eventually find themselves at Luft 7, Haddon and James in *Trupp 47*, the other two in *Trupp 48*.

*

37 Squadron were to lose a second Wimpy, ME880, on the Maribor raid and, as with LP259, only the pilot – P/O Brian Charlton Jeffares RNZAF – was killed with the rest of the crew surviving as POWs. Landing in the mountains of Yugoslavia, they were taken hostage by the *Ustaše*, members of the Croatian Revolutionary Movement who were fighting against Tito's partisans and were therefore on the side of the Germans. Two weeks later they were handed over to the Germans in Zagreb.

Their troubles were now only just beginning. They were placed in cells with wooden partitions, and found that there were several American airmen in the adjoining cells. Eric Scott, ME880's bomb aimer, takes up the story:

'Eventually we all entrained and found ourselves heading for Budapest. On arrival the first shells from Russian artillery started to hit the town and the station. All platforms were choked with both civilian and military trying to get on any train which was capable of leaving the city. We were eventually jammed onto a train with our guards, and once more headed back to Jugoslavia.

'On the following day, whilst travelling just north of Zagreb, the train came to an abrupt halt. I looked out of the window and saw the first of three Typhoons [sic] turning to attack the train. Fortunately the compartment window was large and could be lowered. In a few seconds we were out of the train and clambering up the railway banking. Our guards followed, but more slowly as they were much older and less agile.'

Guard and prisoner alike took shelter behind a stone monument as rockets blasted the locomotive. The train was then plastered by cannon shells, killing and wounding many German army personnel. Scott: 'After the attack we were in a very precarious situation, as the Germans were intent on despatching us "into the next world".' Fortunately, a German officer intervened, but only after the prisoners had been lined up in a field 'for the chop'. Another train appeared and the journey was continued to Vienna.

Their arrival there coincided with the end of a bombing raid, 'which had demolished a large residential area of flats'. The prisoners then had to cross from one station to another: 'We were not at all popular and many bricks, stones and pieces of concrete were thrown at us as we beat the guards quite easily to the railway station.' No further adventures befell the POWs, and Eric Scott and his wireless operator, F/S A.R. Nicol, safely reached Luft 7 in *Trupp 48*.

\*

Also in *Trupp 47* were another eight prisoners from Stalag XIIA (Limburg), including both pilots of a Horsa glider that had descended on Arnhem on 18 September after they had been cast off from their Stirling tug. S/Sgt David S. Broadley (first pilot) and Sgt John R. Horton had brought with them a six-pounder anti-tank gun and its crew. Joining the gunners in the fight, they knocked out an enemy tank on 21 September, the day on which they were captured by men of the Hermann Göring Panzer Division who, after heavy mortar fire, had charged with bayonets fixed.

After a very quick stop at Oberursel the two pilots went to Stalag XIIA, where they arrived on 1 October, the day before a further sixty-three glider pilots joined them. As Newton and Smithson noted, life at Limburg was not pleasant, nor were matters improved when, on 3 October, rations were stopped because beds and a sentry box had been used for firewood! After three weeks at Limburg they were purged on 22 October to Oberursel, to Wetzlar on 26 October and, on 8 November, to Luft 7, where they arrived four days later.

\*

S/Sgt Pat Withnall GPR was on the third lift to Arnhem, on 19 September, on Operation Market, with his second pilot, Sgt Ken Travis-Davison GPR. Towed there in their 'G' Squadron Horsa glider, Chalk Number 139, by Halifax LL409 (F/S R.F. Mackrill) of 298 Squadron, they were cast off from the tug a mile short of the LZ, but made a successful landing with two Jeeps and six troops of the 1st Polish Parachute Brigade:

'We were hit whilst landing and came under fire again as we struggled to unload our Jeeps and to see our Polish passengers on their way. Ken and I were pinned down in a wood. We became separated. He made his way to Arnhem. I came across a German patrol and had to wait until nightfall. I was later joined by another member of the Airborne forces and we began to make our way towards the river [Rhine]. I was picked up about midday on the following morning.'

While Ken Travis-Davison[162] went to Stalag XIIA, Pat went to Luft 7.

*

Armourers LAC Alexander Jardine RCAF and Corporal Eric Maycock were working on Spitfires of 126 (RCAF) Wing's squadrons (Nos. 401, 411, and 412), which were closely supporting the Allied advance through Belgium and into Holland in September and October 1944. Moving forward from one airfield to another, 126 Wing had reached airfield B.84 at Rips on 4 October. On the day before, however, Jardine and Maycock had taken a truck and 'decided to scout around the immediate area to find some suitable material on which to put certain armaments rather than [onto] the damp ground. Unfortunately, the immediate area was also home to the German army, who were not advised of our coming! They demolished the truck, and almost [did] the same to us.'[163] The two armourers were captured at Grave, near Eindhoven, having apparently been mis-directed by a phoney Dutch policeman. They arrived at Luft 7 (Trupp 47) on 12 November.

(Maycock's POW number, 1114, was clearly issued at Luft 7, but Jardine's, 076594, was not. Eight GPR men in Trupp 47, all captured at Arnhem, also unusually had POW numbers beginning with the three digits 075 or 076.)

*

**13 NOVEMBER 1944.** On behalf of the Swiss Protecting Power, Dr Albert A. Kadler made his third visit to Luft 7. He noted that Behr was still commandant; his adjutant was Oberleutnant Owin; Major Peschel was still security officer; and camp officers were Hauptmann Wiener and Zimmerman. Absent was the Medical Officer Stabsarzt Dr. Ebersberger. For the POWs, Thomson, Greene and Walkty were respectively Camp Leader, Man of Confidence, and adjutant. The number of POWs had now risen to 1,363: 984 UK; twenty-two Irish; 193 Canadians; 106 Australians; twenty New Zealanders; fifteen South Africans; ten Gaullists [Free French]; and thirteen others. Included in the total were Padré Collins, and five medical orderlies.

At the time of Kadler's previous visit on 12 September the POWs were in the 'chicken huts'. Now Kadler:

'was glad to find the men in their new quarters… The compound which the prisoners took over is the first of four similar compounds at present under construction. The camp consists of:

8 barracks for men holding 10 rooms of 16, one of 8, and one of 6, a cooking-room and a night-latrine.

1 barrack serving for the camp's administration and all entertainment and studying purposes.

1 large cookhouse with adjoining theatre-room.

1 barrack holding the Revier and some German administration offices.

2 combined latrine- and bath- and washhouses.

In the middle of these barracks is a very large sports- and parade-ground, the whole camp being laid out in a manner to give plenty of moving space to everybody.'[164]

Kadler also noted that 'Interior Arrangements' (bedding, lighting, heating) were 'Adequate', and that 'Bathing and Washing Facilities' were 'Satisfactory'. A 'fairly good stock of Red Cross parcels' was available, with the main store 'at Kreuzburg near the station'. The Revier (sick quarters) was 'wired-off from the other barracks as about half of the barrack is taken up by German officers. There are at present 32 beds available, 18 were occupied on the date of visit. No serious cases here, but six men are at present being treated at the Lazarett at Lamsdorf Stalag 344.' Kadler was also told that, while Bruce Davis (see page 162) 'feels much better', 'there are now quite a number of men in this camp who begin to show signs of mental unbalance. It is therefore absolutely necessary that a British medical officer is being sent to this camp.'

Though the men's religious needs were being taken care of by Captain The Reverend Collins, he was Church of England, while the Roman Catholics 'of which there about 150 in camp have no attendance'. This matter would be addressed with the arrival of Captain John Berry (see page 203).

Overall, Kadler was impressed with the camp: 'Materially speaking it may be considered as the best air-force camp in Germany except perhaps the Dulag Luft at Wetzlar. The Camp Commander takes a personal interest in the welfare of the prisoners of war and is quite proud for being able to build up such a good camp as it really is.'

Compound Capers, the first theatrical production at the camp, was presented at the theatre, with music provided by the Accordian Band and by the Harmonicats. One of the gags was:

'What did the brassière say to the top hat?'
'You go on ahead. I'll bring these two!'

The show was well received, and the feeling was that the performers deserved great credit for their efforts.

**14 NOVEMBER 1944.** There was a lot of snow on the ground when a party of POWs, with a guard called Ludwig, went out of the camp to get some wood. They were gone a couple of hours. Ludwig was in no hurry to get back.

**15 NOVEMBER 1944.** Table Tennis League began. The camp's 'Little Theatre' opened in the dining hall. The stage and scenery were made from odds and ends in the camp, and costumes from old clothes. Rookery Nook was performed, followed by a musical revue by Leo Maki's Hepcats, together with three short sketches. The whole show lasted three hours. More snow fell during the night.

**16 NOVEMBER 1944.** Bitterly cold. Red Cross food parcels cut to one per fortnight. The Germans sensibly held roll-call in the barracks.

**17 NOVEMBER 1944.** Snow still falling. Camp site very wet and muddy. Good news received that a new offensive had started on the Western Front. An air raid in the afternoon. The camp's Dickens Fellowship Society held its first meeting.

*

Deryck Lambert tells an amusing story that, perhaps, took place around this time. One of the POWs in his room told of the time when he and his crew were boarding a Lancaster bomber on a 5 Group airfield in Lincolnshire. One of those climbing aboard was of considerable size, requiring the story-teller to assist the bulky personage into the Lancaster's fuselage, remarking as he did so: 'They want to get some bloody thinner aircrew for this job!' The airman then saw the 'dog collar' round the large person's neck, and promptly fell over backwards!

At this point Deryck, who was listening to this story, announced to the room: 'The rather large person with the "dog collar" trying to get into a Lancaster was my father!' (As Canon of Blackburn Cathedral, Deryck's father had been appointed as the Archbishop of York's Visitor to the Royal Air Force). 'This resulted in considerable hilarity, in fact uncontrollable laughter – made even less controllable when I disappeared through the scanty bed boards and appeared on the bunk below!'

Deryck explained the reason for the lack of bed boards. In the huts:

> 'we slept in bunk-beds – an upper and a lower – which consisted of the frame with 6-inch wide loose boards forming the base for a straw filled "mattress". As the winter progressed these boards became a source of fuel to keep the stove satisfied and the room warm. It was, of course, more and more difficult to balance on them to sleep at night – and sit during the day.'

*

**18 NOVEMBER 1944.** Weather was so bad that *Appell* was held indoors. Rookery Nook was performed for the third time.

**19 NOVEMBER 1944.** *Trupp 48* (forty-five men) arrived.

*

Having survived thirty operations since joining 640 Squadron from 1652 OCU (Marston Moor) on 15 July 1944, Dutchman 'Kees' Goemans and his crew were on the trip to the Nordstern oil refinery in the Ruhr on 13 September, when their flight engineer, Sgt L.W. Tratt, was hit in the right hand by a splinter, and Kees landed at Horham in Suffolk, home of the 95th Bomb Group, 8th USAAF.

On the night of 4/5 November 1944 (Bochum), luck ran out for F/O Cornelius Jacobus Maria 'Kees' Goemans (pilot); Sgt Patrick Finnigan (flight engineer, replacement for Sgt Tratt); F/S R.G. Purcell (navigator); F/S H.D. Patterson (bomb aimer);[165] F/S F. Nuttall (wireless operator); Sgt R.R. Heath (mid-upper gunner); and New Zealander Sgt Graham Vincent Korner RAF (rear gunner). They were on their way back from the target when Halifax MZ930 C8-K was hit by a flak shell that 'went right through the nose from starboard to port and beside the pilot, killing him outright'. At the same time the Halifax caught fire. Showing extreme bravery the wireless operator, F/S Freddie Nuttall, 'took over the controls and held aircraft steady although flames [were] blowing back over him. He did not get out.'

That was the simple, short version from Graham 'Kiwi' Korner.[166] The fuller story takes longer to tell, starting with the moment when the two gunners noticed a line of flak bursts across their path, too late to warn Kees Goemans to take avoiding action. Graham Korner counted another three bursts before the fourth struck the cockpit and killed Kees. Amazingly, Freddie Nuttall, who was standing beside his pilot when the shell exploded and was unhurt, instinctively removed Kees and, occupying the empty seat, grabbed the controls to try to bring the stricken bomber under some sort of control.

Kees's lifeless body had fallen down the steps into Jock Patterson and Ron Purcell's compartments, his parachute deploying as he fell. In their confined space in the nose of the aircraft Jock and Ron, considerably hampered by the shrouds of Kees's parachute, tried to put out the fire but were unsuccessful. Due to the lack of oxygen, both briefly passed out. Regaining consciousness at almost the same time, they tried again to dampen the fierce blaze with fire extinguishers, but to no avail and, when Ron tried to throw down the red-hot extinguisher that he had been using, it stuck to his hands. As Jock tugged it away from Ron, it took the skin away from Ron's hands.

Giving up on using the front escape hatch, Jock and Ron made their way to the rear, grabbing a parachute as they passed the stowage. Clipping on his 'chute, Ron looked back and saw Freddie Nuttall still at the controls, his flying suit ablaze. Ron shouted to him to leave the controls and get out, but Freddie just waved at him to go, and stayed there fighting to keep the aircraft as level as he could while the others got out. Ron quickly followed Jock, noticing as he reached the rear hatch that the lower part of his trousers had burnt off and that his legs, too, were burnt. He jumped into space and, though he had to use his arm to open his parachute, had no recollection of having pulled the rip-cord. Both he and Jock landed safely, as did Kiwi Korner and Ron Heath.

When 'Paddy' Finnigan, however, found that his parachute had been burnt, not wishing to chance his luck with a weakened one, he arranged to go out clutching onto Ron Heath's back. Alas, when Ron's parachute snapped open, Paddy lost his tenuous grip, and plunged 10,000 feet to his death. (See the Tom Cloran incident on page 70).

Parachuting down Ron Purcell saw the blazing Halifax suddenly dive and go into a spin, and presumed that this was the moment when Freddie left the controls in an attempt to save himself. If so, it was to no avail, for his body was found in the aircraft's wreckage on the banks of the River Rhine, some 300 yards from the Holy Ghost ferry at Rhein, near Solingen.

Of the four survivors, Ron Purcell landed in the garden of a house near Düsseldorf, his burning parachute (he had never completely managed to extinguish it) having been mistaken for a flare by an old man and a young boy on the ground. With much compassion these two, and an old woman who had joined them, did what they could to ease his burns before he was 'taken to hospital at Gerrisheim, on the outskirts of Düsseldorf, where he underwent a number of skin-graft operations'. These grafts were so good, apparently, that after the war surgeons back in England said that they were some of the best they had seen. When deemed well enough Ron was transferred to Stalag XIIID (Nuremberg) and then to Stalag VIIA (Moosburg), near Munich, where he was liberated by the US Third Army on 29 April 1945.[167]

Graham Korner, having simply turned his rear turret onto the beam, jumped out and landed, he thought, somewhere in a suburb of Düsseldorf. It was, he said, a 'very nice country area with fir tree plantations about. Saw road sign to Solingen and started to walk in this direction when came upon huts at side of road and suddenly challenged by little Volksturmer with very big rifle pointed at me. He was so excited that I think he might have shot me had another Volksturmer not come out!'

For him, Jock Patterson and Ron Heath, there was nothing to look forward to but the long journey to Luft 7, where they arrived on 19 November in *Trupp 48*.

*

The Bochum raid on 4/5 November 1944 had proved costly for RAF Bomber Command, with twenty-three of 749 bombers failing to return, five Halifaxes alone from the French 346 (Guyenne) Squadron, which lost NA121, NA546, NA549, NA558, and NR181. Eight of the captured survivors went to Luft 7, the first being Sergent-Chef Robert H. Vlaminck FAFL, wireless operator of NA558, in *Trupp 48*.

Shortly after leaving the target NA558 was attacked by a night-fighter and set on fire. As the

Halifax went into a dive the pilot, Adjutant Robert A. Hannedouche, gave the order to bale out. The navigator, Lt J. Vles, removed the escape hatch and was about to jump when, through all the smoke in the fuselage, he noticed Robert Vlaminck slumped unconscious over his radio. Without a thought for his own safety Vles went over to Vlaminck, brought him round and, dragging him to the escape hatch, pushed him out, a courageous act that would cost Vles his life.

Seconds later the Halifax exploded. Only three survived – Vlaminck, already on his way down thanks to Vles; the rear gunner Sergent-Chef Henri Olive who had baled out; and the pilot, Hannedouche, who was blown out by the explosion. Olive, though wounded, landed near the village of Burg (seven kilometres from Wermelskirchen). He was taken prisoner but was then killed by German soldiers. Thus, only Vlaminck and Hannedouche (he arrived at Luft 7 in *Trupp 50*, see page 200) lived to see the victory for which they and their compatriots had so gallantly strived.

*

**20 NOVEMBER 1944.** A fine day. Another air raid around noon. American B-17s seen overhead. WO1 Ivan Jervis RCAF 'made a dash for the latrine; a guard took a shot at him. No one has been hit yet, but the shots sure scare hell out of us.' (John McConnell.) See also the incident on 24 September (page 165).

**21 NOVEMBER 1944.** Another fine day. More Red Cross food parcels and musical instruments arrived.

**22 NOVEMBER 1944.** A de-lousing party under the guard Ludwig went to Kreuzburg. 'We enjoyed the walk, and were allowed to stay longer than usual. We all wished we could have kept going.' (John McConnell.)

**24 NOVEMBER 1944.** *Trupp 49* (ten men, mostly ex-hospital cases) arrived.
   Another concert was held, a revue called Dancing Time. The accordian band played popular tunes, and a good impersonation of George Formby was also given. Many were left feeling home-sick after.

*

Ken Dobbs arrived at Kreuzburg with Johnny Hymas, Ernie Stokes, and others, from Meiningen hospital:

> 'We were transported by train, and on arrival found that we had a march of some five miles through thick snow to the camp. My condition was not up to this and I kept falling back on the main party. The German guard at the rear had to keep behind the last man and was eventually jabbing my backside with his bayonet, shouting "Schnell!" If I could have just laid down in the snow and gone to sleep I would have done so, I was so exhausted.'

Though Ken made it in the end, he was not a well man. He collapsed whilst watching a boxing match, and was taken to the camp Lazarett.

He had spent much of the last nine months in a Lazarett of one sort or another, starting in Lille, France, where he shared a room with Johnny Hymas, a Spitfire pilot shot down in January 1944. One of Ken's thumbs was badly broken, so badly that he thought it would have to be amputated, until a German surgeon asked him what he did in civilian life. Ken replied 'Concert pianist', which was bending the truth, though he could play a piano. 'We must try and save your thumb,' said the surgeon, 'and when you are able you can come and play for us.' Ken kept his thumb, but had left Lille before it had healed. His next hospital was Obermassfeld, where he suffered blood poisoning, 'which did make me very ill'. Eventually, he was moved to Meiningen and, briefly, to Luft 7.

*

Experts have long pondered over who it was who caused the death of the Luftwaffe's top-scoring night-fighter pilot, Major Heinrich Prinz zu Sayn-Wittgenstein, on the night of 21/22 January 1944 (Magdeburg). His Ju88, coded R4+XM, was unquestionably hit by fire from an enemy aircraft, possibly from a Mosquito or from a Lancaster, resulting in his death, though the two others of his crew were to survive.

After the war, the family of F/Sgt Albert Williston RCAF, the rear gunner of Lancaster LL672, 514 Squadron, received a letter from the bomb aimer, F/O Earl Clare RCAF, in which he said that they had twice been attacked on the Magdeburg raid by a night-fighter, and that their Lancaster had been set on fire on the first attack. In his book *Through Footless Halls of Air* author Floyd Williston, brother of Albert, suggests, after much careful research, that their assailant *could* have been, perhaps, zu Sayn-Wittgenstein.[168] Both LL672 and R4+XM apparently crashed not far from each other, near a place called Stendal.

Whether or not it was Albert and Sgt Jack Brewer, the mid-upper gunner, who in return shot down Ju88 R4+XM, will never be known, for Albert perished along with flight engineer Sgt Pete McQueeney, though the other five crew survived. One of them, Sgt Ronald L. Smith, was badly burned. After several months at the Obermassfeld Lazarett he arrived at Luft 7 with *Trupp 49*, though later transferred to another camp, possibly for repatriation.

Another of the wounded from Obermassfeld to arrive in *Trupp 49* was TSM Basil Lancelot Baugh RM. He probably should never have been sent to Luft 7 as he was a Royal Marine commando. In his report to MI9 made on 14 May 1945 he declared that the military unit to which he belonged was part of 1st Special Service Brigade (1st SS Bde), and that he was wounded and captured near the River Orne, France, on 12 June 1944. After several months in hospital he was sufficiently mended to be sent to a permanent camp.

1st SS Bde was raised by Brigadier the Lord Lovat DSO MC, specifically for the Normandy landings in June 1944, with Nos. 3, 4, 6 and 45 (Royal Marine) Commandos. Having landed on Sword Beach on D-Day, 6 June, the Brigade, together with airborne troops, held the Allies' eastern flank along the River Orne. They were, however, at a strategic disadvantage given that the Germans' 346th Infantry Division were lodged on higher ground in the village of Bréville-les-Monts.

On 12 June, therefore, 12th Parachute Battalion (350 men) and 'D' Company 12th Battalion Devonshire Regiment (86 men) were ordered to capture Bréville in an attack commencing at 2200 hours. It was preceded by an artillery barrage, one shell from which fell short, killing the CO of 12th Parachute Battalion (Lt Col A.P. Johnston) and seriously wounding Lord Lovat and Brigadier H. Kindersley (6th Airlanding Brigade). For this attack, 'A' Troop (Captain E. E. Grewcock), 45 (RM) Commando was asked to supply one officer and twenty other ranks. The attack, now referred to as the Battle of Bréville, was successful, and ensured that the eastern flank of the landing area was secure. It is conjectured that Basil Baugh may have been captured during the battle.

**26 NOVEMBER 1944.** Sunny day. A musical was staged. The sex-starved prisoners were enthralled by the performance of Freddy Jones as 'Geraldine': 'The boys all hooted and whistled. Freddy sure made a good-looking girl.' As was usual, the front seats were occupied by the Germans who, when the show was over, 'gave the boys a standing ovation'.

Another prisoner gave a talk about a voyage to the moon, and landing on it. The audience thought that he was a comedian and laughed at him to start with.

**27 NOVEMBER 1944.** The Germans kept the prisoners waiting on parade because, they said, 'we have consistently kept him waiting'.

**28 NOVEMBER 1944.** *Trupp 50* (forty-five men) arrived, as did the promised medical officer, Captain D.G. Howatson RAMC (99321).[169]

Bitterly cold again, freezing hard and a slight fog.

\*

When intelligence was received that the German minelayer *Zeus* (the former Italian merchantman *Francesco Morosini*, 2,423 tons) was on her way down the Aegean Sea from the northern Greek port of Salonika to Piraeus, near Athens, W/C C. Foxley-Norris, 603's squadron commander, set off with ten of his own Mk.TFX Beaufighters and two more from 252 Squadron to sink her.

Taking off at around midday on 3 October 1944 from Gambut III airfield, some fifty miles east of Tobruk in the North African desert, the Beaufighters failed to locate the *Zeus*, but they did come across a convoy of five small, heavily-armed vessels to the east of Athens. The 'Beaus' went in firing their rockets and cannons, but the ships' gun crews gave a good account of themselves. They shot down two of 603's Beaufighters – aircraft NT893 'P' and NV205 'W' – and damaged four more. Only three of the vessels were damaged, and there were no reports of any sinking.

The pilot of Beaufighter 'P', Sgt D. Harrison, was killed, but his navigator, Sgt D.V. Bannister, was reported to be in safe hands. Both the crew of 'W' survived their ditching – F/O C.M. de Bounevialle (pilot) and F/Sgt A.E. Potter (navigator). They were seen to go down with their starboard engine on fire. Albert Potter – always called 'Gillie' by his pilot after the radio comedian of the time – thought that they might have hit a cable suspended from a balloon above the ship that they attacked. As he said: 'Never really discussed it. Just glad to get out of the water.' This was their second ditching. Barely ten weeks earlier, on 23 July 1944, they had been rescued from the sea off the island of Mykonos by a Greek caique, eventually rejoining their squadron via Turkey, Syria, and Cairo.

F/O Casimir Marmaduke de Bounevialle, known as 'Cas', had already flown a tour on 227 Squadron, and had been awarded the DFC on 7 December 1943:

> 'This officer has participated in a large number of sorties, involving attacks on roads, airfields and on shipping. On one occasion he took part in an attack on shipping off the Tunisian coast. During the action a large motor vessel and an F-boat were destroyed. On other occasions, Pilot Officer Bounevialle has attacked two large motor vessels, an F boat and a schooner with damaging effect. In air combat, he has assisted in the destruction of 2 enemy aircraft. This officer has displayed great skill, courage and devotion to duty.'[170]

Prior to the war Cas had been an examiner in the Aeronautical Inspection Directorate, before becoming a garage proprietor in Luton. Things didn't work out for him financially, and a petition for bankruptcy was filed against him on 17 August 1939. With far weightier matters about to muddy the legal waters the petition was suspended *sine die* on 22 September 1939.

Now down in the Aegean drink for the second time, he and Albert were fished out of the water by the crew of a German vessel, and taken to Dulag Luft (Athens) for interrogation. They left on 10 October by train for Skopje, Yugoslavia, but progress was slow, their journey being restricted to daylight hours only as partisans had a tendency to attack trains at night. It was more than a week later before they reached Skopje. From there they were flown by Junkers Ju52 to Zagreb. A train took them via Budapest to Vienna, where they were split up, Cas going on to Stalag Luft III. Albert was placed in a civilian jail for a further week before being sent to Dulag Luft (Oberursel). He was there for the best part of a month before heading off with *Trupp 50* for Luft 7.

It was on 30 January 1945, while they were being evacuated from Luft 7, that 1395820 F/Sgt Albert Edward Potter was commissioned (188632), seniority back-dated to 2 October 1944, the day before his second 'swim' in the Aegean. Albert: 'I was wounded on 252 Squadron earlier in the year and they told me that I was being recommended while I was in hospital at Mersa Matruh. I didn't know of my exalted rank until arrival in UK at end of war.'

*

Arriving at Bankau in *Trupp 50* with Adjutant Hannedouche was mid-upper gunner Sergent Marcel A. Debroise FAFL, one of only two survivors of Halifax LW443, 346 Squadron, lost on 2/3 November 1944 (Düsseldorf). The other survivor, rear gunner Sgt Guy Soury-Lavergne FAFL, successfully evaded capture, gaining the American lines after he had walked through a mine field.

Two more 346 Squadron FAFL aircrew arrived with *Trupp 50*, Adjutant Jean A. Cloarec (wireless operator) and Adjutant Jacques Manfroy (rear gunner), both from Halifax NA549, one of the five lost on the Bochum raid in November. All seven crew baled out, but two of them were killed before reaching the ground. Captain A. Beraud (pilot) crashed onto the roof of the church at Stommeln (north west of Cologne) after his parachute had been torn, and Lt P. Raffin (navigator) was electrocuted when he fell onto high-tension cables.

*

**30 NOVEMBER 1944.** 'Went to the show at night – Leo Maki's "Dancing Time". It was marvellous – I couldn't wish to see a better show in "civvy" street. There was George Formby, "Geraldine", Leo Maki's Accordian Band etc. Oh boy, what a laugh and what a swing.' (Tom Glenn.)

## CHAPTER TEN

# DECEMBER 1944, *TRUPPEN 51-56*

**1-19 DECEMBER 1944.** *Truppen 51-54* arrived. German records are, at this point, again obscure, and it has not been possible to identify who arrived with which *Trupp* on which date.

**2 DECEMBER 1944.** Very cold. Over 250 American B-17 Flying Fortress bombers were counted by the prisoners as they flew over the camp at barely 10,000 feet. 'It lifted our morale. No flak, no fighters.' (Fred Brown), but one was seen to lag behind with engine trouble.

An International Trial soccer match between England and Scotland ended in a 0-0 draw.

**3 DECEMBER 1944.** A lot of activity was observed on the railway, and the sounds of gunfire could be heard away to the east. Surely the Russians were getting closer? Morale took another upward turn.

Great Britain lost 0-4 to the Dominions at rugby.

Padré Captain Collins gave a talk on the University Boat Races 1928-30.

The 1933 film The Private Life of Henry VIII was shown. Starring Charles Laughton, Merle Oberon and others, the many scenes of feasting proved too much for the hungry prisoners – 'we all felt worse after seeing it'.

**4 DECEMBER 1944.** Rained for twenty-four hours. The Little Theatre put on a play reading of Journey's End. It was banned by the Germans because one of the actors said 'Boche' instead of 'Jerry'.

**5 DECEMBER 1944.** Second reading of Journey's End.

**6 DECEMBER 1944.** Very cold. It took the POWs a long time to get out of bed in the morning. A number of them were also suffering from 'flu.

Three films arrived with mini-projector. First film shown – The Corsican Brothers (1941), with Douglas Fairbanks Jnr and Ruth Warwick. Apart from the sound apparatus not working properly due to insufficient power and, again, too much food on display in the movie, it was much enjoyed. The film was shown again over the next two days.

**7 DECEMBER 1944.** Very cold. Parcel situation apparently becoming grim. Potato ration cut by a quarter.

**9 DECEMBER 1944.** Getting colder and colder.

**11 DECEMBER 1944.** England beat Canada 6-0 at rugby.

**12 DECEMBER 1944.** An air raid was heard in the morning, bombs exploding.

**13 DECEMBER 1944.** Second film – Life Begins For Andy Hardy (1941), starring Mickey Rooney and Judy Garland – given its first showing.

At evening *Appell*, the Camp Leader, adjutant, and Man of Confidence announced that they had resigned. No reason was given, but the prisoners held a meeting and a vote of confidence in their leaders was passed.

**14 DECEMBER 1944.** It had been freezing hard all night, and a gale was blowing from the east. Going outside the huts in the very low temperature was not recommended. By tea-time the temperature was minus 5° C.

By mid-December the total of POWs in the camp had risen to 1,475.

**15 DECEMBER 1944.** Again very cold, with snow all night. Temperature down to minus 18° C. The Canadians built two ice rinks, which were well used despite the cold. A party of kriegies left the camp to gather wood for the stoves.

**16 DECEMBER 1944.** The show Moods Modernistic was put on by Bob Burns and his orchestra. The feeling was that there was a big improvement thanks to the addition of new instruments and more time in which to practise. Some of the POWs, however, preferred Leo Maki's band, and one thought the performance was 'bloody awful'.

**17 DECEMBER 1944.** SS officers arrived early in the morning to carry out an inspection, but did not complete it because of an air raid. '36 Forts circled the camp at about 8,000 feet and dropped leaflets. All kriegies were already inside. Ferrets and goons came into the compound to pick up the leaflets that landed within the camp.' (Fred Brown.) Another aircraft jettisoned bombs on Bankau village, killing six people and destroying their farm.

Unrest amongst the POWs resulted in accusations being made against the Man of Confidence, W/O Richard Greene RCAF, and the adjutant. The charges, amongst others, included slackness, inability, using YMCA and Red Cross equipment that did not belong to them, the mis-use of personal property, and Greene not giving proper attention and courtesy to those wanting advice. Matters came to a head when, after the Germans had mistakenly confiscated a number of personal blankets, Greene allegedly did nothing to get them back. The owners of the blankets retrieved them themselves, but in the process discovered that Red Cross receipts had not been checked for two months and other details had not been notified to the Red Cross in formal reports. Those charged agreed to resign from their posts, but it was decided that they should remain in office until word had been received from the Red Cross in Geneva as to what should be done.

**18 DECEMBER 1944.** More air raids heard to the south. Snow thawing.

**19 DECEMBER 1944.** After the 'All Clear' had sounded after yet another air raid, two shots were fired at someone looking out of a lavatory window. Two holes were found at the end of the building near the roof. Camp guards now had orders to shoot to kill: 'Tensions and uncertainties continue to grow. The guards were very much on edge. Perhaps the Russians were closer than we thought.'

A Vote of Confidence was taken on the leaders. Camp Leader, Peter Thomson, was voted back into office by a vast majority of 971. The Man of Confidence lost the vote by 750 to 560.

**20 DECEMBER 1944.** Bitterly cold. Third and last film shown – Dixie Dugan (1943), starring Lois Andrews and James Ellison. Also shown was a reel of the USAAF Band which had somehow been passed by the German censor.

*Trupp 55* (fifty-five-eighty men?) arrived. Captain The Reverend John Berry, a Roman Catholic padré, also arrived at this time. He had been captured in Greece on 27 April 1941, the day on which German forces entered Athens. He had been at Stalag VIIIB (Lamsdorf) until transferred to Luft 7.

*

On the night of 16/17 August 1944 Johnny Shields and crew, in Lancaster, PB384, 57 Squadron, were laying mines in the Stettin/Swinemünde channel to prevent German troops from being evacuated by sea from East Prussia to Stettin when they were shot down. Brief details of the Bomber Command operation were recorded by 97 (PFF) Squadron:

'At 1:01 the flare force came in and dropped their blind bombing apparatus over the channel. Illumination was hardly necessary as the Germans had guessed what was happening and had criss-crossed the bay with searchlights... In the face of great batteries of light flak guns from all sides of the bay, although they were coned the whole time, they [the 97 Squadron crews] located the buoys and flew down the channel...'

It was to prove a costly operation, with several aircraft from other squadrons failing to return.

Johnny Shields (mid-upper gunner) landed in a tree and split his pelvis. He had a spell in a hospital before arriving at Luft 7 in *Trupp 55*. The nineteen-year-old flight engineer, Malcolm Crapper, baled out and landed in the sea. Swimming ashore, he was picked up by a flak-gun crew, and went to Luft 7 in *Trupp 28*. There was only one other survivor, F/O Ron Trindall (bomb aimer), who went to Stalag Luft III.

*

Operation Dragoon, the Allied landings on the south coast of France which had begun on 15 August 1944, was called 'The Champagne Campaign' on account of the apparent lack of enemy resistance to it. Ten days later, good progress northwards having been made by the Allies, F/O Mead, 2788 Squadron, RAF Regiment, and his small force of two armoured cars and a truck carrying twelve men ran into strong German opposition near the town of Valence (Drôme), and were captured. Some escaped from the train taking them north and had rejoined their unit within days.[171] But eleven of the non-escapers eventually arrived at Luft 7, eight with *Trupp 37*, two more with *Trupp 38*, and, lastly, Sgt Myrddin L. Davies with *Trupp 55*.

Another member of the RAF Regiment, LAC R.H. Hutchison, had already been at Bankau for four months before Myrddin Davies's arrival. His active service had come to an abrupt end on 3 October 1943 on the Greek island of Kos, when it was attacked by a strong German force. Robert Hutchison was on 2901 Squadron, RAF Regiment, which had been flown to Kos from Beirut, in the British Mandate of Palestine, with 2909 Squadron on 15 September 1943. The two squadrons were armed with Hispano-Suiza HS.404 guns for anti-aircraft defence in support of 1 Battalion, Durham Light Infantry.

At 4.30 am on the morning of 3 October the German invasion of Kos began. By midday, 1,200 Germans, well-armed with light artillery and armoured cars, were ashore, supported by Ju87 dive-bombers, and by the evening German strength had been increased to an estimated 4,000 men. By 6 am on 4 October 1,388 British and 3,145 Italians (of the island's original garrison) had been taken prisoner, including Robert Hutchison, who arrived at Luft 7 in *Trupp 27* on 22 August 1944 from Stalag Luft VI.

*

'About ten minutes after leaving the target I heard the rear gunner's voice over the intercom giving the order to "Corkscrew Starboard". At the same time he opened fire with his guns. A few seconds later both our starboard engines were hit by cannon fire from an e/a. They both caught fire and the plane went into a dive.' This was the beginning of the end of Halifax MZ806, 192 (Special Duties) Squadron, that had been flying in support of main force on 21/22 November 1944 (Aschaffenburg marshalling yards).

Four of the crew baled out. The aircraft 'kept on its course for about thirty seconds then turned to port, and then to an uncontrolled diving turn to port again. It crashed into the ground about a mile from me and immediately exploded.' The witness to the end of MZ806 was its wireless operator, F/S J.G. 'Jack' Smith RAAF, who, a few seconds later, found himself standing in the middle of a wood: 'The trees had broken my fall and the 'chute had caught in the branches just high enough to allow me to touch the ground.'

Walking for a few hours in a westerly direction, despite a twisted ankle and knee, he was crossing a road when he 'ran into a patrol of Wehrmacht [soldiers]', who called on him to halt. Pretending not to hear them he carried on, but they were already after him, and easily caught him. On 23 November he was taken to a railway station, where he was joined by his navigator, Sgt Stan Wharton. They were briefly taken to Darmstadt hospital but Stan, who had also injured himself landing, was not treated – they 'only looked at him'.

At Dulag Luft Jack was told that the rest of the crew were dead: 'It seems incredible that I was the only one to escape alive and uninjured out of eight.' Along with Jack and Stan, however, F/S A.P. Bloomfield (bomb aimer) and Sgt R.B. Hales (flight engineer) had also safely baled out, but were murdered by local police, one of whom, Friedrich Horn, hanged himself ten days before his trial for the murders. On 9 June 1945 the bodies of Bloomfield and Hales were exhumed. An examination by an officer of the US Army Medical Corps revealed that Hales had probably been wounded in the aircraft – a metal fragment was found in his left thigh – and had then been killed by a pistol shot to the chest, fired from a distance of no greater than three feet. Bloomfield, wounded in the left foot and ankle, had been shot four times. For their complicity in the murders four Germans received terms of imprisonment ranging from five to fifteen years. Two more were killed in a car crash before the end of the war, and one was never traced. (For further details of this incident see *Footprints on the Sands of Time*, pages 208-9).

Jack and Stan, after six days and nights on the train, arrived at Luft 7 on 20 December.

\*

When the German army was preparing to retreat from the Balkans in late 1944 it was clear that they would have to use the railway through the Hungarian town of Szombathely, a dozen kilometres east of the Austrian border. On the night of 22/23 November 1944 seventy-nine Halifaxes, Wellingtons and Liberators of 205 Group RAF were despatched from Italian airfields to bomb its marshalling yards and railway junction.

The attack got off to a bad start when the town was found to be blanketted by mist: 'No target indicators were dropped, and the bombing was very scattered. A few aircraft identified the town and river, and eight claimed to have located and bombed the target, but the majority aimed at flares and the glow of incendiaries.'[172] Luftwaffe night-fighters took advantage of the prevailing conditions of moonlight above and haze below and shot down six of the bombers, including Halifax JP323, 'I', 614 Squadron, based at Amendola (Foggia), Italy. Skippered by P/O John L. 'Nick' Nicholson the five other crew were (there was no mid-upper turret): F/S R.B. Hitchings (navigator); F/S R.R. Cartwright (bomb aimer); F/S Sydney Barlow (wireless operator); F/S J. Wiles (flight engineer); and F/S R.A. Bennett (rear gunner).

They were an experienced crew, having flown bombing raids over the eight previous months from North Africa, firstly on 150 Squadron in Wellingtons and then in Halifax B.IIs on 614, and had attacked targets in Tunisia, Sicily, Italy, Yugoslavia, Greece and now all the way to Hungary.

At 11.30 am on the morning of 22 November, the Nicholson crew read on the operations board that they were detailed to lead the Pathfinder Force to Szombathely that night with the responsible duty of 'target marker'. This would be the last operation of their tour, their thirty-seventh altogether. Roy Bennett (rear gunner): 'There were a number of crews standing by and remarks were made, "Sod your luck, they don't want us tonight", from those who were not going.'

In Roy Bennetts's words, the crew then went to their tent:

> 'to prepare for the night and get a couple of hours sleep. Just before five that afternoon the twenty-odd crews from 614 Squadron were on the 'drome checking the plane, guns, bombs, flares and every piece of equipment, because for the next few hours this plane was to be our pigeon there and back.
>
> 'Our turn for take-off, we lined up at the end of the runway, but a fuel pipe burst, we had to change kites… We took off twenty minutes behind the others, and from then on it was flat out until we got in front, as the bombing force had to wait until we had marked the target. We were also carrying 10 x 1,000lb bombs…
>
> 'About thirty miles to go and as black as your hat outside, from out of nowhere came a burst of machine-gun fire. The plane shuddered – I yelled down my intercom – violent weaving and the skipper really threw that plane around. We all took up our attack positions. I was sitting there with four machine-guns that could knock the guts out of any other plane, but what could I see? Sweet ---- ---. We jettisoned our bombs and turned for home as the old kite was not acting too well to the controls. There was a strange silence even above the roar of the engines.
>
> 'Then once again the bullets came into the plane, tearing her to pieces. She staggered like a half knocked-out boxer and both starboard engines burst into flames. The skipper and engineer tried to put them out, but without success. Nick then gave the order "Prepare to abandon aircraft"…
>
> 'I moved back into the fuselage, the engineer opened the exit, and the flames came belting through. I sat on the edge [of the escape hatch] and stuck my feet out, then turned around to plug in the intercom to see if there were any more orders, but at that moment the starboard wing came off the plane. All my training was then forgotten. I went out like a ball and not waiting to count three I pulled the ripcord straight away.'

Sydney Barlow and John Wiles recall that they were shot down by an FW190.

The loss of a target marker was most unfortunate, as the recommendation for the award of the DFC to W/O T.C. Shiel, pilot of a 37 Squadron Wellington on the same raid, explains:

> 'One of the target-marking aircraft having been shot down by night-fighters, the bombing aircraft were forced to locate the target for themselves and it was soon evident that there was considerable night-fighter activity in the area, no fewer than five aircraft were seen to be shot down. Warrant Officer Shiel, however, remained in the target area and eventually bombed as accurately as he could under the very poor conditions of illumination and visibility.'[173]

Roy Bennett landed flat on his face in a muddy field, but was not injured. Burying his equipment, including his .38 revolver which, he said, was 'no good to me as I could not hit a barn door with it!', he heard a dog barking. Walking towards the sound he saw an old man come out of a small house.

Explaining as best he could who he was, the man took Roy indoors. The 'house' was just a single room, with three women in it, 'all the wrong ages! The old man then gave me a glass of wine and offered me his bed, which I took as I was pretty tired by then.'

In the morning Roy was joined by John Wiles, the flight engineer, and they were just debating what to do next 'when the door flew open and in came a bayonet followed by Hungarian soldiers, who chained us together and led us to the remains of our crashed plane, and there we saw the skipper's body – a sight that will always stay in my memory'. Twenty-three-year-old Pilot Officer John Leonard Nicholson (179800), the only one to be killed, now rests in Budapest War Cemetery.

While Roy and John were standing by the wreckage:

'a young Hungarian girl offered us a bottle of wine. By signs we got the guards to unchain our hands so that we could drink in comfort. We both noticed that the guards were more interested in the girl than us, so we took a chance and calmly walked away. Approximately three hours later, walking through a small village we turned a corner and ran smack into the SS who, with drawn revolvers, made short work of our freedom.'

Sydney Barlow was captured on 23 November near Zalaegerszeg, some fifty kilometres south of the target, by 'two teenaged LDV types'. Cartwright and Hitchings were also caught, and at some point the five survivors were taken to the civilian jail in Budapest. Not long afterwards they were on the last train to leave the Hungarian capital before the bridge across the Danube was blown up. Within a week or so they had arrived at Luft 7.

At Luft 7, Sydney Barlow met a rear gunner on 150 Squadron, Sgt A.P. 'Mac' McTeer, who had also been flying from Italy. Explaining that he was on 614 Squadron Sydney asked Mac when he had been shot down. When he heard that it was on 3 April Sydney replied: 'Your pilot was Sergeant Pemberton, and I slept in your bed.' Sydney explained to the suitably amazed gunner that the Nicholson crew had ferried a brand new Wellington from the Hawarden works, England, to the aircraft pool at Foggia, Italy, before being posted to 150 Squadron: 'The first night we slept in the parachute room as there were no more tents available, but after the first night 150 lost a crew. The pilot was Sgt Pemberton, whose crew's tent we took over.'

Mac McTeer had indeed been flying on 150 Squadron with F/S George Gordon Pemberton, pilot of Wellington LN858, when it went missing. It was one of the seventy-nine Wimpys and eight Liberators detailed to bomb the Manfred Weiss armaments factory on Csepel Island, just to the south of Budapest, on the night of 3/4 April 1944. As LN858 was approaching Lake Balaton[174] shortly before midnight it was attacked by a Do217 flown by Oberleutnant Hans Krause, 6./NJG101. McTeer managed to hit Krause's aircraft in its port wing, but not fatally. LN858, however, was finished, and Pemberton decided to ditch the stricken Wellington on Lake Balaton. Pemberton had been hit in the leg by Krause's bullets so severely that he bled to death. He, too, now lies in Budapest War Cemetery.

Anthony 'Mac' McTeer was wounded in the attack, when a bullet shot off his left ear before lodging in his head (where it stayed until the day he died). Following hospitalisation in Budapest, he went for further treatment to Lazarett IXC before being sent to Luft 7 in *Trupp 3*.

Also wounded in LN858 was F/S Harry Redpath RAAF, who lost an eye. Initially held for a week at a 'Jewish-Communist concentration camp' in Budapest he was moved, after a fortnight at Hildburghausen, Germany, to the eye-specialist hospital at Lazarett IXB (Bad Soden – the 'Braille School'), under the care of the Scottish ophthalmic surgeon Major David L. Charters RAMC (captured in the Greek campaign in 1941), where he was given a glass eye. Five months later he arrived at Luft 7 in *Trupp 37*. The two others of the crew, F/S W.R. Bennett and F/S L.L. Taylor, were taken prisoner and went to Stalag Luft VI (Heydekrug).

Map from 'RAF Mediterranean Review No. 10', August 1945.

Another victim of the Szombathely raid on 22/23 November was Wellington LP547, 37 Squadron. Attacked by fighters after bombing the target, with both engines out of action, the aircraft on fire, and the bomb aimer and rear gunner killed, the pilot, F/O J.H. Sutcliffe RNZAF, gave the order to bale out. At 6,000 feet, only W/O W.A.H. Board RAAF (wireless operator) and F/O W.F. Woolfrey (navigator) were able to do so. In the words of Bill Board: 'When I left the aircraft the skipper was the only one alive and he was still at the controls. I saw the plane explode just as I left it and am sure he never got out. Plane crashed approx. 20 miles south of the target. I was told three bodies were found in the wreckage of the plane.'

Injuring his legs on landing and unable to walk, Bill was picked up by Hungarian police. A few days later he was at Luft 7 in *Trupp 55*. Woolfrey was captured, and went to Stalag Luft I (Barth).

*

**21 DECEMBER 1944.** Seven candidates had been put forward for the post of Man of Confidence to fill the vacancy caused by the resignation of W/O Greene RCAF. W/O Ron Mead was duly elected after he had received 1,017 of the 1,250 votes cast. He was to remain in that post until the camp was evacuated on 19 January 1945.

Dixie Dugan film shown again.

**22 DECEMBER 1944.** The camp awoke to a temperature of minus 10° C.

*

In December 1944 five American aircrew arrived at Luft 7 from Stalag XIB (Fallingbostel): T/Sgt James E. Swanson; T/Sgt Charles E. Patterson; S/Sgt George S. Burford; S/Sgt Osbon M. Malone; and S/Sgt Eugene H. Shabatura.

Douglas C-47 Skytrain 43-15098, 442nd TCG/306th TCS, was hit by flak at around 2,000 feet, some twenty kilometres south west of Eindhoven, whilst on Operation Market on 17 September 1944. The pilot of 43-15098, 1st Lt John Corsetti USAAF, remained at the controls to allow the four others of his crew to jump, but paid for his gallant action with his life.[175] Swanson, the Skytrain's crew chief, was first to jump, and was captured. The three who baled out after him were hidden in a nearby village, and were liberated a week later by British troops.

Charles Patterson was also a crew chief of Douglas C-47 Skytrain 42-93098, 439th TCG/94th TCS, flown by Major Joseph A. Beck II USAAF, CO of the 94th TCS. With him, as co-pilot, was Captain Fred O. Lorimor, the 94th's operations officer. They were on the second Market lift, on 18 September 1944, towing a Waco CG-4A glider flown by 2nd Lt George T. Hall USAAF and carrying men of the 82nd Airborne.

Slightly off course approaching the Dutch coast, Major Beck made a slight correction, but no sooner had he done so, at around 1420 hours, than 42-93098 came under accurate fire from flak batteries near Haamstede on Schouwen Island. Damage to the Skytrain's port engine was sufficient for the glider to be cast off. Both aircraft made safe landings on Schouwen Island.

Major Beck made a perfect wheels-up landing in the middle of a large field:

> 'After landing we were fired upon from bunkers. T/Sgt Charles E. Patterson – the crew chief – was lying beside Captain Lorimor and after we were captured Sgt Patterson told me that Captain Lorimor had been hit by mortar or artillery shell and had died in a few minutes. I did not see Capt Lorimor's body myself but after we had been captured and taken into the bunkers, the Germans told me that the other officer was dead. This was about twenty minutes after the crash.'

Beck went to Stalag Luft III, and the navigator, Lt Vincent J. Paterno, to Stalag Luft I. Patterson and the wireless operator, Sgt Vernon E. Gillespie, went to Stalag XIB, though Gillespie, hit in his left side by rifle fire, was first taken to the hospital on Schouwen Island, where a doctor pronounced that the wound was not very serious.

Burford, Malone and Shabatura were, respectively, right waist, tail, and left waist gunners of B-24J 42-100416 *Baggy Maggy*, 93rd BG/409th BS, lost on a supply drop to the US Airborne forces in the Nijmegen-Eindhoven area on 18 September.[176] They came down near Castelré, just to the north of Hoogstraten, in Belgium, and very close to the Dutch border.

At Luft 7 the five Americans shared the same room in Hut 49-13, before being moved to another camp, possibly Stalag XIIID (Nuremberg), sometime prior to Luft 7's evacuation in January 1945.

*

**24 DECEMBER 1944.** Great was the elation when a truck arrived loaded with Argentine Red Cross food, mainly cheese and sugar. The cheeses, which were about 12 inches high and 'round in proportion', were distributed one to approximately every thirty prisoners: 'With great ceremony we gathered round the table to make the share between the combines. In went the knife, and then, to our shock and utter dismay, the cheese had a huge cavity in the centre and only a 3-inch skin of cheese.' (Fred Brown.)

Mass was held at 8 pm in the library and at 10.15 pm in the theatre. As a concession, lights stayed on in the barracks until 1.30 am on Christmas Day.

**25 DECEMBER 1944.** A number of POWs went to Midnight Mass. The only parade of the day took place at 0800 hours. The ice rink was again well used, and a football match took place between 'Best 11' and 'The Rest'.

Padré John Collins wrote home to tell his family about Christmas at Luft 7:

> 'It was not at all a bad one considering that Xmas parcels had not arrived. The weather was bright & frosty, with a little snow on the ground, & every room seemed to have its home-made cake, some of which had a disastrous effect on the eaters! For me it was a busy time, which kept me from dwelling too much on the might-have-beens. On Xmas Eve we had a carol service, on the lines of the broadcast from King's Chapel, Cambridge & then someone had asked for a midnight communion, which I arranged at first in our little chapel; after a bit we thought this might not be big enough & decided on the quiet room; then at the last moment we transferred it to the theatre. Eventually, to my dismay, 200 turned up & I had to get through this number single-handed in time for the R.C's to hold theirs too! It was an inspiring service; we had candles from the local church & one of our fellows had made a lovely cross & candlesticks; another had made paper flowers & 2 more a crib, on which they had directed the stage lighting. The effect was lovely.'[177]

There were rumours that the Germans' Ardennes offensive had been stopped, and that the Russians had taken Kraków. Lights out at 10 pm 'after a most enjoyable day'.

**26 DECEMBER 1944.** Parade was held at 10 am. An arts and crafts exhibition was held in the morning. Exhibits included water colours, pencil drawings, oil paintings, models made of soap, wood and tin, embroidery and clothwork, etc. The Australians beat the South Africans 2-0 at soccer.

*Trupp 56* (forty to forty-four men) arrived, bringing the total of POWs to 1,508.

*

F/S Paul Decroix was on an armed reconnaissance on the morning of 3 November 1944 looking for active German guns between the waters of the Hollands Diep and Oude Maas. He was flying in Spitfire PV134 in Blue Section of 349 (Belgian) Squadron when the section flew into a heavy flak barrage over Strijensas, a few miles south of Dordrecht in Zuid-Holland. A 20mm shell hit PV134 fair and square in the oil tank and propeller, forcing Paul to land. Captured within half an hour, having been fired at by machine guns and rifles, German troops took him to a Dutch farm, where he was attacked again, this time by RAF rocket-firing Typhoons. His own side had not yet finished trying to eliminate him, for he was then shelled at another farm by British guns.

Paul Hippoliet Decroix, born in Courtrai, Belgium, on 23 March 1921, had moved with his family to Canada in 1929 before settling in the USA. On 28 September 1941 he enrolled in the Belgian Fusiliers (Canada) as a private soldier. Soon on his way to England, he arrived aboard the SS *Orcades* at Liverpool on 24 November 1941. On 10 June 1942 he joined the RAF as an aircraftman 2nd class, but early in 1943 was back in Canada learning to fly. On 1 February 1944 he was in England again at the AFU at Ternhill, Shropshire, before being posted to 349 (Belgian) Squadron on 1 August 1944, then stationed in Sussex.

Three months later he was a prisoner of the Germans in Holland who, on the night of 3 November, moved him over the River Maas to Dordrecht, and locked him up in a cellar. Taken to a schoolhouse on 4 November, he received the same rations as the soldiers. From there, at 11.30 pm on the night of 6 November, he and eighteen guards walked in torrential rain to Rotterdam, several kilometres away. Soaked to the skin he was given nothing on arrival but half a cup of lukewarm coffee. Put in another, ice-cold, schoolroom, he was held there for the next fortnight, existing on meagre rations of half a loaf of bread, soup at noon, and two cups of coffee per day. Moved to Utrecht, where he was given his first decent meal, he was put in a car with another POW on 21 November and driven to Amersfoort.

Next day they and twenty-seven other prisoners were put on a goods wagon in a space 'about eight foot square with a bit of dry bread'. A hole was made in the wagon, and five of the prisoners squeezed through, but they made so much noise getting out that the guards heard them and raised the alarm. Paul, sixth in line, never got out, perhaps just as well, for he was told that three of the escapers had been caught and shot.

Twenty-four hours later they were in Oldenzaal, and locked up in a shirt factory. Paul was searched for the third time: 'Rations were ⅛ of a loaf of bread and as much potato soup as one can eat at noon.' On 26 November the prisoners were:

> 'put on a bus and crossed border into Germany at Gronau. Got on train and went to Dortmund. Saw real bomb damage here. Every building as far as one could see was gutted. Rode through Ruhr changed trains seven times to reach Oberursel... Took thirty hours to do 300 kilo. Here was searched again, given shower, deloused and locked in solitary. Ration two slices bread and jam and cup of coffee in morning, plate of thin soup at noon and two slices of bread and marge and cup of coffee for tea. Was interrogated every day and always kept in solitary. Not allowed to wash or anything.'[178]

At Dulag Luft Paul met another 349 Squadron pilot, W/O Ken Brant, who had been shot down on 6 October. Also looking for enemy transport Ken, having dived onto a target, pulled-up directly over a gun-post. At barely 200 feet he was a sitting duck for the German gunners. With his propeller also drilled through, Ken landed his badly-vibrating Spitfire in a narrow Dutch field. After a series of close calls with the Dutch underground, he was one of the many evaders and escapers gathered together after the failure at Arnhem to make the crossing of the River Rhine in Operation Pegasus I. Although nearly 140 men were ferried across to safety on the night of 22/23 October 1944 Ken was not one of them, though he did try to swim the cold river. Later captured, he arrived at Dulag Luft on 31 October, though it is unclear why he and others were detained there for the unusually long time of over a month. He went on to Wetzlar on 8 December, two days before Paul.

Germany's transportation system was under such strain by this time that it took Paul and others fifteen hours on 10 December to reach Wetzlar, having had to change trains four times to cover the sixty kilometres from Oberursel. Compared to his earlier, poor diet, Paul was now well fed: 'Had food parcels here and got ten cigs a day and a bar of chocolate once a week. Felt better than since I was POW.'

Ken was in the group released to Bankau on 14 December. They were at Kassel on 15 December when the US 8th Air Force paid the place a visit. The POW's train was moved out of the town and, locking the wagon doors, the guards left the prisoners to their fate. The bombing was uncomfortably close, with explosions violently shaking the wagons, but more terrifying was the fact that the Americans were dropping their bombs through overcast skies.[179] Happily, the shaken prisoners reached the safety of Luft 7 five days later in *Trupp 55*.

Paul began the last leg of his long journey to Luft 7 on 23 December. Christmas Day was spent on the train: 'Very crowded but we had half an American parcel each and were able to make coffee. Did about 400 kilo through southern Germany. Arrived at Bankau on Boxing Day. Were left in station locked in train during air raid. Searched again on arrival at Bankau, Stalag Luft 7.' *Trupp 56* had made it at last.

*

Heilbronn was visited by RAF Bomber Command for the first and only time during the war on the night of 4/5 December 1944. The job of flattening a relatively unimportant place on a main railway line was given to 282 Lancasters and ten supporting Mosquitos of 5 Group. In the event, the raid was vastly destructive – over 350 acres of the built-up area were destroyed and over 7,000 inhabitants killed. The damage was not one-sided, though, as thirteen Lancasters failed to return, including PB740, 'O-Oboe', 467 (RAAF) Squadron.

O-Oboe had taken off from RAF Waddington, Lincolnshire, at 1642 hours on 4 December, an all-RAAF crew bar the RAF flight engineer: P/O J.B. 'Jack' Plumridge (pilot); Sgt J.L. 'Johnny' Wood (flight engineer) RAF; F/O G.F. Sinden (navigator); F/S J.E. Penman (bomb aimer); F/O G.D. Rawson (wireless operator); F/S C.L. 'Charlie' George (mid-upper gunner); and F/S G. 'Happy' Hayman (rear gunner).

The bombers' route to Heilbronn, a few kilometres north of Stuttgart, took them over Strasbourg in liberated France. John Penman:

'We crossed the lines into German territory in the Strassburg [sic] area shortly after 7 pm and at 7.15 pm, right on zero hour, I saw the illuminating flares and TIs lighting up Heilbronn, our target. About ten minutes from the target we had our first attack, Happy giving us a corkscrew. I heard him firing over the intercom. The fighter broke away and I put Jack onto the "Reds". We were attacked again. I didn't hear much but both Happy and Charlie were on the intercom, but after the fighter broke away I never heard Happy again.

'I put Jack back onto our markers and once again we were attacked, Charlie giving the commentary. After the breakaway I put Jack quickly back onto the TIs and we got a good release. There was a bit of natter all this time and I could see tracer shooting past. We must have got our packet then. I did my panel check and sent Johnny back and resumed windowing. Meanwhile I could hear George Sinden counting off the seconds for the camera steady, when George Rawson's voice rather urgently started talking about the port motors. I didn't make out what he said but I put on my 'chute just in case. Then came Jack's voice "Abandon aircraft – abandon aircraft". I didn't delay but it took an interminable time to get the hatch clear and I dived out, forgetting the instructions re helmet etc.

'I pulled and the 'chute opened – I ripped off my helmet and mask which had twisted around my face and looked around. I could see burning Heilbronn and a kite burning on the ground – I guess it was poor old O-Oboe. Then I saw the ground and prepared for it and landed safely and rolled in a ploughed field – it was just before 8 pm.'

John Penman was not to know it at the time, but he was the only survivor. Gone in an instant were his six comrades, their average age only twenty, shot down at 7.33 pm, ten to fifteen kilometres south of Heilbronn, by Oberleutnant Peter Spoden, Stab II./NJG6, for his fifteenth victory. Spoden would claim two more Lancasters – PD373 (44 Squadron) and LM259 (227 Squadron) – within the next nine minutes.

John Penman had lost one of his flying boots when his parachute opened and, having hidden his equipment under a bush, fashioned a slipper out of his surviving boot for the other foot. At a village a few hundred yards away, most of its inhabitants were out in the street watching the end of the raid on Heilbronn and, though John attracted a few glances, he was nearly clear of the far end of the village when 'I found my way barred again by two bods in NFS outfit. I had no alternative but to try and brazen it through in the dark. However, I must have been conspicuous abroad during the alert, because they challenged me. I grunted in reply and apparently aroused suspicion as I was immediately seized and taken into the nearest house.'

He was not badly treated, indeed he was given a glass of lager, and as he was being taken outside indicated that he wezlud like one of the buns that he saw on a nearby tray. Instead of a bun he 'received half a dozen hefty kicks in the pants from an evil-looking, black-haired brute who later similarly treated me'. He was marched down the road to the Bürgermeister's office and thrown into the gaol. One German who had learnt a little English when he was a prisoner in the First World War tried to question John, who kept repeating "*Nix verstehn*" ("Don't understand"). The Germans gave up at this point 'and left me alone. I had a straw mattress on a cot, two light blankets and some canvas. I rolled myself in these coverings and slept well!'

John spent the next six days in the gaol, and was usually well treated, except by the black-haired brute who gave him 'a hefty sock over the head' for refusing to answer questions. On the evening of 9 December the gaol's caretaker secretly took John back to his house 'for supper with him and his wife. I shared their meal – soup, a square inch of meat, helped myself to bread, butter and jam, and then some white "cake" loaf. *Café au lait* and some red wine. I stayed listening to the radio until about 9pm.' For a nation that had been so utterly brainwashed into such a brutal hatred of the *Terrorflieger*, this was a truly remarkable act of kindness by the caretaker and his wife.

On 11 December, as two Luftwaffe men collected him from the gaol, John was told by the German former POW that his aircraft 'had been found with five bodies'. On that sad note John and his Luftwaffe escort walked to Heilbronn, a distance of about ten kilometres, 'pretty grim in the snow in my slippers'. At the Bürgermeister's office, whither taken, he met Sergeant John J. Willis.[180] The two guards then took the two airmen through the ruins of Heilbronn to the damaged railway station, where they caught a train to Hessenthall, several kilometres north. From the station it was a mile or so to the nearby Luftwaffe aerodrome, where they were locked into cells for the night: 'Here we got bread and soup, interrogated at 8pm and 1am – unsuccessfully. Each cell had a heater, stool and board bed – no palliasse or blankets.' Also there was another POW, simply referred to by John as 'Ted' (possibly F/S Edward L. Wolff).

After a hasty meal of bread and margarine the three airmen were 'rushed off to the station with three guards'. They travelled through the night and on through the next day (13 December) until, after 'nine trains in twenty-four hours' they reached Oberursel. After a depressing time there John Penman was moved to Wetzlar on 17 December 'with thirty-eight others, mainly Yanks', and on 23 December entrained, with forty-two RAF NCOs (including John Willis, Edward Wolff, and Paul Decroix), for Bankau.

*

Another to leave Wetzlar on 23 December was F/S H.W. 'Hank' Pankratz RCAF. He was on his sixth operation when shot down on 6/7 December 1944 (Osnabrück) in Halifax NP945, 424 Squadron. He and his crew were on their way home from the target when a night-fighter set the Halifax on fire.

The skipper, F/O D.L.C. McCullough RCAF, gave the order to bale out. Third to leave was Hank, but only after his parachute had opened inside the aircraft. Nevertheless, he managed to jump from the aircraft, which was now effectively out of control: 'I hung in the air, stationary it seemed, for a long time. Falling not far away from me was a big ball of fire. It was the aircraft I had just vacated, and a moment later it blew up and went hurtling to the ground.'[181] It took with it the pilot and both gunners.

Hank, landing in the darkness and the cold December rain with a bit of a thump, wrapped his parachute around him, and decided to stay put until daylight. He had a vague idea that he must have fallen near the German-Dutch border, for he remembered the navigator saying as much to the pilot just before the fighter attack. Going to a nearby farmhouse German-speaking Hank was welcomed by the farmer and his family, who told him that he was near the town of Uelsen, half a dozen kilometres from the Dutch border. Although the family were Germans, they were fed up with the war and wanted to hide Hank until it was all over. They mentioned, however, that a woman who lived with them was a strong Nazi sympathiser and so, when the decision was taken to hand Hank over to the authorities, the farmer duly escorted him to the police station in Uelsen, just over a kilometre away.

As there was no jail there Hank was marched off past a jeering mob to Hellingo, where there was a prison, and was locked in his own cell. Hearing a voice from a nearby cell shouting "I'm hungry", he recognised it as that of his bomb aimer, F/O A.A.J. Low RCAF. After a loud, shouted conversation – the walls were thick – Hank learnt that Sgt Robert Atkinson, their flight engineer, was also with Low, the two having found each other soon after landing, with both having lost their flying boots. They, nevertheless, managed to walk for five or six agonising miles in their socks before they were captured.

An hour or so later the three airmen were bundled onto the back of a lorry, which they shared with three coffins. Convinced that the coffins were for them, they were driven for miles before turning off the main road. This, they thought, was it! In fact, the Germans were only collecting more coffins which, judging by the effort required to load them, had bodies in them. In due course the airmen were deposited at a Luftwaffe airfield near Lingen, where they were joined by their navigator, F/O A.M. Garner RCAF, who had a badly-sprained ankle, and was all in. When he said that the Germans had told him that three of their crew had been killed, it dawned on Hank that the first three coffins had contained the bodies of his pilot and the two gunners.

With eight others, the prisoners were taken back to Lingen and put on a train. Stopping at Salzbergen, a few kilometres down the line, they had to wait twelve hours for another train, which took them to Minden, over 100 kilometres distant. It was packed, and the airmen were forced to stand all the way – if they tried to sit down German soldiers and other passengers kicked them. Another change of trains at Minden took them to Hannover, where they arrived at around 6 am on the second day of their journey. The city was still in flames in places following earlier bombing, and the locals, decidedly unfriendly, gave the guards a hard time as they protected their prisoners.

Leaving unscathed for Göttingen, a long way south, they again changed trains, at the junction at Bebra, for the final run to Frankfurt-am-Main. It was now about 5 am on the third day of their travels, and they, 'along with a score of other prisoners who had been waiting there, were herded into a street car which took us to a small town called Oberursel'.

Hank recalls that he was interrogated by a German who said that his name was Nicholas Hall. He also told Hank that he had lived in England for fifteen years, had graduated from Oxford and had married an English girl. Furthermore, he had been shot down over England earlier in the war, had been held in a POW camp in northern Ontario, Canada, and had been brought back to Germany in an exchange of prisoners. Whether any of this was true, Hank was unable to tell, but in the course of the interrogation Hank realised that the German seemed to know more about the RAF and RCAF than he did.

With about forty-five others, mostly USAAF NCOs, Hank went to the transit camp at Wetzlar. Four days later, with forty-three others – mostly RAF this time, he headed for Bankau. The journey was, as ever, slow, and it was not until 1 pm on the afternoon of 26 December that the train pulled in to Bankau station.

\*

'It is with the deepest regret that I have to confirm the news already conveyed to you, that your son, A.410929 Warrant Officer R. Whiddon, failed to return from an operational flight over enemy territory. He was the wireless operator of an aircraft which took part in an attack on Osnabrück on the night of the 6th December, 1944. As a result of an emergency which occurred over the target area, your son, together with two of his companions, saw fit to abandon the aircraft. The captain, however, managed to overcome the emergency and landed safely at a British aerodrome with the remaining members of the crew.'[182]

The tone of this letter, to Reginald Whiddon's father, is clear enough, that a dim view was taken of the three crew who 'saw fit to abandon the aircraft' – Halifax NP962, 51 Squadron – leaving the rest to their fate. On 9 December the squadron commander sent a letter to the Under Secretary of State at the Air Ministry in London giving further details of the incident:

'The outward trip was uneventful, but at 19.45 hours whilst running into the target the starboard inner engine began to give trouble. He [P/O F. Fairweather, the pilot] decided not to feather the engine until the bombs had been dropped and in fact the bombs went at 19.46 hours. At 19.47 hours the Captain ordered the Engineer to feather the Starboard Inner. Whilst the Starboard Inner was being feathered the engine over-revved, and while the Captain and Engineer were dealing with this the Captain noticed that a severe draught was blowing through the aircraft, and at 19.48 hours the Engineer reported to the captain that the Wireless Operator [Whiddon], Navigator [F/S David J. Jenkins] and Bomb Aimer [F/S Robert Allen] had left the aircraft and that the main forward escape hatch was open.'

With the hatch closed, Fairweather and the three remaining crew set an emergency course for England, losing height all the way until crossing the English coast at 2,000 feet 'at approximately 22.00 hours' and landing at the first aerodrome they saw. Fairweather reported that he was convinced that, at the time of the short emergency, he had not given any order that might have been misconstrued as an order to bale out. The letter to the Under Secretary of State ended: 'It would seem that the only conclusion that can be drawn is that one or more of the three men who left the aircraft on hearing the Starboard Inner engine over-revving thought that the aircraft was out of control and abandoned without orders.'

Whiddon, Allen and Jenkins also arrived at Luft 7 in *Trupp 56*.

\*

The arrival at Bankau of Warrant Officer David De Renzy RNZAF marked the end, temporarily, of a long journey. Sailing from New Zealand, his native country, he underwent training in Canada before joining 488 (NZ) Squadron at Bradwell Bay, Essex, England. Some while later he collected a new Mosquito aircraft, and he and his navigator, NZ.416214 W/O Rex Frederick Cottrell RNZAF, flew it to Algiers in North Africa, and were thereafter detached to 256 Squadron, with its night-flying Mosquitos, at Alghero on Sardinia. One of the squadron's roles was to hunt for Luftwaffe bombers over France.

On the evening of 2 July 1944 RAF intelligence suggested that David and Rex should make their way to an area near Lyon, France, and patrol a certain wooded area to await returning Ju88 bombers. Taking off at around 7.30 to 8 pm in Mosquito NF.XIII HK399, JT-D, they flew to the suggested location, unaware that the Germans had installed a flak battery in the immediate vicinity. Flying below 500 feet, they presented an easy target to the enemy gunners. With the Mosquito's engines and cockpit ablaze, Rex baled out. David, though, was so busy with the aircraft that he never saw him leave, and by the time he thought about baling out he was too low, and was left with no choice but to effect a landing as best he could in the dark.

Seeing both light and dark patches on the ground, and correctly assuming that the light ones were open ground and the dark ones were trees, David 'headed for the largest light patch and cut my throttles. I touched down quite nicely and was lucky enough to finish just in front of some trees.'

He had landed between the towns of Faramans and Bourg-St Christophe, some thirty kilometres north east of Lyon, in the Ain Département. In his own words he...

'was not in very good shape but I had enough sense to walk away when the cannon shells started exploding. I managed to find a French farmhouse where I was bandaged with torn-up sheets, filled up with wine and put to bed. I woke the next morning feeling it was my duty to escape but only managed to fall down a flight of stairs. The owners were kindness itself, but they insisted that I was in need of hospital treatment.

'I was taken by the Germans to a hospital in Lyon where treatment was minimal in the extreme. After a month I was sent to hospital in Dijon where the German doctor, although lacking in equipment, was at least kindly. When my wounds healed I was sent to Germany, but for some reason I spent a few days in a nunnery at Donaueschingen, where I had my twenty-first birthday.

'I went from there to a holding camp at Rottweil[183] and then the usual places – interrogation at Oberursel, holding camp at Wetzlar, and finally prison camp.'

Rex, however, had been killed after baling out, and was buried in the Lyon-La Guillotière Cemetery, before being re-interred at La Doua national cemetery at Villeurbanne. Rex, too, was only 21.

*

In late August 1944, radar operator 919538 Corporal Albert Austin was posted from an RAF radar station in Norfolk to join a new unit that was forming at RAF Harwell – No. 6080 Light Warning Unit (LWU). Forming at the same time was No. 6341 LWU, both units under the command of W/C John Laurence Brown MBE, known throughout the intimate world of controllers as 'The Great Brown'.

During the planning of Operation Market Garden, intelligence had learnt of the presence in the Arnhem area of German Ju88 night-fighters which, it was thought, would pose a threat to the proposed Arnhem bridgehead. To counter this, therefore, two LWUs with their mobile-radar sets would be flown in by glider on the first lift to act as forward director posts for a flight of night-flying Beaufighters. A landing strip would be built clear of the drop zones used on the first lift and between Wolfheze and Oosterbeek. Once the radar equipment had been brought in by RAF glider, US Waco gliders would then bring in the necessary rolls of wire mesh and engineers to build the airstrip for the Beaufighters. S/Sgt John Kennedy GPR thought that 'the whole operation appeared… to have been very hastily conceived'.

Whether or not a correct summation, matters were certainly not helped when, on 16 September, the day before the first lift to Arnhem was due to take place, forty gliders were earmarked for General 'Boy' Browning's HQ to be flown over on the first lift. Of lower priority, the LWUs were cancelled. This did not please 'The Great Brown', however, who pleaded with General Browning for the two LWUs to be reinstated on the first lift, but the best deal he could get was that they would be included on the second lift, on 18 September.

A highly-experienced radar controller working with ground control interception (GCI) sets, Brown had had a highly successful tour at Sopley GCI, where he controlled the first successful night interception of a German bomber, on the night of 26 February 1941.[184] It was to Sopley on 7 May 1941 that King George VI paid a visit. Brown was concentrating on vectoring the night-fighter of John Cunningham and his radio operator Jimmy Rawnsley onto an enemy bomber when the king leant forward to ask Brown a question – and was promptly told to shut up!

Brown then had a long run of successes with the Beaufighters of 604 Squadron at RAF Middle Wallop, and it was for this that he was awarded the MBE.[185] He joined the Americans in the North African landings in November 1942, before taking part in the invasions of Sicily and Italy in July 1943. Recalled for the Normandy landings on 6 June 1944, he had spent a very uncomfortable time on an American ship that had stuck fast on a sandbank and which had then been shelled for twenty-four hours before it was towed off. Although officially on the Air Staff of 85 (Base) Group (2nd Tactical Air Force), for the impending Arnhem operation he was attached as Liaison Officer to 38 Group (Air Defence of Great Britain).

On 17 September W/C Brown flew to Nijmegen on the River Waal, a dozen kilometres south of Arnhem, not with his LWU personnel but with General Browning's Corps HQ in a GPR 'A' Squadron Horsa glider, which came down in an orchard. It was sheer bad luck that just as W/C Brown had gone back to his glider to retrieve his sleeping-bag a number of Bf109s strafed the landing zone, wounding The Great Brown. Dying of his wounds on the following day thus passed, in the words of a fellow controller, 'probably the most famous GCI controller of the war'.[186]

As for the LWUs themselves, five officers and twenty airmen were flown over in the second lift, in four gliders of 'A' Squadron GPR, the four gliders bearing Chalk Numbers 5000 to 5003 inclusive (the number marked in chalk on the side of the glider for identification). As a result of the day's delay in flying them in they would suffer the catastrophic loss of one officer and eight airmen killed in action. All those aboard Chalk 5003 were killed when the glider's tail was shot off and it plunged into the ground. A further eleven airmen were taken prisoner of war, including Albert Austin, who had been severely wounded. He was in a glider with the officer commanding 6080 LWU, twenty-eight-year-old S/L H.W. Coxon. In the same glider were 1st Lieutenant Bruce Davis USAAF; F/S Semon 'Blondie' Lievense RCAF (from 6110 Servicing Echelon); LAC Roffer James Eden; and LAC G.R. Thomas. Bruce Davis, a ground controller from the US IXth Air Force, who 'decided to go along in case American fighters were used', was there to act as a liaison between the RAF ground stations and their opposite numbers of the 306th Fighter Control Squadron. In the event, only five LWU personnel returned to Allied lines from Arnhem having evaded capture: Coxon and Davis (see below); and three from 6341 LWU – S/L Wheeler; F/L Richardson; and LAC W.H. Scott.

The Stirling tugs for the personnel and heavy wireless equipment of the two LWUs were provided by four crews of 295 and 570 Squadrons from RAF Harwell. Coxon briefly mentioned in his MI9 interrogation report that their 'tug was shot down. We cast off and crash landed at Randwijk.' Coxon and company were aboard glider Chalk 5000, which was flown by S/Sgt 'Lofty' Cummings and Sgt Jimmy McInnes, 'A' Squadron, GPR. Their tug, Stirling LK121, 570 Squadron, flown by P/O

C.W. Culling, crashed near a farm at Opheusden, with all the crew losing their lives.

A dozen kilometres west of Arnhem the Chalk 5000 men joined forces with the personnel of two other gliders that had landed nearby. They had with them 'a field gun, a couple of jeeps and motorcycles'. Unable to move all the heavy LWU material, however, Albert Austin was ordered to destroy the radar equipment by Sten-gun fire. As the other glider similarly loaded with radar parts had been lost when its tail was shot off, there were now no radar units to operate.

With the help of the Dutch Resistance the group, as previously instructed, made their way to division HQ at the Hartenstein Hotel in Arnhem. On the morning of 19 September the Germans began a fearful mortar bombardment. When the radio jeep of the American Air Support team on loan to HQ was damaged, Lieutenant Davis asked thirty-one-year-old LAC Roffer Eden to repair it but, as he did so, another salvo of mortar bombs was launched, and a splinter severed Eden's jugular vein. Davis applied first aid, but to no avail. His wife was now a widow.

Another of several Jews to perish at Arnhem was W/O Mark Azouz DFC, pilot of Stirling LJ810, 196 Squadron, which, hit by flak on 21 September 1944, was then attacked by four or five FW190s: 'He kept the plane in the air whilst all but one of his crew (the rear gunner, [F/S P.H. Bode]) escaped. It being Yom Kippor, he could have taken leave that day but refused as men at Arnhem were waiting for supplies.'[187] He was killed before his DFC was announced in the London Gazette on 27 October 1944.

Moments after Eden had been hit there was a second fatality when F/S Lievense RCAF was hit in the back by three splinters from an 88mm shell burst. The shelling continued, and another burst caught Albert Austin, who 'was hit three times, in the head, the back and the buttocks and had to be taken to a hospital that was in German hands'.[188]

As to the others of Chalk 5000, both Coxon and Davis evaded capture when the time came to evacuate Arnhem on 25 September. Coxon was one of the many waiting on the banks of the Rhine to be ferried across to safety but, as there were insufficient boats, he swam across. Sent to Brussels, he was flown back to England on 28 September, and was debriefed on the following day.

As Bruce Davis had been hit in the foot and had damaged his hip on 20 September, all that he 'could do from now on was to man a Sten gun from a window'. Despite his wounds he, too, found his way to safety when the time came to leave. He had met up with Marek Święcicki, a Polish war correspondent attached to the Polish Parachute Brigade, who had gone in with them on the second Arnhem lift. Święcicki wrote: 'Bruce Davis is an optimist, and a friend of mine. As an optimist he had been declaring for a day or two past that the Second Army was some three miles away. As a friend he had brought me exultantly a single biscuit from an American field ration... We all had thick growths of hair, and Bruce with his beard looked like an old, bearded monk.'[189] On the night of 25/26 September 1944 they withdrew from the north bank of the River Lek under cover of artillery fire from the British Second Army.

LAC Thomas, the last of Chalk 5000 to be mentioned, was also wounded and, captured, went to Stalag IVB (Mühlberg).

Albert Austin, meanwhile, was sent to the hospital at Stalag XIB (Fallingbostel), and then to Luft 7. Joining him there was LAC David Foster, also of 6080 LWU, who had been in the group with Albert and the others when they were shelled. Hit by splinters to his upper right arm, right hand (splinters still there many years later), right knee and back, David Foster was taken to a first-aid post. Though his injuries were not fatal, S/L Coxon had reported at his interrogation after his safe return that David Foster had been killed. As a result, David's mother received a telegram saying that her son had been killed in action on 22 September. It was not until 10 October that she was informed, via the local constabulary, that he was a prisoner of war.

Also turning up at Luft 7 in various Truppen were three of No. 6341 LWU's personnel: Sgt

Edmund 'Ted' Quigley; LAC S. Britland; and LAC B.B. Mowat RCAF. Writing to his brother on 31 May 1945, shortly after his return to England, Ted Quigley briefly described the events leading up to his capture:

'I was in the do at Arnhem last September and now it appears that out of twenty-four of us only five for certain, and possibly three others, remain alive. It was a ghastly experience, and the twenty-seven hours or so I was at large seem like a nightmare now. The Jerries gave us a very hot reception and did their damndest to obliterate the lot of us in record time.'

Having landed in a potato field, Ted dragged a comrade, LAC Young, who had been wounded in the leg, to the safety of a hedge, but they were caught next morning when German tanks appeared over the field. In the confusion, Ted can be forgiven for believing that LWU casualties were so high.

Back in England after his evasion LAC W.H. Scott contacted William Samwells, father of LAC Eric A. Samwells, to ask for Eric's whereabouts, saying that he 'was with Eric four days & then lost contact with him. After a patrol they went on, he seems to think the last he saw of Eric he was bending over a chap who had been hit, as he (Eric) was carrying the first-aid kit.'

Then, early in June 1945, Ted Quigley, who had managed to get home a little earlier than some of the others, received a letter from William Samwells, asking about Eric:

'I was very pleased to hear you are safely back in the old country & free from hateful captivity. I only wish I could tell you the same about Eric. Unfortunately he is completely untraceable. I believe they accounted for every one of the crew, except him, either POW or killed in action… I still clung to the hope that Eric might turn up when the ex POW were brought back, but I am afraid that hope has gone now. I only hope if he has been taken it was quick.'

One cannot even begin to imagine the anguish that must have been felt by William Samwells and his wife who had heard nothing about their son's fate for nine months. Desperate for any news of him, William wrote: '…anything is better now than this awful suspense'. Sadly, Eric had long since been killed, on 22 September 1944, the very day on which LAC Scott last saw him.

\*

**27 DECEMBER 1944.** Cold, but bright and sunny. There was another air raid just after midday. As ordered, all POWs were confined to their huts until the all clear had sounded. At around 12.30 pm the wail of air raid sirens was heard in the distance. Believing that that was the all clear for the camp, twenty-year-old Sergeant Leslie Howard Stevenson RCAF left barrack 52, Room 14, apparently to go to the latrines. But what he and everyone else had heard was the all clear sounding at Kreuzburg, some seven or eight kilometres away.

Two fellow prisoners, realising this, tried to attract Stevenson's attention, but were too late. Camp Leader Peter Thomson was standing at the west-facing window of his barrack hut when he:

'heard one of the guards, standing on the road outside the camp, call out and at the same time he raised his rifle and fired. I immediately looked through the other [south-facing] window in my room and saw a body, later found to be Sgt Stevenson, lying on the ground about thirty feet or maybe more from the door of one of the barracks. The guard raised his rifle to fire again and I called through the window and told him to stop at once. Stevenson managed to get on to his hands and knees and crawl back to the steps of the barracks where he was helped in by some of the inmates.'[190]

Den Blackford was reading by the window of his hut when he heard the shot. Looking out, he 'saw a chap lying outside on the ground, over by 8 Division. As we watched him he lifted his head and then rolled over and started to crawl. He got to his feet and sort of staggered towards 8 Division. One of the chaps in the building ran out waving a white handkerchief and reached him just as he was falling.'

Syd Barlow was another witness to the shooting: '1 was only 6 feet away, and also running to go to the toilets on the other side of the parade ground. The cold-water pipes had frozen on our side of the camp... When the all clear went most of us dashed out to pay a call, but for two or three days the only ablutions were on the far side of the square.'

As soon as they could, Den Blackford and several others went to try to help Stevenson, only to find 'that the bullet had gone through his chest on the left side and out again underneath his right shoulder blade'. With Stevenson's chest opened by the fatal bullet, part of his right lung was hanging out, both lungs having been pierced. Captain Howatson RAMC, who had been hastily summoned to Hut 52 by Peter Thomson, found the still-conscious Canadian lying on a bed with some of the men endeavouring to give him first aid. The padré was there, too, and Stevenson asked him to pray for his family, especially his mother and father, saying: 'I send my love to mother, father, and brothers and sisters. Tell her I love her.'

While Thomson went to ask the Germans for an ambulance, Stevenson was removed on a stretcher to the camp's Revier (hospital), but died half an hour later. No ambulance was forthcoming. Stevenson's personal effects, just one fountain pen, were sent to the camp at Meiningen. His parents were informed that he had died in an air raid.

From enquiries made by Peter Thomson it was discovered that the guard's name was Dollesal, and that he was from Dortmund, but no description of the man was ever forthcoming. Apparently, to avoid any retribution from the prisoners, the Camp Commandant told the POWs that Dollesal was to be immediately posted.

As one of the Canadians said: 'This latest incident has shook up the whole camp.'

**28 DECEMBER 1944.** Weather fine and cold. 500 Argentinian Red Cross parcels issued.

There was yet another local air raid. When the all clear sounded in the camp, none of the POWs dared to leave his barrack hut: 'Our Confidence man finally came around and said it was okay. Even then we didn't trust the Jerries. Tensions in the camp continued to increase. We didn't know what to expect.' (John McConnell.)

**29 DECEMBER 1944.** A post mortem examination of Stevenson revealed that 'death was due to being shot through the right breast, left epigastrium [upper central region of the abdomen], with injuries to the liver, stomach, spleen and diaphragm.' (Library and Archives Canada.)

**30 DECEMBER 1944.** Heavy snow; very cold. A short service for Stevenson was held in the open at 7.30 am at Kreuzburg Cemetery. The funeral party comprised, inter alia, Frank Bishop, Bill Chandler RCAF, and Allan MacNaught RCAF. The guard Ludwig brought a wreath. The bugler tried to play The Last Post, but his spit froze in his bugle. Snow fell on bowed heads as Stevenson was buried in Field 10, Grave 68, Kreuzburg Cemetery.

After the war, no trace of the grave could be found. The cemetery had been obliterated by 'vandals, believed to be either Russian or Polish. All crosses and grave markings had been removed and cemetery records destroyed.'[191] Stevenson is now commemorated on Panel 255 of the Runnymede Memorial.

**31 DECEMBER 1944.** Heavy snow all day. The Germans wanted to put all Jewish prisoners in a hut by themselves. The whole camp said 'No', and for the time being the *status quo* prevailed.

Lights remained on in the barracks until 1 am on New Year's Day.

## CHAPTER ELEVEN

# THE LAST *TRUPP*; THE CAMP IS STRUCK, JANUARY 1945

'*RAF aircrew had not been trained or prepared on the promenade in Blackpool or Brighton for the rigours of an Eastern European winter. But somehow we survived.*'

Sgt J.A. Davies
(*A Leap in the Dark*)

\*

**1 JANUARY 1945.** 'So we start the new year with snow and bitter cold, but much optimism… Received an issue of Argentine jam, honey, corned beef and Irish stew. From the Jerries we got molasses and sugar… Only one parade today, at 9 o'clock.' (George Kilbryde.)

**2 JANUARY 1945.** Snowed all day. Everybody late on parade. Extra parades called at midday and 3.30 pm. With everything frozen over it at least gave the Canadians the chance to complete two ice-rinks, and much good skating was observed.

POWs were locked in their huts from 10 pm until 6 am. Failure to comply brought down the wrath of the guards. Everybody was very much on edge.

**3 JANUARY 1945.** No coal or wood left for many. Bed boards used for firewood. Snowing again by nightfall.

**4 JANUARY 1945.** Parade was held in deep snow, which continued to fall. Snowball fights erupted as the men waited for the headcount.

'Then as one man, as though obeying an order, we made a pile of snowballs. When the Camp Commandant and his staff took their place, filling their appropriate spot in the hollow square, they were bombarded with snowballs, thousands of snowballs in the air at one time. It was a laugh, good fun, which the Commandant took in good part. The goons who counted us got their share too – from very close quarters. It snowed all day.' (Fred W. Brown.)

498 Red Cross parcels arrived, 'just in time to keep the wolf from the door for a little while longer'. Also received were 4,000 pairs of laces and 500 pairs of gloves.

**5 JANUARY 1945.** Some POWs were late on parade again at 9 am, and were kept outside in the freezing cold while their billets were searched. By way of a punishment for the men being late, three further parades were held, at 11 am, 2 pm, and 3.30 pm.

**6 JANUARY 1945.** Snow continued to fall. The last *Trupp* (*Trupp 57*? – sixty-five men approximately) was believed to have been admitted on this day. Camp strength now officially stood at 1,601.

S/Sgt Jock Thomson was due to go to Kreuzburg hospital, while some of the more seriously injured POWs – including 'Ginger' Cleary, Stan Silver RAAF, John 'Tom' Vidler, Ken Dobbs, Anthony Shearman and Harold Grill in FAA – were evacuated to Stalag 344 (Lamsdorf). Those staying behind watched as they left, shouting messages until they were out of sight. Fred W. Brown noted that Stan

Silver's arm was still 'long and useless. He stood up to it well and always had a ready smile.'

Ken Dobbs: 'We had an overnight stay, and this appeared to be an asylum of sorts occupied by prisoner civilians, probably political.' These people, whom Ken reckoned had seen no-one from the outside for years, 'could not do enough to make us comfortable. One chap gave up his bunk for me, and knelt by my side all night holding my hand. I daren't go to sleep!'

They had not been at Lamsdorf for long when the German guards, hearing news of the Russian advance, left the POWs to fend for themselves. Thoughts of the POWs escaping were not entertained for long, as 'temperatures here were so low that escape would have been suicide'. Then the guards returned unexpectedly, to evacuate the wounded POWs, who were pushed 'into cattle trucks, forty of us to half a truck. No room to even lie down. Given one-third of a bread loaf. We endured this for seven days, travelling through Czechoslovakia into Bavaria. We were twice let out of the truck, and on each occasion toilet requirements were the main thought.'

On 5 April they were moved to Stalag VIIB (Memmingen) 'in Bavaria with some 9 inches of snow on the ground and, to our horror, saw our accommodation – TENTS... Once again we were moved, a little nearer Nuremberg', to Stalag 383 (Hohenfels). On 17 April 1945, the Germans marched out most of the fit and able-bodied men, leaving behind approximately 1,600 sick and unfit POWs under a Major Neal, the senior British medical officer. Left behind, too, was a number of fit men who had managed to avoid the march by hiding in various places throughout the camp.

Stalag 383 was liberated by the Americans on 22 April, by which time Stan Silver was long gone. Acquiring 'an Opel panel van at a village close to camp three of us drove to Paris. On the way picked up a Frenchman', and met 'Americans going in direction from which we had come'. Further contact was made with the US authorities in Paris, 'and, after several days, [we] were repatriated back to England'. On 9 May, Stan was directed to the Australian No. 11 PDRC at Brighton – 'where I had arrived three years before'.

After almost a year in hospitals at Llandudno and Hoylake, he went to RAF Wroughton hospital for a further assessment: 'Since the last board he has been at a rehabilitation centre having exercises etc. There has been some little improvement in the function of the [left] arm.' Group Captain Scott, an orthopædic specialist, also noted: 'The prognosis for further spontaneous recovery is not good. I suggest that before any surgical procedure is contemplated he should be repatriated and given full opportunity [of] taking his arm out and to see just how much disability the lack of abduction is to him.'

If that was hardly good news, Stan suffered a further injury while waiting for the boat back to Australia in March 1946: 'This injury was a septic foot due to radiator burn, through loss of feeling in leg caused by war injury.'

What was very much good news, on the other hand, was his marriage to Kathleen in Hove. Sailing on HMS *Indomitable* on 3 April Stan arrived back in Australia on 3 May 1946. He and Kathleen were to be happily married for the next forty-seven-and-a-half years, until Stan's death on 19 October 1993. Of course, she missed him terribly: 'He really was a wonderful man and, despite all his frustrations through disability, never complained.'

*

On the afternoon of 12 September 1944 (Münster) Halifax MZ935, 77 Squadron, was hit by flak over the target and blew up.[192] Sgt Anthony Shearman (mid-upper gunner) remembered nothing more until he regained consciousness in a field surrounded by German civilians, who asked him if he was '*ein flieger Tommy*' or '*Americano*'? 'When I told them I was a "*flieger Tommy*" they shook hands with me. I was placed on a cart and taken to a village where I was attended to by a lady doctor.' Here, too, he met his bomb aimer, F/O W.C. Page. Once patched up, Anthony was removed to the local jail, where he joined his wireless operator (Sgt W. Wilks) and rear gunner (Sgt W.K. Pritchard), both of whom were also wounded. Pritchard reached Luft 7 (in *Trupp 34*), but it is not known to which camp Page and Wilks were sent.

After a spell at the Hohe Mark hospital in November, Anthony was passed on to the Lazarett at Stalag IXC (Mühlhausen) in December, and from there purged to Luft 7. He was one of the 'walking wounded' evacuated to Stalag 344 (Lamsdorf) on 6 January 1945, moving to Stalag XIIID (Nürnberg) in March, where he was liberated by the Americans on 14 April 1945.

\*

From the cold, snowy mountains of Norway three of the crew of Stirling LK203, 8E-P, 295 Squadron – W/O John Butcher (navigator), Sgt Gerald Hulbert (flight engineer), and Sgt Vic Stone (wireless operator) – came to Luft 7 in *Trupp 57*. A fourth crew member, F/O Ron Stancombe (bomb aimer), was also taken prisoner (camp not known).

On the night of 29/30 November 1944, flying on Operation Crupper 9A, they were to drop eighteen containers and three packages of supplies to the Norwegian Home Forces (formerly MILORG, or Military Organisation) somewhere near Vikerfjell, eighty kilometres or so north west of Oslo. They circled what they thought was the drop zone for twenty-eight minutes but, as there was 10/10ths cloud cover, never saw the signal from the Norwegians on the ground, if it was ever given, and set course for base (Rivenhall).

As LK203 headed more or less south down Norway the engines malfunctioned, possibly due to icing. Only hundreds of feet from the ground the pilot, F/O Finlay, concerned about the aircraft icing up, gave the order to the crew to prepare to bale out. Whether or not they misheard the order to stand-by is unclear, but four of them went anyway. Finlay wrote in his report: 'They did not acknowledge instructions and just baled out without a word.' They jumped out more or less in pairs – Butcher with Hulbert, and Stone with Stancombe. The rear gunner, Sgt Bill Brown, remained aboard and flew back to base with his skipper.

With little idea of his location Vic Stone had in fact landed in trees in the mountains near Iveland, forty to fifty kilometres north of Kristiansand. A few hours later, having failed to find anyone to help him, he met up with Ron Stancombe. They survived on the rations from their escape kits, but with the temperature as low as *minus* 32°C at one point, they went to 'a log house where we sought sanction'. However, 'the occupants did not want to speak at all, and when we were finally captured by the German Wehrmacht and taken by staff car to their headquarters we were convinced that the driver of the car was the man who we had previously sought help from'.

John Butcher and Gerald Hulbert were captured a few hours after landing. Gerald, turning up at a farm near Mølland, asked how far it was to Sweden. On being told that it was 800 kilometres, he asked to be handed over to the Germans, and the police at Iveland were notified accordingly. A few minutes later the police received another call, from Øystein Fidjeland, a farmer in Nateland, to the effect that 'a strange person had arrived saying that he was an Englishman'. This was John Butcher.

So from Norway came three more NCOs to swell Luft 7's population.

\*

Given the scale of some of the atrocities committed throughout the war, the brutality that was meted out to Canadian airman Myron Williams barely caused a ripple on the surface of the vast bog of evil that was Nazi Germany.

Shot down in Lancaster ME649, 103 Squadron, on 12 December 1944 (Essen), Myron parachuted onto German soil and, despite the cold weather, survived for a week or so on his own by living off the land until caught sheltering in a barn. His interrogators, probably Gestapo, were convinced that he could not have survived in such a sensitive, high-security area as the one in which he was caught without having had some assistance. They were determined, by whatever means, to discover who had helped him. They deprived him of sleep, kept him in solitary confinement without washing or toilet facilities and, during interrogation, physically assaulted him with blows to the head and with rifle butts smashed onto his bare feet, breaking bones. His jaw was also broken by repeated blows, the interrogator deriving much pleasure from seeing the pain on Myron's face each time he hit the sensitive part.

When the Nazi thugs failed to get anything out of him, Myron was taken into a yard and tied to a post. Waiting for the execution squad of six soldiers to be given the order to fire, he collapsed. He remembered little of events over the next few days, but via Dulag Luft he finally arrived at Luft 7 early in January 1945 in *Trupp 57*, a broken man who trusted no-one.[193]

*

The railway installations at Soest, to the east of Dortmund, were the target for Bomber Command on the night of 5/6 December 1944. One of the three Halifaxes lost on the raid was LW204, OW-K, 426 (Thunderbird) Squadron RCAF. The crew were on their third operation when hit by flak during the bombing run – straight and level for an eternity. All were RCAF except for the flight engineer: F/L P.G. Chipman (pilot); Sgt Henry 'Dusty' Rhodes RAF (flight engineer); F/O C.L. Shipman (navigator); F/O P.H. Harris (bomb aimer); Sgt D.N. McLaren (wireless operator); Sgt Joe Knoke (mid-upper gunner); and F/S John 'Pop' Popadiuk (rear gunner). Neil McLaren's commission came through on the very day on which they were shot down, but he never knew about it until he got back. Pop Popadiuk and Joe Knoke were similarly commissioned.

On 25 November the crew had been given a new Halifax, coded OW-H, which 'Chip' Chipman took for an air test. Deciding that it needed some adjustment, it was flown off to another base for the necessary repairs. For the Soest raid, therefore, the crew were in OW-K. After a few delays they were airborne at 6.45 pm and had an uneventful trip as far as the target. Neil McLaren was in his 'office' copying a message from base when the flak hit them on the bomb run: 'There was a loud thump and the plane went into a very steep turn and then finally levelled out somewhat.' When the order was given to bale out Neil reached over and lifted his parachute 'out of its storage place and snapped it on my chest and followed the engineer out'.

Neil did not see the flight engineer, Dusty Rhodes, again until after the war, when Dusty told him briefly what had happened to him. His parachute had been holed by the flak burst whilst still in the aircraft 'so he had to hold it from unfolding while he baled out. It didn't open properly but, lucky for him, he landed in a tree. Next morning the Jerrys found him and thought he was dead, so cut him down, heard him groan, so took him to hospital. He said that his ankles gave him the most discomfort because they just cut him out of the tree and let him drop. Shortly after the war he got a letter from a German soldier saying that he had saved his life by getting him to a hospital and keeping the SS from getting him.'

When Neil visited Dusty in England in 1958 he was shown Shipman's navigation maps and, amazingly, Dusty's parachute, all of which the soldier had sent to him post war. The German soldier also wrote that he had found their Halifax that night with Joe Knoke's body still in it. Joe was the only one of the seven to lose his life, probably killed by the flak burst that brought down the Halifax.

As Neil floated down after baling out he noted that it was very windy as he descended through the clouds. More alarmingly, he realised that he was being blown 'towards the flak which was coming up like the fireworks at the Saskatoon exhibition'. Manipulating the parachute shrouds, he 'soon floated away where it was a little quieter. It was a very dark, cloudy night so didn't see the ground until about one second before I hit, but I sure saw lots of stars.' Though he had hurt his back in the landing, he set about walking in a north-westerly direction toward the Allied lines in Holland.

Raised on a farm, he reckoned that he wouldn't have any trouble milking a cow to get some milk. It would not prove so easy in the event, as the local farmers kept their cows in heavily-padlocked barns, usually with a German shepherd dog on guard for good measure. Nevertheless, using the rubber bag provided with the escape kit, he did manage to get a good drink every now and then. In one of the barns he found a heavy coat, and put it on. It felt wonderfully warm, especially as he was cold and wet, 'but I had never stolen anything in my life (unless milk enters that category), so I took it off and left. I figured the farmer needed it pretty bad and I would get caught soon and lose it anyway.' Neil was not to know that it would be a fortnight before capture came.

He should have been caught on several occasions, once when he got bitten on his backside by a guard dog – 'He tore the seat out of my pants and got a nip of hide, which stung for a long time' – which had alerted its master. Neil got away then in the pitch dark by hiding in some straw. Another time, in a village near a railway crossing, three soldiers suddenly turned a corner and walked towards him. Quickly turning onto the railway track he hoped that they wouldn't follow. One of them did, though, and as he approached started talking to Neil. Acting surprised, Neil pointed to his ears and mouth, 'shook my head and carried on. He turned and went back.'

A third time he got away with it. Walking along a path beside a railway line that was heading in the direction of Münster, he saw a guard outside a hut at a road crossing. The problem of how to get past the guard and across the road without being seen was solved when a train appeared. Running for all he was worth alongside the train, which he hoped would be a long one, he managed to flop down in a ditch on the other side without having been seen: 'After I got my wind back I got up and carried on.'

Neil eventually reached Münster, and located the marshalling yards. As it was German practice to lable every truck with its intended destination, Neil searched around for one going to Holland. He was able to use his torch – 'the best flashlight I have ever seen' – but found nothing suitable, having to dodge guards all the while. When he found some wagons being joined-up he climbed up the ladder into one and hid in a small space at the end behind boxes of ammunition. The train moved off, and was going faster and faster when Neil thought that it was time to leave, 'so I got out and hung onto the ladder. Just then it [the train] hit something, which stopped it dead. I looked over the top of the car and the ammo had slammed up tight against where I had just vacated. I figured I would have been flattened to the thickness of a postage stamp.'

Deciding that it was probably safer, and faster, to walk, he left the Münster rail yards and set off in the direction of the Rhine. Although the Dutch border was only some thirty-five to forty kilometres away, the mighty River Rhine was the same distance beyond the border. Helping himself to apples and carrots along the way, he kept going. Resting in a barn one day he was found by two old ladies: 'They immediately took me in the house, which was attached to the barn, and gave me a couple of slices of black bread. I ate one slice, but it was very hard to swallow, so I put the other slice in my pocket. They didn't want me to go, but I didn't think I was ready to give up yet.'

Not long afterwards, early in the morning of 21 December, he entered the town of Salzbergen, barely a dozen kilometres from the Dutch border. Here the railway branched, one track going north to Lingen, the other west to Bad Bentheim (which is only four kilometres from the border). He chose to go west but, as dawn was not far off, made himself comfortable in a barn with hay piled up on either side. This had a passage through the middle big enough for a horse and cart. On one side there was only a little hay, while the other was full. Reasoning that the farmer would take hay from the low side, he went to the full one, and managed to get some rest. 'In the afternoon I heard a team and wagon drive in the driveway. Did they take hay off the low side? Oh no!'

When Neil thought that surely they must have a full wagon load he felt a pitchfork taking the hay that was covering his feet, 'so I pulled my feet up as far as possible. The next fork full was off my middle and the tine touched my hip.' Realising that the next fork full might well hit him in the face, he got up. 'It was a man and his wife, and they were so startled I had to smile, and calmly started pulling on my flight boots.' Climbing down, Neil was taken to the farmhouse, and again given some black bread. He asked for a drink and was given a jug of milk. Several people had now gathered at the farm and one of them, a school teacher, told him that the police had been summoned.

By way of a postscript, Neil returned to Germany in 1980 to try to find the couple who had been so kind to him. With the help of a friend they made their back to Salzbergen, only to find that the town had changed beyond recognition. But when they saw a woman standing by a house they went to talk to her: 'It turned out to be the same lady who dug me out of the hay. Her husband had died, and also the school teacher. She was eighty years old, but remembered digging me out of the hay.'

Back in December 1944, however, Neil was taken by a policeman to the local jail, where he spent a very cold night. He was removed to Dulag Luft forthwith, and spent Christmas Day 1944 in solitary confinement. Three days later a batch of fifty or so POWs left for Wetzlar, where he spent the New Year. After a four-day train journey 'in very crowded box cars' Neil and the others arrived at Luft 7.[194]

\*

The 'Unternehmen Wacht am Rhein'[195] offensive began on 16 December 1944 (and officially lasted until 25 January 1945). This was also the day on which RAF Bomber Command sent 3 Group on an all-Lancaster G-H daylight raid to the railway yards at Siegen. Only Lancaster LL944, 115 Squadron, was lost of the 108 aircraft despatched.

After an early-morning wake-up call on 16 December the crew of LL944 enjoyed a delicious breakfast of bacon and eggs – F/O David Robertson RCAF (pilot); Sgt Eddie Hutchinson (flight engineer); P/O P. Smith (bomb aimer); Sgt John Trumble (navigator); F/S R.G. Cornwell RAAF (wireless operator, who had come in as a last-minute replacement for the regular W/OP who was ill); Sgt R.D. Roberts (mid-upper gunner); and Sgt D.W. Roberts (rear gunner).

John Trumble:

> 'After briefing we were transported to our aircraft, where we carried out the usual routine tests and discovered that the upper gun turret was faulty. Transferred to a reserve aircraft and were late taking off, [shortly after midday]... We reached the target area without incident and bombed the target at an altitude of about 24,000 feet. At this point the port outer engine was hit by anti-aircraft flak and caught fire. One bomb was not released due to icing. Flying on three engines, and air-speed reduced, we gradually lost sight of the main bomber stream and were on our own without any fighter escort.
>
> 'The mid-upper gunner and rear gunner both spotted two Me109s coming in to attack. Our plane was hit, almost immediately killing the wireless operator sitting next to me and the two gunners. There was an explosion and my pilot gave the order to bale out. The bomb aimer and flight engineer got out safely, and David, my pilot, was still trying to keep it on an even keel even though he was surrounded by flames; but the plane was now going down in a steep dive.'

John Trumble struggled to get to the escape hatch and passed out, possibly through a lack of oxygen. The 'next thing I remember was coming down on the end of the parachute. I had no recollection of pulling the release handle. One of the German fighters was circling and firing at me. I saw the red tracer bullets come pretty close and could clearly see the pilot.'

Falling unconscious again, John recovered his senses when he was still 1,000 feet or so from the ground. Landing in a ploughed field in bare feet, he was seized by 'German farm workers and frog-marched through a small village where the people were very hostile. A German soldier on a motorbike eventually came, and I was taken to a fighter station where I was given an inner pair of American flying boots.'

On the following day he 'was taken by train to a place rather like Colditz'. This may have been Dulag Luft (Oberursel), where he spent six days in solitary confinement, being interrogated at various times of the day or night. He was taken to see Eddie Hutchinson, and was given the news that P/O Smith, the bomb aimer, was in hospital with leg injuries, and also that the pilot, wireless operator, and the two gunners had been killed. On Christmas Eve John and a group of fellow POWs were sent to Wetzlar, before being transported in cattle trucks (twenty-five men in each) to Luft 7, a journey that took four days.

*

523 RAF heavy bombers gave Duisburg a pounding on the night of 17/18 December 1944, causing severe damage to the town. On the other side of the equation, eight of the 418 Halifaxes despatched failed to return, with a ninth crashing in England at RAF Manston. One of the Halifaxes lost was NR248, MH-A, 51 Squadron. Of the seven aboard, only Sgt Henry Wagner (navigator) survived.

NR248 had taken off from Snaith, Yorkshire, shortly before 3 am on 18 December, and made its way with main force down to Reading, crossing out over Beachy Head. Over France the weather began to deteriorate, with a westerly wind rising to over 100 knots, and the bomber stream was all over the place. When NR248 reached Duisburg, as no marker flares were seen, bombs were dropped using 'Gee'. They were on their way home when attacked somewhere to the north east of the Dutch town of Venlo by a Bf110 flown by Leutnant Rolf Ramsauer, 4.NJG/1, for his second night victory. After his attack had set the bomber on fire, the order to bale out was given.

Henry Wagner, closest to an escape hatch, was the only man to get out. None of the other six stood a chance when the blazing aircraft blew up. W/O W.A. Bates (pilot); Sgt E. Berry (flight engineer); F/S L.G. Roberts (bomb aimer); F/S J.A. Jones (wireless operator); Sgt T.W. Worthington (mid-upper gunner); and Sgt R. Thomas (rear gunner) now rest in Venray War Cemetery in southern Holland.

Henry guessed from his navigational calculations that when NR248 was attacked it was over British-held territory, and that he had therefore baled out over friendly lines. But so strong was the westerly wind that he was blown back over German lines. He landed in the branches of an apple tree in the back garden of a house near Geldern, only a few kilometres east of the Dutch border, with his parachute spread over the tree. With someone watching him from an upstairs window, he decided not to hide his silken canopy and headed off for the open spaces.

He walked for eight or ten kilometres until dawn, spending the rest of the day in a fir plantation. As soon as it was dark he set off again, but fences and water-filled ditches constantly barred his way. Around 4 am on 19 December, very wet and very cold, he stumbled across a barn. Only when it was light did he notice that it was full of hay: 'Took off wet clothes, stuffed them with hay, burrowed under & went to sleep. Woke when it was dark, put on wet clothes again, & set off, stumbling over waterlogged fields.'[196]

As it began raining again at daybreak on 20 December, he sheltered in another fir plantation. He was unable to sleep due to the cold and his 'general discomfort', and though children and their dogs passed within a few yards, he was not seen. 'Opened escape-pack & ate three Horlicks tablets, one piece of nut toffee & one barley-sugar... Drank from streams or troughs at night, using rubber flask and Halazone tablets. Set off again at dusk.' Next day, 21 December, he came across a dilapidated farmhouse, in which he decided he would sleep, 'but an old woman came out, and from her I got some apples, two slices of bread & two cups of coffee'.

Sleeping rough, walking in the rain, was more or less the pattern for the following day, but at some point he helped himself to some milk from a churn in a village. On 23 December, it was so cold that his clothes froze on him. 'Severe cramp. On again at night, breaking ice on puddles to drink. Weak and light-headed by this time. Walked through a village after curfew instead of going round it, & was captured by a German sentry.' Having been relieved of his revolver, the guard – 'he was a decent old chap' – took Henry to a dugout, hung up his wet clothes in front of a fire, and gave him a blanket, followed by a bowl of soup. He then indicated to Henry that he could get some sleep.

By Christmas Day Henry was at Dulag Luft, Oberursel, where he suffered the usual series of day and night interrogations, lack of decent food, and a lack of warmth. Then, on 30 December: 'Roused 2 am & departed 4 am. Marched with about fifty others, nearly all Americans, to the station. Hung about for two hours in the cold. Train to Wetzlar. Air raid on the way. Walked four kms to the camp. Searched, got POW capture parcel, & a billet. Found my bunk was just underneath John Trumble.'

After six days at Wetzlar the prisoners were off to Luft 7 in cattle trucks.

*

Christmas Eve 1944 would prove to be anything but a festive time for 102 (Ceylon) Squadron at RAF Pocklington, Yorkshire, when two of its Halifaxes – LW168 and MZ871 – failed to return from a daylight attack on Mülheim airfield. A third (MZ827) crashed at RAF Carnaby's extra-long and wide runway on its return, though without any casualties.

Of the seven crew of LW168 five became POWs and two were killed. It is believed, however, that all seven of MZ871's crew baled out alive, but that three were murdered by Germans soon after they had landed. F/S James George Williams (rear gunner), aged twenty-three, from Chatham in Kent, was captured by policeman Wilhelm Niessen, and taken by car to the *Kreisleitung* (District Office), where Kreisleiter Johannes Esser berated him for the destruction of the town. After beating him, Esser drew his pistol and shot him in the head. The body was wrapped up, put in a car, and taken away by Esser and a man called Pfeiffer, who threw it into a stream running into the Rhine. Esser was sentenced to death by a Military Court on 28 September 1946, and hanged in Hameln prison at 1102 hours on 23 January 1947.

It is also possible that F/O E. Roberts (pilot) and F/S J.L. Simpson (mid-upper gunner), also of MZ871's crew, were murdered on that same day. Details of their deaths are not known, but a letter to Simpson's family from the Ministry of Defence in 1982 suggested that a war crime had been committed against them, and that four Germans had been tried for the killings in 1948.

As for the five POWs from LW168, four reached the safety of Luft 7, while the fifth possibly went to Stalag Luft I (Barth). The pilot, P/O Edward Hislop, was killed in the aircraft, but some doubt exists as to the circumstances of the death of the bomb aimer, F/S Kevin Patrick 'Lindy' Lindenboom. As seen, airmen who had baled out safely were not always safe from vengeful German civilians, and it is supposed that Lindy also suffered at their hands and was murdered. It is odd that his fellow NCO crewmen never saw him again, and that he has no known grave, unlike his pilot who now rests in the Reichswald Forest War Cemetery.

Sgt Arnie 'Indy' Coope, LW168's flight engineer, counted five other parachutes as he floated down. Clearly visible to those on the ground he was shot at in the air and, once on the ground, manhandled by civilians before being passed to the German army. The mid-upper gunner, F/S Dennis Worthing, landed on the edge of an airfield, and was captured. One of his guards struck him in the face with his rifle butt, and knocked him out. Dennis came round to find the guard stealing his watch and other valuables.

Indy Coope, Dennis Worthing and the other two of their crew – F/S R.G. Clements (wireless operator) and Sgt J. 'Shirley' Temple (rear gunner) – were taken from the airfield jail in which they had been confined, via Frankfurt, to Luft 7 in the last *Trupp*.

*

**7 JANUARY 1945.** 'Food getting short, living on Jerry rations soon... Life is pretty boring now. There are various bets as to when the war will end.' (J.G. 'Jack' Smith RAAF.)

**8 JANUARY 1945.** Dysentery broke out in the camp. Captain Howatson did what he could for the sick, mostly putting them on a milk diet.

At around 11 pm the 'ferrets' found a big tunnel in progress in 8 Division. A massive search was then undertaken, lasting until 12.30, 9 January. 'All the chaps in one room were up on the carpet and I understand they are going to get a severe sentence.' (Tom Glenn.)

**9 JANUARY 1945.** Argentinian Red Cross parcels ran out. 4,000 more Red Cross parcels arrived. Issue of one per two men for four weeks. George Kilbryde noted in his diary that 'fifty-two new chaps arrived... Some of them were shot down on bombing raids on Christmas Eve, hard luck.'

It was very good luck, however, that saw F/S F.D. Green RAAF survive to reach Luft 7 on this day. His Lancaster, ME725, 61 Squadron, was shot down at 8.35 pm local time on 6 December 1944 near Hachborn, a few kilometres north east of the target (Giessen railway yards). ME725 had been blasted by cannon shells from a German night-fighter. With the hydraulics cut, the rear of the fuselage was a blazing inferno within seconds, and ammunition exploded from the heat. The pilot, F/O C.A. Donnelly RAAF, gave the order to bale out.

Meanwhile, F/S Francis Green, the wireless operator, seeing that the severely wounded mid-upper gunner was in danger of being consumed by the fire, tried to extinguish the flames, but was driven back by the heat and the fumes. Moving to the front of the aircraft to make his exit Green noticed that Donnelly was semi-conscious in his seat, asphyxiated by the fumes. Donnelly takes up the story: 'Instead of making an immediate escape he [Green] wasted valuable seconds in endeavouring to arouse me. About that time the aircraft exploded projecting both of us into the safety of space.' The flight engineer and the mid-upper gunner both perished, and were buried in the parish cemetery at Hachborn.

Despite his injuries Green tried to evade capture in the cold and rainy weather, but on the second night, having taken too many benzedrine tablets, he 'was heard falling from a fence into a border as I dropped unconscious'. (F.D. Green.) He was captured and taken to a nearby Luftwaffe airfield, where he was re-united with his skipper and with three others of their crew – F/L J.H. Vincent RAAF (navigator), F/S R.G.D. Brock (bomb aimer), and Sgt T.J. Kerrigan (rear gunner) – Donnelly noting that Green's 'nose, cheek and ear were severely burnt. And his cheek was also minus several square inches of skin... Shreds of skin hanging from one ear indicated the intensity of the heat to which he had exposed himself. His voice was barely audible due to seared throat and lungs.'

For his bravery, not least in trying to save his pilot rather than himself, Donnelly wrote to the

RAAF on 24 October 1945 suggesting that Green 'should be highly commended for his actions and deserves some form of recognition'. A search of Green's RAAF records suggests that none was forthcoming.

**10 JANUARY 1945.** A frost. Very cold. The prisoners stood in nearly a foot of snow during the parade, until the Germans gave up counting. An issue of parcels was made.

**11 JANUARY 1945.** Weather getting worse, very windy. The Germans found an escape tunnel under the theatre.

The Dramatic Club put on Pantomania, a new production that brought much-needed humour to the kriegies. It should have been performed on Christmas Day, but the theatre was too cold. The Germans had insisted that the script be submitted to them before the show went on, the guidelines being that the show could be as 'blue' as the producers wanted but that there should be no derogatory remarks about either Hitler or the German people. 'The script was duly submitted, and the Camp Commandant passed everything except for the incidental music, the overture to Merrie England. "We must have something else", he said. "England was no more merry than Germany!" This childishness put everyone's hump up.'

The producers were not to be put off by this pettiness and, when someone spotted that the composer's name at the top of the sheet music supplied by the Red Cross was a certain E. German, they pointed this out to the Commandant. 'In that case,' he said, 'it can be allowed.' Exit several senior POWs in hysterical laughter.[197]

**12 JANUARY 1945.** Another parcel issue. A 12-foot long tunnel was found by the Germans in Room 13, Hut 52, 8 Division, dug by Sgt Reg Styles. It was not his first attempt apparently. See similar entry for 8 January above.

**13 JANUARY 1945.** A new type of Red Cross parcel was issued, which contained dates amongst other items.

**14 JANUARY 1945.** Some of the younger German guards were sent away. Rumour was that they were off to the Eastern Front, as news had been received that 'Joe' had begun his long-awaited offensive.

**15 JANUARY 1945.** Bitterly cold. The ground had now been frozen for nearly seven weeks. Camp strength 1,617. 'No news today. We had an issue of Jerry tea [in the afternoon]. All the Red Cross parcels are done, so are the cigs. The tea isn't worth drinking so the boys are smoking it.' (Jack Smith RAAF.) According to Dick Nutter 'it smokes very well in a pipe'.

Early in the evening, news of the Russian advance was picked up from the BBC on the 'canary' (the hidden wireless set) claiming 'that the Russians have captured Kielce, which is about 100 miles due east of here'. (Elwyn Healy.)

*Though Europe lay in the grip of an iron winter the Allies, despite the unexpected German counter-attack through the Ardennes in December 1944, were slowly making gains on the Western and Southern Fronts in January 1945. On the Eastern Front, however, to prevent their lines of communication from becoming too stretched, the Russians had halted their advance in October 1944, waiting until supply lines into Poland from Russia and the Ukraine had been repaired and extended. By January 1945 the Russians, along a 1,000-kilometre front, had brought forward five Army Fronts (their word for an Army Group). From north* to south these five Fronts were:- 3rd Belorussian, 2nd Belorussian, 1st Belorussian, 1st Ukrainian, and 4th Ukrainian. The first two were heading for East Prussia, the 1st Belorussian for Berlin, the 1st Ukrainian for Breslau (Wroclaw) and, in the far south, the 4th Ukrainian heading for Slovakia. Opposing over 2,200,000 men in 180 Divisions were just seventy-five under-strength German Divisions.

By the second week of January 1945, nine of the ten armies that made up the 1st Ukrainian Front,[198] under the command of Marshal of the Soviet Union Ivan Stepanovich Konev, had established themselves across the Vistula river in the Baranov bridgehead, based on the town of Sandomierz approximately 180 kilometres south-south east of Warsaw. Facing them was the German Fourth Panzer Army (Generalleutnant Fritz-Hubert Gräser), comprising LXII Corps (Generalleutnant Hermann Recknagel), XXIV Panzer Corps (General Walther Nehring), and XLVIII Panzer Corps (General Maximilian Reichsfreiherr von Edelsheim).

At 0500 hours on the morning of 12 January, with over 250 guns per kilometre on a front measuring barely thirty-two kilometres, the 1st Ukrainian Front unleashed the great winter offensive with a massive artillery bombardment. No sooner had the guns stopped than the first wave of Soviet troops poured forward from the bridgehead: 'The weight and ferocity of the first attack shook the Germans so badly that they thought they were dealing with the main assault, and not just a reconnaissance in force. They were unprepared for the principal attack...' Leading the way across the German minefields were the Russian Penal Battalions, which took little time in overrunning the German front-line defences. 'At 1000 [hours] the Russian artillery received the order to open fire once more.'[199] There was nothing that the Germans could do to stop the onslaught. By evening on that first day the Russians had advanced over twenty kilometres on a forty-kilometre front and were beginning to swing past the town of Kielce.

In an attempt to stop the 1st Ukrainians' advance the Germans made an armoured counter-attack. With over a hundred Panther and Tiger tanks between them 16 and 17 Panzer Divisions, and 20 Panzergrenadier Division of XXIV Panzer Korps were ordered to Kielce. The Russian 3rd Guards and 4th Tank Armies went to meet them. What followed was 'one of the biggest tank engagements since the Battle of Kursk'.[200] After three days of bitter fighting the Russians had taken Kielce, and XXIV Panzer Korps had practically ceased to exist.

By 17 January the 3rd Guards and 4th Tank Armies had swept past Częstochowa and were across the Warthe (Warta) river. While the 4th Tank Army kept to the north, 3rd Guards Tank Army (Colonel-General Pavel Semenovich Rybalko) made for Breslau, Brieg and Oppeln. Rybalko was considered to be 'a masterly tactician and a brave soldier. Whenever this army went into action he rode in the leading tank and took direct charge in the field.'[201] Close on their heels were the infantry of the 5th Guards Army (Colonel-General Aleksei Semenovich Zhadov). Barely fifty kilometres to the north west of Częstochowa, directly in the path of the Russian tanks of the 3rd Guards Tank Army, lay Bankau.

**16 JANUARY 1945.** Still snowing... Weather improved, clear but cold. Much excitement when dozens of Luftwaffe aircraft flew low over the camp, 'the most we have ever seen in one bunch'.

All personnel unfit to march were told to report to the medical room. Some of the POWs were taken to Kreuzburg for a shower and to have their clothes fumigated.

Heading towards Kreuzburg are units of the 1st Ukrainian Front, some of whose 'armoured and mechanised units had reached objectives that had been set for much later in the operation... The rates of advance during the pursuit were the highest achieved by the Soviets in the war so far. The rifle forces moved at up to thirty kilometres every twenty-four hours, and the tank and mechanised forces at between forty-five and seventy.'[202]

On the night of 16/17 January the last German forces escape from Kielce.

In Stockholm, the Military Attaché, Colonel R. Sutton-Pratt, sent a report to various interested parties, in which he said that he had that very day received a visit from Mr Henry Soderberg, 'a Swedish YMCA camp visitor' who 'has been in Germany two years… He is one of the seven area inspectors of the YMCA… The camps within his area are Stalag 344, Lamsdorf, which now contains 24,000 prisoners…, Stalag VIIIB (Teschen) which contains 15,000 prisoners; Stalag VIIIA and VIIIC, also Stalag Luft 3 which now contains 11,000 prisoners… ; and Stalag Luft 7, Bankau, which now contains 8,000 [sic] prisoners with an ultimate capacity of 15,000.'[203]

**WEDNESDAY, 17 JANUARY 1945.** Sgt Peter H. Craig:

'It was just like any other winter morning behind barbed wire, bitterly cold, with a fresh fall of snow blanketing the ground. Alec was duty man in the room and at half past seven when the cookhouse bugle blew, he reluctantly crawled out from beneath his blankets, dressed, not without grumbling, and went out to get our breakfast from the Third Reich – a can of hot water. In ten minutes he returned. "Bloody water's only tepid," he moaned. "Well hurry up and make the coffee before it's stone cold" said Nic', turning over in his bunk.

'Soon we were all sitting up in our bunks eating breakfast, two slices of black bread and butter and a mug of coffee, whilst Alec told us what exactly he thought of the cookhouse staff. He was summing up each member's personal history as each one of us snuggled down under the blankets again in a vain endeavour to snatch another hour's sleep before roll call.

'At a quarter to nine the bugle sounded the quarter. None stirred. At nine o'clock it blew again for roll call. Immediately the billet awoke. Everyone jumped out of bed, swearing and grumbling, and proceeded to put on those clothes, if any, which they had deemed not necessary to wear whilst in bed, pulled on overcoats, gloves and varied assortments of head gear, lit up cigarette ends – the cigarette shortage was acute – and went out to roll call.

'On the parade ground "Rommel" (so called because of his resemblance to the famous general), the German warrant officer who practically ran the camp on his own, was shouting and jumping up and down in front of the Camp Leader and Man of Confidence, but these two, familiarised to his ways by now, just let him rave. It was his way of letting off steam. Presently, he subsided and started the count. Naturally enough the conversation among the ranks was of the new Russian offensive across the Vistula. In his Order of the Day, Stalin had said Breslau was the objective. Our Stalag lay seventy miles south east of Breslau and right in the path of the Red Army. This information was received on the hidden wireless set. From this source we knew that Częstochowa had fallen.

'Roll call correct, we were dismissed and meandered back across the snow to our billets. Back in our room the regular daily routine began. Half the barrack discarded their boots and crawled back into bed; two went off to classes at the school; Alec cleaned up the room, broke up a stool for firewood and lit the stove, while the remainder huddled round it for warmth and talked about what they would do if and when we were released by the Russians. At ten o'clock the news came in. This was strictly BBC and was taken down in shorthand from a receiver hidden in the camp.

'The Germans had suspicions that there was a wireless, but numerous scrupulous searches had failed to reveal its whereabouts. As a precaution against careless talk it was never referred to as "news" or the "wireless", but by a code word, "canary". Reception had been poor and there was nothing startling. The German army was in full retreat before the new Russian offensive. Częstochowa, in Poland, had definitely fallen. There was something about the counter offensive in the Ardennes, and the RAF and the US Army Air Forces had both been out in strength again.

'About eleven o'clock, a row started down the corridor and Bill went to investigate. In a few minutes he was back. "Come on you fellows," he shouted, "We have to evacuate! Be ready in an hour." Immediately he was besieged with questions. Where? Is there transport? How far? Do we walk? "Look, all I know is what I have told you, so we had better start packing."'

'During the next hour chaos reigned in the camp. Kit and bedding was thrown all over the place; stools and tables were piled high in stoves; the ration store was raided; the library, sports store and band room looted. In our room we packed our new meagre Red Cross food – enough for two days – into a wooden box and attached two wooden handles so that it could be carried easily. By midday no order to move had come. One o'clock passed. Two o'clock came and went, and at 3.30 pm we went out again for roll call. We might move tonight but Jerry was non-committal.'

'Rommel', possibly Oberfeldwebel Frank, informed the prisoners that for every man who fell out on the march five more would be shot. This order was never put in writing, and was never to be carried out anyway. As would be seen, Frank was not such a bad chap after all. The prisoners, all packed and ready to go, spent much of the day watching masses of German men and machines moving along the road to Breslau. In the distance the rumble of battle could be heard.

*Częstochowa falls to the Russians in the evening. Konev is directed to make for Breslau (Wrocław) on the Oder river, and to bring up the 59th and 60th Armies.*

*The man blamed for the decision to evacuate the POW camps in the face of the Soviet advance was SS-Obergruppenführer Gottlob Berger. Though he had been in charge of all POW camps since the autumn of 1944, it is not clear who actually made the decision to evacuate Stalag Luft VII. Berger was arrested in 1946 and put on trial in 1947, the indictment against him being: 'that between September 1944 and May 1945, hundreds of thousands of American and Allied prisoners of war were compelled to undertake forced marches in severe weather without adequate rest, shelter, food, clothing and medical supplies; and that such forced marches, conducted under the authority of the defendant Berger, chief of Prisoner-of-War Affairs, resulted in great privation and deaths to many thousands of prisoners.'*

*He was sentenced on another charge, however, namely the killing of European Jews, and was sentenced to twenty-five years' imprisonment, reduced to ten years only because he had refused a direct order from Hitler to kill the Prominente, the high-ranking and high-born POWs who had been held as hostages at Colditz. In the event, he was released in 1951, and died on 5 January 1975 aged seventy-eight.*

**THURSDAY, 18 JANUARY 1945.** Sergeant Ben Couchman, having packed his kit the previous day, woke up 'shivering as my blankets had remained packed overnight'.

Peter Craig:

'On Thursday morning we rose at the usual time allowing a couple of minutes to dress and dash out on parade. Again there was no definite news. The camp was rife with rumours. The wireless set had been dismantled and the parts distributed among several men. Consequently, we lived on rumours. Our souls craved to hear a rumour and then to spread it. You heard someone saying something utterly impossible and absurd, but you had to listen. You could not drag yourself away until he had finished. Then you told it to someone else, consciously or unconsciously altering or exaggerating certain points. Your listener laughed at you, asked how such a thing could happen, said you were a rumour monger, and then went off to tell it to someone else. Just as prison life would become unendurable without Red Cross food, so could it become unbearable without rumours.

'On the afternoon roll call the Camp Leader said it was quite probable that we would wait several days for a train. That was at 3.30 pm. At four o'clock the alarm went. "Prepare to march!" By 5.15 pm everybody was out, lined up in fours, sixteen hundred strong. Darkness had fallen and a bitterly cold wind was blowing from the east. I had on every stitch of clothing including two sets of long underwear, yet the wind went right through, freezing my bones until my body was numb. "To think," said Nic', "that a year ago I was probably basking in the sun in a Palestine orange grove."

'We stood there for an hour but there was no sign of the guards or of the march commencing. In ones or groups, the men started going back to the barracks. I went back with Alec, Nic' and Bill. We piled wood and odd bits of coal high in the stove until the fire was roaring up the chimney. I could feel my cheeks tingling as the heat thawed out the cold. The padré came round and asked us to go out and form up again, and Nic' said we would go but only when the Germans came. It was ridiculous standing out there in the cold. The padré nodded sympathetically and went. We had a brew on the stove when the barrack leader came round to say we would move off at 5 am the next morning. We tidied up the room, untied our blankets which had been rolled then knotted in a horseshoe so as to be easy to carry, and decided to cook the remainder of the German barley for breakfast as it would be impossible to cook on the march. The barley was almost on the boil and someone was pouring out the coffee when there was a terrifying screech and then the crump of a bomb exploding very close by.

'Immediately the lights went out. Then again came the ear-splitting nerve-shattering screech of high-velocity bombs. Everyone flung themselves on the floor. The barley went flying. Crump, crump, cru.....mp, crump went the bombs. The flimsy wooden barracks shivered and shook with the blast. "Christ! That was close!" "Who the hell upset the barley? I'm covered in the bloody stuff!" Bombs and barley. Barley and bombs. Suddenly there was a louder explosion. The building seemed to disintegrate around us. The percussion from the blast seemed to tear through the wooden barrack in waves. I felt my bowels move. I was covered in dust and barley. Everything was quiet now. The bombers had gone. I thought I had better go to the lavatory. There was a queue there.'

Joe Walkty:

'We returned to the barracks with the shriek of sirens in our ears. Faintly but ever louder, we heard the approach of Allied aircraft. The lights were turned out just as they seemed to be overhead. The Russian compound across the road turned off their lights half a minute later amidst the swearing and cursing of the men. Then, in rapid succession, six bombs fell with a blinding flash, an echoing crash, and a shaking of all the buildings. We hit the floor. Our first thoughts were that a part of the camp had been hit. Through the windows we could see a column of smoke rising into the air. We breathed a sigh of relief. The Russians had hit the neighbouring German fighter drome.'

Deryck Lambert also remembers the bombing by Russian aircraft: 'Our room [50/8] was at the end of the block, looking out onto open country. To everyone's dismay a stick of bombs began to fall in a direct line with our room – each one getting nearer and nearer. There was a mad scrambling dive to get under the bunks and onto the floor. I fully expected a direct hit on us, but the bomb never arrived!'

That night, sixty-eight sick men were evacuated to Ilag XVIIIZ (*Internierungslager* – civilian internment camp) at Kreuzburg. The word was that they were later moved to Stalag 344 (Lamsdorf), another camp that was to endure a terrible march away from the Russians.

## FRIDAY, 19 JANUARY 1945.
*1st Ukrainian Front captures Łódź to the north and Kraków to the south of Bankau. The first units of the 3rd Guards Tank Army cross the German border east of Breslau.*

Little sleep was had that night before the lights came on at 3.30 am. Peter Craig:

> 'We were awakened at 3.30 am to the familiar sound of "*Raus! Raus! Aufstehen!*" and warned to be ready to move in an hour and a half. Breakfast was a cup of coffee and one slice of bread. Rations had been issued. Thirteen-fifteenths of a loaf, two tins of bully beef, a small quantity of honey and some inedible cheese (known as fishheads) between eight men. We also got five cigarettes each and two ounces of tobacco between eight. It was still dark when we went outside at five o'clock, with a cold wind blowing from the east. At 5.30 am the guards appeared, scores of them, some with dogs, all with heavy rucksacks and blankets and clothed in heavy greatcoats, mittens, and balaclavas. The men divided into three companies of approximately 500 men each. I was in the first division, right at the front with Bill, Alex and Nic' and the rest of the boys. We marched through the gate and down the road about fifty yards, halted for about five or ten minutes, then on again another few yards, then a halt while Jerry counted, recounted and rechecked. We got under way at 6.30 am.'

Lined up in fives, it took an hour and half for the entire compound – 1,565 men – to leave, those at the back having to stand still in the freezing cold until it was their turn to move off. With them went two field kitchens, each capable of cooking for only 200 men at a time. The only medical equipment taken was carried by the medical officer, Captain Howatson RAMC, and three orderlies.

One of the POWs, Jack Broad, raised a laugh when his 'hat' was spotted: 'Some of the POW's had visited the sports store and one was wearing a football as headgear with flaps suitably cut to cover the ears.' (Alan Clarke.)

Aussie Fred Brown noticed as he left his hut that someone had scrawled on a corridor wall: "come on Joe," to which someone else had added: "too fucking late." That just about summed it up.

CHAPTER TWELVE
# 19 JANUARY-5 FEBRUARY, 1945: EVACUATION

The following table, showing the route of the march from Bankau to Goldberg, is largely based on 'best evidence' from a number of diaries kept by the POWs, and from a 2009 Michelin map of Poland (scale 1:300,000). The times given for departures and arrivals are approximate, and vary according to a person's position in the long column of march – those at the front obviously left a lot earlier, and arrived earlier, than those at the rear. Where there was insufficient room for the entire column to stay the night in a certain place, other accommodation was found as close by as possible, as would appear to have been the case on the night of 21/22 January 1945. Distances, too, vary, with some diaries giving a total walked of 256 kilometres (160 miles).

| Date/day | Departed | Time | Arrived | Time | Kms | Details |
|---|---|---|---|---|---|---|
| **January** | | | | | | |
| 19  Friday | Bankau | 0330 | Winterfeld | 1700 | 28 | Via Kreuzburg, Konstadt. |
| 20  Saturday | Winterfeld | 0500 | Karlsruhe | 1100 | 13 | Stopped at brick factory. |
| 20  Saturday | Karlsruhe | 2100 | Karlsmarkt | | 12 | Short stop. Overnight march. |
| 21  Sunday | Karlsmarkt | | Buchitz | 0900 | 20 | Crossed Oder. Some at Dom Waldhaus. |
| 22  Monday | Buchitz | 0500 | Gr Jenkwitz | 1530 | 20 | Schönfeld also a stopping place. |
| 23  Tuesday | Gr Jenkwitz | 0500 | Wansen | 1600 | 24 | Via Konradswaldau, Zindel, Bankau, Köchendorf. |
| 24  Wednesday | *Rest day* | | | | | |
| 25  Thursday | Wansen | 0400 | Heidersdorf | 1400 | 32 | Via Strehlen, Karzen, Rothschloss. |
| 26  Friday | *Rest day* | | | | | |
| 27  Saturday | Heidersdorf | 1100 | Pfaffendorf | 1630 | 19 | Nine inches of snow on the road. |
| 28  Sunday | Pfaffendorf | 0500 | Standorf | 1300 | 18 | |
| 29  Monday | Standorf | 1800 | | | | Overnight march. Terrible blizzard. |
| 30  Tuesday | | | Peterwitz | 0400 | 22 | |
| 31  Wednesday | *Rest day* | | | | | |
| **February** | | | | | | |
| 1  Thursday | Peterwitz | 0830 | Prausnitz | 1330 | 12 | |
| 2  Friday | *Rest day* | | | | | |
| 3  Saturday | *Rest day* | | | | | |
| 4  Sunday | *Rest day* | | | | | |
| 5  Monday | Prausnitz | 0645 | Goldberg | 0845 | 8 | Boarded train to Luckenwalde. |

Estimated distance on foot: 228-256 kilometres (142½-160 miles).

There is consensus as to the route taken on the first day, but that taken on the second and third days is less clear, as some of the diaries tend to differ one from the other not only as to dates and times but also as to place names. One author, for example, noted Beurich and Akzleuz, neither of which appears on the modern map, but which may have been Buchitz and Alzenau. The picture becomes less clear beyond Karlsruhe late on the evening of 20 January (Day 2). Most diarists mention the short halt at Karlsmarkt (Karłowice in Polish), and it is more or less clear that, once across the Oder river, the next stop was at Buchitz (Buszyce) and also at Dom Waldhaus, on 21 January (Day 3). The Oder was crossed by the bridge between Alt Poppelau (Popielów) and Nikoline (Mikolin).

The march continued on the morning of 22 January (Day 4). The Thomson/Howatson joint report[204] mentions stopping at Schönfeld (Obórki) on the evening of 22 January, others that the stop was at Gross Jenkwitz (Jankowice Wielkie), three kilometres to the south. The likely route for the column to have taken from Nikoline to Schönfeld was via Schurgast, Buchitz, Lossen, Johnsdorf (Janów), Alzenau (Olszanka), and Kreisewitz (Krzyżowice). The distance from Karlsruhe (Pokój) to Schönfeld was (and still is) around thirty-seven kilometres.

Some of the column passed *through* Schönfeld on 23 January (Day 5), which suggests that they spent the night elsewhere (i.e. Gross Jenkwitz) before going via Konradswaldau (Przylesie), Zindel (Mlodoszowice), another Bankau, and Körchendorf (Kucharzowice) to Wansen (Wiązów).

The route from Wansen to the train at Goldberg (Złotoryja) – with stops at Heidersdorf, Pfaffendorf, Standorf, Peterwitz and Prausnitz – is not in dispute, nor is the track taken by the train to Luckenwalde in Germany.

*

**FRIDAY, 19 JANUARY 1945 – DAY 1.** A bitterly cold wind blew from the south-east when the camp was paraded at 4 am in readiness for the evacuation. The men were to march off in 'divisions', each hut being a division. With the sound of gunfire in the distance to the east, the head of the 1,565-strong column of prisoners shuffled out of the camp two or three hours later, pulling their precious food ration and other treasured possessions on hastily-prepared sledges or carrying them in packs and sacks. Leading the way were the cookhouse staff, pulling a sled with emergency Red Cross rations and the POW records on it. Some of the musicians, Bob Burns among them, took their musical instruments. With guards counting the prisoners as they left, it took over an hour and a half for the last man to clear the camp gates, by which time those at the front were already a mile up the road. With guards and dogs every twenty yards or so, the Germans were taking no chances, though anyone foolish enough to escape in the harsh winter conditions would have stood little chance of surviving for long on his own. Heading in the same direction as the prisoners were scores of refugees, fleeing before 'Uncle Joe', and these poor souls, too, were pushing, pulling or carrying all their last remaining worldly possessions.

*

Back at the camp the guards had failed to notice in all the confusion that Sergeants Winton and Darwin, crew mates shot down in September 1941, were missing. When two recent arrivals had died and graves had been dug for them, Peter Darwin and Andrew Winton came up with the idea of having two extra 'graves' dug: 'Such was the shambles generally around us, with the wounded being carried to over-loaded wagons and the walking wounded being helped to the parade for counting, that we were able to slip our gear into the graves, slide in ourselves, were covered, and the grass sod carefully laid on top.'[205] It was bitterly cold under the earth.

Only when he heard the guards opening and closing doors to the huts, and then silence, did Andrew push away the covering clods of earth 'and looked at the sky… I eased my cold body out into the warm air. There was no movement from Pete.' No wonder, for he was frozen stiff. Quickly pulling him out, Andrew rolled him on the grass until there was some sign of life. Regaining some feeling in their limbs the two made their way to the cookhouse, reasoning that that would be the warmest place in the camp. After a long, warm drink, and having each donned a pair of overalls to make themselves look like workmen, they headed out of the camp.

After five kilometres or so they came to a house. A knock on the door was answered by a woman to whom nothing they could say in English, French or German had any effect. But when Andrew took a calculated gamble and quietly said 'Baranowski', she suddenly sprang into action. Shouting to someone in the house, her husband and daughter appeared, and the two airmen were pulled inside.

W/O Tadeusz 'Baron' Baranowski PAF had been with Andrew and Pete at Stalags VIIIB and 383 before they all moved to Luft 7 on 30 July 1944. Baranowski, a Polish Spitfire pilot on 317 Squadron, had been shot down into the English Channel on 30 December 1941. He described his subsequent capture in a rubber dinghy thus: 'I sit on the water. Water is all I see. I listen. What do I hear? A *ploop, ploop*. I move my foot. A hole in the boat! I put my finger in the hole... water stops. Then I think, what if little fish come and bite my finger? Then boat comes and here I am.'[206]

As it happened, Luft 7 was not all that far from his parents' home. Understandably anxious to see how they were, 'Baron' planned to escape, with Andrew's help. They selected a spot in a corner of the wire, 'where two poles were only two yards apart. This meant that the position of the watchtower lights threw a heavy shadow under the double wire lasting for forty-seven seconds before swinging away and then coming back.' (Winton, p.123). Despite a patrolling guard with his dog, Baron temporarily escaped, while Andrew covered his tracks by bending the cut wire back into place.

By chance it would seem that Andrew and Pete had stumbled upon a Polish family who knew, or who knew of, the Baranowski family. In due course the two escapers were escorted to Warsaw and, with the help of Polish railway workers, were put onto a goods train. After several hours travelling hopefully in the direction of the Black Sea port of Odessa, they got off when the train came to a halt in a siding in the middle of nowhere. Spending the night in a hay barn, they awoke in the morning to see a Russian armoured column heading towards them, and joined it in the advance to the Oder river. A female Russian tank commander insisted that Andrew, a Scotsman, celebrate Burns Night by reciting The Bard's poetry, which she translated to an approving gallery of hardened tank men.

After the column's tanks and assorted vehicles had been ferried across the Oder by barge, the two RAF men were in a van looking for working parties to join when, as they entered a small town looking for something to eat, shots rang out, and their Russian van driver was killed. Discretion being the better part of valour Andrew and Peter rapidly abandoned the vehicle. After three days hiding in a cellar they had had enough, and on 1 February joined a long column of resting prisoners at Peterwitz. To their amazement, they had rejoined the column from Bankau!

*

The main column, meanwhile, having left Bankau, plodded on in the icy wind through Kreuzburg (Kluczbork) to Konstadt (Wołczyn), walking past dead horses, shattered tanks and vehicles. It was not long before tired men began to discard much of their unwanted impedimenta: 'It was impossible to keep in line and march steadily. The roads were coated with ice and the wind kept blowing across the road' (Keith Campbell). There was a brief stop at 11.30 am, long enough to eat some bread and jam or whatever was at hand, and to smoke a cigarette. As these were beginning to run out, some resorted to the German tea leaves, better smoked than drunk.

At Konstadt the column turned south-west, away from Brieg and towards Winterfeld (Zawiść). At around 5 pm that evening, having covered some twenty-eight kilometres, they halted, having walked 'under extremely trying weather conditions and severe cold'.[207] Most of the men, packed into sheds and barns, burrowed into what little straw there was in an attempt to warm up. George Cross and about fifty others were put into a barn which they thought was rather crowded but would just about do – until another 150 were pushed in.

Sgt Doug Grant RCAF recalled that he and his mates couldn't 'find room to get in out of the snow' so knocked on the door of a house. The lady of the house, knowing perfectly well who they were, let them in. She was sympathetic, even though she 'had lost two sons over London'. She made them sleep in the loft, and fed them gruel, but insisted that they kept absolutely quiet as Major Peschel was billetted in the house too! As Doug said: 'Now there was a very brave woman and God bless her!'

Less fortunate were Harold Bennett and W/O Harold 'Ginger' Holmes. Finding the barn they were in to be too crowded they 'slept in snow outside – boots wet and frozen solid'. And Bill Cleeve, unable to get into the barn to which he had been allocated, 'spent the night huddled up in the doorway absolutely frozen'. Ben Couchman 'slept (?) sitting up'.

**SATURDAY, 20 JANUARY – DAY 2.** Gunfire could still be clearly heard when the second day began in a howling gale at around 4 am (it had subsided by noon). After a rough count of the POWs the guards realised that six men were missing. Just in case they were still hiding in the barns, they gave them a good burst of machine-gun fire, but the six were long gone.[208] They were soon caught by members of the Volkssturm and sent to Stalag VIIIC at Brieg. It was not long, though, before that camp, too, was evacuated, and they escaped once again by hiding in a cellar. Soon liberated by the Russians, they were repatriated in due course to the UK via Odessa.[209]

Another man, unidentified, was apparently left behind with a broken leg when the bulk of the frozen POWs, their clothes covered in frost, and with no issue of food or drink, set off at around 6 am on the short march into about six inches of snow. Even though it was only ten kilometres from Winterfeld to Karlsruhe-im-Oberschlessien (Pokój), it still took five or six hours to cover that distance. By 11 am the men were billetted in a disused brick factory where, for the first time since leaving Luft 7, they were allowed to light fires for a brew. The field kitchen that accompanied the column produced, for some, welcome cups of acorn coffee. Norman Oates, though, has no recollection that he ever received any food: 'All I can remember was wandering aimlessly round the brickyard trying to find somewhere to rest.'

Everyone was feeling sorry for himself, including the guard dogs which 'covered the farm entrance. Who wanted to escape?'

Later in the day Oberstleutnant Behr informed the Camp Leader, Peter Thomson, that they had to cross the Oder (Odra) river that same night as sappers were preparing to blow it up early next morning. Thomson and Howatson 'protested against further marching until the men were adequately fed and rested'. But the Germans were in no mood for arguing, and said 'that it was an order and must be complied with'.

Canadian Laird MacLean noted: 'At the moment we are stopped in a factory in Carlsruhe [sic]. Tonight we hit the road again. We have no smokes or food, so we can just pray that something turns up. Most of the boys are half dead now.'

David De Renzy, still suffering from burns incurred when his Mosquito had crashed in flames (see page 215), found the going hard: 'On the march I had quite a bit of difficulty in keeping up as, like many others, I had not fully recovered and, in addition, I had effective use of only one arm.' It was a measure of his poor condition that, as soon as he had been returned to England, he was sent to the famous burns unit at East Grinstead, 'where the treatment was wonderful and I made many friends. I also got into quite a lot of mischief during the convalescent periods.' It wasn't until January 1946 that he was back in New Zealand.

During the halt at Karlsruhe a horse and cart was commandeered for transporting the sick. The cart was big enough to carry only six sitting men.

The POWs were preparing to set off again in the evening, when an air-raid alarm sent them back inside, everyone fervently hoping that the Russians would not be tempted to bomb the place. Their prayers were answered, and two hours later, at around 7 to 8 pm, the prisoners were forced to their feet again and set off into the freezing cold night.

With the rumour flying around that the Russians were close by, Peter Thomson 'spread the word by mouth that we were to walk as slowly as possible and so enhance our chances of being recaptured'.

Keith Campbell reckoned that what followed, 'was one of the worst experiences I ever hope to go through'.

*

For a few, though, the opportunities for escaping were too tempting to be ignored, and three GPR men, according to Ron Watkinson, bricked themselves in 'until all the rest and guards had gone and then sat back to wait for the Russians'. They were found by the Russians, given passes, and told to make their own way down to Odessa: 'They had to live off the land or scrounge or beg food and a few lifts on Russian transports.' But they made it.

Two more men – Sgt T.W. Greene and F/S Donald Meese – decided to escape from the brickworks. Tom Greene was recaptured in the afternoon of the following day by a German patrol: 'The Germans took me to Brieg, but when Brieg was evacuated a few days later I hid under a sort of stage with several others. The Germans did not discover us and we remained in Brieg until the Russians liberated us on 6 February 1945.'

Donald Meese managed to reach the Russian lines and freedom. Falling in love with a nineteen-year-old German girl, they were married by a Polish priest on their way to Odessa.

Nine more POWs also decided to escape. In one group of six were W/O A.D. Naysmith, Flight Sergeants W.S. McPhail, F.J. Such and Albert Tweddle, Sgt F.R.W. Waters, and F/S D.R. Grant RCAF; in the other F/S W. Dyson, and Warrant Officers M.J. Muirhead RAAF and J.H. Marini RCAF. Ron Mead, in charge of escaping, gave them the go-ahead, and said that he would juggle the count when the time came to leave.[210]

Making their way up to the top floor of the brick factory, the nine men crawled on top of the large ovens in the hope that they would not be noticed when the column moved off. McPhail: 'We were dressed in RAF uniform, but for the purposes of bettering the chances of our escape we took off our NCO badges and took officers' rank.' Fortunately the dust, which lay everywhere an inch thick, was covered in boot tracks, and when the guards returned that night their dogs were unable to find any scent in all the dust.

The group of six was found next morning by Polish workmen, who told the airmen to stay in hiding as there were still German patrols in the area. They returned with blankets and food, and were back again in the evening with the news that Dyson, Muirhead and Marini were outside with a Russian tank. With all nine airmen aboard the tank headed back towards Karlsruhe: 'The tanks were firing all the time, engaging the fast-retreating enemy.' Spending the night in a large house in Karlsruhe, they had an interview on the following day with 'high staff officers including a general (name unknown), who treated us very politely'. That morning they were put in a truck and driven to Laski, 100 kilometres east of Breslau. On 26 January they left for the POW collection centre that had been established by the Russians at Lublin, not far from Majdanek concentration camp.[211]

Before he left Lublin F/S McPhail was handed a roll of 'undeveloped film containing photographs of Mydanik [sic] (murder) camp in Lublin, portraying human remains, shoes of all description, and various parts of the camp'. On his return to England McPhail handed over the film to the RAF photographic section, 'but [it] proved too fogged to be printable'. Another escaped POW, British soldier Sam Kydd, also visited Majdanek: 'We saw the ovens, the gas chambers, the bleached bones and the dentures, but even with all this evidence I don't think the enormity of it hit us until some time afterwards.'[212]

On 23 February 1945 some 500 escaped POWs were sent by train from Lublin to Odessa. The officer in charge, F/O P.J. Anderson RCAF, described it as a journey made 'in bitter cold that took six days and nights'.

Anderson was the navigator of Halifax JP162, 148 (Special Duties) Squadron, that had taken off from Campo Casale airfield at Brindisi, Italy, on the night of 4/5 August 1944 with supplies for the *Armia Krajowa* (AK, Polish Home Army) on DZ *Kanarek 211* at Miechowa near Kraków. On the way home, after a successful drop, JP162 was attacked and shot down by a German Bf110 night-fighter. Though the pilot, rear gunner, and despatcher were killed, Anderson, Sgt A. Jolly (wireless operator), Sgt R.G. Peterson RCAF (bomb aimer), and F/S W.C. Underwood (flight engineer) survived, and fought with the AK until the Russian advance put an end to their activities.

On arrival at Odessa, on 28 February 1945, the officers and men from Lublin were separated and, according to Anderson:

> 'were issued with one blanket apiece and were deloused – showers and baths were available. Three American Liberty ships in port provided us with what food they could to supplement the Russian ration. Members of the British Military Mission arrived on 1 March and on 3 March British personnel were transferred to what was designated the British camp. It then appeared that the Russians were giving the Americans preferential treatment as the Russian ration provided in the British camp was not as good as that in the American camp nor were the messing facilities as good.'

On 7 March F/O Anderson and 'about 1,700 all ranks' – which total must have included a second train-load of Allied ex-POWs from Kraków – embarked on the *Moreton Bay*. Anderson was appointed messing officer, and was assisted in his duties by Naysmith, Dyson, McPhail, and Such: 'These NCOs,' in Anderson's words, 'while acting in the capacity of officers during our stay in Lublin and until we reached Port Said did outstanding work. They were excellent in maintaining the morale of the men, showed a great deal of initiative, and were a credit to the air force.'[213]

Making friends with McPhail aboard the *Moreton Bay* was WO1 Hubert Brooks RCAF, 419 (RCAF) Squadron. Shot down on 8/9 April 1942 (Hamburg) Brooks had been on the run since escaping from a work party at Tost on 10 May 1943, and had fought with the AK. So distinguished was his service with them that he was awarded the Polish Cross of Valour. He was later Mentioned in Despatches (1/1/46) and awarded the MC (8/10/46) for his escape.

Sailing across the Black Sea the *Moreton Bay* reached Port Said on 12 March, via the Bosporus, the Sea of Marmara, the Dardanelles, the Aegean Sea, and the Mediterranean. Its passengers, though, were not allowed to disembark until 15 March, 'when the RAF personnel were taken off and sent to Cairo. We remained in Cairo until 18 March and were housed at No. 22 PTC under canvas.' From there aircrew were dispersed to their respective countries, for most of them their war done.

**SUNDAY, 21 JANUARY – DAY 3.** Some time in the small hours there was a short stop at the village of Karlsmarkt (Karłowice). The men rested for a while before continuing towards the frozen River Oder. Everyone was affected by the extreme cold, and many were hallucinating. At around 1 am 'the temperature really plumetted – to about 35-40° below' (Bill Cleeve), and by 2 am or so was reckoned to have fallen to 42° below.[214] Eventually the vague outlines of the bridge, estimated to be about 500 yards long, could be seen in the eerie, misty white light of dawn. They 'crossed the bridge at a place called Nikolas Ferry [sic]. Not much could be seen of the river though on the further bank you could make out the dim outline of trenches and concrete pillboxes.' (Joe Walkty.)

'About 5 am we reached the Oder river and they made us line up in single file in order to cross the bridge on the side walk. You can imagine the amount of time this took, [as] there were fifteen hundred men. We finally started across the bridge, [and] as we were crossing I noticed on the road itself there were large holes with bars of metal across, and at each of these holes they had a guard. I found out later the reason for this. The bridge was mined, and if the Russians came before they had a chance to blow it up, when the wheels of their vehicle hit the bars in the road it would blow up. At 9.30 am we had finished our march of forty-one kilometres and stayed in big barns (500 men in each) at Lossen. Here the cookhouse got busy and made a brew of coffee. We got equivalent to a cup per man ...' (Bill Niven RCAF).[215]

As the POWs trudged across, the surface full of holes 'possibly made by small bombs', they were watched by the German engineers, who had everything in readiness for the bridge's demolition. Joe Walkty again: 'On the further side of the bridge we met one solitary, dejected-looking army corporal. He was armed with a gun, and at his feet he had two German anti-tank rocket bombs. With this he was to guard the further approaches of the bridge against attack by the Russians.'

At some point after the crossing Bruce Smith RAAF decided to rest his back-pack on one of the white posts that marked the side of the road: 'I selected one such post and rested myself by standing with my back to that post and taking the weight of my load on it. Some time after doing that I was awakened by our Roman Catholic padré [John Berry], who was picking up stragglers. I had, quite clearly, been sound asleep, standing up, and might well have frozen stiff where I was if I had not been roused by that padré, who walked with me for a kilometre or so to be sure that I was awake.'

Across the Oder, at Schurgast (Skorogoszcz), the men stood about in the freezing cold for an hour or more until it was decided that there was nowhere there for them to stay. It was 9 am before the column stopped at Waldhaus (Buszyce), five kilometres down the road.[216] Oberfeldwebel Frank was keen to get everyone settled so that he too could have some time in which to relax. All by now were feeling the strain, and when Frank gave some of the kriegies a push to hurry them up one of them, who spoke German well, took exception to being pushed and told Frank that he would not tolerate being manhandled. At this Frank 'became very agitated indeed, took his sidearm out of its holster, and fired two rounds into the air'. This had little effect but, now safely across the Oder, the men were given the rest of the day off. Bill Cleeve noted that their 'billet proved to be a state farm, and here we shared the barn with the cows and other animals, but no one minded as the atmosphere, although a trifle "high", was warm especially after the arctic temperatures experienced during the previous night'.

Once over the river, Neil Ostrom recalls 'feeling sorry for a column of, they even looked young to us, Germans going the other way, and spoiling their day with remarks such as "Joe Stalin kommt" and pointing to the front we had been marching from'.

It was about now that Captain Howatson carried out an examination on Sgt Jim Morgan, who had a large boil on his leg: 'I with five other chaps were marched to a military hospital where I had it lanced.' After what Jim described as a long trek the six arrived at Stalag Luft III (Sagan): 'Fortunately for me, I left there with quite a large stock of cigs. The hut was half full of the remains of parcels sent to these chaps (officers). They must have lived like lords, which even included silk swimming shorts.' The six were eventually evacuated to Stalag IIIA, where they 'were bundled in with the Irish boys (all army and navy). I saw more fights there than in the whole of the war!'

\*

After Captain Howatson had made strong representations to Behr, fourteen of the men, suffering with badly-blistered feet, swollen knees, or dysentery, were given transport to the *schloss* (castle) at Lossen (Łosiów), which Behr knew was a German army command post. Howatson and a German medical orderly accompanied the men with instructions from Behr that the fourteen sick men were to be taken from the castle to an SS field hospital at Schurgast in the morning.

At the SS field hospital they found numerous German wounded, casualties of the fierce fighting across the Oder beyond Oppeln (Opole). Before long nine more Luft 7 prisoners, who had been unable to continue, were given permission by Behr to join the fourteen now at Schurgast. Captain Howatson returned to the main column.

Thanks in part to the research undertaken by author Michael Hingston for his gripping book *Into Enemy Arms*, the names of twenty-one of the twenty-three are known: J.A. Cakebread; K. Chapman; G.R. Claydon; C.M. Dawson; G. Fallon; F.A. Giles; P.P. Hardwick RAAF; F. Jenkinson; C.S. Joce; T.W.M. Kemp; T.B. Lewis; L.R. Maki RCAF; W.J. McCoombs RCAF; R. Mead; C.A.F. Murray RAAF; M.J. O'Leary RAAF; W.A. Poulton; S.W. Simes; J.G. Slowey (Michael Hingston's uncle); D. Yardley; and Petty Officer Victor Smyth. The other two men may have been S/Sgt Hugh C. 'Paddy' Clenaghan and S/Sgt Herbert Ranfield, two of the three glider pilots mentioned by Ron Watkinson (see page 241), who were evacuated via Odessa. According to Vic Smyth the 'Roman Catholic padré, Father Berry' was also in the party.

With the rapid advance of the Russian forces, these twenty-three men were uncomfortably close to the front line, and in the immediate vicinity of units of an SS Division, whose commander ordered the non-combatant airmen to be taken to the civilian hospital in Brieg. Ron Mead somehow persuaded their driver to return to the castle at Lossen because, he said, a few of the sick were so ill that they were in danger of dying from the cold. The castle had by now been evacuated by the German troops, and so the 'sick' personnel 'settled down there pretty well'. (Vic Smyth.)

Vic Smyth also said that it was Father Berry who then made contact in Lossen with the local Roman Catholic priest. This was Father Richter, 'who promptly took us to his house and gave us the best meal we ever had in Germany'. Word of the presence of the twenty-three came to the ears of retreating SS soldiers, who had taken over the castle. According to Vic Smyth, Father Richter told the escapers that the SS 'wanted to shoot us as escapees. A service was actually held in the [Lossen] church for us and the priest, with several women, approached the officer in charge to ask him to spare our lives as we were all sick men.' The next few days in Lossen were tense for the twenty-three as they waited to see what their fate might be.

Father Berry probably returned to the main column of POWs, for his name appears on the nominal roll compiled at Stalag IIIA in April, though how he accomplished this is unclear.

Fortunately for the twenty-three in Lossen there were two people who were prepared to help them – Ditha Bruncel, the nineteen-year-old daughter of hotelkeepers in Lossen, and Gefreiter Krumpeck, an Austrian soldier in the German army. Krumpeck was in charge of a working party of twenty-one Frenchmen billetted on the village inn at Lossen. On 26 January, after Ditha Bruncel had spoken with him, Krumpeck appeared at the house. He told the twenty-three that he was taking them to join the French, where they would be under his protection and where he would be better able to provide food and medication, however meagre. The French, even though they would now become very cramped in their quarters, welcomed the twenty-three 'airmen', and even found jackets for some to cover their uniforms.

As the fighting approached the SS unit that was dug in at Schurgast, some ten kilometres away, not then knowing of the presence of the 'RAF' prisoners, ordered Krumpeck to evacuate Lossen. This, to his eternal credit, he refused to do.

On the afternoon of 1 February, Lossen came under Russian attack, first from relays of aircraft that shot at everything in sight, and then from the artillery that pounded away all through the night and on into the next day. Finally, at around 4.30 am on 4 February, Russian T-34 tanks arrived. The twenty-three men warily left their refuge, a cellar, and made themselves known to a Russian officer, who fortunately spoke good German. But there was a serious moment when the Russians discovered a radio that the group had hidden in the cellar: 'As most of us were telegraphists we were able to fix it up so as to listen to the BBC news… When the Russians found it they thought we were spies and treated us very suspiciously at first. But when a Russian major came along we were able to establish our identity.' (Vic Smyth.)

With other matters to attend to, the Russians left the group to its own devices. Having fallen in love with Ditha (and vice-versa), Gordon Slowey found a hiding space for her in their quarters in the village inn. The dangerous nature of the men's position was highlighted when two of the French workers appeared with tears in their eyes. They had gone back to their own quarters after visiting their Polish girlfriends only to find that the rest of their group had been shot. It was not the Russians, they believed, but the SS.

Sad to relate, also killed was Father Richter. There is a somewhat confused story about the shooting of a 'monk', who may well have been Father Richter, that was told by Dave Yardley when he was at RAF Cosford after repatriation. Bumping into Bill Taylor, he told him about the shooting of a monk at Lossen. Dave and some of the others had been put into a cellar which had a small grill looking out 'at ground level onto a lawn. Dave saw the SS put the monk against a wall and shouted at him to tell them where the British prisoners were. He refused and they shot him.'

*

Fate was also to decree that The Reverend John Berry would not live to see old age. On 14 August 1959, then the Rector of St Mary's Monastery at Kinnoull, in Fife, Scotland, and aged forty-eight,[217] he was with a group from the monastery who went for a swim near the small fishing village of East Haven. When one of the novices got into difficulties in the rough sea, the Very Reverend John Berry, as he had now become, unhesitatingly plunged into the sea to rescue the novice, and took him to shallower water. A few moments later John Berry 'was seen to be floating head downwards in the water'. A doctor who was summoned too late to help 'gave his opinion that death was due to a heart attack… The certificate [of death] issued later gave asphyxia as the immediate cause of death.'

*

On 11 February, after the Russians had made arrangements, the twenty-three at Lossen were ordered to pack and to be ready to go within a few hours. When three open lorries appeared the men, and Ditha, piled aboard one, while the surviving French and Krumpeck boarded the other two. The lorries made for the Oder river which, in the absence of any bridge, was crossed by the simple expedient of driving across its frozen waters. That night they were in Oppeln, and on the following day were formally registered by the Russians. After a stay of two or three days the group continued to Gleiwitz and, after a further two days, to Katowice in Poland. Their next move came on 23 February, to Kraków, having been joined by a dozen more stragglers – either evaders or escapers – bringing the size of the party to around thirty-five.

Already working in Kraków was F/O Wlodzimierz Bernhardt, 301 Squadron, a Polish airman who had been shot down in his Halifax by three Ju88s on 16 August 1944 and who had managed to evade capture. The Russians had set him up in an office to register POWs as and when they arrived.

Another party from Częstochowa was soon to arrive at Kraków, in the charge of F/L A.H. Hammet

DFM, RAAF (see page 158 and Appendix IV). Being of higher rank than Bernhardt, Allan Hammet became the senior officer in charge of the escaped POWs at Kraków.

On 25 February the British joint party was put aboard a long train of coaches and, after a tediously slow journey, finally reached Odessa on 3 March. The rest of their journey back to their home countries was much as recorded by Doug Grant in Appendix III.

For their comrades left behind on the march from Luft 7, however, freedom was still a long way off…

*

**MONDAY, 22 JANUARY – DAY 4.** Having been roused at 1.30 am – the Germans said that the Russians had crossed the Oder to the north of them – the men were on the road by 5 am, as they made the long haul to Gross Jenkwitz. A further thirty-one sick men were evacuated to, it was thought, Stalag 344 (Lamsdorf). Just after setting off, two large explosions were heard seconds after flashes had been seen to the north. Most reckoned that it was the bridge over the Oder being demolished.

Meanwhile Oberfeldwebel Frank had made a point of finding the kriegie who had resented being pushed and apologised for his unsoldierly behaviour on the previous day. As Bruce Davis said, 'that incident enhanced the respect which we already had for that man'. Frank's stock would rise further with the prisoners over the coming days. Another of the Germans to impress the prisoners was 'Otto', the interpreter (Richard Erffinger), who was a kindly and thoughtful man. Bruce Davis, on behalf of his food 'syndicate', mentioned to Otto that they were in need of a kitchen knife to help 'with the preparation of food. A day or two later Otto called me aside and handed me just such an item, simply as a friendly gesture, and certainly without any thought of any requirement for recompense.'

Gross Jenkwitz was reached by early afternoon, a distance of seventeen kilometres having been covered. Billetted in large barns, the men received a meagre food ration – 'one biscuit between two and a pound of margarine to last five days. We dug in the frozen earth and found pieces of potatoes, carrots and peas and made ourselves a cup of soup, and then to our blankets. We had two blankets and slept fully dressed with every bit of clothing we possessed.'[218]

At Schönfeld Bill Taylor sneaked out into a cow byre and helped himself to a Klim tin of milk from the cows' full udders. He was filling up his tin for a second time 'when a guard came in and fired his rifle at me. He chased me round the cows until I finally escaped through the door as he fired again. I managed to get most of the milk back to my friends.'

Meanwhile, four more POWs had slipped away during the night of 21/22 January. The first two to leave, accompanied by a hail of bullets, none of which hit their mark, were W/O E.E. East and F/S R.J. Hansford, followed by W/O M. Holloway and F/S W.F. Sutherland RAAF. East and Hansford were recaptured on the following morning, having spent the night lying in the snow. They managed to escape a second time shortly afterwards, and this time gained the Russian lines.

Holloway and Sutherland stayed for a fortnight in the roof of the barn where they had all been resting. They survived by drinking melted snow (of which there was plenty) and a little milk brought for them by a forced labourer. They narrowly escaped death when the barn was shelled by the Russians, to whom they surrendered.

**TUESDAY, 23 JANUARY – DAY 5.** *Konev's forces reach the Oder river.*

The call of "*Raus!*" came at 6 am. The temperature during the night had, apparently, fallen to *minus* 25° C. The column was on the move two hours later. Not only the prisoners were feeling the pace, for one of the German guards collapsed. These were mostly elderly and, as such, unfit for front-line service. But they were fed better than the prisoners, whom they goaded with promises of better billets and good food at the end of each day. Few were surprised, therefore, when they reached their destination, Wansen (Wiązów), to find that the billets were 'more big cold barns', and the food a cup of tea and a cup of soup.

Some believed that the man responsible for the guards' behaviour was Sgt R.D. Hughes, who was, some of his fellow prisoners believed, 'obviously working with the Germans'. Given his earlier track record, it is easy to see why they thought this.[219]

In a small town near Wansen the prisoners, who had had to pass a column of German tanks that were waiting down a side road, were being jeered at by the locals and by the tank crews when, suddenly, someone started singing the popular 1939 song You are my Sunshine. The prisoners, without any order being given, formed into column of threes, straightened their shoulders and, with heads held high, marched through the town in a wonderful show of defiance.

When the column had reached Wansen, Captain Howatson put Hughes, because he spoke German, in charge of a party of thirty-one sick prisoners to be taken by rail in cattle trucks from Wansen to Stalag Luft III (Sagan). After only five or six days at Sagan Hughes was ordered to take another group of over fifty officers and NCOs from there to Stalag IIIA (Luckenwalde). Hughes: 'I had difficulty getting them decent rail travel but eventually succeeded. We arrived at Luckenwalde and I remained in the camp until it was liberated on 22 April 1945.'

**WEDNESDAY, 24 JANUARY – DAY 6.** *The 1st Ukrainian Front captures Oppeln (Opole), forty kilometres south west of Kreuzburg.*

On the sixth day they rested. 400 loaves of bread were issued, a quarter per man. Ben Couchman and friends made a fire 'and roasted a few spuds. Supplied with two half-cups of soup and quarter loaf of bread from the field kitchen.'

**THURSDAY, 25 JANUARY – DAY 7.** It was another early rise, this time at 1.30 am, and the column was off two hours later. The temperature was a little warmer now, the icy snow turning to slush, but walking was still difficult. They passed through Strehlen (Strzelin) (7.45 am), Niklasdorf (Mikoszow), Nass Brockguth (Brochocinek), Karzen (Karczyn) (11 am) and Rothschloss (Białobrzezie), before halting at Heidersdorf (Łagiewniki) after another thirty weary kilometres. Ben Couchman was issued 'with a cup of soup and a fifth of a loaf'. He also noted that, according to some French POWs, 'the Russians were nearer to Sagan than we were'.

Fourteen German tanks passed the prisoners, heading for the ever-closer Eastern Front. As Fred Brown said: 'None of us wished to swop places with them. Theirs was a one-way ticket job.'

George Cross noted: 'Saw here a batch of [British] army types. They were from Lamsdorf, had been on the road three days and still had rations.'

*Units of 1st Ukrainian Front establish bridgeheads across the Oder south of Breslau.*

**FRIDAY, 26 JANUARY – DAY 8.** The men enjoyed another rest day, and were issued with 600 loaves, to last for two days. Ben Couchman: 'Scrounged some spuds and beans and made some stew. Issued with two half-cups of soup from field kitchen and a seventh of a block of margarine. I went to bed.'

**SATURDAY, 27 JANUARY – DAY 9.** The prisoners had something of a 'lie in', not having to rise until, for them, quite late. There was a further issue of bread – half a loaf each – to last two days.

Laird MacLean:

'It is now Saturday morning and it has been snowing all night. A bunch of us slept all night in a barn with some cows. The Germans have told us to be ready to march again at eleven o'clock. I saw the doctor yesterday about my feet because my big toe is swollen up and all black from the frostbite. He put me down for transport if they can get a train for the sick and, if not, I have to ride in a wagon because I can't walk any more.'

The trek continued shortly before midday. The roads were crammed with refugees. Passing through Langseifersdorf (Jaźwina) around 3.30 pm, it was dark by the time the prisoners arrived at Pfaffendorf (Książnica) around 6 pm after nineteen kilometres. They were put into the ubiquitous, cold barns, though there was an unseemly rush by several POWs to get into a warm cattle byre. Half a cup of soup was issued at around 8.30 pm.

**SUNDAY, 28 JANUARY – DAY 10.** No lie in today, the call of 'Raus! Raus!' coming at 3.30 am. An hour and a half later they were off. It was snowing again, and the wind was bitterly cold, but at least the slush had hardened. Nevertheless, it was still twenty-one or more kilometres to their destination, Standorf (Stanowice). The temperature continued to drop, and more POWs suffered from frost-bitten feet caused by inadequate footwear. When they reached Standorf at 1.30 pm, even though it was still very cold, they were not allowed to light fires. Some found room in an old prison camp.

There was an issue of twenty-four cartons of knäckerbrot, 150 kilograms of margarine, and fifty kilograms of sugar.

*

Twenty-two of the sick, including Laird MacLean and Bill Taylor (hernia), were marched off with two guards, Otto and Franz, to a hospital at Schweidnitz (Świdnica). After a long wait outside, they were admitted and examined, their spirits rising when they thawed out. They were given a cup of soup, a slice of bread, and a cup of coffee – 'it was like manna from Heaven'. In the morning, however, it was back to reality. Told to leave, they were given a third of a loaf and some margarine to help them on their way. Snow was falling as they trudged to Schweidnitz railway station, outside the town on a flat, endless, snow-covered plain. Here they had an interminable wait in the cold.

With the German railway system in chaos and priority being given to the hospital trains bringing back the wounded from the Russian Front, the guards eventually took the sick POWs into an air-raid shelter below a beer cellar. An English-speaking German civilian, as Laird MacLean noted, 'brought us some beer and meat sandwiches. I managed to scrounge a couple of fat cigars, so we were all right for a while.' That night the men slept as best they could. Bill Taylor put three chairs together for his 'bed'.

On the following morning, 30 January, at around 4 am they rushed to the station to catch a train, only to find that it had gone. In the dark and freezing temperatures it was another two hours before the next one arrived, packed with German soldiers. With no room inside, the prisoners and their guards were put onto open, flat wagons: 'I had been cold before, but never experienced a cold so intense. There was no protection from the wind in this flat, open countryside. We were numbed through and through. Ice caked on our faces, hair and clothing.' (Bill Taylor.) Luckily, after only ten kilometres or so, the train stopped. Everyone, including the guards, was fed up, and they left the train.

They had to wait until the late afternoon for another. It was snowing heavily again as they piled aboard the French railway wagon – forty men or eight horses – that was to be their carriage. During the night a number of German soldiers pushed their way in. They 'were pretty crowded all night and it was cold, but it was better than walking'. At Gorlitz, Otto was ordered to take the prisoners to Sagan. At around 11 am on 31 January the sick men arrived at Stalag Luft III. Here they joined not only the 500 or so sick RAF officers who had been left behind when the camp was evacuated a few days earlier but also a party of sick who had left the Bankau column at Wansen.

After his foot had been seen to by a doctor, Laird MacLean's only regret was 'that I can't help the other fourteen hundred boys on the road somewhere. God help them.' He also noted that about '200 of the gang has dropped out already and we don't know how many were lost in the snow. Up to now we have had no news or food, so we are in a pretty bad way.' Many of those on the march were led to believe that dozens of their comrades had perished before they reached Stalag IIIA. Surprisingly, this was not so.

**MONDAY, 29 JANUARY – DAY 11.** Most of the men stayed wrapped up in their blankets until soup – half a cup – was served. Ben Couchman noted that they also received 'seven biscuits, 1 oz margarine and one tenth of a tin of bully beef'.

The order to prepare to depart from Standorf was given at 4 pm, with the usual German promise of transport when they reached their next stop. At 5.30 pm, in the dark, they moved off. The weather then took a turn for the worse, if that were possible, the men having to stagger through an horrendous blizzard which, very quickly, had deposited two or three feet of snow on the ground. A convoy of vehicles passing them on the road only made things worse, as the prisoners were forced to pass them in single file through the deep snow drifts on the side.

Tom Trimble:

'When German transport started to pass, at one point some of this transport got snow bound on road and we were held up for about two hours. At this point the storm was at its very worst and it cost some of our chaps very dear. They were utterly exhausted and yet could not drop out as they would freeze in less than five minutes. When eventually the road was clear and we got past we found a jerry dead (frozen solid) by the roadside. The fact that a jerry was frozen by the wayside will give some idea of the storm. About half way along this road one of the jerry transports hit my sleigh on purpose and smashed it to pieces, also spilling the kit all over the place. Luckily he missed hitting anyone else. Actually, it is impossible to put the facts of this night on paper – it had to be experienced to be believed.'

Jack Smith RAAF noted that 'Jerry got annoyed when we refused to help him drag his trucks out of the jam. A lot of hope he had. Stan [Wharton] and I could hardly pull our own sledge, never mind a truck.'

One of those caught in the two-hour hold up was Joe Walkty. They had been climbing up 'a hill that stood out much higher them the others. As the front of the column reached the top we came to a halt. The officer went forward to see what was the matter. It seemed we had run into the tail end of a traffic jam caused by the snow storm.' There was no way past, with a hundred-foot sheer drop one side and a thick forest on the other. Joe 'was one of the unfortunate ones who stood on the crest of the hill. There was no cover, and the wind blew from the direction of the sheer drop. The snow, a powdery snow, soon covered us from head to foot.'

And Harold Bennett: 'We walked all night in the worst blizzard I've ever experienced – terribly cold (30 below according to guards) – German civvies lying dead from the cold on side of road – everyone just a pillar of white – wet and frozen to the skin.'

Maybe it was now that Padré Collins, suffering with a cold, tried to blow his nose with his handkerchief, only to find that it had frozen solid in his pocket.

At 0230 hours the precious field kitchen overturned.

As the column staggered on through the night men lost contact with those behind or in front of them:

'...the road was distinguishable only by the flattened snow – the whole country was one featureless white landscape. I became aware of the fact that I could see no other marchers ahead, so I turned around and strained my eyes into the distance – again no marchers in sight. There I was, plodding along, alone and cold and hungry. A small village eventually came into sight, and there standing in the village square was a guard, with an electric torch, reading the name of the village from a signpost. I approached and in my "best" German said: "Was name?" He replied: "*Es ist Rosen!*", then turning and seeing me he grabbed his rifle and started to shout: "*Mach schnell. Schnell. Schnell...*" I plodded along!' (Stan Zucker.)

**TUESDAY, 30 JANUARY – DAY 12.** The men were utterly exhausted when they arrived at Peterwitz (Piotrowice) at around 4 am, the whole time fighting their way through the blizzard, all twenty-one kilometres of it. The Germans tried to cram the prisoners into two small barns, but they were inadequate, and even though a small loft was opened up as extra accommodation it was a good three hours later before all were packed in. A Polish worker gave George Cross and his pals 'a drink of Jerry tea which was very much appreciated, the drink situation being very grim on the march'.

A tragedy now befell Ben Couchman. Having 'to go outside for two minutes' he got back to his space to find that someone had stolen his two, precious blankets. In the circumstances, there could have been no more serious a crime, except possibly the theft of food.

The good news, such as it was, was an issue of 104 kilograms of meat, one sack of salt, twenty-five kilograms of coffee, and 100 of barley. A further issue was made later – 296 loaves of bread, fifty kilograms of oats, and thirty-five-and-a-half kilograms of margarine.

**WEDNESDAY, 31 JANUARY – DAY 13.** The POWs were given a lie-in until *Appell* at 11 am. Having survived the theft of his blankets, Ben Couchman roasted 'a few spuds I had scrounged from a Polish girl, and made a brew of tea'. In one of the barns thirty-one POWs from Stalag 344 were discovered. Too sick to continue with the rest of their column they had been left behind after their guard had disappeared during the night.

Further rations were issued – 300 kilograms of oats, fifty of coffee, and forty of margarine. The men were also given the news that the camp at Sagan, possibly their destination, had been evacuated: 'Now we had nowhere to go.'

A soft rain was falling by bedtime. In the distance 'flashes of artillery fire heralded the approach of the Russian juggernaut'.

**THURSDAY, 1 FEBRUARY – DAY 14.** During the night a thaw had set in, and it was still raining. George Cross was 'very warm in bed, in fact so warm that I took off my cap and scarf in the middle of the night for the first time'.

The rain had stopped by the time that the POWs were awakened at 6 am. Two hours later they left Peterwitz. The overnight rain had melted the snow, leaving large puddles, but at least the roads were clear of refugees. After only a dozen kilometres the column stopped at Prausnitz (Prusice). Ben Couchman, unable to find any room in the authorised barns, 'slept at a cowshed further down the road, after fencing off the cows and spreading straw over the dried cowdung'.

From their allotted rations the men received two-fifths of a loaf, half an ounce of margarine, and half a cup of oats. New rations issued amounted to 680 loaves, and thirty-seven-and-a-half kilograms of margarine.

Re-joining the column were the sick prisoners from Sagan.

**FRIDAY, 2 FEBRUARY – DAY 15.** At 3.30 pm, still at Prausnitz, the prisoners were ordered to put out all fires, as Oberstleutnant Behr had received a bill of 4,000 marks for damage caused at the last stop. In the evening the farmer whose yard had been commandeered complained that five of his chickens were missing. The Germans promptly warned the prisoners that anyone caught stealing would be shot.

An offer was then made 'to move ten men by passenger train. This was said to be in appreciation of our good behaviour on the march. The doctor suggested eight sick and the two that the Germans had nominated for services rendered in the past for our common good.' (Joe Walkty.)

**SATURDAY, 3 FEBRUARY – DAY 16.** Still at Prausnitz, the rest of the farmer's chickens disappeared, as did one of his wooden sheds, which re-appeared in the form of firewood.

Food issued – 112½ kilograms of margarine, 250 loaves, 100 kilograms of sugar, 200 of flour, and 150 of barley.

*The Yalta Conference begins (concluding on the 11th). A communiqué is issued which, though emphasising the military necessity of destroying German militarism and Nazism, adds that 'it is not our purpose to destroy the people of Germany…'*

**SUNDAY, 4 FEBRUARY – DAY 17.** Still at Prausnitz. 150 loaves issued.

Padré Collins held a service in the yard, taking his lesson from the 23rd Psalm – 'The Lord is my shepherd, I shall not want…'. It was attended by a large percentage of the POWs.

In the evening the prisoners were told that they would be put on a train of cattle trucks on the following day. Then came the unexpected news from Oberstleutnant Behr himself, who 'read out an order from the OKW to the effect that five men were to be released and would be liberated at the first opportunity. The purpose of this we were unable to understand.' The actual message, translated from the German, read:

> 'For appreciation of your conduct on the march and for the fortitude you have shown
> in overcoming all hardships, the OKW has decided to liberate five men. These five men
> have been picked out by you and now they are free men. As soon as possible they are to
> be sent to a neutral country.'

One of the five was an American, one a Canadian, one an Australian, and two English. The rest of the prisoners were then informed that their destination was Stalag IIIA (Luckenwalde).

*

Aussie F/S C.R. 'Bob' Richardson RAAF had been hugely impressed by the courage and devotion shown by two of the men on the awful march. One was The Reverend Captain Collins: 'During the march, when a rest period was given, Captain Collins would walk back from the front of the column, checking the chaps to see that everyone was OK, and encouraging them to keep going. The distance from front to rear was quite some walk, and in snow this gave him little rest. The captain was one of the finest men I have known.'

Bob's second nomination was a fellow Aussie, F/S Johnny Shields RAAF, 'whose pelvis was smashed when he was shot down. He had difficulty walking at the best of times, but in the winter, if he stopped, he could hardly move again. During the march Johnny would start from the front of the column, and by the time the next rest period came, he would have fallen to the rear. While everyone else had a rest, Johnny would keep going and, when the rest resumed, he would be at the front again.'

Johnny Shields was a few years older than most (born 11 September 1913), and had an early service number (19790) and before the war had been a professional boxer with the Jimmy Sharman Boxing Troupe. His ability to look after himself came in handy when back in England in Brighton. He was in the gents of the Regent Ballroom when a large civilian picked on the small Aussie airman. When Johnny told the man to pick on someone his own size, the man swung a punch at him, which Johnny easily avoided. In return Johnny hit the would-be assailant with a mighty blow to the body, leaving the wretched civilian to be carted away on a stretcher.

*

Far, far less impressive on the march were the contemptible actions of two of the guards, who were seen by Bill Knox to strike prisoners:

> 'On one occasion we passed a water pump in a village. Some of the prisoners tried to get some water from it but were ordered back into the column and one prisoner was struck by a guard with a rifle butt. On another occasion passing through a village the villagers had put out some pails of water. Again we were stopped from having the water and a prisoner was struck by a guard with a rifle butt.' The guard at the water pump incident 'was aged about thirty but young looking, height about 5 foot, weight about 9 stone, hair grey at sides and bald on top, ruddy complexion, round clean-shaven face, small and slight build. His rank was Gefreiter. He was a Luftwaffe guard and on the staff of Stalag Luft VII where he had a bad reputation.'

The other offender, an older man who spoke good English, was an Unteroffizier interpreter on the Luft 7 staff.

*

**MONDAY, 5 FEBRUARY – DAY 18.** Somewhat inconsiderately the cows in Ben Couchman's quarters broke loose at around 2 am 'and trampled all over our beds. We managed to get them out, but were awakened at 4 am, and we were on the road at 6 am.' First, there was yet another food ration to be distributed – 500 loaves, ninety-six kilograms of margarine, and 530 tins of meat.

The short march that followed, eight kilometres to Goldberg (Złotoryja), was to be the POWs' last, not counting the even shorter march to their next camp at the end of the rail journey. They reached the railway sidings at around 9 am. Norman Oates remembered little of the long march but:

> 'suddenly, I have a very clear memory of the railway marshalling yards at Goldberg. A train crossing a few lines of rail for some reason caught my eye and attracted my interest. I walked across and looked into the open door of a cattle truck and found it full of bunks holding German wounded. I climbed into the truck, took a packet of cigarettes out of my battle-dress – the last I had – and showed them to the nearest soldier so that he would understand, and slipped them under his pillow. I then realised our guards were shouting so hurried back to where our men were milling about.'

In the confusion Jack Stead and his GPR 'oppo' Ron Watkinson 'were able to fill our greatcoat pockets with grain from a sack that was on a handcart near the station. A couple of RAF chaps also helped themselves to a half-filled 10-gallon churn of milk.'

Fifty-five men on average were crammed into each cattle truck, which measured approximately 30 feet long by 8 feet wide. With insufficient room for all to sit down at the same time, democracy prevailed in most of the trucks, and they took it in turns to share the floor space.

One-twelfth of a loaf was issued at 11.30 am. Jack Stead and Ron Watkinson were in the same truck as the two RAF milk thieves, but the milk soon went. Handfuls of grain were shared with those within reach: 'This we just chewed and chewed, including the husks.' The milk churn was quietly deposited during one of the many stops.

It was not long before 'there were numerous cases of dysentery, and facilities for men to attend to personal hygiene were inadequate. The majority had no water on the train journey for two days. When the men were allowed out of the trucks to relieve themselves, numerous of the guards ordered them back inside again and we had to be continually getting permission for the men to be allowed out.'[220] This was often not allowed, though, and the men had to cope as best they could with the disposal of their bodily waste.

When the train was at one halt Bruce Davis asked the guards to open the door of their wagon so that they could eject the particularly vile excreta from one of their number who was suffering badly with dysentery. He shouted through a crack in the wagon's walls: "*Posten! Posten! Öffnen die Tür! Eine Mann sehr Krank!*" ("Guard! Guard! Open the door! Very sick man!") Bruce kept this up for several hours to no avail until, in the darkness of night, he at last heard what he thought was the sound of boots on the gravel by the track. At that moment someone handed him a full, very foul-smelling tin. Taking careful aim – he was after all a bomb aimer – he threw out the contents of the tin hoping to hit the guard. This he most certainly did: "You bastard! I was coming to help in answer to your calls, and that's the third time that's happened to me tonight! Your sick man can stay that way now so far as I'm concerned." The prisoners recognised the voice of the interpreter Otto.

As this trainload of POWs, however 'Krank' they might be, was not accorded high priority, it did not leave Goldberg until 1.15 pm. It passed through Leignitz (Legnica) at 3.30 pm but, with a 'flat' wheel, came to a halt in a siding near Sagan (Żagań) at 7 pm, after only some 80-100 kilometres had been covered, remaining in the siding overnight.

**TUESDAY, 6 FEBRUARY – DAY 19.** At around 6 am the train pulled out: 'All of us,' wrote George Cross, 'very thirsty having had nothing to drink for over a day.' Stopping what seemed like every quarter of an hour, the train came to a halt at 10 am, resuming slowly towards Cottbus (Chóśebuz) after a three-hour halt. Having got to Cottbus around 12.20 pm the train stuck fast for a while, enabling the prisoners to have some sort of drink in the station. The journey continued westwards past Calau (2.45 pm), then south-west along the line to Finsterwalde and on to Falkenberg where, once again, the train ground to a halt. Captain Howatson came round with water at 10.30 pm and told the men that they could be there for twenty-four hours.

By the end of the day most of the prisoners had finished their meagre ration of food, and were grateful for the earlier encouragement from Padré Collins, who told them that there was only another sixty or seventy kilometres to go. Tempers, however, were becoming frayed.

**WEDNESDAY, 7 FEBRUARY – DAY 20.** To everyone's intense relief, the train set off at 11.30 am, but after forty-five minutes came to a halt yet again – the railway had been bombed. George Cross noted: 'Strange aroma in truck due to bods smoking tea and coffee etc. Got half cup [acorn] coffee at 3.30 and gen that we have three hours travelling ahead of us but several other trains have to pass through a junction ahead of us before we do.' Progress was resumed at about 6 pm, for two-and-a-half hours. No food rations had been issued for days, and some of those who had eaten what little they had had when they boarded the train were now fainting from a lack of nourishment.

**THURSDAY, 8 FEBRUARY – DAY 21.**

*The 1st Ukrainian Front breaks out of the Oder bridgehead north of Breslau.*

At 8.30 am the train pulled in to Luckenwalde station, fifty kilometres south of Berlin. 'Everyone awoke very weak and shaky', and were ordered off the train. George Cross, who had managed to hoard one last slice of bread, felt very dizzy and almost passed out when he tried to stand up. He quickly polished off the last slice. George Kilbryde noted 'a funeral-like march up to Luckenwalde camp. It is over at last, 500 kilometres, over half on foot, in twenty-one days exactly.' George's measurements were close enough, though the total distance may have been nearer 550 kilometres, with just under half of that on foot.

From Luckenwalde station, 1,493 prisoners walked the final few kilometres to their new home, Stammlager IIIA (Luckenwalde), and were very happy to get behind the wire again: 'Never was the sight of a POW camp so welcome to 1,400 odd half-starved, foot-sore, dejected kriegies.' (Jack Smith RAAF.) The short walk was more of a stagger, as men's legs slowly recovered the ability to walk after three, cramped days in the filthy cattle trucks. Fred Brown was reeling about when one of his pals said: '"Can't you walk straight, Fred?" I was doing a drunken reel.'

Passing a row of huts in a wired compound, Fred commented that they didn't look too bad, to which 'Paddy Trimble, never one to mince words, said "You stupid bastard. They're the guards' quarters."'

## CHAPTER THIRTEEN

# STALAG IIIA (LUCKENWALDE) AND LIBERATION

*'Luckenwalde was a thoroughly disorganised camp. Our hopes were high but our stomachs were empty.'*

Sergeant Jim Palmer, 83 Squadron

\*

Stalag IIIA was 'home' for POWs of several nations: French, Belgian, Italian, Yugoslav, Romanian, Norwegian, Russian, American, and British. The camp had opened in 1939 to house Polish prisoners taken during the invasion of their country. They were followed by over 40,000 French POWs captured after their country had fallen in June 1940. A large contingent of Italians, some 15,000, arrived after the September 1943 armistice. It is estimated that over 4,000 prisoners died whilst at or attached to the camp. Most were Russians, who were buried without identification in mass graves. Around 200 Italians lost their lives.

The Camp Commandant was Oberst Lutter, his deputy Oberstleutnant Löhr, and the camp officer for the officers' section Obertsleutnant König, while the OKW representative was a Major Bosenberg. The camp's Abwehr officer was Hauptmann von Canitz, and the senior doctor was Oberstabsarzt Dr. Dunsing. The Germans had the gall to appoint two so-called welfare officers, Sonderführer Braune and Jenke.

Although an IRCC delegation that arrived on 8 February 1945 seemed to paint the Camp Commandant in a good light, some of his subordinates were a very unpleasant bunch. The senior Allied officer issued a statement, when it was all but over in May 1945, in which he named these rotten Germans. Hauptmann Bemann, for example, was 'charged with the deliberate destruction and theft of clothing and food belonging to British officers'. Major Sturzkopf, known by the prisoners as 'Bulk Issue', was a liar to the detriment of the welfare of prisoners, and 'encouraged his soldiers to be as vicious and ruthless as possible during searches and thus caused wanton looting and destruction of their property'. Earlier in the war he had been the deputy commandant at Oflag VIB (Warburg), where he had been given the name. He was, according to one of the authors of *Escape to Freedom* (1953), 'a gross, revolting, twenty-stone caricature of a German' and a figure of fun.

Another German officer on the senior officer's report was Hauptmann Rademacher. He had also been at Warburg with Sturzkopf as head of the *Abwehr* staff, but was altogether different from his corpulent comrade. He was a:

'good-looking man aged around fifty, he not only had a pathological hatred of insolence, especially when shown by enemy officers, but also an alarming habit, whenever the slightest sign of it was shown, of hopping about and screaming with excitement. Worse, he would usually take his pistol out of its holster and fire it into the air. He also carried a sword which, when unable to find anything illegal during a search of prisoners' effects, he would use to spear any inanimate and spearable object within reach'.[221]

At Luckenwalde he 'incited his soldiers to strike British officers with their rifle butts, he displayed a violent and uncontrollable temper and drew and fired off his revolver on numerous occasions... He lost no opportunity of humiliating and ill-treating British officers.' Clearly he had not improved over the past three or four years.

'Last but not least there is Hauptmann Simm, the hotel manager, who probably achieved a greater personal loathing among Allied prisoners than any other of his colleagues. Possessed of a mean and spiteful nature, he did everything possible to make us uncomfortable or to humiliate us.'

But probably the nastiest of all was Obergefreiter Gisevius who, though only the equivalent of a corporal, was considered to be more powerful than the commandant himself. To the senior Allied officer he was 'perhaps typical of the whole Nazi system… He dictated his wishes and commands to his superiors whenever he chose to do so. He was responsible for keeping many prisoners in the cells for months at a stretch without trial and doing his best to deprive them of their food.'[222]

A 'very comprehensive list of the principle Nazis of Luckenwalde' was prepared at Luckenwalde by W/O Walter Henderson, British Man of Confidence.

For the Allies, the SBO was G/C A.H. Willetts,[223] while the Americans' senior officer was Lt Col Roy J. Herte. American Man of Confidence for Compound 1 (holding men from Stalag IIIB) was S/Sgt J.C. Gasperich, and for the Luft 7 contingent in Compound 2 it was still F/O Peter Thomson RAAF.

Each nation was divided into its own quarters, either side of a road running roughly east-west. To the south was the camp's *Friedhof* (cemetery), and to the south-west the Lazarett.

Also present in their own compound close to the Luft 7 NCOs were some 1,400 Irish soldiers, mostly regulars in the Irish Guards captured in 1940. 660 of them were out on nineteen local work detachments (*Arbeitskommandos*) when the Luft 7 contingent arrived. The Germans had segregated them from other POWs in camps elsewhere in the hope that they would fight against the Russians on the Eastern Front. Some hope! Their Camp Leader was W/O Walter Henderson, assisted by RSM William Strawbridge. Bruce Davis met one of them who had been a private all his adult life in the Guards, and had no desire ever to rise above that lowly rank. Well into his fifties the guardsman had spent nearly four years as a POW of the Germans in the First World War and now almost five more in the Second having been captured at Dunkirk. 'He was always quite cheerful, and gave every sign of being a contented man. Undoubtedly a survivor!'

These Guardsmen took great pride in their regiment, as the scruffy RAF types observed:

> 'A squad of about forty Irish Guards in an adjoining compound used to parade twice a day for counting by the Germans. Their turnout was unbelievable, battledresses although worn were pressed with immaculate creases, highly-polished boots and caps at correct angles, their RSM gave orders as though they were on duty at Buckingham Palace, and the resulting drill movements were perfect.' (Peter Wilmshurst.)

Once in the camp the Luft 7 men were given a cigarette each, followed by a hot shower – it took until 5 pm before some of the prisoners had had their shower – and a cup of soup and potatoes, their first real food for nearly three days. George Cross: 'The padré was still coming round cheering everyone up and organising. He and the MO [Captain Howatson] have been our saviour on this march, the MO especially, who has constantly been on to Jerry for more food. If he had not been with us we would have had a far, far worse time.'[224] One who had had a bad enough time, though, was Jock Patterson, 640 Squadron. Suffering severe frostbite to both feet, he was to spend the rest of the time in the Luckenwalde Lazarett.

After their shower the tired men were shown to their quarters, usually in a block holding 400 men, which were, as George Cross said: 'A bit cramped, but nothing like the trucks.' Morale was briefly boosted by an issue of 'soup and spuds from camp kitchen and some wizard soup with noodles of pork in it from our field kitchen'. It was, as George noted: 'The best I have ever tasted.'

Visiting the camp on 8 February were Doctors Marti and Lehner, a Swiss delegation from the International Red Cross, who reported:

*Top left:* WO2 Norman H. Swale SAAF in March 1944. [*N.H. Swale*]

*Top right:* Sgt Bill Oakes GPR arrived at Luft 7 with John F. MacDonald and others in *Trupp 38*. [*W.A. Oakes*]

*Above left:* Padré John Collins, standing, 4th from left at Oflag VA, end of March 1944. [*Richard Collins*]

*Above right:* 'B' Squadron, Glider Pilot Regiment, at No.15 MU, RAF Wroughton, Wiltshire, Octo-ber 1943. Four identified in the back row are: 1st left, S/Sgt W.K. Marfleet (killed in Normandy, 6 June 1944); 2nd left, S/Sgt C.R. Watkinson DFM; 7th left, S/Sgt J.J. Thomson; 8th, Sgt A.J. Dallimore (killed at Arnhem, 21 September 1944). Watkinson and Thomson survived to become POWs at Luft 7. [*C.R. Watkinson*]

*Inset:* Crew of Lancaster PB436. Standing: Wilson, Winkley, Bragg. Seated: Finch, Loneon, Longhurst. Missing: Sgt Evris Harris. [*Photo via Ole Kraul*]

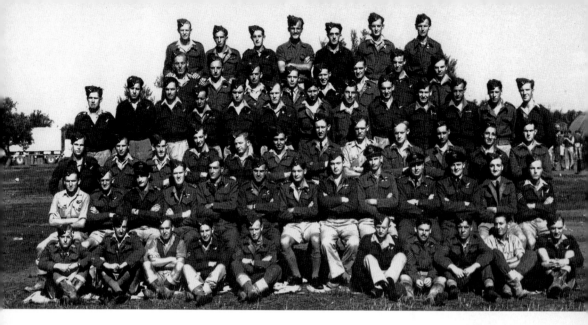

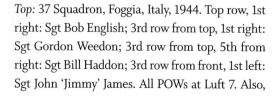

killed in action Sgt Ken Saxton (3rd row from top, 3rd from right).

*Above left:* 'B' Flight, 614 Squadron, Italy, 1944. John Nicholson sitting 2nd from left; Syd Barlow 2nd row 6th from left; John Wiles 3rd row just to Nicholson's right; Roy Bennett 2 rows behind Nicholson's left shoulder; Cartwright 3rd row 1st from right; Hitchings 4th row 1st from right.

*Above right:* Crew of Mitchell FW106, 226 Squadron. Standing (left) Douglas Backhouse; (right) Jimmy Warren. Seated (left) Freddie Turner; (right) Keith Pendray. [*K. Pendray*]

*Left:* The accordian band with, far right, the lovely 'Geraldine'. [*Pat Batt*]

*Top:* 37 Squadron, Foggia, Italy, 1944. Top row, 1st right: Sgt Bob English; 3rd row from top, 1st right: Sgt Gordon Weedon; 3rd row from top, 5th from right: Sgt Bill Haddon; 3rd row from front, 1st left: Sgt John 'Jimmy' James. All POWs at Luft 7. Also,

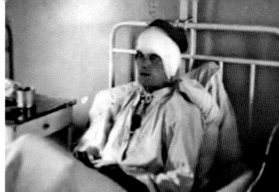

*Above left:* Left to right, four of the crew of Halifax JP323, 614 Squadron: F/Sgts R.B. Hitchings; R.R. Cartwright; J. Wiles; S. Barlow. [*S. Barlow*]

*Top right:* 'Mac' McTeer in hospital, Budapest; photo from a Hungarian newsreel. [*Nigel McTeer*]

*Above right:* Paul Decroix with Spitfire. [*John Skinner*]

*Below:* Ken Brant with Hurricane. [*K. Brant*]

*Inset:* An uncommon photograph of a rare aircraft – Halifax JP323 with four-bladed propellers. [*Tom Scotland*, via http://myweb.tiscali.co.uk/hphalifax/614plane.htm]

*Top left:* 'Hank' Pankratz RCAF. [*H. Pankratz*]
*Top right:* Crew of Halifax LW204, taken at 1664 HCU Dishforth, October 1944: (left to right) Neil McLaren RCAF; Henry 'Dusty' Rhodes RAF; John 'Pop' Popadiuk RCAF; Percy 'Chip' Chipman RCAF; Joe Knoke RCAF; Percy Harris RCAF; Lee Shipman RCAF.

*Above right:* Remains of Halifax LW204 lost 5/6 December 1944. [*H. Bürmann, via Henry Rhodes*]
*Below:* Lancaster LM259, 227 Squadron, shot down by Oberleutnant Peter Spoden on 4 December 1944. Four of its crew – T.R. Aspinall; W. J.J. Hudson; J.D.W. Maxwell; and W.R. Whitbread – went to Luft 7. [*W.J.J. Hudson*]

# THE BURIAL OF FLIGHT SERGEANT L.H. STEVENSON RCAF

*Above left:* Flight Sergeant L.H. Stevenson RCAF.
*Top right:* In the Kreuzburg church attended by his comrades.

*Above right:* Leaving the church; Padré Collins on the right.
*Below:* The funeral service; Padré Collins on the left.

Schloß

*Top left:* Crew of Halifax LW168, RAF Pocklington. Top (left to right): R.G. Clements (POW Luft 7); A. 'Indy' Coope (Luft 7); D. 'Taffy' Worthing (Luft 7). Middle (left to right): F/S K.P. Lindenboom (KIA); R. Hawthorne RCAF (POW, camp not known); ground crew; J. Temple (Luft 7); P/O R. Hislop (KIA). Front: two ground crew. [*A. Coope*]

*Top right:* An old postcard of the *Schloss* at Lossen. [*Vic Smyth*]

*Above left:* A drawing of the march by Ted Milligan. The tall figure to the left is Padré Collins. [*By kind permission of Mrs Milligan, via Jon England*]

*Above right:* Stalag IIIA. The main road dividing the compounds. (The wavy lines are caused by degradation on original photo.) [*Arthur E. Seller*]

*Left:* Captain Howatson (left) and F/S F. Stead, at Stalag IIIA. [*F. Stead*]

*Above:* 405 Squadron Halifax B.II (the squadron began converting to Lancasters in August 1943) and crew, RAF Gransden Lodge. Back row (left to right): F/O A.B. Durfee RCAF (POW Luft 3); WO1 R.H. Rafter RCAF (evaded); Sgt A.C.D. Budd RCAF (evaded); P/O P.A. Musgrave RCAF (KIA). Kneeling (left to right): Sgt Jim Umscheid RCAF (POW Luft 7, *Trupp 28*); F/O R.C. Wiens RCAF (evaded); P/O B.H. Walter RCAF (evaded). [*Denis Budd*]

*Inset:* Stalag IIIA (Luckenwalde). Left to right: J. Shore; H.P Christenson; J. Hislop; John Ackroyd; Ray Lord; F. Curtis. [*John Ackroyd*]

*Below:* Stalag IIIA. POWs listening to US war correspondents. Circled in centre is Keith Prowd RAAF. [*Keith Prowd*]

*Left:* Allen R. MacNaught RCAF at the graves of Crosswell and Johnson. Behind him are the graves of French prisoners. [*Via Alex Jardine*]

*Above:* Percy Bruce Crosswell RCAF. [*Library and Archives Canada, via Dave Champion*]

*Below left:* With good reason to smile, these former Aussie Luft 7 POWs, en route for Sydney, are nearly home. Photograph taken at Wellington, New Zealand at the end of August 1945. Standing (left to right): Gwynne 'Tassie' Thomas; Gerry Poulton; Ross Breheny; Brian Halligan; Willard Fethers ('with fag'); unknown -; 'Pop' Lister. Squatting (left to right): Harry 'The Boong' Whiting; Collin Sheel.

*Inset:* Stalag IIIA (Luckenwalde), 8 April 1945. [*Air Photo Library, Dept. of Geography, University of Keele*]

'This large camp seems to have become the assembly and transit camp for prisoners evacuated from the central region of the Eastern Front. Prisoners of all nations have lately arrived there from the Wehrkreis XXI, III and VIII… On the day of the visit, delegates noted a general strength of 38,413 prisoners, of which 24,136 belonged to the normal camp strength before the arrival of the evacuees… Barbed-wire separations have been put up to separate newly-arrived prisoners of various nations. The camp is divided by a large central alley, half being used for the former camp occupants and the other has become an Oflag followed by a field of tents.'

The delegates also noted that on the previous day the numbers of prisoners had been swollen by 4,600 American NCO's from Stalag IIIB (Fürstenburg). Their evacuation, too, had been no picnic. They had had to leave behind 'their reserve of 11,600 parcels stored outside the camp… The prisoners had to travel on foot, nearly all day and all night for a week receiving practically nothing from their escort except bread. They slept two nights in schoolhouses and only one night in good quarters.'

On 2 February 6930568 S/Sgt Karl B. Johnson, (POW no. 20290, Stalag IIIB), was shot by a guard during the march. Stopping for a moment to adjust his kitbag, the 'sentry shouted to him, and as the man did not hurry enough, shot him through the head'.

The plight of these Americans at Luckenwalde was woeful. All of them were exceedingly tired, cold and hungry, and their only available accommodation was in tents (400 men in each), with damp straw for bedding. The American compound became known as 'Tentsville'. This compares with the conditions of the British contingent whose quarters 'were in a large wooden hut where we slept on the wooden floor with a palliasse of wood shavings'. (John Trumble.)

The Swiss delegation noted, too, that it was fortunate that the weather was not so cold lately – only two degrees below zero! – and also that the Camp Commandant, Oberst Lutter, was 'trying to procure wood shavings to replace the straw but is encountering insuperable difficulties'.

One of the Swiss delegates, who was on his way to Lübeck from Luckenwalde, 'was requested to have 80,000 parcels sent immediately to Stalag IIIA – this number corresponds to two parcels per man for a strength of 40,000 prisoners of all nations'. In the meantime, though, as the days passed, men were fainting from near-starvation, but food was available, albeit in small quantities. Norman Oates was one of the many close to death. Collapsing with dysentery on arrival, he remembers 'crawling time and time again to the toilets, too weak to walk, and sitting propped up by a wall outside a building, past caring, hearing two Australian voices complaining about the Germans and saying they had a lot to answer for'. Norman received no help of any kind, but he survived.

**9 FEBRUARY 1945.** On the day after their arrival, the Luft 7 contingent heard a rumour that Red Cross food parcels would be arriving within two to five days.

**10 FEBRUARY 1945.** Fred Brown's toes were so painful that he decided to go sick:

'The sick bay was in another barrack, just as cold and just as crude as the others. The MO's surgery was divided off by a few blankets hung up around a table and a couch… The sick bay was packed with bods lying on the floor with just one blanket covering them… no heating anywhere. Eventually my turn to see the MO came. He looked at my toes, said they were slightly frostbitten. I knew that.'

The POWs were treated to a film show – a short, silent German film on animal life, and a silent Laurel and Hardy one filmed in 1924. Total one hour.

*The 1st Ukrainian Front reaches the Neisse river, encircling Glogau and capturing Liegnitz.*

**11 FEBRUARY 1945.** Everyone still very hungry; the soup due to be issued at midday was very late. As it was a Sunday it was supposed to be 'special soup' – pea soup – but no-one could find a pea.

Captain Collins held a service in a small hut. He told those present how disturbed he had been at the way some aircrew had behaved on the march, in particular the fighting for cattle fodder.

**12 FEBRUARY 1945.** 'A lot of stealing of fellows' bread rations has been going on since we left Bankau. Today two men were caught. First of all they were paraded in front of all of us. Then a summary of evidence was taken and is going to the protecting board – to be used in a court martial when we get back to England. To my mind nothing is too bad for those two – stealing a chum's only piece of bread.' (Paul Decroix.)

**12 -16 FEBRUARY 1945.** As the British and US Protecting Power under the Geneva Convention, a Swiss Delegate, Fritz Dasen, 'representative of the Swiss Legation at Berlin', arrived to inspect the British and American section of the camp. His report differed little in substance to that of the IRCC visit four days earlier, but he did mention that the 'new American POWs in tents have only a make-shift latrine about twenty-five yards from their tents. These places have absolutely no cover or protection from the weather.'

Under the section 'Medical Attention' Dasen recorded: 'The staff is composed of 1 British Medical Officer (Cpt. Headon) 3 NCO and 10 protected personnel mainly unit medical orderlies, R.A.S.C. drivers. All these men are employed as medical orderlies in the camp revier.' Dasen was handed a report from the British MO:

> 'The revier is housed in a half barrack inside the British Compound. Total number of beds available for patients seventy-two, sixty of these beds are ordinary barrack beds, twelve are iron bed frames with iron springs. Bed linen is not supplied. Cooking facilities are nil, and preparation of special foods for patients is carried out on small coal fires in the Revier. Patients requiring special diets can be issued with one and a half litres of German porridge, which is prepared in a German diet kitchen outside the Compound.'

The MO's report listed further problems and lack of medical equipment. Everywhere, Dasen observed, not just in the Revier, there were problems, usually brought on by a lack of something, be it clothing, heating fuel, or food.

**13 FEBRUARY 1945.** Midday soup ration was late again – issued at 3.30 pm. Peter Thomson was so incensed at the poor rations that he complained to the Camp Commandant, and took with him several POWs to illustrate the point. Stripped to the waist, they were just skin and bones.

**14 FEBRUARY 1945.** *The 6th Army's 22nd and 74th Rifle Corps, and other units of the 1st Ukrainian Front, encircle Breslau (Wroclaw), which has been declared a fortress (Festung Breslau), under the command of Gauleiter Hanke. Such was the German resistance here that the city did not fall until 6 May, after an eighty-two-day siege. An estimated 6,000 German soldiers and 170,000 civilians perished, with a further 45,000 German troops taken prisoner.*

**15 FEBRUARY 1945.** Henry Wagner bumped into two men from his squadron, 51, who had recently arrived at the camp. One of them, F/S Jeff Orr RAAF, had been shot down on the night of 5/6 January 1945 (Hanover) in Halifax MZ767, one of three aircraft lost by the squadron on that raid. The other was mid-upper gunner Sgt Norman Wilcock, one of three survivors of Halifax MZ811 (P/O S.J. Bunn) lost on 6/7 January 1945 (Hanau).[225] Henry noted in his diary that F/S Ralph Smith, also from MZ811, turned up later at Stalag IIIA having been 'left behind at Wetzlar. These three chaps often came to see me and sit and natter in days following, and we dreamed of squadron life, and food and home, and wondered how long it would be.'

**16 FEBRUARY 1945.** Food was the priority for all in the camp, but during the night two men were caught stealing Red Cross parcels from the store. Their crime was reported to the Swiss delegate, who passed it on to the authorities in England. The Swiss delegate's general view of Stalag IIIA was that it:

> 'made a sorry impression. Through the sudden arrival of several thousands of new POW from other camps, the Stalag authorities were confronted with immense difficulties which they tried to overcome to the best of their ability. It must be borne in mind that all measures taken were of a temporary nature and will be improved within a short time.'

The Swiss delegate promised the POWs that things would improve, but they 'took that with the non-existent pinch of salt. Bread rations cut to a one-seventh of a loaf per man. Better conditions the Protecting Power said!'

> 'Today we got 200 grams of bread for the first time (about three medium slices). We got a spoonful of sugar, about ¾ oz. of marge, six little potatoes, and a cup of soup. That is what we live on in future. The Protecting Power also came and inspected us. Goodness knows what they can do. We can only wait and see. At least the news is good. That is something.' (Paul Decroix.)

**17 FEBRUARY 1945.** A German medical officer carried out an inspection of a hundred or so of the prisoners, and declared that ninety-eight per cent were undernourished. Although only a small sample of the 2,500 officers and 9,000 NCOs in the camp, it was enough for Captain Howatson to say that, if they were ordered to march somewhere there and then, half would drop out on the first day and one in six would die. The German commandant was sympathetic but, with regard to the necessary supplies, was unable to do anything about it.

The Polish compound received a delivery of US and British Red Cross parcels. The US and British POWs – those most in need – got none.

**SUNDAY, 18 FEBRUARY 1945.** Padré John Collins held an ecumenical service in which he urged everyone to hold on.

**20 FEBRUARY 1945.** Air-raid sirens woke up the camp early. The sound of bombing was heard close by – 'very good for our morale'.

Group Captain Willetts issued a statement that the Norwegian prisoners in the camp had donated 500 parcels to the RAF officers. It was not practicable, he said, for them to be shared amongst the NCOs, but 100 parcels had been allotted to the RAF and USAAF sick NCOs. 'It was a splendid gesture for which we shall never cease to be grateful to our Norwegian friends.' (*The Log*, page 157.)

**21 FEBRUARY 1945.** The Norwegian contingent's Danish Red Cross parcels were shared one between five men. There were three air raid warnings after dark.

*The 1st Ukrainian Front captures Guben.*

**23 FEBRUARY 1945.** POWs were on parade for over an hour. There were numerous re-counts. A partial Red Cross parcel issue boosted morale a fraction. Lack of food amongst the NCOs was so bad that some men would fall over when they tried to stand up. The last two issues of soup, which usually looked no better than washing-up water, were reckoned to be worse than usual. The potatoes were bad, too.

**24 FEBRUARY 1945.** An election was to be held in the afternoon for a new Man of Confidence, but it was called off for lack of interest. W/O John Snowden AFM was appointed to fill the vacancy. The rumour was that during the march from Luft 7 he had bought an Alsatian dog – and cooked it.

**26 FEBRUARY 1945.** The market rate for coffee was twenty cigarettes for 250 grams. There were many cigarettes, but no coffee. An air raid in the direction of Berlin was heard at lunchtime.

**27 FEBRUARY 1945.** Parade lasted about an hour in the morning as five men were missing. Oberfeldwebel 'Frank' eventually gave it up as a bad job. After the afternoon parade at 5 pm there was a Red Cross parcel issue, but only one parcel per four men. 'Morale went up 100 per cent.'

**28 FEBRUARY 1945.** Rumour was that two men had been shot, and a third seriously wounded, during a night raid on the Serbs' Red Cross parcel store. Another version of the rumour was that two men had been shot and two were in the cooler, having been caught raiding the French parcel store. There had been a wave of stealing – mainly bread rations – in the barracks, forcing POW guards to be posted at all times. Paul Decroix noted in his diary: 'Two of our boys were shot last night trying to get into the Polish Red Cross store. Hungry men will do some queer things! No porridge this morning. It looks as though it may be all off. Time will tell. Bread three loaves for sixteen again.'

**1 MARCH 1945.** The German army took over administration of the camp from the Luftwaffe. *Appell* was held earlier than usual, at 0715 hours. There were six re-counts before the POWs were dismissed. This made the day long and tempers short.

The French POWs received 20,000 American No. 10 Red Cross parcels, universally acknowledged to be the best type of parcel. Peter Thomson asked the French Man of Confidence if they would be prepared to share these parcels with POWs of all nationalities. He refused. Thomson thereupon saw the Camp Commandant and was told that there would be a further issue of parcels either tomorrow or the next day.

**2 MARCH 1945.** Weather still very cold, with a strong wind blowing: 'Everyone is half frozen – no fires – nothing at all – everyone is very miserable.' Most prisoners lay on their beds all day wrapped in their blanket.

**3 MARCH 1945.** Famous heavyweight boxer and former World Champion Max Schmeling paid the camp a visit (though another diarist noted that he visited on 18 March). No-one knew why, and most couldn't even be bothered to go and see him, though Sam Malick RCAF got his autograph. Schmeling, a Fallschirmjäger wounded when parachuting onto Crete in 1941, thereafter retired from active service, but from time to time made propaganda visits to POW camps, usually ones containing American prisoners. (He died seven months short of his 100th birthday in February 2005.)

**4 MARCH 1945.** Snowed hard in the morning. The Luft 7 POWs were issued with one parcel between four. 'To cap the day off, the RAF put on a raid. We watch the red and green target indicators fall and kites coned by searchlights. What a day!' (Fred Brown.)

*To the north of the Eastern Front, 1st and 2nd White Russian Armies reach the Baltic.*

**5 MARCH 1945.** The German army guards sealed off the compounds from one another.

**6 MARCH 1945.** Snowed during the night. Very cold. Wind, rain and snow. Theft of goods continued, one man having twenty cigarettes stolen from a case by his head. Never heard a thing.

*US First Army captures Cologne, while 2nd White Russian Army takes Polish city of Graudenz (Grudziadz).*

**7 MARCH 1945.** Sunshine. The first in a long time. Another daylight-bombing raid lasted for most of the afternoon, thereby delaying the soup issue. Morale was further boosted by the Man of Confidence announcing the arrival in the camp of 80,000 Red Cross parcels – each man would be issued with one tomorrow. A force of eighty Mosquitos raided Berlin again during the night.

**8 MARCH 1945.** Snowed again. Bitterly cold. A memorable day among many others to be forgotten. Henry Wagner: 'Issued today with one American Red Cross No. 10 food parcel each, tins unpunctured. John [Trumble] and I are keeping one intact in case we have to march again, or for when parcel supplies run out, although we have been promised one each for next five weeks. We are living pretty well now, and time is passing very quickly…'

**9 MARCH 1945.** More food parcels arrived. Food was no longer the main topic of conversation, with news being received via the 'canary' that the Allies had crossed the Rhine: 'We all become generals and win the war!' (Fred Brown.) Fountain pens and lighters that had been confiscated at Bankau were returned to their owners.

POWs noted the eighteenth successive raid on the Berlin area.

**10 MARCH 1945.** Weather continued to be very cold. Cigarettes that had recently been used for barter rather than for smoking were now being smoked. Eighteen lorry-loads of Red Cross food parcels arrived.

**11 MARCH 1945.** With more food the prisoners turned to cooking their own again, using home-made 'blowers'.

**12 MARCH 1945.** With fuel in greater demand for the 'blowers', the Russians, the main suppliers, raised the price to five cigarettes per small bundle of wood. A further seven lorry-loads of food parcels arrived.

**13 MARCH 1945.** Another issue of one American No. 10 Red Cross parcel each.

Twenty-year-old F/S Alan Leslie Midlane was brought into the camp hospital on a stretcher with severe stomach pains. An operation, which he somehow survived, revealed a twisted bowel and a 'gangrenous' stomach.

**14 MARCH 1945.** Though critically ill, Alan Midlane survived two further operations.

**15 MARCH 1945.** *The 1st Ukrainian Front begins an offensive in the Ratibor area of Upper Silesia.*

Although the weather was not as cold as before, the men in the camp were still on a near-starvation diet, and most were ill to some degree or other. The tireless Captain Howatson continued to do what he could for his Luft 7 boys.

The POWs enjoyed the sight of the US air force bombing the Berlin area around lunchtime. (Their main target was a German army HQ at Zossen, some twenty kilometres to the north east of Luckenwalde, which received the attention of 308 B-24 Liberators and 276 B-17 Flying Fortresses, which between them dropped 1,373 tons of bombs. One B-24 was lost.)

**16 MARCH 1945.** For Alan Midlane there was nothing more that anyone could do for him. His friends, particularly his best pal Bill Rowe, were shocked to learn that he had died on this day.

**17 MARCH 1945.** Midlane and an 'Irish private soldier' who had died on the same day (5337669 Private John A.J. Sawyer, R. Berkshire Regiment) were buried in the camp cemetery. (Both were later re-interred in the Berlin 1939-1945 War Cemetery.) Ironically, today was St Patrick's Day: 'The Irish boys celebrated their day with football and made cakes.'

George Kilbryde noted: 'It is a dismal day and not many chaps are out.'

**18 MARCH 1945.** Bread rations were cut to one-seventh of a loaf per man. Soup ration also reduced.

**20 MARCH 1945.** A further parcel issue – one per man. Three wagons of Canadian parcels also arrived, as well as a wagon of bulk cheese and one of blankets.

**21 MARCH 1945.** A cold day, with a strong wind blew dust all over the camp.

**22 MARCH 1945.** The RAF played the army at football, and lost 2-4.

*1st Ukrainian Front opens offensive in Upper Silesia, south west of Oppeln, and captures Neustadt on the Czechoslovakian border.*

**24 MARCH 1945.** 'For the past three days it has been really beautiful weather, clear blue sky and lots of warm sunshine. A nice change but the sirens are going all day long.' (Paul Decroix.)

*Operation Varsity, the Allied crossing of the Rhine, begins. Its specific target is: 'To disrupt the hostile defences of the Rhine in the Wesel sector by seizure of the key terrain by airborne attack, in order rapidly to deepen the bridgehead to be seized in an assault crossing of the Rhine by British ground forces, and in order to facilitate further the offensive operations of the [British] Second Army.'*

In support of Varsity were close to 1,000 US B-17s, some of which were visible to those at Luckenwalde, as they went about their business of bombing German airfields.

*The 1st Ukrainian Front captures Neisse in Upper Silesia.*

**27 MARCH 1945.** Another issue of one American No. 10 Red Cross parcel per man. A number of Red Cross vehicles seen in the camp, taking away the sick and injured.

**28 MARCH 1945.** The American POWs cut a hole in the wire between their compound and the British. The goons were not bothered enough to do anything about it. Trading and gambling rose dramatically.

**29 MARCH 1945.** A German pilot landed his Fieseler Storch light aircraft just outside the RAF's compound: 'We were all so impressed with the airmanship, we raise a cheer and clap, even though the pilot was a German.' (Fred Brown.)

*3rd Ukrainian Front reaches the Austrian border, capturing Köszeg.*

**31 MARCH 1945.** Wet and cold. RAF v Ireland rugby match ended in a 14-0 win for the Irish.

\*

One of the Luft 7 airmen, Irishman Sgt Pat Nolan, met up with the Irish soldiers, who 'gave me a good haircut and a shave, bath and food'. But then, in April, Pat was hospitalised with ulcerations of the cornea of his right eye, and was to lose most of the sight in it. He tried to return to flying duties on repatriation, but was deemed unfit to do so.

\*

**2 APRIL 1945.** High winds created yet more dust. The attitude of the German guards was noticeably more couldn't care less: 'He hardly bothers to count us and never worries if we are all on parade or not.' (Jack Smith.)

**4 APRIL 1945.** Another issue of an American No. 10 Red Cross food parcel per man.

**5 APRIL 1945.** April showers interspersed with periods of sunshine.

**8 APRIL 1945.** A Mosquito aircraft released thousands of leaflets at 20,000 feet near the camp. According to the camp's intelligence they said that the Russian POWs would be liberated within ten to fifteen days.

**9 APRIL 1945.** Late in the evening the Germans announced that the camp was to be moved by rail to Munich on the 11th. POWs reckoned that it would be a miracle if the train got there without having been strafed by Allied fighters. Aircraft were constantly observed, and the POWs started to note Russian ones, 'not advanced types like the Allies' aircraft, but they looked old and lumbering in the air'.

**10 APRIL 1945.** A further issue of one American No. 10 Red Cross food parcel per man.

**11 APRIL 1945.** It was announced in the camp that 1,200 POWs – 800 officers and 400 NCOs – were to be evacuated on the following day to a camp near Munich, probably Stalag VIIA (Moosburg). John Trumble and Henry Wagner volunteered to go with the thirty-three selected from Barrack 7 'because we thought others might not get transport and we would have to march'.

**12 APRIL 1945.** Those detailed for evacuation, some 400, were called at 11 am, and four hours later were marched the two kilometres to Luckenwalde railway station. The Man of Confidence handed out forty cigarettes to each man, who were packed forty to each cattle truck. Trumble and Wagner bought coal brickettes from some French, and stole porridge oats from a nearby train. The Germans were persuaded to provide paint and to give permission for the POWs 'to embellish the tops of the carriages with the letters "RAF – POW" in yellow'. German railway staff thought the whole matter a huge joke as there was never any hope of a locomotive arriving to pull them to Moosburg.

*President of the USA, Franklin Delano Roosevelt, dies of a massive brain hæmorrhage aged sixty-three.*

**FRIDAY, 13 APRIL 1945.** After *Appell* the entire camp – including the German guards, who were about to leave – stood to attention and observed two minutes' silence in memory of the late President Roosevelt.

At around 11 pm, during an air raid on Potsdam, three airmen, against the advice of the Escape Committee, attempted to escape through the wire on the north side of the camp: F/O P.B. Crosswell RCAF, Sgt Allan MacNaught RCAF, and nineteen-year-old F/S G.R. Johnson. They were seen and shots were fired. Allan MacNaught managed to get back to his billet undetected, but Johnson was killed immediately. Percy Crosswell did not die until 1 pm on 14 April. A Canadian airman 'spoke to the German guard who shot him [Crosswell], a rather old fellow, and asked why he had done it with the war's end so close and the guard just burst into tears and said "Why did he try and escape? The war is over".'[226] The rumour was that Johnson had attacked a guard with a bottle, and had been shot as a result. One unsympathetic wing commander commented: 'Bloody fools.'

After the war Karel Valášek, one of Johnson's room mates, went to Crewe to see his parents. His mother told Karel that their son was under age when he enlisted.

Those still in the cattle trucks at Luckenwalde station were informed by the wing commander in charge of the party that there appeared to be little chance of them moving off within the next four or five days. Later it was announced that the entire party would return to the camp next day. Jack Smith and Stan Wharton, having traded cigarettes and soap for potatoes, carrots, onions, and bread, thought it was 'just like a picnic here today. Everybody is in the best of spirits. Had another half food parcel issued.'

On the train Henry Wagner met F/O Anthony Arthur Griffiths, an old friend whom he had not seen since 1934. Griffiths was flying on Ramrod 385 over France on 21 December 1943 in Spitfire EP559, 501 Squadron, when he was shot down by a USAAF P-47. Taken prisoner, he went to Stalag Luft III, and was in the evacuation to Stalag IIIA at the end of January 1945.

**14 APRIL 1945.** The train party returned to camp later in the day. American Sgt R.S. 'Bob' Hall RCAF noted: 'It was a swell forty-eight-hour leave. The siding that we were parked on was very close to the street where the civilians were going to and from work. The difference in language didn't hinder us at all.'

*The 1st Belorussian and 1st Ukrainian Fronts begin reconnaissance in force along their main axes in preparation for the advance towards Berlin.*

**14/15 APRIL 1945.** During the night, a force of sixty-two Mosquitos raided Berlin. At more or less the same time 500 Lancasters, led by twelve Mosquitos of RAF Bomber Command, blasted the German army barracks and railway facilities at Potsdam, the first time that RAF four-engined bombers had been near Berlin since 24/25 March 1944.

With Potsdam only forty kilometres from Stalag IIIA, and Berlin a similar distance, the POWs at Luckenwalde had a grandstand view of the raids. One of the observers of the night's goings-on was Bob Hall:

'The nite Bomber Command had a target just fifteen miles from here – a huge force were in on the attack around midnight. I have never seen anything to compare with it – it was very much too close for comfort. I was scared stiff and don't mind admitting it. It's much safer upstairs… We saw one of them go down in flames.'

This was Lancaster RF143, 138 Squadron, which had only recently converted from SOE duties to bomber operations. Six of the seven-man crew were killed, the seventh simply being noted as 'Safe'. On the same Potsdam raid, Lancaster PB377, 35 Squadron, was also hit, but the pilot, F/O U.B. Bowen-Morris, flew the aircraft back to the Dutch/Belgian border, where he baled out, landing not far from the Belgian town of Vosselaar. What happened to the flight engineer is unclear, but he was never seen alive again. The other five of the crew baled out over enemy-occupied territory, where four of them became POWs. The fifth man, F/S J.W. Tovey, evaded capture but, cold and hungry, found shelter in a POW work camp for four or five days without the Germans' knowledge.

**15 APRIL 1945.** *The Oder line opposite Berlin and Dresden breaks into action.*

**16 APRIL 1945.** An early morning air raid was very close, presumed to be the Russians. There was an unconfirmed report that one aircraft had been shot down.

The funeral for Johnson and Crosswell was held at 10.30 am at the camp cemetery. Among those in the funeral party were Frank Bishop, Jack Danes, Arthur Seller RCAF, Bill Chandler RCAF, 'Norm', Keith Wynn RCAF, Jim Umscheid RCAF, and Allan MacNaught RCAF. The trusty German guard Ludwig brought two wreaths.

**17 APRIL 1945.** In the morning, a large formation of USAAF B-17 bombers – on their way to several railway targets – passed overhead, accompanied by their 'little friends', the long-range P-47 and P-51 fighters.

Last issue of American No. 10 Red Cross parcels – the camp's entire stock – with half a parcel per man. Most of the parcels were delivered to the 4,000 or so POWs from Stalag IIA who had arrived at Luckenwalde in the previous week. They were living in the open with no food supplies and no medical attention. Accompanying the parcels were two doctors and medicine.

*The battle for Berlin escalates. A breakthrough is made by the 1st Ukrainian Front.*

**18 APRIL 1945.** *The 1st Ukrainian Front captures Forst on the Neisse river, north of Frankfurt.*

**19 APRIL 1945.** *At Gresse, near Hamburg, RAF Typhoons mistakenly strafe a column of British prisoners of war. Many killed and wounded, including at least one who had been a POW since 1940.*

**20 APRIL 1945.** Hitler's last birthday. Fine day. Heavy bombing by the Americans over Berlin clearly seen. Russian artillery also clearly heard.

*Soviet forces, having crossed the Oder river, fan out into a wide bridgehead, and get within forty kilometres of Berlin.*

**21 APRIL 1945.** At 0100 hours a German aircraft strafed the main road of the camp, though causing little or no damage, most of his shells hitting only the road. It was amusing, however, according to *The Log*, 'to see people baling out of top bunks and landing on the people who were simultaneously baling out of the tier below'.

At 0200 hours a Dutch girl reported that a Marine Artillery Division from Berlin had arrived at Luckenwalde in twenty-five railway wagons.

During the night most of the German staff moved out with lorries, cars and tractors. POWs woke up to find the camp virtually free of German guards. One of the guards, whom some of the prisoners were sorry to see go:

'was a large rotund man who had been an opera singer, a tenor, and fond of singing a few bars of various operas as he approached each hut in the morning and, unlike his compatriots whose yells of "*Raus! Raus!*" greeted every morning, held open the door and said "Please Mr Gentlemens – Out! Out!". He it was who showed his pistol to some of the prisoners demonstrating that it was empty and that it had no ammunition... I think he was a gentle person and I hoped that no harm came to him.' (Emrys T. Williams.)

The camp's defence scheme now came into operation, as noted in the British Intelligence Summary, *Stalag IIIA*, which also reported:

'In the woods near the Lazarett, there is a party of Germans consisting of seven or eight SS troops and 100 other soldiers. They have visited the Lazarett, and state that anyone outside the camp after dark will be fired upon, and reprisals will be taken for any overt acts of hostility. The German general commanding Light Artillery threatened to open fire upon this camp unless eight rifles taken from his men were immediately returned to him. The rifles were found and returned.'

During the afternoon Russian aircraft bombed the town of Luckenwalde, causing several fires in buildings and factories. At 7.35 pm it was reported that 'Russian artillery at Waltersdorf, two-and-a-half miles north east of Luckenwalde, was shelling the town'. An hour and a half later it was further 'reported that only about 1,000 Volkssturm and Hitler Youth, armed with Tommy guns, rifles, and panzerfaust, are defending Luckenwalde. Rumours say that American and Russian troops have linked up in Trebbin, eight miles north of here.' See diary entry below for 28 April.

*First Russian troops – 1st Mechanised and 12th Guards Tanks Corps of the 2nd Guards Tank Army – cross Berlin's boundary. 3rd Guards Army, 1st Ukrainian Front, captures Cottbus, 110 kilometres south east of Berlin.*

**22 APRIL 1945.** At 0030 hours a delegation from the ex-mayor of Luckenwalde visited the camp offering to hand over the town to the camp authorities 'for subsequent surrender to the Russian army'.

At 0115 hours nine German soldiers moving north-west past the camp said that the front line was four kilometres to the south-east and about six north east of Luckenwalde.

At 0600 hours the first Russian armoured car entered the camp. It left half an hour later, taking three men to Luckenwalde: the Norwegian General Otto Rüge (1882-1961); the US senior officer; and an interpreter. When the armoured car was fired upon near the camp the latter two 'ended their journey rapidly, returning to the camp on foot while the car proceeded to Luckenwalde'.

At 0815 hours Russian infantry were seen from the Norwegian compound moving into the woods to the west of the camp to deal with the remnant of an SS unit that had shelled the camp earlier, without causing any casualties.

At 1000 hours Russian tanks and armoured cars of the 83rd Guards entered the camp. A group of German soldiers opened fire with a machine gun, but caused no casualties. Between 10 and 11 am huge numbers of Russian troops passed through Luckenwalde. After they had gone the civilians began looting the shops. White flags appeared in large numbers.

For the 17,489 POWs of all nationalities confusion reigned, but within hours the Russian barracks in the camp had been emptied of their 9,000 prisoners. Without the protection of the Geneva Convention, these men 'were helpless, underfed, denied medical attention, and forced to do hard labour. Their death rate was staggering.' Day after day the other comparatively healthy prisoners had watched in horror as 'a truck collected its daily quota of corpses'. Free now to enter the Russian compound, the other prisoners found:

> 'a scene of incredible horror. But at its heart they had wrought a miracle – they had built a church. We stood breathless. A golden crucifix flashed from the altar... chandeliers hung the length of the nave. The windows were a splendour of stained glass... How could dying men have created such a magnificent place of worship?'[227]

Closer inspection revealed the truth, that these were all marvels of the Russians' own handiwork using nothing more than pieces of wood and coloured paper salvaged from wherever they could find it.

**23 APRIL 1945.** Well and truly in the centre of the battle, frightened POWs were badly shaken by Russian artillery shells flying over the camp towards the German lines.
*Street fighting takes place in Berlin. Other Soviet forces are fifty kilometres north west of Dresden.*

**24 APRIL 1945.** The officers' and the Americans' compounds were opened up to all POWs, thereby giving the effect of greater freedom.
Despite orders not to do so, many of the POWs wandered off into the surrounding area, usually on the scrounge for food, but always just to get a taste again of what freedom felt like. Fred Brown left the camp on his own, and came across a sandpit full of water:

> 'On the bank was an RAF bod trying his hand with a line and a bent pin. I went round to ask him the usual question "Had any luck?" To my surprise it was Donaghue, the F/Lt I had shared a cell with in Antwerp. We exchanged a few words, but I got the impression he wasn't keen on talking to other ranks. I thought snobby bastard and left.'

Fred had the last laugh when he learnt that the pond had been fished out using hand grenades!

**25 APRIL 1945.** Today was 'Anzac Day, and all the Aussies and Kiwis held a church service this morning. It went off well.' (Jack Smith RAAF.)
*Units of the 1st Belorussian Front's 47th Army and the 1st Ukrainian Front's 4th Guards Tank Army meet at Ketzen, to the west of Berlin. The encirclement of Berlin is complete. US and Russian forces meet at Torgau, on the Elbe river, fifty kilometres north east of Leipzig.*

**26 APRIL 1945.** Major-General Famin of the Repatriation Board on Konev's staff visited the camp. He said that, owing to the congestion to the Soviet's lines of communication, it was most probable that the POWs would return home via the west. He also gave assurances that everything was being done to expedite their return.

**27 APRIL 1945.** Still heavy artillery and small arms fire all around the camp. A major of the Russian repatriation board arrived in the camp in the morning. The senior British officer met with the Russians to request transport to British and American lines. Officers of the US First Army were reported to be in Luckenwalde, but American war correspondents (one female) were found there on their way to Berlin, and promised to visit the camp on their way back.

**28 APRIL 1945.** *In a desperate attempt to split the Allies, Germany offers unconditional surrender to*

*Britain and the USA only. The offer, recognised for what it is, is rejected.*

Late in the night, under the command of the Russian Captain Medvedev, a convoy of fifty lorries carrying food and clothing arrived with staff to look after the camp. Medvedev 'comes from the Caucasus, is twenty-four years of age and wears the Stalingrad Defence medal and the Soviet Cross for gallantry. Above these decorations are three wound stripes...' (*The Log.*)

**29 APRIL 1945.** Rained all day. Unloading of the lorries continued in the morning. NCOs, some from Luft 7, beat the officers 4-2 in a football match.

**30 APRIL 1945.** *Hitler commits suicide. The Allies enter Munich, Turin, Venice and Milan.*

**1 MAY 1945.** The camp's population, due to the constant influx of POWs and refugees, had risen to an estimated 30,000. In the prevailing chaos it was not difficult to slip away, and just after 7 am Sgt Wacław 'Wally' Dworakowski and a POW referred to only as Pat made their way out of the camp. They had had enough of the Russians' obfuscation.

F/S Dave Berrie was ordered to attend the funeral of a Polish officer. As he had been on 300 (Polish) Squadron (also Dworakowski's squadron) it was assumed that he could speak Polish. At least he knew more than the young American officer in charge of the funeral party, to whom Dave had to whisper the English equivalent of the Polish commands.

Heavy fighting was heard all around the camp during the night.

**2 MAY 1945.** Fighting flared up in the area of the camp in the morning. POWs were told to keep under cover.

*The garrison in Berlin surrenders to the 1st Belorussian and 1st Ukrainian Fronts at 3 pm local time, a few hours after German radio had announced the deaths of Hitler and Göbbels.*

**3 MAY 1945.** More Italians arrived, with their horses. The camp began to resemble a large stable in places. The Italians were keen to sell their horses to the POWs, who were able to buy them for a song.

Two US war correspondents, Bob Vermillion of the *United Press* and Louis Azrael of the *Baltimore News-Post*, appeared with the news that they had known nothing about the camp until four days earlier, when four Americans from the camp had reached the Elbe river. Also present in the camp was Captain Edward William Beattie jnr, also of the *United Press*, who had himself been a prisoner of the Germans. The three war correspondents said that they would be leaving next day, and would take with them various particulars, including POW nominal rolls.

Despite their 'freedom' morale was, generally, low. The men were fed up with waiting, and rations were beginning to get very poor indeed. Many more were thinking of going off on their own.

**4 MAY 1945.** Lt Col Anthony F. Kleitz, commanding 125th Cavalry Squadron, US 83rd (Infantry) Division, arrived in the camp with the news that the evacuation of US, British and Norwegian POWs would begin on the next day, but with the caveat that Russian agreement to this had not yet been obtained.

**5 MAY 1945.** *Unconditional surrender of all German forces in The Netherlands, North-west Germany, and Denmark.*

Excitement mounted when it looked to the POWs as if they would really be moving off with the Americans. Paul Decroix:

'This morning the first parties are standing by waiting for the first convoy. I am in the third party to go. Hope to go tomorrow if the first leave today. Hope the Russians do not interfere. It looks like the real thing this time. Yet I can hardly believe it till I'm on the way! 1.00 pm the first trucks have started to arrive. There are ambulances for the sick. 10.00 pm the sick are all gone. We are waiting for the main convoy which they expect tomorrow. We heard of our own liberation for the first time from the BBC today. The Yanks have brought us K-rations – mighty good!'

At 1 pm a convoy of twenty-three US Army ambulances had arrived at Luckenwalde. The surgeon in charge of the convoy, Lt Col D. Clotselter, 83rd Infantry Division, told the senior Allied officer of the camp that evacuation of the bulk of the British, American and Norwegian sick would begin on this day, and that the remainder would be evacuated tomorrow. He also said that a large convoy of lorries was on its way, but could not be certain of either its size or time of arrival as they were busy with the evacuation of the liberated camp at Altengrabow (Stalag XIA). The majority of the lorries for Stalag IIIA were coming from Hildesheim, to the south of Hannover, about 215 kilometres away. They would be bringing a large quantity of K-rations for distribution throughout the camp. (The K-ration was an individual package of three basic meals, designed to provide enough daily calories – around 2,830 – for a person to live on.)

Four lorries did indeed arrive later, bringing a supply of K-Rations. A small number of American ambulances also arrived and took away all the sick Americans and six British POWs.

**6 MAY 1945.** A notice in the camp announced that the US convoy would arrive later that day. No one really believed it, having been let down so many times before but, to most people's surprise, the promised trucks did appear, nineteen of them with an American liaison officer, Captain John G. Sinkavitch. The Americans began the evacuation of POWs, but were stopped by Captain Tchekanov, a Russian officer deputising for the sick Captain Medvedev. Tchekanov announced that he had no orders to hand over the prisoners to the Americans and, furthermore, the prisoners were to be repatriated in the Russians' own time via Russia.

The Russians were clearly in no hurry, even though negotiations for the POWs' release had been underway for some time. After a conference at the camp, that evening G/C J.C. MacDonald sent a letter to the Russians 'to avoid misunderstanding'. After making it clear that the situation inside the wire was all of the Russians' making, he continued:

'The food situation, up to yesterday, was precarious, and the daily ration, even though assisted by American supplies, is still grossly inadequate… No doubt this whole affair is due to a misunderstanding but the situation created is extremely serious. In spite of assurances that we were to be repatriated with the least possible delay we now see the Russians actively preventing such repatriation. It is impossible for me to explain or justify such action in the eyes of the officers and men. I warned Capt. Medvedev on 4th May that such a situation was likely to arise, and that if it did I could not be responsible for the consequences… I therefore demand that the position may be clarified without delay and that our repatriation may [be] proceeded with immediately… Finally, I must point out that the present situation renders my position as senior Allied officer untenable. I therefore resign my position and from now must be regarded as responsible only for the British.'

**7 MAY 1945.** *At 2.41 am General Alfred Jodl, the representative of the OKW, and Grand Admiral Karl*

*Dönitz, the designated head of the German state, sign the Act of Military Surrender in Reims, France. The first part of the second clause reads:*

> 'The German High Command will at once issue orders to all German military, naval and air authorities and to all forces under German control to cease active operations at 2301 hours Central European time on 8th May 1945, to remain in all positions occupied at that time and to disarm completely, handing over their weapons and equipment to the local allied commanders or officers designated by Representatives of the Allied Supreme Commands.'

More US trucks arrived, but the Russians had still not given permission for their departure with POWs. An American officer and the Russian officials went to Marshal Konev's HQ to try to resolve the problem.

**8 MAY 1945.** *The unconditional surrender is ratified in Berlin by the Germans. Hostilities in Europe cease at one minute after midnight (0001 hours).*

The fact that the war was now over made no difference to those in the camp. In the morning the US trucks were told to leave empty. Some of the frustrated POWs took the opportunity of jumping aboard, but their departure was spotted by Russian guards, who opened fire in their general direction. With bullets flying over their heads the truck drivers had no option but to turn back. Dropping off those passengers who had not managed to 'escape', they returned empty to their own lines.

Earlier in the morning a number of airmen POWs, including Bruce Smith RAAF, went out of the camp through one of the many holes in the wire: 'Several kilometres west of Luckenwalde, while on a straight stretch of road, we saw a Jeep round a bend ahead of us, followed by a second Jeep and a number of army trucks. We stood in the centre of the road and waved our arms to stop the leading Jeep, which was occupied by an American captain, a driver and an orderly.' Enquiries of the captain elicited the fact that the US convoy was bound for the 'god-damned prison camp at Luckenwalde, to find out what has happened to our detail which was sent there yesterday to evacuate American and Limey prisoners'.

Bruce Smith and company explained who they were, and told the captain that if they continued to the camp they might not get back. It was suggested to the captain that, if he halted his convoy where it was, he would soon have every seat in every truck filled by the POWs. An American went to the camp and passed the word that trucks would be waiting three or four miles from the camp, and would leave at 4 pm. There were many takers, among them Paul Decroix.

The trucks were soon full, and the good captain headed off with his ex-POWs to Schönebeck, a few kilometres south of Magdeburg, on the River Elbe. Although the Germans had destroyed the bridge over the river, US engineers had constructed a pontoon bridge to replace it, which the convoy 'proceeded to negotiate (carefully) to the left bank. As we came onto the track which had been built to give access to the pontoon, an American officer came out of a nearby building and shouted, "It's all over, boys. Germany has just capitulated and is now *kaput!*" We proceeded into the town of Schönebeck with a sense of some euphoria.'[228]

It was also on this momentous day that F/S Kenneth Slack RCAF lost his life whilst trying to save a German guard from drowning in the River Elbe. The details of this sad event are not known, but Slack must have been one of the many to have left Luckenwalde without Russian permission.

**9 MAY 1945.** Many Russian trucks arrived.

**10 MAY 1945.** Peter Broadribb, having slipped out of the camp, found himself in the town of Hildesheim:

> 'when, with a party of ten or so airmen – and perhaps twenty-four soldiers, we were put on a Dakota and flown to Le Havre. Here we were put under canvas but, because more and more POWs were continuing to come in, some 400 of us during the evening were taken down to the harbour and placed on an American Liberty ship. Again the treatment extended to us was superb, and overnight we sailed across to Southampton, arriving at around 0800 hours to be met by Red Cross women throwing oranges up at the ship.'

**11 MAY 1945. FRIDAY.** By evening, Peter Broadribb was at RAF Cosford for a medical check up. Two days later he was sent home on six-weeks' leave: 'almost unbelievable how quickly things moved from the previous Tuesday morning. My leave I found was difficult getting adjusted to home and family.'

Maj-Gen Famin returned to the camp and, in a meeting lasting from 2300 hours until 0200 hours on 12 May 'expressed the greatest dis-satisfaction over the unofficial evacuation from this camp, and demanded from the senior British officer a written report there and then.' Famin also stated that he was not pleased at the way in which his staff had looked after the POWs, particularly in the matter of food, and added that Captain Medvedev would be court-martialled.

**12-18 MAY 1945.** Little happened during this period of any note. The Russians had tightened the cordon round the camp, and any former POWs found wandering about outside the camp were brought back under armed guard with the demand that they should be disciplined. This did not, however, prevent more former POWs from getting through to American lines, and the number of personnel within the camp's confines was noticeably dwindling. For those left behind, time hung heavily on their hands.

**19 MAY 1945.** At last, more Russian trucks arrived: 'When the siren goes we were to climb on. The Russians would take us to the Elbe and turn us over to the Yanks. This was to be an exchange: us for theirs. Rumour said we were going to Leipzig. We didn't care. We were finally heading west.' (John McConnell.)

**20 MAY 1945.** The convoy of Russian trucks departed Luckenwalde for the Elbe, where the ex-POWs changed over to US trucks: A 'big cheer went up. We were now with our own people.' The US convoy then made its way via Bitterfeld to Halle, where the ex-POWs were de-loused, given a good wash, and fed.

**22 MAY 1945.** *Negotiations begun earlier in the month between SHAEF and the Soviets resulted in the so-called Halle Agreement. Allied POWs could now be repatriated with little hindrance. Operation Exodus, the repatriation by air of former POWs from camps in the Reich, had begun seven weeks earlier, on 3 April. After many thousands had been flown back – some 354,000 by the end of May – General Dwight D. Eisenhower expressed SHAEF's gratitude on 15 June 1945 to ACM Sir Arthur Harris for RAF Bomber Command's prodigious efforts: 'It was a contribution to human happiness of which the air force can remain forever proud.'*

**22-25 MAY 1945.** The former POWs were airlifted, usually by Dakota, to Brussels.

**26 MAY 1945.** Many of the ex-POWs were then flown to England. John McConnell and his pals were on Lancaster JO-B$^2$, 463 (RAAF) Squadron: 'We were rather quiet on the flight to England. Each with our own thoughts. I realised I had been rather lucky. Our bunch had been through some trying times but we had hung together… A great bunch of guys… We touched down at Dunsfold in the south of England… Our last trip was finally over.'

*

Fred Brown came back on a Lancaster from an airfield in northern France: 'As it came to our turn [to board] I saw the letters on the aircraft, JI, my squadron letters, 514 Squadron at Waterbeach.' Soon they were approaching the White Cliffs of Dover, the sight of which almost had Fred in tears: 'When I thought of Vera Lynn and her song… The sun was shining, and it was a beautiful day when we landed.'

# POSTSCRIPT

It would be neither right nor proper to compare the grimness of the forced march undertaken by the Luft 7 kriegies with that undertaken by kriegies from other camps. Conditions in each case were, of course, different, but the Luft 7 men were fortunate to have with them two such fine officers as their padré and medical officer.

Tribute has been paid earlier in this book to Padré John Collins. Strong both physically and mentally, he would prove to be a great example and inspiration to the men during their awful ordeal in January and February 1945 and at Luckenwalde. Here is what a few more kriegies had to say of him:

'I hesitate to suggest it to you – no doubt it is your intention already – but I feel that sufficient tribute has never been paid to the part played by the padré, Captain Collins, in encouraging the strength and morale of prisoners on the march.' (Henry Wagner, letter to author, 31 May 1989.)

'You mention the padré. One memory in particular, which I have related more times than any other, is of a tall padré walking back and forth along the line of frozen bodies lifting our spirits. Walking two kilometres to our one. A tower of strength. I have always recalled that man when spiritually I have needed a lift.' (Harold Bennett, letter to author, 12 September 1989.)

'This was easily the worst part of our march. There was a fifty mph blizzard blowing and men could not stop for a moment otherwise they froze up. The C of E padré really did wonders here to help the men, but of course he did all the way along.' (Tom Trimble, on the blizzard of 29 January 1945.)

Finally: 'He was a wonderful inspiration to us all. Faith is so important when one is liable to crack up. Also John Berry, Peter Thomson and Doug Howatson. These were leaders among men and respected by all.' ('Mac' McMurdon, letter to author, 1 April 1991.)

After the war, about which he seldom if ever spoke, John Collins resumed as vicar at Canford Magna and as chaplain at Canford School, a position he was to finally relinquish in 1947. In that year he became rector at St Gregory's, Marnhull, still in Dorset, and in 1953 went to St Mary's, Market Lavington, Wiltshire.[229] Whilst he was there he was appointed chaplain to Dauntsey's School. One of the Lavington villagers, Tom Gye, remembers that John, having been taught bell-ringing in Dorset, tried ringing at St Mary's. Being so tall, he once took too much rope, got into difficulties, and had to be 'rescued' by Tom. Finally, in 1957, he went to Hever in Kent, before retiring in 1973 to Herefordshire, firstly to Orcop, then Weobley, and finally Leominster in 1988, where he died in October 1992.

For everything he did on behalf of his fellow prisoners Padré Collins received only a Mention in Despatches (gazetted 21 February 1946).

*

The last words rest with Frenchman Henri Bruneau: 'To tell the truth, I think it was a bloody good experience and I sincerely don't regret having gone through it. I'm still in touch with about half a dozen ex-POW chaps around the world and I assure you they count among the best friends I have.' (Letter to author, 28 November 1985.)

To Henri's words Jim Palmer added: 'I think we all know what he meant and I, for one, agree with him.'

*

> "Since you are not certain of an hour
> Throw not away a minute."
> (*Old saying*).

# DATES OF *TRUPPEN* ARRIVALS AT STALAG LUFT VII (BANKAU)

| Trupp | Arrived | Luft 7 POW numbers | Trupp | Arrived | Luft 7 POW numbers |
|---|---|---|---|---|---|
| 1 | 6/6/44 | 1-70 | 27 | 22/8/44 | 541-648 28 |
| 2 | 13/6/44 | 71-105 | 28 | 29/8/44 | 649-688 |
| 3 | 18/6/44 | 106-113 | 29 | 3/9/44 | Three men, possibly |
| 4 | 20/6/44 | 114-138 | | | from a Stalag in France |
| 5 | 21/6/44 | 139-140 | 30 | 4/9/44 | 689-727 |
| 6 | 21/6/44 | 141 | 31 | 13/9/44 | 728-735 |
| 7 | 28/6/44 | 142-202 | 32 | 18/9/44? | One man, from |
| 8 | 3/7/44 | 203-247 | | | hospital |
| 9 | 9/7/44 | Ten men from Stalag | 33 | ? | 736-788 |
| | | XIIA | 34 | 25/9/44 | 789-827 |
| 10 | 9/7/44 | Three wounded from | 35 | ? | 828-829? |
| | | Stalag IXC | 36 | ? | 828-829? |
| 11 | 10/7/44 | 248-287 | 37 | 3/10/44 | 830-878 |
| 12 | 13/7/44 | 288-332 | 38 | 7/10/44 | 879-968 |
| 13 | 16/7/44 | 333-344 | 39 | 12/10/44 | 969-1012 |
| 14 | 20/7/44 | 345-378 | 40 | 21/10/44 | 1013-1052 |
| 15 | 26/7/44 | 379-428 | 41 | ? 22/10/44 | Several wounded |
| 16 | 30/7/44 | Ninety-four men from | 42 | ? | |
| | | Stalag 383 (formerly | 43 | ? | |
| | | at Stalag VIIA) | 44 | ? | |
| 17 | 31/7/44 | One man from Stalag | 45 | ? 26/10/44 | |
| | | IVB; six from Stalag | 46 | 28/10/44 | 1053-1088. Actual |
| | | IXC | | | date is uncertain. |
| 18 | 1/8/44 | Nine men from Stalag | 47 | 12/11/44 | 1089-1127 |
| | | XIA; fourteen from | 48 | 19/11/44 | 1128-1171 |
| | | Stalag XIB | 49 | 24/11/44 | Possibly a number of |
| 19 | 3/8/44 | Possibly one man from | | | wounded |
| | | Stalag XIA inc. in Tr.18 | 50 | 28/11/44 | 1172-1215 |
| 20 | 4/8/44 | Ten men from Stalag | 51 | ? 1 or 2/12/44 | |
| | | Luft III; one from | 52 | ? | |
| | | Oflag VIA | 53 | ? | |
| 21 | 5/8/44 | 429-500 | 54 | ? | |
| 22 | 8/8/44 | Three men from Stalag | 55 | 20/12/44 | 1216-1270 |
| | | XIIA. (Note that the | 56 | 26/12/44 | 1272-1310. Note: it is |
| | | date is uncertain). | | | unclear when POW |
| 23 | 11/8/44 | 501-539 | | | number 1271 was |
| 24 | 12/8/44 | 540 | | | allocated. |
| 25 | ? | | 57 | 5 or 6/1/45 | 1311-1358. |
| 26 | ? | | | | |

**NOTE:** The dates of arrival of the *Truppen* shown with a '?' are unclear/unknown. It is also believed that several POWs arrived at Luft 7 after *Trupp 57*, on 9, 10 and 12 January 1945, but apparently with no Trupp number. These latest arrivals may have been ones from other POW camps (who had already been given their POW number), some twenty-one men in total.

APPENDIX II

# OLD GERMAN PLACE NAMES WITH
# MODERN POLISH EQUIVALENT

| Alt Poppelau | *Popielów* | Leignitz | *Legnica* |
|---|---|---|---|
| Bankau | *Baków* | Lossen | *Łosiów* |
| Breslau | *Wrocław* | Oppeln | *Opole* |
| Brieg-am-Oder | *Brzeg* | Peterwitz | *Piotrowice* |
| Buchitz | *Buszyce* | Pfaffendorf | *Ksiaznica* |
| Cottbus | *Chóśebuz* | Prausnitz | *Prusice* |
| Goldberg | *Złotoryja* | Rosenthal | *Różyna* |
| Gross Jenkwitz | *Jankowice Wielkie* | Rothschloss | *Białobrzezie* |
| Heidersdorf | *Łagiewniki* | Sagan | *Żagań* |
| Karlsmarkt | *Karłowice* | Schönfeld | *Obórki* |
| Karlsruhe* | *Pokój* | Schurgast | *Skorogoszcz* |
| Karzen | *Karczyn* | Schweidnitz | *Świdnica* |
| Köchendorf | *Kucharzowice* | Standorf | *Stanowice* |
| Konradswaldau | *Przylesie* | Stoberau | *Stobrawa* |
| Konstadt | *Wołczyn* | Strehlen | *Strzelin* |
| Koppen | *Kopanie* | Waldhaus | *Buszyce* |
| Kreuzburg | *Kluczbork* | Wansen | *Wiazów* |
| Lamsdorf | *Łambinowice* | Winterfeld | *Zawiść* |
| Langseifersdorf | *Jaźwina* | Zindel | *Mlodoszowice* |

\* The full name of Karlsruhe was Karlsruhe-im-Oberschlessien.

# SERGEANT DOUG GRANT'S REPATRIATION VIA ODESSA

*Doug Grant and eight others escaped during the forced march from Bankau after hiding in the disused brick factory at Karlsruhe on 20 January 1945 (see page 241). Doug's account of their travels and adventures thereafter is taken from his* NOTES FOR OVERSEAS, *which are reproduced below just as he wrote it.*

'The brick factory was at cross roads. Some Russian tanks came – Pole managed to flag them down without getting shot – we were with the tanks approx week. Life is dangerous on outside of tank – fight all night then try and hide – rest during day. These tanks were back of Jerry line at this time so had to move fast – no quarter asked – none given – everything was shot – looking back it was out and out luck that they didn't shoot the "Polock" who helped us.

'I think the first venture after leaving brick factory was village of Roseburg – nothing left when we left. Shot – killed – set fire – scorched earth – then on – I am not completely sure of sequence. Latski [Laski] – Wielun – Czestocheva – Radomsko – Mazauiechi – Lodz – Radom and Lublin. Lublin was where the Russians had the head of government. The Warsaw govt. was in London. Just on the outskirts of Lublin was a camp called Majdanek – "the crematorium" over 2 million people went through this place – there is a hell on earth.

'Lublin became a gathering place for troops liberated up north – both Brits and Yanks. I became O/C British personnel. I think it was a case of the youngest – dumbest and the guy with the biggest mouth. Anyway, we "got on with it".

'Thoughts of getting home were always in our mind – couldn't go south to Constanca – Jerries held the mountain passes – thought about Danzig – but it was too cold and no way to live.

'Heard about a Br. Maj. who was making an ass of himself up in Warsaw – a couple of us – 4 or 5? – started out for Warsaw – got stopped at check point – one chap had a non combattant paper – real important looking – so guy at check point held it upside down smiled and let us proceed. Eventually got to Warsaw. Warsaw was flat – smashed – *kaput*. Only life was across wooden bridge to Spraugda.'

'Found Limey Maj – he even had a batman – informed him and everybody else to get down at Lublin forthwith – Russian C.O. backed me up – so it was back to Lublin.'

*During his time in Lublin Doug Grant had become friendly with a member of the Polish Underground Army, Slawomir Litwinski, who had access to a wireless transmitter. Slawomir was familiar with the process for getting names checked, and broadcast the names and numbers of Doug and his comrades from 'a radio shack in Lublin'. Amazingly, the transmission was picked up by a radio 'ham' in Texas, USA, and the relevant information was relayed to the RCAF in Ottawa – 'My dad found out that way. Miracles!'*

'An American Col. – Col. Wilmont – from Moscow came to Lublin – he had a sergeant driver who was of Polish descent so he did the interpreting – also a man from Geneva – Int. Red Cross. The colonel was a menace – big time operator – not a clue. It was brought to his attention damn quickly that we did not come under his jurisdiction.

'The Russians were sending a bunch of tank cars down to Kiev for more fuel and also heard through "reliable sources" that a British freighter would be in Odessa. Got hold of Russian commandant – he said he could hook on some box cars. He assigned a Russian Maj. to be I/C this venture – Maj Alexandria – something like that – anyway, he was ex tank corps and a line major. He helped us a great deal – without him the train trip could have been a disaster.

'We had the Brits and one Yank who was in trouble with the Russians – he became a British pro tem and [there were] at least 85 Yanks so it was a good sized crowd.

'The wind blew the roofs off a couple of boxcars during a snow storm – I was cold as a frog in a frozen pool.

'We finally arrived in Odessa– late afternoon. We were met by one Maj. Hall – Brit – out of Moscow – he wanted us to board ship immediately – I told him No because we had wounded with us and would need a room set aside aboard ship as a First Aid station and also Maj. Alexandria said there would be hot water for showers – hot food and we could have our clothes de-flead and de-loused. It was set up that we would board early next morning – I think the ship's name was "Highland Princess".

*The ship was, indeed, the* Highland Princess. *She had sailed from Liverpool a few days earlier with two other ships, the* Duchess of Bedford *and* Moreton Bay, *bringing with them some 7,000 Russians who were being repatriated under the terms of the agreement struck at the Yalta Conference between Churchill, Roosevelt and Stalin.*[230]

'We formed up at 0800 hours next morning to march to the jetty – I mentioned we would leave here like we owned the place. My God, what a show!! We checked out 120 [*steps*] per minute – dressed in rags and tatters but we looked like the King's Own Guard! When we got to the jetty we were piped aboard. Lt. Col. Rob of the 51st Highlanders was troop master. A really great man. We also had "Dixie" Dean – Sgt. Maj. Dean! Now there was a real RSM.

'Our Yank left us at Istanbul. The Dardanelles were quite a sight!

'On way to Part Said Col. Rob said we could have shore leave – I mentioned that we were all broke – no money – no problem he said. Seeing as I was the C.O. I could sign for the money from Bank of England. I signed for 795 pounds – every one of us received 5 pounds. I was never questioned about that when back in England.

'At Port Said – MI9 or whoever – mentioned that those of us from Luft 7 would fly back to UK – so truck took us up to Cairo and we stayed in a camp – tents, etc at Heliopolis. This is really comic opera stuff. The retards were in charge – they hated and looked down upon transients, which we were. Fortunately, we were just passing through on way home and somewhat put up with them – e.g. – we had an Aussie cpl. to drive us around camp – went to stores to draw blankets, etc. The QM sgt. Wanted to know on who's authority. I told him mine! It was mentioned that I could blow that idea out my ear – told him to get out from behind counter so he wouldn't get hurt. We got our own blankets and Aussie found us a tent all set up. We were in business.

'It was one row after another – a RAF S/L said we had to draw kit up to and including pith helmets – "Baldy" told him to cram it. Broke up sgts mess. Cairo got us transportation back to UK – I think they were glad to see the end of us. Flew via Castel Benito – Marseille – London fogged in so landed at Bristol and took train to London. We still had no papers so a bunch more flak – fortunately the Intelligence types found us and took over. None of the SP's or MP's would touch us – they didn't know who we belonged to. I had Russian hat – calfskin jacket – Br. battle dress pants – we looked what we were – refugees. We were put up at "Escapers Club" in London then to Knightsbridge – Lincoln's Inn Fields and into "the" RAF GHQ – way underground. We were always escorted – sign in and sign out of every room – etc. – debriefing several days – had to sign No Mention statement – last time there – just before going home – went for interview – got my commission!'

*Although perhaps not the most historically accurate picture of events, Doug's account nevertheless gives a certain flavour to the feelings of a POW on return to 'normal' wartime service life.*

There were two main collection centres for Allied ex-POWs who found themselves in Russian-occupied territory in 1945 – one at Lublin, the other at Kraków.

In February 1945 the British Military Mission in Moscow signalled that seventy British and Commonwealth officers and 2,571 other ranks were on their way to Odessa. This total suggests that account had been taken of all ex-POWs at all collection centres. The train from Lublin to Odessa departed on 23 February 1945 with an estimated 500 ex-POWs on board, under the command of F/O P.J. Anderson RCAF (see page 242). Arriving at Odessa on 28 February, they were probably among the first to do so. The second trainload of Allied ex-POWs departed from Kraków on 25 February, and reached Odessa on 3 March.

Sir James Grigg, Secretary of State for War, however, told the House of Commons on 6 March 1945 that only fourteen officers and 464 other ranks had so far reached Odessa. This would suggest that this total of 478 was the Anderson contingent from Lublin. A fortnight later, on 21 March, British Foreign Minister Anthony Eden complained to his opposite number, Soviet Foreign Minister Molotov, that he had 'had no information since February 17th when your authorities told us that 2,611 of our men had been collected and were being sent to Odessa. Only 1,817 of these have arrived in time to be embarked on the ship sent to collect them.' No doubt that these were the lucky ones to sail for Port Said aboard the *Moreton Bay* and *Highland Princess* on 6 March.

It is believed that, eventually, a total of some 36,000 Allied ex-POWs were shipped from Odessa on nineteen British ships between 6 March and 22 June 1945 – 27,500 French; 4,130 British and British Commonwealth; 2,858 American; and 1,500 Belgian.

# F/L A.H. HAMMET DFM, RAAF

Allan Hunter Hammet was born on 24 July 1921. At the start of the Second World War, he was working as a chemist's assistant in Red Cliffs, Victoria, Australia. By the end of the war, still only twenty-three, he had flown thirty-three bomber operations from England, had been decorated with the DFM, had then flown a further thirteen supply missions from Italy, had been shot down and wounded, had spent the best part of six months in Poland on the run with partisans, and had then married a Polish girl.

His RAAF career began quietly enough. Following initial training he embarked at Sydney on 27 November 1940 for further training in Canada, where he arrived on 23 December. At No. 2 Wireless School, and at No. 2 Bombing & Gunnery School, he trained as a wireless operator/air gunner. From 6 July to 29 July 1941 he was at sea on the crossing to the UK.

His first posting in England was to No. 2 Signals School, followed by 27 OTU (23 September 1941-11 March 1942), when he was posted to 12 Squadron at Binbrook, Lincolnshire, which was flying operations with the Mark II Wellington.

Whether or not he shared the Australian serviceman's disdain of authority is not known, but he was absent without leave (AWOL) on 24/25 April 1942, for which he received a 'Severe Reprimand' and forfeited one day's pay. Posted on 16 May to 460 (RAAF) Squadron, at Breighton, Yorkshire, he was AWOL again on 20/22 July 1942. This time he was 'Admonished' and lost three days' pay. On another occasion, he and others of his crew had had a few beers one night in the town of Goole. Not fancying the long eight-mile walk back to Breighton, they 'borrowed' some bicycles but, coming upon an unattended steamroller, agreed that that would be a much better mode of transport.

Ditching the bicycles, they 'climbed aboard, threw some coal into the fire box, and, after some pushing and pulling of levers, the monster began to move. As there was no mutual agreement who would drive, whenever one pulled a lever the other automatically pushed one, consequently a rather erratic course along the road was set. However, a small crowd of bystanders had by this time gathered to watch the spectacle and, with plenty of encouragement being given, they pursued a course for base, travelling at a speed which is not normally expected or required of a steam roller. They drove it for some distance and about a mile short of their destination they took a dive to port, off the road, over a ditch, and through a hedge where the machine stopped and, despite much coaxing, the crew were unable to restart it and reluctantly they abandoned ship.'[231]

Allan Hammet went on to complete a tour on 460 Squadron, and was commissioned on 18 January 1943. On 12 March 1943, whilst having a 'rest' back at 27 OTU, he was awarded the DFM, the citation for which read:

> 'One night, in December 1942, Flight Sergeant Hammet was wireless operator of an aircraft detailed to attack Duisburg [20/21 December 1942]. On the return journey, his apparatus was seriously damaged by gunfire, and became unserviceable. In addition the compass failed but Flight Sergeant Hammet was able to improvise communications which gave the navigator valuable assistance which enabled the aircraft to be flown safely back to base. Throughout, this airman has displayed high courage, efficiency and devotion to duty.'

On 15 October 1943, having been promoted flying officer with effect from 18 July 1943, he was posted to HQ Middle East Air Command. Further promotion to acting flight lieutenant came on 18

September. A posting to 1 RAF Base Area in January 1944 was followed by a move on 1 March to HQ Mediterranean Allied Air Forces, where he spent the next four-and-a-half months. It was not until 14 July 1944 that he was again posted to an operational squadron, in this case 178 Squadron based at Amendola (Foggia) in Italy, which was flying the Mark VI Liberator.

Early in August 1944, despite the impending invasion of the south of France, the decision was made that the two Liberator squadrons of 205 Group RAF – 178 (RAF) and 31 (SAAF) – should, along with the Polish 1586 (SD) Flight, drop supplies to the *Armia Krajowa* (AK) in and around Warsaw. For this, 205 Group aircrew would pay a high price.

Earlier sorties in August had resulted in no losses, but that would change over the four nights of 13/14–16/17 August, when seventeen Polish and sixty-two RAF and SAAF aircraft attempted drops to Warsaw and other parts of Poland. Only fifteen loads reached the AK, at a cost of three Polish, five RAF and seven South African crews. In addition, two RAF and one SAAF aircraft crashed on return, and others came back with wounded aboard.

On 16/17 August 1944, the last night of the four, six aircraft failed to return, three of them SAAF. Morale among the aircrew in Italy was weakened by these losses, and the views of the commander of 1586 Flight, S/L E. Arciuszkiewicz PAF, who had himself made the Warsaw run, are worth noting. The following is from a message sent on 20 August from the Polish base commander at Brindisi to the head of the Polish Sixth Bureau in London:

> 'The commander of 1586 Flight informed me today that in the present state of the anti-aircraft defence of Warsaw, as experience has shown, precision drops from a height of 600-800 ft. are impracticable. In his opinion sending aircraft to Warsaw in practice amounts to the loss of aircraft and crews without any guarantee of supplying the troops in the capital.'[232]

Even though some aircraft were making drops over selected wooded areas (the Kampinos and Kabacki forests especially), losses continued.

F/L Allan Hammet was flying in Liberator KG933 when it was attacked by a night-fighter on 16/17 August 1944. Though hit in the arms and legs during the attack, he baled out. Landing in a field some twenty-five kilometres east of Kraków, and hiding in woods during the day, he walked for the next two nights, until he decided that he needed treatment for his wounds and food. Chancing his luck at an isolated farmhouse, he was taken in by friendly Poles, who treated his wounds, and fed him. In the early hours of 19 August he was moved by horse and cart to a house on a large estate at Kocmyrzów. A doctor was summoned to look at his wounds.

Provided with civilian clothes he was again moved, to Słoboszów, some forty kilometres north east of Kraków, joining a group of some 200 partisans, men and women, armed with weapons dropped by the RAF and with anything else they could capture from the Germans. Hammet began his active service with the partisans by doing simple guard duty. By the middle of September 1944, he was allowed out on patrols and, eventually, on raiding parties, one of which, on about 23 September, was an attack on a sugar factory at Kazimierza: 'We killed eight German guards and removed all the sugar from the factory This was distributed at a later date to Poles by the manager of the factory.'

On about 30 September Hammet, having decided to try to get to Sweden from the port of Gdynia (Gdansk), was escorted in stages by partisans to a place near Warsaw to try to locate a mysterious Englishwoman, Miss Walker. (Though Miss Walker had not been found by Hammet, she made her way to Lublin after the Russians had finally occupied Warsaw, and was taken by train with Allied ex-POWs to Odessa.) After ten fruitless days near Warsaw, he returned to his partisan group in the forest at Słoboszów on 20 October.

At the end of that month Allan and the partisans shot down, with rifles and machine guns, a German Fieseler Storch, a light, spotter aircraft, killing the pilot. As a result, the Germans sent a force of a hundred or so White Russians (Ukrainians) from Miechów to deal with the partisans. Well-armed and resolute, the partisans and Allan, somewhere east of Swiecice, took on their opponents in a fierce gun battle that saw nineteen Ukrainians and nine partisans killed. According to Allan, two of the nine partisans were 'Britishers (escaped POWs further details unknown)' and that they 'were magnificent fighters. One had accounted for about eighty Germans.'

A few days later information was received that 'three Ukrainians in the German forces were in a peasant's hut in Słaboszów. I threw a Mills bomb into the room they were in.' Allan didn't wait to find out their fate, but heard later that they had been killed.

Allan Hammet survived his adventures with the partisans, moving to a large house on the outskirts of Swiecice on 6 November. Early in December two escaped British Army privates, Carter, of The Buffs, and John Williams (unit unknown), moved into a house nearby.

On 11 January 1945, the British Military Mission in Moscow advised the Australian Legation there that Hammet was in Warsaw: 'The mission is taking up with the Soviet General Staff arrangements for the release of this officer with other British prisoners immediately the prison camps concerned fall into the Red Army's control.' Once his release had been agreed, Hammet and his two British Army friends walked to Częstochowa, where another British Military Mission 'placed him in command of Allied prisoners of war released from the German camps'. A month later the Allied ex-POWs were driven to Kraków, and from there sent by train to Odessa.

Reaching England on 26 March 1945, he was put on the strength of 11 PDRC at Brighton, as were all returning Australian aircrew POWs. Finally sailing from the UK aboard the *Stirling Castle* on 4 October 1945, he disembarked at Sydney one month later.

There was, however, the not inconsiderable matter of Allan Hammet's marriage. Little is known of this happy event except that it occurred on 25 February 1945, that the name of his wife was Jadwiga Suchodowska, and that she already had a child. Mother and child were allowed to travel with their husband and father but, in so doing, Mrs Hammet left behind in Poland her father, her sister, and a property. They settled in Australia, where the family grew over the forthcoming years.

# SAS OPERATION MAPLE, 1944

Plans for Operation Maple had been submitted to 15th Army Group on 10 December 1943, and permission to proceed was given on 17 December. The objective of Maple was to cut specific sections of the railway lines north and east of Rome in the Orte-Terni area, and also the line from Ancona to the plain of Lombardy. To achieve this, Maple was divided into two parts – Thistledown (commanded by Lt D.G. Worcester, Highland Light Infantry) and Driftwood (Capt J.St.G. Gunston, Irish Guards).

Thistledown was itself sub-divided into four parties. In charge of No. 2 Party was Jack Lloyd, with Cpl Davis, and Parachutists (Pct) Pepper and Todd. Their task was to cut the railway line between Orvieto and Orte. Party No. 4 was led by Paul Hill, with L/Cpls Roberts and Hughes, and Pct Medlin, their objective being to cut the railway between Terni and Perugia.

After two false starts due to poor weather, the seventeen men of Thistledown and the eight men of Driftwood assembled at Gioia del Colle airfield on 7 January 1944, where three Douglas C-47 *Skytrain* aircraft of 8th Troop Carrier Squadron USAAF were waiting to drop the men behind enemy lines. C-47s number 439 and 681 took the four Thistledown parties to their DZ north west of Aquila at Colle Futa, while number 391 took the two Driftwood parties to a DZ north east of Ancona. In bright moonlight, the Thistledown troops were dropped into four feet of snow near Terni, about 100 miles inside enemy lines.

The deep snow made for heavy going, and it was not until 16 January that Jack Lloyd's party completed its task. Paul Hill's party had, however, reached its objective on schedule on 13/14 January. Lt Worcester's party, having found that their stretch of railway line had already been bombed by the Allies, did what damage they could with their plastic explosives to targets of opportunity, mostly vehicles (twenty-five of which were destroyed) and roads. Once the tasks had been accomplished the SAS were to make their way to a rendezvous on the coast where light coastal craft would wait for them on three consecutive nights. It was winter, very cold, and snow lay deeply all around. Though these inconveniences could be overcome with little difficulty in normal circumstances, the SAS faced the additional hazard of an extremely alert enemy, put on their guard not only by the Anzio landings on 22 January 1944 but also by increased partisan activity and by large numbers of escaped POWs circulating in the area, some of whom were found by the Thistledown parties.

In the event, neither Lt Worcester[233] nor any of the other sixteen men managed to avoid capture, though the last man to stay free did so until the beginning of June. Paul Hill was captured on 5 February 1944 at Artena after he had been betrayed by an Italian farmer, and had had the distasteful sight of watching the farmer being paid off by the Germans. Jack Lloyd, having accumulated a number of POW strays during his wanderings, split them up into smaller groups to give everyone a better chance. He himself headed for Rome, but became embroiled with partisans, and made several attacks with them on the enemy. Continuing on his way to Anzio, he was nearing the British lines when he was found by a British patrol, which he joined. They were on their way back to Allied lines on 24 April 1944 when, within sight of safety, all were captured by a German patrol.

The Thistledown men at least were alive, unlike the eight Driftwood men. On 7 March 1944 Capt Gunston's party left from a point a little south of Porto San Giorgio in a 22-foot boat which, it is believed, was either attacked by Allied aircraft (pilots were instructed to fire on craft off the enemy coast) or capsized and drowned its occupants.

There is, however, a third possibility. *The Times* of 10 November 1945 carried an *In Memoriam* notice for Capt Gunston, which included the words '... previously reported missing in Italy, March,

1944, now believed to have been shot by the Germans after capture'. This would suggest that some, if not all, of the Driftwood men had managed to gain dry land, only to be captured and shot by the Germans. The eight were: Capt John St. George Gunston, Irish Guards (124477); 2043553 Cpl (Bombardier) Albert Henry Pugh, Royal Artillery, age twenty-five; 2135077 Pct. (Sapper) William Dodds, Royal Engineers, age twenty-five; 4698891 Pct. (Private) Herbert Loosemore, Durham Light Infantry, age twenty-one; 4121828 Sgt (Serjeant) Robert Thomas Benson, Cheshire Regiment, age thirty; 1443815 Sgt (Serjeant) William Osborne Glen, Royal Artillery, age twenty-nine; 1987141 Pct. (Sapper) Alan Lockeridge, Royal Engineers, age twenty-four; and 4130239 Pct. (Private) John Evans, Cheshire Regiment, age twenty-six. All are commemorated on the Cassino Memorial, Italy.

If it were indeed the fate of Capt Gunston and his men to have been shot by the enemy, then Lloyd and Hill were fortunate not to have suffered that fate too. Paragraph 3 of Hitler's notorious 'Kommando Befehl' secretly issued on 18 October 1942 stated, inter alia, that:

'Anyone operating against German troops in so-called Commando raids in Europe or in [North] Africa, are to be annihilated to the last man. This is to be carried out whether they be soldiers in uniform, or saboteurs, with or without arms…'

Paragraph 4 continued:

'Should individual members of these Commandos… fall into the hands of the Armed Forces through any other means – as, for example, through the Police in one of the Occupied Territories – they are to be instantly handed over to the S.D.'

The Sicherheitsdienst (SD), a secret police force as brutal as the Gestapo, had, therefore, the authority to execute any 'irregular' soldier without trial.

Paul Hill was held under Gestapo supervision at the Regina Coeli prison in Rome. On 1 April 1944 he and three other 'parachutists' were taken from that prison to the Nahkampfschule (close combat school), fourteen kilometres from Rome on the Via Casilina, to be shot. It was only because they had Red Cross parcels with them – apparently a sign that their capture had been notified to the International Red Cross – that SS-Obergruppenführer Karl Wolff gave them a stay of execution.[234] Hill remained in the prison for several more weeks until, towards the end of May, he was released to Dulag Luft, Oberursel. On 2 June 1944, after eight days there, he was purged to Luft 7.

Jack Lloyd had spent a very unpleasant three-and-a-half weeks (26 April-21 May) in the hands of the Gestapo at their Rome HQ at 145, Via Tasso, before he, too, was released to Luft 7.

APPENDIX VI
# STALAG LUFT VII (BANKAU) PRISONERS OF WAR

The airmen POWs at Luft 7 flew thirty-four different types of aircraft, listed in the table below, including such rarities as the Bristol Bombay and Supermarine Walrus. The USAAF Consolidated B-24 was known to the RAF as the Liberator. The Canso was the Canadian-built Consolidated PBY Catalina. As for the Airspeed Horsa glider, though over 660 were towed into action at Arnhem in September 1944, only two GPR men seem to have noted their aircraft's serial number.

## TYPES OF AIRCRAFT FLOWN BY STALAG LUFT VII POWS:

| | 1940 | 1941 | 1942 | 1943 | 1944 | TOTAL |
|---|---|---|---|---|---|---|
| Albacore | - | 1 | - | - | - | 1 |
| Albamarle | - | - | - | - | 2 | 2 |
| B-24 (USAAF) | - | - | - | - | 3 | 3 |
| Baltimore | - | - | 1 | 1 | 4 | 6 |
| Barracuda | - | - | - | - | 1 | 1 |
| Battle | 1 | - | - | - | - | 1 |
| Beaufighter | - | 1 | - | 1 | 13 | 15 |
| Beaufort | - | 6 | 1 | - | - | 7 |
| Blenheim | 2 | 3 | - | - | - | 5 |
| Bombay | - | 2 | - | - | - | 2 |
| Boston | - | - | 1 | - | - | 1 |
| Canso | - | - | - | - | 1 | 1 |
| Dakota | - | - | - | - | 18 | 18 |
| Fortress | - | - | - | - | 15 | 15 |
| Halifax | - | 4 | 3 | 14 | 396 | 417 |
| Hampden | 1 | 10 | 12 | 1 | - | 24 |
| Horsa | - | - | - | - | 132 | 132 |
| Hudson | - | 5 | - | - | - | 5 |
| Hurricane | 1 | 2 | - | - | - | 3 |
| Kittyhawk | - | - | 1 | - | 6 | 7 |
| Lancaster | - | - | 2 | 14 | 657 | 673 |
| Liberator | - | - | - | 1 | 12 | 13 |
| Manchester | - | 5 | 3 | - | - | 8 |
| Marauder | - | - | - | 1 | 10 | 11 |
| Maryland | - | 3 | - | - | - | 3 |
| Mitchell | - | - | - | - | 14 | 14 |
| Mosquito | - | - | - | 1 | 8 | 9 |
| Mustang | - | - | - | - | 3 | 3 |
| Spitfire | - | 7 | - | 2 | 32 | 41 |
| Stirling | - | 4 | 5 | 3 | 54 | 66 |
| Tempest | - | - | - | - | 2 | 2 |
| Typhoon | - | - | - | 1 | 8 | 9 |
| Walrus | - | - | - | - | 2 | 2 |
| Wellington | - | 21 | 20 | 3 | 48 | 92 |
| Whitley | 1 | 9 | 2 | - | - | 12 |
| **TOTAL** | **6** | **83** | **51** | **43** | **1441** | **1624** |

Re the list of names below, the first three columns are simply Name, Initial, and Rank.

The fourth is Nationality, British unless otherwise stated: AUS – Australian, BEL – Belgian, CAN – Canadian, CZ- Czechoslovakian, EIR – Irish Republic, FRA – French, HOL – Dutch, MAL – Maltese, MAU – Mauritian, NR – Northern Rhodesia, NZ – New Zealand, POL – Polish, SA – South African, SR – Southern Rhodesia, USA – American.

The fifth column is the unique service number; sixth, the squadron on which he was serving, or other unit: e.g. AMES – Air Ministry Experimental Station, BD – Bomb Disposal, BSD – Base Signals Depot, GPR – Glider Pilot Regiment, LWU – Light Warning Unit.

Seventh and eighth columns are the type of aircraft in which he was flying and its unique serial number; ninth, the date on which lost (or captured); tenth, the camp(s) to which sent; eleventh, his POW number; and twelfth, the number of the *Trupp* in which he arrived at Luft 7.

In the final column 'ss' means sole survivor of the crew, the number after it signifying how many in the crew. Re a GPR man the squadron and flight to which he belonged are shown as e.g. F/16 – F Squadron, 16 Flight. Where the attribution is shown with an asterisk, e.g. D/*, the '*' indicates that the flight number is unknown. But note also, e.g., Bayford, G.W. who was attached elsewhere.

The squadron/flight details are taken from Appendix 11 of Glider Pilots at Arnhem. Anything followed by a question mark '?' is unconfirmed or doubtful.

Other, selected, initials are: DMT – Driver Motor Transport; G/G – Ground gunner; LCT – Landing Craft (Tank). n/a – not applicable; n/k – not known; S&T – Supply & Transport column; TCG/TCS – Troop Carrier Group/Squadron (USAAF).

| NAME | INIT | RANK | NAT | SERVICE NO | SQN | AIRCRAFT | NO. | DATE | CAMP(S) | NUM | TRUPP | COMMENTS |
|---|---|---|---|---|---|---|---|---|---|---|---|---|
| Abbott | JR | SGT | | 1803798 | 10 | Halifax | LV906 | 24/05/1944 | L7 | 1 | 1 | F/E. Baled out on 44th operation (2nd tour). Aircraft returned to base. |
| Abbs | KA | SGT | | 959080 | 405 | Lancaster | PB233 | 25/08/1944 | L7 | 736 | 33 | |
| Ackroyd | JO | SGT | | 1043366 | 192 | Halifax | MZ570 | 03/05/1944 | L7 | 830 | 37 | |
| Achim | J | SGT | CAN | R.1912091 | 50 | Lancaster | LL791 | 25/02/1944 | L7 | 248 | 11 | Damaged foot landing. Captured in the Pyrenees 21 April 1944. Savagely beaten by Gestapo. |
| Acworth | GF | SGT | | 1811321 | 622 | Lancaster | LL803 | 02/11/1944 | L7 | 1128 | 48 | |
| Adair | E | SGT | | 1083270 | 630 | Lancaster | JB546 | 22/05/1944 | L7 | 71 | 2 | Born in Belgium; lived in Belfast. |
| Adye | EB | F/S | | 776184 | 112 | Kittyhawk | AK988 | 10/06/1942 | L3/L7 | 1449 | 20 | |
| Agnew | WH | SGT | | 1623139 | 115 | Lancaster | PD274 | 25/08/1944 | L7 | 689 | 30 | |
| Ainley | H | SGT | | 966915 | 106 | Lancaster | NN726 | 18/12/1944 | L7 | 1311 | 57* | |
| Airey | DV | F/S | | 1285074 | 44 | Lancaster | ND976 | 21/05/1944 | L7 | 72 | 2 | |
| Aitken | PB | S/SGT | | 2879361 | GPR | Horsa | n/k | 20/09/1944 | L7 | 831 | 37 | F/16. |
| Aitken | RN | SGT | | 1509571 | 101 | Lancaster | DV267 | 19/02/1944 | L7 | 690 | 30 | Captured Antwerp 10 August 1944 - see *Just a Survivor*, p.72. |
| Alavoine | A | SGT | FRA | 94 | 346 | Halifax | NA121 | 04/11/1944 | L7 | 1216 | 55* | From Arras, Pas-de-Calais, France. |
| Alderson | R | F/S | | 2221636 | 75 | Lancaster | PB520 | 20/11/1944 | L7 | 1217 | 55* | |
| Aldred | CJ | SGT | | 1803014 | 274 | Spitfire | MH935 | 16/06/1944 | L7 | 379 | 15 | Shot down on Ramrod to Alençon. |
| Alexander | GA | SGT | | 1893475 | 630 | Lancaster | LM537 | 18/07/1944 | L7 | 541 | 27 | Captured 10 August 1944. |
| Allan | GE | SGT | NZ | NZ.404489 | 207 | Manchester | L7309 | 14/01/1942 | 7A/383/L7 | 90151 | 16 | Also POW no. 150 (Stalag 383). |
| Alldis | SC | F/S | | 1398378 | 57 | Lancaster | LL939 | 11/11/1944 | L7 | 1219 | 55* | |
| Allen | B | F/S | | 1471159 | 75 | Lancaster | ME702 | 10/06/1944 | L7 | 380 | 15 | ss7. Captured St Paire, 24 June 1944. |
| Allen | C | SGT | | 1898566 | 75 | Lancaster | PB520 | 20/11/1944 | L7 | 1218 | 55* | |
| Allen | R | SGT | | 1471159 | 12 | Lancaster | LL909 | 14/10/1944 | L7 | 1172 | 50 | |
| Allen | R | F/S | | 1563989 | 51 | Halifax | NP962 | 07/12/1944 | L7 | 1272 | 56 | Baled out over target (Osnabrück). Aircraft returned to England. |
| Ames | RL | SGT | | 1805664 | 115 | Lancaster | PD274 | 25/08/1944 | L7 | 691 | 30 | |
| Amos | DL | SGT | | 1591288 | 460 | Lancaster | PB254 | 07/10/1944 | L7 | 1013 | 40 | |
| Anderson | AP | W/O | CAN | R.116051 | 48 | Dakota | KG428 | 20/10/1944 | L7 | 1220 | 55* | Nav shot down over Arnhem on 19 September. Commissioned (J.193689). |
| Anderton | KC | F/S | | 1110429 | 106 | Lancaster | ND680 | 06/06/1944 | L7 | 288 | 12 | |
| Andrews | DE | SGT | | 1892914 | 75 | Lancaster | LL921 | 18/07/1944 | L7 | 429 | 21 | |

| | | | | | | | | | | | | |
|---|---|---|---|---|---|---|---|---|---|---|---|---|
| Andrews | DJL | SGT | | 1636735 | 467 | Lancaster | LM267 | 29/08/1944 | L7 | 728 | 31 | W/OP lost over Arnhem. |
| Andrews | F | F/S | | 1078392 | 620 | Stirling | LJ946 | 20/09/1944 | L7 | 1014 | 40 | Repatriated. |
| Annis | CW | W/O | | 1430265 | 103 | Lancaster | W4364 | 27/08/1943 | 9C/L7 | 43141 | 3 | Captured in the Pyrenees 21 April 1944. Toulouse, Fresnes, and Frankfurt prisons. |
| Ansell | J | F/S | AUS | A.410615 | 50 | Lancaster | LL791 | 25/02/1944 | L7 | 249 | 11 | |
| Applegath | TA | F/S | CAN | R.192919 | 57 | Lancaster | LM580 | 21/06/1944 | L7 | 250 | 11 | Nickname 'Honk'. |
| Appleton | AS | W/O | | 1576662 | 41 | Spitfire | RM699 | 18/12/1944 | L7 | 1312 | 57* | Shot down by flak 15kms NE Münster. |
| Appleton | F | S/SGT | | 5121712 | GPR | Horsa | n/k | 20/09/1944 | L7 | 879 | 38 | F/16. |
| Archer | JT | F/S | | 1131556 | 570 | Stirling | LJ594 | 18/09/1944 | L7 | 880 | 38 | R/G shot down over Arnhem. |
| Archer | JW | SGT | | 1595705 | 578 | Halifax | LL584 | 11/09/1944 | L7 | 881 | 38 | |
| Archer | S | SGT | | 803473 | 407 | Hudson | AM778 | 01/12/1941 | 7A/383/L7 | 90105 | 16 | See Silk and Barbed Wire, p.215. |
| Armstrong | AP | LAC | | 973077 | 235 AMES | n/a | n/a | 21/06/1942 | #/L7 | 140309 | 18 | G/G. Captured at Tobruk. |
| Arrowsmith | HL | F/S | | 571013 | 576 | Lancaster | DV365 | 21/05/1944 | L7 | 73 | 2 | |
| Arsenault | JA | SGT | CAN | R.136822 | 425 | Halifax | LW672 | 18/07/1944 | L7 | 542 | 27 | ss8. Commissioned (J.89926). |
| Ashton | SR | F/S | | 1385518 | 630 | Lancaster | LM117 | 18/07/1944 | L7 | 543 | 27 | |
| Aspinall | JSA | W/O | CAN | R.90453 | 83 | Lancaster | ND963 | 22/05/1944 | 9C/L7/383 | 53418 | 3 | Evacuated to Stalag 383. Repatriated. |
| Aspinall | TR | F/S | | 1385143 | 227 | Lancaster | LM259 | 04/12/1944 | L7 | 1273 | 56 | |
| Atkins | JE | F/S | | 1233521 | 7 | Lancaster | PA964 | 06/10/1944 | L7 | 1089 | 47 | |
| Atkinson | R | SGT | | 1692746 | 424 | Halifax | NP945 | 06/12/1944 | L7 | 1274 | 56 | |
| Auld | WJ | SGT | | 1573465 | 299 | Stirling | EF319 | 19/09/1944 | L7 | 882 | 38 | F/E lost over Arnhem. |
| Austin | AH | CPL | | 919538 | 6080 LWU | Horsa | n/k | 22/09/1944 | 11B/L7 | 117211 | 56 | Radar W/OP. Wounded at Arnhem. |
| Austin | RW | SGT | CAN | R.163476 | 424 | Halifax | LV951 | 12/08/1944 | L7 | 544 | 27 | Commissioned (J.89813). |
| Auty | S | SGT | | 4617488 | GPR | Horsa | n/k | 20/09/1944 | L7 | 969 | 39 | D/5. |
| Aveyard | A | SGT | | 1505664 | 100 | Lancaster | LM542 | 22/05/1944 | L7 | 2 | 1 | |
| Aylmer | AA | SGT | | 2210900 | 102 | Halifax | LW195 | 12/08/1944 | L7 | 545 | 27 | |
| Ayton | R | F/S | | 1394268 | 10 | Halifax | MZ312 | 20/07/1944 | L7 | 430 | 21 | |
| Backhouse | DA | F/S | | 1386717 | 226 | Mitchell | FW106 | 15/10/1944 | L7 | 1090 | 47 | All four crew POW. |
| Badham | JG | LAC | | 958550 | 235 AMES | n/a | n/a | 21/06/1942 | 11B/383/L7 | 140858 | 18 | Captured at Tobruk. Married. From Hereford. |
| Badkin | RW | SGT | | 1385831 | 130 | Spitfire | BM335 | 21/05/1944 | L7 | 74 | 2 | Shot down near Péronne on Ramrod 905. |
| Bagott | RR | F/S | | 1489917 | 7 | Lancaster | PA964 | 06/10/1944 | L7 | 1053 | 45* | |
| Bain | RG | W/O | AUS | A.412879 | 460 | Lancaster | PB152 | 19/10/1944 | L7 | 1091 | 47 | ss7. |
| Baker | C | F/S | | 1384015 | 97 | Lancaster | ND451 | 21/06/1944 | L7 | 203 | 8 | |
| Baker | G | F/S | | 1807820 | 207 | Lancaster | ND567 | 07/07/1944 | L7 | 431 | 21 | Captured Dreux 16 July 1944. |

| Surname | Initials | Rank | Country | Number | Sqn | Aircraft | Serial | Date | Code | | | Notes |
|---|---|---|---|---|---|---|---|---|---|---|---|---|
| Balchin | DH | SGT | CAN | R.218575 | 101 | Lancaster | PB258 | 12/08/1944 | L7 | 546 | 27 | Commissioned (J.89965) |
| Ball | H | SGT | | 2210336 | 12 | Lancaster | LL910 | 29/06/1944 | L7 | 345 | 14 | |
| Ballard | WJS | SGT | | 1853215 | 75 | Lancaster | ND915 | 20/07/1944 | L7 | 692 | 30 | |
| Balloch | F | W/O | NR | 776173 | 165 | Spitfire | MK855 | 07/06/1944 | 12A/L7 | 84256 | 31 | From Broken Hill, N. Rhodesia. |
| Balmanno | DT | F/S | AUS | A.426020 | 50 | Lancaster | LL791 | 25/02/1944 | L7 | 251 | 11 | Captured in the Pyrenees, 21 April 1944. Toulouse, Fresnes, and Frankfurt prisons. |
| Bamford | FB | SGT | | 1452115 | 622 | Lancaster | LM108 | 28/05/1944 | L7 | 649 | 28 | Captured 4 June 1944. Fresnes. |
| Banning | JDJ | WO1 | CAN | R.117093 | 429 | Halifax | LW128 | 07/06/1944 | L7 | 204 | 8 | Commissioned (J.87192). See Failed to Return, pp.159-60. |
| Baranowski | T | W/O | POL | 780443 | 317 | Spitfire | AD306 | 30/12/1941 | 7A/383/L7 | 90107 | 16 | Also POW no. 112 (Stalag 383). Awarded the Krzyz Walecznych on 11 November 1941. |
| Barker | L | SGT | | 1561352 | 57 | Lancaster | JA910 | 29/09/1943 | L3/L7 | 739 | 33 | Also POW no. 2173 (Stalag Luft III). |
| Barkess | P | F/S | | 1591472 | 214 | Fortress | HB763 | 25/08/1944 | 9C/L7 | 52666 | 57* | W/OP flying from Amendola, Italy, to Szombathely, Hungary. |
| Barlow | S | F/S | | 1515040 | 614 | Halifax | JP323 | 23/11/1944 | L7 | 1221 | 55* | |
| Barlow | WG | SGT | | 2206343 | 49 | Lancaster | PB231 | 18/07/1944 | L7 | 547 | 27 | Captured 10 August 1944. |
| Barnes | AT | F/S | | 1579507 | 78 | Halifax | MZ763 | 23/09/1944 | L7 | 1015 | 40 | |
| Barnes | JH | SGT | | 964553 | 467 | Lancaster | LM239 | 26/09/1944 | L7 | 970 | 39 | |
| Barnett | TE | SGT | SR | 777657 | 144 | Hampden | AD804 | 28/12/1941 | 7A/383/L7 | 90137 | 16 | Brother of WD Barnett. Also POW no. 138 (Stalag 383). From Felixburg, S. Rhodesia. |
| Barnett | WD | SGT | SR | 710152 | 44 | Lancaster | LM434 | 21/06/1944 | L7 | 289 | 12 | Brother of TE Barnett? |
| Barr | RMcP | SGT | | 1823151 | 115 | Lancaster | HK549 | 08/08/1944 | L7 | 548 | 27 | A/G. Baled out, Aircraft returned to UK. |
| Barraball | DJ | F/S | | 1315203 | 57 | Lancaster | JB364 | 02/01/1944 | 9C/L7/383 | 39978 | 3 | Seriously wounded. Evacuated to Stalag 383. ss6. Also POW no. 134 (Stalag 383). |
| Barraclough | S | SGT | | 1007462 | 57 | Wellington | Z1097 | 27/12/1941 | 7A/383/L7 | 90133 | 16 | |
| Barrows | SW | SGT | | 1580168 | 576 | Lancaster | LL799 | 28/07/1944 | L7 | 650 | 28 | |
| Barry | MR | F/S | AUS | A.419764 | 463 | Lancaster | DV229 | 10/06/1944 | L7 | 432 | 21 | Captured 7 July 1944. |
| Bartlett | DA | SGT | | 1896762 | 61 | Lancaster | EE186 | 04/07/1944 | L7 | 433 | 21 | |
| Barwise | F | F/S | | 1433271 | 247 | Typhoon | MM973 | 26/09/1944 | L7 | 1092 | 47 | AFM (1/9/44). |
| Batchelor | LG | SGT | | 1735257 | 83 | Lancaster | PB249 | 29/08/1944 | L7 | 749 | 33 | |
| Bateman | GH | F/S | | 1421197 | 83 | Lancaster | PB138 | 12/08/1944 | L7 | 549 | 27 | |
| Bates | JB | S/SGT | | 912044 | GPR | Horsa | n/k | 07/10/1944 | L7 | 1093 | 47 | G/10. |
| Bateson | GW | SGT | | 1147950 | 207 | Lancaster | LM540 | 22/05/1944 | L7 | 142 | 7 | ss7. |
| Batt | CS | F/S | | 1836548 | 420 | Halifax | MZ645 | 28/07/1944 | L7 | 501 | 23 | |

| Surname | Initials | Rank | Nat. | Service No. | Sqn | Aircraft | Serial | Date | Camp | No. | No. | Notes |
|---|---|---|---|---|---|---|---|---|---|---|---|---|
| Baugh | | SGT | | PLY/X1067 | n/a | n/a | n/a | 12/06/1944 | 9C/L7 | 53312 | 49 | Royal Marine commando. Captured near the River Orne, France. |
| Baum | FWA | SGT | | 530379 | 69 | Baltimore | AG699 | 15/06/1942 | 18A/L7 | 9179 | 57* | Pilot flying from Malta. The observer was F/S A. Baum RAAF (who was killed). |
| Bayford | GW | RSM | | 6843827 | GPR | Horsa | n/k | 17/09/1944 | L7 | 883 | 38 | 1 Wing/HQ. |
| Baylis | GS | S/SGT | | 6206242 | GPR | Horsa | n/k | 21/09/1944 | L7 | 884 | 38 | B/19. Taken ill with dysentery on train from Holland. |
| Bazinet | JO | SGT | CAN | R.200004 | 425 | Halifax | MZ674 | 14/10/1944 | L7 | 1222 | 55* | Commissioned (J.93660). |
| Beattie | JW | SGT | CAN | R.204582 | 432 | Halifax | LW616 | 12/06/1944 | L7 | 290 | 12 | Commissioned (J.90065). |
| Beattie | R | LAC | | 1108775 | 520 AMES | n/a | n/a | 21/06/1942 | 11A/L7 | 138831 | 18 | Captured at Tobruk. |
| Bedard | JRA | SGT | CAN | R.220008 | 424 | Halifax | LW460 | 18/03/1944 | 9C/L7 | 52296 | 41* | Commissioned (J.90141). |
| Bedborough | L | F/S | | 1387698 | 70 | Wellington | LN699 | 21/07/1944 | L7 | 434 | 21 | W/AG. |
| Bedford | KA | F/S | | 1399347 | 148 | Halifax | JN926 | 14/08/1944 | L7 | 651 | 28 | B/A lost on trip to Warsaw. See *Hell On Earth*, pp.16-24. |
| Beecroft | JM | F/S | AUS | A.418787 | 102 | Halifax | LW195 | 12/08/1944 | L7 | 550 | 27 | |
| Bell | JS | SGT | | 1821004 | 433 | Halifax | NP992 | 04/11/1944 | L7 | 1173 | 50 | |
| Bell | LW | SGT | | 1896269 | 115 | Lancaster | PD274 | 25/08/1944 | L7 | 693 | 30 | |
| Bell | S | SGT | | 943582 | 106 | Lancaster | ND331 | 29/08/1944 | L7 | 729 | 31 | |
| Bell | T | SGT | CAN | R.166865 | 77 | Halifax | NA524 | 16/06/1944 | L7 | 143 | 7 | |
| Bell | WL | F/S | | 969297 | 57 | Lancaster | ME787 | 23/10/1944 | L7 | 1174 | 50 | DFM (11/2/44). Baled out? Lancaster returned to UK. |
| Bellman | G | SGT | | 2216234 | 630 | Lancaster | ND685 | 06/06/1944 | L7 | 346 | 14 | |
| Belshaw | WD | SGT | | 1808996 | 619 | Lancaster | ME846 | 21/06/1944 | L7 | 381 | 15 | Captured 10 July 1944, Antwerp (?) |
| Belverstone | AWG | SGT | | 1803264 | 40 | Wellington | LP234 | 13/06/1944 | L7 | 144 | 7 | Lost on raid on Munich. |
| Bennett | AR | SGT | | 1893631 | 614 | Halifax | JP323 | 23/11/1944 | L7 | 1223 | 55* | A/G flying from Amendola, Italy, on Szombathely, Hungary. |
| Bennett | HR | SGT | | 1181163 | 603 | Spitfire | R7333 | 08/12/1941 | 7A/383/L7 | 90091 | 16 | Shot down on a sweep to Le Havre. |
| Benson | GE | SGT | | 1465626 | 630 | Lancaster | PB244 | 18/08/1944 | 12A/L7 | 86388 | 31 | 12A? |
| Benson | L | SGT | | 1806151 | 635 | Lancaster | JB728 | 15/06/1944 | L7 | 551 | 27 | Captured 26 June 1944. |
| Benson | LJ | SGT | | 1375555 | 40 | Wellington | X9824 | 10/01/1942 | 7A/383/L7 | 90141 | 16 | Also POW no. 140 (Stalag 383). |
| Bentley | E | F/S | | 2221018 | 83 | Lancaster | ND455 | 25/08/1944 | L7 | 744 | 33 | |
| Beresford | AG | F/S | | 1576595 | 50 | Lancaster | LL840 | 21/06/1944 | L7 | 291 | 12 | |

| Surname | Initials | Rank | Nat. | Service No. | Sqn | Aircraft | Serial | Date | Camp | No. 1 | No. 2 | Notes |
|---|---|---|---|---|---|---|---|---|---|---|---|---|
| Berrie | D | F/S | | 1368457 | 300 | Lancaster | ND984 | 24/07/1944 | L7 | 435 | 21 | |
| Berry | GA | SGT | | 1891300 | 61 | Lancaster | ND867 | 07/07/1944 | L7 | 436 | 21 | |
| Berry | J | CAPT | | P/100651 | n/a | n/a | n/a | 27/04/1941 | 8B/L7 | 23919 | 51 | Roman Catholic padré. |
| Berry | TGW | SGT | | 1168647 | 83 | Hampden | AE123 | 21/01/1942 | 7A/383/L7 | 90121 | 16 | On loan to 106 Squadron. Also POW no. 124 (Stalag 383). |
| Bertuch | FL | F/S | AUS | A.419250 | 460 | Lancaster | LL907 | 07/07/1944 | L7 | 437 | 21 | |
| Bestall | SS | S/SGT | EIR | 7022602 | GPR | Horsa | n/k | 22/09/1944 | L7 | 1054 | 45* | D/*. From Dublin. |
| Bestel | EGR | SGT | CAN | R.70458 | 207 | Manchester | L7309 | 14/01/1942 | 7A/383/L7 | 90149 | 16 | Also POW no. 148 (Stalag 383). |
| Bethel | RH | W/O | AUS | A.412476 | 97 | Lancaster | ND764 | 09/06/1944 | L7 | 145 | 7 | Robert Henderson Bethel. |
| Bilinski | B | SGT | POL | 783406 | 300 | Wellington | R1705 | 07/11/1941 | 8B/L7/L6 | 24513 | 20 | Moved to Luft 6 on 18 August 1944. 8B? |
| Billing | AW | SGT | | 1355714 | 178 | Liberator | EW277 | 13/06/1944 | L7 | 146 | 7 | A/G flying from Foggia No. 1, Celone, Italy. |
| Birch | DH | LAC | | 1470344 | 2788 | n/a | n/a | 25/08/1944 | L7 | 885 | 38 | G/G. RAF Regiment. Captured at Valence after the invasion of the south of France. |
| Bird | BF | F/S | | 1385842 | 166 | Lancaster | ND956 | 21/05/1944 | L7 | 3 | 1 | At 18A first? |
| Bird | FW | F/S | | 1615841 | 158 | Halifax | LW635 | 02/06/1944 | L7 | 106 | 3 | |
| Birds | C | SGT | | 1736716 | 10 | Halifax | MZ312 | 20/07/1944 | L7 | 438 | 21 | |
| Birkett | NT | SGT | | 987156 | 44 | Lancaster | L7548 | 17/04/1942 | 7A/L7 | 138900 | 51 | Captured 1 May 1942. Interned Vichy France and POW in Italy. |
| Birtles | SG | W/O | AUS | A.418049 | 454 | Baltimore | FW701 | 23/08/1944 | 9C/L7 | 52731 | 57* | Wounded in left elbow when shot down by flak. |
| Bishop | F | W/O | | 1378127 | 76 | Halifax | MZ623 | 24/05/1944 | L7 | 4 | 1 | |
| Blackford | DA | W/O | | 1332435 | 10 | Halifax | LV906 | 24/05/1944 | L7 | 6 | 1 | Commissioned 25 July 1944 (177012) wef 22 May 1944. F/O 15 Dec 1944. |
| Blake | WA | F/S | | 917122 | 76 | Halifax | LK795 | 30/03/1944 | L7 | 502 | 23 | Fractured pelvis after falling out of a pine tree. |
| Bland | RW | SGT | | 1892064 | 100 | Lancaster | LM542 | 22/05/1944 | L7 | 5 | 1 | |
| Blattman | LJ | W/O | AUS | A.412369 | 148 | Halifax | JP179 | 04/07/1944 | L7 | 552 | 27 | On SOE drop to Yugoslavia. Landed in Zambor railway station. |
| Blundell | L | SGT | | 2210896 | 578 | Halifax | NA568 | 11/09/1944 | L7 | 763 | 34 | |
| Blunt | LJ | SGT | | 1581776 | 178 | Liberator | KG933 | 18/08/1944 | L7 | 652 | 28 | F/E on trip to Warsaw. Same crew as F/L A.H. Hammet RAAF. |
| Board | WAH | W/O | AUS | A.420855 | 37 | Wellington | LP547 | 22/11/1944 | L7 | 1224 | 55* | W/OP, shot down on Szombathely raid, Hungary. |
| Boddy | W | SGT | | 1577663 | 78 | Halifax | JN974 | 20/12/1943 | 4B/L7 | 269749 | 31 | |
| Boffin | CA | F/S | | 1324613 | 227 | Beaufighter | EL475 | 14/08/1944 | L7 | 730 | 31 | Nav. Ditched in the Adriatic off Yugoslavia. |
| Bommel | DN | SGT | | 1892627 | 299 | Stirling | LK241 | 28/11/1944 | L7 | 1275 | 56 | F/E shot down on SOE op to Norway. |

| Name | Initials | Rank | Nat | Service No. | Unit | Aircraft | Serial | Date | Camp | No. | Ref | Notes |
|---|---|---|---|---|---|---|---|---|---|---|---|---|
| Bond | PJ | SGT | | 14417457 | GPR | Horsa | n/k | 20/09/1944 | L7 | 886 | 38 | F/15. |
| Bonner | IK | SGT | | 14423232 | GPR | Horsa | n/k | 21/09/1944 | L7 | 887 | 38 | D/*. |
| Bonnet | CB | F/S | FRA | 132 | n/k | n/k | n/k | 11/07/1944 | L7 | 426 | 15* | A/G. From Dortan, Ain, France. |
| Boswell | C | SGT | | 10539450 | GPR | Horsa | n/k | 20/09/1944 | L7 | 888 | 38 | D/*. |
| Bott | RL | SGT | | 930272 | 420 | Hampden | AT130 | 21/01/1942 | 7A/383/L7 | 90117 | 16 | Also POW no. 120 (Stalag 383). |
| Bourdat | WL | WO1 | CAN | R.119837 | 420 | Halifax | LW420 | 25/02/1944 | 9C/L7 | 53120 | 57* | Evacuated to Stalag 383. |
| Bourne | HJ | F/S | | 1586150 | 514 | Lancaster | DS818 | 12/06/1944 | L7 | 205 | 8 | |
| Bovill | JM | F/S | AUS | A.428015 | 115 | Lancaster | NF960 | 28/10/1944 | L7 | 1225 | 55* | |
| Bowden | SK | SGT | | 71237 | GPR | Horsa | n/k | 20/09/1944 | L7 | 889 | 38 | F/16. |
| Bower | GE | SGT | | 2203720 | 218 | Lancaster | PD252 | 12/08/1944 | L7 | 553 | 27 | |
| Bowker | C | SGT | | 2211810 | 138 | Stirling | LK131 | 31/08/1944 | L7 | 764 | 34 | ss8. |
| Bowlby | TL | SGT | CAN | R.131006 | 620 | Stirling | BF576 | 27/08/1943 | 9C/L7 | 53200 | 17 | |
| Bowmaster | HF | W/O | CAN | R.126237 | 98 | Mitchell | FW194 | 28/09/1944 | 11B/L7 | 118006 | 51 | W/AG ss4. Shot down 25 September. From Stalag 8C. 11B? Commissioned (J.92229). |
| Bown | LG | SGT | | 860460 | 44 | Lancaster | PB192 | 04/11/1944 | L7 | 1226 | 55* | |
| Boyd | JC | F/S | NZ | NZ.424966 | 76 | Halifax | DK247 | 03/10/1943 | L6/L7 | 3102 | 22 | |
| Boyes | JA | SGT | | 1621546 | 51 | Halifax | MZ349 | 12/08/1944 | L7 | 554 | 27 | |
| Boynton | TS | F/S | | 1622415 | 103 | Lancaster | ME649 | 12/12/1944 | L7 | 1313 | 57* | |
| Bracegirdle | AE | F/S | | 1084585 | 44 | Lancaster | NE138 | 21/06/1944 | L7 | 206 | 8 | Aircraft returned to UK. DFM (25/5/46). See No Time For Fear, pp.183-4. |
| Bradbury | JA | SGT | | 14547304 | GPR | Horsa | n/k | 20/09/1944 | L7 | 890 | 38 | D/22. |
| Bradley | JW | SGT | CAN | R.196716 | 625 | Lancaster | LM427 | 31/05/1944 | L7 | 107 | 3 | |
| Bragg | DA | SGT | | 1864528 | 61 | Lancaster | PB436 | 29/08/1944 | L7 | 731 | 31 | |
| Bramble | RE | F/S | | 1397119 | 142 | Wellington | LN700 | 14/06/1944 | L7 | 147 | 7 | Nav. |
| Branch | HJ | SGT | CAN | R.194624 | 424 | Halifax | LV910 | 28/06/1944 | L7 | 555 | 27 | Commissioned (J.90144). |
| Brant | KR | W/O | | 1575679 | 349 | Spitfire | PT395 | 06/10/1944 | L7 | 1227 | 55 | Caught after failed Rhine crossing on 14 October. |
| Breheny | RTH | W/O | AUS | A.404957 | 145 | Spitfire | ER199 | 27/03/1943 | L3/L7 | 968 | 20 | Shot down near Gabes, Western Desert. |
| Brett | CG | SGT | | 580758 | 37 | Wellington | T1387 | 01/041941 | 11A/L7 | 140848 | 18 | Nav. Reported missing in newspapers on 24 April 1941. |
| Brett | PB | F/S | AUS | A.434238 | 462 | Halifax | LL610 | 02/11/1944 | L7 | 1129 | 48 | |
| Brewer | RH | SGT | | 1353143 | 102 | Halifax | LL552 | 24/07/1944 | L7 | 556 | 27 | ss7. |
| Brice | AR | SGT | | 1577795 | 158 | Halifax | LW720 | 24/05/1944 | L7 | 7 | 1 | |

| | | | | | | | | | | | | |
|---|---|---|---|---|---|---|---|---|---|---|---|---|
| Brickenden | AW | SGT | CAN | R.160205 | 625 | Lancaster | LM513 | 21/05/1944 | L7 | 439 | 21 | Betrayed Antwerp 25 July 1944. Later commissioned (J96549). |
| Bridgeman | RD | F/S | | 1587436 | 57 | Lancaster | ME864 | 28/07/1944 | L7 | 694 | 30 | Ground Radar OP. Captured at Arnhem. |
| Britland | S | LAC | | 1750457 | 634LWU | Horsa | n/k | 29/08/1944 | L7 | 1055 | 45* | W/AG lost on Milan raid. Crashed San Bassano, Italy after collision with Wellington MF120, 142 Squadron. |
| Broad | JD | W/O | | 903310 | 70 | Wellington | LN806 | 14/07/1944 | L7 | 383 | 15 | |
| Broadley | DS | S/SGT | | 1468299 | GPR | Horsa | n/k | 21/09/1944 | 12A/L7 | 075475 | 47 | G/10. 21 September 1944? |
| Broadribb | PF | SGT | | 1399362 | 90 | Stirling | EF294 | 02/06/1944 | L7 | 440 | 21 | Seriously wounded. Captured 5 June 1944. In hospital at Amiens and St Gilles. |
| Broddle | A | SGT | | 1591363 | 640 | Halifax | MZ855 | 12/08/1944 | L7 | 557 | 27 | Nav lost over Arnhem. |
| Bromige | DW | W/O | | 1332853 | 512 | Dakota | KG418 | 20/09/1944 | 11B/L7 | 118153 | 51 | |
| Brook | JH | F/S | | 1575148 | 617 | Lancaster | DV403 | 24/06/1944 | L7 | 347 | 14 | |
| Brookes | CH | F/S | | 1552091 | 158 | Halifax | MZ945 | 25/10/1944 | L7 | 1094 | 47 | |
| Brooks | CJ | SGT | | 7590893 | GPR | Horsa | n/k | 19/09/1944 | L7 | 891 | 38 | D/*. |
| Brooks | WA | F/S | | 1318320 | 10 | Halifax | LV906 | 24/05/1944 | L7 | 8 | 1 | Captured 28 May 1944. Brookes? |
| Brosnahan | JJ | W/O | | 1313253 | 44 | Lancaster | LM171 | 28/07/1944 | L7 | 503 | 23 | |
| Brough | JE | F/S | | 1545826 | 106 | Lancaster | PB359 | 19/09/1944 | L7 | 971 | 39 | |
| Brown | DE | F/S | AUS | A.437332 | 463 | Lancaster | LM375 | 06/10/1944 | L7 | 1016 | 40 | |
| Brown | DWL | SGT | CAN | R.186516 | 138 | Halifax | LL252 | 31/03/1944 | L7 | 148 | 7 | Captured 19 April 1944. Commissioned (J.86785). |
| Brown | FJ | F/S | AUS | A.421787 | 454 | Baltimore | FW300 | 03/03/1944 | 9C/L7 | 43306 | 37* | Lost over Aegean Sea. Six days in dinghy. W/O 5 September 1944. |
| Brown | FM | SGT | CAN | R.169529 | 431 | Halifax | MZ597 | 28/07/1944 | L7 | 441 | 21 | Commissioned (J.92612). |
| Brown | FW | SGT | | 1350401 | 514 | Lancaster | LL739 | 11/05/1944 | L7 | 207 | 8 | Captured 9 June 1944. Betrayed to Antwerp Gestapo by René van Muylem. |
| Brown | GGC | SGT | CAN | R.216314 | 427 | Halifax | LW166 | 04/07/1944 | L7 | 348 | 14 | Commissioned (J.90066). |
| Brown | KH | W/O | | 1027464 | 247 | Typhoon | EK223 | 13/10/1944 | L7 | 1095 | 47 | Shot down by flak. |
| Brown | N | SGT | | 1894304 | 10 | Halifax | MZ773 | 12/08/1944 | L7 | 558 | 27 | |
| Brown | PH | F/S | | 1451938 | 139 | Mosquito | DZ519 | 20/10/1943 | L7 | 75 | 2 | Captured in Pyrenees 6 February 1944. In prisons at Toulouse, Fresnes, Wiesbaden. |
| Brown | RA | SGT | AUS | A.401812 | 460 | Lancaster | W4308 | 23/01/1943 | 9C/L7 | 42732 | 3 | Broke ankle, fractured fibula and tibia. Repatriated. |
| Brown | RL | SGT | CAN | R.197323 | 166 | Lancaster | DV406 | 30/01/1944 | 9C/L7 | 39980 | 3 | 9C ? |

| Surname | Initials | Rank | Country | Service No. | Sqn | Aircraft | Serial | Date | Code | No. 1 | No. 2 | Notes |
|---|---|---|---|---|---|---|---|---|---|---|---|---|
| Browne | EW | S/SGT | | 5730039 | GPR | Horsa | n/k | 20/09/1944 | L7 | 1056 | 45* | G/9. |
| Brownhall | EE | SGT | | 1601501 | 467 | Lancaster | PB234 | 18/07/1944 | 9C/L7 | 53360 | 31 | Broke collar-bone. See Massacre over the Marne. |
| Bruce | N | SGT | CAN | R.136423 | 148 | Halifax | BB431 | 28/04/1944 | #/L7 | 3798 | 3 | DFM (24/3/44). Commissioned (J.89122, 23/3/44). |
| Brulinski | W | F/S | POL | 704290 | 300 | Lancaster | NF959 | 14/10/1944 | L7 | 1057 | 45* | ss7. |
| Brummell | TE | F/S | AUS | A.429213 | 467 | Lancaster | LM205 | 29/06/1944 | L7 | 382 | 15 | |
| Bruneau | H | F/S | FRA | 13161 | GrB1 | Blenheim | V6142 | 28/11/1941 | 7A/383/L7 | 90095 | 16 | GrB1 Lorraine Squadron. From Cavaillon, Vaucluse, France. |
| Bryce | C | S/SGT | | 3254730 | GPR | Horsa | n/k | 19/09/1944 | L7 | 892 | 38 | E/*. |
| Brydon | H | SGT | | 1035149 | 462 | Halifax | LL610 | 02/11/1944 | L7 | 1130 | 48 | |
| Buchanan | AS | SGT | | 1822721 | 44 | Lancaster | LM171 | 28/07/1944 | L7 | 504 | 23 | |
| Buck | K | SGT | | 1867845 | 106 | Lancaster | LM641 | 07/08/1944 | #/L7 | 70446 | 41* | |
| Budd | RA | SGT | | 1626052 | 83 | Lancaster | PB345 | 25/08/1944 | L7 | 695 | 30 | |
| Bulmer | JH | F/S | | 1474195 | 77 | Halifax | MZ698 | 16/06/1944 | L7 | 349 | 14 | |
| Burden | HJ | SGT | | 1581371 | 462 | Halifax | LL610 | 02/11/1944 | L7 | 1131 | 48 | |
| Burford | G | S/SGT | USA | 33629460 | 409BS | B-24 | 42-100416 | 18/09/1944 | 11B/L7 | 117997 | 51 | USAAF. Right waist gunner of Baggy Maggy. Posted to another camp. |
| Burgess | AS | WO1 | CAN | R.134254 | 233 | Dakota | KG586 | 21/09/1944 | L7 | 1017 | 40 | W/OP. |
| Burgess | J | F/S | NZ | NZ.4211088 | 75 | Lancaster | ME752 | 20/07/1944 | L7 | 442 | 21 | |
| Burgess | LG | CPL | | 321601 | n/a | n/a | n/a | n/k | L7 | 149 | 7 | Army? Posted to another camp. |
| Burgess | WJH | F/S | | 1339854 | 7 | Lancaster | PA964 | 06/10/1944 | L7 | 1058 | 45* | |
| Burke | E | F/S | AUS | A.426527 | 463 | Lancaster | LM589 | 24/07/1944 | L7 | 559 | 27 | |
| Burleigh | SC | F/S | | 1711577 | 83 | Lancaster | PB188 | 11/11/1944 | L7 | 1228 | 55* | DFM (12/2/46). |
| Burn | AE | SGT | | 1128244 | 75 | Lancaster | LL921 | 18/07/1944 | L7 | 443 | 21 | |
| Burnett | T | SGT | | 1823259 | 75 | Lancaster | LM104 | 06/10/1944 | L7 | 1059 | 45* | |
| Burns | DR | F/S | | 1525609 | 106 | Lancaster | ND853 | 26/04/1944 | 9C/L7 | 53145 | 17 | Three months in Obermassfeld hospital. |
| Burns | DR | F/S | | 545186 | 514 | Lancaster | DS787 | 11/09/1944 | L7 | 893 | 38 | |
| Burns | JD | WO2 | CAN | R.129859 | 424 | Halifax | LV997 | 28/07/1944 | L7 | 505 | 23 | |
| Burns | JE | SGT | | 567466 | 38 | Wellington | HZ866 | 01/03/1944 | L7 | 560 | 27 | Pilot. JE? |
| Burr | RPV | SGT | | 1337442 | 57 | Lancaster | LM579 | 25/08/1944 | L7 | 765 | 34 | |
| Buswell | EJ | W/O | | 1165208 | 7 | Lancaster | PA964 | 06/10/1944 | L7 | 1175 | 50 | |
| Butcher | JJ | W/O | | 1175415 | 295 | Stirling | LK203 | 30/11/1944 | L7 | 1314 | 57* | Nav. Baled out without orders. Aircraft returned to base. |

| Name | Init | Rank | Nat | Service No | Unit | Aircraft | Serial | Date | Camp | No | No | Notes |
|---|---|---|---|---|---|---|---|---|---|---|---|---|
| Butkewitz | LJ | T/SGT | USA | 10601605 | 432 | Halifax | NP706 | 18/07/1944 | #L7 | 40201 | | American in RCAF. On thirtieth operation. From Naperville, Illinois, USA. |
| Butler | J | LAC | | 1461098 | 2788 | n/a | n/a | 25/08/1944 | L7 | 832 | 37 | G/G. RAF Regiment. Captured at Valence after the invasion of the south of France. |
| Buxey | WT | SGT | | 1876657 | GPR | Horsa | n/k | 22/09/1944 | L7 | 972 | 39 | G/10. On first lift to Arnhem. |
| Byrne | CT | F/S | EIR | 610794 | 190 | Stirling | LJ939 | 19/09/1944 | 11B/L7 | 118691 | 56 | F/E. Broke a leg in landing. Captured 21 September 1944. 11B? From Crumlin, Dublin. |
| Bzowy | MA | WO2 | CAN | R.186848 | 426 | Halifax | NA510 | 12/06/1944 | L7 | 444 | 21 | Commissioned (J.86996). No. R.88848? |
| Cakebread | JA | SGT | | 1801960 | 432 | Halifax | LW616 | 12/06/1944 | L7 | 208 | 8 | |
| Calder | RR | S/SGT | CAN | 3859441 | GPR | Horsa | n/k | 21/09/1944 | L7 | 894 | 38 | E/*. |
| Callaghan | PA | WO2 | CAN | R.174480 | 432 | Halifax | NP695 | 06/12/1944 | L7 | 1315 | 57* | |
| Callingham | J | F/S | CAN | R.156781 | 578 | Halifax | NA568 | 11/09/1944 | L7 | 766 | 34 | Commissioned (J.90377). |
| Camenzuli | AMP | F/S | MAL. | 1818930 | 433 | Halifax | HX291 | 22/04/1944 | L7 | 561 | 27 | Captured Antwerp 3 August 1944. From Malta. |
| Cameron | J | S/SGT | | 7341479 | RAMC | n/a | n/a | n/k | 344/L7/383 | 14874 | 41* | Evacuated to Stalag 383. |
| Campbell | A | S/SGT | | 2694009 | GPR | Horsa | n/k | 18/09/1944 | L7 | 895 | 38 | A/* |
| Campbell | HT | F/S | CAN | R.252789 | 426 | Halifax | LW209 | 17/12/1944 | L7 | 1360 | 57+ | Probably at Luft 7 soon after Trupp 57. |
| Campbell | J | SGT | | 1895819 | 640 | Halifax | MZ579 | 24/05/1944 | L7 | 108 | 3 | |
| Campbell | KW | F/S | AUS | A.423220 | 466 | Halifax | LV833 | 24/07/1944 | L7 | 445 | 21 | On 33rd operation. ss8. Captured after four days. |
| Cancea | SJW | SGT | CAN | 1475709 | 76 | Halifax | LK949 | 03/11/1943 | 4B/L7 | 263400 | 31 | Baled out – aircraft flew back to UK. |
| Capar | NC | F/S | CAN | R.172692 | 50 | Lancaster | PA994 | 29/08/1944 | L7 | 767 | 34 | ss7 |
| Carey | FJ | F/S | | 900040 | 514 | Lancaster | LL727 | 07/06/1944 | L7 | 384 | 15 | With French Resistance until captured 6 July 1944 |
| Carmichael | DA | SGT | NZ | NZ.407980 | 40 | Wellington | HX425 | 16/08/1942 | #L7 | 126549 | 3 | Lost on raid on Tobruk. Hospital. |
| Carragher | WAJ | WO1 | CAN | R.111693 | 183 | Typhoon | JP789 | 17/08/1944 | #L7 | 7078 | 34 | |
| Carrier | JARM | F/S | CAN | R.180936 | 425 | Halifax | LW379 | 01/11/1944 | L7 | 1176 | 50 | Commissioned (J.92917). |
| Carter | JE | F/S | AUS | A.422413 | 21SAAF | Marauder | HD591 | 13/09/1943 | L7 | 833 | 37 | Co-pilot. Commissioned whilst POW. |
| Carter | R | SGT | | 1620578 | 44 | Lancaster | ND517 | 18/07/1944 | L7 | 506 | 23 | |
| Cartwright | GH | F/S | | 1448747 | 37 | Wellington | HF524 | 17/06/1944 | L7 | 350 | 14 | |
| Cartwright | RR | F/S | | 1525358 | 614 | Halifax | JP323 | 22/11/1944 | L7 | 1229 | 55* | B/A flying from Amendola, Italy, on Szombathely, Hungary. |
| Cassell | DB | SGT | | 1473875 | 90 | Lancaster | LM111 | 07/08/1944 | 12A/L7 | 86320 | 31 | |
| Cassidy | C | SGT | | 2208871 | 76 | Halifax | MZ623 | 24/05/1944 | L7 | 9 | 1 | |
| Cermolacce | M | S/C | FRA | 36059 | 341 | Spitfire | PL424 | 14/08/1944 | 12A/L7 | 86288 | 34 | Escaped from France to Spain in 1940. From Marseille, France. |

| Surname | Initials | Rank | Nat. | Service No. | Sqn | Aircraft | Serial | Date | Camp | POW No. | Ref | Notes |
|---|---|---|---|---|---|---|---|---|---|---|---|---|
| Chambers | H | SGT | | 1823907 | 158 | Halifax | MZ734 | 25/10/1944 | L7 | 1096 | 47 | Escaped on march, captured, escaped. To UK via Odessa and Middle East, on 31 March 1945 |
| Chambers | SJ | SGT | | 2209363 | 433 | Halifax | HX353 | 04/07/1944 | L7 | 385 | 15 | |
| Chandler | WP | WO2 | CAN | R.160751 | 166 | Lancaster | NE114 | 22/05/1944 | L7 | 10 | 1 | |
| Chaplin | FJ | F/S | | 1601653 | 76 | Halifax | LW648 | 04/11/1944 | L7 | 1177 | 50 | |
| Chapman | CE | F/S | | 1801069 | 207 | Lancaster | LL973 | 21/06/1944 | L7 | 252 | 11 | |
| Chapman | K | SGT | | 1581545 | 61 | Lancaster | LM518 | 24/06/1944 | L7 | 253 | 11 | ss7. To UK via Odessa and Middle East. |
| Chapman | RJ | F/S | AUS | A.421177 | 622 | Lancaster | LM138 | 23/06/1944 | L7 | 254 | 11 | |
| Chapman | W | SGT | | 1498555 | 102 | Halifax | MZ642 | 16/06/1944 | L7 | 209 | 8 | |
| Chesters | GW | F/S | | 636624 | 83 | Lancaster | PB249 | 29/08/1944 | L7 | 768 | 34 | |
| Chevalier | J | S/C | FRA | C.15569 | 347 | Halifax | NR153 | 06/12/1944 | L7 | 1317 | 57* | Escaped during evacuation. To UK via Odessa and Middle East. |
| Chiasson | JA | F/S | CAN | R.88187 | 408 | Halifax | NP781 | 24/12/1944 | L7 | 1318 | 57* | |
| Christensen | HP | SGT | | 1819753 | 462 | Halifax | LL610 | 02/11/1944 | L7 | 1132 | 48 | |
| Christianson | DR | SGT | CAN | H/440619 | n/a | Horsa | n/k | 11/06/1944 | L7 | 446 | 21 | Canadian Army (1st Canadian Paras). Horsa? |
| Christie | JH | F/S | CAN | R.251732 | 433 | Halifax | NP992 | 04/11/1944 | L7 | 1178 | 50 | |
| Christie | WJ | SGT | | 651450 | 158 | Halifax | HX320 | 24/05/1944 | L7 | 351 | 14 | Betrayed Antwerp 27 June 1944. |
| Christison | JV | AC2 | | 1557381 | 235AMES | n/a | n/a | 21/06/1942 | 11B/L7 | 139510 | 18 | G/G. Captured at Tobruk. POW no.135910? |
| Churchyard | CK | F/S | | 1592517 | 106 | Lancaster | ND339 | 05/06/1944 | 13D/L3/L7 | 15186 | 41* | British Army (1st Gordon Highlanders). |
| Clark | AG | CQMS | | 2884663 | n/a | n/a | n/a | 18/06/1944 | L7 | 150 | 7 | |
| Clark | L | SGT | | 1805832 | 50 | Lancaster | PD294 | 11/09/1944 | L7 | 769 | 34 | Shot down by flak. |
| Clark | P | SGT | | 1801114 | 73 | Spitfire | MJ116 | 18/09/1944 | L7 | 834 | 37 | Rest of crew evaded. |
| Clark | R | SGT | | 1523869 | 138 | Halifax | LL183 | 09/05/1944 | L7 | 109 | 3 | |
| Clark | RT | W/O | NZ | NZ.422369 | 75 | Lancaster | ND802 | 27/05/1944 | L7 | 770 | 34 | Captured Antwerp 23 August 1944. |
| Clarke | AW | F/S | | 1447838 | 271 | Dakota | KG444 | 21/09/1944 | L7 | 973 | 39 | Lost over Arnhem. Co-pilot to Jimmy Edwards. |
| Clarke | WK | SGT | CAN | R.252617 | 405 | Lancaster | PA981 | 12/09/1944 | L7 | 771 | 34 | |
| Claydon | GR | W/O | | 1338856 | 504 | Spitfire | PL385 | 07/08/1944 | L7 | 733 | 31 | Shot down on Ramrod 1175. To UK via Odessa and Middle East. |
| Claydon | LW | SGT | | 1395170 | 571 | Mosquito | MM113 | 06/10/1944 | L7 | 1018 | 40 | |
| Cleary | JP | F/S | | 1454243 | 115 | Lancaster | DS664 | 24/03/1944 | L7 | 653 | 28 | Wounded. Repatriated 6 January 1945. |
| Cleeve | AWJ | SGT | | 1181633 | 101 | Wellington | R3295 | 30/11/1941 | 7A/383/L7 | 90080 | 16 | Also POW no. 92 (Stalag 383). |
| Clement | WJ | CPL | | 1276315 | 2788 | n/a | n/a | 25/08/1944 | L7 | 835 | 37 | G/G. RAF Regiment. Captured at Valence after the invasion of the south of France. |

| Surname | Initials | Rank | Nat. | Service No. | Sqn | Aircraft | Serial | Date | Camp | No. | No. | Notes |
|---|---|---|---|---|---|---|---|---|---|---|---|---|
| Clements | RC | F/S | | 1402056 | 102 | Halifax | LW168 | 24/12/1944 | L7 | 1319 | 57* | B/19. Escaped during the evacuation. Back to UK via Odessa. |
| Clenaghan | HC | S/SGT | | 133139 | GPR | Horsa | n/k | 21/09/1944 | L7 | 974 | 39 | |
| Cliff | W | F/S | | 1503275 | 76 | Halifax | MZ623 | 24/05/1944 | L7 | 11 | 1 | |
| Clifford | JA | F/S | | 1494676 | 218 | Lancaster | PD374 | 08/11/1944 | L7 | 1179 | 50 | |
| Clinton | EO | SGT | CAN | R.220110 | 429 | Halifax | MZ302 | 28/06/1944 | L7 | 292 | 12 | Ran out of fuel on delivery flight UK to Malta. |
| Cloarec | J | ADJ | FRA | 1255 | 346 | Halifax | NA549 | 04/11/1944 | L7 | 1180 | 50 | W/AG. Lost on delivery flight to Middle East. |
| Cloran | TH | SGT | | 144776 | 622 | Lancaster | LL782 | 31/05/1944 | L7 | 151 | 7 | F/16 |
| Cluley | GH | SGT | | 755796 | 114 | Blenheim | T2058 | 26/08/1940 | 11A/L7 | 138568 | 18 | Captured 31 May 1944. In Fresnes prison with Hodgson & Teague. |
| Cobb | FK | W/O | | 911174 | 3RAAF | Maryland | AH281 | 08/05/1941 | 18D/7A/383/L7 | 8183 | 16 | |
| Cobbold | GA | S/SGT | | 2575249 | GPR | Horsa | n/k | 20/09/1944 | L7 | 975 | 39 | |
| Cochrane | AP | SGT | | 1052620 | 90 | Stirling | EF509 | 09/05/1944 | L7 | 210 | 8 | |
| Coedy | HJW | WO1 | CAN | R.131043 | 75 | Lancaster | ND752 | 20/07/1944 | L7 | 562 | 27 | |
| Cohen | S | F/S | NZ | NZ.421023 | 622 | Lancaster | LM108 | 28/05/1944 | 9C/L7 | 53400 | 31 | |
| Cole | AJ | F/S | | 1579246 | 44 | Lancaster | ND517 | 18/07/1944 | L7 | 563 | 27 | |
| Cole | RC | F/S | | 1388659 | 274 | Tempest | EJ632 | 07/11/1944 | L7 | 1230 | 55* | Shot down by FW190 north of Münster. |
| Coleman | EB | W/O | | 655128 | 640 | Halifax | LW464 | 24/07/1944 | L7 | 507 | 23 | |
| Colledge | VG | F/S | AUS | A.426826 | 158 | Halifax | HX334 | 12/05/1944 | L7 | 12 | 1 | |
| Collings | BL | F/S | AUS | A.430853 | 463 | Lancaster | PD338 | 02/11/1944 | L7 | 1181 | 50 | |
| Collingwood | CJ | F/S | | 1115393 | 61 | Lancaster | LM310 | 24/02/1944 | 9C/L7 | 52294 | 32 | Wounded. Arrived at L7 mid September 1944. DFM (21/12/45). |
| Collingwood | F | SGT | | 1623947 | 514 | Lancaster | LL727 | 07/06/1944 | 12A/L7 | 80059 | 9 | 12A? |
| Collins | DJ | LAC | | 1176828 | 211GRP | n/a | n/a | 21/06/1942 | 11B/L7 | 140041 | 18 | DMT, 211 Group. Captured at Tobruk. |
| Collins | JB | CAPT | | 111558 | n/a | n/a | n/a | 21/06/1942 | 5A/17A/L7 | 3014 | 46 | British Army (Chaplain 4th Class). Captured at Tobruk. MID. |
| Collins | L | F/S | | 1375761 | 102 | Halifax | MZ649 | 27/05/1944 | L7 | 386 | 15 | Captured Antwerp 10 July 1944. Commissioned (177370) 25 July 1944. |
| Collins | MWG | F/S | | 1397319 | 622 | Lancaster | LM283 | 19/10/1944 | L7 | 1133 | 48 | Beaten by civilians on landing. Testified at Dulag Luft Trial. Commissioned (185884). |
| Collins | T | SGT | | 6153130 | GPR | Horsa | n/k | 02/07/1944 | 12A/L7 | 83906 | 34 | A/* is a guess. |
| Collis | MA | SGT | | 1324325 | 300 | Lancaster | ND984 | 24/07/1944 | L7 | 447 | 21 | |
| Columbus | GP | SGT | CAN | R.156898 | 428 | Halifax | LK931 | 04/10/1943 | L7 | 352 | 14 | Fought with French Maquis. Captured 2 July 1944. |

| Surname | Initials | Rank | | Number | Sqn | Aircraft | Serial | Date | | | | Notes |
|---|---|---|---|---|---|---|---|---|---|---|---|---|
| Cometti | KA | SGT | NZ | NZ.402225 | 12 | Wellington | W5552 | 12/10/1941 | 8B/L7 | 18670 | 16 | 8B? |
| Comfort | WS | F/S | | 1342606 | 111 | Spitfire | MJ189 | 04/06/1944 | L7 | 152 | 7 | Captured Antwerp 7 August 1944. |
| Connell | V | F/S | AUS | A.424151 | 75 | Lancaster | ND752 | 20/07/1944 | L7 | 696 | 30 | DFM (22/10/40). WOP/AG. Ran out of fuel on delivery flight to Malta. |
| Conner | FR | SGT | | 625341 | 57 | Blenheim | T2176 | 27/09/1940 | 11A/L7 | 138878 | 18 | |
| Connor | AE | SGT | | 970956 | 35 | Halifax | L9582 | 30/11/1941 | 7A/383/L7 | 90087 | 16 | Also POW no. 97 (Stalag 383). |
| Conroy | J | SGT | | 1489747 | 295 | Stirling | LK115 | 21/09/1944 | L7 | 976 | 39 | F/E lost over Arnhem. |
| Conway | WJ | F/S | AUS | A.424978 | 467 | Lancaster | LM450 | 24/06/1944 | L7 | 293 | 12 | Pilot lost on raid to Khalkis Harbour, Greece. |
| Cook | LW | W/O | | 1314478 | 38 | Wellington | JB296 | 02/06/1944 | L7 | 110 | 3 | |
| Cooke | TA | SGT | | 1375885 | 101 | Wellington | R3295 | 30/11/1941 | 7A/383/L7 | 90075 | 16 | Also POW no. 87 (Stalag 383). |
| Coope | A | SGT | | 1815629 | 102 | Halifax | LW168 | 24/12/1944 | L7 | 1320 | 57* | |
| Cooper | A | F/S | | 1398308 | 51 | Halifax | MZ916 | 11/09/1944 | L7 | 836 | 37 | |
| Cooper | DB | F/S | SR | 778207 | 10 | Halifax | HX326 | 26/04/1944 | L7 | 153 | 7 | Captured 15 June 1944 by German patrol looking for saboteurs. |
| Cooper | L | SGT | | 1585673 | 75 | Lancaster | LM104 | 06/10/1944 | L7 | 1060 | 45* | |
| Cooper | PG | SGT | | 1086096 | 514 | Lancaster | DS818 | 12/06/1944 | L7 | 211 | 8 | |
| Cooper | RGS | F/S | AUS | A.434622 | 463 | Lancaster | NF977 | 23/10/1944 | L7 | 1097 | 47 | |
| Cooper | VV | SGT | | 1111806 | 83 | Hampden | AE123 | 21/01/1942 | 7A/383/L7 | 90154 | 16 | On loan to 106 Squadron. Also POW no. 153 (Stalag 383). Vernon Victor Cooper. |
| Cope | DE | F/S | | 1501874 | 83 | Lancaster | ND963 | 22/05/1944 | L7 | 13 | 1 | |
| Coppack | PM | S/SGT | | 937504 | GPR | Horsa | n/k | 22/09/1944 | L7 | 977 | 39 | F/16. |
| Corfield | R | SGT | | 14344873 | GPR | Horsa | n/k | 19/09/1944 | L7 | 896 | 38 | E/*. |
| Cork | CS | F/S | AUS | A.422429 | 77 | Halifax | MZ711 | 16/06/1944 | L7 | 154 | 7 | |
| Cornelius | CB | SGT | CAN | R.210069 | 424 | Halifax | LW121 | 14/06/1944 | 9C/L7 | 53308 | 41* | Commissioned (J.88810). |
| Cornish | D | SGT | | 903724 | GPR | Horsa | n/k | 20/09/1944 | L7 | 897 | 38 | F/15. |
| Cotgrove | WR | SGT | | 1801737 | 70 | Wellington | LN699 | 21/07/1944 | L7 | 448 | 21 | Lost on raid on Pardubice. |
| Cottam | WW | SGT | | 1510799 | 156 | Lancaster | JA702 | 30/01/1944 | L7 | 564 | 27 | Captured Antwerp 7 August 1944. |
| Couchman | WB | SGT | | 1893438 | 300 | Lancaster | ND984 | 24/07/1944 | 9C/L7 | 53390 | 41* | WOP/AG. Baled out over target. Also POW no. 117 (Stalag 383). |
| Coughlan | RM | SGT | | 1101022 | 103 | Wellington | Z1142 | 10/01/1942 | 7A/383/L7 | 90114 | 16 | |
| Cousins | WL | F/S | | 2201368 | 424 | Halifax | LW121 | 14/06/1944 | L7 | 255 | 11 | |
| Cowan | JPC | SGT | | 1390638 | 622 | Lancaster | LM466 | 12/08/1944 | L7 | 565 | 27 | ss7. |
| Cowan | WHJ | SGT | | 1615879 | 253 | Spitfire | JK876 | 18/08/1944 | L7 | 734 | 31 | |

| Surname | Initials | Rank | Nat. | Service No. | Unit | Aircraft | Serial | Date | Camp | No. | No. | Notes |
|---|---|---|---|---|---|---|---|---|---|---|---|---|
| Cox | AJ | SGT | | 613278 | 466 | Halifax | HX267 | 27/05/1944 | L7 | 76 | 2 | ss7. |
| Cox | K | SGT | | 1819033 | 50 | Lancaster | PD294 | 11/09/1944 | L7 | 772 | 34 | Rest of crew evaded. Commissioned (J.86449). |
| Cox | LE | F/S | CAN | R.149319 | 90 | Stirling | EF147 | 05/03/1944 | L7 | 353 | 14 | ss7. Captured after thirty-six hours. |
| Coxhill | LEJ | F/S | AUS | A.431157 | 463 | Lancaster | PB263 | 28/07/1943 | 9C/L7 | 52948 | 57+ | Hospitalised with burns. |
| Coyne | P | SGT | | 972772 | 156 | Lancaster | JA702 | 30/01/1944 | L7 | 566 | 27 | Blown out of aircraft. Captured Antwerp 7 August 1944. |
| Craig | PH | F/S | | 1578239 | 178 | Liberator | EW277 | 13/06/1944 | L7 | 155 | 7 | From Foggia No. 1, Celone, Italy. |
| Cram | A | S/SGT | | 3656512 | GPR | Horsa | n/k | 17/09/1944 | L7 | 898 | 38 | D/13. |
| Crapper | M | SGT | | 1591526 | 57 | Lancaster | PB384 | 16/08/1944 | L7 | 654 | 28 | Baled out at 200 feet. |
| Craven | C | SGT | | 1596016 | 195 | Lancaster | LM743 | 02/11/1944 | L7 | 1134 | 48 | |
| Crawford | IRB | SGT | | 1521647 | 640 | Halifax | LK865 | 27/05/1944 | L7 | 77 | 2 | |
| Croney | L | F/S | | 1672013 | 619 | Lancaster | LM742 | 06/11/1944 | L7 | 1231 | 55* | |
| Cross | G | F/S | | 1540339 | 23 | Mosquito | HR201 | 30/09/1944 | L7 | 1098 | 47 | ss2. On 41st op. Five weeks in solitary at DL. |
| Cross | GH | SGT | | 1197071 | 70 | Wellington | DV570 | 12/10/1942 | 383/L7 | 139 | 5 | A/G. Captured 18 October 1942. 383? |
| Cross | RH | F/S | | 3031311 | 626 | Lancaster | LM137 | 12/09/1944 | L7 | 1099 | 47 | |
| Crosswell | PB | SGT | CAN | R.191256 | 429 | Halifax | LK802 | 03/08/1944 | L7 | 655 | 28 | Commissioned (J.88362). Killed attempting to escape at Stalag IIIA, 13/14 April 1945. |
| Crounkamp | WM | SGT | SA | 48101 | 12SAAF | Maryland | AH287 | 14/11/1941 | 7A/383/L7 | 90074 | 16 | Also POW no. 86 (Stalag 383). Shown as having been killed. |
| Crump | J | SGT | | 1239164 | 77 | Halifax | MZ711 | 16/06/1944 | L7 | 156 | 7 | |
| Cubberley | AN | SGT | | 1819252 | 7 | Lancaster | PB474 | 12/10/1944 | L7 | 1061 | 45* | |
| Cuffe | GL | SGT | CAN | R.250894 | 431 | Halifax | MZ859 | 28/07/1944 | L7 | 508 | 23 | ss7. |
| Culpan | EH | SGT | | 2081536 | GPR | Horsa | n/k | 19/09/1944 | L7 | 899 | 38 | D/*. |
| Cumberlidge | RB | F/S | | 633728 | 550 | Lancaster | NE164 | 28/07/1944 | L7 | 509 | 23 | |
| Cundall | IP | SGT | | 1593070 | 51 | Halifax | MZ349 | 12/08/1944 | L7 | 567 | 27 | |
| Currie | JM | F/S | CAN | R.205609 | 158 | Halifax | MZ945 | 25/10/1944 | L7 | 1100 | 47 | |
| Curtis | FF | LAC | | 1461397 | 2788 | n/a | n/a | 26/08/1944 | L7 | 837 | 37 | G/G. RAF Regiment. Captured at Valence after the invasion of the south of France. |
| Curtis | PJ | SGT | | 576549 | 214 | Fortress | HB763 | 25/08/1944 | L7 | 697 | 30 | |
| Cutting | AMB | F/S | | 1806570 | 103 | Lancaster | ME799 | 28/07/1944 | 9C/L7 | 52466 | 57+ | Broken leg. 9C? See Intercom Winter 1990, p.50, & Lanc 5, p.43. |

| Surname | Initials | Rank | Nat. | Service No. | Sqn | Aircraft | Serial | Date | Camp | No. | Stalag | Remarks |
|---|---|---|---|---|---|---|---|---|---|---|---|---|
| Cutts | VH | F/S | | 955831 | 149 | Stirling | LJ501 | 31/05/1944 | L7 | 157 | 7 | ss7. Verdon Harold Cutts. Commissioned (175928) 20 June 1944. See *No Time For Fear*, pp.175-7. |
| Cytulski | N | SGT | POL | 706767 | 300 | Lancaster | LM141 | 06/11/1944 | L7 | 1233 | 55* | |
| Czura | S | SGT | POL | 706720 | 300 | Lancaster | LM141 | 06/11/1944 | L7 | 1234 | 55* | |
| Dale | ED | F/S | AUS | A.419958 | 467 | Lancaster | LL846 | 25/06/1944 | L7 | 294 | 12 | M/U/G. Baled out after rear turret almost blown off. |
| Dale | H | SGT | | 1512975 | 100 | Lancaster | LM621 | 30/06/1944 | L7 | 295 | 12 | |
| Dale | R | SGT | | 1818765 | 75 | Lancaster | ND802 | 27/05/1944 | L7 | 111 | 3 | |
| Dale | RR | S/SGT | | 5112070 | GPR | Horsa | n/k | 21/09/1944 | L7 | 900 | 38 | B/19. |
| Dalseg | PI | SGT | CAN | R.205026 | 57 | Lancaster | NE127 | 22/05/1944 | L7 | 14 | 1 | |
| Danes | J | SGT | | 1213115 | 76 | Halifax | MZ623 | 24/05/1944 | L7 | 15 | 1 | |
| Darby | PR | SGT | | 924342 | 70 | Wellington | Z8984 | 25/04/1942 | 4B/L3/L7 | 248454 | 55 | Pilot. On Benghazi raid. |
| Dare | SC | SGT | | 1386152 | 44 | Lancaster | ME634 | 07/07/1944 | L7 | 387 | 15 | |
| Darwin | PCP | SGT | | 994782 | 49 | Hampden | AD733 | 28/09/1941 | 8B/383/L3/L7 | 9690 | 16 | |
| Dashwood | WS | W/O | NZ | NZ.401374 | 106 | Hampden | P1341 | 15/01/1942 | 7A/383/L7 | 90099 | 16 | Also POW no. 108 (Stalag 383). |
| Davenport | V | F/S | | 1425262 | 158 | Halifax | MZ367 | 12/08/1944 | L7 | 656 | 28 | |
| Davey | LW | F/S | AUS | A.420457 | 148 | Halifax | JP179 | 03/07/1944 | L7 | 510 | 23 | Shot down over Hungary on SOE drop to Yugoslavia. |
| Davidson | JEL | WO2 | CAN | R.161701 | 425 | Halifax | LW633 | 22/04/1944 | L7 | 256 | 11 | Captured 17 June 1944, Antwerp. |
| Davidson | SF | SGT | | 1356077 | 58 | Whitley | Z6729 | 16/08/1941 | 7A/383/L7 | 90052 | 16 | Also POW no. 65 (Stalag 383). |
| Davidson | T | SGT | CAN | R.202589 | 428 | Lancaster | KB743 | 18/08/1944 | L7 | 657 | 28 | |
| Davies | AB | SGT | | 1650369 | 102 | Halifax | MZ699 | 12/09/1944 | L7 | 773 | 34 | |
| Davies | DM | F/S | CAN | R.164445 | 408 | Halifax | NP761 | 06/11/1944 | L7 | 1236 | 55* | |
| Davies | DS | SGT | CAN | R.204086 | 408 | Halifax | NP773 | 15/10/1944 | L7 | 1062 | 45* | |
| Davies | IG | SGT | | 928736 | 101 | Wellington | R3295 | 30/11/1941 | 7A/383/L7 | 90079 | 16 | Also POW no. 91 (Stalag 383). |
| Davies | JA | SGT | | 1651898 | 101 | Lancaster | DV267 | 19/02/1944 | L7 | 698 | 30 | Captured Antwerp 10 August 1944. Author of *A Leap in the Dark*. |
| Davies | ML | SGT | | 1169790 | 2788 | n/a | n/a | 25/08/1944 | L7 | 1235 | 55* | W/OP. RAF Regiment. Captured at Valence after the invasion of the south of France. |
| Davis | BH | W/O | AUS | A.416563 | 103 | Lancaster | ME722 | 21/05/1944 | L7 | 568 | 27 | In hospital. Repatriated in February 1945. Same crew as ES Moran RCAF. |
| Davis | CGG | WO2 | CAN | R.130464 | 252 | Beaufighter | NE636 | 02/08/1944 | L7 | 699 | 30 | Pilot. Commissioned (J.89774). |
| Davis | FV | SGT | | 1168910 | 7 | Stirling | W7436 | 18/12/1941 | 7A/383/L7 | 90152 | 16 | Also POW no. 151 (Stalag 383). |

| Surname | Initials | Rank | Service No | Country | Sqn | Aircraft | Serial | Date | Camp | POW No | Age | Notes |
|---|---|---|---|---|---|---|---|---|---|---|---|---|
| Davis | GE | S/SGT | 2045543 | | GPR | Horsa | n/k | 20/09/1944 | L7 | 901 | 38 | F/16. |
| Davis | GJ | F/S | 1553150 | | 514 | Lancaster | DS817 | 20/12/1943 | 4B/L7 | 269762 | 31 | ss7. Injured – spent a week in the Hohe Mark. |
| Davis | HA | SGT | 1805997 | | 622 | Lancaster | LM283 | 19/10/1944 | L7 | 1101 | 47 | |
| Davis | KC | SGT | 1877371 | | 10 | Halifax | LW716 | 04/11/1944 | L7 | 1237 | 55* | ss7. |
| Davis | TG | W/O | 923999 | | 31 | Liberator | EW105 | 14/08/1944 | L7 | 700 | 30 | A/G, 31 (SAAF) Squadron. 'Smiler'. |
| Dawson | CM | F/S | 1895949 | | 466 | Halifax | LW116 | 22/06/1944 | L7 | 257 | 11 | M/U/G. Escaped on march. UK via Odessa and Middle East. |
| Dawson | E | SGT | 1590916 | | 625 | Lancaster | LM139 | 10/06/1944 | L7 | 112 | 3 | |
| Dawson | H | F/S | 1515484 | | 429 | Halifax | LW124 | 24/05/1944 | L7 | 78 | 2 | |
| Day | BR | SGT | 2201772 | | 44 | Lancaster | PB751 | 04/12/1944 | L7 | 1276 | 56 | |
| Day | DR | F/S | 1324989 | | 158 | Halifax | LK875 | 02/06/1944 | 12A/L7 | 80013 | 3 | POW no. 80015? 12A? |
| De Kock | DP | WO2 | 542303V | SA | 12SAAF | Marauder | FB518 | 13/07/1944 | L7 | 462 | 21 | A/G. Baled out of aircraft which returned to base. |
| De Luca | JM | F/S | R.186540 | CAN | 426 | Halifax | NP741 | 12/09/1944 | L7 | 838 | 37 | |
| De Renzy | TD | W/O | NZ.415751 | NZ | 256 | Mosquito | HK399 | 02/07/1944 | L7 | 1301 | 56 | ss2. Suffered severe burns when shot down. Hospital. |
| De Viell | WH | F/S | 1384585 | | 619 | Lancaster | LL783 | 06/06/1944 | L7 | 418 | 15 | Captured 9 June. See Flying Into Hell, p.127 & pp.131-3. |
| Deane | JHK | SGT | 902295 | | 58 | Whitley | Z6575 | 30/11/1941 | 7A/383/L7 | 90071 | 16 | Also POW no. 83 (Stalag 383). |
| Debroise | MA | SGT | 942 | FRA | 346 | Halifax | LW443 | 02/11/1944 | L7 | 1182 | 50 | From Saumur, Maine et Loire, France. |
| Decroix | PH | F/S | 1424878 | BEL | 349 | Spitfire | PV134 | 03/11/1944 | L7 | 1277 | 56 | Born in Courtrai, Belgium. Resident in Fulham, London. |
| Dedman | ADC | SGT | 778241 | | 44 | Lancaster | L7548 | 17/04/1942 | 7A/L7 | 333 | 13 | |
| Deeley | G | SGT | 5127622 | | GPR | Horsa | n/k | 22/09/1944 | L7 | 902 | 38 | D/*. Arnhem. |
| Delayen | NP | W/O | 1135619 | | 83 | Lancaster | PB230 | 12/08/1944 | L7 | 569 | 27 | |
| Dennis | F | SGT | 5887705 | | GPR | Horsa | n/k | 21/09/1944 | L7 | 978 | 39 | B/19. |
| Descourtis | Y | ADJ | 31456 | FRA | 341 | Spitfire | PT755 | 10/10/1944 | L7 | 1232 | 55* | From Donzac par Cadillac-sous-Garame, Gironde, France. |
| Devey | JR | S/SGT | 3601654 | | GPR | Horsa | n/k | 20/09/1944 | L7 | 903 | 38 | E/*. |
| Devine | F | F/S | 1496959 | EIR | 405 | Lancaster | ND344 | 11/06/1944 | 9C/L7 | 53309 | 31 | Injured. In RE at Dunkirk with the B.E.F. Re-mustered in RAF as W/OP. |
| Devine | WH | F/S | R.161385 | CAN | 419 | Lancaster | KB719 | 24/07/1944 | L7 | 570 | 27 | |
| DeWitt | JM | CPL | 41878 | SA | n/a | n/a | n/a | n/k | 344/L7 | 80773 | 47 | S. African Army. Evacuated from Luft 7, left at Stalag VIIIB. |

| Name | Init | Rank | Nat | Service No | Sqn | Aircraft | Serial | Date | Camp | POW No | Age | Remarks |
|---|---|---|---|---|---|---|---|---|---|---|---|---|
| Dezellis | A | W/O | FRA | 1515 | 346 | Halifax | NA561 | 17/12/1944 | L7 | 1321 | 57* | Baled out - aircraft returned to UK. See *Night Pilot*, pp.154-7. From Mezergues, Meknes, Morocco |
| Dixon | LW | SGT | | 1538492 | 299 | Stirling | EF267 | 19/09/1944 | L7 | 839 | 37 | B/A lost over Arnhem. |
| Dixon | SC | SGT | | 3006315 | 207 | Lancaster | LM123 | 15/10/1944 | L7 | 1063 | 45* | A/G. Baled out – aircraft returned to UK. |
| Dobbie | WT | F/S | AUS | A.426323 | 3 RAAF | Kittyhawk | FX576 | 12/11/1944 | L7 | 1238 | 55* | ss7. In hospital in Lille for first two months. |
| Dobbs | KA | SGT | | 1218961 | 158 | Halifax | HX322 | 30/03/1944 | 9C/L7/ 344/383 | 53297 | 49 | Evacuated two weeks before the march. |
| Docherty | JP | SGT | | 637870 | 426 | Halifax | NP683 | 28/06/1944 | 12A/L7 | 86289 | 31 | Captured Lisieux 14 August 1944. 12A? Commissioned (55798) 19 September 1944.. |
| Dodds | W | AC2 | | 1557234 | 235AMES | n/a | n/a | 21/06/1942 | #/L7 | 139513 | 18 | G/G. Captured at Tobruk. |
| Doidge | WT | SGT | | 1317136 | 576 | Lancaster | LL905 | 28/07/1944 | L7 | 511 | 23 | |
| Donaldson | KJ | WO2 | CAN | R.130256 | 434 | Halifax | LK801 | 16/06/1944 | L7 | 212 | 8 | |
| Dorman | RA | SGT | | 1813863 | 620 | Stirling | LJ867 | 11/04/1944 | 9C/L3/L7 | 53250 | 41* | F/E lost on SOE supply drop to France. |
| Dossett | KSF | SGT | | 1318986 | 65 | Mustang | FB365 | 03/07/1944 | L7 | 449 | 21 | |
| Dougherty | JH | SGT | CAN | R.64021 | 434 | Halifax | LW433 | 16/06/1944 | L7 | 388 | 15 | |
| Dowdeswell | P | SGT | | 1586209 | 158 | Halifax | LW723 | 10/04/1944 | L3/L7 | 8085 | 57* | To Luft 3 from Buchenwald concentration camp. |
| Dowding | AW | W/O | AUS | A.425139 | 453 | Spitfire | PL313 | 25/07/1944 | L7 | 658 | 28 | Shot down by Bf109 five miles south-west Lisieux. |
| Dowling | PL | SGT | | 1716350 | 625 | Lancaster | LL962 | 28/07/1944 | L7 | 512 | 23 | |
| Downing | EJ | F/S | CAN | R.170649 | 434 | Halifax | LW433 | 16/06/1944 | L7 | 450 | 21 | Captured Antwerp 7 July 1944. Commissioned. ss7. |
| D'Oyley | AA | F/S | | 1803479 | 57 | Lancaster | NG126 | 18/09/1944 | 9C/L7 | 52825 | 41* | ss7. |
| Dransfield | WI | SGT | | 1684242 | 44 | Lancaster | PB266 | 28/07/1944 | L7 | 571 | 27 | |
| Drury | JR | SGT | | 1817351 | 550 | Lancaster | NE164 | 28/07/1944 | L7 | 513 | 23 | |
| Ducharme | AJ | SGT | CAN | R.221243 | 408 | Lancaster | DS634 | 28/07/1944 | L7 | 514 | 23 | |
| Duckham | GR | SGT | | 1255325 | 12 | Wellington | Z8410 | 25/02/1942 | 7A/383/L7 | 90156 | 16 | Also POW no. 154 (Stalag 383). |
| Dudley | S | F/S | | 1480232 | 195 | Lancaster | HK663 | 02/11/1944 | L7 | 1135 | 48 | |
| Duffield | JW | W/O | | 923202 | 76 | Halifax | L9561 | 12/10/1941 | 7A/383/L7 | 90077 | 16 | Also POW no. 89 (Stalag 383). Evacuated back to Stalag 383. |
| Dugdale | G | W/O | | 651166 | 161 | Halifax | LL388 | 28/08/1944 | L7 | 774 | 34 | On SOE Operation Hendrik 1. |
| Dunbar | WS | SGT | | 2572042 | GPR | Horsa | n/k | 26/09/1944 | L7 | 1102 | 47 | E/*. |
| Duncan | GI | F/S | | 1396979 | 190 | Stirling | LJ916 | 21/09/1944 | L7 | 1019 | 40 | Nav shot down on Arnhem supply drop. |
| Dunham | GE | SGT | CAN | R.203997 | 429 | Halifax | MZ302 | 28/06/1944 | L7 | 572 | 27 | |
| Dunkley | D | SGT | | 1016935 | 61 | Lancaster | PA998 | 25/08/1944 | L7 | 701 | 30 | Ribs broken by rifle butt. |
| Dunn | EF | SGT | | 2211106 | 207 | Lancaster | PB765 | 04/12/1944 | L7 | 1278 | 56 | |

| Surname | Initials | Rank | Country | Service No | Sqn | Aircraft | Serial | Date | Camp | POW No | No | Notes |
|---|---|---|---|---|---|---|---|---|---|---|---|---|
| Dupont | LJ | SGT | CAN | R.200175 | 408 | Halifax | NP773 | 15/10/1944 | L7 | 1064 | 45* | Captured 4 August 1944. |
| Durdin | CN | SGT | CAN | R.169692 | 158 | Halifax | HX333 | 28/01/1944 | L7 | 573 | 27 | Wounded. Later commissioned. |
| Durrant | SA | F/S | | 1287908 | 35 | Halifax | HR926 | 22/10/1943 | 9C/L7 | 43181 | 31 | W/OP Obs. Also POW no. 109 (Stalag 383). |
| Durrant | T | F/S | NZ | NZ.415243 | 622 | Lancaster | LM138 | 23/06/1944 | L7 | 258 | 11 | Nickname 'Stumpy'. Repatriated with Stan Aspinall |
| Dutton | JK | W/O | | 966968 | 272 | Beaufighter | T3246 | 06/12/1941 | 7A/383/L7 | 90103 | 16 | |
| Duvall | VR | F/S | | 591384 | 97 | Lancaster | ND440 | 24/03/1944 | 9C/L7 | 53121 | 2* | |
| Dworakowski | W | SGT | POL | 780556 | 300 | Lancaster | LM141 | 06/11/1944 | L7 | 1239 | 55* | |
| Dyer | AJ | LAC | | 1578470 | 313S&T | n/a | n/a | 08/06/1944 | 9C/L7 | 53420 | 31 | DMT on LCT390 caught when landing craft sank off Normandy beaches. |
| Dyson | W | SGT | | 1592140 | 57 | Lancaster | PB425 | 19/10/1944 | L7 | 1183 | 50 | Escaped on 20 January 1945. To UK via Odessa and Middle East. |
| Eadie | RD | SGT | EIR | 1527066 | 462 | Halifax | LL610 | 02/11/1944 | L7 | 1136 | 48 | From Killarney. Joined up in Belfast. |
| East | EE | W/O | | 1388579 | 243 | Spitfire | MJ950 | 14/06/1944 | L7 | 213 | 8 | Escaped on 23 January 1945 with F/S Hansford. To UK via Odessa and Middle East. |
| Eastwood | CE | SGT | | 1624047 | 431 | Halifax | MZ597 | 28/07/1944 | L7 | 451 | 21 | W/AG |
| Eckford | H | SGT | | 1528597 | 297 | Albemarle | V1817 | 29/05/1944 | L7 | 259 | 11 | |
| Ede | DN | F/S | | 1491396 | 626 | Lancaster | ND985 | 27/05/1944 | L7 | 79 | 2 | |
| Eden | F | SGT | | 1755205 | 57 | Lancaster | ME864 | 28/07/1944 | L7 | 702 | 30 | |
| Edwards | GB | SGT | SR | 102517 | 12SAAF | Maryland | AH287 | 14/11/1941 | 7A/383/L7 | 90068 | 16 | A/G. Rank was air sergeant. Also POW no. 81 (Stalag 383). From Cape Town, S. Africa. |
| Edwards | KJ | S/SGT | | 3654436 | GPR | Horsa | n/k | 17/09/1944 | L7 | 904 | 38 | D/13 |
| Egglestone | R | SGT | | 1369656 | 106 | Lancaster | NN726 | 18/12/1944 | L7 | 1322 | 57* | |
| Egri | WE | WO2 | CAN | R.87920 | 514 | Lancaster | LL716 | 03/08/1944 | L7 | 574 | 27 | DFM (15/12/42). Commissioned (J.87632) wef 25 June 1944. Hungarian-born. |
| Elliott | KE | WO1 | CAN | R.158470 | 432 | Halifax | NP706 | 18/07/1944 | L7 | 452 | 21 | Commissioned (J.88058). |
| Ellis | JA | S/SGT | | 1901936 | GPR | Horsa | n/k | 20/09/1944 | L7 | 840 | 37 | E/*. |
| Ellis | L | SGT | | 1033239 | 431 | Halifax | MZ520 | 16/06/1944 | 9C/L7 | 52467 | 41* | ss7. |
| Ellis | RO | F/S | | 1395330 | 609 | Typhoon | JR147 | 17/11/1943 | L7 | 16 | 1 | Worked in the camp hospital. Later evacuated to Stalag 383. |
| Eisliger | JH | SGT | CAN | R.96593 | 420 | Halifax | LW423 | 27/05/1944 | L7 | 354 | 14 | Baled out in error. Captured 16 June 1944. Commissioned. See *Point Blank and Beyond*, p.127. |
| Ely | TR | SGT | | 1892372 | 434 | Halifax | LW713 | 13/06/1944 | 9C/L7 | 53421 | 31 | F/E. Commissioned (177637) 1 August 1944. |

| Surname | Initials | Rank | Nationality | Service no. | Sqn | Aircraft | Serial | Date | Camp | No. | No. | Notes |
|---|---|---|---|---|---|---|---|---|---|---|---|---|
| Embury | CVC | SGT | | 1821623 | 61 | Lancaster | ME595 | 14/10/1944 | L7 | 1065 | 45* | |
| Emmett | WCE | SGT | | 1686014 | 158 | Halifax | MZ945 | 25/10/1944 | L7 | 1103 | 47 | See *The British Airman*, pp. 162-3. |
| Enfield | RG | SGT | | 1876535 | 428 | Lancaster | KB743 | 18/08/1944 | L7 | 659 | 28 | |
| England | N | SGT | | 1217807 | 61 | Lancaster | ME595 | 14/10/1944 | L7 | 1066 | 45* | A/G on raid to Maribor. |
| English | R | SGT | | 1590341 | 37 | Wellington | LP259 | 21/10/1944 | L7 | 1137 | 48 | Nav shot down over Arnhem. |
| English | RE | W/O | AUS | A.409908 | 437 | Dakota | FZ656 | 21/09/1944 | L7 | 979 | 39 | |
| Etheridge | FG | F/S | CAN | R.182140 | 7 | Lancaster | PB241 | 06/10/1944 | L7 | 1067 | 45* | |
| Evans | E | SGT | | 2211558 | 463 | Lancaster | NF990 | 06/11/1944 | L7 | 1240 | 55* | |
| Evans | FN | SGT | | 1321021 | 57 | Lancaster | PB425 | 19/10/1944 | L7 | 1104 | 47 | |
| Evans | HC | F/S | AUS | A.417168 | 466 | Halifax | HX271 | 02/06/1944 | L7 | 158 | 7 | Co-pilot lost over Arnhem. |
| Evans | L | SGT | | 1607215 | 437 | Dakota | FZ656 | 21/09/1944 | L7 | 980 | 39 | W/OP. LAC when shot down. Possibly |
| Evans | TS | W/O | | 536059 | 218 | Battle | P2326 | 10/05/1940 | 8B/L7 | 27365 | 48* | Trupp 51. 8B? |
| Evison | E | SGT | | 1601354 | 625 | Lancaster | LM546 | 28/07/1944 | L7 | 515 | 23 | |
| Fagan | JA | W/O | | 1077128 | 7 | Lancaster | PB466 | 06/09/1944 | L7 | 775 | 34 | DFM (2/11/43). |
| Fallon | EJ | F/S | AUS | A.426565 | 463 | Lancaster | LM589 | 24/07/1944 | L7 | 575 | 27 | |
| Fallon | G | SGT | | 3041124 | 582 | Lancaster | PB523 | 23/12/1944 | L7 | 1323 | 57* | Escaped (see AIR 14/1864). To UK via Odessa and Middle East. |
| Farley | C | SGT | | 1397812 | 166 | Lancaster | LL743 | 03/05/1944 | L7 | 516 | 23 | Captured 13 May 1944. |
| Farrington | CA | SGT | | 964670 | 7 | Lancaster | ND897 | 29/06/1944 | L7 | 355 | 14 | |
| Farrington | DA | F/S | | 1066554 | 90 | Stirling | EH906 | 04/03/1944 | 333/12A/L7 | 80140 | 9 | Captured 11 June 1944. Badly beaten by captors. See *To Hell and Back*, pp.62-9. |
| Farrington | EH | SGT | | 1819957 | 576 | Lancaster | PB400 | 26/08/1944 | L7 | 703 | 30 | |
| Fearn | JE | F/S | | 1549396 | 44 | Lancaster | PB235 | 04/10/1944 | L7 | 1020 | 40 | |
| Federico | JS | F/S | CAN | R.151371 | 425 | Halifax | LW379 | 01/11/1944 | L7 | 1138 | 48 | Commissioned (J.92915). |
| Fenn | CG | SGT | | 1645862 | 9 | Lancaster | JB116 | 07/07/1944 | L7 | 389 | 15 | |
| Fereday | JC | SGT | | 1579620 | 431 | Halifax | MZ537 | 16/06/1944 | L7 | 159 | 7 | |
| Ferguson | AA | SGT | | 1055942 | 22 | Beaufort | N1085 | 12/12/1941 | 7A/383/L7 | 90088 | 16 | W/OP AG. Also POW no. 98 (Stalag 383). |
| Fethers | WN | SGT | AUS | A.401279 | 148 | Wellington | DV562 | 05/10/1942 | O5A/L7 | 2733 | 20 | Also POW no. L7/1316. |
| Finch | FE | SGT | | 1320793 | 61 | Lancaster | PB436 | 29/08/1944 | L7 | 735 | 31 | |
| Finch | RStC | W/O | | 1188016 | 101 | Wellington | R1778 | 30/11/1941 | 7A/383/L7 | 90082 | 16 | Also POW no. 94 (Stalag 383). Evacuated to Stalag 383. |
| Finlay | E | SGT | | 1532438 | 625 | Lancaster | ND636 | 10/04/1944 | L7 | 356 | 14 | ss7. Captured 27 April 1944. |

| Surname | Initials | Rank | Nat. | Service no. | Sqn | Aircraft | Serial | Date | Camp | POW no. | ? | Notes |
|---|---|---|---|---|---|---|---|---|---|---|---|---|
| Finlayson | CW | F/S | | 656903 | 150 | Wellington | HE956 | 21/05/1944 | L7 | 80 | 2 | W/AG. |
| Finnie | JE | SGT | CAN | R.207670 | 427 | Halifax | LW166 | 04/07/1944 | L7 | 357 | 14 | Commissioned (J90273). |
| Firth | JB | SGT | | 1850441 | 50 | Lancaster | LL922 | 07/08/1944 | 12A/L7 | 86332 | 34 | |
| Fischer | JE | F/S | | 1338557 | 207 | Lancaster | LM129 | 04/07/1944 | L7 | 576 | 27 | Captured 7 August 1944. |
| Fisher | CEF | SGT | | 1473246 | 626 | Lancaster | ND952 | 30/06/1944 | 9C/L7 | 53310 | 31 | POW no.53210? |
| Fisher | LS | SGT | | 1091186 | 178 | Liberator | BZ930 | 07/07/1944 | L7 | 390 | 15 | B/A, lost on Feuersbrunn raid, Austria. See Sgt LJ Hall. |
| Flay | GA | F/S | NZ | NZ.421694 | 489 | Beaufighter | LZ543 | 14/06/1944 | L7 | 160 | 7 | Pilot ss2. |
| Flear | C | SGT | | 2220385 | 207 | Lancaster | LM123 | 15/10/1944 | L7 | 1068 | 45* | Baled out – aircraft returned to UK. |
| Fletcher | LR | WO2 | CAN | R.103746 | 103 | Lancaster | ME738 | 27/04/1944 | L7 | 113 | 3 | Blown out at 6,000 feet. |
| Flint | G | SGT | | 1824180 | 97 | Lancaster | PA398 | 25/08/1944 | L7 | 704 | 30 | Escaped on march, captured, escaped. To UK via Odessa and Middle East. |
| Flintoft | GH | SGT | CAN | R.197596 | 180 | Mitchell | FW175 | 09/08/1944 | L7 | 577 | 27 | W/OP. Hands and face burned during bale out. Nose broken. Legs injured. |
| Flower | GW | SGT | EIR | 1798759 | 195 | Lancaster | HK663 | 02/11/1944 | L7 | 1139 | 48 | From Dublin. |
| Fogg | JVO | SGT | | 533457 | 218 | Stirling | N3714 | 01/09/1942 | 8B/344/L7 | 26858 | 42/45* | |
| Ford | CW | SGT | CAN | R.223422 | 427 | Halifax | LV987 | 07/06/1944 | L7 | 161 | 7 | |
| Ford | RE | SGT | CAN | R.69494 | 425 | Halifax | MZ831 | 04/11/1944 | L7 | 1184 | 50 | Commissioned (J93006). |
| Foreman | TR | F/S | | 1477011 | 90 | Stirling | LJ460 | 10/04/1944 | L7 | 841 | 37 | Captured Romorantin 26 May 1944. |
| Forrest | JFJ | SGT | | 1583098 | 619 | Lancaster | LL783 | 06/06/1944 | L7 | 391 | 15 | See Flying Into Hell, pp.126-134. |
| Forster | JG | SGT | | 1078097 | 7 | Lancaster | PB241 | 06/10/1944 | L7 | 1021 | 40 | |
| Forward | J | SGT | | 1666426 | 57 | Lancaster | PD264 | 06/12/1944 | L7 | 1279 | 56 | |
| Foster | DW | LAC | | 1652764 | 6080LWU | Horsa | n/k | 22/09/1944 | 11B/L7 | 117862 | 56 | MT mechanic. Captured at Arnhem. |
| Fowler | F | F/S | | 1144830 | 57 | Lancaster | ME864 | 28/07/1944 | L7 | 705 | 30 | |
| Frais | EB | SGT | | 985776 | 103 | Wellington | Z1142 | 10/01/1942 | 7A/383/L7 | 90115 | 16 | A/G. Baled out over target. Also POW no. 118 (Stalag 383). |
| Francis | JG | F/S | | 982830 | 83 | Lancaster | PB138 | 12/08/1944 | L7 | 578 | 27 | |
| Franczak | A | SGT | POL | 783443 | 306 | Spitfire | P8524 | 16/08/1941 | 8B/L7/L6 | 24761 | 20 | Moved to Luft 6 on 18 August 1944. 8B? |
| Fraser | BAM | SGT | CAN | R.192908 | 51 | Halifax | LK885 | 24/05/1944 | L7 | 358 | 14 | Captured 8 July 1944, Tilburg. |
| Fraser | G | SGT | | 1822053 | 61 | Lancaster | PB725 | 06/11/1944 | L7 | 1140 | 48 | |
| Freeman | JS | SGT | | 619413 | 6225BD | n/a | n/a | 08/06/1944 | L7 | 296 | 12 | Armourer, BD Flight. On LCT390. Captured on French coast. Born Nottingham 7 November 1918. |

| Surname | Init | Rank | Nat | Service No | Sqn | Aircraft | Serial | Date | Camp | No. | | Notes |
|---|---|---|---|---|---|---|---|---|---|---|---|---|
| French | FM | SGT | | 1868666 | 115 | Lancaster | ND805 | 14/10/1944 | L7 | 1105 | 47 | |
| French | WE | SGT | | 1872129 | 7 | Lancaster | PA964 | 06/10/1944 | L7 | 1106 | 47 | |
| French | WF | SGT | | 1152939 | 75 | Wellington | X9628 | 08/11/1941 | 7A/383/L7 | 90083 | 16 | Also POW no. 93 (Stalag 383). |
| Friday | JW | F/S | CAN | R.186609 | 419 | Lancaster | KB726 | 12/06/1944 | L7 | 214 | 8 | Commissioned (J.92337). 186609? |
| Frost | AGA | SGT | | 1603739 | 76 | Halifax | LW648 | 04/11/1944 | L7 | 1185 | 50 | |
| Fuller | H | W/O | | 1515746 | 582 | Lancaster | PB523 | 23/12/1944 | L7 | 1324 | 57* | |
| Fullum | JEM | WO2 | CAN | R.108486 | 425 | Halifax | LW431 | 25/02/1944 | 9C/L7 | 43346 | 31 | On 1st op. Fell out of a tree and broke his back. |
| Fulmore | PA | W/O | CAN | R.114706 | 48 | Dakota | KG428 | 19/11/1944 | 11B/L7 | 53692 | 57* | Arnhem 18/9/44. POW no. 53690? Commissioned (J.90936). 11B? Died 22 March 1994. |
| Furness | DH | SGT | | 571405 | 158 | Halifax | W1215 | 05/08/1942 | 8B/344/L7 | 25640 | 56 | |
| Gale | LJ | F/S | CAN | R.202678 | 425 | Halifax | MZ831 | 04/11/1944 | L7 | 1186 | 50 | |
| Gallagher | JDF | F/S | | 1522873 | 142 | Wellington | LN318 | 29/05/1944 | L7 | 81 | 2 | Obs. |
| Gallivan | WF | SGT | | 1613986 | 90 | Lancaster | NE177 | 10/06/1944 | L7 | 842 | 37 | Captured 25 August 1944. |
| Galloway | AB | SGT | | 1559085 | 625 | Lancaster | LM163 | 03/08/1944 | L7 | 579 | 27 | |
| Gamble | JD | SGT | | 1818577 | 24SAAF | Marauder | HD490 | 02/09/1944 | L7 | 776 | 34 | W/OP. Landed wrong side of lines. See Eagles Victorious p.282. |
| Gannon | RF | SGT | | 1665853 | 630 | Lancaster | LM117 | 18/07/1944 | 12A/L7 | 70445 | 29 | 12A? |
| Gardner | A | S/SGT | | 6018981 | GPR | Horsa | n/k | 14/06/1944 | 12A/L7 | 81288 | 22 | D-Day Operation Tonga. |
| Garland | EF | F/S | CAN | R.153444 | 514 | Lancaster | LL692 | 28/07/1944 | L7 | 580 | 27 | Commissioned (J.88157). |
| Garrard | SW | SGT | | 10577268 | GPR | Horsa | n/k | 20/09/1944 | L7 | 843 | 37 | F/* |
| Garratt | H | SGT | | 1591218 | 9 | Lancaster | LL853 | 24/06/1944 | L7 | 359 | 14 | |
| Gascoigne | J | SGT | | 1584618 | 101 | Lancaster | LM508 | 21/06/1944 | L7 | 453 | 21 | Captured Antwerp 24 July 1944. ss4. Nav lost over Arnhem. Two Air Despatchers also survived. |
| Gaydon | LC | F/S | | 1319434 | 271 | Dakota | FZ626 | 19/09/1944 | L7 | 905 | 38 | |
| Gerrard | DB | F/S | | 974222 | 35 | Lancaster | ND734 | 23/06/1944 | L7 | 215 | 8 | DFM (23/5/44, 10 Sq). On 48th op. |
| Getty | E | F/S | | 1490674 | 12 | Lancaster | ND627 | 04/07/1944 | L7 | 360 | 14 | Ernest Getty was from Belfast. |
| Gibbens | GHP | WO2 | CAN | R.157979 | 214 | Fortress | HB763 | 25/08/1944 | L7 | 706 | 30 | |
| Giblett | RL | SGT | | 1893705 | 434 | Halifax | LW175 | 12/08/1944 | L7 | 581 | 27 | |
| Gibson | HR | F/S | | 1316931 | 192 | Halifax | MZ570 | 03/05/1944 | L7 | 114 | 4 | |
| Gilbert | M | SGT | | 1040779 | 10 | Halifax | MZ773 | 12/08/1944 | L7 | 582 | 27 | |
| Gilbey | W | SGT | | 1281641 | 144 | Hampden | AD804 | 28/12/1941 | 7A/383/L7 | 90136 | 16 | Also POW no. 137 (Stalag 383). |
| Gilchrist | AA | W/O | AUS | A.409105 | 156 | Lancaster | NE143 | 31/05/1944 | L7 | 162 | 7 | |
| Giles | CH | F/S | AUS | A.437917 | 463 | Lancaster | LM242 | 11/09/1944 | L7 | 844 | 37 | |

| Surname | Initials | Rank | Nat. | Service No. | Sqn | Aircraft | Serial | Date | Code | No. | Col | Notes |
|---|---|---|---|---|---|---|---|---|---|---|---|---|
| Giles | FA | F/S | | 1322679 | 77 | Halifax | MZ748 | 28/06/1944 | L7 | 583 | 27 | To UK via Odessa and Middle East. |
| Gill | A | SGT | | 955101 | 78 | Halifax | LK840 | 22/06/1944 | 9C/L7 | 53361 | 49 | F/E. In hospital in France first. |
| Gill | RHJ | F/S | | 1333854 | 35 | Lancaster | ND734 | 23/06/1944 | L7 | 216 | 8 | DFM (25/1/46). |
| Gillespie | IM | SGT | | 979940 | 115 | Lancaster | ND745 | 22/05/1944 | L7 | 17 | 1 | |
| Gillow | C | S/SGT | | 894370 | GPR | Horsa | n/k | 21/09/1944 | L7 | 906 | 38 | D/*. |
| Gilmore | H | F/S | | 1045143 | 514 | Lancaster | LL716 | 03/08/1944 | L7 | 584 | 27 | |
| Giloran | AJ | F/S | AUS | A.26853 | 463 | Lancaster | LM375 | 06/10/1944 | L7 | 1022 | 40 | |
| Girvin | R | S/SGT | | 7022767 | GPR | Horsa | n/k | 21/09/1944 | L7 | 907 | 38 | B/19. From Belfast. |
| Gledhill | DG | SGT | | 1603852 | 139 | Mosquito | KB198 | 12/08/1944 | L7 | 660 | 28 | |
| Glenn | TD | F/S | | 1516970 | 214 | Fortress | SR384 | 24/05/1944 | L7 | 18 | 1 | |
| Glew | CA | SGT | | 578398 | 9 | Lancaster | ME704 | 21/06/1944 | L7 | 454 | 21 | Captured 21 July 1944. |
| Goheen | AL | F/S | CAN | R.62230 | 426 | Halifax | NP775 | 04/11/1944 | L7 | 1187 | 50 | Commissioned (J.92957). |
| Goldwyn | L | SGT | | 1391262 | 83 | Lancaster | R5630 | 17/01/1943 | 4B/L7 | 222700 | 31 | |
| Gooch | E | SGT | | 1862966 | 115 | Lancaster | NF960 | 28/10/1944 | L7 | 1107 | 47 | |
| Good | GF | SGT | | 1796603 | 514 | Lancaster | DS787 | 11/09/1944 | L7 | 779 | 34 | |
| Goodall | H | F/S | | 1382888 | 100 | Lancaster | ME677 | 21/05/1944 | L7 | 19 | 1 | ss7. |
| Goodbourne | PD | W/O | | 571487 | 15 | Stirling | BF329 | 13/08/1942 | 8B/L7 | 25673 | 56 | ss7. |
| Goode | RJ | W/O | | 574067 | 35 | Lancaster | ND731 | 04/07/1944 | L7 | 392 | 15 | DFM (20/4/43, 76 Sq). |
| Goodman-Jones | A | F/SGT | AUS | A.414786 | 40 | Wellington | LP234 | 13/06/1943 | L7 | 163 | 7 | Nav. Shot down on Munich raid. |
| Goodsell | HR | F/S | AUS | A.423709 | 466 | Halifax | MZ368 | 09/08/1944 | L7 | 585 | 27 | |
| Goodwin | JA | SGT | | 1398401 | 150 | Wellington | JA191 | 03/07/1944 | L7 | 297 | 12 | Nav lost on Feuersbrunn raid 29/30 June 1944. |
| Gordon | JA | F/S | CAN | R.91186 | 37 | Wellington | HD963 | 19/09/1942 | 7A/L7 | 334 | 13 | A/G. |
| Gordon | JA | F/S | CAN | R.201055 | 196 | Stirling | EF248 | 19/09/1944 | L7 | 908 | 38 | A/G lost over Arnhem. Captured 25 September 1944 Commissioned (J.90607). |
| Gore | DW | SGT | | 1624691 | 75 | Lancaster | ME691 | 20/07/1944 | L7 | 455 | 21 | ss7. |
| Gorman | WM | F/S | CAN | R.84878 | 405 | Lancaster | LM345 | 27/09/1943 | L7 | 260 | 11 | Captured in Pyrenees 21 April 1944. Toulouse (11 days) & Fresnes (4 weeks) prisons. |
| Gotham | ER | F/S | | 1583724 | 578 | Halifax | NA501 | 22/12/1944 | L7 | 1325 | 57* | |
| Goudy | GH | SGT | CAN | R.215417 | 619 | Lancaster | ND932 | 04/12/1944 | L7 | 1280 | 56 | ss7. |
| Gould | RE | SGT | | 1028246 | 115 | Lancaster | DS668 | 19/06/1943 | 9C/L7 | 43279 | 2 | Posted. Repatriated? |
| Gowing | RW | LAC | | 546430 | 216 | Bombay | L5847 | 16/11/1941 | 7A/383/L7 | 90089 | 16 | Rigger/flight engineer. Later W/O. Also POW no. 99 (Stalag 383). |

| Name | | Rank | Nat | Service No | Sqn | Aircraft | Serial | Date | Camp | | | Notes |
|---|---|---|---|---|---|---|---|---|---|---|---|---|
| Grace | CH | W/O | | 613809 | 77 | Whitley | Z6596 | 27/12/1941 | 7A/383/L7 | 90132 | 16 | Also POW no. 133 (Stalag 383). |
| Graham | HJ | WO2 | CAN | R.155227 | 432 | Halifax | NP801 | 09/10/1944 | L7 | 1023 | 40 | Nav. |
| Grainger | CP | F/S | | 1341067 | 252 | Beaufighter | NE546 | 19/06/1944 | L7 | 586 | 27 | A/G. |
| Grant | A | F/S | | 615683 | 37 | Wellington | HF524 | 16/06/1944 | L7 | 261 | 11 | ss8. |
| Grant | A | SGT | | 1105073 | 10 | Halifax | LV912 | 20/07/1944 | L7 | 456 | 21 | A/G. |
| Grant | CA | F/S | | 1851087 | 30SAAF | Marauder | HD596 | 04/09/1944 | L7 | 777 | 34 | A/G. 30 SAAF? |
| Grant | DR | SGT | CAN | R.210613 | 9 | Lancaster | LL970 | 25/06/1944 | L7 | 262 | 11 | ss7. Shot down near Calais. Escaped. Repatriated via Odessa. |
| Grant | HRC | S/SGT | | 2342594 | GPR | Horsa | n/k | 20/09/1944 | L7 | 909 | 38 | E/*. |
| Grant | RS | S/SGT | | 6474934 | GPR | Horsa | n/k | 20/09/1944 | L7 | 910 | 38 | A/1. |
| Grant | WA | SGT | CAN | R.116118 | 432 | Wellington | HE817 | 27/09/1943 | 11B/L7 | 117717 | 33 | Commissioned (J.18813). |
| Gray | DG | F/S | | 1282892 | 50 | Lancaster | R5546 | 30/03/1944 | 9C/L7 | 43390 | 3 | Kept a diary in captivity. |
| Gray | J | SGT | | 1777605 | 75 | Lancaster | ND911 | 20/11/1944 | L7 | 1241 | 55* | ss7. |
| Gray | RWS | SGT | CAN | R.259653 | 428 | Lancaster | KB737 | 25/10/1944 | L7 | 1188 | 50 | ss7. |
| Greay | LE | F/S | | 1399095 | 97 | Lancaster | PB510 | 11/09/1944 | L7 | 845 | 37 | ss7. |
| Green | FD | F/S | AUS | A.432170 | 61 | Lancaster | ME725 | 06/12/1944 | L7 | 1326 | 57* | Severe burns to hands and face. Arrived L7 9 January 1945. |
| Green | G | SGT | | 1579028 | 166 | Lancaster | LL954 | 22/05/1944 | L7 | 20 | 1 | |
| Green | JB | W/O | USA | 702081 | 86 | Beaufort | AW207 | 20/11/1941 | 7A/383/L7 | 90054 | 16 | W/AG. Also POW no. 67 (Stalag 383). |
| Green | KW | SGT | | 1582088 | 44 | Lancaster | LM638 | 12/07/1944 | L7 | 737 | 33 | Captured 17 August 1944. See Massacre over the Marne p. 124. |
| Greenbaum | FA | SGT | | 14417002 | GPR | Horsa | n/k | 22/09/1944 | L7 | 981 | 39 | A/*. On second Arnhem lift. Born Stepney, London, 23 December 1924. |
| Greene | RA | W/O | USA | R.66340 | 1 OADU | Wellington | HX580 | 30/07/1942 | PG66/PG59/7A/L7 | 141 | 6 | From 99 Squadron. Shot down en route to ME. American in RCAF. |
| Greene | RAF | SGT | SA | 212243 | 24SAAF | Boston | Z2294 | 17/08/1942 | 344/L7 | 25695 | 56 | WOP AG lost on Mersa Matruh raid. Rank was air sergeant. From Durban. |
| Greene | TW | SGT | | 1550195 | 250 | Kittyhawk | FT923 | 14/10/1944 | L7 | 1189 | 50 | Shot down by flak dive-bombing. Escaped 20 January 1945. Recaptured, to Stalag VIIIC (Brieg). |
| Greenhalgh | WD | F/S | | 748670 | 126 | Hurricane | Z2491 | 24/11/1941 | 7A/L7 | 335 | 13 | See photos of Z2491 on p.337 Malta: The Hurricane Years 1940-41. |
| Greenslade | GC | S/SGT | | 6086559 | GPR | Horsa | n/k | 21/09/1944 | 12A/L7 | 075462 | 47 | G/10. |

| Name | Initials | Rank | Nat | Service No | Sqn | Aircraft | Serial | Date | Camp | POW No | Age | Notes |
|---|---|---|---|---|---|---|---|---|---|---|---|---|
| Greeves | AJ | SGT | | 1802620 | 83 | Lancaster | ND740 | 11/09/1944 | L7 | 778 | 34 | |
| Gregory | NE | SGT | | 1473815 | 101 | Lancaster | LM395 | 23/05/1944 | L7 | 587 | 27 | B/A. |
| Greig | CFJ | F/S | NZ | NZ.422281 | 75 | Lancaster | ND756 | 28/07/1944 | L7 | 588 | 27 | |
| Grenfell | RC | SGT | | 1590721 | 148 | Halifax | EB147 | 05/08/1944 | L7 | 661 | 28 | A/G lost on supply mission to Warsaw. |
| Grice | J | SGT | | 1577822 | 57 | Lancaster | ND954 | 31/07/1944 | L7 | 589 | 27 | |
| Griffin | HCG | LA | | FX77190 | 827 | Albacore | N4389 | 30/07/1941 | 322/9C/8B/383/L7/344/7B/383 | 294 | 20 | Leading airman. Lost on Fleet Air Arm attack on Kirkenes harbour, Norway. |
| Griffith | RO | SGT | | 14625110 | GPR | Horsa | n/k | 28/09/1944 | L7 | 982 | 39 | E/*. |
| Griffiths | NDR | SGT | | 755823 | 9 | Wellington | R1335 | 27/03/1941 | L1/L3/L7 | 548 | 20 | L1? |
| Griffiths | RL | SGT | | 3976492 | GPR | Horsa | n/k | 26/09/1944 | L7 | 911 | 38 | B/20. |
| Griffiths | RL | F/S | | 639470 | 83 | Lancaster | JA928 | 26/04/1944 | L7 | 217 | 8 | Captured 11 May 1944. |
| Griffiths | RW | F/S | | 938582 | 37 | Wellington | LN643 | 11/05/1944 | L7 | 21 | 1 | Nav. |
| Griffiths | WG | S/SGT | | 4192348 | GPR | Horsa | n/k | 21/09/1944 | 12A/L7 | 075510 | 47 | G/10. |
| Grimwood | C | SGT | | 1378601 | 99 | Wellington | BB475 | 27/02/1942 | 7A/L7 | 336 | 13 | 1 OADU. Ran out of fuel en route Malta. |
| Groendyk | WM | Pt/Off | HOL | 906042 | 320 | Mitchell | FR151 | 20/06/1944 | L7 | 298 | 12 | Petty officer in RNNAS. Real name Theunissen - used nom de guerre Groendyk. |
| Grubb | DW | SGT | | 1323923 | 112 | Kittyhawk | FX544 | 22/05/1944 | L7 | 22 | 1 | Sports officer at Luft 7. |
| Guerin | M | SGT | | 1394415 | 166 | Lancaster | ED372 | 27/09/1943 | 9C/L7 | 43132 | 3 | Posted. Repatriated? |
| Guest | DW | WO1 | CAN | R.134604 | 421 | Spitfire | MK421 | 06/08/1944 | 12A/L7 | 86367 | 33 | Shot down ten miles east of Caen. |
| Gundy | RY | F/S | NZ | NZ.42663 | 214 | Fortress | SR384 | 24/05/1944 | L7 | 23 | 1 | |
| Guy | TC | SGT | CAN | R.213001 | 76 | Halifax | MZ531 | 07/06/1944 | L7 | 662 | 28 | Captured 22 June 1944. Fresnes & Wiesbaden prisons. |
| Haddon | WR | SGT | | 1650725 | 37 | Wellington | LP259 | 21/10/1944 | L7 | 1108 | 47 | B/A on raid to Maribor. Captured in Yugoslavia. |
| Haggett | R | SGT | | 925435 | 107 | Blenheim | Z7800 | 13/12/1941 | 7A/383/L7 | 337 | 13 | Obs. Also POW number 132004 (Stalag VIIA). |
| Haill | RCH | SGT | | 1806542 | 431 | Halifax | MZ597 | 28/07/1944 | L7 | 457 | 21 | |
| Hainey | T | F/S | | 1370651 | 570 | Stirling | LJ913 | 18/09/1944 | 11B/L7 | 117435 | 55* | W/AG lost on Arnhem 18 September 1944. Commissioned (185103). |
| Haldenby | JF | F/S | CAN | R.155154 | 434 | Halifax | LW433 | 16/06/1944 | L7 | 299 | 12 | Commissioned (J.87396). |
| Hale | AF | SGT | | 1809797 | 463 | Lancaster | PD338 | 02/11/1944 | L7 | 1141 | 48 | |
| Hall | AE | F/S | | 1388156 | 148 | Wellington | T2749 | 11/07/1942 | 8B/18A/L7 | 9278 | 57* | |
| Hall | FWW | SGT | | 1296692 | 158 | Halifax | MZ367 | 12/08/1944 | L7 | 663 | 28 | |
| Hall | JWG | W/O | | 754778 | 220 | Hudson | AM678 | 23/12/1941 | 7A/383/L7 | 90124 | 16 | Pilot shot down off Norway. Also POW no. 127 (Stalag 383). |

| Surname | Initials | Rank | Nat. | Service No | Sqn | Aircraft | Serial | Date | Code | POW No | Seq | Notes |
|---|---|---|---|---|---|---|---|---|---|---|---|---|
| Hall | LJ | SGT | | 1603774 | 178 | Liberator | BZ930 | 07/07/1944 | L7 | 393 | 15 | A/G lost on Feuersbrunn raid, Austria. See Sgt LS Fisher. |
| Hall | RS | SGT | USA | R.158758 | 432 | Halifax | LK811 | 27/05/1944 | L7 | 115 | 4 | Pilot. American in RCAF, from Normal, Illinois. |
| Hallett | WW | SGT | | 1587281 | 214 | Fortress | SR384 | 24/05/1944 | L7 | 24 | 1 | |
| Halliday | JJ | SGT | | 1681765 | 103 | Lancaster | PB303 | 18/08/1944 | L7 | 707 | 30 | |
| Halligan | BT | F/S | AUS | A.434208 | 142 | Wellington | LN318 | 29/05/1944 | 17B/L7 | 104259 | 7 | A/G lost on Feuersbrunn raid. At Stalag 17B (Krems) from 31 May-17 June 1944. |
| Hamilton | AF | SGT | | 1895854 | 460 | Lancaster | ND674 | 11/05/1944 | L7 | 218 | 8 | Captured Ghent 13 May 1944. In St Gilles prison for six weeks. |
| Hamilton | J | F/S | | 1338203 | 38 | Wellington | JB296 | 02/06/1944 | L7 | 116 | 4 | 2nd Pilot lost on raid to Khalkis Harbour, Greece. |
| Hamilton | JC | F/S | | 969499 | 35 | Halifax | L9582 | 30/11/1941 | 7A/383/L7 | 90072 | 16 | Also POW no. 84 (Stalag 383). |
| Hammond | FW | SGT | | 1287892 | 467 | Lancaster | DY240 | 30/03/1944 | DL/L7 | 16 | 1 | On permanent staff at DL. |
| Hammond | TE | SGT | | 1852312 | 148 | Halifax | EB147 | 05/08/1944 | L7 | 664 | 28 | F/E lost on supply mission to Warsaw. |
| Hannedouche | R | ADJ | FRA | 3052 | 346 | Halifax | NA558 | 04/11/1944 | L7 | 1190 | 50 | From Salammbo, Tunisia. |
| Hansford | RJ | F/S | | 1337128 | 622 | Lancaster | LM138 | 23/06/1944 | L7 | 263 | 11 | Escaped with W/O E.E. East on 23 January 1945. |
| Hanson | RE | SGT | | 14323788 | GPR | Horsa | n/k | 26/09/1944 | L7 | 983 | 39 | F/*. |
| Hardie | RS | SGT | | 1549463 | 9 | Lancaster | ME704 | 21/06/1944 | L7 | 219 | 8 | |
| Hardwick | PP | F/S | AUS | A.427323 | 467 | Lancaster | LM450 | 24/06/1944 | L7 | 264 | 11 | Wounded by flak – see Silk and Barbed Wire, p.279. Out via Odessa and Middle East. |
| Hardy | HD | F/S | CAN | R.218193 | 408 | Halifax | NP750 | 04/11/1944 | L7 | 1191 | 50 | From Liège, Belgium. |
| Hardy | HPL | F/S | BEL | 1424855 | 61 | Lancaster | LL777 | 06/12/1944 | L7 | 1282 | 56 | Nav/B lost on SOE drop to France. |
| Hargreaves | HJ | F/S | | 639702 | 620 | Stirling | LJ867 | 12/04/1944 | L7 | 82 | 2 | |
| Hargreaves | JW | F/S | | 644906 | 77 | Halifax | MZ748 | 28/06/1944 | 12A/L7 | 86199 | 33 | Captured near Caen 13 August 1944. |
| Harrington | DFL | F/S | | 1334114 | 37 | Wellington | HF524 | 16/06/1944 | L7 | 265 | 11 | W/OP. |
| Harrington | MA | F/S | CAN | R.255124 | 432 | Halifax | NP801 | 09/10/1944 | L7 | 1024 | 40 | |
| Harris | C | LAC | CAN | 955625 | 2788 | n/a | n/a | 25/08/1944 | L7 | 912 | 38 | G/Dr RAF Regiment. Captured at Valence after the invasion of the south of France. |
| Harris | E | SGT | | 1081196 | 61 | Lancaster | PB436 | 29/08/1944 | L7 | 740 | 33 | Committed suicide in 1950. |
| Harris | FM | SGT | | 1850150 | 75 | Lancaster | ND802 | 27/05/1944 | L7 | 300 | 12 | Betrayed and captured Antwerp 28 June 1944. |
| Harris | HH | SGT | | 1610165 | 57 | Lancaster | PB425 | 19/10/1944 | L7 | 1109 | 47 | |
| Harris | T | W/O | | 1387023 | 605 | Mosquito | NS878 | 31/08/1944 | L7 | 741 | 33 | ss2. |
| Harrison | CG | F/S | | 1430582 | 300 | Lancaster | ND984 | 24/07/1944 | L7 | 458 | 21 | |

| Surname | | Rank | Nat | Number | Sqn | Aircraft | Serial | Date | Camp | | | Notes |
|---|---|---|---|---|---|---|---|---|---|---|---|---|
| Harrison | FG | SGT | | 323314 | n/a | n/a | n/a | n/k | L7 | 164 | 7 | British Army (Royal Armoured Corps). Moved to another camp. |
| Harsley | RB | SGT | | 1495739 | 61 | Lancaster | LL777 | 06/12/1944 | L7 | 1283 | 56 | |
| Hartgroves | RS | SGT | | 917378 | 106 | Hampden | AE151 | 21/12/1941 | 7A/383/L7 | 90128 | 16 | Also POW no.130 (Stalag 383). |
| Harvey | EG | SGT | CAN | R.150730 | 424 | Halifax | LV951 | 12/08/1944 | L7 | 590 | 27 | |
| Harvey | RA | SGT | CAN | R.148411 | 415 | Halifax | LW595 | 28/07/1944 | L7 | 517 | 23 | ss9. |
| Hather | G | F/S | | 1578914 | 630 | Lancaster | ND788 | 24/03/1944 | 9C/L7 | 53401 | 17 | |
| Hattey | DH | SGT | CAN | R.112861 | 431 | Halifax | NA514 | 16/06/1944 | L7 | 220 | 8 | |
| Haughton | R | SGT | | 954638 | 40 | Wellington | LP234 | 13/06/1944 | L7 | 165 | 7 | A/G. Shot down on raid on Munich. |
| Hayes | BDB | WO1 | SA | 580059V | 24SAAF | Marauder | HD465 | 14/08/1944 | L7 | 665 | 28 | |
| Hayes | HB | F/S | CAN | R.204430 | 419 | Lancaster | KB718 | 04/07/1944 | L7 | 361 | 14 | |
| Hayes | PFJ | SGT | EIR | 1875976 | 50 | Lancaster | LL840 | 21/06/1944 | L7 | 221 | 8 | Born in Dublin. |
| Hayes | TE | F/S | CAN | R.204051 | 12 | Lancaster | PB247 | 12/08/1944 | L7 | 591 | 27 | |
| Hayman | WC | SGT | NZ | NZ.403448 | 57 | Wellington | W5445 | 30/09/1941 | 7A/383/L7 | 90078 | 16 | Broke ankle landing. Also POW no. 90 (Stalag 383). See Silk and Barbed Wire, p.88. |
| Hayward | N | SGT | | 1239056 | 161 | Halifax | LL388 | 28/08/1944 | L7 | 780 | 34 | Lost on SOE Operation Hendrick 1. |
| Haywood | JA | SGT | | 939402 | 463 | Lancaster | NF990 | 06/11/1944 | L7 | 1242 | 55* | |
| Hazlehurst | WB | W/O | | 1187336 | 582 | Lancaster | PB184 | 11/09/1944 | L7 | 781 | 34 | |
| Hazzard | SB | SGT | | 1588124 | 640 | Halifax | MZ406 | 12/09/1944 | L7 | 782 | 34 | Author of They're Not Shooting At You Now, Grandad. |
| Head | RJ | SGT | | 1853252 | 76 | Halifax | MZ622 | 24/05/1944 | L7 | 222 | 8 | ss7. |
| Healey | E | S/SGT | | 3775315 | GPR | Horsa | LH288 | 17/09/1944 | L7 | 1025 | 40 | B/19. 1st pilot. Captured 21 September 1944. |
| Healy | E | SGT | | 1836017 | 90 | Stirling | EF294 | 02/06/1944 | L7 | 117 | 4 | Shot down near Amiens, France. |
| Heard | RP | W/O | | 751885 | 216 | Bombay | L5847 | 17/11/1941 | 7A/383/L7 | 90073 | 16 | Nav. Also POW no. 85 (Stalag 383). |
| Heasman | R | SGT | | 1600293 | 57 | Lancaster | LM115 | 21/06/1944 | L7 | 301 | 12 | Came down near Antwerp. |
| Heath | ALR | SGT | | 1167938 | 101 | Wellington | R3295 | 30/11/1941 | 7A/383/L7 | 90081 | 16 | Also POW no. 93 (Stalag 383). Noted post-war abstract artist. |
| Heath | PF | SGT | | 1935490 | 57 | Lancaster | LM579 | 25/08/1944 | L7 | 708 | 30 | Shared his parachute with the flight engineer, who fell off and was killed. |
| Heath | RR | SGT | | 1395933 | 640 | Halifax | MZ930 | 04/11/1944 | L7 | 1142 | 48 | |
| Hector | FA | SGT | CAN | R.114679 | 419 | Lancaster | KB715 | 24/12/1944 | L7 | 1327 | 57* | |
| Heddle | GC | SGT | CAN | R.163712 | 76 | Halifax | MZ531 | 07/06/1944 | 12A/L7 | 80153 | 9 | 12A? |
| Hedgecock | HE | SGT | | 1394818 | 115 | Lancaster | ND745 | 22/05/1944 | L7 | 25 | 1 | |

| Surname | Initials | Rank | Nat. | Service No. | Sqn | Aircraft | Serial | Date | Camp | No. | Ref | Notes |
|---|---|---|---|---|---|---|---|---|---|---|---|---|
| Helme | F | F/S | | 1675318 | 178 | Liberator | KG933 | 30/07/1944 | L7 | 666 | 28 | A/G on trip to Warsaw. Same crew as F/L A.H. Hammet RAAF. |
| Hendery | ARC | SGT | CAN | R.216270 | 77 | Halifax | NA524 | 16/06/1944 | L7 | 166 | 7 | Commissioned (J.89074). |
| Henry | RJ | F/S | CAN | R.70957 | 431 | Halifax | LK968 | 03/12/1943 | 11B/L7 | 117121 | 33 | |
| Heron | J | LAC | | 1115357 | BSD Helwan | n/a | n/a | 23/06/1942 | #/L7 | 138933 | 18 | DMT. Captured at Tobruk. |
| Herrick | VR | SGT | CAN | R.225262 | 432 | Halifax | NA516 | 16/06/1944 | L7 | 167 | 7 | |
| Herron | J | SGT | | 1532782 | 77 | Halifax | NA524 | 16/06/1944 | L7 | 168 | 7 | |
| Hewitt | GA | SGT | | 1594150 | 77 | Halifax | MZ711 | 16/06/1944 | L7 | 169 | 7 | |
| Hewitt | I | F/S | CAN | R.64413 | 97 | Manchester | R5795 | 18/12/1941 | 7A/383/L7 | 90129 | 16 | Also POW no.? (Stalag 383). |
| Hewlett | KJR | SGT | | 1852573 | 550 | Lancaster | PA991 | 28/08/1944 | L7 | 783 | 34 | |
| Higginbotham | J | S/SGT | | 905927 | GPR | Horsa | n/k | 21/09/1944 | 12A/L7 | 984 | 39 | B/19. |
| Higman | FJ | SGT | | 1587565 | 102 | Halifax | MZ646 | 28/06/1944 | L7 | 303 | 12 | |
| Hill | J | F/S | | 1467922 | 103 | Lancaster | ME741 | 22/04/1944 | 6J/9C/L7/ 344/7B/383 | 7069 | n/k | DFM (16/11/43; 12 Sq). On second tour. |
| Hill | LG | F/S | NZ | NZ.426997 | 75 | Lancaster | ND802 | 27/05/1944 | L7 | 170 | 7 | |
| Hill | P | SGT | | 5550150 | 2SAS | n/a | n/a | 05/02/1944 | L7 | 26 | 1 | SAS (transferred from Hampshire Regiment). Removed to Stalag 383. |
| Hillyard | LG | SGT | | 1818509 | 190 | Stirling | LJ943 | 21/09/1944 | L7/L3 | 1026 | 40 | F/E hit by flak after Arnhem. Injured. |
| Hislop | J | LAC | | 1347549 | 2788 | n/a | n/a | 25/08/1944 | L7 | 846 | 37 | G/G. RAF Regiment. Captured at Valence after the invasion of the south of France. |
| Hitchcock | FN | F/S | NZ | NZ.4310172 | 489 | Beaufighter | NT926 | 30/08/1944 | L7 | 742 | 33 | Nav. Pilot F/Sgt C.I. Lyell RNZAF. |
| Hitchings | RB | F/S | | 1578091 | 614 | Halifax | JP323 | 23/11/1944 | L7 | 1243 | 55* | Nav flying from Amendola, Italy, on Szombathely, Hungary. |
| Hodgkinson | BG | SGT | CAN | J.38649 | 401 | Spitfire | W3955 | 27/10/1941 | 7A/383/L7/L3 | 90144 | 16 | Commissioned. Transferred to Stalag Luft III in August as F/O. Also POW no. 143. (Stalag 383). MiD 28/12/45. |
| Hodgson | RY | WO1 | CAN | R.128401 | 426 | Halifax | LW199 | 02/11/1944 | L7 | 1193 | 50 | |
| Hodgson | W | F/S | AUS | A.415900 | 90 | Stirling | EF509 | 09/05/1944 | L7 | 266 | 11 | Captured 31 May 1944. Fresnes prison. Author of Bombs and Barbed Wire. |
| Hogan | JK | P/O | CAN | R.223544 | 582 | Lancaster | PB149 | 09/11/1944 | L7 | 1192 | 50 | A/G. Commissioned wef 8 November 1944. |
| Holcroft | D | SGT | | 1622307 | 76 | Halifax | LW648 | 04/11/1944 | L7 | 1244 | 55* | |

| Surname | Initials | Rank | | Service No. | Sqn | Aircraft | Serial | Date | Stalag | POW No. | Notes |
|---|---|---|---|---|---|---|---|---|---|---|---|
| Holden | AJ | F/S | | 1178754 | 405 | Lancaster | LM345 | 27/09/1943 | L7 | 667 | 28 | Captured near Fos, France 8 May 1944. Toulouse, Fresnes, Wiesbaden prisons. |
| Hollinrake | R | SGT | | 1893307 | 426 | Halifax | NP775 | 04/11/1944 | L7 | 1194 | 50 | |
| Holloway | ME | F/S | | 1315065 | 37 | Wellington | HF524 | 16/06/1944 | L7 | 304 | 12 | Shot down over Yugoslavia. Repatriated to UK via Odessa and Middle East. |
| Holmes | HR | F/S | | 926487 | 83 | Hampden | AE133 | 10/01/1942 | 7A/383/L7 | 90150 | 16 | W/AG. Also POW no. 149 (Stalag 383). |
| Holmwood | AA | F/S | | 1320871 | 103 | Lancaster | ME799 | 28/07/1944 | 9C/L7/383 | 53392 | 41* | Evacuated to Stalag 383. See *Intercom* Winter 90, p.50, & *Lanc at War*:5, p.43. |
| Holt | E | SGT | | 1109174 | 455 | Hampden | P1201 | 07/11/1941 | 7A/383/L7 | 90113 | 16 | Captured 21 December 1941, but see *Silk and Barbed Wire*, p.90. Also POW no. 116 (Stalag 383). |
| Holt | GM | SGT | | 2212994 | 514 | Lancaster | LM265 | 12/08/1944 | L7 | 592 | 27 | ss8. |
| Hooker | F | SGT | | 1850487 | 102 | Halifax | MZ699 | 12/09/1944 | L7 | 784 | 34 | |
| Hooper | JM | S/SGT | | 2584037 | GPR | Horsa | n/k | 19/09/1944 | L7 | 913 | 38 | B/20. |
| Hope | R | S/SGT | | 325601 | GPR | Horsa | n/k | 20/09/1944 | L7 | 914 | 38 | F/16. Date is a guess based on other F/16 men. |
| Hormfleck | PW | SGT | | 1337114 | 207 | Lancaster | PD322 | 06/12/1944 | L7 | 1284 | 56 | |
| Horn | G | SGT | | 978849 | 217 | Beaufort | AW342 | 21/06/1942 | 7A/L7 | 338 | 13 | W/AG. |
| Horner | WR | F/S | | 1318192 | 35 | Lancaster | ND846 | 04/07/1944 | 9C/L7 | 52625 | 41* | ss8. |
| Hornsby | NW | SGT | | 107881 | GPR | Horsa | n/k | 09/06/1944 | 12A/L7 | 80162 | 9 | D-Day Operation Tonga. 2nd pilot. 12A? |
| Horrigan | LVH | SGT | | 1577094 | 101 | Lancaster | LM508 | 21/06/1944 | L7 | 223 | 8 | |
| Horseman | AW | W/O | | 1164562 | 106 | Hampden | P1341 | 15/01/1942 | 7A/383/L7 | 90100 | 16 | W/AG. Also POW no.106 (Stalag 383). |
| Horton | JR | SGT | | 14413159 | GPR | Horsa | n/k | 21/09/1944 | 12A/L7 | 075482 | 47 | G/10. |
| Horton | WHA | SGT | | 1581905 | 195 | Lancaster | HK697 | 12/12/1944 | L7 | 1328 | 57* | |
| Howard | H | F/S | AUS | A.430260 | 463 | Lancaster | LM309 | 23/09/1944 | 9C/L7 | 52795 | 57* | N/B. Fractured arm and back. Three months in hospital. Repatriated. |
| Howard | LE | S/SGT | | 6207012 | GPR | Horsa | n/k | 20/09/1944 | L7 | 915 | 38 | E/*. |
| Howarth | BJ | SGT | | 575933 | 15 | Lancaster | NF958 | 12/09/1944 | L7 | 847 | 37 | |
| Howarth | GT | W/O | | 1062415 | 77 | Halifax | LL138 | 22/05/1944 | L7/8B | 83 | 2 | Badly injured. Repatriated from Stalag 8B on *Letitia*, arriving Liverpool on 2 February 1945.See *Men of Air*, pp. 231-5, & *D-Day Bombers: The Veterans' Story*, pp. 106-8. |
| Hoyle | H | F/S | | 1067690 | 70 | Wellington | LN699 | 21/07/1944 | L7 | 540 | 24 | Nav lost on raid on Pardubice. |
| Hudson | AL | SGT | | 1896263 | 77 | Halifax | MZ711 | 16/06/1944 | L7 | 171 | 7 | |
| Hudson | P | F/S | | 1474650 | 10 | Halifax | LV906 | 24/05/1944 | L7 | 27 | 1 | |

| Surname | Initials | Rank | Nat. | Service no. | Sqn | Aircraft | Serial | Date | Grid | No. | Age | Notes |
|---|---|---|---|---|---|---|---|---|---|---|---|---|
| Hudson | WJJ | SGT | | 1586412 | 227 | Lancaster | LM259 | 04/12/1944 | L7 | 1285 | 56 | |
| Hughes | AM | F/S | AUS | A.417845 | 467 | Lancaster | LM239 | 26/09/1944 | L7 | 1069 | 45* | Repatriated? |
| Hughes | EL | SGT | | 1312705 | 10 | Halifax | W7852 | 01/10/1942 | #/L7 | 1480 | 3 | Splinter wounds to face, abdomen and left shoulder. |
| Hughes | JM | F/S | AUS | A.418418 | 467 | Lancaster | LM450 | 24/06/1944 | L7 | 305 | 12 | Frostbitten toe amputated during evacuation, January 1945. |
| Hughes | K | F/S | | 1457564 | 9 | Lancaster | ND948 | 24/06/1944 | L7 | 306 | 12 | |
| Hughes | RD | SGT | | 1697212 | 467 | Lancaster | ED764 | 17/08/1943 | #/L7 | 12821 | 29 | Court-martialled for working for the enemy. |
| Hulbert | GA | SGT | | 1860229 | 295 | Stirling | LK203 | 01/12/1944 | L7 | 1329 | 57* | F/E. Baled out without orders. Aircraft returned to base. |
| Hull | FG | F/S | CAN | R.206554 | 425 | Halifax | LW379 | 01/11/1944 | L7 | 1143 | 48 | Mid-under gunner. |
| Hulse | RJ | SGT | | 1578581 | 93 | Spitfire | n/k | 31/08/1944 | L7 | 848 | 37 | Aircraft serial number not known. |
| Hume | W | SGT | | 1567551 | 299 | Stirling | EF267 | 19/09/1944 | L7 | 849 | 37 | F/E lost over Arnhem. |
| Humes | EAL | SGT | | 642170 | 514 | Lancaster | LL639 | 11/04/1944 | 9C/L7 | 52732 | 49 | ss7. |
| Hunt | PR | SGT | CAN | R.176092 | 76 | Halifax | MZ531 | 07/06/1944 | 12A/L7 | 80028 | 9 | 12A? |
| Hunter | D | SGT | | 1479638 | 550 | Lancaster | NE164 | 28/07/1944 | L7 | 518 | 23 | |
| Hunter | WH | W/O | | 941800 | 97 | Lancaster | NE121 | 30/07/1944 | L7 | 668 | 28 | |
| Huntley | N | SGT | | 1592382 | 161 | Halifax | LL388 | 28/08/1944 | 9C/L7 | 52826 | 57* | On SOE Operation Hendrick 1. |
| Hurley | JA | SGT | | 1866943 | 44 | Lancaster | ME628 | 24/06/1944 | L7 | 307 | 12 | |
| Hutchinson | CG | SGT | | 1874806 | 50 | Lancaster | LM676 | 06/10/1944 | L7 | 1027 | 40 | A/G. |
| Hutchinson | ED | SGT | | 1595455 | 115 | Lancaster | LL944 | 16/12/1944 | L7 | 1330 | 57* | |
| Hutchinson | KW | SGT | | 1826348 | 432 | Halifax | NP801 | 09/10/1944 | L7 | 1028 | 40 | |
| Hutchison | RH | LAC | | 1053031 | 2901 | n/a | n/a | 03/10/1943 | L6/L7 | 2967 | 27* | RAF Regiment, captured on Greek island of Kos. |
| Hyde | EH | F/S | CAN | R.217237 | 426 | Halifax | NP775 | 04/11/1944 | L7 | 1195 | 50 | Captured 7 November 1944. |
| Hydes | AG | F/S | | 1577072 | 57 | Lancaster | LM580 | 21/06/1944 | L7 | 224 | 8 | Escaped on march, captured, escaped. To UK via Odessa. |
| Hymas | JH | SGT | | 1321217 | 91 | Spitfire | MB832 | 23/01/1944 | 9C/L7 | 53294 | 49 | Shot down on Ramrod 472. Injured; hospitalised. |
| Illingworth | AW | F/S | | 904903 | 233 | Dakota | KG329 | 06/06/1944 | 12A/L7 | 80163 | 9 | |
| Imart | P | S/C | FRA | 13481 | 346 | Halifax | NA549 | 04/11/1944 | L7 | 1245 | 55* | From Chambéry, Savoie, France. |
| Indge | RC | SGT | | 2203016 | 578 | Halifax | NA568 | 11/09/1944 | L7 | 785 | 34 | |
| Inglis | AA | SGT | | 1678502 | 547 | Liberator | EV897 | 18/06/1944 | L7 | 362 | 14 | F/E shot down off French coast. |
| Inglis | ER | SGT | CAN | R.159493 | 207 | Lancaster | ND570 | 04/07/1944 | L7 | 394 | 15 | |
| Ireland | JR | SGT | | 1645994 | 570 | Stirling | LJ594 | 18/09/1944 | L7 | 985 | 39 | F/E shot down over Arnhem. |
| Irwin | KH | SGT | CAN | R.177874 | 44 | Lancaster | LM171 | 28/07/1944 | L7 | 519 | 23 | |

| Surname | Initials | Rank | Country | Service No. | Sqn | Aircraft | Serial | Date | Camp | No. | Age | Notes |
|---|---|---|---|---|---|---|---|---|---|---|---|---|
| Jack | PD | SGT | | 1821450 | 466 | Halifax | LW372 | 06/10/1944 | L7 | 1029 | 40 | Punched in the face by three German civilians. |
| Jackson | CW | F/S | | 1433366 | 76 | Halifax | LW629 | 01/03/1944 | L7 | 267 | 11 | ss7. Nav. Captured in the Pyrenees 21 April 1944. |
| Jackson | J | SGT | | 2206208 | 550 | Lancaster | LL747 | 16/06/1944 | L7 | 459 | 21 | |
| Jackson | JL | SGT | | 1543931 | 640 | Halifax | NA560 | 09/08/1944 | L7 | 669 | 28 | |
| Jackson | S | F/S | | 1316398 | 35 | Lancaster | ND734 | 23/06/1944 | L7 | 225 | 8 | |
| Jacobs | ID | F/S | | 1395210 | 101 | Lancaster | LM395 | 22/05/1944 | L7 | 84 | 2 | |
| Jakeman | APA | WO1 | CAN | R.157995 | 428 | Lancaster | KB749 | 15/08/1944 | L7 | 709 | 30 | |
| James | DWM | S/SGT | | 944489 | GPR | Horsa | n/k | 20/09/1944 | L7 | 916 | 38 | E/11. |
| James | EW | SGT | | 1653092 | 450 | Kittyhawk | FX789 | 04/09/1944 | L7 | 786 | 34 | Shot down near Ravenna, Italy. |
| James | JH | SGT | | 1480087 | 37 | Wellington | LP259 | 21/10/1944 | L7 | 1110 | 47 | A/G on raid to Maribor. |
| James | LP | SGT | | 1872732 | 104 | Wellington | MF350 | 21/08/1944 | L7 | 743 | 33 | |
| James | WM | SGT | | 1817311 | 195 | Lancaster | HK689 | 04/11/1944 | L7 | 1196 | 50 | ss7. |
| Jameson | EH | SGT | | 1320456 | 640 | Halifax | MZ939 | 06/12/1944 | L7 | 1331 | 57* | |
| Jansen | ICJ | F/S | SA | 280690V | 24SAAF | Marauder | HD465 | 14/08/1944 | L7 | 670 | 28 | W/AG. From Transvaal, S Africa. |
| Jardine | AE | AC1 | CAN | R.153782 | 12AF HQ | n/a | n/a | 03/10/1944 | 12A/L7 | 076594 | 47 | Armourer. |
| Jarvis | NE | F/S | AUS | A.410413 | 61 | Lancaster | EE186 | 04/07/1944 | 12A/L7 | 86119 | 34 | |
| Jeacocke | S | F/S | AUS | A.425310 | 150 | Wellington | MF240 | 30/06/1944 | L7 | 520 | 23 | W/OP. Commissioned. |
| Jeary | GH | SGT | | 1610626 | 622 | Lancaster | LM477 | 24/07/1944 | L7 | 460 | 21 | ss7. |
| Jeffrey | CW | SGT | | 656342 | 37 | Wellington | LN853 | 03/04/1944 | L7 | 85 | 2 | Removed to Stalag 344. |
| Jenkins | DJ | F/S | | 1650738 | 51 | Halifax | NP962 | 06/12/1944 | L7 | 1286 | 56 | Nav. Baled out over target (Osnabrück). Aircraft returned to England. |
| Jenkins | JS | SGT | | 1324768 | 550 | Lancaster | LL747 | 16/06/1944 | L7 | 593 | 27 | Captured Antwerp 27 July 1944. |
| Jenkinson | F | SGT | | 971969 | 149 | Wellington | X9878 | 07/11/1941 | 8B/L7 | 6439 | 16* | ss6. Repatriated via Odessa. 8B? |
| Jennings | NE | F/S | CAN | R.219640 | 426 | Halifax | NP775 | 04/11/1944 | L7 | 1197 | 50 | |
| Jervis | IH | WO1 | CAN | R.103353 | 433 | Halifax | NP992 | 04/11/1944 | L7 | 1144 | 48 | |
| Joce | CS | SGT | | 1881284 | 61 | Lancaster | LM729 | 17/12/1944 | L7 | 1332 | 57* | ss7. Escaped on march. Repatriated via Odessa |
| Joel | WV | WO2 | CAN | R.180404 | 405 | Lancaster | ND526 | 24/05/1944 | L7 | 268 | 11 | Captured 20 June 1944(?), Brussels. |
| Johnson | GR | SGT | | 3050454 | 158 | Halifax | MZ734 | 25/10/1944 | L7 | 1111 | 47 | Aged nineteen. Killed escaping from Stalag IIIA 13 April 1945. MID (13/6/46). |
| Johnson | WL | SGT | USA | R.64415 | 101 | Wellington | R3295 | 30/11/1941 | 7A/383/L7 | 90092 | 16 | Pilot. In RCAF. From Freeport, New York. Also POW no. 101 (Stalag 383). |
| Johnston | GN | W/O | CAN | R.108304 | 424 | Halifax | LV910 | 28/06/1944 | 12A/L7 | 85730 | 33 | Badly beaten up by Gestapo in Reims. Commissioned (J.92609). |

| Surname | Initials | Rank | Nat. | Service No. | Sqn | Aircraft | Serial | Date | Camp | | | Notes |
|---|---|---|---|---|---|---|---|---|---|---|---|---|
| Johnston | MM | F/S | | A.426421 | 466 | Halifax | MZ368 | 09/08/1944 | L7 | 594 | 27 | |
| Johnston | V | F/S | AUS | 793627 | n/k | n/k | n/k | 21/05/1944 | L7 | 118 | 4 | Pilot. Lived at 251 Renfrew Street, Glasgow. AHB(5) RAF can find no record of him. ss7. |
| Johnstone | AI | F/S | CAN | R.145475 | 635 | Lancaster | ND924 | 12/05/1944 | L7 | 28 | 1 | |
| Jolivet | MS | SGT | FRA | n/k | n/k | n/k | n/k | 11/07/1944 | L7 | 427 | 15* | A/G. Service no. given same as Vaissade's. From Poitiers, Vienne, France. |
| Jonas | JG | SGT | | 1851378 | 432 | Halifax | NP695 | 06/12/1944 | L7 | 1287 | 56 | |
| Jones | E | W/O | | 745248 | 32 | Hurricane | N2533 | 11/06/1940 | L1/L3/L7/344 | 21 | 20 | Shot down over France. Caught on Jersey on 1 July 1940. To Stalag 344 in October 1944. Trupp 20? |
| Jones | FH | F/S | | 1395269 | 295 | Stirling | LK115 | 21/09/1944 | L7 | 986 | 39 | W/AG lost over Arnhem. Frederick H. Jones. |
| Jones | FH | F/S | | 1435330 | 233 | Dakota | KG586 | 21/09/1944 | L7 | 1030 | 40 | Pilot. Frank H. Jones. |
| Jones | H | SGT | | 2210970 | 625 | Lancaster | LM163 | 03/08/1944 | L7 | 595 | 27 | |
| Jones | JD | F/S | | 573430 | 15 | Lancaster | NF958 | 12/09/1944 | L7 | 850 | 37 | |
| Jones | L | SGT | | 2209587 | 630 | Lancaster | JB546 | 22/05/1944 | L7 | 29 | 1 | |
| Jones | N | SGT | | 2209235 | 625 | Lancaster | LM546 | 28/07/1944 | L7 | 461 | 21 | |
| Jones | TS | SGT | | 1016799 | 144 | Hampden | AD804 | 28/12/1941 | 7A/383/L7 | 90134 | 16 | Also POW no. 135 (Stalag 383). |
| Jones | W | SGT | | 1575502 | 158 | Halifax | LW634 | 30/03/1944 | L7 | 30 | 1 | Captured Etalle 18 May 1944. |
| Jones | WS | S/SGT | | 1910052 | GPR | Horsa | n/k | 06/06/1944 | L7 | 363 | 14 | B/*. |
| Kebbell | RF | F/S | | 1295606 | 199 | Stirling | EF295 | 06/06/1944 | L7 | 364 | 14 | W/AG lost on pre-D-Day para drop. |
| Kedie | JR | SGT | | 1672630 | 241 | Spitfire | PL323 | 20/10/1944 | L7 | 1145 | 48 | Pilot. |
| Keeler | PH | F/S | | 1388476 | 576 | Lancaster | ND859 | 12/07/1944 | L7 | 745 | 33 | Captured 16 August 1944. |
| Keeling | CT | SGT | | 1579149 | 101 | Lancaster | PB258 | 12/08/1944 | L7 | 596 | 27 | |
| Keil | J | SGT | | 1372964 | 626 | Lancaster | PA989 | 25/08/1944 | L7 | 710 | 30 | |
| Keirle | SA | SGT | | 1335551 | 550 | Lancaster | LM425 | 30/03/1944 | L7 | 119 | 4 | Wounded. In hospital at Aachen. |
| Kellard | A | SGT | | 2205580 | 462 | Halifax | MZ401 | 02/11/1944 | L7 | 1146 | 48 | |
| Kelly | CJ | SGT | CAN | R.54380 | 51 | Whitley | Z6839 | 07/11/1941 | 7A/383/L7 | 90061 | 16 | Also POW no. 74 (Stalag 383). |
| Kelly | G | SGT | | 1825685 | 50 | Lancaster | LM212 | 23/09/1944 | L7 | 1246 | 55* | ss7. Captured 23 November 1944. |
| Kelly | GHR | SGT | | 1588762 | 578 | Halifax | NA501 | 22/12/1944 | L7 | 1333 | 57* | |
| Kelly | LC | F/S | | 1339986 | 578 | Halifax | MZ563 | 22/04/1944 | L7 | 120 | 4 | |
| Kemp | AE | F/S | NZ | NZ.414638 | 47 | Beaufighter | JM323 | 02/08/1943 | 7A/L7 | 339 | 13 | Pilot. Ditched off Sardinia. In Campo 54 briefly. Escaped in September 1943. On the run until 5 May 1944. From Hamilton, NZ. |

| Surname | Initials | Rank | Nat. | Service No. | Sqn | Aircraft | Serial | Date | Camp | POW No. | Section | Notes |
|---|---|---|---|---|---|---|---|---|---|---|---|---|
| Kemp | TWM | F/S | | 1605894 | 466 | Halifax | MZ299 | 15/10/1944 | L7 | 1112 | 47 | ss7. Escaped from march. Repatriated via Odessa. |
| Kendall | RPE | F/S | | 1457152 | 15 | Lancaster | NF958 | 12/09/1944 | L7 | 851 | 37 | |
| Kenley | CJ | F/S | AUS | A.419372 | 622 | Lancaster | LM108 | 28/05/1944 | L7 | 852 | 37 | Captured 3 June 1944. Bayonne prison for thirty days, then in Fresnes and Wiesbaden prisons. |
| Kennedy | J | SGT | | 1796561 | 431 | Halifax | NA514 | 16/06/1944 | L7 | 269 | 11 | F/E. 5' 3" tall. |
| Kennedy | R | F/S | AUS | A.420224 | 299 | Stirling | LK241 | 27/11/1944 | L7 | 1288 | 56 | W/OP on SOE op to Norway. Captured 29 November 1944. |
| Kent | GE | SGT | | 1231765 | 466 | Halifax | LW116 | 22/06/1944 | L7 | 270 | 11 | |
| Kenworthy | J | F/S | | 1672259 | 12 | Lancaster | ND342 | 12/12/1944 | L7 | 1289 | 56 | |
| Kenyon-Ormrod | H | SGT | | 659144 | 578 | Halifax | LW503 | 24/02/1944 | L7 | 521 | 23 | |
| Kerrigan | TJ | SGT | | 1537753 | 61 | Lancaster | ME725 | 06/12/1944 | L7 | 1290 | 56 | |
| Kershaw | C | F/S | | 1143375 | 190 | Stirling | EF260 | 20/09/1944 | L7 | 917 | 38 | A/G lost over Arnhem. |
| Kilbryde | GH | SGT | | 4922900 | GPR | Horsa | n/k | 19/09/1944 | L7 | 853 | 37 | C/*. 2nd pilot. |
| King | AJ | WO2 | CAN | R.144492 | 427 | Halifax | LV938 | 28/06/1944 | L7 | 308 | 12 | Possibly escaped after camp evacuated in January 1945. Commissioned (J.87598). |
| King | GJ | SGT | | 1321205 | 90 | Stirling | EF294 | 02/06/1944 | L7 | 121 | 4 | Captured 5 June 1944. Chief medical orderly. |
| King | GW | F/S | AUS | A.426352 | 463 | Lancaster | DV229 | 10/06/1944 | L7 | 309 | 12 | Captured 19 June 1944. |
| Kirby | PS | SGT | | 1450081 | 40 | Wellington | LP234 | 13/06/1944 | L7 | 172 | 7 | W/OP shot down on raid on Munich. |
| Kirkby | GJ | F/S | | 1623229 | 166 | Lancaster | NE112 | 31/08/1944 | L7 | 787 | 34 | |
| Kirkpatrick | S | F/S | | 1827066 | 415 | Halifax | MZ603 | 02/11/1944 | L7 | 1147 | 48 | |
| Kirwan | KPJ | F/S | AUS | A.419366 | 57 | Lancaster | JB370 | 07/07/1944 | L7 | 395 | 15 | Landed near German guard billet. |
| Klatt | HW | F/S | CAN | R.157721 | 570 | Stirling | EH897 | 19/09/1944 | L7 | 918 | 38 | B/A. See his photo in The Royal Air Force at Arnhem, p.153. |
| Kneil | HC | SGT | | 1187608 | 44 | Lancaster | PB266 | 28/07/1944 | L7 | 597 | 27 | |
| Knott | HW | SGT | | 1895617 | 466 | Halifax | LV936 | 04/11/1944 | L7 | 1148 | 48 | Captured 8 November 1944 trying to cross the Rhine. |
| Knowles | JAE | SGT | | 1595230 | 227 | Lancaster | NG296 | 06/12/1944 | L7 | 1291 | 56 | |
| Knox | WH | SGT | | 11000594 | GPR | Horsa | n/k | 20/09/1944 | L7 | 1070 | 45* | A/1. 2nd pilot. |
| Konarzewski | S | SGT | POL | 784818 | 300 | Wellington | R1705 | 07/11/1941 | 7A/383/L7 | 90062 | 16 | Also POW no. 75 (Stalag 383). |
| Korner | GV | SGT | NZ | 1392129 | 640 | Halifax | MZ930 | 04/11/1944 | L7 | 1149 | 48 | Shot down on 31st op. Transferred to RNZAF (no. 44769) after the war, then back to the RAF. |

| Name | Init | Rank | Nat | Service no | Sqn | Aircraft | Serial | Date | Camps | POW no | Block | Notes |
|---|---|---|---|---|---|---|---|---|---|---|---|---|
| Kydd | G | F/S | CAN | R.220333 | 115 | Lancaster | PD274 | 25/08/1944 | L7 | 711 | 30 | |
| La Pointe | HD | SGT | CAN | R.187666 | 429 | Halifax | HX352 | 24/05/1944 | L7 | 46 | 1 | ss7. |
| Ladkin | AH | SGT | | 1860013 | 49 | Lancaster | NE128 | 21/06/1944 | L7 | 226 | 8 | |
| Laffin | MA | WO1 | CAN | R.124642 | 434 | Halifax | LK801 | 16/06/1944 | L7 | 227 | 8 | |
| Laing | KN | SGT | CAN | R.61468 | 609 | Spitfire | AD507 | 15/11/1941 | 7A/383/L7 | 90053 | 16 | Also POW no. 66 (Stalag 383). |
| Laing | RC | SGT | CAN | R.223741 | 78 | Halifax | MZ340 | 28/07/1944 | L7 | 463 | 21 | |
| Laing | TD | F/S | | 1561720 | 463 | Lancaster | NF977 | 23/10/1944 | L7 | 1113 | 47 | |
| Laird | R | SGT | | 1825466 | 149 | Lancaster | HK645 | 12/12/1944 | L7 | 1334 | 57* | Lanc HK645 (or NF934?). |
| Lambert | DMD | F/S | | 1494741 | 35 | Lancaster | ND702 | 11/09/1944 | L7 | 788 | 34 | MB, ChB, FRCGP. MBE (1/1/93). |
| Lambert | JAJ | F/S | CAN | R.185327 | 424 | Halifax | LW131 | 02/11/1944 | L7 | 1198 | 50 | Commissioned (J.92976). |
| Lamont | JW | SGT | | 987184 | 101 | Wellington | R1778 | 30/11/1941 | 7A/383/L7 | 90076 | 16 | Also POW no. 88 (Stalag 383). |
| Lane | KA | W/O | | 1314755 | 83 | Lancaster | ND963 | 22/05/1944 | L7 | 31 | 1 | DFC (19/5/44). Deputy Camp Leader. Commissioned (177324) 25 July 1944. Flying officer 24 November 1944. |
| Larkin | CF | F/S | AUS | A.427387 | 467 | Lancaster | PB299 | 19/09/1944 | L7 | 987 | 39 | Landed in a forest in Belgium. |
| Latchford | P | F/S | | 1451333 | 90 | Stirling | LJ460 | 10/04/1944 | L7 | 32 | 1 | Captured 20 April 1944. |
| Lauder | WR | F/S | NZ | NZ.424480 | 9 | Lancaster | ME724 | 22/04/1944 | 9C/L7 | 53141 | 49* | Pilot. Commissioned. |
| Law | AC | SGT | | 1434905 | 460 | Lancaster | ND674 | 11/05/1944 | 9C/L7/7A | 53362 | 49* | Jaw broken by parachute harness; lacerated nerves. In hospital in Brussels. |
| Lawlor | JJ | SGT | CAN | R.103379 | 426 | Halifax | LW199 | 02/11/1944 | L7 | 1150 | 48 | Nav lost on night intruder mission. Pilot killed (F/L DH McLeod RAF). |
| Lawson | AJ | F/S | | 1578235 | 487 | Mosquito | HR144 | 20/11/1944 | L7 | 1247 | 55* | |
| Le Heup | KLG | SGT | | 1896608 | 158 | Halifax | LV792 | 02/06/1944 | L7 | 302 | 12 | Baled out in error. See Nachtjagd, p.180. |
| Lea | H | SGT | | 1895544 | 61 | Lancaster | ND988 | 23/09/1944 | L7 | 919 | 38 | ss7. |
| Leadbeater | R | F/S | | 1433570 | 214 | Stirling | EH895 | 23/08/1943 | 4B/L7 | 267166 | NK | Badly damaged ankles on landing. Unclear how/when arrived at L7. From Bristol. |
| Leak | LC | F/S | AUS | A.417087 | 460 | Lancaster | LL957 | 18/07/1944 | L7 | 464 | 21 | ss7. Evacuated to Stalag 383. |
| Leaney | WH | SGT | | 1182065 | 460 | Lancaster | LL951 | 21/05/1944 | L7 | 173 | 7 | |
| Leason | TH | SGT | | 2321469 | 467 | Lancaster | LM205 | 29/06/1944 | 9C/L7/L3 | 53341 | 41* | Evacuated to Luft 3? |
| Lee | BA | SGT | | 1338225 | 78 | Halifax | DT768 | 15/07/1943 | 12A/L7 | 80123 | 9 | Captured near Romorantin 9 or 11 June 1944. 12A? |
| Lee | HE | SGT | | 1891948 | 463 | Lancaster | PD259 | 23/10/1944 | L7 | 1151 | 48 | |
| Lee | SK | SGT | | 1863003 | 218 | Lancaster | PD374 | 08/11/1944 | L7 | 1199 | 50 | |
| Leigh | JCL | F/S | | 1322733 | 166 | Lancaster | ME639 | 25/02/1944 | 9C/L7 | 53402 | 57* | |

| Surname | Initials | Rank | Nat. | Service No. | Unit | Aircraft | Serial | Date | Camp | No. | Age | Notes |
|---|---|---|---|---|---|---|---|---|---|---|---|---|
| Leppington | GW | WO1 | CAN | R.144385 | 431 | Lancaster | KB817 | 01/11/1944 | L7 | 1200 | 50 | Shot down by bomber. Commissioned (J.91189). |
| Lewis | D | SGT | | 2203739 | 207 | Lancaster | LM123 | 15/10/1944 | L7 | 1071 | 45* | Baled out - aircraft returned to UK. |
| Lewis | OD | SGT | CAN | R.55041 | 432 | Lancaster | DS831 | 16/12/1943 | 9C/L7 | 43348 | n/k | Wounded? 9C? |
| Lewis | PA | SGT | | 1318024 | 103 | Lancaster | ME649 | 12/12/1944 | L7 | 1335 | 57* | |
| Lewis | RE | SGT | | 1893895 | 44 | Lancaster | ND517 | 18/07/1944 | L7 | 598 | 27 | |
| Lewis | TB | SGT | | 1381322 | 103 | Wellington | R1395 | 15/01/1942 | 7A/383/L7 | 90125 | 16 | ss6. Also POW no. 128 (Stalag 383). Escaped on march 21 January 1945. |
| Lewis | TV | SGT | | 1313601 | 623 | Stirling | EF155 | 18/11/1943 | 9C/L3/L7 | 43163 | 4 | Evacuated to Stalag 383. |
| Lewis | WE | WO1 | CAN | R.65518 | 61 | Lancaster | PA998 | 25/08/1944 | L7 | 712 | 30 | |
| Lidbury | RL | F/S | | 1585512 | 76 | Halifax | MZ736 | 28/06/1944 | 12A/L7 | 86387 | 34 | |
| Lillywhite | FC | F/S | AUS | A.426625 | 44 | Lancaster | ME634 | 07/07/1944 | 12A/L7 | 86398 | 34 | |
| Limacher | AR | F/S | CAN | R.258284 | 425 | Halifax | MZ831 | 04/11/1944 | L7 | 1201 | 50 | |
| Limet | HJR | F/S | BEL | 1299911 | 349 | Spitfire | MH610 | 28/04/1944 | 9C/L7 | 53403 | 41* | Shot down escorting B-26 bombers to Paris. Killed in DC-4 crash 13/14 May 1948. |
| Lindsay | JD | F/S | AUS | A.419074 | 625 | Lancaster | ED938 | 12/06/1944 | L7 | 174 | 7 | |
| Lister | FK | SGT | AUS | A.402512 | 7 | Stirling | W7436 | 18/12/1941 | 7A/383/L7 | 90148 | 16 | Also POW no. 147 (Stalag 383). |
| Little | A | AC1 | | 1558393 | 235AMES | n/a | n/a | 21/06/1942 | 11A/L7 | 140101 | 18 | G/G. Captured at Tobruk. |
| Little | GB | SGT | CAN | R.265557 | 419 | Lancaster | KB715 | 24/12/1944 | L7 | 1336 | 57* | |
| Little | RRA | SGT | | 1342079 | 77 | Halifax | JD301 | 23/09/1943 | L7 | 365 | 14 | Broken limbs. At Hohe Mark for seven months. |
| Little | TG | SGT | | 1459875 | 75 | Lancaster | HK569 | 20/07/1944 | 9C/L7 | 52469 | 49* | B/A. |
| Lloyd | A | F/S | | 1443304 | 226 | Mitchell | FW127 | 17/08/1944 | 12A/L7 | 86372 | 34 | Nav. Commissioned (184801) 31 October 1944 (seniority 21/7/44). F/O 23 February 1945. |
| Lloyd | J | SSM | | 5882820 | 2SAS | n/a | n/a | 24/04/1944 | L7 | 33 | 1 | SAS (transferred from Northamptonshire Regiment) captured in Italy. |
| Lloyd | RF | SGT | | 2211370 | 214 | Fortress | SR384 | 24/05/1944 | L7 | 34 | 1 | |
| Loakes | PG | SGT | | 1868416 | 207 | Lancaster | LL973 | 21/06/1944 | L7 | 271 | 11 | |
| Locke | JB | F/S | CAN | R.79194 | 149 | Stirling | BF312 | 16/07/1942 | 344/L7 | 24957 | 57* | Pilot. 344? |
| Loftus | A | F/S | | 1569758 | 158 | Halifax | LK787 | 18/03/1944 | 9C/L7 | 53140 | 49* | A/G. Adrift in dinghy for eighty hours. |
| Lonergan | TP | F/S | AUS | A.432828 | 463 | Lancaster | NF977 | 23/10/1944 | L7 | 1152 | 48 | Eye injured by shattered Perspex. Landed on island of Vlissingen. |
| Long | HJ | W/O | AUS | A.417091 | 460 | Lancaster | ND674 | 11/05/1944 | L7 | 396 | 15 | Stomach wound and bullet in right hip. In hospital at St Gilles prison, Brussels. |
| Long | RA | S/SGT | | 10538193 | GPR | Horsa | n/k | 19/09/1944 | L7 | 920 | 38 | D/5. |

| Surname | Initials | Rank | Nat. | Service No. | Sqn | Aircraft | Serial | Date | Camp | | | Notes |
|---|---|---|---|---|---|---|---|---|---|---|---|---|
| Longhurst | JC | SGT | | 189/250 | 61 | Lancaster | PB436 | 29/08/1944 | L7 | 746 | 33 | |
| Lord | RA | SGT | | 1575194 | 44 | Lancaster | PB192 | 04/11/1944 | L7 | 1153 | 48 | |
| Lovatt | EN | SGT | | 1590361 | 214 | Fortress | SR384 | 24/05/1944 | L7 | 35 | 1 | |
| Lovatt | JW | SGT | | 1583191 | 101 | Lancaster | PB258 | 12/08/1944 | L7 | 600 | 27 | |
| Loveridge | A | SGT | | 2210265 | 626 | Lancaster | PA989 | 26/08/1944 | 9C/L7 | 52691 | 49* | F/E. |
| Lovett | J | S/SGT | | 128577 | GPR | Horsa | n/k | 17/09/1944 | L7 | 854 | 37 | E/11. Pilot towed by Dakota. |
| Low | WD | F/S | | 1232330 | 106 | Lancaster | ND680 | 06/06/1944 | L7 | 465 | 21 | See No Time For Fear, p.178. |
| Lowe | JJ | SGT | | 1818999 | 190 | Stirling | LJ916 | 21/09/1944 | L7 | 1031 | 40 | F/E shot down on Arnhem supply drop. |
| Lowe | KR | SGT | CAN | R.204449 | 434 | Halifax | LW175 | 12/08/1944 | L7 | 599 | 27 | Commissioned (J.88084). |
| Lowrey | A | SGT | | 1111840 | 10 | Halifax | MZ312 | 20/07/1944 | L7 | 466 | 21 | |
| Ludwig | JA | SGT | CAN | R.192407 | 432 | Halifax | MZ601 | 12/06/1944 | L7 | 175 | 7 | |
| Lund | R | S/SGT | | 2005243 | GPR | Horsa | n/k | 19/09/1944 | L7 | 921 | 38 | D/5. From India. His father, Lt Col The Rev Lund was Senior United Board Chaplain at Kasauli. |
| Lusted | RB | F/S | AUS | A.419880 | 466 | Halifax | MZ368 | 09/08/1944 | L7 | 601 | 27 | A/G. |
| Lyall | RT | F/S | AUS | A.421541 | 214 | Fortress | SR384 | 24/05/1944 | L7 | 36 | 1 | |
| Lydford | PF | SGT | | 1801914 | 293 | Walrus | L2223 | 05/08/1944 | L7 | 602 | 27 | Pilot. Crashed rescuing Sgt K Etchels, Spit JF351, 241 Squadron. |
| Lyell | CI | F/S | NZ | NZ.413866 | 489 | Beaufighter | NT926 | 30/08/1944 | L7 | 747 | 33 | Pilot. |
| Lynch | WH | SGT | | 1894983 | 100 | Lancaster | LL887 | 22/04/1944 | L7 | 122 | 4 | Captured c. 6 June 1944, Brussels or Antwerp. |
| Lyon | ABD | SGT | | 14216954 | GPR | Horsa | n/k | 20/09/1944 | 13D/L7 | 15246 | 55 | F/16. |
| Lyons | R | SGT | | 1798263 | 635 | Lancaster | ND703 | 06/12/1944 | L7 | 1292 | 56 | |
| MacDonald | AH | F/S | | 1604307 | 166 | Lancaster | ME829 | 23/09/1944 | L7 | 923 | 38 | Landed on roof-top near Düsseldorf. |
| MacDonald | CD | F/S | CAN | R.164366 | 432 | Halifax | NP185 | 06/11/1944 | L7 | 1155 | 48 | |
| MacDonald | JF | SGT | | 2881342 | GPR | Horsa | n/k | 19/09/1944 | L7 | 924 | 38 | E/11. |
| MacDonald | WA | F/S | CAN | R.176660 | 100 | Lancaster | PB172 | 28/07/1944 | L7 | 603 | 27 | B/A. ss7. Captured 3 August 1944. Commissioned (J.90609). |
| Macey | MEF | SGT | | 1801876 | 127 | Spitfire | NH600 | 14/08/1944 | L7 | 748 | 33 | Shot down by flak near Falaise, France. |
| MacGregor | AJ | SGT | | 14615855 | GPR | Horsa | n/k | 26/09/1944 | L7 | 988 | 39 | A/*. |
| Maciej | L | SGT | POL | 792369 | 300 | Wellington | W5666 | 11/06/1941 | 9C/L3/L7/L6 | 39140 | 20 | Moved to Luft 6 on 18 August 1944. |
| MacLean | DL | SGT | CAN | R.183260 | 433 | Halifax | HX353 | 04/07/1944 | L7 | 399 | 15 | A/G lost over France. Commissioned (J.90246) |
| Macleod | JT | F/S | CAN | R.153205 | 417 | Spitfire | JF874 | 26/07/1944 | L7 | 467 | 21 | HF Mk.VIII Spitfire captured in Italy. |
| MacNaught | ARR | SGT | CAN | R.181619 | 428 | Lancaster | KB743 | 18/08/1944 | L7 | 672 | 28 | Tried to escape from Stalag IIIA with Crosswell and Johnson. |

| Surname | Initials | Rank | Nat | Service No | Sqn | Aircraft | Serial | Date | Code | No | Age | Notes |
|---|---|---|---|---|---|---|---|---|---|---|---|---|
| MacTaggart | DA | F/S | | 1564919 | 103 | Lancaster | ND613 | 14/08/1944 | L7 | 789 | 34 | ss7 hit after bombing at only 2,100 feet. |
| Madelaine | A | SGT | | 1892568 | 12 | Lancaster | PD273 | 29/08/1944 | L7 | 790 | 34 | See Flying into Hell, pp. 46-54, & Men of Air pp. 389-91. |
| Magill | SM | SGT | | 1796525 | 102 | Halifax | LW195 | 12/08/1944 | L7 | 604 | 27 | Exchanged identities at Stalag XI A. |
| Maguire | TL | F/S | AUS | A.430548 | 462 | Halifax | MZ401 | 02/11/1944 | L7 | 1249 | 55* | Evaded for twelve days. Captured when close to the US lines. |
| Mahon | R | LAC | | 999852 | 235AMES | n/a | n/a | 21/06/1942 | #/L7 | 140106 | 18 | Trade C/B. Captured at Tobruk. Also POW no. 1812. |
| Maki | LR | SGT | CAN | R.172398 | 424 | Halifax | LV951 | 12/08/1944 | L7 | 671 | 28 | Escaped during evacuation. Repatriated via Odessa. |
| Malick | S | WO2 | CAN | R.179512 | 619 | Lancaster | NE151 | 21/06/1944 | L7 | 273 | 11 | ss7. Commissioned (J.88281). |
| Maling | HJ | F/S | | 1431250 | 10 | Halifax | MZ574 | 23/09/1944 | L7 | 927 | 38 | Commissioned (185040) 7 November 1944. |
| Malone | OM | S/SGT | USA | 34183882 | 409BS | B-24 | 42-100416 | 18/09/1944 | 11B/L7/# | 117985 | 51/55* | USAAF tail gunner Baggy Maggy. Posted to another camp. |
| Manfroy | J | ADJ | FRA | 6707 | 346 | Halifax | NA549 | 04/11/1944 | L7 | 1202 | 50 | From Châlons-sur-Marne, Marne, France. |
| Manick | N | SGT | FRA | 1022 | 346 | Halifax | NA555 | 06/10/1944 | L7 | 1033 | 40 | From Champagnac-La-Rivière, Haute Vienne, France. |
| Mannion | FP | F/S | | 1678638 | 10 | Halifax | MZ574 | 23/09/1944 | L7 | 928 | 38 | |
| Mansbridge | ME | SGT | | 1852202 | 619 | Lancaster | LL808 | 21/06/1944 | L7 | 176 | 7 | |
| Mansfield | JJ | S/SGT | | 2065026 | GPR | Horsa | n/k | 20/09/1944 | L7 | 929 | 38 | D/*. |
| Manson | KW | F/S | AUS | A.408375 | 467 | Lancaster | LM376 | 30/03/1944 | L7 | 522 | 23 | Captured Belgium 28 April 1944. In Liège prison. |
| Mantle | A | SGT | | 925315 | 75 | Lancaster | ND802 | 27/05/1944 | L7 | 469 | 21 | Captured Antwerp 17 July 1944. |
| Marcham | J | F/S | | 1585721 | 570 | Stirling | EH897 | 19/09/1944 | 11B/L7 | 117985 | 49 | W/OP lost over Arnhem. 11B? |
| Marchant | HW | F/S | | 1547845 | 460 | Lancaster | PB407 | 07/10/1944 | L7 | 1034 | 40 | |
| Margerison | R | SGT | | 2204613 | 625 | Lancaster | LM513 | 21/05/1944 | L7 | 397 | 15 | Betrayed Antwerp 11 July 1944. Author of Boys at War. |
| Marini | JAH | F/S | CAN | R.162818 | 432 | Halifax | LW682 | 30/03/1944 | DL/L7 | 9 | 50 | Escaped on march 20 January 1945. To UK via Odessa. Commissioned (J.89209). |
| Marley | GRG | SGT | | 909805 | 78 | Halifax | MZ340 | 28/07/1944 | L7 | 605 | 27 | |
| Marriot | RA | SGT | | 1190134 | 427 | Halifax | EB242 | 30/07/1943 | 4B/L7 | 222464 | 33 | |
| Marris | WJ | F/S | AUS | A.428535 | 462 | Halifax | LL604 | 09/10/1944 | L7 | 1073 | 45* | Captured 5 October 1943. MID (13/6/46). |
| Marshall | JF | SGT | | 2201694 | 12 | Lancaster | LL910 | 29/06/1944 | 9C/L7 | 53340 | 33 | |
| Marshall | VL | F/S | CAN | R.183838 | 57 | Lancaster | LM115 | 21/06/1944 | L7 | 310 | 12 | |

| | | | | | | | | | | | | |
|---|---|---|---|---|---|---|---|---|---|---|---|---|
| Martin | D | F/S | | 655033 | 190 | Stirling | EF260 | 20/09/1944 | L7 | 989 | 39 | B/A lost over Arnhem. |
| Martin | DC | SGT | | 3225017 | 51 | Halifax | MZ916 | 11/09/1944 | L7 | 791 | 34 | From Belfast. |
| Martin | GI | SGT | | 1048607 | 619 | Lancaster | LL808 | 21/06/1944 | L7 | 228 | 8 | |
| Martin | HA | SGT | AUS | A.407506 | 108 | Wellington | DV873 | 19/10/1942 | PG57/18C/L7 | 39171 | 2 | WOP/AG. Captured 25 October 1942 after walking for six days in the desert. |
| Masdin | T | SGT | CAN | R.193919 | 431 | Halifax | NA514 | 16/06/1944 | L7 | 470 | 21 | Captured Antwerp 22 July 1944. |
| Mash | GH | LAC | | 1473755 | 2788 | n/a | n/a | 25/08/1944 | L7 | 855 | 37 | DMT. RAF Regiment. Captured at Valence after the invasion of the south of France. |
| Masters | SC | F/S | | 1323009 | 7 | Lancaster | ND744 | 15/06/1944 | L7 | 311 | 12 | See D-Day Bombers: The Veterans' Story, passim but particularly pp. 262-5. |
| Mate | HE | F/S | | 1052215 | 148 | Halifax | BB341 | 28/04/1944 | L6/L7 | 3797 | 3 | Nav. L6? |
| Matthews | DC | SGT | | 983449 | 178 | Liberator | KG938 | 20/08/1944 | L7 | 792 | 34 | ss7 Nav. Two broken ribs & dislocated shoulder. Captured near Linz, Austria. See To Hell and Back, pp.116-123. |
| Matthews | J | SGT | | 1518211 | 550 | Lancaster | LL747 | 16/06/1944 | L7 | 177 | 7 | |
| Maughan | AS | SGT | | 4270235 | GPR | Horsa | n/k | 20/09/1944 | L7 | 930 | 38 | F/15. |
| Maxwell | AW | F/S | CAN | R.206220 | 625 | Lancaster | LL962 | 28/07/1944 | L7 | 471 | 21 | |
| Maxwell | JDW | SGT | | 1570342 | 227 | Lancaster | LM259 | 04/12/1944 | L7 | 1294 | 56 | |
| Maycock | EA | CPL | | 650516 | 000 | n/a | n/a | 03/10/1944 | L7 | 1114 | 47 | Armourer. Unit not known. |
| Mays | WT | SGT | | 1717384 | 76 | Halifax | MZ623 | 24/05/1944 | L7 | 37 | 1 | |
| McAllister | RB | SGT | CAN | R.174878 | 514 | Lancaster | LL625 | 24/03/1944 | 9C/L7 | 53122 | 41* | ss7. Commissioned (J.92512). |
| McAlpine | W | SGT | | 1824486 | 424 | Halifax | LV997 | 28/07/1944 | L7 | 713 | 30 | |
| McBurney | WR | SGT | CAN | R.132139 | 138 | Halifax | LL252 | 31/03/1944 | L7 | 86 | 2 | Commissioned (J.86786). |
| McCahon | FJ | F/S | CAN | R.210088 | 166 | Lancaster | NF974 | 12/09/1944 | L7 | 793 | 34 | |
| McCann | FT | F/S | | 1438842 | 576 | Lancaster | LL905 | 28/07/1944 | L7 | 523 | 23 | |
| McCann | J | SGT | | 978471 | 86 | Beaufort | AW207 | 24/11/1941 | 7A/383/L7 | 90066 | 16 | W/AG. Broken collar bone. Also POW no. 79 (Stalag 383). |
| McCarney | LF | F/S | | 1532536 | 166 | Lancaster | ME638 | 30/03/1944 | 9C/L7 | 53245 | 57* | |
| McClafferty | J | SGT | | 1825703 | 578 | Halifax | NA501 | 22/12/1944 | L7 | 1337 | 57* | |
| McConnell | JR | F/S | CAN | R.167547 | 425 | Halifax | LK798 | 08/05/1944 | L7 | 38 | 1 | Commissioned (J.87052). |
| McCoombs | WJ | WO2 | CAN | R.88234 | 9 | Lancaster | JA679 | 15/07/1943 | 7A/L7 | 340 | 13 | Shot down over Italy. Escaped on the march. Repatriated via Odessa. |
| McCorkindale | W | SGT | | 1568425 | 462 | Halifax | MZ401 | 02/11/1944 | L7 | 1154 | 48 | |

| Name | Initials | Rank | Nat. | Service No. | Sqn | Aircraft | Serial | Date | Code | | | Notes |
|---|---|---|---|---|---|---|---|---|---|---|---|---|
| McCourt | TC | F/S | AUS | A.423168 | 640 | Halifax | MZ939 | 06/12/1944 | L7 | 1338 | 57* | A/1. |
| McCracken | MR | S/SGT | | 2929859 | GPR | Horsa | n/k | 20/09/1944 | L7 | 922 | 38 | |
| McCutchan | JE | SGT | CAN | R.178606 | 214 | Fortress | SR384 | 24/05/1944 | L7 | 39 | 1 | |
| McElroy | GFJ | F/S | CAN | R.169230 | 625 | Lancaster | LM513 | 21/05/1944 | L7 | 87 | 2 | 12A? |
| McGarvey | JF | F/S | CAN | R.169176 | 76 | Halifax | MZ531 | 07/06/1944 | 12A/L7 | 80135 | 9 | |
| McGeachin | WQ | F/S | AUS | A.409730 | 644 | Halifax | LL403 | 05/10/1944 | L7 | 1293 | 56 | Nav on SOE Op DODEX III. Captured 19 November 1944. |
| McGiveron | JN | SGT | | 2203805 | 10 | Halifax | MZ574 | 23/09/1944 | L7 | 925 | 38 | |
| McGowan | R | SGT | CAN | R.193475 | 425 | Halifax | LK810 | 23/05/1944 | 9C/L7 | 53389 | 57* | A/G ss7. Commissioned (J.83716). |
| McGraw | RW | SGT | USA | R.83846 | 7 | Stirling | BF379 | 11/12/1942 | 7A/L7 | 140 | 5 | In Italian camps until May 1944. American in RCAF. Nickname 'Spike'. |
| McKay | JM | S/SGT | | 2823181 | GPR | Horsa | n/k | 20/09/1944 | L7 | 926 | 38 | D/*. |
| McKibben | A | W/O | CAN | R.97019 | 66 | Spitfire | ML123 | 06/07/1944 | L7 | 398 | 15 | Shot down escorting Mitchells to Chartres. Commissioned (J.86858). |
| McLaren | DN | SGT | CAN | R.196937 | 426 | Halifax | LW204 | 05/12/1944 | L7 | 1339 | 57* | Captured 21 December 1944. |
| McLean | RB | F/S | AUS | A.420035 | 12 | Lancaster | JB358 | 27/01/1944 | 9C/L7 | 52254 | 3 | Aircraft ran out of fuel. Evacuated to Stalag 383. 9C? |
| McLeod | TG | F/S | CAN | R.256282 | 408 | Halifax | NP761 | 06/11/1944 | L7 | 1203 | 50 | |
| McMillan | RG | SGT | CAN | R.134302 | 61 | Lancaster | LM452 | 28/07/1944 | L7 | 750 | 33 | |
| McMullen | AE | F/S | CAN | R.211660 | 424 | Halifax | LW131 | 02/11/1944 | L7 | 1156 | 48 | |
| McMurdon | AO | SGT | SR | 778964 | 266 | Typhoon | MN483 | 09/05/1944 | L7 | 40 | 1 | Involved with Luft 7 tunnels. From Salisbury, Rhodesia. |
| McNiffe | FA | WO1 | CAN | R.93099 | 429 | Halifax | LW127 | 18/07/1944 | L7 | 468 | 21 | A noted drummer. Escaped on march 20 January 1945. UK 18 March 1945 via Odessa. |
| McPhail | WS | F/S | | 1125822 | 106 | Lancaster | LL975 | 24/06/1944 | L7 | 272 | 11 | |
| McPhee | JA | SGT | CAN | R.220193 | 408 | Halifax | NP810 | 21/11/1944 | L7 | 1248 | 55* | ss7. Blown out of rear turret. |
| McQueen | JF | F/S | CAN | R.250547 | 419 | Lancaster | KB754 | 09/10/1944 | L7 | 1032 | 40 | Pilot. Commissioned (184350, 24/10/44, seniority 11/8/44). Promoted F/O 9 March 1945. |
| McRae | D | W/O | | 1372020 | 7 | Lancaster | PA964 | 06/10/1944 | L7 | 1072 | 45* | On 31st op. Aircraft hit by flak. Intercom failed. Baled out. Aircraft returned to UK. Note 5-digit service number. |
| McRostie | AG | F/S | AUS | A.27306 | 617 | Lancaster | DV393 | 25/07/1944 | L7 | 524 | 23 | |

| Surname | Initials | Rank | Nat. | Service No. | Sqn | Aircraft | Serial | Date | Ref | No. | Age | Notes |
|---|---|---|---|---|---|---|---|---|---|---|---|---|
| McStay | RJL | F/S | AUS | A.426661 | 576 | Lancaster | LL799 | 28/07/1944 | 9C/L7 | 52473 | 49 | In hospitals at Strasbourg (29 Jul-29 Aug) and Meiningen (7 Sep-24 Nov). |
| McTeer | AP | SGT | | 1676580 | 150 | Wellington | LN858 | 03/04/1944 | 9C/L7 | 53123 | 3 | R/G. Shot down over Hungary. 'Mac'. |
| McWilliam | JRM | W/O | AUS | A.418907 | 463 | Lancaster | PD259 | 23/10/1944 | L7 | 1157 | 48 | |
| Mead | FH | SGT | | 1880117 | 640 | Halifax | MZ406 | 12/09/1944 | L7 | 794 | 34 | |
| Mead | R | SGT | | 759170 | 70 | Wellington | T2891 | 24/02/1941 | 7A/11A/L7 | 140519 | 18 | Lost on Tripoli raid. Escaped on march. To UK via Odessa and Middle East. UK on 30 March 1945. |
| Meader | CG | F/S | | 961018 | 22 | Beaufort | L9793 | 27/11/1941 | 7A/383/L7 | 90094 | 16 | W/AG shot down off French coast. Also POW no. 103 (Stalag 383). |
| Meadows | FCN | SGT | | 1896521 | 640 | Halifax | NA560 | 09/08/1944 | L7 | 673 | 28 | |
| Medland | CJ | W/O | | 1337754 | 514 | Lancaster | LL695 | 21/05/1944 | L7 | 123 | 4 | DFM (2/6/44). |
| Meehan | MJ | SGT | | 1798317 | 57 | Lancaster | PB425 | 19/10/1944 | L7 | 1074 | 45* | A/G |
| Meese | D | SGT | | 2201408 | 622 | Lancaster | LM138 | 23/06/1944 | L7 | 274 | 11 | Escaped 20 January 1945. Evacuated through Odessa. |
| Meggs | AM | F/S | AUS | A.419412 | 467 | Lancaster | LM239 | 26/09/1944 | L7 | 990 | 39 | |
| Melrose | WG | S/SGT | | 1464667 | GPR | Horsa | n/k | 19/09/1944 | L7 | 991 | 39 | E/11 |
| Mercer | J | SGT | | 939719 | 207 | Manchester | L7309 | 14/01/1942 | 7A/383/L7 | 90146 | 16 | Also POW no. 145 (Stalag 383). ss8. |
| Merrion | HN | SGT | | 1318979 | 101 | Lancaster | LM417 | 03/05/1944 | L7 | 88 | 2 | |
| Middleton | HHW | SGT | | 543851 | 44 | Lancaster | ND520 | 25/02/1944 | #/L7 | 606 | 27 | F/E. Also POW no. 3444. |
| Midlane | AL | SGT | | 1852348 | 51 | Halifax | MZ507 | 24/03/1944 | L7 | 89 | 2 | Died at Stalag IIIA on 15 March 1945 during operation. |
| Mignot | R | S/C | FRA | 269 | 346 | Halifax | NR181 | 04/11/1944 | L7 | 1250 | 55* | From French Algeria. |
| Millar | DL | W/O | | 1344400 | 83 | Lancaster | PB138 | 12/08/1944 | L7 | 607 | 27 | |
| Miller | AE | SGT | | 1308689 | 2788 | n/a | n/a | 25/08/1944 | L7 | 856 | 37 | G/G. RAF Regiment. Captured at Valence after the invasion of the south of France. |
| Miller | BA | F/S | | 1430469 | 148 | Halifax | EB147 | 05/08/1944 | L7 | 674 | 28 | AG/despatcher lost on supply mission to Warsaw. |
| Miller | GF | SGT | | 1562235 | GPR | Horsa | n/k | 21/09/1944 | L7 | 931 | 38 | B/19. |
| Miller | J | F/S | | 656301 | 103 | Lancaster | ND417 | 25/02/1944 | L7 | 400 | 15 | Captured Antwerp 6 July 1944. |
| Milliard | GL | SGT | CAN | R.189561 | 425 | Halifax | LL594 | 05/08/1944 | L7 | 608 | 27 | Commissioned (J90960). |
| Milligan | EA | SGT | | 1579064 | 49 | Lancaster | LM572 | 24/06/1944 | L7 | 312 | 12 | Sketch artist of some note. |
| Millington | A | SGT | | 580352 | 10 | Whitley | N1497 | 15/08/1940 | 7A/L7 | 341 | 13 | Shot down in Italy in August 1940. |
| Mills | JA | LAC | | 932993 | 520AMES | n/a | n/a | 21/06/1942 | 11B/L7 | 138832 | 18 | ACH. Captured at Tobruk. |

| Surname | Initials | Rank | Nat | Service no | Sqn | Aircraft | Serial | Date | Camp | POW no | Notes |
|---|---|---|---|---|---|---|---|---|---|---|---|
| Mills | JW | F/S | | 928841 | 619 | Lancaster | LL919 | 26/04/1944 | L7 | 124 | 4 | ss7. Blown out of aircraft. Suffered fractured jaw, broken ribs, cracked vertebræ. |
| Mills | R | SGT | | 1254702 | 460 | Lancaster | ND654 | 20/07/1944 | L7 | 714 | 30 | Captured Ypres 21 August 1944. Betrayed by 'The Captain'. |
| Millward | GE | CPL | | 955192 | 2788 | n/a | n/a | 25/08/1944 | L7 | 857 | 37 | G/G. RAF Regiment. Captured at Valence during the invasion of the south of France. |
| Milne | W | F/S | | 1557821 | 214 | Fortress | SR382 | 21/06/1944 | L7 | 472 | 21 | Captured 11 July 1944. |
| Milton | S | SGT | | 1822938 | 10 | Halifax | MZ773 | 12/08/1944 | L7 | 609 | 27 | |
| Minifie | KC | SGT | CAN | R.192847 | 51 | Halifax | LK885 | 24/05/1944 | L7 | 90 | 2 | |
| Mitchell | A | SGT | | 10538003 | GPR | Horsa | n/k | 20/09/1944 | L7 | 858 | 37 | A/1. |
| Mitchell | JA | SGT | | 1567016 | 37 | Wellington | MF241 | 07/07/1944 | L7 | 473 | 21 | WOP/A/G. ss5. Shot down over Hungary. Serious burns to arms. |
| Mitchell | JA | F/S | | 1812446 | 227 | Lancaster | NG296 | 06/12/1944 | L7 | 1295 | 56 | W/OP. |
| Mitchell | SM | F/S | | A.419197 | 9 | Lancaster | JB116 | 07/07/1944 | L7 | 474 | 21 | |
| Moal | JC | SGT | FRA | 3222 | n/k | n/k | n/k | 11/07/1944 | L7 | 428 | 15* | F/E. From Plougastel-Daoulas, Finistère, France. |
| Molloy | BP | F/S | AUS | A.419472 | 467 | Lancaster | LL846 | 28/07/1944 | L7 | 610 | 27 | Captured 31 July 1944 after three days in dinghy. |
| Monk | DE | SGT | | 1134580 | GPR | Horsa | n/k | 17/09/1944 | L7 | 992 | 39 | A/*. |
| Monk | KNT | F/S | | 1890479 | 7 | Lancaster | ND852 | 25/08/1944 | L7 | 715 | 30 | DFM (12/2/46). |
| Monteith | GIW | SGT | | 1518174 | 61 | Lancaster | EE186 | 04/07/1944 | L7 | 475 | 21 | |
| Montgomery | VGF | F/S | AUS | A.423291 | 463 | Lancaster | LM242 | 11/09/1944 | L7 | 795 | 34 | Captured 14 September 1944. |
| Montwill | J | SGT | POL | 704317 | 300 | Lancaster | LM141 | 06/11/1944 | L7 | 1251 | 55* | |
| Moore | EA | SGT | | 1161448 | 106 | Hampden | P1341 | 15/01/1942 | 7A/383/L7 | 90101 | 16 | Also POW no. 107 (Stalag 383). |
| Moran | ES | WO2 | CAN | R.74523 | 103 | Lancaster | ME722 | 21/05/1944 | L7 | 275 | 11 | Same crew as BH Davis RAAF. |
| Morgan | EJ | SGT | | 1835337 | 550 | Lancaster | LL747 | 16/06/1944 | L7 | 178 | 7 | |
| Morgan | H | SGT | | 1583624 | 427 | Halifax | LV938 | 28/06/1944 | L7 | 313 | 12 | |
| Morgan | J | SGT | | 1836566 | 51 | Halifax | MZ916 | 11/09/1944 | L7/L3 | 859 | 37 | To Stalag Luft 3 on 24 January 1945. |
| Morgan | JL | SGT | | 1836448 | 576 | Lancaster | ME800 | 29/08/1944 | L7 | 751 | 33 | |
| Morneau | WL | F/S | CAN | R.168348 | 103 | Lancaster | JB746 | 31/07/1944 | L7 | 611 | 27 | |
| Morris | A | SGT | | 994380 | 77 | Whitley | Z6578 | 17/05/1941 | 18A/L2/L3/L6/L7 | 32 | 1 | MBE (1/10/46) for POW activities. |
| Morris | DE | SGT | | 1836702 | 408 | Halifax | NP773 | 15/10/1944 | L7 | 1075 | 45* | |
| Morris | NP | F/S | | 1480801 | 16 | Spitfire | MK723 | 22/07/1944 | L7 | 525 | 23 | Shot down on first operational sortie – low level to Doullens. |

| | | | | | | | | | | | | |
|---|---|---|---|---|---|---|---|---|---|---|---|---|
| Morris | TV | SGT | | 1817517 | 61 | Lancaster | LL777 | 06/12/1944 | L7 | 1296 | 56 | ss7. Commissioned (J.91170). |
| Morrisey | FP | SGT | CAN | R.166374 | 424 | Halifax | LV780 | 22/04/1944 | L7 | 91 | 2 | |
| Morrison | JE | F/S | AUS | A.32691 | 463 | Lancaster | LM597 | 24/06/1944 | L7 | 314 | 12 | |
| Morrison | WE | SGT | CAN | R.188162 | 426 | Halifax | NP771 | 01/11/1944 | L7 | 1297 | 56 | |
| Moscrop | R | SGT | | 993844 | 106 | Lancaster | PB359 | 19/09/1944 | L7 | 993 | 39 | |
| Mosley | HM | F/S | CAN | R.256245 | 426 | Halifax | NP800 | 04/11/1944 | L7 | 1204 | 50 | |
| Mowat | BB | LAC | CAN | R.168468 | 6341LWU | Horsa | n/k | 20/09/1944 | 11B/L7 | 118704 | 56 | R/Mech. Captured at Arnhem. |
| Mowbray | RE | F/S | | 1577274 | 427 | Halifax | LV938 | 28/06/1944 | L7 | 315 | 12 | Commissioned (178761) 15 August 1944. |
| Mucha | S | F/S | POL | 792823 | 301 | Wellington | Z1333 | 10/04/1942 | #/L3/L7/L6/L4 | 6444 | 20 | Moved to Luft 6 on 18 August 1944. |
| Muirhead | MJ | F/S | AUS | A.427136 | 467 | Lancaster | LM267 | 29/08/1944 | L7 | 796 | 34 | Captured on 2 September 1944. Escaped on march 20 January 1945. |
| Muirhead | WD | SGT | | 988131 | 51 | Whitley | Z9424 | 15/01/1942 | 7A/383/L7 | 90112 | 16 | Also POW no. 115 (Stalag 383). |
| Mulhall | JE | SGT | | 2202223 | 75 | Lancaster | PB520 | 20/11/1944 | L7 | 1252 | 55* | |
| Mullan | E | SGT | | 1822831 | 570 | Stirling | LJ913 | 18/09/1944 | L7 | 860 | 37 | Lost over Arnhem 18 September 1944. Scotsman British Army (The Highland Light Infantry). |
| Munachen | J | CPL | | 3318575 | n/a | n/a | n/a | n/k | 7A/383/L7 | 90059 | 16 | Also POW no. 72 (Stalag 383). |
| Munro | EG | WO1 | CAN | R.2174 | 433 | Halifax | NP992 | 04/11/1944 | L7 | 1158 | 48 | Commissioned (J.92474). |
| Munroe | CL | SGT | | 1570200 | 102 | Halifax | MZ699 | 12/09/1944 | L7 | 861 | 37 | |
| Munson | CR | WO2 | CAN | R.116469 | 427 | Halifax | DK180 | 25/06/1943 | 9C/L7 | 43239 | 41* | |
| Murphy | F | SGT | | 1694010 | 195 | Lancaster | LM743 | 02/11/1944 | L7 | 1159 | 48 | |
| Murphy | JP | F/S | | 1421522 | 102 | Halifax | MZ871 | 24/12/1944 | L7 | 1340 | 57* | |
| Murphy | VJ | L/CPL | | 2653598 | n/a | n/a | n/a | 14/06/1944 | L7 | 276 | 11 | British Army (RAMC). Captured in Italy |
| Murray | CAF | F/S | AUS | A.426648 | 454 | Baltimore | FW701 | 23/08/1944 | L7 | 752 | 33 | Escaped on the march. Repatriated via Odessa and Middle East. |
| Murray | J | SGT | | 1595009 | 625 | Lancaster | LM163 | 03/08/1944 | L7 | 612 | 27 | |
| Murray | RA | F/S | | 1231291 | 48 | Dakota | FZ620 | 22/09/1944 | L7 | 932 | 38 | Co-pilot, 48 Squadron, lost over Arnhem 21/9/44? |
| Murray | TY | SGT | | 1822582 | 640 | Halifax | MZ579 | 24/05/1944 | L7 | 125 | 4 | |
| Mylchreest | WE | F/S | CAN | R.214600 | 424 | Halifax | LV997 | 28/07/1944 | L7 | 526 | 23 | |
| Nagley | LW | SGT | | 1676957 | 57 | Lancaster | LL939 | 11/11/1944 | L7 | 1253 | 55* | |
| Nagy | AJ | F/S | CAN | R.68629 | 69 | Baltimore | AG739 | 25/01/1943 | 7A/L7 | 342 | 13 | W/AG. |
| Nathanson | S | F/S | | 1334086 | 7 | Lancaster | ND744 | 15/06/1944 | L7 | 316 | 12 | Captured 19 June 1944. |

| Surname | Initials | Rank | Nat. | Service no. | Sqn | Aircraft | Serial | Date | Camp | No. | Age | Notes |
|---|---|---|---|---|---|---|---|---|---|---|---|---|
| Naylor | L | SGT | | 2206023 | 625 | Lancaster | LM546 | 28/07/1944 | L7 | 476 | 21 | Captured 28 June 1944. Escaped to Russian lines. UK 19 March 1945 via Odessa. |
| Naysmith | AD | F/S | | 1336555 | 57 | Lancaster | LM115 | 21/06/1944 | L7 | 277 | 11 | |
| Neal | D | F/S | | 1398484 | 550 | Lancaster | PA991 | 28/08/1944 | L7 | 797 | 34 | |
| Needham | HC | SGT | | 1193496 | 51 | Whitley | Z9424 | 15/01/1942 | 7A/383/L7 | 90109 | 16 | Also POW no. 114 (Stalag 383). |
| Needham | JW | F/S | | 1459553 | 77 | Halifax | MZ698 | 16/06/1944 | L7 | 179 | 7 | |
| Neeves | GL | W/O | | 904170 | 407 | Hudson | AM778 | 01/12/1941 | 7A/383/L7 | 90086 | 57* | Stalag 383? |
| Neills | RA | F/S | | 1801181 | 7 | Lancaster | ND744 | 15/06/1944 | L7 | 180 | 7 | |
| Neilson | JF | F/S | | 1346150 | 640 | Halifax | LW464 | 24/07/1944 | L7 | 613 | 27 | Captured 30 July 1944. |
| Nelson | RE | F/S | CAN | R.212425 | 429 | Halifax | MZ377 | 21/11/1944 | L7 | 1254 | 55* | |
| Nettell | RF | SGT | | 913978 | GPR | Horsa | n/k | 26/09/1944 | 12A/L7 | 076317 | 47 | D/*. |
| Newberry | TA | SGT | | 1602063 | 619 | Lancaster | ME846 | 21/06/1944 | L7 | 317 | 12 | |
| Newton | A | S/SGT | | 913044 | GPR | Horsa | n/k | 18/09/1944 | L7 | 1076 | 45* | G/10. |
| Newton | NE | W/O | AUS | A.408286 | 460 | Lancaster | PB254 | 07/10/1944 | L7 | 1115 | 47 | |
| Nicholls | NA | SGT | | 581004 | 105 | Blenheim | Z7503 | 11/08/1941 | 11B/L7 | 145850 | 18 | Nav on raid on Cretone from Malta. POW number possibly 140850. |
| Nicklin | FH | F/S | | 1431710 | 250 | Kittyhawk | FX635 | 24/04/1944 | L7 | 41 | 1 | |
| Nicol | AR | F/S | | 1370377 | 37 | Wellington | ME880 | 22/10/1944 | L7 | 1160 | 48 | W/OP. Commissioned (187952, 2/1/45). |
| Nicol | IL | F/S | | 1545322 | 603 | Beaufighter | NE651 | 29/08/1944 | L7 | 1116 | 47 | Nav. |
| Nicol | JP | F/S | | 1564242 | 106 | Lancaster | ND331 | 29/08/1944 | L7 | 798 | 34 | |
| Niven | WM | SGT | CAN | R.148100 | 431 | Halifax | NA550 | 28/07/1944 | L7 | 477 | 21 | MUG shot down on Hamburg raid. Commissioned (C.90054). |
| Noel | JH | F/S | CAN | R.171310 | 51 | Halifax | LK885 | 24/05/1944 | L7 | 92 | 2 | |
| Nolan | MJ | F/S | AUS | A.7188 | 44 | Lancaster | PB266 | 28/07/1944 | L7 | 478 | 21 | Note short but correct service no. Born in Ireland on 4 August 1918. |
| Nolan | PJ | SGT | EIR | 1796249 | 635 | Lancaster | ND693 | 26/08/1944 | L7 | 799 | 34 | ss8. Captured Denmark 30 August 1944. From Annborough, County Down. |
| Noon | HC | F/S | | 1295792 | 115 | Lancaster | ND754 | 21/05/1944 | L7 | 42 | 1 | ss8. |
| Norris | FGD | SGT | | 573714 | 37 | Wellington | LN643 | 11/05/1944 | L7 | 43 | 1 | B/A. Lost on raid to Leghorn. |
| Norrish | GH | SGT | | 1338827 | 51 | Halifax | MZ916 | 11/09/1944 | L7 | 800 | 34 | |
| Notton | LP | SGT | | 1416687 | 138 | Halifax | LL276 | 31/05/1944 | L7 | 93 | 2 | |
| Nuttall | REG | F/S | | 1483234 | 57 | Lancaster | ND671 | 29/03/1944 | 9C/L7 | 53298 | 17 | Nav. |
| Nutter | R | S/SGT | | 4537370 | GPR | Horsa | n/k | 20/09/1944 | L7 | 933 | 38 | D/*. |

| Surname | Initials | Rank | Nat. | Service No. | Sqn | Aircraft | Serial | Date | Camp | No. | Ref | Notes |
|---|---|---|---|---|---|---|---|---|---|---|---|---|
| Oakes | WA | SGT | | 14573970 | GPR | Horsa | n/k | 20/09/1944 | L7 | 934 | 38 | E/11. 2nd pilot. |
| Oates | NF | F/S | | 1555705 | 9 | Lancaster | ME833 | 18/07/1944 | L7 | 614 | 27 | Captured 10 August 1944. |
| Ocelka | A | F/S | CZ | 787772 | 312 | Spitfire | MK682 | 18/09/1944 | L7 | 935 | 38 | A/1. |
| O'Donnell | E | SGT | | 7013133 | GPR | Horsa | n/k | 24/09/1944 | L7 | 995 | 39 | A/1. |
| O'Farrell | JEE | F/S | CAN | R.178953 | 576 | Lancaster | PB400 | 26/08/1944 | L7 | 716 | 30 | Baled out & aircraft returned to UK? |
| Offierski | M | SGT | POL | 783676 | 300 | Wellington | Z1382 | 09/06/1942 | L3/L7/L6 | 346 | 20 | Moved to Luft 6 on 18 August 1944. |
| Offley | WEL | SGT | | 2218499 | 462 | Halifax | NP990 | 06/10/1944 | L7 | 1035 | 40 | Baled out as ordered. Aircraft landed at RAF Woodbridge. |
| Ogden | JA | SGT | | 975784 | 10 | Halifax | W1042 | 30/05/1942 | 8B/383/L7 | 12678 | 16 | Also POW no. 524 (Stalag 383). 8B? |
| Oger | RN | ADJ | FRA | C.3231 | 347 | Halifax | NA606 | 11/09/1944 | L7 | 994 | 39 | ss7. R/G. Married. From Boufarik, Algeria. |
| Ogilvie | WD | F/S | | 1313470 | 635 | Lancaster | JB706 | 30/03/1944 | 9C/L7 | 43395 | 4 | Broke ankle. At Hohe Mark, Obermassfeld & Meiningen hospitals. |
| O'Hagan | J | SGT | | 1076857 | 44 | Lancaster | PB751 | 04/12/1944 | L7 | 1281 | 56 | |
| O'Leary | LS | SGT | CAN | R.174641 | 429 | Halifax | LW128 | 07/06/1944 | L7 | 181 | 7 | See Failed to Return, pp.159-60. |
| O'Leary | MJ | F/S | AUS | A.426379 | 467 | Lancaster | LL846 | 28/07/1944 | L7 | 527 | 23 | Captured 31 July 1944 after three days in dinghy. Escaped during evacuation. Repatriated via Odessa and Middle East. |
| Olivier | JE | WO2 | CAN | R.130151 | 432 | Halifax | LW616 | 12/06/1944 | L7 | 318 | 12 | |
| Olsen | RP | F/S | AUS | A.429479 | 640 | Halifax | LK865 | 27/05/1944 | L7 | 94 | 2 | |
| Olver | AC | SGT | | 7949749 | GPR | Horsa | n/k | 14/06/1944 | 12A/L7 | 81323 | 23 | D-Day Operation 'Tonga'. |
| Oram | AW | SGT | | 14416890 | GPR | Horsa | n/k | 17/09/1944 | L7 | 936 | 38 | D/13. |
| Orford | BH | SGT | | 1511963 | 10 | Halifax | LV870 | 28/06/1944 | L7 | 319 | 12 | |
| Orwin | CW | F/S | | 577085 | 3 | Tempest | EJ540 | 10/09/1944 | L7 | 801 | 34 | Shot down on armed recce off Dutch coast. |
| Osborne | RF | S/SGT | | 922174 | GPR | Horsa | n/k | 24/09/1944 | L7 | 996 | 39 | A/*. Horsa pilot. Carried a Jeep and General Browning's personal staff. |
| O'Shea | JO | SGT | EIR | 1798349 | 576 | Lancaster | ME800 | 29/08/1944 | L7 | 753 | 33 | |
| O'Shea | PE | SGT | EIR | 1813944 | 61 | Lancaster | EE186 | 04/07/1944 | L7 | 401 | 15 | |
| Osmond | NHA | SGT | | 1621871 | 103 | Lancaster | PB303 | 18/08/1944 | L7 | 717 | 30 | |
| Ostrom | NJE | F/S | | 1452355 | 156 | Lancaster | ND929 | 06/10/1944 | L7 | 1036 | 40 | A naturalised Swede. |
| Owen | AJ | W/O | | 818146 | 77 | Halifax | MZ715 | 16/06/1944 | L7 | 182 | 7 | ss7. |
| Owst | K | SGT | | 1774018 | 100 | Lancaster | LM542 | 22/05/1944 | L7 | 44 | 1 | |
| Oxford | CJ | SGT | | 4859963 | GPR | Horsa | n/k | 20/09/1944 | L7 | 862 | 37 | E/*. |

| Surname | Initials | Rank | Country | Service No. | Sqn | Aircraft | Serial | Date | Camp | POW No. | Age | Notes |
|---|---|---|---|---|---|---|---|---|---|---|---|---|
| Page | NF | F/S | AUS | A.417974 | 44 | Lancaster | ND517 | 18/07/1944 | L7 | 615 | 27 | Shot down by bomber. |
| Page | RB | WO2 | CAN | R.188830 | 431 | Lancaster | KB817 | 01/11/1944 | L7 | 1205 | 50 | |
| Page | RE | W/O | | 1578086 | 83 | Lancaster | PB292 | 26/08/1944 | L7 | 802 | 34 | |
| Pagett | FH | SGT | | 1863239 | 467 | Lancaster | LM450 | 24/06/1944 | L7 | 320 | 12 | |
| Paisley | FN | SGT | CAN | R.181549 | 35 | Halifax | JP121 | 20/02/1944 | 9C/L7 | 43350 | 41* | R/G. |
| Pallett | CG | WO2 | CAN | R.141179 | 424 | Halifax | LW121 | 14/06/1944 | L7 | 616 | 27 | Captured 9 August 1944. |
| Palmer | AE | SGT | | 4803786 | GPR | Horsa | n/k | 22/09/1944 | L7 | 937 | 38 | D/*. 2nd pilot Horsa glider. |
| Palmer | BJP | SGT | | 1254963 | 83 | Hampden | AE123 | 21/01/1942 | 7A/383/L7 | 90126 | 16 | On loan from 83 to 106 Squadron. Also POW no. 129 (Stalag 383). |
| Palmer | GA | SGT | | 1823501 | 300 | Lancaster | ND984 | 24/07/1944 | L7 | 479 | 21 | |
| Palmer | JE | SGT | | 1548066 | 626 | Lancaster | LL895 | 28/07/1944 | L7 | 528 | 23 | ss7. |
| Pankratz | HW | F/S | CAN | R.193542 | 424 | Halifax | NP945 | 06/12/1944 | L7 | 1298 | 56 | Captured at Ülzen. Later commissioned (J.91073). |
| Paquette | RA | WO1 | CAN | R.130121 | 102 | Halifax | MZ699 | 12/09/1944 | L7 | 803 | 34 | |
| Paradise | LE | F/S | | 1318259 | 626 | Lancaster | LM599 | 12/08/1944 | L7 | 617 | 27 | |
| Pare | JLM | SGT | CAN | R.185125 | 425 | Halifax | MZ674 | 14/10/1944 | L7 | 1077 | 45* | |
| Parham | RD | SGT | | 1600512 | 83 | Lancaster | ND740 | 11/09/1944 | L7 | 997 | 39 | |
| Parker | DS | SGT | | 5886465 | GPR | Horsa | n/k | 23/09/1944 | L7 | 1078 | 45* | D/5. 2nd pilot Horsa glider. |
| Parker | DVA | SGT | | 1315573 | 166 | Lancaster | LL954 | 22/05/1944 | L7 | 45 | 1 | |
| Parker | FC | SGT | | 6469399 | GPR | Horsa | n/k | 19/09/1944 | L7 | 938 | 38 | A/1. |
| Parker | TW | SGT | | 1256785 | 40 | Wellington | Z1046 | 24/11/1941 | 7A/L7 | 343 | 13 | Lost on raid on Benghazi. |
| Parker | WRM | AC2 | | 1577513 | 235AMES | n/a | n/a | 21/06/1942 | 11A/L7 | 140153 | 18 | ACH. Captured at Tobruk. |
| Parkin | W | F/S | CAN | R.200096 | 7 | Lancaster | PA964 | 06/10/1944 | L7 | 1079 | 45* | |
| Parkinson | RC | F/S | NZ | NZ.425193 | 44 | Lancaster | PB192 | 04/11/1944 | L7 | 1206 | 50 | |
| Parry | DAE | F/S | | 1577455 | 544 | Mosquito | NS633 | 14/09/1944 | L7 | 939 | 38 | Nav. |
| Parry-Jones | RH | CPL | | 323569 | 000 | n/a | n/a | 13/06/1944 | L7 | 183 | 7 | British Army (Royal Armoured Corps). |
| Parsons | WJ | SGT | | 1398268 | 97 | Lancaster | PB510 | 11/09/1944 | L7 | 804 | 34 | |
| Patterson | CE | T/SGT | USA | 15330569 | 94TCS | Dakota | 42-93098 | 18/09/1944 | 11B/L7 | 118586 | 55 | 94th Troop Carrier Squadron, USAAF. Moved to other camp. |
| Patterson | HD | F/S | | 1583662 | 640 | Halifax | MZ930 | 04/11/1944 | L7 | 1161 | 48 | Suffered severe frostbite to both feet. |
| Patterson | JT | WO2 | CAN | R.162269 | 431 | Lancaster | KB817 | 01/11/1944 | L7 | 1207 | 50 | Shot down by bomber. |
| Patterson | LE | SGT | CAN | R.151464 | 44 | Lancaster | LM171 | 28/07/1944 | L7 | 618 | 27 | |
| Pattinson | R | SGT | | 526296 | 75 | Wellington | X9951 | 07/11/1941 | 7A/383/L7 | 90118 | 16 | Also POW no. 121 (Stalag 383). |
| Peakman | KL | F/S | | 1575557 | 10 | Halifax | LV870 | 28/06/1944 | L7 | 321 | 12 | |

| Surname | Initials | Rank | Nat. | Service No. | Sqn | Aircraft | Serial | Date | Code | No. | Age | Notes |
|---|---|---|---|---|---|---|---|---|---|---|---|---|
| Pearce | CFR | F/S | CAN | R.257188 | 101 | Lancaster | PB258 | 12/08/1944 | L7 | 619 | 27 | B/A lost on Feuersbrunn raid 29/30 June 1944. |
| Pearce | GM | SGT | | 1432075 | 150 | Wellington | JA191 | 01/07/1944 | L7 | 322 | 12 | Nav. |
| Pearce | RH | F/S | | 1323762 | 12 | Lancaster | ND325 | 01/01/1944 | 9C/L7 | 43351 | 3 | |
| Pearson | W | SGT | | 2208874 | 630 | Lancaster | JB288 | 30/03/1944 | #/L7 | 15143 | 41* | Repatriated 6/2/45 on Arundel Castle. |
| Peart | J | SGT | | 1520024 | 626 | Lancaster | LM137 | 12/09/1944 | L7 | 940 | 38 | |
| Peek | EC | SGT | | 1302650 | 207 | Lancaster | LM671 | 18/12/1944 | L7 | 1341 | 57* | |
| Peers | TH | SGT | | 545691 | 405 | Lancaster | PA981 | 12/09/1944 | L7 | 805 | 34 | Nav. |
| Pendleton | HV | F/S | | 1322937 | 150 | Wellington | LP505 | 21/08/1944 | L7 | 718 | 30 | All four crew POW. |
| Pendray | KJ | F/S | | 1321286 | 226 | Mitchell | FW106 | 15/10/1944 | L7 | 1117 | 47 | ss7. Beaten up on landing by two local Nazi leaders. Born in Dunedin, New Zealand. |
| Penman | JE | F/S | AUS | A.428930 | 467 | Lancaster | PB740 | 04/12/1944 | L7 | 1299 | 56 | |
| Penney | WH | LAC | | 1458665 | 2788 | n/a | n/a | 25/08/1944 | L7 | 863 | 37 | G/G. RAF Regiment. Captured at Valence after the invasion of the south of France. |
| Pepper | MR | SGT | | 7595239 | GPR | Horsa | n/k | 20/09/1944 | L7 | 864 | 37 | B/3. |
| Perera | TH | SGT | | 1579145 | 106 | Lancaster | ND339 | 04/07/1944 | L7 | 402 | 15 | |
| Perini | EE | F/S | CAN | R.202891 | 405 | Lancaster | PB413 | 02/11/1944 | L7 | 1208 | 50 | Baled out. Aircraft crashed in UK. |
| Perkins | JW | SGT | | 1802778 | 158 | Halifax | MZ703 | 18/07/1944 | L7 | 620 | 27 | |
| Perry | JFL | SGT | CAN | R.112020 | 431 | Halifax | LK842 | 27/04/1944 | L7 | 621 | 27 | |
| Peterkin | WA | F/S | | 636801 | 625 | Lancaster | LM546 | 28/07/1944 | L7 | 480 | 21 | DFM (14/11/44). |
| Pett | JT | F/S | CAN | R.220749 | 419 | Lancaster | KB727 | 04/07/1944 | L7 | 403 | 15 | Captured 8 July 1944. |
| Pettit | CC | SGT | | 1800865 | 550 | Lancaster | LL747 | 16/06/1944 | L7 | 184 | 7 | |
| Peyton | AC | SGT | | 1866687 | 101 | Lancaster | ME613 | 21/06/1944 | 9C/L7 | 52470 | 49 | |
| Philippe | AJM | W/O | FRA | Fr.25430 | 346 | Halifax | NA555 | 06/10/1944 | L7 | 1037 | 40 | W/OP. From Agadir, French Morocco. |
| Phillips | AC | SGT | | 1604824 | 432 | Halifax | LW592 | 27/04/1944 | L7 | 404 | 15 | |
| Phillips | CJ | F/S | | 1376122 | 44 | Lancaster | LL938 | 21/06/1944 | L7 | 229 | 8 | Captured 27 June 1944. |
| Phillips | PG | SGT | | 989770 | GPR | Horsa | n/k | 06/06/1944 | 12A/L7 | 80904 | 22 | D-Day Operation 'Tonga'. |
| Phillips | RS | W/O | AUS | A.417112 | 49 | Lancaster | NE128 | 21/06/1944 | L7 | 481 | 21 | |
| Phillipson | AB | SGT | | 1283237 | 195 | Lancaster | LM743 | 02/11/1944 | L7 | 1118 | 47 | |
| Phillipson | GE | SGT | | 1821668 | 640 | Halifax | LW464 | 24/07/1944 | L7 | 482 | 21 | |
| Philpot | JA | SGT | | 1723659 | 300 | Lancaster | ND984 | 24/07/1944 | L7 | 483 | 21 | |
| Phipps | LHT | WO2 | CAN | R.165050 | 408 | Lancaster | DS634 | 28/07/1944 | L7 | 529 | 23 | |
| Picken | JA | SGT | | 1434038 | 106 | Lancaster | W4118 | 04/02/1943 | 9C/L7 | 43274 | 3 | Posted. Repatriated? Pickan? |
| Pinkney | J | F/S | | 1387346 | 83 | Lancaster | JA928 | 26/04/1944 | L7 | 865 | 37 | Captured Châtillon 19 May 1944. |

| Surname | Initials | Rank | | Service No. | Sqn | Aircraft | Serial | Date | Camp | | | Notes |
|---|---|---|---|---|---|---|---|---|---|---|---|---|
| Pitchford | JEM | F/S | | 746311 | 214 | Fortress | HB763 | 25/08/1944 | L7 | 754 | 33 | 12A? Commissioned (183106). |
| Pole | C | F/S | | 1582362 | 181 | Typhoon | MM961 | 19/08/1944 | 12A/L7 | 86397 | 37 | |
| Polson | EW | SGT | | 1823200 | 57 | Lancaster | PD212 | 28/07/1944 | L7 | 622 | 27 | |
| Pons | L | S/C | FRA | 81052 | 346 | Halifax | NA555 | 06/10/1944 | L7 | 1255 | 55* | Wounded. From Puivert, Aude, France. |
| Popadiuk | J | F/S | CAN | R.270205 | 426 | Halifax | LW204 | 05/12/1944 | L7 | 1342 | 57* | |
| Pope | KW | F/S | | 1890795 | 10 | Halifax | MZ312 | 20/07/1944 | L7 | 484 | 21 | |
| Poppa | V | F/S | CAN | R.165480 | 424 | Halifax | HX313 | 27/05/1944 | L7 | 126 | 4 | |
| Porrett | GM | SGT | | 947543 | 51 | Whitley | Z6874 | 24/10/1941 | 7A/383/L7 | 90106 | 16 | Also POW no. 111 (Stalag 383). |
| Porter | JA | W/O | | 1074969 | 635 | Lancaster | ND819 | 21/05/1944 | L7 | 278 | 11 | Captured 16 June 1944. |
| Postlethwaite | G | F/S | | 1483130 | 213 | Mustang | HB854 | 21/10/1944 | L7 | 1256 | 55* | Shot down by flak over Kutina, Yugoslavia. |
| Potter | AE | F/S | | 1395820 | 603 | Beaufighter | NV205 | 03/10/1944 | L7 | 1209 | 50 | Nav. Shot down off Kea. Commissioned (188632) 30 January 1945. |
| Potts | JD | SGT | | 5391776 | GPR | Horsa | n/k | 05/06/1944 | L7 | 366 | 14 | D-Day Operation Deadstick. See One Night in June |
| Potts | PJ | SGT | | 1601357 | 103 | Lancaster | PB363 | 18/08/1944 | L7 | 719 | 30 | Author of Just a Survivor. See also No Time for Fear, p.195-6. |
| Poulter | GA | SGT | | 1323162 | 106 | Lancaster | ME831 | 07/07/1944 | L7 | 405 | 15 | |
| Poulton | FG | SGT | AUS | A.404261 | 455 | Hampden | AT119 | 21/01/1942 | 7A/383/L7 | 90116 | 16 | ss4. Also POW no. 119 (Stalag 383). Born Preston, England. |
| Poulton | WA | SGT | | 1575535 | 51 | Halifax | JD244 | 21/06/1943 | L7 | 485 | 21 | Betrayed to Gestapo in Antwerp 16 August 1944. To UK via Odessa. See Hell On Earth pp.43-51. |
| Povey | JF | F/S | | 1320674 | 190 | Stirling | LJ916 | 21/09/1944 | 11B/L7 | 117913 | 47 | A/B shot down on Arnhem supply drop. 11B? |
| Powell | FG | SGT | | 190364 | GPR | Horsa | n/k | 26/09/1944 | L7 | 1080 | 45* | D/5. |
| Preece | FL | SGT | | 1487510 | 192 | Halifax | MZ570 | 03/05/1944 | L7 | 755 | 33 | |
| Preston | F | F/S | | 1436954 | 44 | Lancaster | LM434 | 21/06/1944 | L7 | 323 | 12 | |
| Preston | RS | WO1 | SA | 328339V | 24SAAF | Marauder | n/k | 14/08/1944 | L7 | 675 | 28 | A/G. From Port Elizabeth, S. Africa. |
| Price | FW | LAC | | 1351623 | 235AMES | n/a | n/a | 21/06/1942 | 11B/L7 | 140434 | 18 | G/G. Captured at Tobruk. |
| Price | JE | F/S | | 1339561 | 156 | Lancaster | JB230 | 23/06/1944 | L7 | 279 | 11 | ss7. |
| Price | JH | F/S | | 1324364 | 97 | Lancaster | ND451 | 21/06/1944 | L7 | 230 | 8 | |
| Price | N | SGT | | 1880863 | 195 | Lancaster | HK663 | 02/11/1944 | L7 | 1162 | 48 | |
| Price | SJ | SGT | | 923203 | 220 | Hudson | AM678 | 23/12/1941 | 7A/383/L7 | 90130 | 16 | W/AG shot down off Norway. Also POW no. 131 (Stalag 383). |
| Price | SR | SGT | | 2388139 | GPR | Horsa | n/k | 20/09/1944 | L7 | 941 | 38 | E/11. 2nd pilot carrying one officer & twenty-one men of 181 Field Ambulance. |

| Surname | Initials | Rank | Nat. | Service no. | Sqn | Aircraft | Serial | Date | Camp | POW no. | Age | Notes |
|---|---|---|---|---|---|---|---|---|---|---|---|---|
| Prince | J | W/O | | 1456135 | 622 | Lancaster | LM283 | 19/10/1944 | L7 | 1119 | 47 | ss8. Aircraft's 4,000lb bomb exploded. Suffered broken arm, injuries to face and left shoulder. |
| Pring | BRJ | SGT | | 1853987 | 467 | Lancaster | LL846 | 28/07/1944 | L7 | 623 | 27 | |
| Pringle | GH | W/O | AUS | A.425213 | 106 | Lancaster | ME790 | 22/05/1944 | L7 | 95 | 2 | |
| PDistupa | G | SGT | CZ | 654758 | 312 | Spitfire | ML240 | 11/08/1944 | 9C/L7 | 52472 | 41* | |
| Pritchard | HJ | F/S | | 1259238 | 620 | Stirling | LJ946 | 20/09/1944 | L7 | 998 | 39 | A/G lost over Arnhem. |
| Pritchard | WK | SGT | | 1520995 | 77 | Halifax | MZ935 | 12/09/1944 | L7 | 806 | 34 | |
| Proud | EAJ | SGT | | 545163 | 420 | Halifax | MZ687 | 16/08/1944 | L7 | 676 | 28 | ss7. Adrift two days in dinghy. |
| Prowd | K | W/O | AUS | A.425052 | 196 | Stirling | EF248 | 19/09/1942 | L7 | 942 | 38 | Pilot lost over Arnhem. Awarded Netherlands Flying Cross. |
| Pulbrook | LJ | F/S | AUS | A.430299 | 466 | Halifax | HX271 | 02/06/1944 | L7 | 677 | 28 | Captured 10 June 1944. |
| Purnell | WA | F/S | AUS | A.422810 | 626 | Lancaster | LM633 | 20/07/1944 | L7 | 486 | 21 | Captured 30 July 1944. Betrayed in Brussels. |
| Quick | EE | SGT | | 1605066 | 49 | Lancaster | ND647 | 03/05/1944 | DL/L7 | 10 | 57* | Baled out in error. On permanent staff at Dulag Luft. |
| Quigley | E | SGT | | 1149134 | 6341LWU | Horsa | n/k | 19/09/1944 | 12A/L7 | 943 | 38 | R/MECH. Captured at Arnhem. Born 30 April 1912. Died 1 May 1960. |
| Quinn | HC | F/S | CAN | R.150272 | 432 | Halifax | NP695 | 06/12/1944 | L7 | 1300 | 56 | Also POW no. 113 (Stalag 383). |
| Quinn | J | SGT | | 759133 | 407 | Hudson | AM778 | 01/12/1941 | 7A/383/L7 | 90108 | 16 | |
| Raffill | EJ | SGT | | 1652906 | 57 | Lancaster | LM580 | 21/06/1944 | L7 | 231 | 8 | |
| Rampley | AJ | SGT | | 1261153 | 57 | Lancaster | LM579 | 25/08/1944 | L7 | 756 | 33 | |
| Ramsbottom | WJ | S/SGT | | 920299 | GPR | Horsa | n/k | 26/09/1944 | L7 | 1038 | 40 | D/13. |
| Rancom | HA | S/SGT | | 6402120 | GPR | Horsa | n/k | 10/06/1944 | 12A/L7 | 80971 | 22 | D-Day. His glider was towed by F/L Jimmy Edwards. See One Night in June. 12A? |
| Ranfield | H | S/SGT | | 3448888 | GPR | Horsa | n/k | 18/09/1944 | L7 | 999 | 39 | A/17. Escaped during the evacuation. Back to UK via Odessa. |
| Ranger | JA | WO2 | CAN | R.158728 | 425 | Halifax | LW379 | 01/11/1944 | L7 | 1257 | 55* | |
| Rathband | HH | SGT | | 1544344 | GPR | Horsa | n/k | 26/09/1944 | L7 | 1039 | 40 | C/*. |
| Rawcliffe | J | F/S | | 1589261 | 582 | Lancaster | ND969 | 12/08/1944 | L7 | 624 | 27 | |
| Rawlings | HS | F/S | | 1577450 | 90 | Stirling | BF524 | 08/05/1944 | L7 | 185 | 7 | On SOE op BOB 183. Lost an eye. Given a glass one to replace it. |
| Raymond | RF | F/S | | 1701179 | 83 | Lancaster | ND963 | 22/05/1944 | L7 | 47 | 1 | |
| Reardon | MPP | S/SGT | | 934721 | GPR | Horsa | n/k | 21/09/1941 | L7 | 1081 | 45* | G/10. |

| Surname | Initials | Rank | Nat. | Service No. | Sqn | Aircraft | Serial | Date | Camp | No. | Page | Notes |
|---|---|---|---|---|---|---|---|---|---|---|---|---|
| Reaume | BA | SGT | CAN | R.201470 | 419 | Lancaster | KB723 | 04/07/1944 | L7 | 367 | 14 | |
| Redding | HJ | F/S | | 1247519 | 83 | Lancaster | PB362 | 18/08/1944 | 12A/L7 | 86349 | 34 | |
| Redpath | HC | F/S | AUS | A.410285 | 150 | Wellington | LN858 | 03/04/1944 | 9B/L7 | 877 | 37 | W/OP. Lost an eye. At 9B (Bad Soden Lazarett) with POW no. 53124. |
| Rees | JI | F/S | | 1281572 | 405 | Lancaster | ND526 | 24/05/1944 | L7 | 324 | 12 | Captured 16 June 1944, Erquennes, near Turnhout, Belgium. |
| Rees | WN | SGT | | 1418676 | 576 | Lancaster | LM122 | 02/11/1944 | L7 | 1258 | 55* | |
| Reeves | RE | F/S | | 1317854 | 625 | Lancaster | LM513 | 21/05/1944 | L7 | 406 | 15 | Betrayed & captured at Antwerp 15 July 1944. |
| Reid | W | SGT | | 1553112 | 97 | Lancaster | ND451 | 21/06/1944 | L7 | 232 | 8 | |
| Reilly | JJ | WO2 | CAN | R.156923 | 7 | Lancaster | PA964 | 06/10/1944 | L7 | 1082 | 45* | |
| Relf | AC | L/CPL | | 7348669 | n/a | n/a | n/a | n/k | L7 | 530 | 23 | RAMC. |
| Rennick | WH | F/S | AUS | A.40974 | 467 | Lancaster | LM226 | 12/09/1944 | L7 | 807 | 34 | |
| Reynolds | MJN | F/S | AUS | A.424317 | 51 | Halifax | MZ916 | 11/09/1944 | L7 | 808 | 34 | |
| Rhodes | L | W/O | | 1379166 | 619 | Lancaster | LM446 | 09/05/1944 | L7 | 127 | 4 | ss8. |
| Rhodes | R | F/S | | 1831840 | 35 | Lancaster | ND702 | 11/09/1944 | L7 | 809 | 34 | See We Act With One Accord, p.194. |
| Richards | HW | WO2 | CAN | R.150920 | 57 | Lancaster | ME668 | 07/07/1944 | L7 | 407 | 15 | |
| Richardson | CR | F/S | AUS | A.436701 | 463 | Lancaster | LM242 | 11/09/1944 | L7 | 810 | 34 | Charles Robert Richardson was born in March 1913. |
| Richardson | EEL | SGT | | 1604583 | 207 | Lancaster | DV369 | 14/01/1944 | 9C/L7 | 43819 | 3 | Evacuated. Left at Stalag 344. |
| Ridge | RF | F/S | AUS | A.417891 | 625 | Lancaster | ED938 | 12/06/1944 | L7 | 233 | 8 | Briefly in Luftwaffe Hospital, Amsterdam. |
| Ridgway | W | S/SGT | | 959272 | GPR | Horsa | n/k | 02/07/1944 | 12A/L7 | 84108 | 34 | D-Day. |
| Rigby | AA | SGT | | 5833342 | GPR | Horsa | LH288 | 17/09/1944 | 12A/L7 | 1000 | 39 | B/19. Captured by Panzer Grenadiers near the Rhine on 21 September 1944. |
| Rigden | RJ | F/S | | 1231758 | 514 | Lancaster | LL731 | 12/09/1944 | L7 | 944 | 38 | |
| Riley | TH | F/S | | 1451040 | 640 | Halifax | LK865 | 27/05/1944 | L7 | 128 | 4 | Captured 5 June 1944. |
| Rimmon | CI | L/SGT | | 2360183 | n/a | n/a | n/a | n/k | L7 | 186 | 7 | British Army (Royal Corps of Signals). Moved to another camp. |
| Rix | JA | SGT | | 1174910 | 578 | Halifax | NA568 | 11/09/1944 | L7 | 811 | 34 | |
| Robbins | LW | SGT | CAN | R.209918 | 299 | Stirling | EF267 | 19/09/1944 | L7 | 866 | 37 | A/G lost over Arnhem. |
| Roberts | AC | F/S | | 1473119 | 70 | Wellington | LN806 | 14/07/1944 | L7 | 408 | 15 | A/G lost 13/14 July 1944 (Milan). Crashed San Bassano, Italy after collision with Wellington MF120, 142 Squadron. |
| Roberts | DJ | SGT | | 2220345 | 75 | Lancaster | LM104 | 06/10/1944 | L7 | 1040 | 40 | |

| Surname | Initials | Rank | Nat. | Service No. | Sqn | Aircraft | Serial | Date | Ref | No. | No. | Notes |
|---|---|---|---|---|---|---|---|---|---|---|---|---|
| Roberts | JE | SGT | CAN | R.65957 | 162 RCAF | Canso | 9842 | 22/06/1944 | L7 | 409 | 15 | F/E. ss8. Note that 162 was a Canadian squadron NOT RAF. The Canso was a Catalina. |
| Roberts | TW | SGT | | 1595067 | 158 | Halifax | MZ337 | 13/09/1944 | L7 | 812 | 34 | |
| Robertson | J | SGT | | 1568799 | 35 | Lancaster | ND701 | 09/04/1944 | L7 | 813 | 34 | Captured 30 August 1944. |
| Robertson | JA | WO2 | CAN | R.144404 | 433 | Halifax | MZ816 | 28/07/1944 | L7 | 487 | 21 | |
| Robertson | P | F/S | | 1820743 | 570 | Stirling | EH897 | 19/09/1944 | L7 | 945 | 38 | A/G lost over Arnhem. |
| Robinson | CL | SGT | CAN | R.195309 | 514 | Lancaster | DS787 | 11/09/1944 | L7 | 814 | 34 | Commissioned (J.92951). |
| Robinson | GF | SGT | | 652896 | 514 | Lancaster | LM206 | 28/07/1944 | L7 | 625 | 27 | |
| Robinson | J | SGT | | 2201636 | 166 | Lancaster | ME775 | 19/05/1944 | L7 | 48 | 1 | |
| Robinson | NW | W/O | AUS | A.404682 | 463 | Lancaster | DV229 | 10/06/1944 | L7 | 325 | 12 | Captured 19 June 1944. |
| Robinson | RC | F/S | CAN | R.127012 | 408 | Halifax | NP761 | 06/11/1944 | L7 | 1210 | 50 | |
| Robson | JE | S/SGT | | 3963615 | GPR | Horsa | n/k | 23/09/1944 | L7 | 946 | 38 | A/*. |
| Robson | WA | F/S | | 956452 | 415 | Hampden | P1258 | 18/08/1943 | 4B/L7 | 222549 | 49 | Pilot. Shot down off Dutch coast. |
| Roche | FJ | SGT | AUS | A.423897 | 630 | Lancaster | ND685 | 06/06/1944 | L7 | 326 | 12 | Baled out at 1,500 feet, just before aircraft exploded. |
| Rodgers | A | F/S | | 1064159 | 405 | Lancaster | ND526 | 24/05/1944 | L7 | 49 | 1 | DFM (6/8/43, 408 Sq). |
| Rogers | GE | SGT | | 1896391 | 424 | Halifax | LV959 | 04/08/1944 | L7 | 626 | 27 | ss7. Surname given in official records as Rodgers. |
| Rogers | RC | F/S | | 1587087 | 463 | Lancaster | NF990 | 06/11/1944 | L7 | 1259 | 55* | |
| Rogerson | SD | SGT | | 1567332 | 101 | Lancaster | LM508 | 21/06/1944 | L7 | 234 | 8 | |
| Rose | HP | SGT | | 1654274 | 426 | Halifax | NP741 | 12/09/1944 | L7 | 815 | 34 | |
| Rourke | L | SGT | | 1041971 | 408 | Lancaster | DS634 | 28/07/1944 | L7 | 531 | 23 | |
| Rowan | WS | F/S | | 1344656 | 432 | Halifax | LK811 | 27/05/1944 | L7 | 129 | 4 | Captured Antwerp 6 June 1944. |
| Rowe | FJ | F/S | | 1191426 | 76 | Halifax | MZ578 | 22/04/1944 | 9C/L7 | 53246 | 17 | See *Halifax Down!*, pp. 145-7. |
| Rowe | FR | SGT | | 1301361 | 196 | Stirling | LJ937 | 12/05/1944 | L7 | 96 | 2 | A/G. Baled out & aircraft returned to UK? |
| Royle | RG | SGT | | 1278347 | 44 | Lancaster | LM638 | 12/07/1944 | L7 | 410 | 15 | See *Massacre over the Marne* p. 124. |
| Rudland | WP | SGT | | 1284078 | 70 | Wellington | LN699 | 21/07/1944 | L7 | 488 | 21 | A/G lost on raid on Pardubice. |
| Russell | PR | F/S | | 1392240 | 233 | Dakota | KG586 | 21/09/1944 | L7 | 1083 | 45* | Pilot. Lost on Arnhem supply. |
| Rutland | TW | SGT | | 1621874 | 158 | Halifax | MZ734 | 25/10/1944 | L7 | 1163 | 48 | |
| Sales | AA | SGT | | 1800282 | 142 | Wellington | LN700 | 14/06/1944 | L7 | 187 | 7 | A/G. Lost on Munich raid. |
| Samways | RC | F/S | | 1324626 | 148 | Halifax | JN926 | 14/08/1944 | L7 | 678 | 28 | Nav lost on trip to Warsaw. See *Hell On Earth*, pp. 17, 18, 20-4. |
| Sanderson | E | SGT | | 937039 | GPR | Horsa | n/k | 20/09/1944 | L7 | 947 | 38 | D/*. |
| Sanderson | JA | F/S | NZ | NZ.424525 | 166 | Lancaster | LL743 | 03/05/1944 | L7 | 235 | 8 | |

| Surname | Initials | Rank | Nat | Service No | Sqn | Type | Serial | Date | Camp | | | Notes |
|---|---|---|---|---|---|---|---|---|---|---|---|---|
| Sargant | RR | SGT | | 4617321 | GPR | Horsa | n/k | 26/09/1944 | L7 | 1041 | 40 | G/9. Married. From Sheffield. |
| Sargeant | AJ | W/O | AUS | A.410098 | 44 | Lancaster | LL938 | 21/06/1944 | L7 | 236 | 8 | |
| Sargeant | E | F/S | | 1410601 | 132 | Spitfire | NH476 | 27/09/1944 | L7 | 1001 | 39 | Captured in Germany. |
| Sargent | LS | SGT | | 1546217 | 619 | Lancaster | NE151 | 21/06/1944 | 9C/L7 | 53424 | 28 | |
| Sawyer | E | SGT | | 1853704 | 427 | Halifax | HX279 | 18/03/1944 | 9C/L7 | 53103 | 10 | |
| Sayles | B | S/SGT | | 850767 | GPR | Horsa | n/k | 20/09/1944 | L7 | 948 | 38 | F/16. |
| Schofield | DC | W/O | | 1500434 | 233 | Dakota | KG586 | 21/09/1944 | L7 | 1042 | 40 | N/B lost on Arnhem supply. POW no.40042? |
| Schofield | DR | CPL | | 552953 | 211GRP | n/a | n/a | 21/06/1942 | 11B/L7 | 140042 | 18 | W/OP Mechanic. Captured at Tobruk. On strength of 211 Group. |
| Schott | RC | WO1 | CAN | R.147452 | 44 | Lancaster | LM434 | 21/06/1944 | L7 | 327 | 12 | Commissioned (J.88038). |
| Scopes | DR | SGT | | 1391038 | 635 | Lancaster | ND450 | 21/05/1944 | L7 | 50 | 1 | Baled out. Aircraft returned to UK. |
| Scott | D | SGT | | 1061574 | 408 | Lancaster | LL687 | 28/07/1944 | L7 | 489 | 21 | ss8. |
| Scott | EW | F/S | | 1425752 | 37 | Wellington | ME880 | 22/10/1944 | L7 | 1164 | 48 | B/A on 60th op. Lost on Maribor raid. Commissioned. |
| Scott | GL | SGT | NZ | NZ.401721 | 97 | Manchester | L7424 | 12/08/1941 | 7A/383/L7 | 90063 | 16 | A/G. Broke leg on landing. Also POW no. 76 (Stalag 383). See Silk and Barbed Wire, p.88. |
| Scott | JJ | F/S | CAN | R.207973 | 433 | Halifax | NP949 | 21/11/1944 | L7 | 1260 | 51/55* | |
| Scott | JS | SGT | | 1544210 | 640 | Halifax | LW499 | 12/05/1944 | L7 | 51 | 1 | ss7. |
| Scott | WB | F/S | AUS | A.424825 | 463 | Lancaster | PD338 | 02/11/1944 | L7 | 1165 | 48 | |
| Scully | HV | SGT | | 1681512 | 37 | Wellington | LN643 | 10/05/1944 | L7 | 188 | 7 | W/AG. Lost on Leghorn raid. |
| Scully | J | SGT | | 1546284 | 514 | Lancaster | LL716 | 03/08/1944 | L7 | 627 | 27 | |
| Seaman | FG | SGT | | 876231 | GPR | Horsa | n/k | 20/09/1944 | L7 | 949 | 38 | F/16. |
| Sedgwick | FH | F/S | | 1516657 | 299 | Stirling | LK645 | 21/09/1944 | L7 | 950 | 38 | A/B lost over Arnhem. |
| Seeley | CAR | F/S | CAN | R.77145 | 415 | Halifax | MZ603 | 02/11/1944 | L7 | 1120 | 47 | Commissioned (C.90966). |
| Sekine | PY | SGT | | 1375192 | 83 | Hampden | AE133 | 10/01/1942 | 7A/383/L7 | 90145 | 16 | Also POW no. 144 (Stalag 383). Japanese father. |
| Seller | AE | W/O | CAN | R.143073 | 412 | Spitfire | MH754 | 28/06/1944 | L7 | 411 | 15 | Commissioned (J.88527). |
| Selwyn | EG | SGT | | 1640729 | 622 | Lancaster | LM108 | 28/05/1944 | L7 | 867 | 37 | F/E. Captured near Dax 4 June 1944. |
| Semple | DG | SGT | | 1305104 | 420 | Hampden | AT130 | 21/01/1942 | 7A/383/L7 | 90122 | 16 | Also POW no. 125 (Stalag 383). |
| Shabatura | EH | S/SGT | USA | 37557519 | 409BS | B-24 | 42-100416 | 18/09/1944 | 11B/L7 | 117987 | 55 | Left waist gunner B-24 Baggy Maggy 93BG/409BS. Posted to another camp, 11B? |
| Sharpe | AG | WO2 | CAN | R.161485 | 432 | Halifax | NP801 | 09/10/1944 | L7 | 1043 | 40 | Commissioned (J.87263). |
| Sharpe | BT | F/S | AUS | A.423486 | 462 | Halifax | LL610 | 02/11/1944 | L7 | 1166 | 48 | |

| Surname | Init | Rank | Nat | Service No | Sqn/Unit | Aircraft | Serial | Date | Camp | POW No | Page | Notes |
|---|---|---|---|---|---|---|---|---|---|---|---|---|
| Sharpe | GW | | | R.135683 | 433 | Halifax | HX282 | 18/03/1944 | 9C/L7 | 53100 | 10 | Not real surname. Washed out as pilot, went AWOL and re-enlisted. Commissioned (J.86557). |
| Shaw | C | SGT | | 543888 | 156 | Lancaster | ND929 | 06/10/1944 | L7 | 1044 | 40 | F/E. Baled out & aircraft returned to UK? |
| Shaw | GM | F/S | | 1395561 | 57 | Lancaster | JB370 | 07/07/1944 | L7 | 412 | 15 | ss7. |
| Shean | HJ | F/S | | 1320051 | 103 | Lancaster | LL941 | 24/07/1944 | L7 | 490 | 21 | |
| Sheard | F | SGT | | 1591133 | 101 | Lancaster | LM508 | 21/06/1944 | L7 | 237 | 8 | |
| Shearman | AE | F/S | | 971580 | 77 | Halifax | MZ935 | 12/09/1944 | 9C/L7/344/13D | 53755 | 57* | Wounded. At Dulag Luft and Stalag IXC. (Mühlhausen) hospitals. |
| Sheel | KC | F/S | AUS | A.428801 | 463 | Lancaster | LM597 | 24/06/1944 | L7 | 328 | 12 | |
| Sheldon | S | SGT | | 1399935 | 44 | Lancaster | PB192 | 04/11/1944 | L7 | 1211 | 50 | |
| Shelshar | RL | SGT | | 1614247 | 78 | Halifax | LW266 | 23/09/1943 | L7 | 368 | 14 | Broken limbs. At Hohe Mark for seven months. |
| Shenton | JA | SGT | | 1307260 | 10 | Halifax | LV906 | 24/05/1944 | L7 | 52 | 1 | |
| Shetler | LM | WO2 | CAN | R.150081 | 429 | Halifax | LW124 | 24/05/1944 | L7 | 280 | 11 | Captured 15 June 1944, Antwerp. Commissioned (J.86643). |
| Shields | J | F/S | AUS | A.19790 | 57 | Lancaster | PB384 | 16/08/1944 | L7 | 1261 | 55* | Born 11 September 1913. Baled out at 200 feet. Smashed pelvis. In hospital. |
| Shillito | KB | SGT | | 1509115 | 142 | Wellington | LN700 | 14/06/1944 | L7 | 189 | 7 | A/G. Lost on Munich raid. |
| Shilstone | AN | SGT | | 1808652 | 460 | Lancaster | PB469 | 21/11/1944 | L7 | 1262 | 55* | ss7 |
| Shirley | HV | F/S | AUS | A.419905 | 51 | Halifax | MZ319 | 11/09/1944 | L7 | 816 | 34 | Wounded in head by flak. Born Ireland 5 April 1922. |
| Shore | JE | SGT | | 1852444 | 158 | Halifax | LK841 | 02/06/1944 | L7 | 130 | 4 | |
| Short | GT | F/S | | 621194 | 619 | Lancaster | ME855 | 12/08/1944 | L7 | 679 | 28 | |
| Sidebottom | JR | SGT | | 1860962 | 49 | Lancaster | LM572 | 24/06/1944 | L7 | 281 | 11 | F/E. |
| Silver | SA | F/S | AUS | A.419348 | 49 | Lancaster | LM539 | 21/05/1944 | L7/344/383 | 238 | 8 | ss7. Injured arm baling out. Moved in December 1944. Born on 13 May 1910. |
| Simes | SW | F/S | | 1802065 | 106 | Lancaster | JB567 | 22/04/1944 | 9C/L7 | 53104 | 10 | Repatriated via Odessa. |
| Simons | DH | S/SGT | | 119641 | GPR | Horsa | n/k | 24/09/1944 | L7 | 1002 | 39 | F/*. |
| Simpson | A | S/SGT | | 856791 | GPR | Horsa | n/k | 19/11/1944 | L7 | 1263 | 55* | D/*. |
| Simpson | MJ | F/S | CAN | R.184155 | 207 | Lancaster | ND522 | 21/05/1944 | L7 | 532 | 23 | Wounded by bullet in rectum. Came down in the sea . Had to swim ashore. |
| Simpson | PS | F/S | | 9112650 | 126 | Hurricane | Z3158 | 12/11/1941 | 7A/11A/L7 | 138872 | 18 | Captured off coast of Sicily. To Campo PG78 first. |
| Simpson | RF | LAF | | FX101457 | n/k | n/k | n/k | 19/09/1944 | L7 | 951 | 38 | Fitter, Fleet Air Arm. |

| Surname | Initials | Rank | Service No. | Nat. | Sqn | Aircraft | Serial | Date | Camp | | | Notes |
|---|---|---|---|---|---|---|---|---|---|---|---|---|
| Sindall | RAJ | SGT | 1385988 | | 626 | Lancaster | NE118 | 22/05/1944 | L7 | 53 | 1 | Shot down 5 Feb 1944. In Fresnes prison. Commissioned (171383). |
| Slack | DA | F/S | 1078063 | | 175 | Typhoon | JP369 | 29/04/1944 | L7 | 868 | 37 | Drowned 8 May 1945 rescuing German guard. No known grave. |
| Slack | KEC | F/S | R.123313 | CAN | 433 | Halifax | MZ284 | 21/11/1944 | L7 | 1302 | 56 | W/OP. |
| Slater | JA | F/S | 1067480 | | 293 | Walrus | L2223 | 05/08/1944 | L7 | 628 | 27 | |
| Slattery | JP | F/S | 620746 | | 626 | Lancaster | LM599 | 12/08/1944 | L7 | 629 | 27 | |
| Sloane | AR | F/S | A.434538 | AUS | 463 | Lancaster | LM309 | 23/09/1944 | L7 | 952 | 38 | |
| Slowey | JG | SGT | 516838 | | 44 | Hampden | L4088 | 21/04/1940 | L7 | 413 | 15 | From permanent staff, Dulag Luft. Escaped during L7 evacuation. Repatriated via Odessa. UK 30 March 1945. See his biography Into Enemy Arms. |
| Smalley | WC | F/S | 1577526 | | 158 | Halifax | MZ367 | 12/08/1944 | L7 | 680 | 28 | |
| Smart | A | SGT | 14588092 | | GPR | Horsa | n/k | 20/09/1944 | L7 | 953 | 38 | D/*. |
| Smart | HW | SGT | 1627476 | | 640 | Halifax | MZ675 | 24/05/1944 | L7 | 54 | 1 | ss7. |
| Smart | RS | F/S | R.170560 | CAN | 547 | Liberator | EV897 | 18/06/1944 | L7 | 369 | 14 | Wop/AG shot down off French coast. |
| Smit | C | Pt/Off | 90549 | HOL | 320 | Mitchell | FR149 | 12/06/1944 | 12A/L7 | 80164 | 9 | Dutch Fleet Air Arm petty officer. |
| Smith | AC | F/S | 1092340 | | 214 | Fortress | HB763 | 25/08/1944 | L7 | 720 | 30 | |
| Smith | AK | SGT | 949366 | | 463 | Lancaster | DV229 | 10/06/1944 | L7 | 329 | 12 | Captured 19 June 1944. |
| Smith | DS | WO2 | R.148505 | CAN | 426 | Halifax | MZ690 | 07/06/1944 | L7 | 190 | 7 | |
| Smith | EV | SGT | 1162802 | | 7 | Stirling | W7436 | 18/12/1941 | 7A/383/L7 | 90120 | 16 | Also POW no. 123 (Stalag 383). |
| Smith | FJJ | F/S | 920522 | | 42 | Beaufort | AW243 | 11/12/1941 | 7A/383/L7 | 90102 | 16 | WOP/AG. Captured after two days in dinghy. Also POW no. 108 (Stalag 383). |
| Smith | G | SGT | 1621399 | | 12 | Lancaster | NE134 | 22/05/1944 | L7 | 55 | 1 | Baled out - aircraft landed in Allied territory. |
| Smith | GH | SGT | 570259 | | 460 | Lancaster | LL907 | 07/07/1944 | L7 | 491 | 21 | |
| Smith | GH | SGT | 1803973 | | 57 | Lancaster | LM579 | 25/08/1944 | L7 | 721 | 30 | Baled out as ordered. Aircraft landed at RAF Woodbridge. Born 12/12/12. |
| Smith | JA | SGT | 2211862 | | 462 | Halifax | NP990 | 06/10/1944 | L7 | 1045 | 40 | |
| Smith | JG | F/S | A.429256 | AUS | 192 | Halifax | MZ806 | 21/11/1944 | L7 | 1264 | 55* | |
| Smith | OH | SGT | 1567092 | | 582 | Lancaster | PB141 | 23/12/1944 | L7 | 1343 | 57* | |
| Smith | P | SGT | 1833626 | | 428 | Lancaster | KB756 | 04/07/1944 | 9C/L7 | 53391 | 41* | |
| Smith | RL | F/S | 1322308 | | 514 | Lancaster | LL672 | 21/01/1944 | 9C/L7/L3 | 39982 | 49 | Evacuated to Luft 3 (?). See Through Footless Halls of Air. |
| Smith | SN | SGT | 1576444 | | 142 | Wellington | LN700 | 14/06/1944 | L7 | 191 | 7 | N/B. Lost on Munich raid. |

| Surname | Initials | Rank | Nat. | Service No. | Unit | Aircraft | Serial | Date | Camp | No. | No. | Notes |
|---|---|---|---|---|---|---|---|---|---|---|---|---|
| Smith | WBR | F/S | AUS | A.421419 | 622 | Lancaster | LL803 | 02/11/1944 | L7 | 1167 | 48 | |
| Smith | WL | F/S | CAN | R.70871 | 160 | Liberator | AL620 | 16/01/1943 | 7A/L7 | 344 | 13 | W/AG. Lost near Tripoli. |
| Smithson | DG | SGT | | 1886189 | GPR | Horsa | n/k | 18/09/1944 | 12A/L7 | 075465 | 47 | G/10. |
| Smyth | V | Pt/O | | FX.86754 | 831 | Barracuda | LS547 | 16/05/1944 | L7 | 97 | 2 | Petty officer, Fleet Air Arm. Captured 16 May 1944 in Norway. |
| Snowden | JWB | W/O | | 364766 | 115 | Wellington | X9873 | 31/10/1941 | 8B/L6/L7 | 24467 | 28* | AFM (24/9/41), MiD (31/1/47). |
| Solberg | BAJ | WO2 | CAN | R.176229 | 626 | Lancaster | ND952 | 30/06/1944 | L7 | 370 | 14 | Commissioned (J.89289). |
| Sorenson | H | F/S | | 1028119 | 271 | Dakota | KG444 | 21/09/1944 | L7 | 1007 | 39 | Nav lost over Arnhem. Pilot was Jimmy Edwards. |
| Sorzano | AL | SGT | | 1802334 | 40 | Wellington | LP234 | 13/06/1944 | L7 | 192 | 7 | B/A. Shot down on raid on Munich. |
| Souci | H | SGT | MAU | 1685986 | 57 | Lancaster | LM278 | 26/08/1944 | 9C/L7 | 52692 | 41* | ss7. |
| Spagatner | I | SGT | | 1896294 | 15 | Lancaster | NF958 | 12/09/1944 | L7 | 817 | 34 | Not listed on L7/3A Nominal Roll. |
| Sparks | TS | SGT | | 1685161 | 214 | Fortress | SR382 | 21/06/1944 | L7 | 414 | 15 | Betrayed and captured 8 July 1944. |
| Spencer | JH | F/S | | 658681 | 50 | Lancaster | LL842 | 24/07/1944 | L7 | 630 | 27 | |
| Spier | D | SGT | | 1803322 | 582 | Lancaster | PB141 | 23/12/1944 | L7 | 1344 | 57* | |
| Spite | DCG | SGT | | 1322215 | 640 | Halifax | LW464 | 24/07/1944 | L7 | 533 | 23 | |
| Spriggs | FA | F/S | | 1628363 | 158 | Halifax | LV918 | 24/05/1944 | L7 | 56 | 1 | |
| Stapleford | WR | SGT | | 569963 | 35 | Halifax | L9582 | 30/11/1941 | 7A/383/L7 | 90084 | 16 | Also POW no. 96 (Stalag 383). See We Act With One Accord, p.231. |
| Stapleton | RJ | SGT | | 1375337 | 83 | Hampden | AD794 | 23/12/1941 | 7A/383/L7 | 90143 | 16 | Baled out & aircraft returned to base? Also POW no. 142 (Stalag 383). |
| Stapley | FH | SGT | | 1539742 | GPR | Horsa | n/k | 17/09/1944 | L7 | 954 | 38 | D/22. |
| Starr | JM | SGT | CAN | R.196174 | 101 | Lancaster | ME613 | 21/06/1944 | 9C/L7 | 53425 | 41* | Evacuated to Stalag 383. Commissioned (J.92649). |
| Staunton-Smith | MR | F/S | AUS | A.428029 | 463 | Lancaster | NF977 | 23/10/1944 | L7 | 1168 | 48 | On 27th op. Right arm hit by flak splinters; became infected. |
| Stead | F | F/S | | 1432844 | 138 | Halifax | LL276 | 31/05/1944 | L7 | 98 | 2 | |
| Stead | JE | S/SGT | | 794717 | GPR | Horsa | n/k | 20/09/1944 | L7 | 955 | 38 | A/*. BEM (1/1/51) as BQMS, RA, TA. Born 7 August 1913. |
| Steggell | SCR | F/S | | 1865807 | 102 | Halifax | MZ871 | 24/12/1944 | L7 | 1345 | 57* | F/E. |
| Stephenson | JA | SGT | | 4616329 | GPR | Horsa | n/k | 21/09/1944 | L7 | 1003 | 39 | D/*. |
| Stephenson | WE | SGT | | 1580892 | 9 | Lancaster | LM519 | 22/05/1944 | L7 | 58 | 1 | ss7. |
| Stevens | DT | F/S | | 1808171 | 570 | Stirling | LJ913 | 18/09/1944 | L7 | 956 | 38 | R/G lost over Arnhem 18 September 1944. |
| Stevens | TB | SGT | | 3713627 | GPR | Horsa | n/k | 25/09/1944 | L7 | 957 | 38 | G/*. |

| Surname | Initials | Nat. | Rank | Service No. | Sqn | Aircraft | Serial | Date | Camp | | | Notes |
|---|---|---|---|---|---|---|---|---|---|---|---|---|
| Stevens | WH | | F/S | 1620362 | 254 | Beaufighter | LZ318 | 15/10/1944 | L7 | 1121 | 47 | Nav. Lost on ship attack off Wangerooge. |
| Stevenson | LH | CAN | SGT | R.171883 | 576 | Lancaster | PB400 | 26/08/1944 | L7 | 757 | 33 | Leslie Howard Stevenson. Aged twenty, shot dead 27 December 1944. |
| Stewart | DA | CAN | F/S | R.176832 | 158 | Halifax | LV918 | 24/05/1944 | L7 | 57 | 1 | Commissioned (J.86835). |
| Stewart | J | | SGT | 1330546 | 148 | Halifax | EB147 | 05/08/1944 | L7 | 681 | 28 | W/OP lost on supply mission to Warsaw. |
| Stewart | JG | | F/S | 1564631 | 299 | Stirling | LK241 | 29/11/1944 | L7 | 1303 | 56 | Nav on SOE operation to Norway. |
| Stewart | W | | F/S | 1076921 | 106 | Lancaster | ME789 | 07/07/1944 | L7 | 492 | 21 | |
| Stockdill | RG | AUS | F/S | A.427957 | 467 | Lancaster | LM267 | 29/08/1944 | L7 | 758 | 33 | |
| Stokes | HMcL | | SGT | 627443 | 104 | Wellington | Z8568 | 24/07/1942 | 4B/L7 | 226415 | 49 | ss6. Lost on Tobruk. The 2nd Pilot, Sgt G.L. Eke, survived the crash but died later. |
| Stone | VH | | SGT | 1602259 | 295 | Stirling | LK203 | 30/11/1944 | L7 | 1346 | 57* | W/OP. Baled out without orders. Aircraft returned to base. |
| Stoner | BW | | SGT | 1891903 | 207 | Lancaster | PD267 | 12/09/1944 | L7 | 818 | 34 | ss7. |
| Stones | HR | | SGT | 4537089 | GPR | Horsa | n/k | 20/09/1944 | L7 | 958 | 38 | D/22. |
| Strang | JC | | F/S | 1896559 | 622 | Lancaster | LM283 | 19/10/1944 | L7 | 1122 | 47 | |
| Stuart | AR | AUS | SGT | A.402141 | 452 | Spitfire | P8703 | 18/09/1941 | 8B/L7 | 9693 | 16 | Came down in sea after collision with Me109. In abortive escape with Sgt K.B. Chisholm RAAF in May 1942 |
| Stubbs | RE | | SGT | 1803616 | 158 | Halifax | HX320 | 24/05/1944 | L7 | 330 | 12 | Captured 26 June 1944(?), Wuustwezel. |
| Sturgess | FA | | F/S | 658974 | 44 | Lancaster | ND520 | 25/02/1944 | L7 | 131 | 4 | Nav. |
| Styles | RG | | SGT | 657885 | 103 | Lancaster | ND417 | 25/02/1944 | L7 | 59 | 1 | Later in Stalags 13D and 7A. |
| Such | FJ | | SGT | 625821 | 44 | Lancaster | LL938 | 21/06/1944 | L7 | 239 | 8 | Escaped on 20 January 1945 during the evacuation. To UK via Odessa. |
| Surgeoner | G | AUS | F/S | A.421414 | 466 | Halifax | MZ368 | 09/08/1944 | L7 | 631 | 27 | Born on 9 October 1913. |
| Sutherland | WF | AUS | F/S | A.428623 | 57 | Lancaster | PB425 | 19/10/1944 | L7 | 1123 | 47 | Escaped during evacuation. Repatriated via Odessa. |
| Swale | NH | SA | W/O | 212201V | 21SAAF | Marauder | HD591 | 13/09/1944 | L7 | 959 | 38 | W/OP. From Durban, S. Africa. |
| Swanson | JE | USA | T/SGT | 6561236 | 306TCS | Dakota | 43-15098 | 17/08/1944 | 11B/L7 | 117991 | 55 | 442TCG/306TCS. Posted to another camp. 11B? |
| Sweet | WH | | F/S | 1651741 | 7 | Lancaster | PB241 | 06/10/1944 | L7 | 1084 | 45* | |
| Swinton | WJ | NZ | F/S | NZ.414598 | 486 | Typhoon | JP689 | 10/02/1944 | L7 | 632 | 27 | On Rodeo to Chartres. |
| Swolf | RA | | SGT | 502316 | 97 | Lancaster | ND807 | 26/08/1944 | L7 | 819 | 34 | ss8. |
| Szadkowski | JS | POL | F/S | 780622 | 302 | Spitfire | MJ945 | 31/07/1944 | L7 | 633 | 27 | On armed recce south-west Falaise. |
| Tait | FJ | AUS | SGT | A.426928 | 158 | Halifax | HX334 | 12/05/1944 | L7 | 60 | 1 | Handed over to the Germans by Belgian farmer. |
| Tait | HJH | | F/S | 1896656 | 619 | Lancaster | LM742 | 06/11/1944 | L7 | 1212 | 50 | |

| Surname | Initials | Rank | Nat. | Service No. | Sqn | Aircraft | Serial | Date | Camp | No. | Col | Notes |
|---|---|---|---|---|---|---|---|---|---|---|---|---|
| Tames | JS | F/S | CAN | R.155727 | 408 | Lancaster | LL632 | 19/02/1944 | L7 | 829 | 35* | Lost toes to frostbite – fell asleep after landing. Also POW no. 2172. Commissioned (J.86781). |
| Tannen | PA | SGT | | 1323466 | 640 | Halifax | MZ677 | 02/06/1944 | L7 | 193 | 7 | |
| Tarleton | W | F/S | | 1539931 | 103 | Lancaster | ME649 | 12/12/1944 | L7 | 1347 | 57* | |
| Tarlton | PA | SGT | | 1891813 | 158 | Halifax | MZ703 | 18/07/1944 | L7 | 634 | 27 | |
| Tate | KE | WO2 | CAN | R.124433 | 576 | Lancaster | PB400 | 26/08/1944 | L7 | 759 | 33 | |
| Taylor | ER | SGT | | 2928549 | GPR | Horsa | n/k | 19/09/1944 | L7 | 960 | 38 | B/*. |
| Taylor | JD | SGT | | 1549741 | 77 | Halifax | LL138 | 22/05/1944 | L7 | 61 | 1 | |
| Taylor | JF | SGT | | 1591448 | 207 | Lancaster | PD322 | 06/12/1944 | L7 | 1304 | 56 | |
| Taylor | KG | W/O | CAN | R.150962 | 635 | Lancaster | ND450 | 21/05/1944 | L7 | 62 | 1 | Baled out. Aircraft returned to UK. Commissioned (J.90126). |
| Taylor | LEJ | F/S | | 1585057 | 619 | Lancaster | ME846 | 21/06/1944 | L7 | 282 | 11 | |
| Taylor | LF | SGT | | 934153 | 578 | Halifax | MZ556 | 20/07/1944 | L7 | 493 | 21 | |
| Taylor | R | F/S | | 1585691 | 90 | Stirling | LJ460 | 10/04/1944 | L7 | 682 | 28 | Captured 26 May 1944. |
| Taylor | R | F/S | AUS | A.422742 | 455 | Beaufighter | LZ194 | 06/07/1944 | L7 | 371 | 14 | Nav. Shot down into N. Sea at fifty feet. Pilot killed. |
| Taylor | RG | F/S | | 1321710 | 98 | Mitchell | FW211 | 25/09/1944 | 9C/L7 | 52951 | 57* | Shot down by FW190s over Holland. |
| Taylor | TJ | SGT | | 1677773 | 50 | Lancaster | LL791 | 25/02/1944 | L7 | 283 | 11 | Captured in the Pyrenees 21 April 1944. Toulouse, Fresnes, and Frankfurt prisons. |
| Taylor | W | SGT | | 1558719 | 70 | Wellington | LN806 | 17/07/1944 | L7 | 415 | 15 | B/A lost 13/14 July 1944 (Milan). Crashed San Bassano, Italy after collision with Wellington MF120 142 Squadron. |
| Taylor | WH | F/S | | 2214212 | 103 | Lancaster | ME773 | 14/07/1944 | L7 | 494 | 21 | ss7. |
| Teague | TR | F/S | NZ | NZ.427082 | 622 | Lancaster | LM108 | 28/05/1944 | L7 | 240 | 8 | Poitiers prison. Fresnes. |
| Tee | W | F/S | AUS | A.418988 | 299 | Stirling | EF267 | 19/09/1944 | L7 | 869 | 37 | W/OP hit by flak at 300 feet over Arnhem. |
| Temple | J | F/S | | 2218557 | 102 | Halifax | LW168 | 24/12/1944 | L7 | 1348 | 57* | |
| Templeton | LRS | F/S | | 1099268 | 576 | Lancaster | PA997 | 16/06/1944 | L7 | 194 | 7 | |
| Tennant | J | SGT | | 999234 | 515 | Mosquito | PZ163 | 04/09/1944 | L7 | 820 | 34 | |
| Thomas | GP | F/S | AUS | A.400298 | 97 | Manchester | R5795 | 18/12/1941 | 7A/383/L7 | 90119 | 16 | Also POW no. 122 (Stalag 383). |
| Thomas | GR | SGT | | 1836202 | 297 | Albemarle | V1817 | 28/05/1944 | L7 | 99 | 2 | A/G. |
| Thomas | L | SGT | | 1682665 | 233 | Dakota | KG329 | 07/06/1944 | 12A/L7 | 80160 | 9 | W/OP. Shot down by flak on supply drop, Ranville, France. |
| Thompson | RB | F/S | | 542696 | 24 | Marauder | HD433 | 04/07/1944 | L7 | 416 | 15 | A/G. |

| Surname | Initials | Rank | Nat | Service No. | Sqn | Aircraft | Serial | Date | Camp | No. | No. | Notes |
|---|---|---|---|---|---|---|---|---|---|---|---|---|
| Thompson | VH | SGT | | 1333663 | 625 | Lancaster | ND461 | 27/01/1944 | L7 | 284 | 11 | Commissioned (170455) 22 February 1944. Captured 10 April 1944. |
| Thompson | WL | SGT | | 1155659 | 158 | Halifax | MZ703 | 18/07/1944 | L7 | 495 | 21 | |
| Thomson | GB | SGT | | 1572977 | 15 | Lancaster | NF958 | 12/09/1944 | L7 | 870 | 37 | |
| Thomson | JJ | S/SGT | | 3194205 | GPR | Horsa | n/k | 18/09/1944 | L7 | 961 | 38 | B/19. |
| Thomson | JMcV | F/S | | 1343681 | 222 | Spitfire | MH429 | 31/08/1943 | 9B/L7 | 43272 | 42/45* | Lost on Ramrod S16. Face badly burned. Arrived on 26 October 1944 after plastic surgery. |
| Thomson | PA | F/O | AUS | A.415285 | 622 | Lancaster | LL828 | 15/03/1944 | L7 | 100 | 2 | Fresnes. Frankfurt. DL 18 May 1944. L7 Camp Leader. Commissioned after he was shot down. |
| Thornton | A | F/S | | 1232135 | 295 | Stirling | LK115 | 21/09/1944 | L7 | 1004 | 39 | A/B lost over Arnhem. |
| Tidbury | L | F/S | | 1338719 | 184 | Typhoon | MN642 | 07/06/1944 | L7 | 496 | 21 | Shot down by flak. |
| Tiller | HS | W/O | AUS | A.417677 | 97 | Lancaster | PB409 | 23/09/1944 | L7 | 1046 | 40 | ss7. DFM (30/6/44). |
| Tode | GW | SGT | | 1375355 | 40 | Wellington | X9824 | 10/01/1942 | 7A/383/L7 | 90142 | 16 | Also POW no. 141 (Stalag 383). |
| Tolhurst | EJH | SGT | | 907789 | 104 | Wellington | MF350 | 21/08/1944 | L7 | 722 | 30 | A/G. |
| Tomblin | BA | SGT | | 14259326 | GPR | Horsa | n/k | 24/09/1944 | L7 | 1005 | 39 | E/11. |
| Tomei | VP | F/S | | 1802293 | 57 | Lancaster | NG145 | 04/12/1944 | L7 | 1349 | 57* | ss7. |
| Tommis | AE | SGT | | 1675574 | 578 | Halifax | MZ556 | 20/07/1944 | L7 | 497 | 21 | |
| Tomney | JF | SGT | | 1801828 | 166 | Lancaster | ND956 | 21/05/1944 | L7 | 63 | 1 | |
| Tonkin | AJ | SGT | | 922736 | 22 | Beaufort | L9793 | 26/11/1941 | 7A/383/L7 | 90093 | 16 | W/AG shot down off French coast. Also POW no. 102 (Stalag 383). |
| Tonner | PB | W/O | CAN | R.126335 | 512 | Dakota | KG418 | 20/09/1944 | L7 | 1047 | 40 | W/OP lost over Arnhem. Commissioned (J.89757). Died 17 October 1945 of acute TB and meningitis. |
| Toomey | RGE | SGT | CAN | R.82585 | 428 | Lancaster | KB751 | 16/08/1944 | L7 | 683 | 28 | ss7. Commissioned (C.90314). |
| Townshend | FC | SGT | | 1615097 | 514 | Lancaster | DS815 | 22/03/1944 | 9C/L7 | 52298 | 42/45* | 9C? |
| Towse | B | SGT | | 1892647 | 101 | Lancaster | LM474 | 16/06/1944 | 9C/L7 | 53426 | 57* | |
| Tranent | KM | F/S | AUS | A.426402 | 466 | Halifax | MZ313 | 18/07/1944 | L7 | 498 | 21 | Ordered to baled out. Aircraft got back to UK. |
| Tranter | EH | F/S | | 1577056 | 619 | Lancaster | LL808 | 21/06/1944 | L7 | 241 | 8 | |
| Treadgold | FG | SGT | | 576363 | 106 | Lancaster | PB359 | 19/09/1944 | L7 | 1006 | 39 | Escaped on march, captured, escaped. To UK via Odessa and Middle East. |
| Tregoning | JM | F/S | | 1586154 | 578 | Halifax | NA568 | 11/09/1944 | L7 | 821 | 34 | |
| Trimble | T | F/S | EIR | 631467 | 69 | Wellington | MF231 | 14/06/1944 | L7 | 242 | 8 | A/G. From Swanlinbar, Co. Cavan, Ireland. |

| Surname | Initials | Rank | Nat. | Service No. | Sqn | Aircraft | Serial | Date | Camp | No. | No.2 | Notes |
|---|---|---|---|---|---|---|---|---|---|---|---|---|
| Trumble | AHJ | SGT | | 1587423 | 115 | Lancaster | LL944 | 16/12/1944 | L7 | 1350 | 57* | Commissioned (188961) 30 January 1945. Flying officer 1 June 1945. |
| Trussler | JWA | SGT | | 1893139 | 419 | Lancaster | KB734 | 16/06/1944 | L7 | 243 | 8 | |
| Tuck | LJ | SGT | | 1323367 | 10 | Halifax | LV906 | 24/05/1944 | L7 | 64 | 1 | |
| Tuckwell | TH | SGT | | 1876211 | 619 | Lancaster | LL808 | 21/06/1944 | L7 | 195 | 7 | |
| Tudor | FJ | W/O | | 1063420 | 35 | Lancaster | ND762 | 22/05/1944 | L7 | 132 | 4 | DFM (15/2/44). Wounded. See We Act With One Accord pp.178-9 & p.203. |
| Tufnell | HD | SGT | | 1399977 | 253 | Spitfire | JK941 | 27/05/1944 | L7 | 101 | 2 | Mk.Vc Spitfire. |
| Tunstall | AJ | SGT | | 4206290 | AAC | n/a | n/a | n/k | L7 | 196 | 7 | Army Air Corps. At Feldpost 31979, N. Italy. Sent to another camp. |
| Turner | FF | W/O | | 1030201 | 226 | Mitchell | FW106 | 15/10/1944 | L7 | 1124 | 47 | Pilot. All four crew POW. |
| Turner | HF | SGT | | 2214239 | 7 | Lancaster | PB474 | 12/10/1944 | L7 | 1085 | 45* | |
| Turner | HH | F/S | | 1384962 | 12 | Lancaster | ND627 | 04/07/1944 | L7 | 372 | 14 | |
| Turnquist | DE | F/S | CAN | R.192114 | 426 | Halifax | LW197 | 30/09/1944 | L7 | 1048 | 40 | Commissioned (J.89355). |
| Turtle | RJ | SGT | | 1353039 | 626 | Lancaster | NE118 | 22/05/1944 | L7 | 65 | 1 | |
| Turton | HW | W/O | | 1001026 | 83 | Lancaster | PB188 | 11/11/1944 | L7 | 1271 | 55* | Commissioned (188227) 9 January 1945. |
| Tweddle | A | SGT | | 1593423 | 207 | Lancaster | LM671 | 18/12/1944 | L7 | 1351 | 57* | All seven crew POW. |
| Tweed | JF | SGT | | 744733 | 102 | Halifax | MZ642 | 16/06/1944 | L7 | 635 | 27 | |
| Twynam | PS | F/S | | 1800367 | 426 | Halifax | NP741 | 12/09/1944 | L7 | 871 | 37 | |
| Umscheid | JL | SGT | CAN | R.149240 | 405 | Lancaster | PA988 | 16/08/1944 | L7 | 684 | 28 | Commissioned (C.88014). |
| Unknown | | | | | | | | | L7 | 732 | 31 | |
| Unknown | | | | | | | | | L7 | 828 | 35* | |
| Unknown | | | | | | | | | L7 | 876 | 37 | This number was possibly given to Sgt HC Redpath RAAF . |
| Unknown | | | | | | | | | L7 | 878 | 37 | This number was possibly given to F/S FJ Brown RAAF. |
| Unknown | | | | | | | | | L7 | 1359 | 57+ | Probably at Luft 7 soon after Trupp 57. |
| Upton | HR | WO2 | SA | 337598V | 31SAAF | Liberator | EW105 | 13/08/1944 | L7 | 723 | 30 | A/G. From Durban, S. Africa. Committed suicide in 1950s. |
| Urquhart | JA | S/SGT | | 5185152 | GPR | Horsa | n/k | 27/09/1944 | L7 | 1008 | 39 | F/*. |
| Vaissade | JN | SGT | FRA | C.4778 | 347 | Halifax | NA616 | 03/09/1944 | L7 | 822 | 34 | Three of his crew murdered on the ground. From Marseille, France. |

| Surname | Initials | Rank | Nat. | Service No. | Sqn | Aircraft | Serial | Date | Camp | No. | Age | Notes |
|---|---|---|---|---|---|---|---|---|---|---|---|---|
| Valášek | K | P/O | CZ | 787485 | 310 | Spitfire | MJ663 | 21/05/1944 | L7 | 823 | 34 | Commissioned (176089) one month before shot down. Born 21 March 1917. |
| Vale | N | SGT | | 1457575 | 77 | Halifax | NA524 | 16/06/1944 | L7 | 197 | 7 | |
| Van Beers | RL | F/S | HOL | 1814965 | 322 | Spitfire | MJ232 | 26/08/1944 | L7 | 738 | 33 | POW no. 373 in AIR 20/2336. From Batavia. |
| Van der Heyden | JAMA | SGT | HOL | 12623 | 320 | Mitchell | FR149 | 12/06/1944 | 12A/L7 | 84057 | 33 | Shot down by flak over Grimbecq forest. |
| Van der Velde | C | SGT | | 1583073 | 576 | Lancaster | ME586 | 03/05/1944 | L7 | 373 | 14 | With French partisans. Captured 19 June 1944. |
| Van Rooyen | DJ | CPL | SA | 41880 | n/a | n/a | n/a | | L7/7B | 31397 | 47 | South African Army. Evacuated Luft 7, left at Stalag VIIB. |
| Vause | CW | SGT | | 1473602 | 44 | Lancaster | PB235 | 04/10/1944 | L7 | 1049 | 40 | |
| Vautard | JA | SGT | FRA | 549 | 346 | Halifax | NA121 | 04/11/1944 | L7 | 1265 | 55* | From Neuilly, Seine-et-Marne, France. |
| Veitch | TE | SGT | | 1897547 | 640 | Halifax | MZ406 | 12/09/1944 | L7 | 824 | 34 | |
| Venus | LJ | F/S | | 1430699 | 514 | Lancaster | LL695 | 21/05/1944 | L7 | 417 | 15 | Captured 13 July 1944. |
| Vermeulen | PJ | SGT | | 1322766 | n/k | n/k | n/k | n/k | L7 | 872 | 37 | No trace in RAF records. |
| Vero | EW | SGT | | 1811230 | 75 | Lancaster | LM104 | 06/10/1944 | L7 | 1086 | 45* | |
| Vickery | NF | LAC | | 1155793 | 235AMES | n/a | n/a | 21/06/1942 | 11A/L7 | 140844 | 18 | DMT. Captured at Tobruk. |
| Vidler | JE | SGT | | 1698472 | 405 | Halifax | HR810 | 05/09/1943 | 9C/L7 | 43124 | 4 | Evacuated on 6 January 1945 for repatriation on the *Letitia* on 2/2/45. |
| Vigars | RE | SGT | | 1852652 | 419 | Lancaster | KB726 | 12/06/1944 | L7 | 244 | 8 | |
| Vivash | JM | F/S | AUS | A.432023 | 466 | Halifax | LV936 | 04/11/1944 | L7 | 1266 | 55* | Fractured right leg. See *Escape to Danger*, pp.211-18. Killed in motor-cycle accident 1949. |
| Vlaminck | RH | S/C | FRA | 412 | 346 | Halifax | NA558 | 04/11/1944 | L7 | 1169 | 48 | From Calais, France. |
| Vogel | HB | WO1 | SA | 577528V | 21SAAF | Baltimore | FA461 | 21/05/1944 | L7 | 133 | 4 | A/G. Captured in Italy. From Orange Free State, S. Africa. |
| Wade | TM | SGT | AUS | A.402293 | 97 | Manchester | R5795 | 18/12/1941 | 7A/383/L7 | 90153 | 16 | Also POW no. 152 (Stalag 383). |
| Wadsworth | PO | SGT | | 1891750 | 463 | Lancaster | LM589 | 24/07/1944 | L7 | 636 | 27 | Captured in Paris on 25 July 1944. |
| Wagner | HW | SGT | EIR | 1604744 | 51 | Halifax | NR248 | 17/12/1944 | L7 | 1352 | 57* | Nav ss7. |
| Wainwright | EW | SGT | | 903679 | 40 | Wellington | X9824 | 10/01/1942 | 7A/383/L7 | 90140 | 16 | Also POW no. 139 (Stalag 383). |
| Wainwright | WI | SGT | | 1540707 | 44 | Lancaster | LM434 | 21/06/1944 | 9C/L7 | 53363 | 42/45* | Captured 21 July 1944. |
| Walker | B | AC2 | | 1238311 | 235AMES | n/a | n/a | 21/06/1942 | 11A/7A/L7 | 140152 | 18 | ACH. Captured at Tobruk. |
| Walker | FW | F/S | CAN | R.214688 | 166 | Lancaster | NF974 | 12/09/1944 | L7 | 1009 | 39 | Captured after a month on the run. |
| Walker | RG | W/O | CAN | R.77823 | 180 | Mitchell | FW113 | 09/08/1944 | L7 | 637 | 27 | W/AG. Commissioned (J.88494). |

| Surname | Initials | Rank | Nat. | Service No. | Sqn | Aircraft | Serial | Date | Camp | No. | No. | Notes |
|---|---|---|---|---|---|---|---|---|---|---|---|---|
| Walkty | JJ | F/S | CAN | R.166166 | 576 | Lancaster | ME811 | 06/06/1944 | L7 | 198 | 7 | |
| Wall | II | SGT | CAN | R.213532 | 434 | Halifax | LW175 | 12/08/1944 | L7 | 638 | 27 | Commissioned (J.87808). |
| Wallace | KES | F/S | AUS | A.424073 | 467 | Lancaster | LM205 | 29/06/1944 | L7 | 419 | 15 | |
| Waller | GN | SGT | | 1399595 | 252 | Beaufighter | NE636 | 01/08/1944 | L7 | 724 | 30 | N/WOP. Ditched after flak damage from ship. ss5. Two days in dinghy. Also POW no. 80 (Stalag 383). See *Silk and Barbed Wire*, pp.80-106. |
| Walley | BS | SGT | | 1062112 | 51 | Whitley | Z9130 | 07/11/1941 | 7A/383/L7 | 90067 | 16 | |
| Wallis | GL | WO2 | CAN | R.155734 | 432 | Halifax | LW616 | 12/06/1944 | L7 | 374 | 14 | Commissioned (J.87360). |
| Walsh | GD | SGT | | 1417720 | 460 | Lancaster | NE144 | 29/08/1944 | L7 | 760 | 33 | |
| Walsh | HJ | SGT | | 14421175 | GPR | Horsa | n/k | 20/09/1944 | L7 | 963 | 38 | F/16. He possibly escaped during the evacuation in January 1945. |
| Walters | RG | SGT | | 1577984 | 619 | Lancaster | LM742 | 06/11/1944 | L7 | 1215 | 50 | Escaped from forced march 20 January 1945. To UK via Odessa. |
| Walton | CJ | SGT | | 1264944 | 106 | Hampden | P1290 | 07/11/1941 | 7A/383/L7 | 90060 | 16 | Also POW no. 75 (Stalag 7A). |
| Wand | NCT | F/S | | 1603399 | 106 | Lancaster | ME831 | 07/07/1944 | L7 | 420 | 15 | |
| Warburton | KC | SGT | | 1435351 | 112 | Kittyhawk | FR857 | 08/04/1944 | L7 | 639 | 27 | Shot down attacking Rieti airfield. |
| Ward | KA | SGT | | 904302 | 207 | Lancaster | LM129 | 07/07/1944 | L7 | 421 | 15 | |
| Ward | WJ | F/S | | 1576902 | 156 | Lancaster | ND559 | 21/05/1944 | L7 | 134 | 4 | ss7. Badly wounded? Handed over by Dutch to Germans. |
| Wareham | RGW | SGT | | 1650652 | 12 | Lancaster | PB247 | 12/08/1944 | L7 | 640 | 27 | |
| Warr | DWG | F/S | | 1314358 | 576 | Lancaster | PA997 | 16/06/1944 | L7 | 199 | 7 | |
| Warren | B | SGT | | 1200072 | 576 | Lancaster | LM471 | 24/03/1944 | 9C/L7 | 43396 | 3 | A/G. |
| Warren | JF | F/S | | 1222140 | 226 | Mitchell | FW106 | 15/10/1944 | L7 | 1125 | 47 | W/AG. All four crew POW. |
| Warrington | J | SGT | | 636911 | 429 | Halifax | MZ302 | 28/06/1944 | L7 | 331 | 12 | |
| Waterman | CE | SGT | | 1895269 | 102 | Halifax | MZ699 | 12/09/1944 | L7 | 825 | 34 | |
| Waters | FRW | F/S | | 1876128 | 44 | Lancaster | PB266 | 28/07/1944 | L7 | 534 | 23 | Escaped on march. Repatriated to UK via Odessa and Middle East. |
| Watkins | H | S/SGT | | 3660659 | GPR | Horsa | n/k | 20/09/1944 | L7 | 873 | 37 | E/11. |
| Watkins | JC | SGT | | 1320857 | 102 | Halifax | MZ646 | 28/06/1944 | L7 | 641 | 27 | Captured 10 August 1944 – see *It's Suicide but it's Fun*, pp.123-4. |
| Watkinson | CR | S/SGT | | 809931 | GPR | Horsa | RJ221 | 18/09/1944 | L7 | 962 | 38 | B/3. DFM (11/4/46). Born 3 April 1913 in Adelaide; died 24 October 1994. |
| Watolski | EG | F/S | POL | 783288 | 308 | Spitfire | W3940 | 27/09/1941 | 8B/L3/L7/L6 | 9680 | 20 | Moved to Luft 6 on 18 August 1944. |
| Watson | CG | SGT | | 1591231 | GPR | Horsa | n/k | 22/09/1944 | L7 | 1010 | 39 | A/2. |

| Surname | Initials | Rank | Nat. | Service No. | Sqn/GPR | Aircraft | Serial | Date | Camp | No. 1 | No. 2 | Notes |
|---|---|---|---|---|---|---|---|---|---|---|---|---|
| Watson | FC | SGT | | 2082989 | GPR | Horsa | n/k | 25/09/1944 | 13C/L7 | 15356 | 55* | A/*. Blinded in one eye, jaw broken, teeth missing, most of nose missing. |
| Watson | RW | W/O | AUS | A.418600 | 166 | Lancaster | ME749 | 23/09/1944 | L7 | 964 | 38 | Evaded capture after lost 3/4 May 1944 (Mailly-le-Camp). |
| Webb | JC | SGT | | 530869 | 7 | Stirling | W7436 | 18/12/1941 | 7A/383/L7 | 90123 | 16 | Also POW no. 126 (Stalag 383). |
| Webb | RH | SGT | | 915486 | 207 | Lancaster | LM671 | 18/12/1944 | L7 | 1353 | 57* | |
| Webster | F | SGT | | 997227 | 49 | Hampden | AT190 | 10/04/1942 | L3/L6/17B/L7 | 187 | 7 | MID (13/6/46) for his escape activities. |
| Webster | G | SGT | | 1320114 | 576 | Lancaster | DV365 | 21/05/1944 | L7 | 422 | 15 | Captured Antwerp 10 July 1944. |
| Weedon | JG | SGT | | 1806562 | 37 | Wellington | LP259 | 21/10/1944 | L7 | 1170 | 48 | Nav on raid to Maribor. Same crew as English, Haddon & James. |
| Weeks | C | F/S | | 1319454 | 158 | Halifax | LW720 | 24/05/1944 | L7 | 66 | 1 | |
| Wegrzynski | M | SGT | POL | 703812 | 300 | Lancaster | LM141 | 06/11/1944 | L7 | 1267 | 55* | |
| Weir | J | SGT | | 545829 | 433 | Halifax | MZ284 | 21/11/1944 | L7 | 1305 | 56 | |
| Wellein | JC | F/S | CAN | R.195385 | 49 | Lancaster | PB231 | 18/07/1944 | L7 | 642 | 27 | Captured 10 August 1944. Commissioned (J.98060). |
| Wells | EH | F/S | | 1216905 | 630 | Lancaster | LM117 | 18/07/1944 | L7 | 643 | 27 | Changed surname from Swinfield-Wells to join RAF despite his father. |
| Wells | F | F/S | | 1582186 | 106 | Lancaster | ME668 | 07/07/1944 | L7 | 375 | 14 | |
| Welsh | J | SGT | | 1591578 | 102 | Halifax | MZ649 | 27/05/1944 | L7 | 245 | 8 | Captured Antwerp 13 June 1944. |
| West | AG | F/S | | 1626719 | 190 | Stirling | LJ916 | 21/09/1944 | L7 | 1050 | 40 | A/G shot down on Arnhem supply drop. |
| West | P | SGT | | 957498 | 101 | Lancaster | LM474 | 16/06/1944 | L7 | 285 | 11 | |
| Westbrook | LE | F/S | | 1544372 | 218 | Lancaster | PD252 | 12/08/1944 | L7 | 685 | 28 | DFM (13/6/44). |
| Weston | EW | SGT | | 927326 | 51 | Halifax | MZ916 | 11/09/1944 | L7 | 826 | 34 | |
| Westwood | J | SGT | | 1568565 | 90 | Stirling | EF294 | 02/06/1944 | L7 | 135 | 4 | |
| Wetherall | FG | W/O | CAN | R.160570 | 253 | Spitfire | MJ248 | 11/12/1944 | L7 | 1354 | 57* | Shot down attacking MT north of Sarajevo. |
| Wetherall | JAB | SGT | | 1414511 | GPR | Horsa | n/k | 20/09/1944 | L7 | 1087 | 45* | F/16. To Stalag 383. |
| Wharton | S | SGT | | 1622354 | 192 | Halifax | MZ806 | 21/11/1944 | L7 | 1268 | 55* | Nav. |
| Whatton | JH | F/S | | 1384559 | 214 | Fortress | SR382 | 21/06/1944 | L7 | 423 | 15 | Captured Antwerp 8 July 1944. |
| Wheldon | AE | SGT | | 1521246 | 77 | Halifax | NA524 | 16/06/1944 | L7 | 200 | 7 | |
| Wheldon | RA | S/SGT | | 3715219 | GPR | Horsa | n/k | 20/09/1944 | L7 | 965 | 38 | D/22. |
| Whiddon | RH | W/O | AUS | A.410929 | 51 | Halifax | NP962 | 07/12/1944 | L7 | 1306 | 56 | W/AG. Baled out over target (Osnabrück). Aircraft returned to England. |
| Whippy | JW | SGT | | 2044661 | GPR | Horsa | n/k | 20/09/1944 | L7 | 1011 | 39 | D/8. |

| Surname | Initials | Rank | Nat | Service No. | Sqn | Aircraft | Serial | Date | Stalag | POW No. | | Notes |
|---|---|---|---|---|---|---|---|---|---|---|---|---|
| Whitbread | WR | SGT | | 1187771 | 227 | Lancaster | LM259 | 04/12/1944 | L7 | 1307 | 56 | |
| White | JD | SGT | | 576906 | 619 | Lancaster | ND935 | 25/07/1944 | L7 | 644 | 27 | |
| White | MHJ | SGT | | 1323675 | 44 | Lancaster | ND517 | 18/07/1944 | L7 | 535 | 23 | |
| White | RA | SGT | | 1626053 | 630 | Lancaster | LM262 | 07/08/1944 | L7 | 645 | 27 | |
| White | TS | SGT | CAN | R.190509 | 640 | Halifax | LK865 | 27/05/1944 | L7 | 102 | 2 | |
| Whiteley | TP | F/S | AUS | A.437918 | 463 | Lancaster | LM375 | 06/10/1944 | L7 | 1051 | 40 | |
| Whiting | HD | SGT | AUS | A.404422 | 103 | Wellington | Z1142 | 10/01/1942 | 7A/383/L7 | 90147 | 16 | W/OP. Baled out, aircraft returned to UK. Also POW no. 146 (Stalag 383). |
| Wicks | WF | F/S | | 1432836 | 148 | Halifax | JP179 | 04/07/1944 | L7 | 536 | 23 | N/B. See Blattman and Davey – same crew. Also POW no. 132 (Stalag 383). |
| Wiggins | AB | SGT | | 1201732 | 77 | Whitley | Z6956 | 27/12/1941 | 7A/383/L7 | 90131 | 16 | |
| Wilcox | DJR | F/S | NZ | NZ.421244 | 75 | Lancaster | LM268 | 11/09/1944 | L7 | 966 | 38 | |
| Wild | SR | SGT | | 2203758 | 460 | Lancaster | NE144 | 29/08/1944 | L7 | 761 | 33 | |
| Wiles | J | F/S | | 991732 | 614 | Halifax | JP323 | 23/11/1944 | L7 | 1269 | 55* | F/E based at Amendola, Italy, lost on Szombathely, Hungary. Captured 19 April 1944. |
| Wilkinson | E | SGT | | 2211329 | 138 | Halifax | LL252 | 31/03/1944 | L7 | 136 | 4 | |
| Wilks | BCH | F/S | | 1578690 | 578 | Halifax | MZ556 | 20/07/1944 | L7 | 499 | 21 | |
| Williams | E | F/S | | 1480802 | 640 | Halifax | MZ345 | 12/08/1944 | L7 | 646 | 27 | |
| Williams | E | SGT | | 1836732 | 103 | Lancaster | ME649 | 12/12/1944 | L7 | 1355 | 57* | |
| Williams | ET | F/S | | 1097712 | 65 | Mustang | FX988 | 24/06/1944 | L7 | 376 | 14 | |
| Williams | H | SGT | | 1503581 | 405 | Lancaster | JA924 | 30/01/1944 | L7 | 874 | 37 | |
| Williams | I | F/S | | 1418060 | 254 | Beaufighter | LZ318 | 15/10/1944 | L7 | 1126 | 47 | Pilot. Lost on ship attack off Wangerooge. Also POW no. 8124? |
| Williams | JF | SGT | | 3858326 | GPR | Horsa | n/k | 22/09/1944 | L7 | 875 | 37 | E/* |
| Williams | MA | F/S | CAN | R.113236 | 103 | Lancaster | ME649 | 12/12/1944 | L7 | 1356 | 57* | Savagely treated by interrogators. See We Flew, We Fell, We Lived. |
| Williams | W | F/S | | 994884 | 97 | Lancaster | NE124 | 24/06/1944 | L7 | 332 | 12 | |
| Williams | WT | SGT | | 2225296 | 158 | Halifax | MZ734 | 25/10/1944 | L7 | 1127 | 47 | |
| Williamson | CF | F/S | CAN | R.94468 | 425 | Halifax | MZ674 | 14/10/1944 | L7 | 1088 | 45* | Commissioned (J.92205). |
| Williamson | J | SGT | | 1378999 | 102 | Whitley | Z6800 | 30/11/1941 | 7A/383/ 8B/L3/L7 | 90069 | 16 | ss5. Escaped four times, three times in 1942. Also POW no. 82 (Stalag 383). |
| Willington | N | F/S | AUS | A.436767 | 467 | Lancaster | PB299 | 19/09/1944 | L7 | 1012 | 39 | |
| Willis | JJ | SGT | | 1852373 | 44 | Lancaster | PB751 | 04/12/1944 | L7 | 1308 | 56 | |
| Willis | RO | SGT | | 1629806 | 61 | Lancaster | LM454 | 11/05/1944 | L7 | 67 | 1 | ss7 |

| Surname | Initials | Rank | Nat. | Service No. | Sqn | Aircraft | Serial | Date | Camp | No. | No. | Notes |
|---|---|---|---|---|---|---|---|---|---|---|---|---|
| Willson | FA | SGT | | 1612607 | 550 | Lancaster | LL747 | 16/06/1944 | L7 | 201 | 7 | Broke right leg landing. In hospital at Wissen for over four months. |
| Wilmshurst | PGG | SGT | | 1337270 | 76 | Halifax | LK795 | 30/03/1944 | L7 | 537 | 23 | |
| Wilmot | N | F/S | | 1473354 | 10 | Halifax | LV881 | 30/03/1944 | 9C/L7 | 43397 | 3 | Head injuries. Unconscious/semi-conscious for ten days. |
| Wilson | GW | F/S | CAN | R.143388 | 51 | Halifax | LW498 | 24/05/1944 | L7 | 286 | 11 | |
| Wilson | JH | SGT | | 1567315 | 158 | Halifax | LW720 | 24/05/1944 | L7 | 103 | 2 | |
| Wilson | JL | SGT | | 1675969 | GPR | Horsa | n/k | 17/09/1944 | L7 | 967 | 38 | E/*. |
| Wilson | RJ | SGT | | 7368948 | GPR | Horsa | n/k | 19/09/1944 | L7 | 968 | 38 | D/*. |
| Wilson | S | W/O | | 1381243 | 76 | Halifax | MZ736 | 28/06/1944 | L7 | 647 | 27 | |
| Wilson | S | SGT | | 1594900 | 76 | Halifax | LW648 | 04/11/1944 | L7 | 1213 | 50 | |
| Wilson | TAF | F/S | | 1431649 | 49 | Lancaster | NE128 | 21/06/1944 | L7 | 246 | 8 | |
| Wilson | W | SGT | | 533348 | 9 | Lancaster | LL853 | 24/06/1944 | L7 | 377 | 14 | |
| Winchester | LED | WO1 | SA | 187540V | 31SAAF | Liberator | EW105 | 14/08/1944 | L7 | 725 | 30 | A/G (waist). From Brighton Beach, Durban, S. Africa. ss7. |
| Winchester | RG | F/S | CAN | R.217851 | 101 | Lancaster | LM755 | 29/11/1944 | L7 | 1270 | 55* | |
| Winkley | WG | SGT | | 1836247 | 61 | Lancaster | PB436 | 29/08/1944 | L7 | 762 | 33 | |
| Winskill | WW | F/S | CAN | R.119411 | 97 | Lancaster | PB510 | 11/09/1944 | L7 | 827 | 34 | |
| Wintemute | JD | F/S | CAN | R.210669 | 420 | Halifax | MZ645 | 28/07/1944 | L7 | 538 | 23 | Commissioned (J.90309). |
| Winter | HT | SGT | | 1337706 | 427 | Halifax | LK633 | 22/10/1943 | 9C/L7 | 53202 | 17 | Broke femur landing. At Hohe Mark 28 October 1943-9 June 1944. |
| Winton | AS | SGT | | 995694 | 49 | Hampden | AD733 | 28/09/1941 | 8B/383/L7 | 9673 | 16 | MID (13/6/46). Author of Open Road to Faraway. |
| Withnall | PB | S/SGT | | 2332442 | GPR | Horsa | n/k | 21/09/1944 | 12A/L7 | 075480 | 47 | G/10. |
| Wolff | EL | F/S | | 1611111 | 180 | Mitchell | FW209 | 03/12/1944 | L7 | 1309 | 56 | W/AG. |
| Wood | RC | SGT | | 1812663 | 158 | Halifax | LV771 | 04/11/1944 | L7 | 1310 | 56 | |
| Wood | W | F/S | | 749510 | 97 | Manchester | L7384 | 16/08/1941 | 8B/L7 | 23625 | 34 | Date of arrival uncertain, but probably with Trupp 34. |
| Woods | WA | SGT | CAN | R.97182 | 408 | Halifax | NP761 | 06/11/1944 | L7 | 1214 | 50 | |
| Woodward | J | F/S | | 520106 | 103 | Lancaster | ND417 | 25/02/1944 | L7 | 68 | 1 | F/E. |
| Woodward | JS | F/S | | 1338115 | 78 | Halifax | LV939 | 27/04/1944 | L7 | 137 | 4 | Baled out, aircraft returned to base. Captured 19 May 1944. Commissioned (175839). |
| Woodward | LA | W/O | AUS | A.417257 | 75 | Lancaster | ND915 | 20/07/1944 | L7 | 726 | 30 | Betrayed and captured 11 August 1944, Antwerp. Required hospital treatment at Luft 7. |

| Surname | Initials | Rank | Nat. | Service No. | Sqn | Aircraft | Serial | Date | Camp | No. | No. | Notes |
|---|---|---|---|---|---|---|---|---|---|---|---|---|
| Wooldridge | DA | WO | SA | 328413V | 12SAAF | Marauder | FB471 | 18/08/1944 | L7 | 686 | 28 | A/G. Shot down by flak. |
| Woolmer | EA | F/S | AUS | A.432327 | 463 | Lancaster | NF990 | 06/11/1944 | L7 | 1171 | 48 | Captured 3 July 1944. |
| Woosnam | RJ | F/S | | 1804303 | 514 | Lancaster | LL727 | 07/06/1944 | L7 | 424 | 15 | |
| Worthing | D | SGT | | 1834665 | 102 | Halifax | LW168 | 24/12/1944 | L7 | 1357 | 57* | |
| Wray | NW | SGT | | 964639 | 625 | Lancaster | LM427 | 31/05/1944 | L7 | 138 | 4 | |
| Wright | BH | SGT | | 1339374 | 640 | Halifax | MZ677 | 02/06/1944 | L7 | 202 | 7 | |
| Wright | CH | SGT | | 1608844 | 78 | Halifax | MZ692 | 22/06/1944 | L7 | 287 | 11 | |
| Wright | JA | SGT | CAN | R.87125 | 166 | Wellington | HZ280 | 13/05/1943 | 9C/L7 | 42786 | 3 | Wounded. Repatriated. |
| Wright | JF | SGT | | 1673145 | 103 | Lancaster | PB303 | 18/08/1944 | L7 | 687 | 28 | |
| Wright | SD | SGT | CAN | R.164205 | 432 | Halifax | NP706 | 18/07/1944 | L7 | 500 | 21 | Commissioned (J.88504). |
| Wright | SW | SGT | | 1894352 | 428 | Lancaster | KB749 | 15/08/1944 | L7 | 688 | 28 | |
| Wright | WD | PTE | | 4914625 | n/a | n/a | n/a | n/k | #/L7 | 16631 | 47 | British Army (RAMC). Evacuated to Stalag 383. |
| Wulff | ER | F/S | CAN | R.198758 | 408 | Lancaster | DS634 | 28/07/1944 | L7 | 539 | 23 | Commissioned (J.90074). |
| Wyatt | ATJ | SGT | | 547863 | 570 | Stirling | EH897 | 19/09/1944 | 11B/L7 | 117303 | 50 | F/E lost over Arnhem. |
| Wykes | AE | F/S | | 1579856 | 207 | Lancaster | LM671 | 18/12/1944 | L7 | 1358 | 57* | |
| Wynn | KC | SGT | CAN | R.190166 | 166 | Lancaster | NE114 | 22/05/1944 | L7 | 69 | 1 | |
| Wynne-Cole | B | SGT | | 1608600 | 149 | Stirling | LJ621 | 05/06/1944 | 12A/L7 | 70217 | 29 | 12A? |
| Yardley | D | SGT | | 1583633 | 550 | Lancaster | JA712 | 27/05/1944 | L7 | 247 | 8 | Survived his aircraft's crash. Escaped on march. UK via Odessa and Middle East. |
| Yearsley | K | SGT | | 1485103 | 38 | Wellington | MF153 | 04/08/1944 | L7 | 727 | 30 | W/AG ss6 shot down on Keos Island. |
| Yearsley | R | SGT | | 999352 | 106 | Hampden | AE151 | 21/12/1941 | 7A/383/L7 | 90135 | 16 | Also POW no. 136 (Stalag 383). |
| Yeo | ER | SGT | | 1399011 | 142 | Wellington | LN318 | 29/05/1944 | L7 | 104 | 2 | W/AG. |
| Yorke | HE | F/S | | 1615279 | 603 | Beaufighter | NE595 | 19/07/1944 | L7 | 648 | 27 | Pilot. Damaged by flak and ditched. |
| Youle | DR | CPL | | 644871 | 235AMES | n/a | n/a | 21/06/1942 | 11A/L7 | 138584 | 18 | Ground radar operator. Captured at Tobruk. |
| Young | A | W/O | | 563811 | 207 | Lancaster | ME827 | 21/06/1944 | L7 | 378 | 14 | ss7. |
| Young | GJH | SGT | | 1801860 | 44 | Lancaster | ND976 | 21/05/1944 | L7 | 70 | 1 | |
| Yvars | RF | SGT | FRA | 114 | 346 | Halifax | NA555 | 06/10/1944 | L7 | 1052 | 40 | From Rabat, French Morocco. |
| Zado | AF | F/S | CAN | R.79971 | 98 | Mitchell | FW184 | 11/06/1944 | L7 | 425 | 15 | Lost on night intruder mission. |
| Zeff | M | W/O | SA | 135082V | 12SAAF | Marauder | FB425 | 14/07/1944 | 11A/L7 | 138899 | 18 | W/OP. From Johannesburg, S. Africa. |
| Zucker | VSJ | F/S | AUS | A.420792 | 630 | Lancaster | JB546 | 22/05/1944 | L7 | 105 | 2 | Captured 28 May 1944. |

# ENDNOTES

## INTRODUCTION

1 Later promoted *General-Feldmarschall*, Keitel, also Hitler's deputy, was found guilty of war crimes at the Nuremberg Trials, and was hanged on 16 October 1946.

2 So appointed with effect from 19 July 1940.

3 Stalag Luft VI would briefly re-appear in August 1944 in a large, former garage at St Wendel, Germany for a few USAAF POWs.

4 It has been calculated that, from August 1943 to May 1945, of the 350,000 aircrew who flew with the Eighth Air Force, approximately 26,000 were killed and 23,000 became POWs.

## CHAPTER 1

5 From a declaration that he made on 27 October 1944 at Stalag 383. TNA file WO 344/144/2.

6 Roy Goldenberg was the navigator of B-24 bomber *The Comanche*, 42-64447, 448th BG/712th BS. Shot down by flak twenty-three kilometres south east of Dieppe on 20 March 1944, one of the ten-man crew evaded capture, the rest were POWs.

## CHAPTER 2

7 Fred Singh went to Stalag 6J (Dorsten). He was repatriated with a serious leg injury, and was hospitalised for three years in England and Australia. Later changing his surname to Stuart, he retired from the RAAF with the rank of squadron leader in 1973.

8 This may have been Leutnant Karl-Heinz Grunert, 6./NJG6, who claimed a victory, his second of the war, south west of Aachen at approximately 0130 hours. See also endnote 12.

9 For further details of Dulag Luft and its transit camps see *Footprints on the Sands of Time*, Chapter 2.

10 Their attacker was Major Walter Borchers, Stab/NJG5, who claimed his twenty-first victory.

11 Cyril Weeks stayed in the RAF until 1949, as a wireless operator instructor at No. 2 Air Navigation School, Middleton St George. He returned to Puffendorf with Bill Graham and Arthur Brice in 1991.

12 The pilot of the Bf110 who attacked them may have Leutnant Karl-Heinz Grunert, 6./NJG6, who claimed a 'Lancaster' over Aachen at a height of 4,800 metres at 0132 hours. See endnote 8.

13 In early 1944, 83 Squadron had decreed that all its pilots should wear the seat-type parachute. This order undoubtedly saved Ken Lane's life, as there would not have been time for another crew member to have handed him an observer-type parachute.

14 Don Cope died in the mid-1970s after falling 16 feet from a ladder.

15 In east Holland, close to the German border.

16 425 (Alouette) Squadron was the only French-Canadian squadron in the RCAF. Ninety-one of its aircrew were to become POWs (one escaped), while a further fifty-three evaded capture.

17 The USAAF grade of flight officer was established on 8 July 1942. On graduation, aviation (flying training) cadets who had not qualified for a commission as 2nd lieutenant could be appointed flight officer with a status equivalent to that of warrant officer, junior grade. Promotion from flight officer to 2nd lieutenant was permitted.

18 Their assailant was Leutnant Friedrich Potthast, 11./NJG1. LK798 was his tenth victory.

19 For his adventures see *RAF Evaders*, pages 315-6.

20 According to *2nd TAF*, Volume 1, p.104, 'Mac' was flying Typhoon MN483.

21 ND450 survived the war before being scrapped in May 1946.

22 Oberleutnant Wilhelm Henseler, 1./NJG1, was their probable attacker, claiming his seventh victory.

23 Mid-upper gunner Leslie Jones said they were attacked by a FW190, but who the pilot was is unclear, as five claims were made by pilots of JG300, which was flying the FW190 at the time.

24 See *RAF Evaders*, p.154, for more on this episode.

25 Lambert's DFC was gazetted on 16 November 1943, when he was on 10 Squadron.

26 Osbourn's DFM was gazetted on 26 September 1941, when he was a flight sergeant (528527) on 47 Squadron.

27 The castle is known in Flemish as Kasteel van de Hertogen van Brabant.

28 A further two Fleet Air Arm personnel, and one Royal Marine, would later arrive at Luft 7 – A/Ldg.Air. Harold

C.G. Griffin, and LAF (A) Ronald F. Simpson (both transferred from Luft 3) and A/CSM (Ty.) Basil L. Baugh RM (from Stalag IXC Lazarett). Harry Griffin retired from the Royal Navy with the rank of lieutenant commander (O) in the 'early 1970s'.

29 It was one of its Halifaxes, L9613, NF-V, that on 28/29 December 1941 dropped the Czech agents who carried out the assassination of General Reinhard Heydrich in Prague on the mission codenamed 'Anthropoids'.

30 *Bombers Over Sand and Snow*, p. 121.

31 Most equipment was provided by the YMCA and International Red Cross.

## CHAPTER 3

32 Of the 795 participating aircraft (572 Lancasters, 214 Halifaxes, nine Mosquitos) sixty-four Lancasters and thirty-one Halifaxes were lost.

33 It had 502 flying hours and over forty ops under its belt.

34 W/O A.D. Hall RNZAF, sole survivor of Lancaster LL738, 514 Squadron, also lost on the Nuremberg raid, went to Stalag Luft 3 (Sagan) via Stalag Luft 6.

35 Norman Jackson was remembered by Private Bert Martin RAMC, one of the orderlies who selflessly tended to the sick and wounded in Germany for over five years: '"Jacko" Jackson… was one of a line of burn cases onto whom we poured gallons of home brewed saline week in and week out to cleanse the raw tissues in preparation for skin grafting which, even there, was often carried out successfully.' *Lasting Impressions*, p.63, H.L. Martin (privately, 1990).

36 In 1963, Norman Wilmot joined 201 (Macclesfield) Squadron, Air Training Corps, and eventually became its commanding officer, remaining in that post until he retired.

37 The 90 Squadron Operations Record Book shows that F/L H.C. Adams (136190), was a replacement bomb aimer with this crew on a mining sortie to Kiel on 18 April, which could be the operation in question.

38 This airstrip, in Suffolk, had been specially enlarged to take the lame ducks such as the 90 Squadron aircraft.

39 In fact they evaded capture, being liberated some two months later.

40 They were at the Luftwaffe's Rosières-en-Santerre airfield which, ironically, had been constructed for the RAF during the 1939-40 'Phoney War'. For over a year, up to summer 1944, the resident unit on the airfield was I.Gruppe/ Schlachtgeschwader 10 with FW190 aircraft.

41 Sergeant (later P/O) R.S. 'Bob' Hall, pilot, 432 (Leaside) Squadron, RCAF. Shot down 27 May 1944 (Bourg-Léopold).

42 John Edward Blair had won his DFM on 24 October 1941 on 103 Squadron, and his DFC as A/F/L on 12 November 1943 on 97 Squadron. He would have been on his third 'tour of operations' when killed aged thirty-two.

43 Medland, born in Exeter and brought up in Torquay, was a police constable before enlisting in 1941.

44 Drewes survived the war with a total of fifty-two victories.

45 F/O P.J.K. Hood 125519, 514 Squadron, Lancaster LL696, JI-A. Shot down 30/31 March 1944 (Nuremberg). POW Stalag Luft 1 (Barth). Five others of his crew survived to be POWs; only the mid-upper gunner was killed.

46 The two Americans were shot down in B-17 bomber 42-38029, 381BG/682BS on 8 March 1944 (Berlin/Erkner).

47 Weert, in The Netherlands, is south of Eindhoven and south west of Venlo.

48 See Andrew McMurdon's version of this incident on page 21.

49 *The Bomber Command War Diaries*, p. 500.

50 It was on this raid that flight engineer Sergeant Norman C. Jackson, 106 Squadron, was awarded the Victoria Cross. See page 48 & endnote 35.

51 Ogilvie and Cytulski were probably accompanied on the forced march by three other Poles from the same crew – Sergeants Stanislaw Czura, Jan Montwill, and Mieczyslaw Wegrzynski. Shot down in Lancaster LM141, 300 (Masovian) Squadron, on the Gelsenkirchen (daylight) raid of 6 November 1944, they arrived together at Luft 7 on 20 December 1944.

52 Aircrew received their Pathfinder Force badge after completing their tour.

53 S/L D.B. Everett DFC and 2 Bars (no DSO, though he had flown nearly ninety operations) was killed with all his crew in Lancaster ME361. His third DFC was gazetted on 27 March 1945, three weeks after his death.

54 Oberleutnant Hans-Heinz Augenstein, 12./NJG1, alone claimed ND762 for his thirty-first victory.

## CHAPTER 4

55 Jaggar was commissioned on 27 November 1942. (Information gratefully received from Errol Martyn).

56 For some unknown reason McGraw's POW record card shows him as 'Observer'.

57 By this time 'Spike' had been promoted to Warrant Officer II (2nd Class).

58 'Robbie' was Lieutenant Eugene Robarts SAAF (206857v). He was flying Spitfire MH538.

59 Corporal Robert H. Parry-Jones of Chester, Royal Armoured Corps, was attached to the Long Range Desert Group. His rank on the Stalag IIIA Nominal Roll was given as sergeant.

60 Peter Craig's account is reproduced with his kind permission.

61 LN318 was a veteran, having flown a number of operations on 40 Squadron in 1943.

62 *Out of the Italian Night*, p.99, Maurice Lihou (Airlife Publishing Ltd, Shrewsbury, 2003).

63 Australian Air Vice-Marshal D.C.T. Bennett RAF, became officer commanding 8 (PFF) Group.

64 The authors are most grateful to John Grogan, Ronald's son, for permission to quote from his father's diary.

## CHAPTER 5

65 From: http://www.550squadronassociation.org.uk/documents/public/Rebecq-Memorial-Project/TheRebecqStory.pdf

66 F/O Riding was flown back to Northolt on 27 August. F/O Prentice followed him back to England three days later.

67 This may well have been one of the Mosquito 'nuisance' raids, several of which took place at the end of June.

68 *Men of Air*, p.322.

69 Either destroyed or very seriously damaged, these houses were rebuilt after the war.

70 From Arthur Beresford's personal account, courtesy of the Beresford Society BFS030.

71 Modrow scored four victories on this night. He died in Kiel on 10 September 1990, aged eighty-two.

72 Five of *Karen B*'s crew, including Nelson, were to evade capture, with the other five becoming prisoners of war.

73 Much of the information courtesy of Jelle Reitsma.

74 Quotes from records held by the Australian National Archives.

75 Quotes from US Archives http://media.nara.gov/nw/305270/EE-714.pdf.

76 In fact the V1 site was at Moyenneville, half a dozen kilometres south west of Amiens.

77 *Nachtjagd War Diaries*, Volume Two, page 67.

78 Acting S/L Cedric Alexander Fraser-Petherbridge was awarded the DFC on 14 November 1944, and a Bar on 4 December 1945.

79 George Lambert had apparently joined the RAF as a clerk before the war, and was a sergeant when commissioned on 2 May 1941. Shot down over France on 10/11 April 1943, he evaded capture via neutral Switzerland, reaching England towards the end of February 1944.

80 The pilot was probably Unteroffizier Heinrich Schultz, 6./NJG2, scoring his first night victory. He was killed in action on 17 August 1944.

81 *'We Act With One Accord'*, p.187, Alan Cooper (J&KH Publishing [1998], Hailsham, 1998).

82 *Halifax for Liberté*, p. 182, Louis Bourgain (Compaid Graphics, Preston).

83 Gerrard's pilot, S/L G.F.H. Ingram DFC, was one of two to lose his life in Lancaster ND734 on 23/24 June.

84 Peter Reeve was Mentioned in Despatches on 1 January 1946. He died suddenly on 1 September 1951, aged twenty-nine.

85 *Fighters Over the Desert*, p.70.

86 *The Middle East Commandos*, p.105, Charles Messenger (William Kimber, Wellingborough, 1988).

87 The Bombay had a crew of six: two pilots; navigator; wireless operator; fitter/air gunner; and rigger/air gunner. Powered by two 1,010 hp Bristol Pegasus XXII radial engines it had a top speed of 192 mph (310 km/h), with a ceiling of 25,000 ft (7,620 m), and a range of 2,230 miles (3,590 kms). It was armed with four 0.303 machine guns – one each in the nose and tail turrets, and two that could be fired from hatches amidships. It could be fitted with up to twenty-four seats.

88 There was a joke amongst the SAS that the twin-engined Bombay was so slow that, whilst it was in flight, you could open the door, go outside and have a piss, run back after it and climb in again. *Stirling's Men* p.23 – Gavin Mortimer (Weidenfeld & Nicolson, London, 2004).

89 Martin's commission (111325) was gazetted on 19 December 1941, with seniority dated 12 August 1941.

90 The authors are most grateful for these figures to Alan Orton, whose father was in the David Stirling group.

91 Of German descent, Bonington had changed his name from Bonig. His son is the legendary climber Sir Chris, CBE.

92 Their attacker, in his Bf110, was pilot Oberleutnant Reinhold Knacke, II./NJG1. They were his twelfth victory. Knacke was killed by return fire from a Stirling bomber on the night of 3/4 February 1943 with forty-four victories

to his name.

93 Hall went to Stalag Luft III, where he became involved with the 'Great Escape' and was valued for his knowledge of meteorology. One of the escapers, he was recaptured near Sagan, and murdered on 30 March 1944.

94 *The Barbed-Wire University*, p.85.

95 Ibid., p.86.

96 Letter courtesy of Richard Collins.

97 The Hampden crashed at 9.50 pm at a place called Nørregård, owned by farmer Johannes Lauridsen, in Hostrup east of Nordenskov.

98 The authors are most grateful to Søren Flensted for permission to use information from his website www. flensted.eu.com/194201.shtml.

99 *Nachtjagd War Diaries Volume Two*, p.30 and p.379. The *Führer Kurier Staffel*, Hitler's personal flight based at Berlin-Tempelhof airfield, was commanded by Heinz Baur.

100 This bombing may well have occurred on or near 20 July 1944, the day on which 134 B-24 bombers of the US 8th Air Force attacked the airfields of Erfurt Nord (near the north of the town) and Erfurt/Bindersleben (a Luftwaffe base five kilometres east of Erfurt).

101 Bob Burns – letter of 30 December 1994 to Ray Crompton. Born in Spain, Xavier Cugat (1900-90) was a successful band leader in New York, and had a 'hit' in 1940 with his recording of *Perfidia*.

102 W/O T.C. Stanley, 61 Squadron, had been shot down on 25/26 March 1942 (Essen) in Manchester L7518, only he and the mid-upper gunner surviving. For his service to others he would be awarded the MBE (28 December 1945) and the Bronze Star Medal (USA) (19 November 1946).

## CHAPTER 6

103 The diesel-engined *Rangitata* was built in 1929. The *Elisabethville* was built in 1921 by John Cockerill Shipyards, Hoeboken, Belgium for the Compagnie Belge-Maritime Du Congo, Antwerp.

104 *Havock* ran aground in the Strait of Sicily on 6 April 1942 and was wrecked. *Decoy* was transferred to the RCN as HMCS *Kootenay* on 12 April 1943.

105 They were fortunate not to have been aboard the ship when, on 17 August, on her way from Italy loaded with urgent supplies for the Afrika Korps, she was torpedoed and damaged by two 39 Squadron Beauforts crewed by 86 Squadron personnel. That night she was finished off by torpedoes fired by HM Submarine *United*.

106 Information courtesy of Caroline Barnard – www.burningblue.co.za.

107 WO1 J.L.W. Rodgers is buried at Florence War Cemetery.

108 Before it was lost on 1 January 1943, N9029 evacuated King Peter of Yugoslavia from his country on 18 April 1941.

109 W/C Brown now lies in Catania War Cemetery, Sicily. His DFC was gazetted on 30 July 1940, and his Bar on 23 May 1941 whilst CO of 1(F) Squadron. Part of the citation for his Bar read: 'He has destroyed a further two enemy aircraft bringing his total victories to at least 18.'

110 Jopling was to escape from his Italian POW camp on 9 September 1943, the day after the Italian armistice, and successfully reached Allied lines. Manning ended up at the camp for naval officers near Westertimke, north Germany.

111 *Bombers Over Sand and Snow*, p.278.

112 Dawson Wright – letter to Raymond Crompton, 8 November 1988.

113 Leo Joseph Butkewitz, aged seventy-eight, tragically died of smoke inhalation in a fire at his home on 16 November 2000.

114 As neither the RAF nor USAAF had deliberately attacked Wilhelmshaven it is possible that any damage to the port had been caused by aircraft from the previous night's raid to Hamburg.

115 The *London Gazette* No. 36745, 13 October 1944. F/S Clay was presented by King George VI with his medal on 13 July 1947.

116 Fred Heathfield, letter of 23 January 1984 to Allan Poulton's widow.

117 Née Bagshaw, she was born in Birmingham on 31 May 1899.

118 Said to have been Leutnant Heinz Bock, 6./NJG101.

119 They all successfully evaded, Agur and Schwilk at the camp in Fréteval forest.

120 Perhaps the surgeon was the Australian Sir Hugh Cairns, professor at Oxford, who in 1948 visited Adelaide whilst on a travelling professorship to Australia and New Zealand? Sir Hugh died in Oxford on 18 July 1952, aged fifty-six.

121 Rossel's report in TNA file WO 224/66.

122 Ken Lane quoted in Bob Burns's letter to Ray Crompton, 18 September 1996.

123 *Poland, SOE and the Allies*, Josef Garlinski (George Allen and Unwin Ltd, London, 1969), p.187.

124 'RAF' in this instance includes SAAF and PAF crews.

125 *Bombers Over Sand and Snow*, p.283. All six of the Halifaxes on this raid returned.

126 Twenty-year-old P/O Good is buried in Sage War Cemetery.

## CHAPTER 7

127 Twenty-four of 109 Lancasters were lost. For the full story of the three Revigny raids see *Massacre over the Marne*.

128 *To Hell and Back*, p.69.

129 The German pilot, Unteroffizier Egon Engling, 8./NJG2, claimed his seventh victory, and his second that night.

130 *Poland, SOE and the Allies*, op. cit, pp.208-9.

131 Sadly, in the mid 1950s Henry Upton, his mind apparently unbalanced by his POW experiences, took his own life.

132 S/L Blackburn, also a POW, went to Stalag Luft I (Barth). He retired from the RAF as a wing commander with effect from 26 December 1962.

133 From his postwar interrogation report in TNA file WO 208/3337.

134 Information courtesy of Søren Flensted and his website http://www.flensted.eu.com/1944127.shtml

135 *Nuits de Feu Sur l'Allemagne*, p.178 – Louis Bourgain (PANDA, Noisy-le-Sec, 1991).

136 http://fcafa.wordpress.com/2011/06/19/karel-valasek-evasion-and-pow/.

137 This was probably S/L František Fajtl, shot down over Belgium on 5 May 1942.

138 Brannagan, CO of 441 (RCAF) Squadron, was shot down south west of Vimoutiers on 15 August in Spitfire NH233.

139 MacAleavey was awarded the DFC on 15 September 1944.

140 They were Bomber Command's last fatalities on the V1 sites campaign (*The Bomber Command War Diaries* p.574).

## CHAPTER 8

141 *The Brereton Diaries*, p.343, Lewis H. Brereton (William Morrow & Co, New York, 1946). See also, for example, *Glider Pilots at Arnhem and Arnhem 1944*.

142 *The History of the Glider Pilot Regiment*, p.107, Claude Smith (Leo Cooper, London, 1992).

143 In the *London Gazette* of 6 June 1947 it was announced that Robert Henson Killoran of 2 Dashwood Road, Gravesend, Kent, a lieutenant in the Glider Pilot Regiment and a natural-born British subject, had renounced and abandoned the surname of Conchie. With effect from 15 November 1948 R.H. Killoran was transferred to the RAF as a flying officer (500293) on short service (seven years on the active list), seniority back-dated to 15 January 1946.

144 The American Waco CG-4A glider of 7,500 lbs gross weight was used by the RAF as the 'Hadrian'. CG stood for 'cargo glider'.

145 7 KOSB went in 765 men strong. 112 were killed, seventy-six were evacuated, and the rest, 577, were missing (POWs etc).

146 *Eagles Victorious. A History of the S.A.A.F.*, page 283, Lt. Gen. H.J. Martin and Col. N. Orpen (Purnell, Cape Town, 1977).

147 *The Royal Air Force at Arnhem*, p. 149. Much of the information on Arnhem air losses comes from this superb reference book.

148 'Trader' after the 1931 film *Trader Horn*. Horn had been commissioned (110872) in December 1941.

149 TNA file AIR 27/1647.

150 See the GPR Association's magazine *The Eagle*, December 1989.

151 Ocelka was born on 27 May 1913 at Lipník nad Bečvou, actually a long way to the south of their track to Bankau.

152 Jimmy Edwards, the future actor and comedian, wrote of his war in his book *Six of the Best*.

153 The authors are most grateful to Søren Flensted and to his website http://www.flensted.eu.com/1944131.shtml.

154 Ostrom, Swedish by birth, took British nationality in 1936.

155 *Halifax For Liberté*, p.186, Louis Bourgain (Compaid Graphics, Preston, no date but not earlier than 1997).

156 Only one of the seven crew was killed.

157 LJ943 returned to base, but was lost on 21 September on a supply flight to Arnhem. P/O Berger and four others

of his crew were killed. One of the two survivors, Sergeant L.G. Hillyard, was taken prisoner, ending up at Luft 7.

158 From website http://www.pegasusarchive.org/pow/douglas_smithson.htm.


**CHAPTER 9**

159 Letter to Raymond Crompton, undated but 1987.

160 See *The Barbed-Wire University*, p.228, Midge Gillies (Aurum Press Ltd, London, 2011).

161 The *London Gazette*, 9 January 1940.

162 In 1973 Ken became Lord Mayor of Leeds.

163 Alex Jardine, letter to Ray Crompton, 9 January 1992.

164 From TNA file FO 916/842 10013.

165 1473698 Ronald Gerald Purcell was commissioned (186255) on 5 December 1944 (*London Gazette*). 1583662 Howard Disney Patterson was commissioned (186094) on 28 November 1944 (*London Gazette*).

166 Although born in Christchurch, New Zealand, his family moved to Southgate, London in the early 1930s when he was seven. After the war he enlisted in the RNZAF, but came back to England to fly until demobbed on 20 June 1950.

167 The authors are most grateful to Bill Norman for his account of the loss of MZ930 in *No.640 (Halifax) Squadron RAF Leconfield*, pages 107-110, (Compaid Graphics, Warrington, 1999).

168 *Through Footless Halls of Air* (General Store Publishing House, Burnstown, Ontario, Canada, 1996).

169 He was captured at St Valéry-en-Caux, France, in May 1940.

170 The *London Gazette* No. 36276. Cas had been commissioned on 4 May 1943.


**CHAPTER 10**

171 Details from http://www.rafweb.org/Regiment2.htm.

172 *Bombers Over Sand and Snow*, p.298.

173 Recommendation by W/C H.A.Langton, CO of 37 Squadron, dated 3 January 1945.

174 Lake Balaton, the 'Hungarian Sea', approximately 77 by 14 kilometres, is the largest lake in Central Europe. For a photograph of LN858 see *Wellington. The Geodetic Giant*, p.145, Martin Bowman (Airlife Publishing, Shrewsbury, 1989).

175 Corsetti was awarded the DSC (US), the second highest military award after the Medal of Honor. The DSC was awarded 'For extraordinary heroism in connection with military operations against the enemy.'

176 Replacing the B-24's usual ball gun-turret under the fuselage was a 'Joe hole' through which the packages were ejected. On this day, 248 B-24s of the US Eighth Air Force dropped 782 tons of supplies to the US Airborne troops, losing seven of their number to ground fire.

177 Letter courtesy of Richard Collins, The letter, incidentally, was not received by the Collins family until January 1946.

178 The authors are most grateful to John Skinner for permission to quote from Paul Decroix's diary.

179 Such was Allied air superiority at this time that none of the 318 effective B-17 bombers on the Kassel raid was lost.

180 Also shot down on the Heilbronn raid, in Lancaster PB751, 44 Squadron.

181 From his article *Road Back Complicated*, in the Canadian *Air Force* magazine, March 1983.

182 From Australian National Archives.

183 Donaueschingen is in the south of Germany, not far from Switzerland. Rottweil is some 20 kms north east of Donau.

184 Roderick Chisholm briefly mentions this incident in *Cover of Darkness*, p.48 (Chatto & Windus, London, 1953). The successful crew were S/L M.F. Anderson and Sgt B. Cannon, later DFC and DFM.

185 Gazetted on 24 September 1941. Brown was also Mentioned in Despatches three times.

186 S/L John Kemp, *Off to War with '054'*, p.108 (Merlin Books, Braunton, 1989).

187 http://www.jewishvirtuallibrary.org/jsource/ww2/Arnhem.html.

188 *Air Mail*, Winter 1994, p.15.

189 *With the Red Devils at Arnhem*, pp.83-4, Marek Święcicki (MaxLove Publishing Co. Ltd., London, 1945).

190 Answer 13 of Recorded Evidence of 415285 F/O Peter Thomson, RAAF, Wednesday, 11 July 1945.

191 Letter of 5 October 1989 from Personnel Records Centre, National Archives of Canada.

## CHAPTER 11

192 The pilot (F/O R. Cave) and two others were killed.

193 Myron's story is told in *We Flew, We Fell, We Lived*, pp.72-80. In it, the author writes that he was brutally questioned at Dulag Luft. This is most unlikely, as these authors are not aware of a similar case ever occurring there.

194 Neil says that he arrived on 9 January 1945, having left Wetzlar on the 5th.

195 Commonly known as the 'Battle of the Bulge'.

196 Quotes are from the diary that Henry managed to keep.

197 Sydney Barlow, letter of 9 June 1989. Edward German's opera originally opened, in London, in April 1902.

198 The ten Armies were: 3rd Guards; 13th; 52nd; 5th Guards; 59th; 60th; 6th; 3rd Guards Tank; 4th Tank; and in reserve, to the east of the Vistula, the 21st.

199 *Red Storm On the Reich*, p. 68.

200 *Armageddon Ost*, p. 81. The Kursk battle was fought in July and August 1943.

201 True or not, it's a good story. *I'll Never Go Back*, p.63, M. Koriakov (Harrap & Co Ltd, London, 1948).

202 *Red Storm On the Reich*, p.87.

203 TNA file AIR 40/280.

## CHAPTER 12

204 Peter Thomson and Captain Howatson wrote a report of the forced march, dated 15 February 1945, which was marked 'For the attention of the Swiss Commission as the Protecting Power', who were visiting the camp on that date.

205 *Open Road to Faraway*, p.126.

206 *Open Road to Faraway*, p.123. Baranowski had been up before the law in England for stealing a goose, which he wanted as the squadron's mascot. The animal was stolen from a policeman who, on hearing in court that Baranowski had just shot down a German aircraft, asked the court to close the case, shook the Pole's hand, and said "sorry!"

207 From the joint Captain D.G. Howatson RAMC/P/O P.A. Thomson RAAF report.

208 The six were: Flight Sergeants G. Flint, A.C. Hydes; Sergeants H. Chambers, F.G. Treadgold; and two of the GPR men from Arnhem.

209 *Into Enemy Arms*, p. 150.

210 The adventures of the escapers from the brick factory are told in Doug Grant's inimitable style, exactly as he wrote it, in Appendix III.

211 On 1 October 1941 the Nazis had established Majdanek concentration camp on the outskirts of Lublin. Though not an extermination camp, it is, nevertheless, estimated that by the time that it was overrun by the Russians on 22 July 1944 over 79,000 people had died there.

212 *For You the War is Over*, p. 308.

213 From Appendix C of Anderson's report M.I.9/S/P.G.(-) 2931 in TNA file WO 208/3326.

214 Minus 24° Celsius equals minus 11° Fahrenheit.

215 From his diary, with kind permission of his son, Ron Niven.

216 Waldhaus, or Domwaldhaus, appears in some POW diaries as Buchitz. The Polish name today is Buszyce.

217 John Berry was born at Padiham, near Burnley, Lancashire on 2 September 1910.

218 From Ben Couchman's diary.

219 See Hughes's story in Chapter 8.

220 Howatson/Thomson report.

## CHAPTER 13

221 *Footprints on the Sands of Time*, p.58.

222 *The Log*, p.198.

223 G/C Willetts had come from Luft 3. He was shot down on 23/24 August 1943 (Berlin).

224 For his selfless work, Captain Howatson received only a Mention in Despatches (gazetted 20 December 1945). He died in Canada, where he had been in practice, on 24 August 1972.

225 From the four 51 Squadron Halifaxes lost on these two nights, eighteen were killed and ten taken POW.

226 Information gratefully received from Dave Champion.

227 Art Kinnis, via Frank Wells, in letter of 7 November 1990.

228 Quotes from Bruce Smith's unpublished memoirs *The Airforce Years*.

## POSTSCRIPT
229 Coincidentally where one of the authors now lives.

## APPENDIX III
230 In return for the Anglo-American promise, Stalin agreed to hold free elections in liberated Poland as soon as possible, though it is clear now that he had no intention of ever doing this.

## APPENDIX IV
231 From http://www.460squadronraaf.com/crews.html, with kind permission of Laurie Woods.
232 *Poland, SOE and the Allies*, p.193, Garlinski, op.cit.

## APPENDIX V
233 Lieutenant David Grey Worcester (232585) was awarded the MC on 29 November 1945.
234 Karl Friedrich Otto Wolff (13 May 1900-17 July 1984), who ended the war as the Supreme Commander of all SS forces in Italy, negotiated the early surrender of all German forces in Italy, which ended the war in Italy on 2 May 1945.

# BIBLIOGRAPHY

*Against The Sun* – Edward Lanchberry (Cassell and Co Ltd, London, 1955)

*A Leap in the Dark* – J.A. Davies (Leo Cooper, London, 1994)

*Armageddon Ost. The German Defeat on the Eastern Front 1944-5* – Nik Cornish (Ian Allan Publishing, Hersham, 2006)

*Barbed Wire. Memories of Stalag 383* – M.N. McKibbin (Staples Press, London, 1947)

*Barbed-Wire University, The* – Midge Gillies (Aurum Press Ltd, London, 2011)

*Berlin 1945. End of the Thousand Year Reich* – Peter Antill (Osprey Publishing Ltd, Oxford, 2005)

*Bomber Command War Diaries, The* – Martin Middlebrook and Chris Everitt (Penguin Books Ltd, Harmondsworth, 1985)

*Bombers Over Sand and Snow. 205 Group RAF in World War II.* Dr Alun Granfield (Pen & Sword Books Ltd, Barnsley, 2011)

*Bombs and Barbed Wire* – Wilf Hodgson (W Hodgson, Attadale, Perth, Australia, 2000)

*Boys at War* – Russell Margerison (Ross Anderson Publications, Bolton, 1986)

*British Airman, The* – Roger A. Freeman (Arms and Armour Press, London, 1989)

*D-Day Bombers: The Veterans' Story* – Stephen Darlow (Grub Street, London, 2004)

*Escape to Danger* – F/L Paul Brickhill and Conrad Norton (Faber and Faber Ltd, London, 1946)

*Failed to Return* – Bill Norman (Leo Cooper, London, 1995)

*Fighters Over the Desert* – Christopher Shores & Hans Ring (Neville Spearman Ltd, London, 1969)

*Flying Into Hell* – Mel Rolfe (Grub Street, London, 2001)

*Footprints on the Sands of Time* – Oliver Clutton-Brock (Grub Street, London, 2003)

*For you the War is over* – Sam Kydd (Bachman & Turner, London, 1973)

*Glider Pilots at Arnhem* – Mike Peters & Luuk Buist (Pen & Sword, Barnsley, 2009)

*Halifax Down!* – Tom Wingham (Grub Street, London, 2009)

*Hell On Earth* – Mel Rolfe (Grub Street, London, 1999)

*Into Enemy Arms* – Michael Hingston (Grub Street, London, 2006)

*It's Suicide but it's Fun* – Chris Goss (Crécy Books Ltd, Bristol, 1995)

*Just a Survivor* – Phil Potts (Woodfield Publishing, Bognor Regis, 1999)

*Massacre over the Marne* – Oliver Clutton-Brock (Patrick Stephens Ltd, Sparkford, 1994)

*Men of Air. The Doomed Youth of Bomber Command* – Kevin Wilson (Weidenfeld & Nicolson, London, 2007)

*Nachtjagd War Diaries Volume One September 1939-March 1944* – Theo E.W. Boiten (Red Kite, Walton-on-Thames, 2008)

*Nachtjagd War Diaries Volume Two April 1944-May 1945* – Theo E.W. Boiten and Roderick J. Mackenzie (Red Kite, Walton-on-Thames, 2008)

*Night Pilot* – Colonel Jean Calmel DFC (William Kimber, London, 1955)

*Not All Glory!* – Victor F. Gammon (Arms & Armour Press, London, 1996)

*No Time For Fear* – Victor F. Gammon (Arms & Armour, London, 1998)

*One Night in June* – Kevin Shannon and Stephen Wright (Airlife Publishing, Shrewsbury, 1994)

*Open Road to Faraway* – Andrew S. Winton (Cualann Press, Dunfermline, 2001)

*Point Blank and Beyond* – Lionel Lacey-Johnson (Airlife Publishing, Shrewsbury, 1991)

*P.O.W. Wartime Log of F/Sgt. T.D.Glenn* – Rosamund Glenn (compiler) (Wild Wolf Publishing, 2010)

*RAF Evaders* – Oliver Clutton-Brock (Grub Street, London, 2009)

*Red Storm on the Reich. The Soviet March on Germany, 1945* – Christopher Duffy (Castle Books, Edison, USA, 2002)

*Regiment, The. The Real Story of the SAS* – Michael Asher (Penguin Books, London, 2008)

*Royal Air Force at Arnhem, The* – Luuk Buist, Philip Renders, Geert Maassen (The Society of Friends of the Airborne Museum Oosterbeek, Oosterbeek, 2005)

*Silk and Barbed Wire* – edited by Brian Walley (Sage Pages, Warwick, Australia, 2000)

*The Log, Stalag Luft III, Belaria Sagan* – Bryce Cousens (editor) (Bryce Cousens, Cheltenham, 1947)

*They're Not Shooting At You Now, Grandad* – B. Hazzard (S.B. Hazzard, privately, 1991)

*To Hell and Back* – Mel Rolfe (Grub Street, London, 1998)

*War in the Air, The* – Gavin Lyall (editor) (Hutchinson & Co (Publishers) Ltd, London, 1968)

*War is Half Luck* – Charles J.L. Bonington (unpublished typescript, c.1960)

*We Act With One Accord* – Alan Cooper (J&KH Publishing (1998), Hailsham, 1998)

*We Flew, We Fell, We Lived* – Philip Lagrandeur (Grub Street, London, 2007)

*Wingless. A Biographical Index of Australian Airmen detained in Wartime* – Tom Roberts (Thomas V. Roberts, Ballarat, Australia, 2011).

# INDEX

Abbott, Sgt J.R. 25-27, 286
Abbott, Sgt N. 119
Ackerman RA, Gnr D. 177
Ackroyd, Sgt J.O. 182, 286
Acthim RCAF, Sgt J. 109, 110, 286
Adair, Sgt E. 37, 38, 286
Adams, F/L H.C. 349 (en37)
Agur RCAF, F/O P.G. 154, 351 (en119)
Aitchison SAAF, Major R.U. 175
Akins USAAF, 1st Lt Francis E. 165
Aldous, Sgt R. 130
Allègre FAFL, Lt 118
Allen,F/S J. 190
Allen, F/S R. 215, 286
Almanzora 140
Alpe, Charles 140
Anderson RCAF, Sgt A.A. 36
Anderson DFC, S/L M.F. 353 (en184)
Anderson RCAF, F/O P.J. 242, 278
Ansell RAAF, F/S J. 109, 287
Arciuszkiewicz PAF, S/L E. 280
Arnold RCAF, F/O R.S. 164
Arundel Castle 70, 329
Ashton, F/S S.R. 160, 287
Aspinall RCAF, WO1 J.S.A. 30, 45, 287, 302
Atkinson, Sgt R. 214, 287
Aubossu family (French) 115
Aubrey RCAF, Sgt J.A.A. 32, 132
Auchinleck, Gen Sir Claude 126
Augenstein, Oberleutnant Hans-Heinz 349 (en54)
Austin, F/O A.E. 118
Austin RAF, Cpl A.H. 216-218, 287
Azouz DFC, W/O M. 218
Azrael, Louis (US war correspondent) 268

Backhouse, Sgt D.A. 191, 287
Badham, LAC J.G. 138, 287
Bad Soden hospital 163
Bailey, F/S J. 163
Baillie, F/O C.W. 33
Baldwin DFM, F/S C.F. 184

Balmanno RAAF, F/S D.T. 109, 288
Bament RAAF, Don 123
Bannister, Sgt D.V. 200
Baranowski PAF, W/O T. 124, 239, 288, 354 (en206)
Barber, Sgt D. 104
Barkess, Sgt P. 160, 288
Barley RAMC, Capt (Aus) 163
Barlow, F/S S. 7, 205-207, 220, 288, 354 (en197)
Barnard SAAF, Lt D.W. 140
Barnett, Sgt T.E. (Rhodesian) 131, 288
Barraclough, Sgt S. 130, 131, 288
Bartleet, F/L J.P.D. 168
Bastiaans, L.J. (student) 106
Bates, W/O W.A. 228, 288
Baugh RM, A/CSM (Ty.) B.L. 199, 289, 349 (en28)
Bauldie, Sgt D. 150
Baur, Heinz 351 (en99)
Bayford GPR, RSM G.W. 285, 289
Bayley, F/L A.F. 112
Beattie jnr, Capt E.W. (US war correspondent) 268
Beatty RCAF, F/O A.M. 41
Beck II USAAF, Major J.A. 209
Becker, Oberleutnant Martin 48
Beech RCAF, Sgt S.P. 42
Beeson, P/O S.C. 169
Behr, Oberstleutnant 20-22, 63, 162, 189, 194, 240, 244, 251
Bell RCAF, F/O C. 86, 89
Bell RCAF, Sgt T. 137, 289
Beluse RCAF, Sgt J.E.M 32
Belverstone, Sgt A.W.G. 84, 289
Bemann, Hauptmann (IIIA) 255
Bennett, AVM D.C.T. 350 (en63)
Bennett, Sgt H.R. 133, 240, 249
Bennett, F/S R.A. 205, 206
Bennett, F/S W.R. 207
Benson (SAS), Sjt R.T. 283
Beraud FAFL, Capitaine A. 201
Beresford, F/S A.G. 105-107, 289

Beresford, Sgt W.C. 147, 148
Berger, SS-Obergruppenführer Gottlob 234
Bernhardt PAF, F/O W. 245, 246
Berrie, F/S D. 268, 290
Berry, Sgt E. 228
Berry, Capt the Reverend J. 195, 203, 243-245, 273, 290, 354 (en217)
Berry, Sgt T.G.W. 132, 133, 290
Bettington RAAF, W/O M.M. 85
Bicknell, F/S D.G. 34
Bidwell RNZAF, Sgt N.S. 125
Billing, Sgt A.W. 73, 74, 290
Birch RAAF, F/S E.H. 49
Bird, F/S B.F. 36, 290
Bishop, W/O F. 19, 24, 220, 265, 290
Bitter, Joke (Joop) (civilian) 107
Bitter-van de Noordaa, Juliana 107, 108
Blackburn, S/L J. 162, 352 (en132)
Blackford, W/O D.A. 20, 25-27, 45, 161, 183, 220, 290
Blair DFC DFM, S/L J.E. 58, 349 (en42)
Blake, F/S W.A. 150, 290
Blakemore DFM, F/O E.J. 105, 107
Bland, Sgt R.W. 36, 290
Blattmann RAAF, W/O L.J. 151, 152
Blew, F/O D. 135
Bloomfield, F/S A.P. 205
Blunt, Sgt L.J. 158
Board RAAF, W/O W.A.H. 208, 290
Bock, Leutnant Heinz 351 (en118)
Bode, F/S P.H. 218
Boffin, F/S C.A. 162, 290
Bond SAS, Sgt Ernie 128
Bonington SAS, Lt C.J.L. 127-129, 350 (en91)
Booth, P/O J. 34
Borchers, Major Walter 348 (en10)
Bornschein, Hauptmann Walter 137

Bosenberg, Major (IIIA) 255
Bostridge, F/S I.W. 49
Bouché (French policeman) 115
Bowen-Morris, F/O U.B. 265
Bowes, Bill (cricketer) 139
Bowlby RCAF, Sgt T.L. 136
Bracegirdle, F/S A. 102, 291
Bradburn, F/O G. 165
Bragg, Sgt D.A. 164, 291
Brannagan RCAF, S/L T.A. 168, 352
Brant, W/O K.R. 211, 291
Braune, Sonderführer (IIIA) 255
Bray, F/S J. 164
Breheny RAAF, W/O R.T.H. 142, 291
Brereton, Maj. Gen. Lewis H. (USA) 170, 171, 352 (en141)
Brewer RCAF, F/S H.R. 121, 291
Brewer, Sgt J. 199
Brice, Sgt A.R. 26, 27, 291, 348
Brinkmann, Oberleutnant Arnold 179
Britchford, F/S A.T. 166
Britland, LAC S. 219, 292
Broad, W/O J.D. 98, 120, 292
Broadley GPR, S/Sgt D.S. 193, 292
Broadribb, Sgt P. 49, 52, 271, 292
Brookes, F/S W.A. 25, 26, 292
Brooks RCAF, WO1 H. 242
Brooks RCAF, Sgt L. 164
Brown RCAF, Sgt D.W.L. 292
Brown, Freddie (cricketer) 139
Brown RAAF, F/Sgt F.J. 186
Brown, Sgt F.W. 180, 202, 203, 210, 222, 236, 247, 254, 263, 267, 272
Brown, Sgt J. 163
Brown MBE, W/C J.L. 216
Brown DFC*, W/C M.H. 141
Brown, F/S P.H. 39, 40, 157, 292
Brown RCAF, Sgt R.C. 32
Browning, Lieutenant-General 'Boy' 170, 217
Bruncel, Ditha 244
Bruneau FAFL, F/S H. 125, 126, 135, 273, 293
Bryce GPR, S/Sgt C. 173, 293
Buchenwald camp 118, 120, 301
Bunn, P/O S.J. 259
Burford USAAF, S/Sgt 209, 293

Burnell DFC, F/L C.J. 143
Burns, F/S D.R. (545186) (musician) 137, 203, 238, 293
Burns, F/S D.R. (1525609) 136
Burns RCAF, F/L J.C. 86, 89, 293
Burton RCAF, F/S R.E. 143
Buschmann, Hauptmann Franz 151
Butcher, W/O J.J. 224, 293
Butkewitz USAAF, T/Sgt L. 143, 144, 294, 351 (en113)
Butler, Sgt P.G. 122, 123, 294

Cairns, Professor Sir Hugh 351 (en120)
Cakebread, Sgt J.A. 244, 294
Calder, S/L C.C. 117, 294
Cameron RCAF, F/O A.L. 145
Cameron, Sgt P. 73
Cammish, Sgt H.S. 109, 110, 294
Campbell RAAF, F/S A.D. 46, 47, 294
Campbell RAAF, F/O D.R. 85
Campbell, Sgt J. 294
Campbell RAAF, F/S K.W. 144, 239, 241
Campo (Italy):
  Dulag 339 (Mantua) 68, 315
  PG 19 (Bologna) 176, 190
  PG 47 (Modena) 190
  PG 54 (Fara Sabina) 113, 114
  PG 57 (Gruppignano) 44
  PG 59 (Servigliano) 69
  PG 63 (Aversa) 190
  PG 66 (Capua) 44, 69
  PG 75 (Torre Tresca, Bari) 142, 190
  PG 78 (Sulmona) 68, 139, 141, 142
  PG 82 (Laterina) 114
Cann DFC, F/O L.N.B. 185
Cannon DFM, Sgt B. 353 (en184)
Carey, F/S F.J. 70, 122, 123, 294
Carrington RAAF, P/O H.J. 102
Carter, P/O A. 125
Carter RAAF, F/S J.E. 174, 294
Carter (The Buffs), Pte N. 175, 281, 294
Cartwright, F/S R.R. 205, 207, 294
Cass, Sgt E.G. 64
Cave, F/O R. 354 (en192)

Chalkley, F/O F.D. 177
Chambers, Sgt H. 295
Chambers, Sgt S.J. 120-122, 295
Champness RAAF, P/O E. 37
Chandler RCAF, WO2 W.P. 220, 265, 295
Chant, Sgt J.H. 32
Chaplin RASC, Driver W.J. 177, 295
Chapman, F/S J. 163
Chapman, Sgt K. 244, 295
Charlish, Sgt M. 73
Charters RAMC, Major D.L. 163, 207
Chiles, Sgt K. 168
Chipman RCAF, F/L P.G. 225
Chittleburgh GPR, Lt K.T. 187
Christie DFM, F/L W.T. 68, 295
Clare RCAF, F/O E. 199
Clark, CQMS A.G. (Army) 85, 295
Clarke, F/S A.D. 158
Clarke, F/S A.W. 179, 236, 295
Clarke RA, Sgt H.P. 177
Clay DFM RCAF, F/S F.J. 145, 147, 351 (en115)
Claydon, W/O G.R. 244, 295
Cleary, F/S J.P. 222, 295
Cleeve, Sgt A.W.J. 131, 132, 240, 242, 243, 295
Clegg, F/S T.R. 91, 92
Clements, F/S R.G. 230, 296
Clenaghan GPR, S/Sgt H.C. 244, 296
Cliff-McCulloch, Sgt A.P. 43
Cloarec FAFL, Adjutant J.A. 201, 296
Cloran, Sgt T.H. 70, 197, 296
Clotselter US Army, Lt Col D. 269
Cluley, W/O G.H. 141, 296
Cobb, W/O F.K. 131, 296
Cockbain DFC, S/L S.L. 102
Codner, Lt M. 26
Cole DFC, S/L T.B. 104-106
Coleman DFC, P/O D.E. 66, 67, 296
Collingwood, F/S C.J. 163, 296
Collingwood, Sgt F. 123, 160
Collins, Capt the Rev J.B. 133, 190, 194, 195, 202, 210, 249, 251, 253, 258, 259, 273, 296
Comète escape line 40
Comfort, J. (Army) 70
Comfort, F/S W.S. 297

Compiègne camp 123, 154, 160
Conchie GPR, Lt R.H. 172, 173, 352 (en143)
Conner DFM, W/O F.R. 141, 297
Cook, Sgt L.W. 52, 297
Cooke, Sgt T.A. 131, 132, 297
Cooney, Sgt F. 73
Coope, Sgt A. 230, 297
Cooper USAAF, 2/Lt H.F. 60
Cooper DFC RCAF, F/L J.H. 143, 144
Cooper, Sgt R. 147, 148, 163
Cooper, Sgt V.V. 132, 133, 297
Cope, F/S D.E. 30, 297, 348 (en14)
Corbet RCAF, F/O C.M. 159
Cork RAAF, F/S C.S. 89, 90, 297
Cornier RCAF, WO2 A.A. 32
Cornwell RAAF, F/S R.G. 227
Corsetti USAAF, 1st Lt. J. 209, 353 (en175)
Cosgrove RCS, Sgt J. 141
Costello RAAF, P/O J. 115
Cottrell RNZAF, W/O R.F. 216
Couchman, Sgt W.B. 234, 240, 247, 249, 250, 297
Coverley, F/L H.D. 149
Cox, F/S A.W. 66, 298
Coxon, S/L H.W. 217, 218
Craig, Sgt P.H. 73, 233, 234, 236, 298, 350 (en60)
Crapper, Sgt M. 204, 298
Craven DFC, F/O J. 105, 107, 298
Crawford, Sgt I.R.B. 40-41, 298
Crompton, Sgt C. 40
Crompton RAAF, Sgt G.W.S. 69
Cronin RNZAF, Sgt M. 130
Cross, F/S G.H. 68, 190, 247, 250, 253
Crosswell RCAF, F/O P.B. 264, 265, 298
Crump, Sgt J. 89, 90, 298,
Cuffley RAMC, Major 163
Cugat, Xavier 137, 351 (en101)
Cullen, F/O 101
Culling, P/O C.W. 218
Cumberlidge, Sgt R.B. 152, 298
Cummings GPR, S/Sgt 217
Cursiter, Sgt J.R. 66
Curtis, Sgt P.J. 160, 298
Cusson, P/O T.F. 89, 90
Cytulski PAF, Sgt M. 65, 299, 349 (en51)

Czura PAF, Sgt S. 299, 349 (en51)
Dahms, Oberfeldwebel Helmut 116, 158
Dalhuisen, Willem (civilian) 106
Danes, Sgt J. 265, 299
Darwin, Sgt P.C.P. 238, 299
Dasen, Fritz (Swiss delegate) 258
Dashwood, RNZAF, W/O W.S 134, 135 299
Davey RAAF, F/S L.W. 151, 152, 299, 345
Davidson RCAF, Sgt T. 159, 299
Davies, Sgt D. 27, 299
Davies, F/S E.A. 30
Davies, Sgt I.G. 132
Davies, Sgt J.A. 222, 299
Davies RAF Regt, Sgt M.L. 204, 299
Davis USAAF, 1st Lt B. 218
Davis RAAF, W/O B.H. 155, 162, 195, 217, 218, 246, 253, 256, 299
Davis, W/O T.G. 161, 162
Davis (SAS), Cpl 282
Dawson, F/S C.M. 244, 300
Dawson RCAF, F/O E. 145, 164, 300
Deane, Sgt J.H.K. 125, 300
de Boer, Henk (civilian) 106
de Bounevialle, F/O C.M. 200
Debroise FAFL, Sergent M.A. 201, 300
Decroix, F/S P.H. (Bel) 210, 213, 258, 259, 260
Deere, Sgt A. 132, 133
de Ghetto USAAF, Sgt R.D. 157
De Kock SAAF, WO2 D.P. 140, 300
den Hollander RNethAF, Kpl-sch L. 111
den Tex Bondt RNethAF, Of-vl2 C.J. 111
De Renzy RNZAF, W/O T.D. 215, 240, 300
de Saint-Marc FAFL, Lt L. 186
De Viell, F/S R. 116, 300
de Vries, Meijer (civilian) 107
Denson RAAF, P/O M.R. 84, 85
Dezitter, Prospère Valère (Bel) 148
Dinney RCAF, F/O W. 152
Dissard, Françoise (PAT line) 109

Dobbs, Sgt K.A. 198, 222, 223, 301
Dodds (SAS), Pct. W. 283, 301
Dollesal, (German guard) 220
Donaghue, F/L 220, 367
Dönitz, Grand Admiral Karl (German navy) 270
Dothie, P/O H.J. 147, 148
Drake RAAF, C. 122, 123
Drewes, Hpt Martin 58, 349 (en44)
Drury, Sgt J.R. 152, 301
Dryden RCAF, F/O R. 143, 144
Duchess of Bedford 277
Duckworth, Padré J.N. 190
Dufau, Obergefreiter Adolf 136
Dunkley, F/S D. 161, 301
Dunsing, Oberstabsarzt Dr. (IIIA) 255
Dupureur, Doctor 98
Durand, Robert (French Resistance) 109
Dutch-Paris escape line 40
Duvall, F/S V.R. 45, 302
Dworakowski PAF, Sgt W. 268, 302
Dyson RAAF, F/S D.J. 99
Dyson, F/S. W. 241, 242, 302

Easson DFC RAAF, F/O R. 65
East, W/O E.E 246, 309
Ebersberger, Stabsarzt Dr. 194
Eden, Anthony (British Foreign Minister) 217, 218, 302
Eden, LAC R.J. 217, 218, 302
Edwards, Sgt E.W. 114
Edwards SAAF, W/O G.B. 157, 302
Edwards DFC, F/L J.K.O. 179, 295, 331, 337, 352 (en152)
Egri RCAF, F/S W.E. 153, 154, 302
Eisenhower, General Dwight D. 271
Elizabethville 138, 351 (en103)
Elliott RCAF, WO1 K.E. 143, 144, 302
Ellis, F/S R.O. 43, 302
Emmerson DFM, F/S F. 163
Empress of Britain 114
Enfield, Sgt R.G. 159, 303
Engling, Unteroffizier Egon 352 (en129)
English, Sgt R. 192, 303
Erffinger, Richard ('Otto') 21, 246

Esser, Kreisleiter Johannes 229
EVA organisation 157
Evans RAAF, F/S H.C. 85, 303
Evans (SAS), Pct J. 283
Everett DFC**, S/L D.B. 66,
  349 (en53)

Fairweather, P/O F. 215
Fajtl, S/L František (Czech) 352
  (en137)
Falconer, P/O J.A.R. 134
Falkingham DFM, F/S O. 68
Fallon, Sgt G. 244, 303
Famin, Major-General (USSR)
  267, 271
Farrington, F/Sgt D.A. 160, 303
Faul SAAF, 2nd Lt A. 161
Fawkes, F/O S.G.H. (S. African)
  134
Feakins, Sgt F.J. 165, 166
Feindell RCAF, Sgt L. 64
Felix escape line 157
Fereday, Sgt J.C. 86, 87, 303
Fethers RAAF, W/O W.N. 142,
  303
Fielitz, SS-Hauptsf Karl 107
Finch, Sgt F.E. 164, 303
Finlay, F/O (295 Sqdn) 107
Finlayson, Sgt C.W. 39, 304
Finnigan, Sgt P. 196, 197
Fisher GPR, S/Sgt C. 112, 187
Fisher, Sgt R. 113
Fisher DFM, Sgt R.V. 185
Flay RNZAF, F/S G.A. 91, 304
Fletcher RCAF, WO2 L.R. 48,
  49, 304
Flint, F/S G. 304, 354 (en 208)
Ford USAAF, Sgt D.S. 127, 136
Forrest, Sgt J.F.J. 116, 304
Foster, LAC D. 218, 304
Fowler, Sgt C.R. 179
Fox DFM, F/L C.C. 27
Fox, F/S R. 123
Foxley-Norris, W/C C. 200
Frame RCAF, WO2 J.H. 42
Frank, Sgt K. 64
Frank, Oberfeldwebel (German
  guard) 21, 22, 234, 243, 246
Franklin, F/S T.G. 36
Fraser RCAF, Sgt B.A.M. 42,
  304
Fraser GPR, Sgt R.A. 171
Fraser-Petherbridge DFC*, F/L
  C.A. 117, 350 (en78)

Fresnes prison, Paris 39, 101,
  110, 115, 118, 119, 167, 287,
  288, 292, 296, 306, 308,
  311, 312, 316, 336, 339, 340
Fréteval Forest, France 154, 351
  (en119)
Frost, T. 124
Fyfe, Sgt W. 104

Gallagher, Sgt J.D.F. 84, 305
Galloway, Brigadier Sandy 127,
  305
Gannon, Sgt R.F. 160, 305
Gardener, F/S J. 35
Gardner GPR, S/Sgt L.J. 171
Gardner, F/S R. 59
Garner RCAF, F/O A.M. 214
Garnham, Sgt J.S. 147
Gasperich US Army, S/Sgt J.C.
  256
Gavin, Brig. Gen. James M.
  (USA) 170
George RAAF, F/S C.L. 212
'Geraldine' – see 1395269
  Jones, F/S F.H.
Gerrard, F/S D.G. 119, 305
Gibbens RCAF, WO2 G. 160, 305
Gibbs RCAF, F/O R.C. 177
Gibson RCAF, Sgt W.R. 119,
  305
Gilbey, Sgt W. 131, 305
Giles, F/S F.A. 244, 306
Gill, Sgt S.T. 73, 75
Gillespie USAAF, Sgt V.E. 209
Gilmore, F/S H. 154, 306
Gilson, Sgt K.E. 109
Gippard, Wim (Dutch
  Resistance) 59
Gisevius, Obergefreiter (IIIA)
  256
Glen (SAS), Sjt W.O. 283
Glenn, F/S T.D. 30, 31, 98, 124,
  149, 162, 163, 172, 180, 201,
  230
Godard, Sgt D. 131
Goemans RNethAF, F/O C.J.M.
  196
Goldenberg USAAF, 2nd Lt R.
  23, 348 (en6)
Good RCAF, P/O R.E. 159, 352
  (en126)
Goode DFM, W/O R.J. 117, 118,
  155, 306
Goodman, F/L F.V.S. 89, 90
Goodman-Jones RAAF, F/S A.
  84, 85

Gordon RCAF, F/S J.A.
  (R.201055) 68, 176, 177, 306
Göring, Reichsmarschall
  Hermann 15, 16, 158, 193
Gorlia, Mme Mariette 148
Gorman RCAF, F/S W.M. 110,
  306
Gosway, Sgt W. 42
Gowing, LAC R.W. 128, 130,
  306
Graham RCAF, F/O W.C. 27,
  348 (en11)
Grant, Sgt J. 46
Grant RCAF, Sgt D.R. 239, 241,
  246, 276, 307
Grant RCAF, Sgt W.A. 136, 137
Gräser, Generalleutnant Fritz-
  Hubert 232
Gray, W/O D.G. 46, 47, 135, 307
Green, F/S F.D. 230, 231, 307
Green, Sgt K.W. 164
Greene RCAF, W/O R.A. (USA)
  22, 24, 69, 194, 203, 208
Greene, Sgt T.W. 241
Greiner, Oberleutnant Georg-
  Hermann 40
Griffin FAA, A/Ldg.Air. H.C.
  142, 308, 349 (en28)
Griffiths, F/O A.A. 264
Grigg, Sir James (Secretary of
  State for War) 278
Gripsholm 136
Grisdale, F/S E. 59
Groendyk, H – see Theunissen
Grogan, F/O R.J. 89-91
Grunert, Leutnant Karl-Heinz
  348 (en8, en12)
Guest, Sgt L.J. 143
Gundy RNZAF, F/S R.Y. 30, 31,
  308
Gunston (Irish Guards), Capt
  J.St.G. 282, 283
Gunzi, F/L G.G.C. 64

Habgood, Sgt F.H. 152
Hablot FAFL, Lt J. 186
Haddon, Sgt W.R. 192, 308
Hale, Sgt C.T. 42
Hales, Sgt R.B. 205
Hall RNZAF, W/O A.D. 47, 349
  (en34)
Hall, P/O C.P. 131, 351 (en91)
Hall, F/L D.R. 118
Hall USAAF, 2nd Lt G.T. 209
Hall RCAF, Sgt R.S. (USA) 131
Hall DFM, F/S S.J. 30

Hallett RCAF, F/O W.A.M. 164
Hallett, Sgt W.W. 30, 309
Halligan RAAF, F/S B.T. 84, 309
Hamilton, W/O B. 155
Hamilton, Sgt A.F. 98, 99, 309
Hamilton, Sgt J. 52, 309
Hammet DFM RAAF, F/L A.H. 158, 245, 279-281, 290, 311
Hanneck, Oberleutnant Gottfried 152
Hannedouche FAFL, Adjutant R.A. 198, 201, 309
Hansford, F/S R.J. 246, 302, 309
Hardwick RAAF, F/S P.P. 27, 244, 309
Hardy, Mme Edith 148, 351 (en117)
Harris, ACM Sir Arthur T. 271
Harris, Sgt E. 164
Harris RCAF, F/O P.H. 225
Harrison, Sgt D. 200
Harrison RCAF, P/O J.R. (USA) 136
Hartgroves, Sgt R.S. 125, 310
Haughton, Sgt R. 84, 310
Hayes, Eva M. (civilian) 104
Hayes, H.A. (civilian) 104
Hayes, Sgt P.F.J. 103-105, 107
Hayes USAAF, W. 113
Hayman RAAF, F/S G. 212
Headon RAMC, Capt 258
Healey GPR, S/Sgt Edwin 171, 310
Healy, Sgt Elwyn 49, 50, 51, 54, 170, 180, 189, 231, 310
Heard, W/O R.P. 126-130
Heasman, Sgt R. 112, 310
Heath, Sgt A.L.R. 124, 131, 132, 134, 310
Heath, Sgt R.R. 169, 197, 310
Heathfield, Sgt F.J.H. 147, 351 (en116)
Helme, Sgt F.W. 158, 311
Henderson RAMC, Major 162
Henderson RNVR, Sub Lt T.McK. 42, 43
Henderson, W/O W. 256
Hendrickson USAAF, S/Sgt W.B. 110
Henseler, Oberleutnant Wilhelm 348 (en22)
Herger RCAF, P/O R.B. 188
Herte US Army, Lt Col R.J. 256
HM ships & boats:
    Decoy 138, 351 (en104)
    Havock 138, 351 (en104)
    Porpoise 129
    United 351 (en105)
Hewitt, Sgt G.A. 89, 91, 311
Hewlett, Sgt K.J.R. 169, 311
Heydrich, General Reinhard 349 (en29)
Highland Princess 140, 277, 278
Higman, Sgt F.J. 154, 311
Hill (SAS), Danny 129
Hill (SAS), Sgt P. 22, 23, 124, 282, 283, 311
Hill RCAF, F/O A.L. 34
Hillyard, Sgt L.G. 355 (en157)
Hingston, Michael (author) 244
Hislop, P/O E. 229, 311
Hitchings, F/S R.B. 205, 207, 311
Hitler, Adolf 15, 16, 21, 22, 80, 86, 119, 127, 231, 234, 266, 268
Hockley RAAF, P/O A.J.N. 30, 31
Hodgson RAAF, F/S W. 23, 311
Hohe Mark Lazarett 48, 65, 135-137, 163, 180, 224, 300, 318, 327, 335, 346
Holden, F/S A.J. 157
Holden DFC RCAF, F/O R.G. 145-147
Holloway, W/O M. 246, 312
Holmes DFC, F/L E. 240, 312
Holmes, F/S H.R. 66, 67, 240, 312
Hood, F/O P.J.K. 58, 349 (en45)
Hooker FAA (RNAS), Air Mech. 2nd Cl. L.A. 177
Hooks RCAF, Sgt J. 42
Horn, F/L S.F. 177
Horscroft SAAF, WO1 H.E. 175
Horton GPR, Sgt J.R. 193, 312
Hounam DFM, F/O J.E. 27, 29
Howarth, W/O G.T. 312
Howatson RAMC, Capt D.G. 200, 220, 230, 236, 238, 240, 243, 247, 253, 256, 259, 262, 273, 353 (en169), 354 (en 204, en 207, en 224)
Hoyle, F/S H. 153, 312
Hudson, Sgt A.L. 89, 91, 312
Hudson, F/S P. 25-27, 312
Hughes, Sgt E.I. 48
Hughes, Sgt R.D. 156, 157, 182, 247
Hughes (SAS), L/Cpl 282
Hulbert, Sgt G.A. 22, 313
Humphries, AC1 W. 128
Hunter, Sgt D. 152, 313
Hurley USAAF, 2nd Lt J.E. 154
Husemann, Hpt Werner 30
Hutchinson RCAF, Sgt A.R. 121, 122
Hutchinson, Sgt E.D. 227, 228, 313
Hutchinson RCAF, F/S J.A. 44
Hutchinson RNVR, Sub Lt V.H. 42
Hutchison RAF Regt, LAC R.H. 313
Hydes, F/S A.C. 313, 354 (en208)
Hymas, Sgt J.H. 198, 313

Ilag Kreuzburg 236
Ingram DFC, S/L G.F.H. 350 (en83)
Ingram, F/S K.H.C. 105, 107
Irving, F/S G.R. 190, 191
Ittershagen, Obersarzt Dr Ernst Waldemar 135, 136
Ivins, F/O F. 125

Jabin FAFL, W/O R. 126
Jackson, F/S C.W. 109, 314
Jackson, F/S J. 92, 314
Jackson VC, Sgt N. 48, 349 (en35, en50)
Jaggar RNZAF, P/O W.R. 68, 349 (en55)
James, Sgt J.H. 192, 314
James, Sgt R.G. 41
James RCAF, F/O R.W. 144, 145
Jandrell SAAF, Lt Col A.C. 175
Jardine RCAF, LAC R. 194, 314, 353 (en163)
Jeffares RNZAF, P/O B.C. 192
Jeffrey, F/S D.S. 54, 56, 57
Jeffreys, F/S J.C. 68
Jeffries, F/S A. 54, 57
Jenke, Sonderführer (IIIA) 255
Jenkins, F/S D.J. 215, 314
Jenkins, F/S J.S. 92
Jenkinson, Sgt F. 244, 314
Jervis RCAF, WO1 I.H. 198, 314
Joce, Sgt C.S. 244, 314
Jodl, General A.J.F. (Wehrmacht) 270
Johns DFC RAAF, F/O S. 152
Johnson, F/S G.R. 364, 365, 314
Johnson US Army, S/Sgt K.B. 257
Johnson RCAF, Sgt W.L. (USA) 131, 132

Johnstone RCAF, F/O G. 145
Johnstone, Sgt J. 37
Johnstone RCAF, F/L M.M. 86, 89
Jolley DFC RAAF, W/O K.A. 65
Jolly, Sgt A. 242
Jones, F/S A. 30
Jones GPR, Sgt A.L. 177
Jones, W/O E. 142
Jones, 1395269 F/S F.H. 199, 315
Jones, F/O H. 152, 315
Jones, F/S J.A. 228
Jones, Sgt L. 37, 38, 315, 348 (en23)
Jones, Sgt T.S. 131, 315
Jopling FAA, PtOff A. 141, 351 (en110)

Kadler, Albert A. 16, 17, 19, 20, 162, 194, 195
Keane, Sgt D.G. 147, 148
Keen RAAF, F/O H.B. 84
Keighley, F/O C.W. 143
Keirle, Sgt S.A. 54, 57, 315
Keitel, General Wilhelm 15, 348 (en1)
Kemp RNZAF, F/S A.E. 112, 114, 180
Kemp, F/S T.W.M. 244
Kempnich RAAF, F/Sgt A.W.J. 186
Kennedy GPR, S/Sgt J. 217, 316
Kesselring, Generalfeldmarschall Albert 129, 174
Kilbryde GPR, Sgt G.H., 172-174, 187, 222, 230, 254, 262, 316
Kiltie, Sgt J. 36
King, Sgt G.J. 49, 57, 316
Kinney USAAF, Sgt W.C. 60
Kirby, Sgt P.S. 84, 85, 316
Kleitz US Army, Lt-Col A.F. 268
Klette SAAF, 2nd Lt R. 161
Knacke, Oberleutnant Reinhold 350 (en92)
Knoke RCAF, Sgt J. 225
Knox GPR, Sgt W.H. 21, 187, 316
Konev, Marshal I.S. 232, 234
König, Obertsleutnant (IIIA) 255
Korner, Sgt G.V. 196, 197, 316, 353 (en166)
Krause, Oberleutnant Hans 207

Kristopher, Leutnant 86
Krumpeck, Gefreiter (German army) 244, 245
Kutzner, Unteroffizier Otto 149

La Grange SAAF, Lt A.F. 140
Lamb RCAF, Sgt W.A. 164
Lambert, F/S D.M.D. 165, 166, 235, 317
Lambert DFC, S/L G.F. (Aus) 117, 350 (en79)
Lambert DFC, F/O K. 40, 348 (en25)
Landis, C. (USA) 72
Lane, W/O J.F. 105, 106
Lane DFC, W/O K. 19, 24, 29, 30, 317, 348 (en13), 352 (en122)
Langton, W/C H.A. 353 (en173)
Lauridsen, Johannes (farmer) 351 (en97)
Laurie RAMC, Capt 65
Law, Sgt A.C. 99, 317
Lawes, Sgt A. 49
Lawson RCAF, P.O C. 42
Lazarett IXB (Bad Soden) 207
Leake RAMC, Capt (Aus) 163
l'Ecluse, Willem (civilian) 107
Lee, W/O J.R. 160
Lees SAAF, W/O J. 140
Lefebvre RCAF, F/S J.R. 32
Lehner IRCC, Dr 256
Leschalles GPR, Major E.H. 172
Lester, Sgt A. 104
Leube, Oberlt Hermann 31
Lewes SAS, Lt J.S. 127
Lewis, P/O L.W.C. 122
Lewis, Sgt T.B. 244, 318
Lievense RCAF, F/S S. 217, 218
Lihou, F/S M.G. 85, 350 (en62)
Liles USAAF, 2/Lt J.L. 110
Lindenboom, F/S K.P. 229
Lippert, Hauptmann 129
Little, Sgt R.R.A. 136, 318
Litwinski, Slawomir (Polish underground) 276
Liversidge RAAF, A/S/L J.P. 158
Lloyd (SAS), SS-M J. 22, 23, 282, 283, 318
Lloyd, Sgt R.F. 30, 98, 160
Lockeridge (SAS), Pct A. 283
Löhr, Oberstleutnant (IIIA) 255
Loneon RAAF, F/S B.F. 164
Longhurst, Sgt J.C. 164
Loosemore (SAS), Pct H. 283
Lorenz, Hpt Herbert 123

Lorimor USAAF, Captain F.O. 209
Louis Pasteur 86
Lovatt, Sgt E.N. 30, 319
Low RCAF, F/O A.A.J. 214
Ludwig, (German guard) 195, 198, 220, 265
Lüschen RNethAF, Of-zee3 H. 111
Lutter, Oberst (Commandant IIIA) 255, 257
Lyall RAAF, F/S P.T. 30, 31
Lynch, Sgt W.H. 149

MacAleavey, S/L K. 169, 352 (en139)
MacDonald, G/C J.C. 269
MacDonald, F/L K.J. 49
MacGregor, F/S J. 34, 319
Mackrill, F/S R.F. 193
MacLean RCAF, Sgt D.L. 121, 165, 190, 240, 247, 248, 319
MacNaught RCAF, Sgt A.R.R. 159, 220, 264, 265, 319
MacPherson RCAF, F/O N.C. 151
MacTaggart, F/S D.A. 168, 320
MacVean USAAF, 2nd Lt P.D. 154
Madelaine, Sgt A. 189, 320
Majdanek concentration camp 241, 276, 354 (en211)
Majeepa, Wilson (SA Army) 48
Maki RCAF, Sgt L.R. 244, 320
Malick RCAF, WO2 S. 260, 350
Malone USAAF, S/Sgt O.M. 209, 320
Manfroy FAFL, Adjutant J. 301, 320
Manick FAFL, Sergent N. 186, 320
Manning RN, Lt J.S. 141, 351
Mannion, F/S F.P. 176, 320
Marini RCAF, W/O J.H. 241, 320
Marshall RCAF, F/S V.L. 112, 320
Marti IRCC, Dr 256
Martin, Sgt D. 125, 321
Martin, Sgt D.S. 128, 350 (en89)
Martin RAAF, F/S H.A. 44, 45, 48, 321
Martin RAMC, Pte H.L. 349 (en35)
Martineau RCAF, F/O W.A. 144, 145

Maskell, F/O A.T. 66
Masters RCAF, Sgt R.H. 147, 148
Matthews, Sgt D.A. 177
Matthews, Sgt D.C. 158, 321
Matthews, F/S J. 92, 321
Maugham, Sgt D. 46
Maunsell DFC, F/O J.R. 112
Mauthausen concentration camp 148
Maycock, Cpl E. 194, 321
Mayne SAS, Lt R.B. 127
McAuley DFC, S/L V.C. 68
McCluskey, Sgt T. 43
McConnell RCAF, F/Sgt J.R. 18, 19, 32, 165, 176, 198, 220, 271, 272, 321
McCoombs RCAF, WO2 W.J. 114, 244, 321
McCullough RCAF, F/O D.L.C. 214
McCutchan RCAF, Sgt J.E. 24, 30, 31, 322
McDonald, F/S I. 68
McDonald SAAF, George 113
McGindle DFC RAAF, F/O E. 184
McGonigal SAS, Lt E.C. 127, 129
McGraw RCAF, Sgt R.W. 57, 68, 322, 349-350 (en56, en57)
McInnes GPR, Sgt J. 218
McLaren, F/S A.S. 225, 322
McLaren RCAF, Sgt D.N. 73, 322, 354 (en194)
McLean, Sgt R. 73, 322
McMahon USAAF, Capt 109
McMurdon, Sgt A.O. 21, 32, 33, 183, 273, 322, 349 (en48)
McPhail, F/S W.S. 241, 242, 322
McQueeney, Sgt P. 199
McTeer, Sgt A.P. 207, 323
Mead, W/O R. 139, 208, 241, 244, 323
Mead RAF Regt, F/O 204
Medland DFM, F/S C.J. 64, 323, 349 (en43)
Medlin (SAS), Parachutist 282
Medvedev, Captain (USSR) 268, 269, 271
Meese, F/S D. 241, 323
Meiningen Lazarett 48, 49, 65, 186, 198, 199, 220, 323, 327
Meister, Hauptmann Ludwig 187

Mellor, F/L A. 39, 40
Merrill RCAF, F/O C.L. 99, 101
Messenger, Sgt H. 40, 41
Michaud, Pierre (French surgeon) 150-151
Midlane, Sgt A.L. 187, 261, 262, 323
Milligan, Sgt E.A. 190, 323
Mills, P/O J. 44, 57, 64
Mills, F/S J.W. 324
Minifie RCAF, Sgt K.C. 42, 324
Miranda de Ebro camp (Spain) 111
Mitchell, Sgt J.A. 143, 324
Modrow, Hauptmann Ernst-Wilhelm 106, 350 (en71)
Molloy RAAF, F/S B.P. 152, 324
Molnar RCAF, Sgt E.J. 98
Montwill PAF, Sgt J. 324, 349 (en51)
Moore, Sgt E.A. 126, 134, 135, 324
Moorhead, F/O P. 117, 118
Moran RCAF, WO2 E.S. 155, 299
Moreton Bay 242, 277, 278
Morgan, Sgt E.J. 92, 324
Morgan, Sgt J. 243
Morlock, Feldwebel Wilhelm 43
Motts, Sgt G.E. 150
Mowat RCAF, LAC B.B. 219, 325
Muir GPR, Capt I.C. 178
Muirhead RAAF, W/O M.J. 241, 325
Murray RAAF, F/S C.A.F. 244, 325
Murray, W/O H.G.F. 43

Naugler RCAF, Sgt G. 37
Naysmith, F/S A.D. 112, 241, 242, 326
Neal, F/S D. 169
Neal RAMC, Major (SBMO at Stalag 383) 223
Nehring, General Walther 232
Newton GPR, S/Sgt A. 188, 193
Newton, Sgt C.C. 145, 146
Nichol, F/L C.W. 187
Nicholls DFC RAAF, F/L J.H. 64, 65, 326
Nicholson, P/O J.L. 205-207, 326
Nicol, F/S A.R. 193, 326
Nightingale, Sgt F.K. 68

Niven RCAF, Sgt W.M. 145, 243, 326
Nock MC, F/O H.A. 147
Noel RCAF, F/S J.H. 42, 326
Nolan, Sgt P.J. 108, 263, 326
Nölle, Major 21
Norgate, Sgt J.K. 169
Norris RCAF, W/O W.W. 49
Notton, F/S L.P. 43, 326
Nuttall, F/S F. 196, 197
Nutter GPR, S/Sgt R. 178, 231, 326

Oakeby, Sgt H. 143
Oakes GPR, Sgt W.A. 171, 327
Oates, F/S N.F. 153, 240, 252, 257, 327
Oates RCAF, F/O R.J. 86, 88, 89
Obermassfeld, Reserve Lazarett IXC 65, 102, 108, 136, 137, 160, 163, 186, 199, 293, 327
Obino, Tenente 113
Ocelka, F/S A. (Czech) 168, 178, 327, 352 (en151)
O'Connell RAAF, P/O F. 117
Offley, Sgt W.E.L. 184, 185, 327
Oflag:
VA (Weinsberg) 142, 190
VIB (Warburg) 225
79 (Braunschweig) 191
Oger FAFL, Adjutant R.N. 166, 167, 327
Ogilvie, F/S W.D. 64, 327, 349 (en51)
O'Leary RAAF, F/S M.J. 109, 152, 244, 327
Olive FAFL, Sergent-Chef Henri 198
Olsen RAAF, F/S R.P. 40, 41, 327
Operation:
101A 151
Crupper 9a 224
Crusader 126
Dragoon 204
Driftwood 282, 283
Garden 170, 216
Goodwood 143
Kanarek 242
Maple 22, 282-283
Market 170, 171, 188, 193, 207, 216
Nida 158
Osric 43
Pegasus I 211

Squatter 126, 129
Thistledown 282
Titanic 160
Varsity 262
*Orcades* 210
Orr RAAF, F/S J.G. 258
Osbourn DFM, F/L B. 40, 348
    (*en26*)
Ostrom, F/S N.J.E. 185, 243,
    327, 352 (*en154*)
Owen, W/O A.J. 85, 327
Owin, Oberleutnant 194

Pace Jnr USAAF, S/Sgt H.G. 154
Packham, F/O G.H. 92
Page, F/O W.C. 224
Palmer, Sgt B.J.P. 124, 132, 133,
    328
Pankratz RCAF, F/S H.W. 213
Parker, F/S H. 35
Parry-Jones RAC, Cpl R.H. 73,
    328, 350 (*en59*)
Parsons SAAF, Lt C.E. 140, 328
PAT escape line 109
Paterno USAAF, Lt V.J. 209
Patey, Sgt F.B. 46
Patrick RCAF, P/O E.R. 44
Patterson USAAF, T/Sgt C.E.
    209, 328
Patterson, F/S H.D. 196, 197,
    256, 328, 353 (*en165*)
Paxton, Sgt R. 54, 57
Pearcey RCAF, F/O J. 43
Peggs RAAF, Sgt R.J. 41
Pemberton, F/S G.G. 207
Pendray, F/S K.J. 191, 192, 329
Penman RAAF, F/S J.E. 212,
    213, 329
Pepper GPR, Sgt M.R. 173
Pepper (SAS), Parachutist 282
Pergantes RCAF, P/O H.P. 121,
    122
Peschel, Major 21, 22, 194, 240
Peter of Yugoslavia, King 351
    (*en108*)
Peterson RCAF, Sgt R.G. 242
Pett RCAF, Sgt J.T. 119, 120, 329
Pettit, F/S C.C. 92, 95, 96, 329
Philippe FAFL, Adj-Chef A.J.M.
    186, 329
Phillips, F/S C.J. 102, 329
Phillips, Sgt D.K.J. 152
Phillips, F/S V.W. 85
Philpot, F/L O.L.S. 26
Pickering, Sgt A. 37
Pickstone, Sgt A. 64

Pickstone, Sgt J. 136
Picton, Sgt H.S. 169
Pique, Monsieur (French Res)
    167
Pitchford, F/S J.E.M. 160, 330
Pius XII, His Holiness Pope 68
Pizey DSC, RN, Lt. Cdr. E.F.
    129
Plumridge RAAF, P/O J.B. 212
Pollard, F/S H. 120
Pommersgaard family (Danish)
    179
Pons FAFL, Sgt-Chef L. 186,
    330
Poole, F/O L. 49
Popadiuk RCAF, F/S J. 225, 330
Pott RAAF, Sgt J.H. 128
Potter, F/S A.E. 200, 201, 330
Potthast, Leutnant Friedrich
    348 (*en18*)
Pougin de la Maisonneuve
    FAFL, Lt C. 126
Poulton, Sgt J. 130
Poulton, Sgt W.A. 147, 148, 244
Powderhill, F/O M. 126
Prentice, F/O K.R. 99, 350
    (*en66*)
Pring, Sgt B.R.J. 152, 331
Pringle RAAF, W/O G.H. 42,
    155, 331
Prístupa, Sgt G. (Czech) 168,
    ¯331
Pritchard, Sgt W.K. 224, 331
Prowd RAAF, W/O K. 176, 331
Prudham RCAF, 119
Pugh (SAS), 283
Pulbrook RAAF, F/S L.J. 85, 331
Punter RCAF, F/S R.H. 59
Purcell RAAF, 'Bluey' 163
Purcell, F/S R.G. 196, 197, 353
    (*en165*)
Purdy DFM, W/O T. 130
Pyle, Sgt J. 25

Quigley, Sgt E. 219, 331

Rackwitz, Oberstleutnant 21
Rademeyer DFC, F/L I. 102
Rademacher, Hauptmann
    (IIIA) 255
Radermackers-Balieux, Mme
    Irène 148
Radusch, Oberstleutnant
    Günther 102
Raffin FAFL, Lt P. 201
Randall, F/S W.J. 179

Ranfield GPR, S/Sgt H. 244,
    331
*Rangitata* 138, 351 (*en103*)
Rauh, Haupmann Hubert 49,
    85
Rauter, SS-Obergruppenführer
    Hanns Albin 107-108
Rawson RAAF, F/O G.D. 212
Raymond, F/S R.F. 30, 126,
    156, 331
Reavill, F/L R. 27
Recknagel, Generalleutnant
    Hermann 232
Reeve RCAF, Sgt P.A. 121, 126,
    156, 331, 350 (*en84*)
Regan, P/O W.T.A. 49
Regina Coeli prison, Rome 283
Reid VC, F/L W. 163, 332
Reilly, F/O J.W. 36, 332
Reinecke, General Hermann 15
Remmer, Leutnant Hans 126
Reneau RCAF, 'Spanky' 112, 113
Rhodes, Sgt H. 225
Rhodes, F/S R. 165, 166
Richardson, F/L 127
Richardson RAAF, F/S C.R.
    251, 332
Richter, Father (German priest)
    244, 245
Riding, F/O R.H. 99, 350
    (*en66*)
Rigby GPR, Sgt A.A. 171, 332
Riley, Sgt T.H. 40, 41, 332
Rippingale, F/S E.G. 123
Rivers, Sgt W.M. 27
Robarts SAAF, Lt E. 350 (*en58*)
Roberts, F/S A.C. 120, 332
Roberts, Sgt D.W. 227
Roberts, F/O E. 229
Roberts RCAF, Sgt J.E. 117, 333
Roberts, F/S J.M. 27
Roberts DFC RAAF, F/O K. 116
Roberts, F/S L.G. 228
Roberts, Sgt R.D. 227
Roberts (SAS), L/Cpl 282
Robertson RCAF, F/O D. 227
Robertson RCAF, WO1 J.A.144,
    333
Robinson, Sgt J. 19, 34, 36, 333
Robinson, F/S P.S.M. 35
Robinson, Sgt R. 43
Rodgers SAAF, WO1 J.L.W. 140,
    333, 351 (*en107*)
Roelofs, Broek (pastor) 106
Rogers, F/O W.J. 27, 333
Rökker, Oberlt Heinz 116

'Rommel' (German guard) 233, 234
Roosevelt, Franklin Delano (US president) 249, 264, 277
*Rosolino Pilo* 139
Rose RCAF, Sgt C.E. 58
Rose, Sgt H.P. 333
Rose, Sgt R.A. 41
Rossel IRCC, Dr M. 156, 352 (en121)
Rousseau RCAF, Sgt R.C.O. 134, 135
Rowan, Sgt W.S. 52, 333
Royle, Sgt R.G. 164, 333
Rüge, General Otto (Norwegian) 266
Russell RCAF, Sgt H. 135
Rybalko, Colonel-General Pavel Semenovich 232

St Gilles Hospital, Brussels 32, 54, 99, 101, 103, 148, 292, 309, 318
Salt, F/L F. 118-120
Samwells, LAC E.A. 219
Sandulak RCAF, Sgt J. 159
Sargeant RAAF, W/O A.J. 102, 334
SAS 'L' Detachment 126, 129
Saunders, Sgt A.G.T. 25
Sawyer, Sgt E. 108
Sawyer, Pte J.A.J. 262
Saxton, Sgt K.W. 192
Sayn-Wittgenstein, Major Heinrich Prinz zu 199
Scarlett RAAF, F/O R. 130
Schade, Hauptmann 21
Schaus, Oberleutnant Jakob 34
Schirmeck Security camp 152
Schmeling, Max (boxer) 260
Schmidt, Oberleutnant Dietrich 64
Schmitz, Leutnant Hans 99
Schofield, LAC B. 138, 139, 334
Schultz, Unteroffizier Heinrich 350 (en80)
Schultz, Hauptmann 182
Schulz, Oberfeldwebel 128
Schwilk RAAF, F/S/ C.W. 154, 350 (en119)
Scopes, Sgt D. 18, 34-36, 334
Scott, F/S E.W. 193, 334
Scott, LAC W.H. 217, 219
Scully, Sgt H.V. 85, 334
Scully, Sgt J. 154, 334
Sealtiel, Sgt A.R. 58, 59

*Sebastiano Venier* 129
Sekine, Sgt P.Y. 124, 163, 334
Seller RCAF, W/O A.E. 265, 334
Seymour RAAF, W/O J.D. 186
Shabatura USAAF, S/Sgt E.H. 209, 334
Sharpe RCAF, WO2 G.W. 108, 335
Shaw, Sgt C. (635 Sq) 35
Shaw, Sgt C. (156 Sq) 185, 335
Shearman, F/S A.E. 223
Shelshar, Sgt R.L. 136
Shenton, F/Sgt J.A. 18, 25, 26
Sherman DFC RCAF, F/O L. 116, 117
Shiel, W/O T.C. 206
Shields RAAF, F/S J. 204, 251, 252, 335
Shimmons, Sgt L. 58, 59
Shipman RCAF, F/O C.L. 225
Shorter, F/S S.H. 105, 106
Silver RAAF, F/S S.A. 102, 162, 222, 223, 335
Simes, F/S S.W. 108, 244
Simm, Hauptmann (IIIA) 255, 335
Simmonds (Aus Army), Pte 44
Simpson, Sgt H. 54, 57
Simpson, F/S J.L. 229
Simpson RCAF, F/S M.J. 150, 151
Simpson, F/S P.S. 140
Simpson, Sgt R. 30
Simpson FAA, LAF (A) R.F. 335, 349 (en28)
Simpson, Sgt W. 44
Sinden RAAF, F/O G.F. 212
Singh RAAF, F/O F.R. 25, 348 (en7)
Sinkavitch US Army, Capt J.G. 269
Slack RCAF, F/S K.E.C. 270, 336
Slowey, Sgt J.G. 244, 245, 336
Smith, F/S A.D. 160
Smith RAAF, P/O A.L. 85
Smith, Sgt D.L. 49
Smith RASC, Driver F.G. 177
Smith, Sgt J.A. 184, 336
Smith RAAF, F/S J.G. 205, 230, 231
Smith, P/O P. 227, 228, 336
Smith, Sgt R.L. 199, 259, 336
Smith, F/S S.A.C. 65
Smith RAAF, F/S W.B.R. 243, 270

Smithson GPR, Sgt D.G. 43, 188, 193, 337
Smyth FAA, A/Pty Off V. 42, 43, 244, 245, 337
Snowden AFM, W/O J.W.B. 181, 182, 260, 337
Soames DFM, Sgt S.L. 184
Soderberg, Henry (YMCA) 17, 233
Sorenson, F/S H. 179, 337
Sorzano, Sgt A.L. 84, 337
Sosabowski, Maj-Gen S. 170
Souillard FAFL, Sgt-Chef 118
Soury-Lavergne FAFL, Sergent G. 201
Sowerby, Sgt F.W. 85
Sparkes, F/S S. 59
Sparks, Sgt T. 119, 337
*Speditørerne* group 164
Spence RA, Driver J. 177, 337
Spencer RCAF, Sgt S.D. 36
Spoden, Oberleutnant Peter 212
Spriggs, F/S F.A. 27, 29, 337
Stalag:
 IIA (Neubrandenburg) 265
 IIIB (Fürstenberg) 256, 257
 IVB (Mühlberg) 68, 148, 186, 218, 274
 VC (Malschbach) 190
 VIG (Bonn) 27, 57
 VIJ (Dorsten) 348 (en7)
 VIIA (Moosburg) 16, 69, 99, 112, 114, 124-126, 130-133, 135, 139, 141, 190, 197, 263, 274, 308
 VIIIA (Görlitz) 233
 VIIIB (Lamsdorf) 16, 130, 203, 239, 300
 VIIIC (Kunau) (Brieg) 233, 240, 307
 IXC (Mühlhausen) 224, 335
 IXC (Obermassfeld) – see Obermassfeld
 XIA (Altengrabow) 139-141, 269, 274
 XIB (Fallingbostel) 139, 140, 209, 218, 274
 XIIA (Limburg a.d. Lahn) 178, 188, 193, 194, 274
 XIIID (Nürnberg) 197, 209, 224
 XVIIA (Kaisersteinbrüch-bei-Brüch) 190
 XVIIB (Krems-Gneixendorf) 84
 XVIIIB (Wagna) 45

XVIIIC (Markt Pongau) 45
XVIIID (Marburg a.d. Drau) 131
344 (Lamsdorf) 23, 38, 42, 68, 103, 114, 142, 155, 162, 195, 222, 224, 233, 236, 246, 250, 332
357 (Fallingbostel) 32, 34, 49, 57, 65, 304
383 (Hohenfels) 23, 124-126, 130-135, 223, 239, 274, 286, 318, 322-331, 334-345, 348 (en5)
Frontstalag 122 (Compiègne) 160
Frontstalag 133 (Chartres) 160
Stalag Luft:
 I (Barth) 16, 122, 145, 160, 352 (en132)
 II (Litzmannstadt) 16
 III (Sagan) 16, 26, 40, 43, 91, 110, 118, 120, 142, 145, 151 152, 168, 243, 247, 248 250, 253, 275, 349 (en28)
 IV (Beninia?) 16
 IV (Gross Tychow) 131, 136, 142
 V (Gröditz) 16
 VI (Heydekrug) 16, 21, 32, 47, 348 (en3)
Stancombe, F/O R. 224
Stanley RCAF, F/O L.O. 86, 88, 89
Stanley, W/O T.C. 351 (en102)
Stapleton RAAF, F/Sgt J.E. 252, 253, 337
Stead, F/S F. 252, 253, 337
Stead GPR, S/Sgt J.E. 252, 253, 337
Steeves RCAF, F/O M.B. 86
Stevenson RCAF, F/O J.M. (USA) 119
Stevenson RCAF, Sgt L.H. 6, 219-221, 338
Stewart RCAF, F/S D.A. 27, 29, 338
Stewart, F/L J.K. 66, 338
Stirling SAS, Capt D. 126, 127
Stirling Castle 281
Stokes, Sgt H.McL. 198, 338
Stone SAS, Sgt S.J. 129
Stone, Sgt V.H. 224, 338
Strawbridge, RSM W. 256
Struthof-Natzweiler extermination camp 152

Stuart, Sgt R. 35
Sturgess, F/S F.A. 149, 157, 163, 338
Sturzkopf, Major ('Bulk Issue') (IIIA) 255
Styles, Sgt R. 231, 338
Such, Sgt F.J. 102, 241
Sutcliffe RNZAF, F/O J.H. 208
Sutherland RAAF, F/S W.F. 246, 338
Sutton, W/O L.J.W. 123
Sutton-Pratt, Colonel R. 233
Swale SAAF, WO1 N.H. 175, 176, 338
Swanson USAAF, T/Sgt J.E. 209, 338
Święcicki, Marek (war correspondent) 218, 353 (en189)
Szewyck USAAF, S/Sgt M. 136

Tames RCAF, F/S J.S. 169, 339
Tanton's Hotel, Bideford 62
Taylor, Sgt J.D. 41, 42, 339
Taylor, F/S J.E. 151
Taylor RCAF, W/O K.G. 35, 36, 339
Taylor, F/S L.L. 207
Taylor, Maj. Gen. Maxwell D. (USA) 170
Taylor RAAF, F/S R. 116, 339
Taylor, Sgt T.J. 109
Taylor, Sgt W. 98, 120, 181, 182, 245, 248
Taylor, F/S W.H. 339
Taylor, P/O W.H. 109, 110
Tchekanov, Capt (USSR) 269
Temple, Sgt J. 34
Terry, Sgt J. 34
Theunissen RNethAF, W.M. 111, 308
Thiryn, Mme Eleuthère 148
Thomas, LAC G.R. 217, 218, 339
Thomas, Sgt R. 228
Thompson, Maj F.C. 127, 129
Thompson, F/S J.Mck.V. 187
Thomson GPR, S/Sgt J.J. 222, 340
Thomson RAAF, F/O P.A. 20 21, 23, 57, 183, 194, 203, 219, 220, 238, 240, 241, 256, 258, 261, 273, 340, 353 (en190) 354 (en204, en207)
Tindall, Sgt R.W. 49
Tirpitz 42
Todd RAAF, F/O W.K. 84

Todd (SAS), Parachutist 282
Tomlinson, Sgt T.W.H. 151
Tomney, Sgt J.F. 6, 19, 36, 124, 160, 340
Topham, F/O J.B. 154
Tovey, F/S J.W. 265
Townshend, Sgt F.C. 187, 340
Tratt, Sgt L.W. 196
Travis-Davison GPR, Sgt K. 188, 193, 194, (en162)
Trayhorn, Sgt J.A. 169
Treadgold, Sgt F.G. 340, 354 (en208)
Trend, Sgt J.M. 59
Trimble, F/S T. 99, 249, 254, 274, 340
Trindall, F/O R. 204
Trumble, Sgt A.H.J. 227-229
Tuck, Sgt L.J. 25
Tucker, F/S J.H. 116
Tudor DFM, F/S F.J. 65, 66, 341
Tungsteen, Operation 42
Turner, W/O F.F. 191, 192, 341
Tweddle, F/S A. 241, 341
Tyson RA, Gnr J. 177

U-boat:
 U-32 (Kap-Ltn Hans Jenisch) 114
 U-480 (Kap-Ltn Hans-Joachim Förster) 117
 U-980 (Kap-Ltn Hermann Dahms) 116
Umscheid RCAF, Sgt J.L. 265, 341
Underwood, F/S W.C. 242
Upton SAAF, WO2 H.R. 54, 56, 57, 352 (en131)
Upton, Sgt W.G. 161, 341
Urquhart CB DSO, Maj-Gen R.E. 170

Vaissade FAFL, Sgt J. 118, 341
Valášek, P/O K. (Czech) 167, 264, 342
Van de Velde, Sgt C. 115
Van Reekum, Doctor 106
van Terwisga, Narda 107-108
van Trotsenburg SAAF, Lt C. 175
Velleman RNethAF, Kpl-sch J.H. 111
Venus, F/Sgt L.J. 22, 58, 59, 64, 342
Vermillion, Bob (US war correspondent) 268

Vidler, Sgt J.E. 222, 342
Vinecombe, Sgt F.S. 119
Vlaminck FAFL, Sgt-Chef R.H. 197, 198, 342
Vlassie RCAF, F/O N. 64
Vles FAFL, Lt J. 198
Vlok SAAF, Lt T.V. 143
Vogel SAAF, W/O H.B. 57, 342
Vogel, Unteroffizier 136
von Canitz, Hauptmann (IIIA) 255
von Edelsheim, General Maximilian Reichsfreiherr 232
von Grävenitz, Generalmajor Hans 15

Wagner, Sgt H.W. 228, 258, 261, 263, 264, 273, 342, (en196)
Walde, Oberst Ernst 16
Walker, Miss (Englishwoman in Warsaw) 280
Walker, F/O D.F. 58-60
Walkins, P/O P. 163
Walkty RCAF, F/Sgt J.J. 21, 194, 234, 242, 243, 249, 251, 343
Wallis RAAF, F/S G. 46, 47, 343
Walshe RNZAF, F/O P. 151
Ward, F/S J.D. 115
Ward, F/S W.J. 58, 343
Warren, F/S J.F. 191, 192, 343
Waters, Sgt F.R.W. 241, 343
Watkins GPR, S/Sgt H. 343
Watkins, Sgt J.C. 154, 155
Watkinson GPR, S/Sgt C.R. 177
Webb DFC, F/L N. 163
Weddle, Sgt L. 123
Weedon, Sgt J.G. 192, 344
Weeks, F/S C. 26, 27, 344, 348 (en11)
Wegrzynski PAF, Sgt M. 344, 349 (en51)
Wells, F/S E.H. 160, 344
Wells RCAF, Sgt R.A. 135
West, F/S C. 127, 128
Westwood, Sgt J. 49, 52, 344
Wharton, Sgt L. 164
Wharton, Sgt S. 205, 249, 264, 344
Whatton, F/S J.H. 119, 344

Wheeler, S/L 217
Whelan DFM RAAF, F/S E.G. 184
Wherry RAAF, P/O J.J. 176
Whiddon RAAF, W/O R.H. 215, 344
White USAAF, Flt/O L. 32
White, Sgt T.S. 40, 41, 345
Whitehead, F/S A. 65
Whitehouse SAAF, Lt G. van der H. 174, 175
Whitley, Sgt J.W. 54, 57
Wicks, F/S W.F. 151, 152, 345
Wieggers, Hendrik 167
Wiener, Hauptmann 21, 22, 194
Wigger, SS-Untersf Hubert 107
Wilcock, Sgt N. 259
Wilcox RNZAF, F/S D.J.R. 179, 345
Wiles, F/S J. 205, 206, 207, 345
Wilhelmina Gestern, Amsterdam 60
Wilks, Sgt W. 224
Willetts, G/C A.H. (SBO, IIIA) 256, 259, 354 (en223)
Williams, Sgt B.R. 58
Williams, F/L Eric 26, 345
Williams, F/S E.T. 266, 345
Williams, F/O F. 40, 41
Williams, F/S J.G. 229
Williams USAAF, Sgt L. 154
Williams DFM, F/O M. 224, 354 (en193)
Williams RCAF, F/S M.A. 345
Williams (Br Army), Pte John 281
Williamson, Sgt A.T.S. 44
Willis, Sergeant J.J. 213, 345
Williston RCAF, F/S A. 199
Wilmot, F/S N. 49, 346, 349 (en36)
Wilmshurst, Sgt P.G.G. 149, 256, 346
Wilson, F/S F.A. 92
Wilson, Sgt H.W.D. 164
Wilson SAAF, WO2 J. 175, 176
Wilson, Sgt J.H. 27, 346
Wilson GPR, Sgt R. 178
Winchester SAAF, WO1 L.E.D. 161, 346

Winfield, Sgt P. 131, 132
Winkley, Sgt W.J. 164, 346
Winter, Sgt H.T. 135, 136, 346
Winton, Sgt A.S. 238, 239, 346
Withnall GPR, S/Sgt P.B. 193, 346
Witzmann FAFL, Sgt-Chef 118
Wolff, F/S E.L. 213, 346
Wolff, SS-Obergruppenführer Karl 283, 355 (en234)
Wolstencroft RCAF, P/O G.A. (USA) 120, 121
Wood, Sgt J.L. 212
Woolfrey, F/O W.F. 208
Woosnam, Sgt R.J. 123, 347
Worcester SAS, Lt D.G. 282, 355 (en233)
Worthing, F/S D. 230, 347
Worthington, Sgt T.W. 228
Wray AFC RCAF, G/C L.E. 108
Wright GPR, Corporal 173
Wright, Sgt B. 46
Wright RCAF, Sgt D. 143, 144, 352 (en122)
Wright, F/L W.D. 158, 347
Wuillemin FAFL, Lt J. 186
Wyand, F/O G. 116
Wynn RCAF, Sgt K.C. 265, 347
Wynne-Cole, Sgt B. 160, 347

Yardley, Sgt D. 98, 244, 245, 347
Yearsley, Sgt R. 347
Yeo, Sgt E.R. 84, 347
YMCA 17, 43, 45, 189, 203, 233, 349 (en31)
Young RCAF, F/O H.J. 103
Young, LAC 219
Yvars FAFL, Sgt R.F. 186, 347

Zacharuk RCAF, W/O A. 143
Zercher USAAF, Sgt R.W. 107
Zerff SAAF, W/O M. 140, 347
Zeus 200
Zhadov, Colonel-General Aleksei Semenovich 232
Zimmerman, Hauptmann 194
Zucker RAAF, F/S V.S.J. 37, 38, 250, 347